KT-198-834

THE
RADICALISM
HANDBOOK

A COMPLETE GUIDE TO THE
RADICAL MOVEMENT
IN THE TWENTIETH CENTURY

JOHN BUTTON

CASSELL

Other titles in Cassell's *Global Issues* Series

Hotspots: The Legacy of Hiroshima and Nagasaki
by Sue Rabbitt Roff

East Timor at the Crossroads: The Forging of a Nation 1974–1994
edited by Peter Carey and G. Carter Bentley

Generations of Resistance: East Timor
by Steve Cox and Peter Carey, with a foreword by John Pilger

Comfort Women:
Korean Survivors of Japanese Forced Prostitution Tell Their Stories
edited by Keith Howard

Silent Revolution: The Rise of the Market Economy in Latin America
by Duncan Green

Re-enchanting Humanity:
A Defense of the Human Spirit against Antihumanism, Misanthropy,
Mysticism and Primitivism
by Murray Bookchin

Crossfire: Turkey and the Kurds
by Jonathan Rugman and Roger Hutchings

Cassell
Wellington House
125 Strand
London WC2R 0BB

© John Button 1995

All rights reserved. No part of this publication may be reproduced
or transmitted in any form or by any means, electronic or
mechanical including photocopying, recording or any storage
information or retrieval system, without prior permission
in writing from the publishers.

First published 1995

British Library Cataloguing-in-Publication Data
A catalogue record for this book is available from the British Library

ISBN   0-304-32713-1 (hardback)   0-304-32711-5 (paperback)

Typeset in Bitstream Amerigo by the author, using Corel Ventura
Printed and bound in Great Britain by Biddles Ltd,
Guildford and Kings Lynn

CONTENTS

ABOUT THE AUTHOR

John Button has been active in environmental politics and radical therapeutic groupwork for more than twenty years and is the author of more than a dozen books, including *A Dictionary of Green Ideas*. His particular interests are the links between human motivation and social action, and the way in which important ideas and tactics are shared and communicated between activists in different areas. He lives and works in the English Cotswold town of Stroud.

INTRODUCTION

Welcome to *The Radicalism Handbook*, a celebration of a century of individuals and groups of people working for a peaceful, just, safe and sustainable world.

There are those who believe that radical activism died with the 1970s, and that as May 1968 and Vietnam became distant memories so materialism, comfort and certainty overtook the idealism and naïveté of those protest years. There are even those who tell us that the world is now moving towards a post-scarcity era of limitless economic progress and social stability for all: this is certainly what many politicians would have us believe.

History is neither so neat nor so accommodating of those who tell us that they know best about what the future holds. The truth is that ours is an age of extremes, of massive inequality and opportunity, of unprecedented destruction and uncertainty. Yet there is much evidence to suggest that an ever-increasing proportion of the world's population is countering this doubt, destruction and uncertainty with heartfelt determination and with positive grassroots activism.

In the mid-1990s nearly ten million US citizens – 5% of the population – are actively supporting organisations dedicated to protecting the environment, working for peace or defending human rights. In Britain the combined membership of environmental organisations alone tops three million, while in the October 1994 national elections Die Grünen (the German Green Party), on a radical platform of environmental and human rights, won 7.3% of the vote with some four million people supporting them. Cooperative working and marketing in the Third World is growing apace, often linking directly with trading cooperatives in the richer countries.

It is all too easy to think that people today would rather sit back and be spoonfed their worldview by television than play an active part in worldshaping. There are many politicians who would like to believe that radical activism has run its course, and that today's more adult and comfortable electorate has no need to be loud and difficult. But there were similar mainstream voices in the late 1930s, heralding the end of communist-inspired radicalism as war loomed and patriotism became the cause of the day. This in turn was a *déjà vu* of the years prior to the first world war, when powerful voices advocating anarchism, suffragism and pacifism were silenced in the blind rush towards international conflict.

If you believe in generation-long cycles of authority and protest then we are certainly due for another era of more public social and political activism. We can be fairly sure, however, that the radicalism of the twenty-first century, while it will echo that of the twentieth, will manifest itself in subtly different ways. Some argue that true radicalism is dying because such tactics of the 1930s and 1970s as mass demonstrations, marches and public displays of civil disobedience are less evident than they were then. Not only will such observers have been troubled by the growing tide of protest in the early 1990s; their analysis would ignore a number of profound changes in the way people learn about and participate in radical movements as the century draws to a close.

The first stage of radical change is knowing that something is very wrong. If you have been made homeless, or are working for pennies an hour on sweated labour, or have been imprisoned for criticising the president, this may be first-hand knowledge. If you are moved to righteous indignation by injustice seen or read about, you will probably want to know more, until you are convinced that something must change.

One of the biggest changes in the last quarter century has been the proliferation – and the more widespread ownership and control – of channels of communication. Those who know something is wrong, unless they have been incarcerated or live in a heavily censored country (of which there are now mercifully few), today have relatively easy access to information and the support of like-minded people. Telephone, radio, easily-printed newsletters and a growing computer network have been added to word of mouth and public meeting. A group in Tonga can monitor closely the strategies and successes of a similar group in Greenland; human rights activists can immediately counter a politician's lies with detailed and accurate information.

Though global inequality is on the increase, a combination of desperation, determination and ingenuity is helping many poor communities to turn their backs on centralised systems and procedures, a trend which many governments ignore since it reduces the drain on official coffers. Hence, in addition to the mainstream economies of the world, an alternative 'rainbow' economy of barter, direct trading, local currencies and gift work is developing rapidly both in poor and in rich nations.

In this way poor communities in many parts of the world are in the process of converting economic and social subservience into sustainable self-determination, and here we have one clue as to the nature of twenty-first-century radicalism: it will be a bottom-up rather than a top-down phenomenon. Radical change needs its leaders and prophets, but it is unlikely that the next cycle of radicalism will either need or produce new Marxes, Pankhursts, Gandhis and Martin Luther Kings. We shall continue to be inspired by those who match vision and action, but there will be many more of them, and we shall value them more for the immediacy of their message for us and our situation than for their towering moral stature. We shall also empathise more with their all-too-human failings.

Another major shift in radicalism comes from the blurring of the left/right divide. It was German green activist Herbert Gruhl who first explained that green politics was neither right nor left, but out in front. Most late twentieth-century radicals share the sense that, while socialist and communist ideas are far from dead, progressive politics has now transcended partisan rhetoric and moved into inspiring new realms of challenge and responsibility.

This trend away from traditional political divisions and towards a new distinction between those who accept and those who protest marks another characteristic of the new radicalism. Perhaps this is too polarised, and it would be more useful to think of those who accept with very little questioning and those who believe in the right to question everything. However we frame it, it is clear that a growing number of those who know something is wrong are prepared to question why it is wrong and how it might be put right. And, as we have already seen, a growing proportion of questioners are prepared to do something to put it right.

A third important trend, in the West at least, is the very recent but rapidly growing abandonment of traditional channels of middle class lobbying in favour of the direct action which has so long been seen as the preserve of the militant left. Mass demonstrations against road building, the trade in live animals, toxic waste dumping and arbitrary political authority are increasingly drawing participation from young and old, left and right, middle and working class.

When you consider the alienation that most citizens feel from the political process, it is hardly surprising that even the most ardent defenders of 'traditional democracy' complain that their views are simply not being taken into account. Even arch-conservative British politician Norman Tebbit told a radio interviewer early in 1995 that 'people have begun to realise that there is no democratic way in which British people can change laws which they find abhorrent and unacceptable'. Yes, he was talking about a particular set of arrangements for greater cooperation with Britain's European neighbours that he, from his xenophobic standpoint, thought objectionable, and wanted everyone to agree with him. But at least he acknowledged the right and the need to protest.

How about some more traditionally radical voices commenting on the status of radical thinking and activism in the 1990s? Here is Noam

Chomsky in a 1992 interview (*Chronicles of Dissent*, Common Courage Press, 1992): 'When I started giving talks back around 1964, it seemed totally hopeless... [Today] the cultural level of the country is much higher. Outside the educated classes, which are not changed, I think the moral and intellectual level of public discourse and public understanding has risen very considerably. I don't doubt that for a moment. And that's encouraging.' And here is peace activist Howard Zinn writing in his autobiographical *You Can't be Neutral on a Moving Train* (Beacon, 1994): 'Going around the country, I was impressed again and again by how favorably people reacted to what, undoubtedly, is a radical view of society – antiwar, antimilitary, critical of the legal system, advocating a drastic redistribution of the wealth, supportive of protest even to the point of civil disobedience... It is this change in *consciousness* that encourages me.'

Radicalism dead? Humbug. We do hope you will find enough time between canvassing for signatures for that petition against nuclear dumping and writing to your politician on behalf of prisoners of conscience to enjoy the many inspiring stories in *The Radicalism Handbook*.

John Button
Stroud, Gloucestershire, England
March 1995

ACKNOWLEDGEMENTS

A book like this, three years in the making, owes an enormous debt of gratitude to those who helped me to compile it. As is customary, I take full and final responsibility for deciding who and what to include, the tone and content, the criteria for inclusion and exclusion, and the typing of most of the words (more than 200,000 of them). I could not have done it, though, without the help and support of the following friends and colleagues.

First I thank my research assistants: Yarrow Cleaves, who researched the North American entries and wrote the drafts of more than fifty of them, and Laura Mahoney, who spent countless hours in Sussex University Library looking for references and elusive articles.

Thanks to those who helped with specific regions and subject areas: Robin Blackburn of *New Left Review* for South-East Asian sources, Chris Church on Friends of the Earth, Steve Cook on gay rights campaigners, Paul Ekins on radical economists, Ken Jones on Buddhist activists, Adrian Jackson of the London Bubble Theatre on radical theatre directors, Adam Keller of the Israeli Council for Israeli-Palestinian Peace on Middle East peace campaigners, Chris Lee of the Latin America Bureau on the Latin American entries, Julia Martin and Mike Cape of Cape Town University on the South African entries, Sara Parkin on environmental campaigners, John Rowan on radical therapists, Ann Waswo of the Nissan Institute of Japanese Studies on the Japanese entries, Beryl Williams and Gordon White of Sussex University on Chinese entries and Rebecca Yeo on African and Central American entries.

Next come my administrative assistants: Lesley Abraham, who wrote to and fielded the responses from many of the entrants in the *Handbook* who are still very alive and active; and Caroline Carless, whose careful eye checked for consistencies, accurate cross-references and accents where (and only where) they should be.

Special thanks to Professor Michael True of Assumption College, Worcester, Massachusetts, for carefully reading the near-to-final version with an expert American eye: it is so simple to overlook small but telling details which a European can easily miss. Charles Mosley cast his historian's eye over the introductory essay, for which I am very grateful.

Thanks as always to my nearest and dearest: to Fran for understanding just how it feels, listening to and being moved by the stories, and being brave enough to pick the introduction apart until it was absolutely right; to Margaret for reading large chunks and being so amazed that I could dream of leaving out Shelley; to Roz and Katy for being really interested in progress.

These days it isn't enough to thank just those people who you know have helped with your research; indeed, it doesn't even feel adequate to thank only human beings. I'm referring (for those who don't sense the same kind of debt) to my faithful friend PET, the Pentium named after my original 1985 Commodore PET, who has sat patiently with me through my darkest – and most triumphant – hours. Technology-by-wire has eased tremendously the compilation of a reference project such as this, and I would like to thank all the invisible people who compiled the online library catalogues and article databases which have made my task so much lighter than it would have been just a few short years ago. Special thanks to MELVYL for being so truly user-friendly even from eight thousand miles away, and to Compuserve's Magazine Database Plus for being so comprehensive.

Last but not least, my thanks to Steve Cook of Cassell for having had the courage and foresight to commission *The Radicalism Handbook*, and to Jane Greenwood for her work with Steve to see the project to completion and always be excited by it. I wish I could say the same of all editors!

CRITERIA FOR INCLUSION

When I started to think about this book I was fairly clear about what I meant by radical. I discuss this at more length in the introductory essay, but I quickly arrived at a working definition which equated 'radical' with 'going to the roots of an issue, examining it thoroughly, questioning everything, and leaving no stone unturned in the quest for respect and justice.'

The next step was to decide which areas of radical endeavour would be covered by *The Radicalism Handbook*, and after a short period of brainstorming I and my researchers came up with the following. We would look at people and groups who had worked or who were working in these areas:

◆ arts and empowerment
◆ civil and human rights
◆ environmental campaigning with a political and social dimension
◆ gay and lesbian rights
◆ labour movements (especially where these have a wider social element)
◆ liberation theology
◆ nonviolent struggle for self-determination
◆ the peace movement
◆ the peaceful anarchist movement
◆ radical education
◆ radical therapy
◆ radical economics
◆ women's rights, including suffrage and equal rights campaigners

We knew (because we had already compiled a draft list containing nearly five hundred individuals and two hundred organisations – many more than we had space for) that we would have to become clearer about our criteria for including people in the 'Biographies' section. Another brainstorming session led to this list:

◆ We would favour people who have been doers as well as thinkers, active in the world at large and not just academic theorists;
◆ We would favour people who have worked all or most of their lives for the radical cause, rather than those who have gained short-lived fame for one action, book or event;
◆ We would favour those who have chosen nonviolent means of protest

over violent ones, though we would recognise the difference between violence against other living things and symbolic destruction
of property, and we would take into account the perceived limits of
nonviolence when human rights are under dire threat;

◆ We would favour people who have become known beyond their own
country or region for what they are doing;

◆ We would favour people whose beliefs and campaigning are not limited to their one area of concern, and who have an integrated radical
worldview;

◆ We would favour people who have provided a real inspiration for
others.

In addition, we felt that it was important from the outset to do what
we could to redress the pro-male and pro-Western bias of the majority
of reference books. In both the 'Biographies' and the 'Groups and
Movements' section, therefore, we attempted to include a representative sample of both male and female endeavour, third world and
first world, north and south, east and west.

In terms of gender balance we have ended up with 58% of the entries
in the 'Biographies' section being men and 42% women; still not an
accurate reflection of the 49%:51% proportion in the world as a whole
but not bad, we feel, given the overwhelming androcentricity of the
century.

When it came to geographical distribution, we knew from the start
that we had an almost intractable problem when it came to the USA.
We discovered that, if you ask historians and social scientists to list the
dozen most influentials radicals of the twentieth century, their list will
almost certainly (especially if they are American themselves) include a
majority of Americans. Thus one of the early decisions we made about
the balance of entries in *The Radicalism Handbook* was to limit the
proportion of US entries in the 'Biographies' section to no more than a
quarter of the total.

It is true that the USA has been the main breeding ground for many
of the radical causes which have gone on to change the whole world,
from women's suffrage and equal rights to labour organisation and
environmental activism. There is a lurking danger, however, that the
primacy of the USA in forming world opinion can be overstated, even
in an area as seemingly beneficial (to fellow radicals!) as pioneering
radicalism.

One reason for limiting the US entries is, therefore, to highlight
radical voices from the rest of the world, and to show Americans how
many of the radical trends in their own history are reflected in other
parts of the world. A second reason (or perhaps justification) for the
decision is that the history of US radicalism is better documented than

that of any other country. It is therefore much easier, especially for readers living in the USA, to find out about the events and characters of their country's radical past than it is for, say, Russians, Chinese, Indians or Latin Americans. What other country would in recent years have produced a weighty volume like Darlene Clark Hine's *Black Women in America: An Historical Encyclopedia* (Carlson, 1993), or Buhle and Georgakas' 900-page *Encyclopedia of the American Left* (Garland, 1990), or Gayle Hardy's *American Women Civil Rights Activists* (McFarland, 1993), or Wayne Dynes' two-volume *Encyclopedia of Homosexuality* (Garland, 1990)?

It is for these reasons you will find just over ninety US names among the 360 radicals featured in the 'Biographies' section. Inevitably this early editorial decision means that there is a long list of radical Americans who do not feature here (though many receive mentions under other entries). Among those we considered were Louisa May Alcott, Nelson Algren, Oscar Ameringer, Maya Angelou, Virginia Apuzzo, Herbert Aptheker, Ti-Grace Atkinson, Emily Greene Balch, James Baldwin, Ruth Benedict, Elizabeth Blackwell, Harriot Stanton Blatch, Kenneth and Elise Boulding, Randolph Bourne, Anne and Carl Braden, David Brower, Lester Brown, Carlos Bulosan, César Chávez, Voltairine de Cleyre, Clarence Darrow, John Dewey, John Dos Passos, Bob Dylan, Marian Wright Edelman, William Z. Foster, John Kenneth Galbraith, William Lloyd Garrison, Eugene Genovese, Carol Gilligan, Woody Guthrie, William ('Big Bill') Haywood, Ammon Hennacy, Aileen Clarke Hernandez, Joe Hill, Langston Hughes, Jesse Jackson, Jane Jacobs, Helen Keller, Abby Kelley, Coretta Scott King, Robert M. La Follette, Fiorello La Guardia, Meridel Le Sueur, Denise Levertov, Jack London, Amory Lovins, Staughton Lynd, Vito Marcantonio, José Martí, Margaret Mead, Bob Moses, Lucretia Mott, John Muir, Ralph Nader, Diane Nash, Clifford Odets, Tillie Olsen, Pat Parker, Rosa Parks, Leonard Peltier, A. Philip Randolph, Walter Reuther, Elizabeth Robins, Eleanor Roosevelt, Muriel Rukeyser, Kathie Sarachild, Sarah Schulman, Barbara Smith, I. F. Stone, Lucy Stone, Anna Louise Strong, Norman Thomas, Carlo Tresca, Mary Heaton Vorse, Ida B. Wells, Claude Williams, William Appleman Williams, Richard Wright and Howard Zinn.

All these people are or were tremendously important in their particular field, and have provided stimulation and motivation to those fortunate enough to know of them. But *The Radicalism Handbook* is more than a reference guide to US radicalism with the rest of the world added for balance. If in making this decision we have omitted some of those people who have particularly inspired you we apologise. So that readers of the *Handbook* can find out more about the people listed above, Appendix C provides a brief listing giving dates, area of involvement, and sources for further information. We will be more than happy to reconsider our policy for future editions, and hope that you can judge the *Handbook* by the ninety Americans included rather than the eighty and more we have reluctantly relegated to an appendix.

On a smaller scale the same policy applies to Western Europe, where we decided to limit British biographical entries to 15% of the whole, and Western European entries (including Britain) to one third. What we hope this has done is left space for radical voices from Russia, China, Japan, Australia, New Zealand, South-East Asia, India, the Middle East, Africa and Latin America to have a much-needed impact on the history of radical activism in the twentieth century.

How the Handbook is Set Out

We have tried to make *The Radicalism Handbook* as easy to use as possible, and there is no reason why a reader should not simply be able to dip into it and find something of interest. We have, however, used a consistent system of indexing, cross-referencing, appendices and bibliographical styles to make things even easier, and it may well be worth taking a few minutes to read this section.

The Main Sections

Following the introductory essay, 'Radicalism in the Twentieth Century', *The Radicalism Handbook* is divided into two main sections: 'Biographies' and 'Groups and Movements'.

The 'Biographies' section is again divided. First is a subsection headed 'Radical Forerunners': this arose from the fact that although the *Handbook*'s focus is the present century, much of the inspiration for modern radicalism came from the lives and writings of earlier pioneers. Here you will find the biographies of 38 people crucial to twentieth century radicalism even though they were dead (or in one or two cases had completed most of their life's work) before 1900.

The 'Groups and Movements' section (which sounds as though it should be related to psychotherapy or the creative arts) is a mixed bag of organisations, cultural and political movements, events and campaigns which have had a marked impact on the development of radical ideas and tactics. We tried, but failed, to find a more elegant name for this section.

Where to Look for What

Because no book like this can be comprehensive, we have done our best to be truly representative and to write each entry within the context of the broad sweep of twentieth century radicalism. Thus one individual or organisation has to represent many others within the same field or country, and a single entry often covers an enormous amount of history.

Thus, for instance, you will find the entire history of modern Haiti telescoped within the entry for Jean-Bertrand Aristide, the vitally important US Catholic Workers Movement enveloped within the entry for Dorothy Day, and many thousands of courageous Czech and Slovak civil rights campaigners subsumed in the entry for Charter 77.

As well as looking in the main alphabetical sequence, therefore, if you know what area you are interested in it is well worth checking the geographical and topical categories in Appendices A and B, and the general index at the end of the book should help you find more obscure references.

ALPHABETICAL ORDER

Not much to say here, except that following the standard conventions the names of Japanese, Chinese, Tibetan, Vietnamese and Burmese radicals included in the *Handbook* appear with their family name first and given name last. Where you might expect to find an entry under another name, like the Dalai Lama (whose personal name is Tenzin Gyatso), you will find them by looking in the general index.

NAMES AND FULL NAMES

The name that people are commonly known by is often not the same as their full given name (the name they were given at birth or when they were renamed at a childhood naming ceremony). In the *Handbook* we give both the most common form of each name (the part which appears outside of any square brackets), and the full given name. The names inside the square brackets are usually additional forenames or women's family names before they were married, but they are occasionally additional names acquired through marriage or personal choice. Thus the entry for **Charlotte Perkins [Stetson] Gilman [Charlotte Anna Perkins]** (one of the most complex) indicates that she was born Charlotte Anna Perkins and first married someone called Stetson, thus becoming Charlotte Perkins Stetson, but then acquired the name Gilman from her second husband, giving her the name – Charlotte Perkins Gilman – by which she is most commonly known.

SPELLING

The transliteration of names from scripts other than those based on the Roman alphabet is fraught with problems. The conventions we have sought to use are as follows. With Chinese we have used the Pinyin system of transliteration for modern Chinese entries (roughly from Mao Zedong onwards), though where most historical sources predate the use of Pinyin transliteration (as with the entry for Sun Yat-Sen for example) we have used the earlier Wade-Giles system. With Japanese we have used the forms as transliterated into English by the *Kodansha Encyclopedia of Japan* (1983). With Cyrillic (Russian) we have followed the slightly amended British Standard transliteration system used and explained in *The Soviet Union: A Biographical Dictionary* (edited by Archie Brown, Weidenfeld and Nicholson, 1990). For names transliterated from other non-Roman languages we have followed most common usage.

British spelling has been used throughout in preference to American (except for book titles and names of organisations), for the simple reason that I am British and the *Handbook* was compiled in rural England.

CROSS-REFERENCES

It is useful and interesting to be able to trace names and affiliations from one entry to another, and to make this possible cross-references from one entry to another are highlighted in **bold type**.

BOOK TITLES

Where we mention the titles of books that people have written we include the date of first publication. If the book was written in French, German or Spanish (and occasionally in other languages too) we have wherever possible given the original title. If there is a translation into English we also give the English title (unless it is obvious) and the year it first appeared in English translation.

SHORT BIBLIOGRAPHIES

The entries in the *Handbook* may well inspire you to want to know more about people, events and movements, and at the end of almost every entry is a short bibliography to assist you in delving deeper. Each bibliography follows the same pattern. First we list, in order of publication, important books by the subject of the entry. Then we list, again by date, useful books about that person.

Each entry in the bibliographies gives author or editor, translator where appropriate, full title, publisher and date of first publication. Where the book was published simultaneously in more than one country (usually Britain and the USA) we usually list the publisher in the country where the author was living and working, though the recent trend towards simultaneous publication means that you may well find that other publishers have issued their own editions of the same title. Where books have been in print for many years and reprinted in numerous editions, we have included the year of first publication and noted that many editions have appeared since then.

APPENDICES AND INDEX

The three appendices at the end of the book are self-explanatory. Appendix A lists the biographical entries by country of birth and activity (the symbols are explained at the beginning of the appendix). Appendix B lists the biographical entries by field of interest and involvement. Appendix C provides a brief listing of a further eighty-odd US radicals, with their dates, field of activity, and suggestions for further reading: for the rationale behind Appendix C see pages xiv-xvi.

Finally, the index should help you find people and subjects not cross-referenced elsewhere. As it explains at the beginning of the index, a reference to a main entry for a person, group or movement is highlighted in bold numerals.

ACCURACY AND FEEDBACK

We have tried very hard to ensure that the information in *The Radicalism Handbook* is accurate. As well as checking and cross-checking with a wide range of reference sources, we have been fortunate to have the input of the many experts listed in the acknowledgements section.

We made an early decision to send (where we could find addresses) draft entries to those entrants who are still alive, asking them for comments and feedback. Of the 136 still alive we wrote to 106 and received 68 replies, which is, we feel, a pretty good response rate for such busy people. A number of other entries were checked by entrants' personal friends and colleagues. Thank you to those who took the time and effort to reply, thus ensuring that the majority of the entries for people who are still alive have been thoroughly checked for accuracy.

In the course of our research we discovered (as I am sure many researchers have discovered to their delight) that even the best reference books sometimes get things wrong. Most encyclopedias have Rebecca West born in rural Ireland (and a few in Edinburgh), when she was in fact born in Notting Hill, near London's Paddington Station. The excellent *Encyclopedia of the American Left* gives Noam Chomsky the wrong birthdate. We are all human. We have no doubt that the *Handbook* also contains unintentional mistakes of fact and errors of judgement, and if you find something which is not the truth, or not the whole truth, we invite you to write to us care of the publishers, whose address appears on the reverse of the title page.

RADICALISM IN THE TWENTIETH CENTURY

What *really* matters? It is a deceptively simple question, but one which provides a highly productive starting point for this exploration of twentieth-century radicalism. The impetus for asking the question comes from a variety of contemporary concerns.

First there is growing clarity that, whatever its advantages to those who benefit from it, capitalism and the market economy are relentlessly widening the resource gap between the haves and the have-nots of our world. Whether within a single small town, a region, or the planet as a whole, the overwhelming evidence is that the haves are growing richer at the expense of the have-nots, and that this process is accelerating. Whatever religious or ethical stance we choose to take, such growing inequality is difficult to justify, and makes it hard for even the most committed supporter of economic trickle-down theory to sound convincing.

Coupled with this is an increasing realisation that many of those who are supposed to be benefiting from capitalism and enjoying the fulfilment of their material requirements are nevertheless lacking when it comes to their mental, emotional, social, inspirational and spiritual needs. In an absorbing 1994 survey of the consumer society, *The Costs of Living*, psychology professor Barry Schwarz describes a worrying reunion with one of his highflying former students: Allen, a lawyer, has realised ten years into his all-too-successful career that he 'mostly just helped rich people get richer', while his equally successful wife Nancy works hard in marketing 'to get people to want things they don't need and can't quite afford.' And these are the 'success stories' of our generation. For many, told that they do not have the skills required to earn a living in the modern world, capitalism has failed to fulfil their most basic needs for both substance and purpose. Before the twentieth century such alienation and purposelessness was rare; today, especially among young people, it is all too common.

A third linked concern is the rapid ascendancy, throughout most of the world, of money as the only valid measure of value. This is another uniquely twentieth-century phenomenon. Although the use of money long predates the present century, a hundred years ago the measurement of wealth in terms only of money was still a minority, élitist concern in most parts of the world. How different it is now, when there is hardly a community or individual for whom money does not hold the power to give life and to destroy it. When money can seemingly buy anything, and lack of money denies the most basic needs, it can easily appear that what matters more than anything else is having enough of it.

As the world's haves have extended their grip on the planet's resources, they have also seen fit to protect 'their interests'. The first half of the century was marked by outward shows of industrial and military prowess; in recent decades overt social and military control has been increasingly replaced with commercial and political tactics which, while less obvious, are equally effective in disempowering the satisfyingly silent majority.

Underlying the trend towards centralised control and massive disempowerment are the same élitist beliefs that have always oppressed those groups of people seen by the power establishment as inferior: women, nonwhites, children, gays and lesbians, the old, the poor, the disabled. Sexism, racism and all the other entwined and overlapping oppressions are still at the core of inequality and injustice in our world, but at least they have now all been named and challenged. Shown to be the result of bigotry and imposed injustice rather than justifiable by the cold reason of science, oppression is today widely accepted as a fact rather than as a partisan perspective.

Many of the certainties of a century ago have been shattered. The great pillars of late nineteenth-century establishment thinking – progress, civilisation, free trade, blind faith in science – are either toppling or have already crumbled into dust. The supremacy of these concepts, virtually unquestioned a century ago, has been rocked by a century of unimagined horror: blind capitalism, fascism, failed communism, two world wars, the gas chambers and countless other acts of genocide, widespread alienation and disempowerment.

Maybe human beings were never very tolerant of new and strange ideas threatening their own certainties. What the late twentieth century has uniquely provided, however, is a potent and potentially lethal combination of blinkered fundamentalism and massively destructive technology. Pressure on land and increasingly scarce natural resources add to the less tangible threats from strange religions and ideologies, and the chief casualties are compassion, understanding and tolerance.

Of course it is not all doom and gloom. The entries in *The Radicalism Handbook* record numerous successes in the struggle for dignity, freedom and self-reliance. As we shall see, at the heart of radicalism lies the belief that realising human beings' creative potential is both possible and achievable. If we didn't think there was a better way to be, if we weren't at least slightly optimistic at least some of the time about the potential for positive change, why would we continue to make the effort?

At the end of the twentieth century, opinions which offer any semblance of certainty about what *really* matters are more divided than ever before. For better or for worse, confusion and chaos appear to be the only common ground. Despite a century of unprecedented economic, political and material change, we appear to have made remarkably little headway towards providing the rich variety of humankind with any semblance of the freedom, equality and compassion promised by bright-eyed eighteenth-century revolutionaries, not to mention the humility and generosity modelled by the buddha and the christchild.

Have we then forgotten what *really* matters?

REFUSING TO BE LIMITED

A ny surveyor of the British political scene in the early 90s will have been amused and perturbed by the hypocrisy of the ruling party's 'back to basics' campaign. When pressed to enumerate which specific basics the British public were to be encouraged to get back to, government ministers listed such principles as honesty, decency, religious principles and family values – easy to say; much harder, as many of those same politicians discovered to their cost, to abide by.

The confusion which followed such 'back to basic' pronouncements, leading eventually to the campaign being quietly dropped, is hardly surprising. It seems blindingly obvious that the promise to encourage 'back to basics' thinking was doomed precisely because of the unwillingness of those in power to question the assumptions implicit in their pronouncements. How can we demand honesty without defining whose truth counts for most? Who can define decency without addressing prejudice, fear, and the weight of conformity? As for religion and the family, who will stop to disentangle the complex strands of fulfilment and dysfunction provided by these pillars of the establishment?

The assumptions underlying 'back to basics' are not hard to pin down. They are, after all, the same assumptions that have kept people 'in their proper place' ever since one group of humans first contrived to control the everyday lives of another. We might usefully call them 'first magnitude' assumptions, since so much else follows from their acceptance or rejection. Every one of the first magnitude assumptions results, more or less consciously, from an answer to an important question.

Some of these important questions have to do with the nature of human nature. Are some people born evil, some geniuses, some gay? Are men naturally more violent than women, and women naturally more caring than men? Are two parents better than one at providing children with what they need? Will people always want more material fulfilment if it is offered to them? Other assumptions have to do with the nature of belief. Is there an external guiding principle affecting our lives? Is there a clear distinction between right and wrong?

Others have to do with our responsibilities as citizens. Do we have a duty to help our family, friends and neighbours? Should we be expected to teach our children what we think they ought to know? Can we safely ignore most of the implications of our actions on people beyond our own community? Do we have a duty to protect our own land, possessions and interests? Yet others arise from technological and economic structures which, though less than a century old, have apparently become vital to our wellbeing. Do people have a right to drive their cars wherever they choose? Should the coin of the realm be the only valid currency? Should people be made to pay their taxes?

Whatever we might think as individuals, it is clear that the vast majority of policy-makers and opinion-formers would answer 'yes' to each of these questions, building an impressive edifice of assumption that is hard to gainsay. If we choose to, as many people do, we can meekly accept all these received assumptions as the firm bedrock on which 'back to basics' can be firmly anchored. After all, agreeing with mainstream wisdom has many rewards.

But what if these big questions had different answers which were every bit as valid as the 'received wisdom'? What if our culture's 'first magnitude' assumptions proved to be based on little more than decisions made a long time ago by a few powerful decision-makers whose primary interest was holding on to their power, and who had stopped listening to those who believed that other answers were possible?

The first response of decision-makers to such suggestions – should they deign to proffer any response at all – has usually been that they are the experts, that they have a popular mandate to make decisions on our behalf, that they are enforcing standards agreed upon by society at large, that they are doing what they are employed to do. So few people question their authority that it is easy to see why their answers to the big questions become accepted as *the* answers, their opinions the standard opinions, their view of the way the world works the official view.

In this way a uniform mainstream of assumption, decision and implementation arises. The term 'mainstream' is telling, for such massive uniformity acts like the current in a wide river, sweeping aside the flotsam of criticism and dissent, leaving it to rot on the banks while the vast bulk of water sweeps irrevocably onwards.

There is, however, a strong and continuous tradition of opposition to the assumptions of 'official' culture. Not only has the alternative, questioning tradition been with us a very long time, it has grown in strength, breadth and volume as the 'mainstream' has extended its influence into virtually every aspect of human life and choice. As we shall see, it is convenient for the mainstream culture to label (and thus attempt to diminish) its opposition as disaffected, stupid, inarticulate, divided, hopelessly idealistic, naïve and misinformed. Yet whatever historians decide, and whatever that opposition itself might feel about its own effectiveness, the tradition which opposes official culture has undeniably grown and flourished throughout the last hundred years, built firmly on the foundations of its antecedents and creating a web, a network, an underground mass of interconnecting roots which continues to resist every weedkiller yet invented.

WHO DEFINES US?

'Radicalism' is a hard word, one to which the Humpty Dumpties among us can have great fun giving whatever meaning we want. But it isn't really that hard to grasp, and the analogy of a mass of roots, striving for life and light and refusing to succumb to poison, is an apt one, especially when we recognise that the word 'radical' comes from *radix*, the Latin word for root. Another inspiring root analogy comes from the conclusion of Charles Reich's 1970 bestseller *The Greening of America*, where he likens the unstoppable force of those who want a better and fairer world to the weeds in a concrete pavement. Though the whole land surface has been covered with a mass of uniform greyness to keep it ordered and tidy, the plants will always find the smallest cracks and send out their green tendrils and bright blossoms, and with time the underground roots will expand and break up the bleak uniformity of the tamed landscape.

As long ago as the 1850s, when American feminist Lucy Stone insisted on keeping her own name because 'my name is the symbol of my identity and must not be lost', it was clear to a few freethinkers that those who took upon themselves the power to bestow names and meanings were thus able to control the masses. It took a long time for this realisation to permeate the radical movement. The doublethink of **George Orwell's** *Nineteen Eighty-Four*, in which democracy is impossible yet the Party is the guardian of democracy, gave a hint of the growing recognition of the power of naming, but it was in the 1970s, when the 'politics of naming' became a more widely understood phenomenon, that the stranglehold of oppressive convention was beheld in its full glory. In 1973 **Mary Daly's** *Beyond God the Father* explained how women 'have had the power of naming stolen from us,' and how the evolving consciousness of women is 'a reclaiming of the right to name'.

Suddenly, it seemed, it became blindingly clear that every attempt by the radical movement to define its own terms had been deliberately – and very successfully – subverted by the reactionary mainstream. Just as Roosevelt had succeeded in reviling 'anarchism' and Churchill 'pacifism', so Joseph McCarthy had turned 'communism' into a term of abuse and loathing – at least among 'rightminded' citizens. It might be gratifying to have others agree with the radical worldview and the names used by the radical movement, but what Mary Daly and others were now saying was that we don't have to be an expert, or one of the power élite, to name things and thus give them meaning and life. And we certainly don't need the agreement of those same experts and powerbrokers about the meanings of those words that hold particular power and meaning.

Thus we have arrived at the end of the twentieth century with two opposed meanings for many of the words that those in the radical movement hold most dear. One meaning belongs to traditional reactionary conservatism, the other to those who see the mess the world is in, want to make it better, and dare to question the status quo. Thus 'anarchism' can mean 'lawlessness, violence and fear' or it can mean 'freedom, choice and harmony'. 'Socialism' can mean 'dogmatism, disrespect and coercion' or it can mean 'equality, sharing and responsibility'. 'Peace' can mean 'deterrence, defence and security' or it can mean 'ease, serenity and interdependence'.

'Radicalism' is no exception, and when we go to the reference shelves to discover its meaning we find that it too has a double life. Thus the *Oxford English Dictionary* gives us, as a political definition of 'radical', 'an advocate of any thorough political or social change; one who belongs to the extreme section of a political party; a member or supporter of a radical movement; a left-winger or revolutionary.' The extremist theme is repeated in the widely respected *Fontana Dictionary of Modern Thought*, which starts its entry for 'radicalism' with 'A tendency to press political views and actions towards an extreme,' and in the widely used American *Grolier Encyclopedia*, which explains that 'Radicalism is a political stance advocating fundamental changes in the existing political, economic, and social order,' and that 'its driving purpose is to force, by whatever means necessary, the status quo to conform to those principles.'

Such definitions serve to underline the official view of radicalism as threat, and since this is how the mainstream will tend to portray challenges to its authority it is hardly surprising that 'official' definitions of radicalism stress its more subversive characteristics. Yet the reinstatement of radicalism onto the political agenda in the 1960s has left its mark, with much more thoughtful definitions also now being offered. Thus **Raymond Williams** suggests in his examination of the concept of radicalism in *Keywords*, it offers 'a way of avoiding dogmatic and factional associations while reasserting the need for vigorous and fundamental change.' Similarly David Robertson's *Penguin Dictionary of Politics* defines a radical as 'anyone who advocates far reaching and fundamental change in a political system. Literally, a radical is one who proposes to attack some political or social problem by going deep into the socio-economic fabric to get at the fundamental or root cause and alter this basic social weakness. As such it can be contrasted with a more "symptomatic" policy cure.'

The twin-track issue of definition depends a great deal on the conventional historical distinction between 'left' and 'right'. A passage from the 'radicalism' entry of the *Grolier Encyclopedia* illustrates the dilemma of many contemporary 'authoritative' sources: 'Although traditionally radicalism has been primarily a movement of the left,' it explains, 'the passionate appeals of the left produced various forms of radicalism of the right. Thus, while the doctrines of the radical left were based on notions of equality, the radicalism of the right espoused élitism. Nazism acclaimed the superiority of the German nation and the so-called Aryan race; fascism was a rightist reaction to the fears of Marxist communism; in the United States radicalism of the right expressed itself particularly through the resurgent Ku Klux Klan of the 1920s and the McCarthyism of the cold-war era.'

What we have here is a misleading attempt to equate two utterly incompatible ideals, and the *Grolier* contributor's contrast between equality and élitism should immediately alert us to the source of the incompatibility. By about mid-century the establishment had so convinced itself of the synonymity of 'radical' and 'extreme' that it came to believe that any form of extremism or fundamentalism could safely be termed 'radical'. Never mind that eminent social scientists like Gunnar Myrdal (in his 1944 *American Dilemmas*) had carefully explained that 'The place of the individual scientist in the scale of radicalism-conservatism has always had strong influences upon both the selection of research problems and the conclusions drawn from research. In a sense it is the master scale of biases in the social sciences.' In popular political usage the so-called 'radical right' rapidly became a potent source of reactionary dogma and cultural inertia, and so it remains today, with everything from neocapitalist dictatorships to gunrunning cartels loosely referred to as 'radical'.

I am sure it will come as no surprise when I emphasise that *The Radicalism Handbook* does not subscribe to this catch-all extremist version of 'radicalism', and you can probably imagine our response to those who asked whether we planned to include radicals like Margaret Thatcher, Saddam Hussein and Pol Pot. Neither do we believe that the parallel existence of widely divergent meanings means that, as in Looking Glass Land, 'radicalism' can mean absolutely anything to absolutely anybody. Within the truly radical tradition there has been remarkably little divergence about the meaning of 'radicalism' in anything but the most trivial sense. It is true that in the past twenty years the word 'radical' appears to have lost much of its bite (and presumably some of its threat), so that in many contemporary instances it means little more than 'different', 'great' or 'risqué'. The same has not yet happened to its cognate 'radicalism', however, and if we reclaim it soon enough we can perhaps help it to avoid the fate of other important ideas like 'development', 'welfare' and 'care'.

There are several compelling reasons for rescuing, reinstating and re-empowering the ideas and traditions underlying 'radical' and 'radicalism'. The first reason is that, for the reasons outlined at the beginning of this essay, we desperately need a word that implies and connotes what 'radical' does, and since we already have such a word, with a long history and a minimum of the political and emotional charge applied to related concepts like 'socialism', 'communism' and 'anarchy', it deserves a new lease of life.

Secondly, as we have seen, the classical derivation of the word 'radical' provides an immensely fruitful metaphor for the complex, tangled, invisible, life-critical network that is the radical movement. As the novelist and poet **Marge Piercy** writes in her poem 'The Seven of Pentacles':

Connections are made slowly, sometimes they grow underground.
You cannot tell always by looking what is happening.
More than half a tree is spread out in the soil under your feet.

Thirdly, 'radical' is a word already in the public domain, a word which, unlike more recent and potentially partisan coinings such as 'green' or 'ecofeminism' or 'new age', can be moulded and interpreted by anyone who resonates with its promises and challenges. Age has given the word generality, variety and breadth, providing a starting point for many productive debates between people embracing different hues of radicalism. Since most radicals would agree that nobody can lay exclusive claim to important ideas, each practitioner's perspective on the concept of radicalism must involve both personal engagement and shared insight; radicalism does not belong to anyone, yet can provide hope for us all.

POWER, CONTROL AND AUTHORITY

On April 3rd 1887 the British peer John Acton wrote a letter to his friend Bishop Mandell Creighton which contained the memorable words 'Power tends to corrupt, and absolute power corrupts absolutely. Great men are almost always bad men.' As professor of modern history at Cambridge and editor of the *Cambridge Modern History* he had plenty of evidence to support his contention. Yet those in power, blinkered by their singlemindedness and seeking rewards primarily in the short term before they are voted out or deposed, almost always forget this unfortunate tendency.

As soon as we speak of power, it is important to recognise that the word 'power' covers a number of overlapping ideas. Most politicians and dictionaries associate 'power' with 'the ability to exact compliance', but radical thinkers from **Rousseau** onwards have questioned this connection. 'The strongest man is never strong enough to be always master unless he transforms his power into right and obedience into duty,' he wrote in the third chapter of *The Social Contract*, establishing the distinction between force and authority.

With the more careful thinking resulting from a century of examining the nature of political power, there is a general consensus that the word 'power' covers at least three linked but quite distinct types of human interaction. First, 'power' is used to describe inner strength and courage, the 'power-within' that taps into innate intelligence and reminds people of what is important to them. Then there is 'power' used in the mainstream political-military sense of 'control' – 'power-over', with all its connotations of property, exclusion, coercion, oppression, armour, rigidity and invulnerability. The third type of power is solidarity, 'power-with', the influence and effort that people can exert when working together in a common cause.

It could be argued that I have missed out the most commonly-accepted sense of the word 'power' (at least in the more comfortable Western 'democracies'), where it is assumed that 'power' is something delegated to elected representatives and their appointees to exert 'on our behalf'. The word is certainly widely used to describe such 'powers' – 'police powers', 'local government powers', 'legal powers' – but this is to blur an important distinction between voluntary delegation, involving consent and full accountability ('power-with'), and any form of authority which takes decision-making away from people and communities without their active agreement and participation ('power-over').

It is convenient to believe that elected, centralised, officially-endorsed authority, 'for the public good', is the most advanced form of human organisation, but it must always be remembered that those who define the rightness and usefulness of mainstream power structures will tend to be those whose ideas and identities depend upon those definitions. Western thinking about the nature of power is permeated by a conviction of the stability of the commentators' own systems, in which power is usually comfortably contained by authority. The apparent stability of a political system, however, does not necessarily validate it, especially when that system contrives, however subtly, to suppress alternative systems. When there is a clear rift between authority and power, especially if it is in a nasty little foreign dictatorship, it is easy to recognise that the two are not synonymous – but the same rift runs through all power relationships from the personal to the planetary. Radicals need constantly to ask who it is that takes the decisions on a particular issue, and whose wishes prevail when conflicts of interest arise.

Oppressive imbalance of political power almost always goes hand in hand with imbalance of economic power, and together they amount to abuse of privilege. In its unadulterated form, 'privilege', from its Latin legal origins, implies the guaranteeing of individual rights and freedoms, and is directly related to the link between basic needs and human rights. In the modern world, however, it is used to describe those who have, or have been given, more than most.

Those who are privileged tend to assume that the problem is the underprivileged, and that the problem will be solved when 'they' are more like 'us'. As many radicals have pointed out, however, this is a distortion. **Paulo Freire** wrote in *The Pedagogy of the Oppressed* in 1970 that 'The oppressors do not perceive their monopoly of having more as a privilege which dehumanises others and themselves,' making it clear that when it comes to inequality the primary problem is overprivilege. Yet as long as privilege appears to provide the overprivileged with what they want, with very few disadvantages, an ever-widening gap between overprivilege and underprivilege appears to be inevitable.

As long as the radical analysis of privilege was rooted in Marxist economic principles there was no real solution to such gross inequality other than revolution from below. Freire and other liberationists, however, were convinced that privilege dehumanises both under- *and* overprivileged, a theme echoed by many feminists and humanistic psychotherapists. As feminist writer and academic Marilyn Frye explains in her 1983 book *The Politics of Reality*, if you are the norm you don't have to think about what you are, whereas if you are marginal you don't have that apparent privilege. However, she goes on to point out that 'This absence of privilege is a presence of knowledge. As such, it can be a great resource.'

If abuse of power and privilege is at the heart of what radicalism works to overcome, what is it that radicalism stands and works *for*? In a word, it stands for empowerment – daring to take matters into our own hands and acting to alleviate the causes of unnecessary suffering. Those concerned with radical change, whatever channel or form they use to work through, do their best to provide the mutual understanding, respect, acknowledgement and practical support which will enable themselves and others to take control of their lives and to be effective in the world. This we are doing in the face of chronic and widespread disempowerment – 'the gravest single illness of our time' as social ecologist **Murray Bookchin** has described it in his 1986 book *The Modern Crisis*. Disempowerment takes many forms, from the absolute disempowerment of the 'wretched of the earth' to the materially comfortable disempowerment of the silent majority in the rich world. It even extends to many of the very wealthy, who, lacking basic life skills and real purpose, experience some of the worst cases of existential angst.

One of the necessary preconditions of disempowerment is the presence of an oppressor or oppressor group, manipulating the political and economic system to maintain their control and asserting the rightness of their worldview. It follows that if empowerment is our aim, we need to do everything we can, both directly and subversively, to stop oppressors oppressing. Alongside this, however, is another vital concern, which is to support those who are oppressed as they learn to appreciate their own power and, as a result, refuse to be oppressed. You might argue that it isn't anything like as easy as that. When you have no resources at all and the threat of a bullet in your head if you move an inch out of line, refusing to be oppressed changes nothing. But most disempowerment is not so stark. Most disempowerment takes the form of a dimly perceived sense that an ordinary, solitary person can have no influence at all over the forces and events shaping their future, that whatever they do it will make no difference whatsoever.

Many millions of the better-off in the world have reached a level of affluence where the majority of their physical needs are being met reasonably comfortably, and where life support systems – food, energy, shelter, transport – for the most part deliver an adequate standard of service. Yet when it comes to active participation in the political and cultural life of the community, the majority appear to be gripped by apathy and inertia. Most people don't bother to attend local events, they don't get together to organise things with their neighbours, they certainly don't bother to vote in local elections. Why? Because it's all too much trouble, and because 'they' can organise things much better than 'we' can. A friend of mine, a district councillor, told me recently how a neighbour, pointing to a pile of soil left by council employees after clearing a drain, declared crossly that 'they' should clear up after themselves. My friend pointed out that his neighbour could use some freshly-dug soil on his roses, went to fetch a spade, and helped both neighbour and garden while they finished their conversation. When the two next met the neighbour still thought that 'they' should have done it.

Disempowerment through inertia is exactly what so-called civilised, democratic governments like best, especially those most intent on maintaining the status quo. It allows them to assert, in the absence of a large-scale and vocal opposition, that they are acting on the behalf of the 'ordinary person in the street'. The 'ordinary person in the street' would never resort to nasty demonstrations or shout at public meetings. Or would they?

In many ways the mainstream economic and political powerbrokers had things much their own way throughout the 1980s. Though there were popular protests about a range of political and environmental issues, coordinated by a growing international network, they tended to be organised and supported by a predominantly middle class, young, educated section of the population. Towards the end of the decade, however, and increasingly as the 1990s progressed, more and more 'ordinary people in the street' felt frustrated enough and informed enough to become actively involved in a range of hands-on campaigns for a more humane, just and caring world.

The main targets of these campaigns have been transnational companies, global organisations like the World Bank and the International Monetary Fund, and the imposed authority of central governments. Whether Indian farmers protesting against the building of destructive dams, Amerindians fighting for their rainforest, Londoners squatting condemned houses to delay the building of urban highways or New Yorkers marching to support women's reproductive rights, a new fearlessness has emerged – a realisation that oppressive centralised power must be resisted and balanced by 'people power'.

And more and more activists are recognising that their concern and their tactics are working. Thanks to the efforts of organisations like **Greenpeace** and **Survival International**, and economists both within and outside the organisation, the World Bank and the IMF have shifted their stance and become more self-questioning. Road protestors in Britain and other countries have forced major rethinks in transport policy and, despite the 'pro-life' backlash in the USA, women's health rights are now a strategic political issue. 'The movement' today is better organised and better informed than ever. It has ample proof that education and persistence do pay, and that although absolute power does indeed tend to corrupt, grassroots power involves, excites, regenerates and enables.

THEORY AND PRACTICE

'It is by their theories far more than by their actions that Western radicals have erected their monument,' writes disenchanted radical Michael Neumann in his 1988 book *What's Left?* 'While their movements, their strategies and enterprises are dead and buried, their thoughts are found all over the earth.' He is writing primarily about the influence and demise of Marxism-Leninism and Maoism, yet it is all too true that abstract theorising has used up a great deal of the energy of a great many twentieth-century radicals. From compulsory readings of **Gramsci** in Communist Party meetings to the endless reworking of Green Party policies, theorising is alive and well.

Why does radical theory carry such weight? Is it because a well-stocked library is the only sure sign of progress towards a brighter future? Is it because radicals are better at thinking than doing? To a large extent the concentration on theory is little more than a reflection of the academic middle class backgrounds and aspirations of those who have chosen the written word as a channel for their message, and in recent decades it has increasingly been the result of the academisation of history and social investigation. With the rapid growth in academic research and publishing, it is not surprising that much of the radical movement's history and rationale is being investigated by professional academics, who tend by their nature and status to be thinkers rather than doers. Since the 1970s several 'schools' of radical social theory have evolved. New Social Movement Theory, the Resource Mobilisation School, New Working Class Theory, the French École de Régulation and others have all developed detailed models of economic and social development to replace increasingly outdated neo-Marxist ideas.

However mangled Marxist thinking became, at its best it resulted in positive action for change, which is a great deal more than can be said for most contemporary radical theory. As Barbara Epstein writes in her survey of political protest in the 1970s and 80s, *Political Protest and Cultural Revolution*, 'The theory has provided some tools for understanding the new movements, but virtually none for advancing movement strategy. It is theory *about* rather than *for*.' It would appear that one reaction to the ascendance of relatively protest-free capitalism during the 1980s was to retreat into social movement theory so as not to become overwhelmed by the apparent demise of radical action.

As with much innovative thinking about radicalism in the 1970s and 80s, some of the best integration of theory and practice came from the women's movement. Here 'theory' and 'practice' became linked in much the same way as the 'political' and the 'personal'. British feminist Gail Chester explained it well in a 1979 essay *I Call Myself a Radical Feminist*: 'Radical feminist theory,' she wrote, 'is that theory follows from practice, and is impossible to develop in the absence of practice.' More and more contemporary radicals are recognising that there is no longer any need for a gulf between theory and practice: we need to think carefully about what we are doing and why, but we know more clearly than ever that theory without practice is moral cowardice and practice without theory doomed to blind fundamentalism.

Theory without practice inevitably leads to untenable conclusions. This is, after all, exactly where the assumptions (the 'theory') of the mainstream political and economic powerbrokers have led us – to an untenable state of affairs which can only be transcended by new assumptions and new ways of living. The inevitable conclusion was summed up by American feminist writer Ti-Grace Atkinson in the introduction to her 1974 *Amazon Odyssey*. 'All that I have said so far is "theory" in the worst sense,' she wrote. 'It assumes concepts as fact, any one of which, if false, would challenge what followed . . . It is one of the many nightmares of feminism that to even conceive of what could count as significant changes for women, one must begin by jumping off one cliff after another.' This is not just the nightmare of feminism: it is the nightmare – and the voyage of discovery – of anyone who is willing and courageous enough to question *everything*.

THE UNITY OF RADICALISM

Perhaps the most universally accepted tenet of the many-faceted contemporary green movement is the ecological principle of inter-dependence. Drawing on insights from fields as varied as quantum physics and traditional Eastern philosophy, meteorology and humanis-tic psychotherapy, a wide range of radical thinkers and activists have homed in on the idea of universal respect and mutuality to underpin the logic of their view of the world.

The act of faith required to convince us that 'everything depends on everything else' is both inspiring and frightening, and the breadth of its implications can as easily numb us into shocked inertia as inspire us to live more responsibly and authentically. The idea that a massacre in a country halfway round the world, or a bank raid in a faraway city, or a famine in a remote part of Africa, can be directly related to choices and actions decided upon by ordinary individuals going about their hum-drum daily lives, can be hard to grasp and harder to accept. Yet the alternative, to say that these things are 'nothing to do with me', is anathema to most radicals. And not just to radicals. Who was it who said, in a much-read passage of one of the world's bestselling books, 'Verily I say unto you, inasmuch as ye have done it unto one of the least of these my brethren ye have done it unto me'?

The principle of universal mutuality – 'everything is connected with everything else' as ecologist Barry Commoner puts it – is perhaps better known to more traditional leftist radicals as 'common cause'. Useful though this principle can undoubtedly be, it is often tempting to take its argument only part of the way. Thus 'everything is connected with everything else' can easily become 'everything is connected with my cause, and that cause must always come first', or 'everything I can understand and accept is connected, but there are things I'm not ready or prepared to look at.'

The potential and the pain of the most radical radicalism lies in its refusal to brush aside the difficult questions, and its insistence on taking its belief in common cause to the limit. This has not always made life easy, especially for those who, rightly and righteously working for liberation in one area, have seen their certainty – and often their popularity – eroded by those calling for parallel and equally important awarenesses and freedoms in another.

At the first annual meeting of the US Equal Rights Association in 1867, for example, all but a handful of the delegates and all the speakers bar one were white and middle class. They cheered loudly, however, when Lucretia Mott introduced ex-slave **Sojourner Truth**, renowned for her début 'Ain't I a woman?' speech at the Akron Women's Rights Convention in 1851. 'My friends,' she started, 'I am rejoiced that you are glad, but I don't know how you will feel when I get through. There is a great stir about colored men getting their rights, but not a word about the colored women: and if colored men get their rights, and not colored women theirs, you see the colored men will be masters over the women, and it will be just as bad as it was before.' She was also convinced that women's rights and black rights were inseparable, and that white women must not ease up until every woman had the same rights. Out of the experience of double oppression she made many of the links between the two, and helped to expose many of the limitations and contradictions of single-issue campaigning.

When black rights resurfaced in the USA as the primary civil rights issue in the late 1950s and 60s, it rapidly became clear that Sojourner Truth's warnings had been ignored by many black male leaders. There were men in the civil rights movement who recognised the importance of the newly emerging women's movement, but there were many more who did not. At the final and faction-torn convention of **Students for a Democratic Society** in June 1969 the women delegates constituted around a quarter of the 1,500 attendance, and a number of groups within the **new left** had prepared tracts on the role of women in the movement. One of the main speakers was Chaka Walls of the Illinois **Black Panthers**. Recalling perhaps his guru Stokely Carmichael's nostrum that 'the only position for women in the movement is prone,' he announced that he was all for having women in the civil rights movement, 'for love and all that – for pussy power.' It is hardly surprising that within a month the famous *Redstockings Manifesto* had appeared. All men, claimed the *Manifesto*, had always oppressed all women.

The realities of multiple oppression and the crying need for common cause seem hard to grasp when there is so much to change on so many fronts, and the blinkers and earplugs of factional self-interest continue to create unnecessary divides in the intrinsic social seamlessness of radicalism. The central Redstockings claim has recently been proven yet again by the more macho spokesmen of the ecoactivist fringe. Though many green-minded men, particularly those who align themselves with the holistic principles of deep ecology, agree with the ecofeminist premise that all exploitation is interlinked, deep ecology sometimes verges on the deeply misogynist – and appears to be proud of it. In the March 1988 issue of the *Utne Reader*, a widely read alternative journal, Edward Abbey, the guru of the **Earth First!** radical green group, publicly criticised social ecologist **Murray Bookchin** for rejecting the truths of deep ecology, writing 'Fat old women like Murray Bookchin have nothing to fear from me.' Throughout most of the 1980s the Earth First! logo was a clenched fist encircled by the motto 'No compromise in defense of Mother Earth', a combination of threat, intolerance and sex stereotyping associated more with Rambo than with raising awareness.

THE WEST AND THE REST

Whenever and wherever there is unwanted and unwarranted control and exploitation of one group of people by another, there will be those of the oppressed who work and fight for freedom. Much of the struggle goes unrecorded, and what records there are are usually those of the oppressive victors who, using the arguments of moral and intellectual superiority, justify their actions in the name of civilisation, progress and order.

With the rapid expansion of European influence throughout the world in the nineteenth century, the assumptions of the European power élite were imposed wherever Western-style administration and trade were introduced. Thus Australasia, India and much of Africa became a series of mini-Britains; north Africa and south-east Asia were reorganised on the French model; much of South America followed Spanish originals; Indonesia became in many respects a Dutch province. Native-born administrators and entrepreneurs who benefited from colonialism quickly adopted the views of their European overlords.

It was not that all of these assumptions and the policies that followed from them were inappropriate or retrogressive. In some areas colonialism brought peace and prosperity to previously wartorn societies, and it can be argued that some of the more humane and sensitive aspects of European culture have been better nurtured in previously colonial societies than they have in Europe. What colonialism did do almost universally, however, was to play down the complex social and political traditions of non-Europeans, and to establish the supremacy of Western concepts and policies.

In many ways this is as true of 'alternative' and 'progressive' thinking as it is of the most reactionary aspects of colonialism, with several important implications for the history of radicalism. The first is that we need to question carefully any tendency to believe that radicalism is a uniquely Western phenomenon, which has only spread to the rest of the world as Western ways have become international cultural currency. There are many non-European precedents for radical ways of looking at and acting in the world.

As far as we can tell from written evidence, the Chinese Taoist writers of the fourth century BC had a wide following for their holistic, anarchist, decentralist philosophies: the Taoist classic, the *Tao Te Ching*, is in many ways a model for practical anarchism and nonviolent direct action. 'A violent man will die a violent death,' it says. 'Nothing is more soft and yielding than water, yet for attacking the solid and strong nothing is better.' The Taoists advocated a free society without government, yet one in which the pursuit of personal goals must involve concern for the wellbeing of others.

There is also a strong libertarian and egalitarian impulse within Buddhism, particularly within its Zen tradition. Human beings are spiritually equal insofar as all are equally capable of attaining enlightenment, and socially equal in both rights and responsibilities: Zen Buddhism in Japan has always rejected that country's caste system. Zen also rejects the idea of private property, seeing it as a barrier to self-understanding and spiritual awareness.

Another recorded outburst of early egalitarianism (for men at least) took place in Persia in the late fifth century, when a pre-Mohammedan prophet called Mazdak preached that all men are born equal but suffer from unequal distribution of wealth and women. His followers, who numbered several thousands between 487 and Mazdak's murder by King Qobbath in 528, proscribed private property and marriage, called for an end to animal slaughter, and urged voluntary poverty and the sharing of resources. Though Mazdak's followers were wiped out in the royal purge, his ideas were revived by later Islamic radicals, most notably the nineteenth-century Ikhwan al-Safa (Brothers of Purity).

Much radical attention is directed towards the failings of impersonal, centralised power structures, and it is usually during periods when such authoritarian structures grow rapidly in significance that radicalism is most needed and most active. For most Westerners, the primary focus of political and economic activity throughout the twentieth century has been national if not international. For the majority of the world's peoples, however, the focus is – as it was throughout Europe and north America two centuries ago – the local community. Until the urban explosion of the last thirty years most non-Westerners' link with the outside world was fully contained within the community. It was here that disputes were settled, economic transactions made, state policies mediated by local representatives.

The decades since most of the world's ex-colonies gained their independence have in many ways been their hardest, partly because traditional economies and infrastructures had been replaced by inappropriate alternatives, partly because any major transition involves stress and uncertainty, but mostly because the rich world, far from leaving the poor world to find its own answers and strategies, used decolonisation as an excuse to push the 'Third World' into ever deeper poverty and dislocation. In the early 1960s the phenomenon of control by other, more devious means, was named 'neocolonialism'. **Kwame Nkrumah** explained this in his 1965 book *Neo-colonialism: The Last Stage of Imperialism*: 'In place of colonialism as the main instrument of imperialism we have today neo-colonialism. The essence of neo-colonialism is that the State which is subject to it is, in theory, independent and has all the outward trappings of international sovereignty. In reality its economic system and thus its political policy is directed from outside.'

By the early 1970s the system was firmly in place, with the rich world milking the poor to sustain its own overconsumption, yet at the same time pleading that all it was trying to do was provide markets, employment and reasonable loan terms. Intelligent Third World observers could see exactly what was happening: 'Must we starve our children to pay our debts?' asked Tanzania's president **Julius Nyerere** in 1975, a *cri de coeur* which was to echo down the years until the late 1980s, when irresponsible lending led to a world banking crisis which only narrowly avoided equalling the 1930s Wall Street crash.

Though the debt crisis has been marginally alleviated in the 1990s, this has often been at the expense of the poorer world's human and environmental health. While the world's richer countries claim to be in the vanguard of progressive welfare and environmental policies, they also continue to make claims on the resources of the poor world which simply cannot be sustained. First World environmentalists and technologists might have useful insights into solutions and technologies appropriate to the world's poor, but the truth is that it is more often the poor that can best teach the rich about sustainable, low-input, human-scale technologies. Many things that Westerners have spent a century forgetting are still part of everyday life in much of Africa, Asia and Latin America.

This insight applies both to material technologies and to human organisation, for one of the crucial things that many Westerners have forgotten – and miss dreadfully – is a sense of community, of belonging in a particular group of people in a particular place. It may be easy to romanticise the social structure of the 'tribe', for tribalism can sometimes set people violently against people. Yet the reality is that, when communities have spent centuries learning the ways of the land and the ways of their neighbours without being exploited by external political, military and economic power, they almost always find satisfying and harmonious ways of ensuring peace and justice.

It is no longer so much a question of 'the West and the rest', especially since 'the rest' comprises the majority of the world's citizens. It is time for the privileged minority to be humble, to listen and to learn, for the poor and the oppressed are the key to the future management of our planet. Here is the Métis Indian writer Lee Maracle explaining what is needed of her country's white majority: 'I have bent my back to this plough for some decades now. It is Canada's turn. In my life look for your complicit silence, look for the inequity between yourself and others. Search out the meaning of colonial robbery and figure out how you are going to undo it all . . . We will take on the struggle for self-determination, and in so doing will lay the foundation. But, so long as your own home needs cleaning, don't come to mine broom in hand.'

RADICAL ANTECEDENTS, 1790–1860

The word 'radicalism' first started to appear in the English language around 1820, and although it was used primarily to refer to the ideas of those who supported thoroughgoing reform of the parliamentary system, it is recorded in 1830 as meaning 'the application of sound reason to tracing consequences to their roots', a wholehearted acknowledgment of its classical lineage. Though the word emerged in the early nineteenth century many of its associated ideas had been gestating for some time. The radical challenge to established privilege, whether such privilege was based on divine authority, nobility of birth or entrenched wealth, had expressed itself in a linked series of events and movements, from the peasant revolts of fourteenth-century England and sixteenth century Germany, through the Diggers and Levellers of seventeenth-century England, to the origins of radical labour movements in the late eighteenth century.

The French and American Revolutions at the end of the eighteenth century paved the way for later radicalism but, although the Jacobins made evangelistic appeals to the dispossessed masses, and Thomas Paine's writings ridiculed the institution of monarchy and asserted the rights of all people to just government, both were essentially bourgeois revolutions. Though they changed dramatically the practice of government, they preserved and enhanced the right of individuals to own and protect their own property. As landowners and investors made full use of new and exciting technological innovations, many thousands from the non-property-owning underclass found what little security had traditionally been provided by social and economic stability pulled from under them.

That underclass did not always sit quietly by while its world disappeared. The Nottinghamshire Luddites of 1811, inspired by the legendary Ned Ludd, who smashed a knitting machine to demonstrate the threat to his traditional security from capitalist technology, mounted a passionate if shortlived rebellion. It was put down, like so many later protests, by a massive show of military might, one of the worst single acts of political repression in British history: within two years more than forty protesters had been hanged.

Thirty years later British working class radicals tried again. In 1838 a group of London working men drew up a six-point People's Charter calling for universal male suffrage and an end to the abuse of parliamentary privilege. When the privileged in parliament peremptorily rejected the charter, riots quickly spread to the Midlands, the North, and South Wales. After the charter was again rejected in 1842 the Chartists threatened a general strike and, though the movement failed to gain widespread organised support from an as-yet inchoate working class, it worried the bourgeoisie. Ironically the final – and decidedly pathetic – Chartist stand took place in London in 1848 just as the spirit of popular revolution was about to sweep through Europe, but almost every one of the Chartists' demands had become law by 1914.

In north America, meanwhile, the radicalism implicit in the preamble to the Declaration of Independence was fiercely defended across the political spectrum. The revolutionary tradition inevitably became tamed to partisan ends, with Jefferson's 'rights of man' supporting Southern sectional interests and the right to own slaves, and Lincoln's 'rights of man' supporting Northern interests and the right to exploit labour. Yet the same untiring radical project supported those undoubted prophets of twentieth-century radicalism, **Eugene Debs** and **W.E.B. Du Bois**, both willing executors of a long and uniquely American tradition which they were proud to inherit and pass on to a new generation of freedom lovers.

European and North American social historians, and particularly labour historians proud of the traditions and heritage of the working class movement in which they took part, tend to regard nineteenth-century radical politics as the process by which a series of popular agitations brought about an extension of the franchise. They also see the identification of social classes and the struggle to assert class-based rights as the most important contribution to the development of the modern social democratic state. Important though these processes were, however, there were other radical ideas which were equally important at the time, many of which had their origins in religious dissidence.

From the perspective of the secular late twentieth century it can be hard to remember that nineteenth-century radical politics were rooted in religion, and that the most important element in the making of the working class was not Christian in any orthodox sense. The radical tradition of **Thomas Paine** was grounded in eighteenth-century deism, and was developed in the nineteenth century by the socialist followers of **Robert Owen**. There were also strong dissenting traditions within Christianity, and many Methodists and Quakers spoke out strongly against slavery and other injustices. In the early nineteenth century, although attendance at church was not as widespread as has sometimes been assumed, religion was still the cement of society, and the churches were powerful supporters of the aristocratic conservative state. As industry spread and towns grew into cities, organised religion was unable to maintain its position in society. Working class movements like the Luddites and the Chartists may have expressed their distaste of privilege in economic terms, but they were equally united in opposition to centrally organised Christianity, which they associated with political oppression. Many ideas which might today be expressed purely in social and economic terms were then often given a religious and sectarian form, and many radical leaders were notoriously antireligious in their opinions.

Whatever radicalism meant in its formative years, very few of its nineteenth-century proponents considered the far-reaching implications of extending the panoply of human rights, privileges and responsibilities to all human beings – even women, even children, even blacks, even heathen foreigners, even the very poor, even people with strange social and sexual proclivities, even criminals. Radicals today recognise that freedom is interconnected and indivisible – how can I be truly free if you are not? A century of growing and widespread activism for equal treatment and half a century of United Nations accord on human rights have had a marked effect on attitudes and policies in many parts of the world. Yet in large parts of the globe the basic human freedoms are far from being respected, and our growing awareness and understanding of oppression and disempowerment only serve to show what elusive goals freedom and self-determination are.

More than half the world's people are women, yet their contribution and achievement, even in the most enlightened societies, is still underacknowledged and undervalued. At the time of the great 'democratic' revolutions of the eighteenth century it was taken for granted that, while women might be useful allies and helpmeets, what every radical was struggling for was the 'true brotherhood of man'. Inspired by the promise of the French Revolution and furious with Edmund Burke's male-dominated *Reflections on the Revolution*, **Mary Wollstonecraft** wrote her spirited essay *A Vindication of the Rights of Women* in 1792, concluding that 'reason demands justice for one-half the human race'. A century later, however, the economic lot of most of the world's women had deteriorated: industrialisation had robbed them of their status as workers, and the new scientism justified their inferiority as part of the 'natural order'. Prevailing wisdom agreed with Queen Victoria that women's rights were a 'mad, wicked folly', but some advances were undoubtedly made, notably as a result of pioneering gatherings like the 1848 Seneca Falls Convention in the USA and the relentless efforts of women's rights activists.

In many ways the early goals of the women's movement, being the most tangible, were the easiest to achieve, though even today these goals have by no means been universally attained. The right of married women to control their own property was enshrined in law in much of Europe and North America by the end of the nineteenth century, and in 1893 New Zealand became the first nation to extend the franchise to women.

Of all the causes that inspired and fuelled the women's movement, the most important, especially in the USA, was the parallel struggle against slavery. In 1794 **Sarah Grimké** was just four years old when she first saw a female slave savagely flogged, and she herself was later beaten for teaching her personal slave to read and write, which was forbidden by law. Her staunch opposition to the uncompromising hostility of masculine society made her a fearless campaigner for both black and women's rights. The British government outlawed the slave trade from the beginning of the nineteenth century, followed by Spain and Portugal in the 1840s. In the USA, however, it took a civil war and nearly a million casualties to decide the issue, and not until the Thirteenth Amendment was passed in 1865 was slavery constitutionally abolished.

As with women's rights, once the most indefensible iniquities were made illegal it was convenient to believe that blacks would be grateful and quiescent with their lot, yet in reality legalised oppression was replaced by social and economic discrimination that was every bit as potent. In the USA, the self-proclaimed birthplace of civil rights, widespread segregation and discrimination continued despite the extension by statute of citizenship and suffrage to everyone born in the country, and it was not until the mid-1950s that the frustration borne of decades of hypocrisy erupted into popular revolt.

MARX, SOCIALISM AND ANARCHISM, 1860–1890

Although little known and read during his lifetime, the German intellectual and professional agitator **Karl Marx** later achieved the rare distinction of having an entire political and economic system named after him. Fascinated by the success of the newly identified phenomenon of capitalism, Marx spent the four years from 1850 sitting in the British Museum reading room devouring everything he could find on the subject. Twenty years later, having experienced the Paris Commune and the birth of the Communist **International**, *Das Kapital* distilled his thinking about the promise and inevitable decline of capitalism.

Following the enthronement of Marxism as Russia's official ideology after the Bolshevik Revolution of 1917, it was the more revolutionary of Marx's ideas that provided the impetus for many activists. With the collapse of official Marxism in the Soviet bloc and the loosening of the stranglehold of socialist dogma throughout the radical movement, however, his writings are today being reassessed and seen in a new light. Beyond the typically Marxist vocabulary of 'labour theory of value', 'constant revolution' and 'dialectical materialism' (a phrase which Marx himself never used), it is possible to see his basic ideas in a more holistic, humanistic light.

Marx's analysis of capitalism stressed the innate creativity of human beings, a creativity which can either be acknowledged and nurtured or stifled and denied. He recognised that the early stages of rapid technological and intellectual progress provided many opportunities for this innate creativity to be unleashed. As long as the owners of the resources needed to fuel productivity refused to share them, however, the creative phase of capitalism would inevitably be followed by the exploitation and alienation of the majority of the population.

Excited as he was by the creativity of capitalism in what he called its 'glorious days', the Marx of the late nineteenth century saw working people everywhere alienated from their own productive power, from a real purpose to their existence. If the 'workers of the world' could organise themselves to produce what ordinary people needed, then, as **Lenin** wrote in *The Immediate Tasks of the Soviet Government* in 1918, 'the majority of the working people would be engaged in independent creative work as makers of history.'

After finishing *Das Kapital* in 1861 Marx travelled to Berlin, where he was impressed with the political awareness of Prussian workers. He was not so pleased that the youthful and charismatic Ferdinand Lasalle had taken his place as the *de facto* figurehead of the continental socialist movement. When Lasalle was killed in a duel in 1864, Marx quickly and opportunistically took over his carefully nurtured socialist power base, slotting himself neatly into the leadership position he had so long coveted. Recognising that words must be linked with grassroots action if he were to maintain any credibility, he now began to attend workers' meetings and nurture friendships with influential labour organisers, to such effect that when the newly formed International Working Men's Association – known retrospectively as the First **International** – was looking for an experienced figurehead, he was in the perfect position to become its most prominent and outspoken member.

The International grew much too slowly for Marx, and he was unhappy about some of the dissident groups who were joining its ranks. In 1868, despite his misgivings, the socialist International absorbed the International Alliance of Socialist Democracy under the leadership of anarchist **Mikhail Bakunin**. Bakunin was an admirer of Marx, but the admiration was not reciprocated. The ideological and organisational gulf between Marx and **Engels** on the one hand and Bakunin's anarchists on the other widened with the surprise victory of Prussia in the Franco-Prussian War of 1870: while the socialists applauded the triumph of an advanced industrial society, Bakunin had serious misgivings about the impact of German victory on the European working class movement.

The split became irreconcileable in March 1871, when a large group of radicals seized control of central Paris, proclaiming themselves an independent entity called the Paris Commune, the greatest urban uprising of nineteenth-century Europe. For two months they withstood the forces of the French central government until, in a wave of terror and counterterror, the Commune was overthrown.

The Paris Commune was not primarily a socialist enterprise, owing far more to the anarchists than to the socialist International, but Marx identified with it as a manifestation of working class solidarity, and his powerful and popular pamphlet *The Civil War in France* ensured that future generations of socialists would link his name with the Commune. Yet his exuberant support of the Paris Commune devalued his position in the International, where many labour leaders recoiled from claiming credit for an episode they considered ill-timed and ill-fated. Marx responded vindictively by moving the International's headquarters to the USA, where it foundered amid factional infighting, and he spent his latter relatively unproductive years knowing full well that he was being increasingly ignored even by those committed to his version of socialism.

Marxism was to emerge as the dominant socialist ideology of the early twentieth century, but the movement based on his 'scientific socialism' was by no means the only influential group seeking the social and economic justice denied by capitalism. From **William Godwin** and **Pierre-Joseph Proudhon** in the 1840s, through Bakunin, to **Errico Malatesta** and beyond, the anarchist movement was, especially during the period from 1870 to the turn of the century, the most visible and controversial manifestation of those who sought to undermine every aspect of oppressive centralised power.

The fiercest controversy centred around the use of terrorist violence to overthrow oppressive regimes. Many anarchists like **Petr Kropotkin** refused to condone the use of violence, yet Kropotkin's ringing assertion that 'A single deed is better propaganda than a thousand pamphlets' was being used throughout the late 1870s and 80s to justify a number of high-profile assassination attempts. Following the killing of Czar Alexander II by a group of Russian populists in 1881 and the Chicago Haymarket massacre of 1886, with the subsequent clampdown on all known anarchists, anarchism became inextricably associated with violence and terror. 'Propaganda by the deed' (a Bakunin extrapolation of Kropotkin's dictum) continued throughout the 1890s, and by the early years of the new century two Spanish prime ministers, an American president (William McKinley), a French president and the king of Italy had all died at the hands of selfstyled anarchists.

Though anarchism continued to develop in subsequent decades, and anarchist thought has played an important part in twentieth-century radicalism, the taint of late nineteenth century terrorism has never again allowed the important anti-authoritarian teachings of anarchism to become common currency among the more reformist elements of the radical movement. On the other hand, anarchism continued to appeal to more radical thinkers and campaigners from **Emma Goldman** to **Paul Goodman**, and inspired a number of practical projects during the 1930s, from anarchist communities in Spain to **Dorothy Day's** 'hospitality houses' for the homeless of New York City.

THE HOPEFUL YEARS, 1890–1920

The rapidly developing socialist movement, meanwhile, carefully distanced itself from the excesses of anarchism. By 1890 the German SPD (Sozialistisches Partei Deutschlands) had gained sufficient popular support to win almost twenty per cent of the votes cast in a parliamentary election, and the following year outlined its distinctly Marxist Erfurt Programme (though Marx, dead for eight years, would almost certainly not have approved of its interpretation of his complex ideas).

Some of the SPD's success derived from circumstances unique to Germany, such as the use of the compulsory block vote, but, despite the vested interests of the wealthy and powerful in maintaining conservative control of governments throughout the western world, socialist parties and pressure groups sprang up across Europe and North America. In France the Marxist Jules Guesde established the shortlived Parti Ouvrier Français in 1879, followed three years later by Paul Brousse's Fédération des Travailleurs de France. Polite middle class British socialists established the **Fabian Society** in 1884, Russian Marxists Georgi Plekhanov and Pavel Akselrod attracted a following (including the student **Lenin**), and in Austria, Italy, Holland and Belgium groups of intellectuals and labour leaders formed groups under the socialist banner.

In 1889, the centennial of the great French Revolution, the international socialist movement regrouped to celebrate the event which had marked the end of feudalism in France and the beginning of the class consciousness that had made Marxism possible. The great socialist congress of July 1889 (typically, given the notorious schismatic tendency of the left, there were actually two rival congresses, with many delegates commuting between them) saw the birth of a new **International**. The Second International united behind the idea of an annual global **May Day** strike of the proletariat, and the celebration of May 1st as a labour holiday became its most lasting monument.

The issue of whether to exclude anarchists from the Second International was summarily dealt with by its London congress of 1896, which decided against militancy and for legislative and parliamentary lobbying. Remembering Marx's mandate (in his inaugural address to the First International) for social democracy rather than militant socialism, and recognising his assurance that historical determinism made socialism an inevitable consequence of capitalism, the mainstream socialist movement now set itself firmly on the path of political legitimacy and acceptability. The Dreyfus Affair of 1894–99, when leading French socialist Alexandre Millerand felt compelled to join the government to support a soldier accused of spying (and for his pains was denounced by Guesde as a defector to capitalism), together with arch-Marxist revisionist Eduard Bernstein's takeover of the leadership of the German SDP, demonstrated that the moderate 'social democratic' brand of socialism was now in the ascendant across northern mainland Europe.

The new century saw the consolidation of socialist parties in other countries. In 1900 the British Labour Representation Committee came into being as the offspring of the Trades Union Congress (established in 1868), the Independent Labour Party (dating from 1893) and **Keir Hardie's** Scottish Labour Party: in 1906 this organisation was renamed the Labour Party. In the USA the Socialist Party was founded in 1901, and in the following decade trade union membership grew from half a million to 2.5 million. By 1913 more than three hundred periodicals were proclaiming the socialist message to newly-politicised American workers, and the radical **Industrial Workers of the World**, established in 1905, claimed 100,000 active members. In Japan the socialist organisation **Heiminsha** was formed in 1903, and despite government repression (especially during the Russo-Japanese War of 1904–05) was an influential voice for labour rights and pacifism. The defeat of Russia by Japan in turn helped to precipitate the first Russian Revolution, that of January 1905, when the threat of escalating uprisings, strikes and mutinies forced major constitutional reforms.

The first decade of the century may have been good for socialism, but in Europe and Asia the economic and political instability resulting from the breakdown of the Austro-Hungarian and Ottoman empires was pushing the Western world inexorably towards international conflict. As Bismarck armed Germany massively against a shifting set of potential enemies, and as those perceived enemies in turn joined the escalating arms race, it seemed that patriotism and survival far outweighed any idealistic radical cause.

There were many influential voices against war in the years immediately before 1914. Keir Hardie, now the leader of British socialism, urged the Labour Party to support a general strike against the impending conflict: the party agreed to inquire into its feasibility, but its leadership saw little point. Lenin and **Rosa Luxemburg** made a successful pacifist appeal to the Second International's 1907 congress, but the war machine rolled on regardless and many national delegations pragmatically changed their tune as conflict became inevitable. **Bertha von Suttner's** pacifist classic *Lay Down Your Arms!* had sold a quarter of a million copies by 1914, but every attempt she made at international mediation failed and she mercifully died a week before war was declared.

American president Theodore Roosevelt had little time for pacifists and doubters: for him the American way of life offered everything for which millions of European emigrants had crossed the Atlantic. He was fond of acclaiming the freedom of thought and action deeply embedded in the American psyche, the freedom for which those settlers had suffered and struggled. As the empty lands filled and the cities grew, however, self-development and material wealth for those who bene-fited from the American dream came to depend more and more on a poorly-paid, heavily exploited underclass.

Roosevelt took every opportunity to praise America's manifold achievements, yet his term of office coincided with an increasing spate of public criticism of the real costs of those achievements. It was Roosevelt who (borrowing from a character in John Bunyan's *Pilgrim's Progress*) labelled as 'muckrakers' journalists like Lincoln Steffens and novelists like **Upton Sinclair**. The high point of the muckraking move-ment was reached with the publication of Sinclair's influential novel *The Jungle* in 1906. The novel recounts the agonies of a Lithuanian family whose men are worn out by overwork in the Chicago meatpacking stations, whose women are forced into prostitution and whose children die on the streets. Because the novel recounted, almost incidentally, the unhygienic conditions of the meatpacking industry and the evasion of health regulations, there was a storm of criticism about health standards and the sale of meat products plunged.

Upton Sinclair wrote *The Jungle* when he was 28, at the start of a long and productive writing career. At almost the same time the 45-year-old Irish labourer Robert Noonan, using the pen-name **Robert Tressell**, was drawing on his experiences of working class England to produce *The Ragged Trousered Philanthropists*. The first version was published in 1914, three years after Noonan's death from tuberculosis, and rapidly became popular in labour circles, though it was not until 1955 that a full edition appeared. Robert Tressell's intricate and compelling novel is a spirited exploration of greed, dishonesty and hypocrisy, and his descriptions of the opposition faced by trade union organisers did much to strengthen the resolve of the early labour movement.

Both novels end on a positive note, with their authors believing that, whatever the challenges faced by ordinary working people, justice and humanity will prevail. In the final scene of *The Jungle*, Jurgis Rudkus listens to a socialist orator proclaiming 'Then will begin the rush that will never be checked, the tide that will never turn till it has reached its flood. Chicago will be ours!'

If the plight of American workers was often dire, in Russia the situation was far worse. Despite the minimal gains made in 1905, the threat of war diverted resources needed for domestic improvements into military production. At the outbreak of hostilities land reform, already pitifully slow, was suspended, and new political restrictions were imposed. Disastrous military defeats sapped public morale, and Czar Nicholas, assuming command of the army in 1915, became identified with its weakness. By the winter of 1916 the country was ripe for widespread revolt. When food shortages provoked street demonstrations in Petrograd (St Petersburg) in February 1917 and soldiers refused to suppress them, Lenin's Bolshevik Central Committee took control. Within months the Romanov dynasty was no more, the aristocracy and its toothless puppet government replaced by an all-powerful Council of People's Commissars. The Soviet Union, soon to become one of the most repressive political regimes the world had yet seen, was born.

The singlemindedness of the first world war, and the patriotic fervour which led to the widespread repression of anti-establishment views in Europe and North America in the postwar period, effectively stopped progressive politics in its tracks. As an ill US president Woodrow Wilson lost his grip on his cabinet in 1919, his attorney general initiated a 'red scare' which led to the widespread repression of 'subversives' and the notorious **Sacco-Vanzetti case**. A devastated Europe mopped up as best it could, trusting in a thoroughly inadequate peace treaty and an ineffectual League of Nations to ensure a better future.

And what of the radical voices that had survived the first world war with their ideals and credentials intact? Much of the passion and idealism of twenty years earlier had now been replaced by the realisation that it would be a long and difficult haul to a more just and humane world. American journalist Lincoln Steffens summed up the postwar demise of many prewar American radicals when he explained in his 1931 *Autobiography* that 'they were all wounded by the fights they fought, the defeats they suffered. Some became cynics, some tired liberals, some dubious radicals, some unhappy fiction writers.'

THE DARK YEARS, 1920–1955

The 1920s and 30s were desperately difficult years in which to be an active radical. As the Western world moved inexorably towards political and economic crisis, so the colonial world moved just as inexorably towards violent confrontation with its dominators, and the combined reactionary power élite of the wealthy, the militarily powerful and the religiously dogmatic took full advantage. Historian **Eric Hobsbawm** has calculated that of the world's sixty-four independent interwar nations, thirty-five had had more or less constitutionally elected governments in 1920. By 1938 there were just seventeen, and following the nazification of much of central Europe the number had dropped by 1944 to just twelve: Britain, Ireland, Finland, Sweden and Switzerland in Europe; the USA, Canada, Colombia, Costa Rica and Uruguay in the Americas; and only Australia and New Zealand in the whole of Africa, Asia and Australasia.

Moreover, the hazard to freedom and democracy did not come from any 'red threat'. Until 1949, despite small-scale annexations, the Soviet Union had relatively little desire or ability to extend its model of state communism, and throughout the interwar period international social-ism, communism and anarchism (not to mention pacifism, feminism and civil rights) became increasingly isolated and marginalised. No, the danger came exclusively from fascistic movements and tendencies, which during the darkest years immediately before the outbreak of war in 1939 threatened to amalgamate into a worldwide force capable of obliterating liberty and justice everywhere.

Lenin's communism soon betrayed its radical origins, and many of its erstwhile Western supporters became disillusioned and highly criti-cal. Within just a few years of the 1917 Russian Revolution, the Bolshevik Party increasingly centralised its power over local soviets throughout the Soviet Union. Lenin's theory of a party of professional revolutionaries led by intellectuals as 'the vanguard of the proletariat' with an 'advanced consciousness' was used to justify ever more bureauc-racy and élitism at the heart of Russian communism. Though he never acknowledged his own theories to be at the root of the problem, in his last years Lenin became painfully aware of the degenerating tendencies in the party, and lamely continued until his premature death to proclaim that state authority would eventually be replaced by a people's socialism.

What emerged in the Soviet bloc was far removed from Marx's vision of the working classes as the principal architects of socialism. Instead, hardline notions of leadership were used to justify ever more harsh dictatorship. After Stalin's rise to power in the 1920s, true grassroots initiatives were discouraged and thwarted, while criticism was severely punished. Resistance to this distortion of the true interpretation of communism surfaced from time to time, coming from the intelligentsia as well as the working class, but each time it was ruthlessly repressed.

What had happened to the voices of reason and understanding? Where had more than a hundred years of the 'self-evident truths' of the French and American Revolutions vanished to? It would be easy, but very probably erroneous, to imagine that the rise of the reactionary right after the first world war was primarily a response to the prewar rise of socialism, the working class labour movement, and events in Russia. The more likely truth is that the physical and emotional anguish and dislocation occasioned by the previously unimaginable horror of continent-wide destruction and bloodshed numbed a generation to the dangers of fascism and totalitarianism. And it was the vacuum provided by material hardship and the subconscious urge for a worthwhile cause that was ruthlessly exploited by devious dictators, racist bureaucrats and power-crazed generals from Japan to Portugal, Nazi Germany to Brazil.

In the few nations where there was still any semblance of liberty and democracy, the common feature of the 1920s and 30s was denial. Scott Fitzgerald (in *The Jazz Age*, his analysis of the 1920s) accurately wrote that most Americans of the period 'had no interest in politics at all'. When the glorious spree of the 1920s ended with the great American crash of 1929, any interest there might have been in international affairs was turned decisively towards domestic problems. With a quarter of American workers unemployed and an economic system on the brink of collapse, social criticism began to revive in the early 30s, but it never regained the vitality or integrity of the prewar period.

The major sources of social criticism in the USA in the 1930s and 40s were not Marxist, even though the Russian economic system did appear to be weathering the crisis as a result of communist planning and China seemed to be enthusiastically following in its footsteps. There was some interest from intellectuals, but nobody else was as enthusiastic about the Soviet 'miracle' as were the British socialists **Sidney** and **Beatrice Webb** in their 1935 eulogy, *Soviet Communism: A New Civilization*. There was growing criticism in the USA of *laissez faire* capitalism, with Thurman Arnold's *The Folklore of Capitalism* (1937) and James Burnham's *The Managerial Revolution* (1941) becoming bestsellers, but the antidote to economic hardship was seen as social planning rather than populist involvement.

Given the economic and social climate of the 1930s, and the fact that the USA was just about the only nation in the world able to offer an independent critique of the growing rightwing threat to global freedom, it is surprising that no coherent radical movement gained ascendancy. Although the need for a 'third party' in American politics was frequently asserted, several 'progressive parties' were founded but quickly declined, and a Third Party Conference in Chicago in July 1935 failed to bear fruit. In many ways the stormclouds of global war united Americans behind conventional policies in the late 1930s, just as they had in 1917.

It would be too easy, however, to imagine that the vision of a better world had entirely failed and forsaken interwar radicals. On the contrary: despite the rightwing clampdown on those who questioned the abuse of power, the working classes did not forget the considerable gains that had been made between 1850 and 1914. Many European countries, even those which by the outbreak of war were firmly under dictatorial control, boasted large working class parties which remained socialist, if not overtly Marxist.

In 1936 the global confrontation between reactionary right and radical left suddenly became polarised when a newly elected leftwing government in Spain was ousted by a military coup led by Francisco Franco. In many ways the **Spanish Civil War** provided a vital outlet for frustrated radicals from all over the world, who saw it both as symbolic of the struggle of good against evil and as a potentially winnable battle in the international war for freedom. In March 1939, however, Spain was lost to a longlived Franco dictatorship, the refusal of any other free nation to support the nationalist cause in Spain (with the dubious exception of the Soviet Union) demonstrating just how little will there was to become involved in the fight against the destructive force of fascism.

The price of denial was high. Hitler's forces continued to occupy country after country with no regard at all for human rights, let alone openness to criticism, and six months after the fall of Madrid to Franco's troops Britain and France were forced to declare war on Germany. By the time Germany and Japan surrendered in 1945 fifty million people had died, thirty-five million of them civilians. Much of Europe, Russia and Japan lay in ruins. Yet despite the tyranny of fascism and the leadership of the free world by élitist statesmen with little sympathy for radicalism, the resistance movements which did so much to secure Europe for the Allies were markedly leftwing. Building on the success of its resistance efforts and its clearly stated internationalism, the European communist movement reached its peak immediately after the war, achieving outstanding successes in the first postwar elections in France and Italy.

As communism swelled in Europe so, at Stalin's express command, it retrenched in the Soviet Union. In order to maintain ironfisted power in his own country *and* appear on the side of the angels 'Uncle Joe' wooed the West by confirming his support for 'socialism in one country', going to the lengths of formally announcing in 1944 the end of Soviet support for Communist Parties outside the USSR, and actively discouraging the successful communist revolutions in Greece, Yugoslavia and Albania. But Stalin's vision of a postwar global alliance of liberal capitalism and communism against fascism was doomed from the start, and in the absence of a common enemy and the presence of a nuclear capability the wartime alliance cooled rapidly. The Cold War, a

8174

thirty-year standoff which consumed massive military resources and fuelled many politicians' worst fears, began in earnest.

While many European countries experienced a postwar communist boom, the British electorate turned massively to a renewed and innovative Labour Party. Increasing its share of the vote by a massive fifty per cent, Labour used its first term to enact a series of major economic and social reforms which turn-of-the-century socialists would have marvelled at. With a decidedly anticolonial administration installed in Britain, the world's largest empire started to succumb to the growing pressure for self-determination. After decades of struggle against colonial rule, a partitioned India/Pakistan was created in 1947 with relative ease. Burma and Israel (formerly the British protectorate of Palestine) followed more painfully in 1948.

By 1950 the decolonisation of Asia was virtually complete. In Africa most of the north had said farewell to European rule by mid-decade, and the stage was set for sub-Saharan independence movements, starting with Nkrumah's Ghana in 1957. Many of the architects of independence had learned both their ideas and their tactics within the more radical reaches of European and American academia, and thus in the Third World, as in the first, it became increasingly clear that idealism and vision had not been murdered by fascism; the roots had been growing steadily in the dark and the green shoots were now ready for the light and fresh air of a new spring.

In the United States, meanwhile, something sinister stirred. The 'red threat' had worried American administrations since the turn of the century, but as the reality of Cold War dawned the Truman administration, under Republican pressure to defend itself against charges of being 'soft on communists', passed an executive order in March 1947 barring 'communists, fascists and totalitarians' from official employment, together with anyone guilty of 'sympathetic association' with such people. The purge of the American left which followed was quickly named McCarthyism, after the Wisconsin senator who dominated the news with his ever more salacious revelations of subversion. Over the next four years many thousands of the country's most able and visionary young people (and many who were not so young) lost their jobs, were harassed to distraction, and suffered social ostracism and economic hardship. In comparison with political repression in other countries McCarthyism was relatively mild: Julius and Ethel **Rosenberg** were the only ones to lose their lives as a result of Joseph McCarthy's ravings and imprisonments were in the low hundreds. The fear of being seen as a 'subversive', however, discouraged the development of an idealistic, activist radical movement in the USA, leaving a decade-long vacuum before the left again felt strong enough to present a united front against injustice and military might.

THE 'REBIRTH', 1955–1975

With the advent of the Cold War and the military potential of the hydrogen bomb, the world's superpowers set themselves on a course of nuclear accumulation which would eventually have the capacity of destroying all human life on the planet, but which also ensured a vital future for an active peace movement. Hundreds of former conscientious objectors were joined by an ever-growing body of people led by intellectuals, scientists and religious leaders appalled by the aftermath of Hiroshima and Nagasaki. US and British nuclear testing in the mid-50s became the main target of SANE in the USA and the **Campaign for Nuclear Disarmament** (CND) in Britain. By 1958 the former boasted 25,000 members, while by 1960 the annual CND pilgrimage from the nuclear weapons base at Aldermaston to London's Trafalgar Square was attracting 60,000 protesters. In Japan, too, the antinuclear group **Gensuikyō** was attracting thousands of supporters following US atomic tests on the nearby Bikini Atoll.

The 1963 Test Ban Treaty came as the initial energy was ebbing from the movement, and further sapped popular support, though in the USA Vietnam soon took over where nuclear testing left off. By 1967, while half a million American soldiers were fighting 'communism' (in reality nationalism with a strong socialist element) in south-east Asia, the Spring Mobilization Committee to End the War in Vietnam was itself able to rally half a million antiwar demonstrators in the largest march ever seen in the USA. The rebirth of radicalism was led from the United States, where leftwing politics was gradually emerging from the darkness of the McCarthy period with a new vigour and purpose. Led by civil rights activists and dubbed 'the movement', a nationwide network of university students developed, supported by a number of powerful intellectual voices. The 'movement' grew out of dissatisfaction with the country's growing involvement in Vietnam and drew strength from huge urban demonstrations against racism, poverty and privilege.

The movement to uproot segregation in the Southern States of the USA was sparked by a 1954 Supreme Court decision that declared segregated schools unconstitutional. Despite the seemingly modest aim of implementing rights already guaranteed by 85-year-old federal law, the movement's goals could not be realised without a fundamental shift in American society. The civil rights movement, inspired by the leadership of **Martin Luther King** and **Malcolm X**, brought a wide range of radical activists into a broad and focused alliance which quickly gained the support of many liberal Americans. Official support came too slowly and too late to avoid anger and frustration spilling over in the riots and rebellions of the mid-60s, and after King's assassination in 1968 the civil rights movement found it hard to regroup and consolidate its hardwon achievements.

Black America and its white liberal allies had, however, learned something of the meaning and implications of true racial equality. This they now concentrated on smaller and more manageable goals. The 1970s saw black mayors and legislators installed across the country. In 1977 Andrew Young, one of King's closest friends, was installed as US ambassador to the United Nations, and in 1984 another of King's protégés, Jesse Jackson, made a strong bid for the presidency.

The postwar left had no problem aligning itself with the civil rights movement, but it had real problems when it came to feminism. From the mid-nineteenth century to the mid-twentieth, many socialists – including some women – tended to dismiss feminism either as a bourgeois reform movement which benefited only white middle class women or as a subsidiary issue which could be looked at after the socialist revolution. The feminist cause was quite definitely secondary, even for many radical women. When she wrote *The Second Sex* in 1949, **Simone de Beauvoir** said that she was not a feminist, believing instead that the class struggle was more important and that women's rights would come with the achievement of socialism. By 1970, however, she had come to a different conclusion. Still calling herself a socialist, she now saw that sexual inequities continued even in the most revolutionary circles.

Although it had been noted by early feminists from **Mary Wollstonecraft** onwards, the primacy of women's oppression by men of all political tendencies was only rediscovered with the publication of **Shulamith Firestone's** *The Dialectic of Sex* in 1970. Appearing four years after the establishment of the **National Organization for Women** in the USA and at the same time as Britain's first National Women's Liberation Conference, her book helped to set a large part of the women's movement on the course of radical feminism.

Opening with the words 'Sex class is so deep as to be invisible,' she outlined how distinctions of gender, based on sex, permeated every aspect of human interaction, and were so pervasive that they almost always went unrecognised. Her class analogy, with women as an underclass serving men's dominance, explained the disempowerment of women in every aspect of their lives. This insight, contradicting the established view that women were born inferior rather than made subservient, allowed the development of a comprehensive critique of women's oppression, while the necessary extension of her probing analysis into the minutiae of everyday life helped the radical movement to understand that personal and political are indistinguishable.

Given that at the time it appeared to be the only populist movement to be having any major effect in the world, it is hardly surprising that

Mao Zedong's 'Great Socialist Cultural Revolution' of the mid-1960s had such a profound effect on newly radicalised young people. With hindsight it is easy to see that singleminded missionary zeal combined with the godlike status attributed to a fallible human being would soon defeat any pretence of true populism, but Mao's stated aim of teaching the masses that it was their right and privilege to criticise those in authority and to take an active part in decision-making struck a strong chord. Never mind that the bulk of the contents of *The Little Red Book* had been written decades earlier, when Mao's gospel of participation and mutual support was truly revolutionary; never mind that the revolution involved widespread violence and destruction, humiliation and persecution; never mind that Mao refused to see how those around him were taking personal advantage of a turbulent era – Mao's China inspired dreams of cultural revolution the world over.

The Little Red Book provided many a late-60s slogan, but the brave hero of the age, prepared to lay down his life for the cause, was **Ernesto 'Che' Guevara**. The Cuban Revolution was inscribed on the heart of the American **new left**. While China was the primary inspiration for European and Japanese radicals, Cuba was on America's doorstep and provided an obvious model for a socialist future. Since 1898 Cuba had been little more than an offshore dependency of the USA, but in 1959 a popular revolution led by Fidel Castro led to a radical socialist regime which, despite hardships and much criticism of its methods, survives to the present under Castro's ageing eye.

The Argentinian-born guerrilla Guevara, who helped Castro achieve the revolution in Cuba and served in Castro's government until 1965, is more famous for his death and his exhortations to armed struggle than for any positive contribution to the radical cause. The bearded revolutionary who died training gunmen in Bolivia in 1967 may have had little in common with the libertarianism espoused by the new left, yet the legend was strengthened by his violent end, and his achievement was eulogised by many influential voices. **Jean-Paul Sartre** described Guevara as 'the most complete person of our age', and who on the left was going to argue with Sartre?

1968 – dubbed by some commentators 'The Year of the Barricades' – saw more turbulent political change across Europe, North America and Japan than any other single postwar year. The power structure was shaken to its roots, and anyone whose activist career spanned the late 60s will remember it with excitement tinged with disappointment. It was perhaps inevitable that a privileged postwar generation's growing sense of unlimited potential would eventually clash with the established hierarchy. The explosion was triggered by anger about the senseless war in **Vietnam** and inhuman repression in Eastern Europe, and it was fuelled by too-rigid authority in the universities and colleges that many of them attended. In the USA an important element within the radical movement was the 'religious left', with leaders like the **Berrigan** brothers and **Thomas Merton** making it clear by their words and actions that 'just war' was a murderous contradiction in terms.

The more newsworthy manifestations of the late 60s had disappeared by the end of 1970, but it would be too easy to imagine that the governments of the 'free world' had triumphed over the forces of chaos. Freedom, even if experienced for only a few fleeting weeks, is not rapidly unlearned, and for many people **May 1968** kindled a flame that would later burn on other parts of the radical stage.

The 'law and order' used to quell the late-60s uprisings drove a few radicals into the use of violence to counter violence. While few in 1968 would have advocated such a stance, organisations like the Weathermen in the USA, Britain's Angry Brigade, the Irish Republican Army, Italy's Red Brigades and Germany's Red Army Faction turned to dynamite and guns to highlight their cause. For reactionary politicians and the media alike it was very convenient to link radicalism and terrorism, and for a decade at least it was hard for proponents of nonviolent revolution to be heard above self-righteous mainstream calls for punitive measures against all would-be radicals.

The 1970s were years of tremendous creative ferment for the European left. The Italian, French and Spanish communist parties were shaking off the burdens of the Soviet model and working on innovative theories for the democratic reworking of capitalism, based on Gramscian and other neo-Marxist principles. 'Eurocommunism', a 'third way' between capitalism and Soviet-style socialism, held out both promise and problems.

By the mid-1970s the contours of the American left had clearly changed. The tenuously united radical front of the 1960s had become a loosely linked network of social movements, each organising around its own issues. The revolutionary ideal had been called into serious question, particularly where it advocated the use of violence, and issue-oriented activism appeared to offer a more peaceful and democratic alternative.

One of the most important realignments of radicalism this century has been the politicisation of environmental issues, a trend that started in the early 60s and gathered unstoppable momentum after the oil crisis of the early 70s and the publication in 1972 of a series of frightening surveys of the global environment, most notably *The Limits to Growth* and *Blueprint for Survival*.

The historical roots of ecological politics are various, tangled, and by no means always entirely healthy. The conservation movement in the USA and elsewhere arose largely from the desire of hunters to preserve tracts of wilderness for their own élitist pleasures. The influential

Germanic notion of life-philosophy, espoused by the interwar generation of nature-loving *Wandervögel* youth, was readily subverted within
the narrow minded territorial nationalism of the Third Reich. Growing
in the same soil, Madame Blavatsky's theosophy and Rudolf Steiner's
anthroposophy linked questionable racism and occultism with practical
and forward-looking ideas about education and the wise use of land
and resources.

The antecedents of green politics were by no means all muddled or
devious. As long ago as the 1890s the American utopian socialist
Edward Bellamy was very clear about the parallels between the exploitation of nature, women and labour. Twenty years later **Industrial
Workers of the World** newspapers were regularly publishing articles
about pollution, noise and environmental devastation, and many of the
leading lights in the Wilderness Society were lifelong socialists. In
Europe, where for the early decades of the century 'natural' ways and
laws were more of an élitist – and blinkered – concern, there was still
some thoughtful experimentation and analysis. The 1930s saw the
growth of Dartington Hall in south-west England, a combination of
cooperative, free school and refuge for radical artists, and in the 1940s
the influential English writer and ruralist **H.J. Massingham** was advocating a Europe based on small regional groupings.

The 1960s saw the environmental shift from a minority concern
ignored or sidelined by political activists to a subject worthy of radical
attention. The publication in 1962 of **Rachel Carson**'s exposé of toxic
pesticides, *Silent Spring*, mobilised a groundswell of popular concern
that was harnessed by activists like the Sierra Club's David Brower, who
was able to boost the organisation's membership from 3,000 to 100,000
within a decade, largely by taking a markedly radical stance on a range
of controversial issues from population to nuclear energy. As a post-
script to the political turmoil of 1968–69 and a hoped-for prelude to a
more peaceful and ecological future, the first **Earth Day** in 1970 enlisted
thousands of people across America and further afield in a celebration
of life on earth. More thoroughgoing leftists kept their distance, pointing out that the event's ideals conflicted with its sponsorship and
endorsement by Coca Cola and the Nixon administration; optimistic
environmentalists considered such carping petty and divisive, especially
given the left's previous indifference towards environmental concerns.

Some on the left, however, were busy surveying and mapping the
common ground between socialism and environmentalism. The neo-
Marxist German activist **Rudolf Bahro** and ex-Trotskyite American anarchist **Murray Bookchin** were laying the foundations for a comprehensive
red-green critique, which within a decade was to become a crucial plank
in emerging green politics.

On a smaller stage, but with no less far-reaching implications, the

60s and early 70s saw a concerted critique of coercive psychiatry under the banner of 'radical therapy'. Paralleling the radical feminist belief that male supremacy is at the heart of women's problems, radical psychologists like **R.D. Laing** and **Thomas Szasz** were convinced that mainstream psychotherapeutic methods, based on the expertise of the therapist and the need for patients to be 'adjusted', were depriving people of their inherent dignity and humanity. A lively debate developed between radical but nonpartisan therapists and their no-less-radical neo-Marxist practitioner-critics, mostly around the issue of personal versus collective responsibility for mental health. As in the emerging green politics, however, they were united on the need for universal empowerment and access to tools for self-reliance.

Empowerment was also the keyword within the burgeoning **gay and lesbian rights movement**. The frustration of many weary decades of struggle for gay acceptance and respectability eventually erupted in the New York **Stonewall Riots** of 1969, so that by the end of the decade gay activism was firmly on the political agenda. The Gay Liberation Front coordinated marches and actions in North America, Europe and further afield, while lobbying organisations like the US Gay Activist Alliance and the British Campaign for Homosexual Equality worked to challenge official discrimination against gays and lesbians.

Given the important role of universities and colleges in the political changes of the late 60s, it was no surprise to find that almost every subject and speciality harboured a radicalising element. It was most noticeable within the newly-emerging social sciences, where throughout the 1960s and early 70s a spate of surveys and anthologies with the word 'radical' in their title rolled off the presses. Radical philosophy, radical sociology, radical political theory, radical economics and radical geography all became topics worthy of academic attention in the more liberal institutions.

In this exciting era it seemed that every institution of the establishment was up for potential radicalisation. Even the Roman Catholic church, seen by many as one of the bastions of universal patriarchal hegemony, was not immune. Many clergy in the Third World, particularly in south and central America, had for decades been concerned that European Catholicism ignored crucial issues of oppression and poverty. Two important gatherings – a 1966 World Council of Churches conference on religion and revolution and a 1968 meeting of Latin American bishops at Medellín in Colombia – provided a forum for concerned activists, and the Peruvian priest **Gustavo Gutiérrez** gave it a name – liberation theology. Throughout the 1970s and 1980s much of the impetus for grassroots change in the developing world, from revolution throughout Latin America to the successful overthrow of the Marcos regime in the Philippines in 1986, had its roots in religious faith.

A potent outpouring of writings about religious and social responsibility included the US bishops' 1983 report *The Challenge of Peace: God's Promise and Our Response* and nonviolence historian Gene Sharp's influential 1973 classic *The Politics of Nonviolent Action*.

FRAGMENTATION AND CONSOLIDATION, 1975–1995

The demise of Marxism is central to an understanding of radicalism in the last quarter of the century. Traditional Marxism looked forward to a universal uprising of the revolutionary working class to overthrow capitalism and establish socialism as the new order. By the late 1970s it was becoming increasingly clear that, in most of the Western world at least, class was no longer the primary social distinction and class action no longer the most important political arena. However hard neo-Marxists tried to expand their definitions of the working class, issues that Marxism signally failed to address – the politics of identity, gender and race issues, nonviolent direct action, environmental and animal rights – were now at the head of the political agenda. Trade union membership in most of Europe and North America fell steeply throughout the 80s, and by the end of the decade militant groupings within the labour movement had largely been sidelined and silenced by the milder and more mainstream majority.

What unifying ideas were to replace Marxist socialism in the radical marketplace? There were almost as many candidates as commentators. Feminism, anarchism, environmentalism, nonviolence, economic cooperation, communal living and spirituality all contained important elements, but none by itself seemed able to provide a central strategic rationale, a coherent intellectual framework at the heart of the radical movement. Thus by the late 1970s it was becoming increasingly pointless – and, as many pointed out, undesirable – to speak of a unified radical movement, united under the banner of a single 'ism'. As **Abbie Hoffman** was fond of stressing to rising radicals in the decade before his death, 'all the isms are wasisms'. Indeed, the social movements of the 1980s frequently challenged a unitary vision of 'the left' as being both totalitarian and élitist. With the stress on identity and diversity, epitomised by the women's movement's slogan 'different, therefore equal', much of the dogmatism that had plagued the movement in earlier decades was swept aside.

Yet growing fragmentation and inclusivity worried many who had sharpened their teeth on leftwing radical solidarity. They felt that a postmodern politics of identity ran the risk of failing to distinguish between individuality and individualism, while 'the cause' was in danger of being lost forever. They felt that were being asked to negotiate an impossible common ground with woolly-minded ecoliberals. A 1989 *Living Marxism* review of my environmental action guide *How To Be Green* typically denounced green activism as 'token gestures and moral platitudes'.

The British 'Beyond the Fragments' initiative in the late 70s and early 80s, established to explore how the **women's movement** and other radical socialist movements were organising for change, illustrates many of the dilemmas of the time. Coming when the centralised structures of the left were being abandoned and grassroots initiatives were having to cope with the implications of working under a far right government, it rapidly became clear that radical socialism had expanded into a very broad church. Some, like politician **Tony Benn**, thought that the electoral process offered the best hope; others like Peter Hain rejected this course of action in favour of political action on all fronts. Some socialist feminists, like Elizabeth Wilson, criticised 'Beyond the Fragments' for not addressing the differences between socialism and feminism; others like **Sheila Rowbotham** saw the link as a way of influencing mainstream socialism for the better. Some red-green activists saw an opportunity to build bridges between socialism and environmental politics, others came away convinced that socialism had hit the buffers. The 'Beyond the Fragments' publications and meetings gave an airing for many points of view, undoubtedly widening the debate and introducing activists to a range of stimulating and provocative ideas. At the same time, such variety tended to confirm many participants in the validity of their own sectarianism and the apparent futility of effective structures and organisation.

The growing international green movement of the 1980s, intent upon finding a voice on the political platform, discovered almost everywhere that as much effort seemed to go into debating internal power structures as into fighting environmental battles. The first 'green' party in the world, New Zealand's Values Party, tore itself apart at its 1979 conference over the issue of campaigning style: was it a 'proper' political party with the 'professionalism' to match, or was it an organic network of individuals free to work towards green awareness in a motley of different approaches? The professionals lost, and left to form – interestingly – the New Zealand Socialist Network. The same pattern was repeated in many green groupings, notably in the German Green Party (**Die Grünen**) in 1984–85 and the UK Green Party in 1986–87.

The debate between professionalism and individuality, leadership and anarchy, structure and structurelessness, ran through every aspect of the radical movement in the 1980s. While there is as a result more clarity about the issues, and in some quarters at least a greater willingness to live with variety and contradiction, these concerns are still being hotly debated today, and are increasingly becoming a topic of interest in more 'mainstream' areas like business management and local government.

Variety and contradiction have been at the heart of the last decade of radicalism, and both can be seen as either negative or positive. Many activists have agitated over the increasing diffusion and fragmentation of the movement and, while they may find comfort in the easily-provable assertion that 'there is an awful lot going on', such widespread activity is often hard to see. Much more visible has been the fact that, throughout most of the decade and in most of the world, it has been the élitist right and its singleminded brand of capitalism that has won power and set the political and social agenda. The right's 'hegemonic project' (to use **Gramsci**'s term) has been to develop a simplistic and dogmatic programme that plays upon popular fears and insecurities, stresses its own blinkered brand of unity and authority, and offers equally simplistic and dogmatic solutions. In apparent contradistinction, the right also has a conspicuous interest in emphasising the 'disunity' of its opposition.

Fortunately for the planet and its inhabitants, however, the supposed disunity of opposition to the status quo has been more a hope in the minds of the powerbrokers than a quantifiable truth. Whether that opposition has been by efficient lobby organisations with years of experience, or by concerned individuals becoming involved in a local campaign, the truth is that 'the movement' is more powerful than ever. In many ways, because they are more focused and less partisan than official channels and sources, those working in the radical tradition can often provide more detailed information and a more balanced critique than those financially and politically beholden to the mainstream.

Thus the Washington-based Worldwatch Institute has become a recognised provider of excellent environmental information all over the world, its annual *State of the World* survey translated into ten languages including Arabic and Chinese. The Stockholm International Peace Research Institute (SIPRI) has become the accepted source of information and new ideas about disarmament and the military threat to world peace. The crucial art of investigative journalism and whistleblowing has never been as vibrant – nor as threatening to the establishment – as in the 1990s, while the opportunities offered by instantaneous (and, given the nature of electronic networking, virtually indestructible) electronic communication are being used to the full by those with radical sympathies. The pioneering San Francisco-based Institute for Global Communications (IGC), funded by the Tides Foundation, has since 1987 been providing a focus for a number of radical computer networks, particularly PeaceNet, EcoNet, ConflictNet and LaborNet: this is a rich resource that anyone with Internet access can plug into (IGC's Internet webserver is at www.igc.apc.org).

Whatever doldrums Western radicals might have experienced in the late 1980s, thousands of courageous activists were ready to challenge arbitrary power in the strongholds of state socialism. During 1989 alone a radical reawakening was evident in a succession of social movements across Asia and eastern Europe, each one carrying major implications for the future of millions of people and the furthering of global democratic reform. In China a student **democracy movement** with remarkable similarities to the 1919 **May 4th Movement** (which was largely responsible for the emergence of modern China) confronted widespread government corruption, nepotism and censorship. Beginning in Beijing, it quickly spread to all the major universities and more than three hundred cities. Although brutally suppressed by Deng Xiaoping, particularly after it spread to workers sympathetic to the students, the democratic uprising of 1989 seriously discredited Deng's regime and led to substantial and ongoing reforms.

In East Germany forty years of effort by a coalition of religious, labour and political leaders helped to bring down the Berlin Wall, for the most part nonviolently. In the former Soviet Union, ordinary citizens successfully resisted an attempted coup against the reform government, winning the army to their side and perhaps averting civil war. Other initiatives associated with a reclaimed 'people power', and informed by pioneers in peace research and international conflict resolution, led to tentative peace agreements between Israelis and Palestinians in the Middle East, between Unionists and Republicans in Northern Ireland, and among warring factions in South Africa. Although old allegiances and antagonisms remain in all these troubled lands, the commitment of the majority to social change offers the bright promise of a more democratic future.

A RADICALISM FOR THE TWENTY-FIRST CENTURY

As the assumptions of the mainstream are increasingly being challenged by events beyond the control of governments and armies, the late 1990s present immense new challenges for the radical movement. That those events are beyond conventional control, and require a previously unimaginable change of policy and action at both local and global level, is now undeniable. Nowhere is now immune from the onslaught of human presence accompanied by ever more destructive technology. Two-thirds of the world's bird species are in decline and a thousand threatened with extinction. The planet's old growth forests are being felled at an alarming rate. Carbon emissions continued to increase annually through the 1980s, peaking in 1991 at 6,000,000,000 tons a year.

Pressure on land for food and energy has put enormous stress on the soil's capacity to provide enough for ever more people to eat. The world grain harvest peaked in 1981, and since then decreasing harvests and a growing population have nearly halved the amount of grain cropland per person. Similarly the global fishery peaked in 1989, and is currently in a rapid decline of nearly two per cent every year. Though scientists and politicians are loath to voice either statement or opinion about the threat of global warming by human agency, the fact is that the planet is on average half a degree celsius warmer than it was a century ago, while in many parts of the world out-of-the-ordinary shifts in weather are becoming increasingly worrying.

Human pressure on land and resources has inevitably played a large part in the conflicts of the last two decades, whether it be the West protecting 'its oil' in Iraq and the Timor Sea or the growing streams of refugees fleeing hunger and tribal territorial rivalry in central and north-eastern Africa. In 1974 the United Nations High Commission for Refugees estimated that two and a half million people were refugees from one country seeking asylum in another; today there are nearly twenty million, including nearly four million in south-eastern Europe and a million in north America. Meanwhile Third World debt has doubled in the last decade, reaching $1,800,000,000,000 in 1994, a phenomenon not unconnected with the rise of anti-Western fundamentalism.

Yet there are hopeful signs too, and the fact that global military spending is in sharp decline, investment in alternative energy is up, and the rate of population increase is on a downward trend all show that common sense may yet avert global catastrophe. It would be convenient for conventional politicians and economists to take the acclaim for these changes, but the truth is that each of these positive trends (and others like them) is due in large part to many thousands of grassroots activists laying the foundations for peaceful coexistence, researching into appropriate technology, and struggling for reproductive rights.

The radicals of any age need to believe that new values and policies are lurking just over the horizon, and that if we work hard enough and passionately enough then we shall surely glimpse the dawn of the new way. Radicals refuse to accept premature claims that we have reached 'the end of history', or that everything we cherished is now lost, or that the closing of the century represents the culmination of progress towards a capitalist heaven for those who most deserve it. Yet we must continue to fight for the right to question, to act, and to force change. But how can the proliferation of radical issues and vital energies that underlie the new 'politics of identity' be preserved, and the links between the various parts be maintained? What kind of radical politics and vision are appropriate to an era which appears to be characterised by claims to be post almost everything – postmodern, postfeminist, post-Marxist, postcapitalist?

We have returned to where we started, to the exploration of what *really* matters. Two centuries on from the great revolutions which ushered in the so-called age of enlightenment, few people would disagree with those who saw the most self-evident truth to be that all people are created equal, and are endowed with the unalienable rights of life, liberty and the pursuit of happiness. Why has it taken so long for such 'self-evident truth' to be taken close to its logical limits?

The simplest explanation is that until such an idea was publicly uttered it was impossible to start exploring the forces that everywhere kept human beings in chains, and when those chains of religion, militarism, privilege, patriarchy and racism (to name but the most obvious) started to be disentangled it thereafter appeared that the tangled knot of oppression and injustice was always more complex and tightly woven than anyone had ever imagined. Thus it took another century to abolish slavery in the USA, and yet another fifty years to take the first major step towards women's rights by confirming that women had a right to vote. It was not until the 1930s that psychology explored the vital links between personal experience and action, not until the 1950s that the right to colonise was actively questioned, and not until the 1970s that new wave feminists could confidently declare the indivisibility of the personal and the political. It has all happened very recently. Despite the speed of change of the modern world, human beings are biological animals as well as programmable intelligences, and take time to adapt to radical ideas as they do to changes in their physical environment.

But a sea-change has taken place. Today's decision-makers grew up in a postcolonial, post-global war world, where women and foreigners and racial minorities and homosexuals and the sick and the disabled and children and old people are known to have rights, even when those rights are deliberately thwarted. The big difference is that until our parents' generation people could be blinkered and still semi-legitimately excuse themselves for being blinkered. 'We didn't know. There wasn't anything we could do. They deserved it.' Having reached the end of a century of extremes we now live in an age where there is no excuse not to know and no excuse not to take a stand.

I would like to think we are on the brink of an age of renewed responsibility, where each of us recognises the part we personally can play in the pursuit of life, liberty and happiness for all. It can be useful to remind ourselves that 'responsibility' comes from the Latin root *respondere*, 'to promise in return', for it helps to underline our essential interdependence and make it clear that responsibility is a promise as well as a burden. As Duane Elgin explained in his 1981 book *Voluntary*

Simplicity, 'We are each uniquely responsible for our response to this time of transition and challenge. There is no one who can take our place.' But this is not the 'me versus the rest' philosophy of individualism so popular in the materialistic 80s. The Italian libertarian Giuseppi Mazzini made it clear as long ago as 1835 that rights must be balanced by responsibilities in order to reflect the interdependent nature of human society, and it is the shared creativity of joint responsibility for important projects that brings out the best in people.

For we now know that we are all in this together. 'My country is the world, and my religion is to do good,' wrote **Thomas Paine** in 1791, a recognition of shared responsibility and destiny repeated by many a radical since, most notably **Virginia Woolf** in *Three Guineas*. Today, when without blinking we buy clothes made half a world away and fresh fruit flown in from another continent, this recognition is all the more poignant. But it need not be a burden. It can also be a shared understanding of the primacy of human dignity for all the world's citizens.

And wherever people work for what they know to be liberating and satisfying, they grow rapidly in understanding, sympathy and courage. Even when they have next to nothing in the way of material advantage (maybe because they have so little to lose), the recognition of self-worth and purpose is truly moving. As a peasant woman from southern India explained to economist Anisur Rahman (recorded in his 1993 book *People's Self-Development*), 'We know that there is no easy and quick solution to our problem of food and clothing. But we as women did not even have the right to speak. In our organisation we can now meet and speak, and share and discuss our problems. We feel that we are now human beings. We look forward to our weekly meetings where we stand up and speak – we can thereby release ourselves as we have never been able to do before, and we now have the courage to speak the truth.'

Not only is it exciting and challenging to question how the world works. Now that we recognise the links between the personal and the political we can also use our radical activism to discover how we work. In a January 1995 review of *The River Stops Here*, Ted Simon's story of how Californian activist Richard Wilson prevented the building of a massive dam on a wild river in the north of the state to provide Los Angeles with water, British environmentalist George Monbiot writes that 'The greatest battle any environmental campaigner faces is the battle with him or herself. At every turn we are taught to fit in, to respect authority, to refrain from rocking the boat. Confronting the state forces us to acknowledge that the maxims we were brought up to follow are false: cheats do prosper, virtue does not triumph of itself, and the truth will out only with the most arduous winkling. Facing this revelation leads swiftly to the questioning of everything one once believed about oneself.'

Until radical thought had reached the depths that we from our end-of-the-century perspective can begin to fathom, such deep personal questioning often led to impenetrable existential angst, madness and ostracism. Today we can dare things which were difficult, even dangerous, to dare in earlier generations. Though the struggle has been hard, I believe we are in a better position than at any other time during the century to envision and create the world that radicals have worked for since the idea first gained currency. When asked by Italian authors Paola Agosti and Giovanna Borgese for a short judgement on the twentieth century, musician Yehudi Menuhin replied 'If I had to sum up the century I would say that it had raised the greatest hopes ever conceived by humanity, and destroyed all our illusions and ideals.' I would like to think that those hopes are as alive today as ever they were, and, having abandoned our illusions and let go of our fixed ideals, we are now in a place of experienced maturity, ready to work in the real world with its real problems and challenges, and understanding deep within ourselves what *really* matters.

SOURCES

Ti-Grace Atkinson, *Amazon Odyssey*, Links, 1974

Murray Bookchin, *The Modern Crisis*, New Society, 1986

Gail Chester, 'I Call Myself a Radical Feminist', *No Turning Back: Writings from the Women's Liberation Movement, 1975–80*, Women's Press, 1981

Mary Daly, *Beyond God the Father, Toward a Philosophy of Women's Liberation*, Beacon, 1973

Duane Elgin, *Voluntary Simplicity*, Morrow, 1981

Barbara Epstein, *Political Protest and Cultural Revolution: Nonviolent Direct Action in the 1970s and 1980s*, University of California Press, 1991

Paulo Freire, *The Pedagogy of the Oppressed*, Herder and Herder, 1970

Marilyn Frye, *The Politics of Reality*, Crossing Press, 1983

Eric Hobsbawm, *Age of Extremes: The Short Twentieth Century*, Michael Joseph, 1994

Lee Maracle, *Bobbi Lee: Indian Rebel*, Women's Press (Canada), 1990

George Monbiot, 'Blasting the Dam Boosters' (review of Ted Simon, *The River Stops Here: How One Man's Battle to Save His Valley Changed the Fate of California*, Random House, 1994), *New Scientist*, 14 January 1995

Michael Neumann, *What's Left: Radical Politics and the Radical Psyche*, Broadview, 1988

Kwame Nkrumah, *Neo-colonialism: The Last Stage of Imperialism*, Oxford University Press, 1965

Marge Piercy, 'The Seven of Pentacles', *To Be of Use*, Doubleday, 1973

Anisur Rahman, *People's Self-Development: Perspectives on Participatory Action Research*, Zed, 1993

Charles Reich, *The Greening of America: How the Youth Revolution is Trying to Make America Livable*, Random House, 1970

Barry Schwarz, *The Costs of Living: How Market Freedom Erodes the Best Things in Life*, Norton, 1994

Raymond Williams, *Keywords*, Oxford University Press, 1985 (rev. edn)

RADICAL FORERUNNERS

Susan B. [Brownell] Anthony
1820–1906
women's rights and women's suffrage campaigner

'Failure is impossible!' was the watchword of Susan B. Anthony's lifelong campaign for women's rights, and she is widely regarded as the most influential American feminist of her era. The daughter of a Quaker abolitionist family, she worked as a teacher and then as a manager with the family firm in upstate New York. Influenced by black rights advocates like **Frederick Douglass**, she became involved in the American Anti-Slavery Society, and also worked for teachers' rights and in the temperance movement, but increasingly experienced sex discrimination within these supposedly egalitarian reform organisations. In 1851 she met **Elizabeth Cady Stanton**, who was to become a lifelong friend and colleague, and her campaigning and lecturing moved into the areas of women's suffrage and property rights. From 1868–70 she edited and published *The Revolution*, a radical women's newspaper, and in 1869 she and Elizabeth Cady Stanton founded the National Woman Suffrage Association. In 1872 she led a group of women to vote – illegally – in the presidential election, and used the trial to make a passionate appeal for universal suffrage. During the 1880s she and Elizabeth Cady Stanton worked with **Matilda Joslyn Gage** to produce the six-volume *History of Woman Suffrage*. Susan B. Anthony went on to cofound the International Council of Women in 1888 and the **International Woman Suffrage Alliance** in 1904. She never married, and always stressed the wisdom of her decision. 'Had I married at twenty-one I would have been either a drudge or a doll for fifty-five years,' she told an interviewer shortly before her death. 'Think of it!'

Katherine Anthony, *Susan B. Anthony: Her Personal History and her Era*, Doubleday, 1954
Alma Lutz, *Susan B. Anthony: Rebel, Crusader, Humanitarian*, Beacon, 1959

Mikhail [Aleksandrovich] Bakunin
1814–1876
anarchist and romantic revolutionary

Mikhail Bakunin, international stirrer and visionary populariser of modern anarchism, inspired many late nineteenth and early twentieth-century radicals the world over, yet **Karl Marx** called him 'a man devoid of all theoretical knowledge', and more recent detractors have questioned his sanity. The eldest son of a large aristocratic Russian family, he spent a short time in the army before studying philosophy in Moscow. His search for political enlightenment soon led him to France and Germany. In 1844 he met both **Proudhon** and Marx, being impressed by the former's fiery politics and the latter's economic insight, though Bakunin's enduring anti-German sentiment put him firmly on the side of romantic revolutionaries, be they Slav, French or Italian, and made him a harsh critic of the 'authoritarianism' of Marxism. He witnessed the French Revolution of 1848 at first hand, and manned the revolutionary barricades at Prague and Dresden in 1848–49; he was sentenced to death, but was reprieved and extradited to Russia. After four years in prison he was on the move again, taking in Siberia, Japan, the USA and England before settling in Italy in 1864. The outbreak of the Franco-Prussian War in 1870 gave him a new purpose for his activism and pamphleteering, that of turning the conflict into a social revolution; even better was the establishment of the French Third Republic, where he played an active part in the Lyon Uprising of 1870 and the Paris Commune of 1871. Mikhail Bakunin was a fluent advocate for mass action against state tyranny, though his speeches and writings (of which he completed very few) were often simplistic and contradictory, especially when he addressed the question of violence as a tool for social and economic change.

Michael Bakunin (ed. Arthur Lehning), *Michael Bakunin: Selected Writings*, Cape, 1973

Edward H. Carr, *Michael Bakunin*, Macmillan, 1937

Aileen Kelly, *Mikhail Bakunin: A Study in the Psychology and Politics of Utopianism*, Oxford University Press, 1982

Aphra Behn
1640–1689
novelist, playwright and poet

'All women together should let flowers fall on the tomb of Aphra Behn,' wrote **Virginia Woolf** in *A Room of One's Own*, 'for it was she who earned them the right to speak their minds.' Born near Canterbury, England, when Aphra was in her early twenties she travelled with her family to Surinam, where she became involved in a slave rebellion, and on her return married a Dutch merchant who died a year later in the great plague. In the mid-1660s she was a government spy in Holland, but was ill rewarded and on her return to Britain was imprisoned briefly for debt. In dire need of financial support, in 1670 she entered the fiercely competitive world of the theatre, becoming the first woman to earn her living as a professional writer. The first of her fifteen plays, *The Forced Marriage or The Jealous Bridegroom*, was performed on September 20th 1670, forcefully presenting a woman's perspective on marriage, a theme she was to return to several times, notably in her most successful play, *The Rover* (1677). During the last years of her life she turned her creative skills to writing novels. The best known, *Oroonoko or The History of The Royal Slave* (1688), drew on her Surinam experience to question slavery, the first time this had been done in the English language. As a successful feminist who vociferously defended her egalitarian views and a sexual pioneer who believed that women and men should live and love as they please (she regularly dressed as a man), she was both admired and reviled. Though buried in Westminster Abbey's famous poets' corner, her work virtually disappeared for more than two hundred years; resurrected by feminist historians and artistes in the 1970s and 80s, however, her plays are now regularly performed and *Oroonoko* is a favourite college text.

Aphra Behn, *Oroonoko: The Royal Slave* (many modern editions)
Angeline Goreau, *Reconstructing Aphra: A Social Biography of Aphra Behn*, Dial Press, 1980

Edward Bellamy
1850–1898
writer and utopian socialist

It was as much a surprise to Edward Bellamy, smalltown American creative writer, as it was to anyone when in 1888 his visionary socialist novel *Looking Backward* became so widely read that a whole social movement developed from it. Within ten years his story about a late nineteenth-century Bostonian who wakes up in a late twentieth-century utopia had sold half a million copies in the USA, been translated into 25 languages, and inspired the formation of Bellamyite societies in a dozen countries. Apart from short periods he lived all his life in his family's home in Chicopee Falls, Massachusetts; here he saw at first hand how industrial change was robbing people of their humanity. After a short unsuccessful period practising law, he thenceforward lived by his pen, writing four important novels and numerous short stories and articles; in 1891 he inaugurated the radical journal *New Nation*. *Looking Backward* and his last novel, *Equality* (1897), envisage a society which has done away with class, exploitation, oppression, censorship, taxation, armed forces and politicians, thus liberating human beings to work together to reach their full potential. Edward Bellamy's conception clearly struck a chord, both with intellectuals and with workers. His vision, which he (unfortunately in the light of later developments) called 'nationalism', quickly rallied mass support, and many contemporary social activists acknowledged a profound debt to him. After a long and debilitating illness he died in May 1898.

Edward Bellamy, *Looking Backward: 2000–1887* (many editions)
Sylvia E. Bowman, *The Year 2000: A Critical Biography of Edward Bellamy*, Bookman, 1958

William Blake
1757–1827
engraver, poet and visionary artist

To many radicals the archetypal creative freethinker, prophet and visionary, William Blake was first and foremost an innovative poet and artist, an independent spirit who resisted many of the strict orthodoxies of his day to present powerful truths in word and image. The third son of a London shopkeeper's family, he was apprenticed as an engraver and studied at the Royal Academy. In 1780, while working for an influential London bookseller, he met his lifelong friend the sculptor John Flaxman, who introduced him to the visionary ideas of the Swedish mystic Emanuel Swedenborg. Flaxman helped to finance Blake's first volume of poetry in 1783, and the next twelve years saw the publication of more than a dozen important works, most of them illustrated with Blake's powerful engravings: the best known are *Songs of Innocence* (1789), *The Book of Thel* (1789), *The Marriage of Heaven and Hell* (1790–93) and *Songs of Experience* (1794). In the early 1790s, after meeting **Thomas Paine**, he produced an important series of revolutionary works, *The French Revolution* (1791), *America: A Prophecy* (1793) and *Vision of the Daughters of Albion* (1793), in which he combined anti-authoritarian fervour with visionary ecstasy. In 1803, while working on his poem *Milton* in Sussex, he was charged with high treason for having been heard uttering the words 'Damn the king; damn all his subjects', but he was acquitted. His later work concentrated on religious themes, though still stressing the rebellious nature of living spirituality. William Blake's radiant poetic vision of a transformed humanity, living harmoniously without the constraints of church or state, has inspired generations of artists and anarchists. His writings had a considerable influence on post-war **Beat** and underground poetry, and more recently his 'new age' vision has resonated strongly with many spiritually-inclined green radicals.

William Blake, *Illuminated Blake: William Blake's Complete Illuminated Works*, Dover, 1993
Peter Marshall, *William Blake: Visionary Anarchist*, Freedom Press, 1988

Thomas Carlyle
1795–1881
essayist, historian and social critic

'There is hardly a superior or active mind of this generation that has not been modified by Carlyle's writings,' wrote **George Eliot** in 1855, and, though his admiration of strong leadership and his obscure prose assisted the waning of his influence as the new century approached, he was nevertheless an important influence for social activists as diverse as **Friedrich Engels**, **William Morris**, **John Stuart Mill** and **Ralph Waldo Emerson**. The son of a religious rural Scottish family, he studied at Edinburgh University; early plans to enter the church soon gave way to more academic inclinations. His marriage to Jane Welsh in 1826 established a long collaboration, and the fact that he wrote little of consequence after her death in 1866 establishes her crucial part in supporting his work; the posthumous publication of her papers and letters, which exposed a certain amount of discord between the Carlyles, caused much late-Victorian controversy, and feminists including **Virginia Woolf** have suggested that the world would have been an even better place if Jane had done the writing while Thomas did the housework. In 1834 they moved from Scotland to London, and the publication of *A History of the French Revolution* in 1837 firmly established his reputation. Although Thomas Carlyle's ideas are often dogmatic and sometimes contradictory, many caught the imagination of his radical contemporaries: in *Chartism* (1839), for example, he deplored the way in which cash payment had become the universally-acceptable unit of exchange between people, while in *Past and Present* (1843) he praised the rapidly-disappearing craftsmanship of the rural artisan.

Thomas Carlyle (ed. Alan Shelston), *Selected Writings*, Penguin, 1971
Fred Caplan, *Thomas Carlyle: A Biography*, Cambridge University Press, 1984
Philip Rosenberg, *The Seventh Hero: Thomas Carlyle and the Theory of Radical Activism*, Harvard University Press, 1975

Kate Chopin [Katherine O'Flaherty]
1851–1904
novelist

Had Kate Chopin not had the courage to publish *The Awakening* in 1899, she might have been remembered only as a minor but entertaining regional novelist. In the event her story of Edna Pontellier, the unfulfilled wife who awakes to self-knowledge and emotional and sexual excitement, which was condemned by many contemporary reviewers for its 'immorality', has since provided generations of readers with a glimpse of the passion and pain of liberated relationships. After her father died in an accident when she was five, Kate Chopin grew up in a predominantly female household in St Louis, Missouri. In 1870 she married businessman Oscar Chopin, by whom she had six children, and after his New Orleans business failed they went to live on his family's plantation in Cane River, where Oscar died of swamp fever in 1882. Kate was already an accomplished writer, but after Oscar's death, in addition to successfully managing the plantation finances until all the debts were paid, she wrote many further poems and short stories, the latter being collected in three well-received volumes between 1894 and 1900. Kate, always her own woman, believed in the importance of self-fulfilment and integrity: to this end, following the publication of a number of short stories on controversial social issues (including infidelity and venereal disease), in 1899 she wrote *The Awakening*, believing that Americans were ready for such insight and artistry from a woman's pen. Though early reviews and friends' opinions were favourable, the establishment press was quick to denounce *The Awakening* as morbid and disgusting (contrary to popular belief, however, the book was never actually banned). Kate was deeply hurt by this response; though she continued to write, her spirit was broken by the experience, and she died of a brain haemorrhage four years later. Despite her detractors' best efforts, however, *The Awakening* remained in print, becoming popular in the 1940s and again with the feminist revival in the 1970s.

Kate Chopin, *The Awakening*, 1899 (many recent editions)
Emily Toth, *Kate Chopin*, Morrow, 1990

Frederick Douglass
1817–1895
antislavery and equal rights campaigner

The most famous black freedom campaigner of the nineteenth-century, Frederick Douglass knew slavery at first hand. His master, Maryland estate owner Hugh Auld, believed that slave literacy threatened the status quo; his wife Sophia's covert teaching and Douglass's determination were to prove him right. In 1838 his future wife Anne Murray, a free black, helped him to escape by providing him with seaman's papers; in New Bedford he came into contact with the antislavery movement, and in 1841, impressed with his power of oratory, the American Anti-Slavery Society enlisted him as an agent. In 1845, partly to counter accusations that he had never been a slave, he published his autobiographical *Narrative of the Life of Frederick Douglass, An American Slave, Written by Himself*, and for two years lectured against slavery in Britain; in 1847 his legal freedom was purchased for £150 by a group of British supporters. Returning to the USA in 1847, he threw himself wholeheartedly into abolitionist speechmaking and journalism. He urged the participation and fair treatment of black soldiers in the Republican Army during the Civil War, and continually stressed the abolitionist cause for that war. With the end of hostilities and of slavery he pushed for black voting rights, and was instrumental in the passage of the Fifteenth Amendment of 1870 which gave black men the vote (he felt that universal suffrage was eventually inevitable, but premature in the prevailing political climate). From 1877 to 1891 he held a number of government posts in the USA, Santo Domingo and Haiti. Always eager to link the black rights cause with women's and labour movement demands, he was at the same time supportive of these movements and critical whenever he witnessed racism within their ranks; he collapsed and died while attending a women's suffrage rally in February 1895.

> Nathan Irvin Huggins, *Slave and Citizen: The Life of Frederick Douglass*, Little, Brown, 1980
> William McFeely, *Frederick Douglass*, Norton, 1991

George Eliot [Mary Ann, later Marian, Evans]
1819–1880
novelist, poet, essayist and social commentator

Having been strongly influenced in her early life by the Coventry freethinkers Charles and Caroline Bray and later by the feminists **Margaret Fuller** and **Mary Wollstonecraft**, George Eliot's powerful novels and stories contain many compassionate and well-observed portraits of radical dissenters and strong women, often being forced to choose between material comforts and social and personal conscience. In her private life she endeavoured to maintain her religious and egalitarian convictions, especially in her often unconventional and misunderstood relationships with men, including her publisher John Chapman, the already-married novelist

George Lewes and, when she was nearly sixty, her forty-year-old financial adviser John Cross. The importance of her work, much admired during her later life, was reinforced by **Virginia Woolf**, who in 1919 wrote of *Middlemarch* that it was 'one of the few English novels written for grown-up people'. Her contribution to the feminist cause has recently been stressed; in an 1885 essay, for example, she 'rescued' Mary Wollstonecraft's *A Vindication of the Rights of Women* from half a century of almost total obscurity.

Thomas Pinney (ed.), *Essays of George Eliot*, Routledge and Kegan Paul, 1963
Gordon Haight, *George Eliot: A Biography*, Oxford University Press, 1978

Ralph Waldo Emerson
1803–1882
transcendentalist philosopher, poet, essayist

Many of Emerson's best-known insights, that 'nature is the incarnation of thought' (from 'Nature', 1836) and that 'nothing can bring you peace but yourself' (from 'Self-Reliance', 1841), still retain the freshness and immediacy that so inspired **Thoreau**, **Whitman**, and subsequent generations of naturalistic artists and freethinkers. A son of the manse, he followed his father into the Unitarian Church, and studied at Harvard before becoming a pastor in Boston in 1829. In 1831 the death of his first wife, Ellen Tucker, precipitated him into a personal and spiritual crisis; he left the church and spent a year in Europe, where he met the poets Samuel Taylor Coleridge and William Wordsworth and established what was to become a lifelong friendship with **Thomas Carlyle**. Returning to Massachusetts in 1833, Ralph Waldo Emerson quickly established himself as a lecturer and writer; remarried (to Lydia Jackson) and revitalised, he fluently articulated the spiritual philosophy of transcendentalism, encapsulated in his 1836 essay 'Nature'. This, together with his optimism about America's role in the arts and his rugged rural imagery, caught the popular imagination. A visit to England in the late 1840s (reviewed in his *English Traits* of 1856) endeared him to a wider readership, and his active engagement in the antislavery campaign of the 1860s showed him to be more than a mere rhetorician.

Ralph Waldo Emerson (ed. Carl Bode and Malcolm Cowley), *The Portable Emerson*, Penguin, 1982
Joel Porte, *Representative Man: Ralph Waldo Emerson in His Time*, Oxford University Press, 1979
Joan McAleer, *Ralph Waldo Emerson: Days of Encounter*, Little, Brown, 1985

Friedrich Engels
1820–1895
socialist-communist writer and philosopher

When Friedrich Engels first met **Karl Marx** in Paris in September 1844 it was the start of a forty-year collaboration that was to change the international political and economic landscape beyond recognition. The joint architects of Marxism, Engels added his quick intelligence and experience of the industrial revolution in Britain to Marx's profound analytical skills. As a young man working in his father's textile firm, first in Wuppertal in German Westphalia and from 1842 in Manchester, Friedrich Engels was much influenced by the libertarian philosophy of Georg Hegel, the anti-religious materialism of Ludwig Feuerbach, and latterly the utopian socialism of **Robert Owen** and **Charles Fourier**. In 1845 he published his first important work, *The Condition of the Working Class in England*, a searing criticism of the capitalist exploitation of labour. Early in 1845 Friedrich Engels read Max Stirner's critique of Feuerbach and started to develop his ideas about class consciousness; for the next five years he devoted himself to working with Marx to rebuild German communism, and on the eve of the 1848 revolution they produced the *Communist Manifesto*, a stirring call to the masses that was to become the blueprint for many late nineteenth-century radicals. After the abortive revolution Engels returned to England to become a partner in the family firm; twenty years later he was able to retire comfortably and move from Manchester to London. Here he helped the ailing Marx to work on *Das Kapital*, and wrote his most important works – *Anti-Dührung* (1873), the first attempt at a general exposition of Marxism, and *The Origin of the Family, Private Property and the State* (1895). The most fluent early populariser of Marxism, Friedrich Engels played a far greater role in its early expansion than did Karl Marx himself.

> Friedrich Engels, *The Condition of the Working Class in England*; *Socialism: Utopian and Scientific* (English trans. of *Anti-Dührung*); *The Origin of the Family, Private Property and the State* (many editions)
> Terrell Carver, *Friedrich Engels: His Life and Thought*, Macmillan, 1989
> J.D. Hunley, *Friedrich Engels: A Reinterpretation of his Life and Thought*, Yale University Press, 1991

[François Marie] Charles Fourier
1772–1837
utopian philosopher and writer

Although for most of his life a travelling textiles salesman who lived in a Besançon boarding house, the original ideas of the French socialist utopian Charles Fourier were to reverberate throughout the world for many decades. In 1902 **Petr Kropotkin** acknowledged him as 'a forerunner of Anarchy', and social ecologist **Murray Bookchin** has described him as 'the most libertarian, the most original, and certainly the most relevant utopian thinker of his day'. From 1808 to 1829 he set out his ideas in a series of pamphlets prefaced *Le nouveau monde* (*The New World*), combining ecological and libertarian awareness with a detailed (sometimes verging on the proscriptive and repressive) blueprint of a new society called 'Harmony', based on communities or 'phalansteries' of around 1,500 people in which the inhabitants are free to work and love in a cooperative, meaningful way. Despite Fourier's concerted efforts to find a benefactor to help him establish such a community, it was only after his death that his ideas started to bear fruit in a series of community experiments in France and the USA.

His protégé Victor Considérant helped Fourierism to become a consider-able political force in the early phase of the 1848 revolution in France, and his American disciple Albert Brisbane successfully used his skills as a publicist to promote Fourier's ideas as the solution for all social problems. During the 1840s more than thirty Fourier-inspired community experi-ments flourished briefly from Massachusetts to Iowa, the best known being Brook Farm near Boston, which became converted to Fourierism in 1844 and thrived for three years before a disastrous fire and financial problems precipitated its dissolution.

Jonathan Beecher and Richard Bienvenu (eds), *The Utopian Vision of Charles Fourier*, Beacon Press, 1971
Jonathan Beecher, *Charles Fourier: The Visionary and His World*, University of California Press, 1987

[Sarah] Margaret Fuller
1810–1850
journalist, literary critic, feminist historian

Despite the best efforts of her male contemporaries, including **Ralph Waldo Emerson** (who succeeded her as editor of the shortlived but influential Boston magazine *The Dial*) and the rewriters of her posthumous *Memoirs* (1852), to portray her as an opinionated, aggressive, unattractive old maid, Margaret Fuller is now widely regarded as one of the best journalists and literary critics of her day. Born in Cambridgeport, Massa-chusetts, her father insisted on her having a rigorous education, which when she grew up and started teaching made her acutely aware of how little educated most of her women friends were. She met Emerson (who found her both frightening and fascinating) in 1836, became an active member of the transcendentalist circle, and in 1839 began holding women-only 'conversations', providing an influential circle of Boston women with the arguments and the skills to present a women-centred world view. She edited *The Dial* for two years from its foundation in 1840, and in 1843 moved to New York to work as literary critic on the *Tribune*; two years later she published *Woman in the Nineteenth Century*, a pioneering tract which skilfully constructed a feminist tradition to balance the male denial of women's contribution to history. In 1846 she travelled to Europe as America's first woman foreign correspondent, and in Italy met, had a child with and married Angelo Ossoli. Both became involved in the Italian revolution of 1848–49 which briefly replaced papal authority with a people's republic, and Margaret began to write a history of the revolution. Her life and her career were cut short when she and her family were drowned in a storm off Long Island while they were returning to America in July 1850.

Margaret Fuller, *Woman in the Nineteenth Century*, 1845 (repr. University of South Carolina Press, 1980)
Marie Urbanski, *Margaret Fuller's 'Woman in the Nineteenth Century'*, Greenwood Press, 1980

Matilda Joslyn Gage
1826–1898
feminist historian, women's rights campaigner

In what is often called 'the triumvirate' of late nineteenth-century American feminists, of which the other two are **Susan B. Anthony** and **Elizabeth Cady Stanton**, Matilda Joslyn Gage often appears the least substantial of the three. Although her contribution, even during her own lifetime, was downplayed in favour of her colleagues, her speeches and writing display a deep knowledge and understanding of women's history and feminist theory which more than equal that of her contemporaries. Matilda Joslyn owed a great deal to her family's insistence on a good education, particularly her Scottish mother's avid interest in history. She married Henry Gage in 1844 and had three children, but let none of this interfere with her lifelong task of searching out women's achievements and cataloguing them, together with forceful descriptions of how they were systematically devalued. Her first major speech, at the Syracuse National Convention of 1852, impressed veteran women's rights campaigner Lucretia Mott, who insisted that it should be printed and circulated. From 1878 to 1881 Matilda Joslyn Gage edited the newspaper of the National Woman Suffrage Association (NWSA), and then joined Anthony and Stanton to work on the multi-volume *History of Woman Suffrage*, for which she contributed much of the historical material and wrote the important introductory chapters. In 1890, when the NWSA decided to merge with the conservative American Woman Suffrage Association, she responded by resigning and establishing the Women's National Liberal Union, with a radical programme including support for native American rights and a call for an end to compulsory religion in schools. Her opposition to organised religion was even stronger than Elizabeth Cady Stanton's, and her *Woman, Church and State* (1893) demonstrated – again using many historical examples – how a patriarchal church conspires to enslave women. Towards the end of her life she felt that many suffragists, including Anthony and Stanton, had betrayed their feminist ideals to the narrow cause of winning the vote; Matilda Joslyn Gage, however, always insisted on the essential unity of feminism.

Matilda Joslyn Gage, *Woman, Church and State*, Persephone Press, 1980 (repr. of 1893 edn with an introduction by Sally Roesch Wagner and a foreword by Mary Daly)
Dale Spender, *Women of Ideas*, Routledge and Kegan Paul, 1982

William Godwin
1756–1836
writer, journalist, anarchist philosopher

The deeply thoughtful son of a family of religious dissenters, William Godwin grew up in the Cambridgeshire town of Wisbech. Following an intensive education he tried to become a minister, but soon gave up the idea in order to make his living in London from his writing. **Jonathan Swift** and **Jean-Jacques Rousseau** were important influences for him in the 1780s, and the vital importance of reason and justice together with the impossibility of creating virtue and happiness using external authority became the cornerstones of his writing. When in 1789 the French followed the Americans into revolution, proclaiming the gospel of liberty, Godwin was among the first to sense the emergence of a new European politic. In considered response to Edmund Burke's jaundiced *Reflections on the Revolution in France* of 1791 he published in 1793 *An Enquiry Concerning Political Justice, and its Influence on General Virtue and Happiness*. The French Revolution had already convinced him of the need for simple government, but he now argued convincingly that people could only be truly free if government was done away with. *Political Justice*, published two weeks after Britain declared war on revolutionary France, became a surprise bestseller, running to two expanded editions in 1796 and 1798 and incurring the wrath of the reactionary establishment. William Godwin had first met **Mary Wollstonecraft** in 1791; in 1796, as she was recovering from a disastrous affair, they became lovers. They had been married only five months when she died, shortly after their daughter, also Mary, was born. Her death was a painful blow to him, and though he married again, had another child, and continued to write successful fiction and philosophy, his happiest and most influential years were over. In 1812 the young rebel poet **Percy Bysshe Shelley** became a disciple, setting Godwin's ideas in verse in poems like *Queen Mab* and *Prometheus Unbound*; Godwin was not so happy when Shelley eloped with his sixteen-year-old daughter.

William Godwin (eds William Godwin and Mark Philp), *Political and Philosophical Writings* , Pickering and Chatto, 1993

Peter Marshall, *William Godwin*, Yale University Press, 1984

Sarah [Moore] Grimké and Angelina [Emily] Grimké
1792–1873 and 1805–1879
civil rights and women's rights campaigners

Daughters of an upper class slaveowning family in Charleston, South Carolina, the Grimké sisters had little radicalism in their blood; what they did have, however, was firsthand experience of the worst excesses of slavery, an understanding of its social context, and a deep moral abhorrence of it. It was the sisters' conversion to Quakerism that took them to Philadelphia (Sarah in 1821, Angelina eight years later), where in 1834 Angelina wrote a strongly-worded letter which was published in the abolitionist magazine *The Liberator*, followed two years later by her *Appeal to the Christian Women of the South* to speak out against slavery. The sisters started to hold public meetings, and as their audiences grew the backlash from clergy and conservative newspapers was quick and vituperative; in 1837 a pastoral letter denounced 'disagreeable women' and the Grimkés in particular. As it became clear that it was as women that the Grimké sisters most threatened the establishment, Sarah and Angelina both turned their attention to the 'woman question': in 1838 Sarah published *Letters on the*

Equality of the Sexes, and the Condition of Women, and Angelina her *Letters to Catherine Beecher in Reply to an Essay on Slavery and Abolitionism*. The abolitionist Theodore Weld had helped to organise many of the Grimkés' lectures, and in 1838 asked Angelina to marry him. This she did but, although it was the intention of neither to let marriage detract from their campaigning, subsequent events had exactly that effect. Three days after the wedding Angelina and Theodore spoke against slavery at Pennsylvania Hall, but even as they were speaking there was a riot, and the next day the brand-new building, specifically designed as a forum for free speech, was burned to the ground. Complications with Angelina's second and subsequent pregnancies caused her much pain and made lecturing impossible, so instead she and Sarah worked with Theodore on *American Slavery as it Is: Testimony of a Thousand Witnesses* – it was published under his name alone. The Grimké sisters continued to work together, raising Angelina's children, teaching, and campaigning for women's suffrage; at the age of 79 Sarah was still travelling the countryside on foot to collect signatures for a suffrage petition to Congress.

Catherine Birney, *The Grimké Sisters: Sarah and Angelina Grimké: The First American Women Advocates of Abolition and Women's Rights* (repr. of 1855 edn), Greenwood, 1969

Gerda Lerner, *The Grimké Sisters from South Carolina: Pioneers for Women's Rights and Abolition*, Schocken, 1971

Henrik [Johan] Ibsen
1828–1906
dramatist

The Norwegian dramatist Henrik Ibsen had an enormous influence on the psychological and social development of the late nineteenth and early twentieth centuries, and the fact that his plays still have such an immediate impact is a tribute to his commitment to social and political realism. Though born into a well-off family, his father's bankruptcy forced Ibsen to fend for himself. He became an apprentice chemist, but failed the entrance examination for the University of Christiania (now Oslo) and turned to journalism, where his efforts came to the attention of writer and theatre director Ole Bull. Working at theatres in Bergen and Christiania, he learned the art of stagecraft at first hand, and in 1858 married Susannah Thoreson: their only son Sigurd was born the following year. From 1864 to 1891 the Ibsens lived abroad, primarily in Rome, Dresden and Munich, and this period saw the tangible fruits of Ibsen's writing skills. His dramatic poems *Brand* (1866) and *Peer Gynt* (1867) were instant successes and provided much-needed financial security but, following a meeting in 1871 with the Danish critic George Brandes, Ibsen became convinced of the need to portray personal psychological, spiritual and political dilemmas in clear and powerful language. The years between 1877 and 1896 saw the production of eleven major plays, including *A Doll's House* (1879), *An Enemy of the People* (1882), *Rosmersholm* (1886), *Hedda Gabler* (1890) and *The Master*

Builder (1892), showing real people in contemporary settings, torn by conflicting loyalties and exploring their personal needs for authenticity and fulfilment. Influential scholars like Edmund Gosse and George Bernard Shaw introduced Ibsen to the English-speaking world, and his widely-read and much-performed plays, though they provoked considerable hostile criticism from reactionary quarters, struck a chord with those readers and theatregoers intrigued and touched by the social and political issues they raised. Ibsen returned to Norway in 1891, suffering in 1900 the first of a series of strokes which were to end his distinguished literary career.

Henrik Ibsen, *A Doll's House*; *An Enemy of the People*; *Rosmersholm*; *Hedda Gabler*; *The Master Builder* (many editions)
Michael Leverson Meyer, *Henrik Ibsen*, Hart-Davis, 3 vols, 1967–71
Lou Andreas-Salome, *Ibsen's Heroines*, Black Swan, 1985
Bernard Frank Dukore, *Money and Politics in Ibsen, Shaw, and Brecht*, University of Missouri Press, 1980

Karl [Heinrich] Marx
1818–1883
historian, social commentator, revolutionary theorist

Because he is the one radical that everyone has heard of, and because regimes using his name have dominated twentieth-century politics, Karl Marx's own contribution to the radical tradition is hard to judge. A man driven by the need to understand the grand patterns of history and philosophy, constantly hounded by fearful establishment forces, obsessed by the idea of mass revolution, he gave his life to the cause of class struggle. Born into a comfortable middle-class family in Trier on the River Moselle, he studied at Bonn and Berlin Universities, becoming immersed in a fashionable mix of romanticism, utopianism and social libertarianism. From 1842 to 1844 he edited a series of radical newspapers in Germany, France and Belgium; in 1843 he married Jenny von Westphalen and in 1844 met **Friedrich Engels**, both of whom were to be lifelong friends and supporters. His first extended works on communism and the materialist conception of history were written during this period, though they were only published much later (as *Economic and Philosophical Manuscripts* and *The German Ideology*). He joined the Communist League, and with Engels was commissioned to write the *Communist Manifesto*; published just as the 1848 wave of revolutions swept Europe, it was the most succinct expression yet of the aims of the communist project. As the revolutionary tide ebbed, Karl and Jenny Marx moved to a small flat in London's Soho. The next two decades were marked by poverty (alleviated by gifts from Engels) and ill health (three of their children died and Karl was frequently confined to his bed), yet he continued to study, write and organise. Of his voluminous writings, *Das Kapital* (in three volumes, 1867–93, completed by Engels after his death) is his greatest achievement, consolidating many influential ideas in a broad historical survey and critique of capitalism. He became one of the early leaders of the International Working Men's Association (the 'First

International') in 1864, and helped to organise six congresses in nine years. From 1868, when the International admitted **Mikhail Bakunin**'s anarchist International Alliance of Socialist Democracy into membership, Marx was suspicious of Bakunin's motives, yet he claimed the Paris Commune of 1871 as a socialist victory rather than an anarchist one, even though its Bakunin-inspired organisers had little to do with the International. In response to the events in Paris Marx wrote *The Civil War in France*, one of his most powerful pamphlets. The death of his wife and his eldest daughter in 1881 clouded his last years, though his other daughters (including his favourite, Eleanor, who continued to strive for the socialist cause) brought him some comfort.

Karl Marx, *Economic and Philosophical Manuscripts*; *The German Ideology*; *The Communist Manifesto*; *The Civil War in France*; *Capital* (many editions)

Isaiah Berlin, *Karl Marx: His Life and Environment*, Oxford University Press, 1978

Tom Bottomore *et al*, *A Dictionary of Marxist Thought*, Blackwell, 1983 (2nd edn 1991)

John Stuart Mill
1806–1873
writer, political and social theorist

John Stuart Mill had little choice about whether or not to become a political thinker. Having recently become a disciple of the ageing Jeremy Bentham, his philosopher father James was at the time of his son's birth an avid propagator of the principles of utilitarianism. He was determined that John should continue his important work, and undertook his son's education himself, starting at the age of three with Greek and Latin, followed closely by philosophy and logic. For a man who escaped the stifling clutches of his family so late (he lived in his parents' house until he was 45 and worked for the same company as his father had until he was 52), his rapidly evolving ideas about freedom and human rights are perhaps surprising, but he was able to balance his welltuned intellect with external stimulation. This came first from the London Debating Society and several study circles of which he became a member in the late 1820s, and more specifically from his growing friendship and collaboration with **Harriet Taylor**, whom he met in 1830. They worked together on several of the books that came out under Mill's name alone, notably *Principles of Political Economy* (1848) and *On Liberty* (1859), the latter being one of the classics of libertarian thought, insisting on the primacy of free enquiry in the pursuit of truth. Twenty-one years after John Stuart Mill and Harriet Taylor first met, and two years after the death of her husband, they married. Neither of them enjoyed good health towards the end of their lives, and after Harriet died in France in 1858 John Stuart Mill spent much time in health resorts. He was elected an independent member of parliament in 1865 and played a prominent part in the passage of the 1867 Reform Bill to extend the British franchise, but did not regret losing his seat in 1868. He returned to Avignon, where Harriet was buried, to write his autobiography and *The Subjection of Women* (1869), which remains one of the best-argued cases for equal rights ever written by a man.

John Stuart Mill, *Principles of Political Economy*; *On Liberty*; *The Subjection of Women*; *Autobiography* (many editions)

Peter Glassman, *J.S. Mill: The Evolution of a Genius*, University Presses of Florida, 1989

William Morris
1834–1896
artist, poet, socialist activist

William Morris's libertarian socialism grew from his love of beauty and craftsmanship, and from his loathing of political and personal constraints which lead to apathy and ugliness. Born into a prosperous middle class Essex family, his education at Marlborough and Oxford gave him access to the classics of art and architecture and early friendships with artists like Edward Burne-Jones and Dante Gabriel Rossetti. One strand of his subsequent life consisted of art and poetry, the other of politics and social awareness, and it is William Morris's legacy to radicalism that he was able to integrate both strands in his own life, projects and writing. While his art, in the form of textiles, furniture, architecture and printing, became ever more closely allied with daily life, his politics and his poetry moved consistently towards practical and utopian socialism. Shortly after his marriage to Jane Burden in 1859 he established a decorating firm which first showed a wide range of household items at the London International Exhibition of 1862; his involvement in what was increasingly being termed 'the arts and crafts movement' continued unabated until his death. His growing politicisation led to his joining the Democratic Federation (the forerunner of the British Socialist Party) in 1882, and by 1889 his socialist vision had expanded to create the utopian world portrayed in *News from Nowhere*, a persuasive glimpse of a post-revolution Britain in which class division no longer holds sway. He read **Marx** and much admired **Kropotkin**, but unlike them he had firsthand experience of manual labour, and was always able to temper his call for social revolution with a deep understanding of the rewards of meaningful work; though he was a man of the world, much of his revolution took place in the workshop and the studio rather than on the international stage.

William Morris, *News from Nowhere* (many editions)

William Morris (ed. A.L. Morton), *Political Writings of William Morris*, Lawrence and Wishart, 1973

E.P. Thompson, *William Morris: From Romantic to Revolutionary*, Merlin, 1977

Roderick Marshall, *William Morris and his Earthly Paradises*, Compton Press, 1979

Fiona MacCarthy, *William Morris: A Life for Our Time*, Faber, 1994

Robert Owen
1771–1858
industrialist, social reformer, utopian socialist

Born just as the industrial revolution was gaining momentum, Robert Owen, the son of a Welsh shopkeeper, took full advantage of the opportunities it offered to better himself. By the age of 28 he had already made a considerable fortune from investing in and managing spinning mills in Manchester, and in 1799 he became manager and joint owner of the New Lanark Mill on the River Clyde near Glasgow. Owen was a friend of **William Godwin**, and was much influenced by Godwin's *Enquiry Concerning Political Justice*, with its call for communism and equity. The appalling conditions he found at New Lanark, with many young children working fourteen hours a day, were so far from his developing utopian vision that he resolved to build a model community. Within fifteen years he had reduced working hours and stopped employing children, and the workers' houses, sanitation, schools and community facilities were much improved; moreover, New Lanark achieved better productivity and quality as a result. Having convinced himself that 'villages of unity and mutual cooperation' worked in practice, he set his ideas out in *A New View of Society* (1813) and distributed it to royalty and nobility throughout Europe. His example helped the passage of the 1819 Factory Act, but he was disappointed by the rate of reform in his home country, and in 1824 sailed for the United States to sell his ideas in this new and idealistic democracy. He conferred with President James Monroe and twice addressed the House of Representatives, and in 1825 was rewarded with the establishment of the first Owenite community in North America, New Harmony in Indiana. Although the experiment failed two years later, Owen's communal vision took root in the American psyche, just as his ideas about cooperation between employers, workers and consumers became an essential element of the growing socialist movement in Britain and Europe. Of the sixteen founder members of the pioneering 1844 Rochdale Cooperative, the first organised cooperative in Britain, six were self-proclaimed Owenite socialists.

> Robert Owen, *Life of Robert Owen, Written by Himself* (rep. of 1857 edn), Kelley, 1980
> G.D.H. Cole, *The Life of Robert Owen*, Frank Cass, 1965
> John Harrison, *Utopianism and Education: Robert Owen and the Owenites*, Teachers College, 1969

Tom [Thomas] Paine
1737–1809
writer, journalist, libertarian

In many of his passionately argued views – political equality, civil liberties, women's rights, tolerance and dignity – Thomas Paine was active at least a century ahead of most radical thinkers, yet the timing of his career, which in its prime took in American independence and the French Revolution, could hardly have been more fortuitous. Ironically it was early misfortune that set him on the international road to fame: his first wife died in premature childbirth, his second left him after the latest of several businesses failed, and he sailed from his home country of England to America in 1774, penniless and with few prospects. He was fortunate enough, however, to have met in London Benjamin Franklin, who gave him a letter of introduction: soon he was successfully editing the *Pennsylvania Magazine* and espousing the nascent idealism of American independence. His January 1776 pamphlet *Common Sense*, with its appeal to replace monarchy and aristocracy with true democracy, exploded in the American consciousness: it sold 100,000 copies in three months, and was instrumental in hastening independence, declared less than six months later. He continued to work for the patriot cause throughout the Revolutionary War, returning to England in 1787. Four years later, incensed by Edmund Burke's criticism of the French Revolution, he published *The Rights of Man*, his best-known libertarian tract, as a result of which he was expelled from England and honoured in France with citizenship and a seat in the French National Convention. Ten months later he was imprisoned during the Reign of Terror of 1793–94, the reactionary backlash which followed the Revolution, yet in the shadow of the guillotine he wrote *The Age of Reason*, a critique of religious institutions which became a primer for nineteenth-century freethinkers. His final major work, *Agrarian Justice* (1797), was a visionary and detailed outline of a socialistic welfare state. His denunciation of organised religion and his criticism of George Washington (for betraying the revolutionary cause) made him many enemies in Europe and America, and when he died in poverty on his farm in New York State, having given most of his income from writing away to radical causes, he was even denied burial in the local Quaker churchyard. His stirring words, however, have inspired many subsequent generations of radicals, who have believed with Tom Paine that 'we have it in our power to begin the world over again'.

Michael Foot and Isaac Kramnick (eds), *The Thomas Paine Reader*, Viking Penguin, 1987
David Powell, *Tom Paine: The Greatest Exile*, Century Hutchinson, 1985

Pierre-Joseph Proudhon
1809–1865
social philosopher, political activist

Pierre-Joseph Proudhon is best known for his eloquent formulations of anarchist belief, 'property is theft' and 'anarchy is order', and his powerful demands for justice and freedom had a considerable influence on radical thought and action in the later nineteenth century. Yet in both his life and his writing – he published more than forty books in his lifetime – he was often contradictory and deliberately outrageous. As the son of a peasant family turned tavernkeepers in the French town of Besançon, his early life was dominated by country life and religion; his puritanical roots coupled with his passionate belief in the need for radical social change provided much of the creative tension in his thinking. When his father was declared bankrupt in 1827 he became a printer's apprentice, supervising among other works the printing of his fellow townsman **Charles Fourier's** *Le nouveau monde*. It was the publication in 1840 of *What is Property?* that set Proudhon firmly on the anarchist road. The book brought him to the attention of **Karl Marx** (who thought it a 'penetrating work', though soon reassessing him as a 'bourgeois socialist'), **Friedrich Engels** and **Mikhail Bakunin**, and in 1844 Proudhon moved to Paris, where he spent much of his time among this circle of protorevolutionary exiles. *What is Property?* clarified both his opposition to capitalism and his understanding of anarchism as natural order, demonstrating that authoritarian government and the inequality of wealth distribution are the root causes of disorder in society. The 1848 revolution provided Pierre-Joseph Proudhon with a popular struggle to engage all his skills and ideals: he published a string of successful newspapers, was elected to the National Assembly, and established a People's Bank offering free credit – he also married (a working girl he met in a Paris street market) and had the first of three daughters. In January 1849, with the coup d'état of Louis Napoleon, he was sentenced to three years' imprisonment, where he took the opportunity to write *Confessions of a Revolutionary* (1849) and *General Idea of the Revolution in the Nineteenth Century* (1851): the latter traces the roots of the authoritarian state within the patriarchal family, demonstrating the inherent contradiction of the concept of democratic government. Of his later works the most important is *Justice in the Revolution and the Church* (1858), where he clarifies the ethical principles implicit in his earlier works.

Pierre-Joseph Proudhon (ed. Stewart Edwards), *Selected Writings*, Macmillan, 1969
Alan Ritter, *The Political Thought of Pierre-Joseph Proudhon*, Princeton University Press, 1969

Jean-Jacques Rousseau
1712–1778
philosopher, social critic

A unique product of the French enlightenment, an unhappy childhood and a determined quest for self-understanding, Jean-Jacques Rousseau earns his place in radical history by stressing liberty and the injustice of oppression while struggling – for the most part markedly unsuccessfully – with those issues in his own life. Brought up by an aunt because his mother died shortly after he was born and his watchmaker father was too busy, Rousseau longed for a truly benevolent authority even while stressing liberty as the noblest human faculty; his ceaseless travelling (from his birthplace in Switzerland to France, Italy and England) paralleled his search for a real home to balance the universality of his vision. His early writings are his most radical: *A Discourse on the Origin of Inequality* (1754) stressed the growing divide between the essential human condition, compassionate and independent, and its constraint by law, government and private property, while *Émile* (1762), much admired by **William Godwin** and **Petr Kropotkin** among others, outlined the aims of education as the excitement of curiosity and the nurturing of considered judgement. In *The Social Contract* (also published in 1762), however, the power had moved away from the individual to a 'general will', and this and his later work provided dictators like Robespierre with the opportunity to distort Rousseau's ideas for their own destructive ends. In his personal life Rousseau was rarely able to live up to his own ideals – his children by his common law wife Thérèse Le Vasseur, whom he treated abominably, were despatched to the public orphanage, and he fell out with several natural allies who objected to his selfishness, yet his posthumously-published *Confessions* (1781–88) and *Reveries of the Solitary Walker* (1782) are, for their time, remarkable exercises in candid and thoughtful self-reflection.

> Jean-Jacques Rousseau, *A Discourse on the Origin of Inequality*; *Émile*; *The Social Contract*; *Confessions*; *Reveries of the Solitary Walker* (many editions)
> James Miller, *Rousseau: Dreamer of Democracy*, Yale University Press, 1984

Percy Bysshe Shelley
1792–1822
poet, novelist

Shelley's romantically tempestuous and tragically short life has led to the legend looming larger than the man, but the variety and eloquence of his passions made him one of the most widely read and influential radical voices of the nineteenth century. The eldest son of a Sussex member of parliament, Percy Shelley was himself destined for Eton, Oxford University and a parliamentary career, but his privileged education (compared with his home life amidst a tribe of adoring younger sisters) made him deeply unhappy and rebellious: in March 1811 he was expelled from Oxford for coauthoring a pamphlet called *The Necessity of Atheism*. After quarrelling with his father he eloped to Scotland with sixteen-year-old Harriet Westbrook, whom he married in Edinburgh despite his disapproval of marriage. The archetypal rebel, he disdained church and royalty, became a vegetarian, and experimented with sharing his wife with his best friend Thomas Hogg. In Dublin in 1812 he advocated political reform and in Devon in 1813 attempted to establish a radical commune, all the time writing widely distributed poetry and pamphlets. In 1814, despite the birth of two children, his marriage collapsed, and Shelley ran away to the Continent with his mentor **William Godwin**'s sixteen-year-old daughter Mary and her younger stepsister Jane: their triangular relationship lasted for eight years. Harriet drowned herself in 1816 and Shelley, now back in England with Mary and their son William, lost a custody battle for their children: the experience shook him deeply. In 1818, harassed by creditors and critics, Shelley again took his ménage abroad, this time to Italy. Despite domestic crises including the death of two children, an affair with an Italian princess and the birth of an illegitimate child, the four years before he died in a boat accident were his most productive. He completed some of his best known short poems, the political odes 'To Liberty' and 'To Naples', essays including 'A Philosophical View of Reform', and numerous other poems and verse dramas. Shelley's outspoken hatred of injustice and oppression, his stirring poetry, and his willingness to match action with belief, inspired libertarians the world over, showing him to be one of the main intellectual bridges between the revolutions of the late eighteenth century and the variety of modern radicalism.

> Percy Bysshe Shelley, *Queen Mab*; *The Masque of Anarchy*; *Ode to Liberty*; *Prometheus Unbound* (many editions)
> Timothy Webb, *Shelley: A Voice Not Understood*, Manchester University Press, 1977
> Paul Foot, *Red Shelley*, Bookmarks, 1984
> Claire Tomalin, *Shelley and His World*, Penguin, 1992

Elizabeth Cady Stanton
1815–1902
women's rights and suffrage campaigner

'I wish you were a boy!' said Elizabeth Cady's lawyer father Daniel on the death of her only brother when she was eleven years old. From then on she did all in her power to demonstrate that women were as capable as men and deserved full recognition as men's equals. In 1840, against her parents' wishes, she married the abolitionist Henry Stanton, and they spent their honeymoon at the World Anti-Slavery Convention in London. Together with other women delegates she was outraged when, by an overwhelming majority, the convention voted to exclude women. It was in London that Elizabeth Cady Stanton met veteran women's rights campaigner Lucretia Mott, and they agreed to organise an American women's rights convention. It was eight years before the Seneca Falls Convention was held, by which time Elizabeth had had two of her seven children: for the event she drafted a Declaration of Sentiments, based on the Declaration of Independence, insisting on women's 'sacred right to the political franchise'. Three years after the 1848 convention she met **Susan B. Anthony**, starting a collaboration crucial to the women's rights movement. In 1860 their efforts were rewarded with the passage of the Married Women's Property Act and, when it became clear that the abolition of slavery was not to be paralleled by women's enfranchisement, they formed in 1869 the National Woman Suffrage Association. In 1878 Elizabeth Cady Stanton proposed an amendment to the US Constitution prohibiting disenfranchisement by sex, but it was only passed, as the Nineteenth Amendment, twenty years after her death. Throughout the 1870s and 80s she lectured widely, and from 1881 worked with Susan B. Anthony and **Matilda Joslyn Gage** on *The History of Woman Suffrage*. From 1883 onward she spent much time in England with her feminist daughter Harriot, speaking out against the patriarchal nature of the church, and in 1895 was chief author of *The Woman's Bible*, a scholarly feminist commentary on the Christian scriptures. Despite support for Elizabeth from many radical thinkers, the Suffrage

Convention of 1896 passed a resolution disavowing any links with its erstwhile mentor.

Elizabeth Cady Stanton, *Eighty Years and More: Reminiscences 1815–1897*, Northeastern University Press, 1992
Elizabeth Griffin, *In Her Own Right: The Life of Elizabeth Cady Stanton*, Oxford University Press, 1984

Jonathan Swift
1667–1745
clergyman and satirist

Following the collapse of the English revolution and the restoration of the monarchy in 1660, there was little encouragement for the development of the libertarian ideas that had fostered so many bold experiments in mid-century, though social criticism did not completely fade away. While the highborn Anglo-Irish Dean Swift was in many ways as reactionary and dilettante as his contemporaries John Dryden (his cousin) and William Congreve (alongside whom he studied at Trinity College, Dublin), he also recognised stupidity and injustice when he saw it. In Book IV of his famous satire *Gulliver's Travels*, where Gulliver visits the land of the Houyhnhnms, Jonathan Swift presents a detailed vision of a society organised according to the principles of rational anarchy, where women and men receive an equal education and the economy runs on communist lines. The anarchist thinker **William Godwin** described the voyage to the Houyhnhnms as 'one of the most virtuous, liberal and enlightened examples of human genius'; in a 1950 essay **George Orwell** called Swift 'a kind of anarchist', though he went on to point out the dangers of a society in which, even if truth is universal and self-evident, there is no dissent (the Houyhnhnms have no word for 'opinion'). The son of English settlers in Ireland, Jonathan Swift nevertheless made several passionate appeals for Irish independence a century before civil war made such a change inevitable. He supported many charitable causes, and his relationships with women (particularly with Esther 'Stella' Johnson, his lifelong companion though they never formally married) were deep and affectionate. In his later years he suffered from Ménière's disease, then widely interpreted as an insanity that 'explained' his forceful ideas.

Jonathan Swift, *Gulliver's Travels* (many editions)
George Orwell, 'Politics vs Literature: An Examination of Gulliver's Travels' (1950), in *Swift*, A. Norman Jeffares (ed), Aurora, 1970
James A. Preu, *The Dean and the Anarchist*, Florida State University Press, 1959

Harriet Taylor [Harriet Hardy]
1807–1858
women's rights advocate

Harriet Taylor is the perfect example of the radical and original woman thinker and writer whose contribution has been almost completely eclipsed by the standing of her male colleague – in this case the economist and philosopher **John Stuart Mill**. Harriet Taylor had been married for two years to druggist John Taylor when she met Mill at a dinner party in 1830, and their mutual attraction and intellectual rapport soon resulted in a deep and loving friendship. John Stuart Mill adored her as much as she admired him, and they were soon working together on a variety of writing projects. Harriet Taylor wrote many cogent essays and articles, and Mill often expressed his great debt to her ideas and inspiration, yet nothing other than a handful of reviews and poems was published under her name – nearly all of her work appeared with Mill's name as author. An important 1851 article, 'On the Enfranchisement of Women', was attributed to her later when he acknowledged that his contribution had been little more than editorial. An important chapter of Mill's *Principles of Political Economy* (1848) was Harriet Taylor's work, *On Liberty* (1859) was clearly acknow-ledged by Mill as 'directly and literally our joint production more than anything else', and his *The Subjugation of Women* (1869) would not have been possible without her contribution. In 1851, two years after John Taylor's death, Harriet Taylor and John Stuart Mill married; she was often ill, and died in Avignon while on a convalescent holiday with her lifelong colleague and companion.

> Alice S. Rossi (ed), *Essays on Sex Equality by John Stuart Mill and Harriet Taylor Mill*, University of Chicago Press, 1970
> Dale Spender, *Women of Ideas*, Routledge and Kegan Paul, 1982

Henry David Thoreau
1817–1862
writer, naturalist, political thinker

In his lifetime Henry David Thoreau was often dismissed as a pale imitator of **Ralph Waldo Emerson**, but his two major contributions to the radical tradition, his ecological tract *Walden* and his powerful treatise on the rationale of civil disobedience, have struck such a strong chord in the late twentieth century that he is now more widely read and admired than his formerly more illustrious compatriot. Thoreau grew up in Concord, Mas-sachusetts, and studied at Harvard; he worked intermittently as a teacher, a labourer and a surveyor, but he was never happier than when observing and writing about the details of the natural and human environment of his chosen corner of the New England countryside. In 1845 he built a wood cabin on land belonging to Emerson near Walden Pond with the purpose of deliberately simplifying his lifestyle and observing nature. In July 1846, as a protest against slavery, he refused to pay his poll tax; he was imprisoned overnight (an aunt, without consulting him, bailed him out), and resolved to write about the injustice of punishment for the infringe-ment of unjust laws: *On the Duty of Civil Disobedience* (1849) quickly became a classic of libertarian activism. The publication in 1854 of *Walden; or, Life in the Woods* consolidated his reputation: his description of the alienation of urban America and the need for a simple life in communion with nature found favour with a growing number of readers, and his timeless prose links many of his ideas almost seamlessly with modern green thinking. Apart from a brief flirtation with the antislavery movement Thoreau was not a political activist; he disliked politicians and described voting as 'a sort of gaming', yet he supported personal acts of rebellion and non-cooperation and was a mentor for **Mohandas Gandhi** and for **Martin Luther King**, who often echoed his vital question (from an 1861 essay 'Life Without Principle'): 'What is it to be born free and not to live free?'

Henry David Thoreau, *Walden; The Duty of Civil Disobedience* (many editions)

Henry Salt, *The Life of Henry David Thoreau* (repr. of 1896 edn), Haskell House, 1982

Edward Wagenknecht, *Henry David Thoreau: What Manner of Man?*, University of Massachusetts Press, 1981

Leo [Lev Nikolaevich] Tolstoy
1828–1910
novelist, essayist, social philosopher

Russia's greatest nineteenth-century novelist, Tolstoy is less remembered as a social innovator and activist who inspired many twentieth-century radicals including **Mohandas Gandhi** and **Vinoba Bhave** in India, **Dorothy Day** in the USA, and the founders of the commune movement in Germany and England. Born into a liberal aristocratic family, Tolstoy lived for most of his life on the family estate at Yasnaya Polyana, 100 miles south of Moscow. His education consisted of private tuition and a short period at Kazan University, followed by several years in the army and travel in Europe; his trilogy *Childhood* (1852), *Boyhood* (1854) and *Youth* (1857) established his literary credentials. In 1863 he married Sophie Behrs, who bore them thirteen children ('Every woman who refrains from childbirth is a whore' he wrote in 1886, shortly before he came to advocate celibacy and sexual abstinence as the solution to uncontrollable passion). Sophie also wrote a considerable amount of work which was published under Tolstoy's name: he was for the most part neither grateful nor kind about the way he used her. The next fifteen years, mostly spent writing *War and Peace* (1865–69; the title was borrowed from **Proudhon**'s 1861 book of the same name) and *Anna Karenina* (1875–77), also witnessed the formulation of Leo Tolstoy's personal philosophy, described in detail in his *Confession* of 1879 and *Memoirs of a Madman* (1884). The cornerstones of his doctrine, which was to exert such an influence on a generation of social activists, were the renunciation of material wealth, self-improvement through manual work, the rejection of violence, opposition to centralised education, and the importance of universal comradeship. By the late 1880s Yasnaya Polyana had become a place of pilgrimage for freethinkers from all over the world, and he did his best to run his own estate in line with his utopian ideals. The Russian government became ever more concerned about the unrest engendered by Tolstoy's ideas, and in 1894 journalists were banned from mentioning his name in foreign dispatches. His practical, anarchist interpretation of Christianity resulted in his excommunication from the Orthodox Church in 1901, but this only served to bolster his reputation. He lent his support to many radical causes and tried hard to live up to his ideals – he refused to be served by servants, gave his fortune to his wife, donated the copyrights on his last books to good causes, and became a vegetarian. Family tensions eventually persuaded him that monastery life was the only way forward, but during the long train journey, at the age of 82, he was taken ill and died.

> Leo Tolstoy, *Confession*; *Memoirs of a Madman* (many editions)
> Ernest Simmons, *Tolstoy*, Routledge and Kegan Paul, 1973
> A.N. Wilson, *Tolstoy*, Hamish Hamilton, 1988

Sojourner Truth [Isabella Bomefree]
*c.*1797–1883
abolitionist, preacher, women's rights campaigner

The myth represented by Sojourner Truth – the lone voice of a courageous, black, ex-slave woman against the might of the nineteenth-century patriarchal establishment – can easily turn her into the token radical of her era. The truth is much more complex, but serves to demonstrate the deep insight the real Sojourner Truth had into the social and political structures of her time, and the intractability of her feminist beliefs. Though she often spoke as a representative of Southern slaves, she was born and grew up on Dutch-speaking farms in New York State, gaining her freedom in 1827 when the state passed abolitionist legislation. Until 1843 she worked as a domestic help in New York City, but in that year she changed her name and started preaching – her strong faith gave her both spiritual purpose and a public platform. As a member of the utopian Northampton Industrial Association she mixed with abolitionists and feminists, and when **Frederick Douglass** published his *Narrative* in 1845 it inspired her to write her own autobiography, *The Narrative of Sojourner Truth*, which appeared in 1850. Her feminist tirade at the Akron Women's Rights Convention of 1851, recorded by Frances Dana Gage, provides the cornerstone of her doctrine, making it clear that black women, and not just black men, deserve full human rights – the famous line 'and ain't I a woman?', while capturing the power of her speech, is almost certainly Gage's and not Sojourner Truth's. The other well-remembered episode of her activist career, baring a breast to prove to a doubting clergyman that she was not a man, showed that she was not afraid to use any tactic that would further her cause. After the Civil War, her uncompromising feminism estranged her from her black abolitionist colleagues, and in 1867 she opposed the ratification of the Fourteenth Amendment because it did not include black women. Throughout the 1870s she worked on a project to provide land in Kansas for freed slaves, which eventually succeeded despite lack of official support; by this time, however, her health was deteriorating, and she died in Battle Creek, the outpost of American radicalism which had been her home for thirty years.

Sojourner Truth, *The Narrative of Sojourner Truth* (with an introduction by Margaret Washington), Vintage, 1993

Jacqueline Bernard, *Journey Toward Freedom: The Story of Sojourner Truth*, Feminist Press, 1990

Harriet Ross Tubman
*c.*1821–1913
civil rights activist and campaigner

Born and brought up a large slave family in Maryland's Dorchester County, Harriet Ross always dreamed of escape, and when she did at last flee slavery in 1849 she created a legend around her courageous exploits as one of the best known 'conductors' on the 'underground railroad' that ran between south and north in the 1850s and 60s, personally delivering more than two hundred other slaves to freedom. In 1844 she had married the free black man John Tubman, but he did not share her anxiety about being sold into the Deep South when their plantation owner died, and refused to escape with her: when she returned for him a few months later he had already remarried. After she had escaped, Harriet Tubman worked as a domestic in Philadelphia to raise money to rescue her sister and her two children. This was the first of more than fifteen such rescue missions, during which Harriet disguised herself and personally accompanied the fleeing slaves to freedom; by 1852 she had a reward of $40,000 on her head, but was never caught and never lost a 'passenger'. She made her last rescue in 1860, by which time she was widely known as 'Moses' and had made strong links with other antislavery campaigners including **Sojourner Truth** and **Frederick Douglass**. When the Civil War began she campaigned hard for President Lincoln to promise an end to slavery, which he eventually did in the Emancipation Proclamation of January 1863, and during the war she acted as a courageous and innovative scout and spy for the Union forces. In 1869 Harriet married Civil War veteran Nelson Davis, and told her life story to her friend Sarah Bradford, resulting in the bestselling *Scenes in the Life of Harriet Tubman*. She spent the remaining years of her long life campaigning for relief for recently-freed slaves and the families of black soldiers, and established a pioneering Home for Aged and Indigent Colored People at Auburn, New York, which is now a National Historic Landmark.

Sarah Hopkins Bradford, *Harriet Tubman: The Moses of her People*, Citadel Press, 1974 (repr. of 1886 edn)

Benjamin Quarles, 'Harriet Tubman's Unlikely Leadership', *Black Leaders of the Nineteenth Century* (ed. Leon Litwack and August Meier), University of Illinois Press, 1988

Darlene Clark Hine, 'Harriet Ross Tubman', *Black Women in America* (ed. Darlene Clark Hine), Carlson, 1993

Walt [Walter] Whitman
1819–1892
poet, journalist, social activist

A courageous experimenter in his personal life and in his art, Walt Whitman's influence has been immense amongst social activists and creative writers alike. North America's first well-known working class writer, he knew from personal experience that the American dream brought hardship as well as freedom: his father's building business on Long Island failed, and for several years he was unable to find work as a printer, his chosen trade. He was an avid and openminded reader, being particularly inspired by **Robert Owen, Fanny Wright, Ralph Waldo Emerson**, and the American Quaker movement. It is as a poet that Walt Whitman is best known, his *Leaves of Grass* growing from a collection of twelve innovative freeform poems in its first edition of 1855 to several hundred poems in its final, ninth, edition. Both his poems and his journalism presented his readers with a vivid contrast to the staid conservatism of late nineteenth-century literary circles: they offered adventure, freedom, excitement, choice and sexual experimentation. Unsurprisingly his honesty offended many of his readers, but established him as an inspiration for future generations of visionary social activists (notably his protégé **Edward Carpenter**) and original writers, especially poets – as Ezra Pound put it, Whitman 'broke the back of conventional metre'. While he was a fervent supporter of women's rights, and one of the first writers to explore the inclusivity of language using phrases like 'the man or the woman', he was particularly outspoken about his love of men. During the Civil War Walt Whitman worked as a clerk and a nurse in Washington; the letters between him and wounded soldiers bear testimony to his empathy and ability to communicate across class barriers. After a stroke in 1873 he lived quietly in Camden, New Jersey, still writing and receiving visitors until the end of his life.

Walt Whitman, *Leaves of Grass* (many editions and selections)
Justin Kaplan, *Walt Whitman: A Life*, Simon and Schuster, 1980
Gay Wilson Allen, *Solitary Singer: A Critical Biography of Walt Whitman*, University of Chicago Press, 1985
Philip Callow, *Walt Whitman: From Noon to Starry Night*, Allison and Busby, 1992

Oscar [Fingal O'Flahertie Wills] Wilde
1854–1900
poet, playwright, social critic

In the early 1890s Oscar Wilde was London's brightest young playwright, his first three satirical plays (*Lady Windermere's Fan*, *A Woman of No Importance* and *The Importance of Being Earnest*) playing to large appreciative audiences. At the height of his career, however, a show trial to test public opinion on homosexuality went against the openly gay Wilde, and he was sentenced to two years of prison with hard labour. Although his experience and eloquent defence of his position provided inspiration for the twentieth-century gay rights movement, it effectively stifled and silenced homosexual writing and activism in Britain for many years. Wilde grew up in Dublin, the son of literary parents, and while at Trinity College Dublin and Magdalene College Oxford won several prestigious poetry awards. In the early 1880s he concentrated on writing mannered poetry in the style of the Pre-Raphaelites, but by 1890, when he published his only novel, *The Picture of Dorian Gray*, his ideas had become markedly radical, and Wilde now considered himself a socialist and social critic. In 1893 Wilde started a relationship with the poet Alfred Douglas, originator of the famous line 'the love that dare not speak its name' – a reference to the recently-enacted amendment which made homosexuality in Britain a criminal act. Douglas's father, the Marquess of Queensberry, angrily accused Wilde of 'posing as a sodomite', whereupon Wilde sued the marquess for libel. The trial was widely reported, with Wilde insisting on the naturalness and nobility of homosexuality, but in the moral climate of the 1890s it was inevitable that he should lose his case. The severity of the sentence shocked liberals and bolstered the views of the reactionary establishment. While in prison from 1895–97 Wilde wrote *The Ballad of Reading Gaol*, which became a battle song of the movement to decriminalise homosexuality, and after his release he wrote the moving autobiographical essay *De Profundis*; within two years of his release, physically and mentally broken, Oscar Wilde died at the age of 44.

Oscar Wilde, *The Ballad of Reading Gaol*, 1898 (many reprints since)
Oscar Wilde, *De Profundis*, 1905 (many reprints since)
Harford Montgomery Hyde, *Oscar Wilde: A Biography*, Eyre Methuen, 1976

Gerrard Winstanley
1609–*c*.1669
anarchist and agrarian reformer

The son of a Lancashire textile merchant, Gerrard Winstanley's own textile business in London failed in the economic turbulence of the 1630s and he became a hired labourer. He started writing mystical tracts, but these soon became imbued with a sharp political edge. For a short period during the English Civil War, as the outspoken leader of the 'digger movement', he achieved a fame and notoriety that has inspired anarchist groups to the present day. Against a background of turbulent social and economic change, rebellion against church and privilege was widespread, especially among the growing class of dispossessed landworkers and itinerant labourers; it was from their ranks that Gerrard Winstanley's Diggers emerged. In a series of important tracts written between 1648 and 1652 he set out the basis for his anarchist vision, calling for universal suffrage, religious equality and the abolition of private land rights. *The True Leveller's Standard Advanced* (sometimes called *The Diggers' Manifesto*, 1649) presents an apocalyptic vision, while *The Law of Freedom in a Platform* (1652) has been described as a proto-Marxist tract. In April 1649 Gerrard Winstanley and a small group of his followers established a Digger colony on common land at St George's Hill near Walton-on-Thames in Surrey. They persevered for a year, digging and manuring the wasteland and growing a wide variety of crops, but continual harassment from government officials and neighbouring landowners forced the end of the experiment. After 1652 Gerrard Winstanley disappeared into obscurity; it is thought that he became a Quaker and a fairly prosperous farmer.

Gerrard Winstanley (ed. G.H. Sabine), *Works*, Cornell University Press, 1941
Christopher Hill, *The World Turned Upside Down: Radical Ideas during the English Revolution*, Temple Smith, 1972

Mary Wollstonecraft
1759–1797
feminist, author

It was the publication in 1792 of *A Vindication of the Rights of Women* that ensured Mary Wollstonecraft a place in radical history as the author of one of the most articulate and best-argued early feminist tracts. Although her formal education had been minimal, she gained much experience from helping to establish a school in London in the 1780s with her childhood friend Fanny Blood. In 1785 she spent time with Fanny in Lisbon, but her friend died in childbirth and Mary returned to Ireland to become a governess. A year later she was dismissed, and determined to make her living as a writer. Her first works were a novel and *Thoughts on the Education of Daughters* (1787), followed by *A Vindication of the Rights of Men* (1790), one of the first of many responses to Edmund Burke's *Reflections on the Revolution in France* (she, unlike Burke, had been in France during the Revolution). Her much-discussed *Rights of Women* exposed the mesh of economic, political and sexual double standards that keep women subservient to men, a theme that reappeared in her posthumous novel *The Wrongs of Women, or Maria*. She strongly refuted **Rousseau's** ideas about the exclusion of women from public life, and constructed a truly feminist identity for women. Her subsequent relationships with men served to underline her arguments. An affair in 1793–94 with an American revolutionary ex-soldier resulted in a child which she was left to care for while he left to live with another woman (Mary twice attempted suicide as a result), and her shortlived marriage to **William Godwin** ended with her death from septicaemia in September 1797, a month after the birth of their daughter Mary (who was to become the author of *Frankenstein* and wife of **Percy Bysshe Shelley**).

Mary Wollstonecraft, *A Vindication of the Rights of Men; A Vindication of the Rights of Women* (many editions)
Claire Tomalin, *The Life and Death of Mary Wollstonecraft*, Penguin, 1992
Gary Kelly, *Revolutionary Feminism: The Mind and Career of Mary Wollstonecraft*, Macmillan, 1992

Fanny [Frances] Wright
1795–1852
utopian socialist, women's rights campaigner

Of the many utopian visionaries of the nineteenth century, Fanny Wright went further than most to see her ideas take physical form. She was born in Dundee, Scotland, but was orphaned young and grew up with relatives in London; in her loneliness she read widely, and by her early thirties had formed a personal belief system which included the abolition of slavery, women's emancipation, the need for birth control and the relaxation of marriage commitments. In 1818–19 she spent two years in America with her sister Camilla, returning in 1824 and spending much time in the southern states. She became convinced that one solution to slavery was to establish a community where black and white could live, farm and administer themselves cooperatively. She bought a property at Nashoba in Tennessee and ten slaves, but within a year the experiment failed, bedevilled by poor management, sexual scandal, and the hostility of neighbouring farmers. Fanny Wright then joined the Owenite community at New Harmony, Indiana, where she edited the community newspaper for two years. In 1828 she embarked on a series of popular lectures on freedom and women's emancipation, which she gave in many American cities over the next decade. Her lectures and a book based on them drew much criticism for their advocacy of 'free love' and their criticism of church and wealth, but they also inspired a network of Fanny Wright societies and centres dedicated to the promotion of her principles. In 1830, finding she was pregnant by New Harmonist William D'Arusmont, she reluctantly married him, but neither marriage nor motherhood suited her; she filed for divorce, became estranged from her daughter Silva (a second daughter died young), and for the last ten years of her life largely lost touch with the radicalism she had worked for so hard.

William Randall Waterman, *Frances Wright*, AMS Press, 1967 (reprint of 1924 edn)

Alice Perkins and Theresa Wolfson, *Frances Wright: Free Enquirer*, Porcupine Press, 1977

Celia Morris Eckhardt, *Fanny Wright: Rebel in America*, Harvard University Press, 1984

TWENTIETH-CENTURY RADICALS

Chinua Achebe [Albert Chinualumgu]
1930–
broadcaster, novelist, journalist, teacher

'It is clear to me that an African creative writer who tries to avoid the big social and political issues of contemporary Africa will end up being completely irrelevant,' wrote Chinua Achebe in 1969, while visiting the USA as a diplomat for the breakaway eastern Nigerian state of Biafra. The massive shifts of culture and politics that have shaped twentieth-century Africa are at the heart of his finely-observed novels, stories and poems, which have established him as one of the continent's best-known writers. His early life embraced the village traditions of Ogidi in eastern Nigeria where he grew up, the educational opportunities offered by a university education (at Ibadan University, where in 1953 he was one of the first graduates, and London and Leeds in Britain), and work with the Nigerian Broadcasting Company during the years around Nigerian independence in 1960. He married Christine Okoli in 1961, and they have four children. His first novel, *Things Fall Apart*, explores the complexities of leadership and mistrust between black and white in colonial west Africa, and gained immediate acclaim; it has since been translated into thirty languages. His next three novels, *No Longer at Ease* (1960), *Arrow of God* (1964) and *A Man of the People* (1966) continue the story of the same black family through to recent times. During the Biafran struggle in 1967–69 Chinua Achebe became a spokesperson for the Ibo people. The war effort concentrated his thoughts on the purpose of African writing and the responsibility of the writer; he continued to write short stories, but also turned to essays, stressing the novelist's role as educator, and children's books, in both English and Ibo. After four years in the mid-1970s spent teaching in the USA, Chinua Achebe returned to the University of Nigeria at Nsukka, where since 1985 he has been professor of literature. 1988 saw the publication of *Anthills of the Savannah*, his first novel for twenty years; again it is set in a fictionalised Nigeria, but the contemporary setting is now informed by the successes and failures of decades of military rule and uneasy peace – Achebe also tackles the thorny subject of sexism and male guilt in present-day Africa.

Chinua Achebe, *Things Fall Apart*, Heinemann, 1958
Chinua Achebe, *Anthills of the Savannah*, Heinemann, 1987
David Carroll, *Chinua Achebe*, St Martin's Press, 1980

Catherine Lynette Innes, *Chinua Achebe*, Cambridge University Press, 1980

Jane Addams
1860–1935
settlement founder, social reformer, pacifist

Jane Addams was the founder of Chicago's famous Hull-House project, a pioneering early twentieth-century inner city community centre, but it took her twenty years of relative aimlessness before she became clear how she wanted to make her mark in the world. She was born in Cedarville in Illinois, the eighth of nine children of whom only four reached adulthood; her mother died when she was two, but her father and stepmother encouraged her education. She went to Rockford Seminary, which special-ised in producing missionaries; she later said that genuine zeal and affectionate solicitude which would have turned her into a Christian missionary were the best possible training for independent thought. For the next twenty years Jane Addams dabbled, spending time in Europe and in Illinois; in April 1888, however, while in Madrid, it suddenly came to her to rent a city house where young women 'who have been given over too exclusively to study' could work together to learn something of real life. A month later she visited Toynbee Hall in London's East End, the university settlement established four years earlier to alleviate the degradation resulting from too-rapid industrialisation. By September 1889 she had returned to the United States and leased the decaying Hull mansion in central Chicago, which was the beginning of more than forty years of a project which would inspire many like it, and attract admirers from the anarchist **Petr Kropotkin** to President Theodore Roosevelt. Her clarity of vision, her talent for attracting able teachers, and her willingness to entertain many divergent points of view, enabled the Hull-House to grow into a wideranging educational and community resource, with a theatre, art gallery, music school, nursery, gymnasium, playground, and coopera-tive boarding house. Much of the Hull-House work was made possible through the collaboration of Mary Rozet Smith, a wealthy young Chicago woman who became Jane Addams' colleague and companion until Mary died in 1933. By 1910 Jane was a sought-after writer and lecturer, and in 1911 became first head of the national Federation of Settlements. As well as her settlement work she worked hard for women's suffrage: as the first vice president of the **National American Woman Suffrage Association** she spoke widely for the cause, and in 1913 she was a leading figure at the Budapest convention of the **International Woman Suffrage Alliance**. She was also a dedicated and outspoken pacifist, and with the outbreak of war in 1914 her whole attention turned to the peace cause. In 1915 she was elected chair of the newly-formed Women's Peace Party, and continued to hold her pacifist line when the United States joined the conflict in 1917. In 1919 she became the first president of the **Women's International League for Peace and Freedom** (WILPF), presiding over the League's conferences in Zürich, Vienna, Dublin and Prague, and the following year was a cofounder of the **American Civil Liberties Union**. In 1931 she shared the Nobel Peace Prize, giving her share to WILPF, but by now her health, never very good, was failing rapidly, and she died two years after suffering a stroke. Thousands of people came to pay tribute as her coffin was displayed at Hull-House, the home of her vision for ordinary people 'attempting to learn from life itself'.

Jane Addams (repr. of 1910 ed. with intro. and notes by James Hunt), *Twenty Years at Hull-House*, University of Illinois Press, 1990
Jane Addams (repr. of 1922 ed. with a new intro. by Blanche Wiesen Cook), *Peace and Bread in Time of War*, Garland Publishing Co., 1972
Allen Freeman Davis, *American Heroine: The Life and Legend of Jane Addams*, Oxford University Press 1973
Daniel Levine, *Jane Addams and the Liberal Tradition*, Greenwood Press, 1980

Theodor [Wiesengrund] Adorno
1903–1969
philosopher, social commentator, music critic

Theodor Adorno, a key member of the later German 'Frankfurt School' of the 1950s and 60s, was in many ways a philosophical iconoclast, having at his disposal a vast store of historical and artistic knowledge as well as experience of the worst excesses of coercion and violence carried out in the name of political and cultural progress. He grew up in Frankfurt, the son of a Jewish father and a Catholic mother, and became a gifted musician as well as a philosopher. He began teaching philosophy at Frankfurt in 1931, but the Third Reich forced him to leave Germany, first for Britain and from 1934 for the USA, where he joined the Institute of Social Research in exile in New York. From 1941–49 he lived in California, working in collaboration with a group of American social scientists on a study of prejudice, *The Authoritarian Personality* (1950). In 1949 Adorno and his friend and colleague **Max Horkheimer** were able to return to Frankfurt and start rebuilding the Institute. Adorno was deeply moved and disturbed by the horrors of the Jewish Holocaust, a subject he was to return to many times in his writing. In the closing sentences of his *Minima Moralia* of 1951 he summed up his moral position thus: 'The only philosophy which can be preached responsibly in the face of despair is the attempt to contemplate all things as they would present themselves from the standpoint of redemption'. His willingness to tackle the bleakness of a world seemingly being overtaken by faceless violence, centralised planning and mass culture has led critics to claim that Adorno's worldview is nothing but an expression of helplessness and despair. His central message, however, is that everywhere freedom and creativity are under threat, and it is vital to create and sustain the capacity for independent criticism and radical social change. In the fullest statement of his ideas, his *Negative Dialektik* (1966, 1973 in English), his central purpose was to dissipate all limiting philosophical distinctions before they harden and prevent flexibility of interpretation and action. He warned against the search for ultimate answers, whatever part of the political spectrum they come from, because such beliefs always tend to result in oppression and totalitarianism. Adorno firmly believed that it is the philosopher's task to negate any theory which claims to have the ultimate answers.

Theodor Adorno, *Minima Moralia: Reflections from Damaged Life*, Verso, 1974 (orig. pub. 1951)
Theodor Adorno, *Negative Dialectics*, Routledge, 1973
Martin Jay, *Adorno*, Harvard University Press, 1984

Saul [David] Alinsky
1909–1972
community organiser and activist

As a young social worker in Depression Chicago, where he had been born and raised, Saul Alinsky saw at first hand how the economic and social turmoil of the 1930s was affecting some of the poorest Americans – and how little effect most of the agencies charged with alleviating the suffering were having. In 1938, when he started working in Chicago's Back of the Yards district (the scene of **Upton Sinclair**'s muckraking novel *The Jungle*), Alinsky soon realised that the district's many social organisations were arranged along ethnic lines, tending to create divisiveness rather than solidarity. Slavs were not speaking to Italians, nor Poles to Germans. The communist-dominated unions had made some headway in overcoming ethnic differences, but were anathema to the church, a crucial influence within the community. Out of this tumultuous flux, Saul Alinsky's achievement was to refine a new concept of social action which built bridges and created leaders at grassroots level to create a true 'people's organisation'. He was able to show churches, unions, local businesses and ordinary people that they shared common concerns, and in July 1939 three hundred and fifty delegates met for the first Back of the Yards Neighbourhood Council: within two years the Council had built a recreation centre, established a credit union, and secured nearly three thousand new jobs. Many community coalitions were subsequently organised along the lines of what came to be called 'The Alinsky Approach', and Saul Alinsky himself continued to work as one of America's first professional 'enablers', committed to empowering those with the least power. His 1945 'textbook' for community action, *Reveille for Radicals*, quickly became a bestseller, and was taken as a model by many populist groups wanting to build a broad consensus for community-based politics. After the war Saul Alinsky turned his attention to residential segregation in Chicago, concentrating on an urban renewal plan to move tens of thousands of poor families in the Hyde Park and Woodlawn areas. In 1961 he launched the Woodlawn Association, which quickly became a model of a new kind of civil rights association in which ordinary people work together to help themselves. In the last decade before his death he was active in a raft of other initiatives to help rich and poor work together for a common future, taking every opportunity to stress that only the sharing of power will solve the problems of inner cities.

Saul Alinsky, *Reveille for Radicals*, University of Chicago Press, 1946
Robert Bailey, *Radicals in Urban Politics: The Alinsky Approach*, University of
    Chicago Press, 1974
David Finks, *The Radical Vision of Saul Alinsky*, Paulist Press, 1984

Salvador Allende [Gossens]
1908–1973
Marxist politician

Among Latin American countries Chile is unique in being the only one in
which the wave of military takeovers of the 1960s and 70s was directed
against a socialist government – that of the Unidad Popular (UP) led by
Salvador Allende. In the mid-1930s, Allende, raised in a middle-class family
in Valparaiso and trained as a doctor, was a founder member of the Socialist
Party, and served from 1939 to 1942 as minister for health in the Popular
Front coalition of Aguirre Cedra. In 1970, as a senator of 25 years standing
who had three times run unsuccessfully as a socialist candidate for the
presidency, he was adopted by the newly-formed UP (an alliance of
socialists, communists and progressives). In a tight threecornered contest
he was elected Latin America's first and only Marxist president. Salvador
Allende's plan was to reconstruct Chilean society and economy along
socialist lines. In order to transfer resources and rewards from wealthy
Chileans and foreigners to ordinary people he redistributed land from large
landowners to peasant cooperatives, legislated large wage increases for
poorly-paid workers, and nationalised the copper industry. As production
fell and prices soared, foreign governments, notably the USA, cut loans and
embargoed Chilean exports. Chilean opinion polarised, but the Allende
government was re-elected in March 1973 with an increased majority. On
September 11th armed forces (many believe with US government support)
occupied the presidential palace in Santiago and murdered the president;
the military junta headed by Augusto Pinochet claimed that Allende had
taken his own life. A fervent believer in his country's ability to provide for
the needs of all its people, Salvador Allende was convinced that Chile's
democratic tradition offered a peaceful route to practical socialism. The
Pinochet dictatorship brutally set out to obliterate that tradition. Between
1973 and 1977 hundreds of UP workers, labour movement leaders and
others opposing Pinochet were murdered, and many thousands more
brutalised and incarcerated. Only in 1990, with a democratic election that
brought to power Patricio Aylwin, the rightwing former opponent of
Allende, did any semblance of democracy return to Chile, by which time
the Chilean left was – perhaps irretrievably – fragmented and divided.

Gabriel Smirnow, *The Revolution Disarmed: Chile 1970–1973*, Monthly Review
    Press, 1979
Brian Loveman, 'The Political Left in Chile, 1973–1990', in Barry Carr and Steve
    Ellner (eds), *The Latin American Left from the Fall of Allende to Perestroika*,
    Westview Press/Latin America Bureau, 1993

Shulamit Aloni
1929–
civil rights campaigner, feminist, politician

Born and brought up in Tel Aviv, Shulamit Aloni is by profession a writer and lawyer. For the last twenty years she has been a courageous and outspoken politician, consistently fighting the rigid control exercised by the orthodox Israeli rabbinate over such issues as education, marriage, divorce, and other areas of personal morality. In 1965 she was elected to the Israeli Knesset on the Labor Party list, but following reactionary pressure was dropped by Golda Meir from the list for the 1969 and 1973 elections. She chose to run for the Civil Rights Movement (CRM) in the 1973 elections, where to many people's surprise it secured three seats. It subsequently joined the coalition government led by Yitzhak Rabin in 1974, in which Shulamit Aloni served as minister without portfolio, but the party withdrew from the coalition in October of that year to protest against the entry into the coalition of the National Religious Party (NRP), on the grounds that the CRM was pledged to a programme of separation of state and religion and that the inclusion of the NRP in the government would lead to a strengthening of religious control over education and morality. Despite the efforts of Jewish fundamentalists, both the Civil Rights Movement (which in the early 1980s linked with other leftist parties to form the secular Meretz) and Aloni have continued their outspoken opposition to religious coercion and their support for civil and women's rights. During the 1980s she led campaigns against corruption in public life and against religious segregation in schools, and became a leading voice within the Israeli peace movement, strongly advocating dialogue and mutually-binding agreement with the Palestinians. The confrontation came to a head during the 1992 Rabin-led coalition government, in which Shulamit Aloni served as minister for education, a post traditionally awarded on religious grounds. In May 1993, threatened with a fundamentalist walkout, Yitzhak Rabin withdrew Aloni's portfolio (at the same time withdrawing that of her Shas opponent Arieh Deri). She has continued to represent Meretz in the Knesset, however, calling for the liberalisation, secularisation and pacification of Israel, and for a closer working relationship with the Palestinians: it seems ironic in the circumstances that it was Rabin and his foreign minister Yitzhak Shamir, together with the Palestinian leader Yasser Arafat, who received the 1994 Nobel Peace Prize.

> Barbara Swirski and Marilyn P. Safir (ed.), *Calling the Equality Bluff: Women in Israel*, Pergamon, 1991

Jessie Daniel Ames
1883–1972
women's rights and civil rights campaigner

Jessie Daniel Ames, born and raised in Texas, became involved in the struggle for women's suffrage in 1916, writing, organising and speaking on behalf of women's rights and helping to ensure that Texas became the first southern state to ratify the Nineteenth Amendment, giving women the right to vote. In 1919 she founded the Texas League of Women Voters and went on to become active in Democratic party politics. Disturbed by the exclusion of black women from the growing women's movement, in 1924 she became a director for the Commission on Interracial Cooperation. Her major contribution in combining antiracist and women's movement issues was as the founder of the Association of Southern Women for the Prevention of Lynching (ASWPL) in 1930. The ASWPL worked through existing women's groups to urge the wives and daughters of the men who took part in lynch gangs to restrain them, bringing pressure on the police to arrest and try those involved in such vicious murders. Since lynch victims were usually black men accused of raping white women, the standard justification for lynching was the protection of white women from black male violence, but Jessie Daniel Ames showed that only a quarter of lynch victims had any record of crimes against women. She urged women to reject the stereotype of vulnerable white women in need of strong male protection. Despite her efforts, antilynching legislation was consistently opposed throughout the 1930s and 40s; it was not until civil rights legislation in the 1960s outlawed all forms of discrimination that lynching stopped completely.

Jacqueline Dowd Hall, *Revolt Against Chivalry: Jessie Daniel Ames and the Campaign against Lynching*, Columbia University Press, 1993

Elizabeth Garrett Anderson
1836–1917
physician, health and women's rights campaigner

Elizabeth Garrett, the first British woman to qualify as a doctor, was born in London, the second of a family of ten children. Her father was a successful merchant and shipowner, and the family moved to Aldeburgh on the Suffolk coast when she was five; he encouraged all his children in their education, including Elizabeth and her younger sister Millicent (later, as Millicent Garrett Fawcett, to become a leading suffrage campaigner). Elizabeth was determined to train in medicine, but in the 1860s no medical school would accept female candidates, so in 1860 she started as an unofficial student at the Middlesex Hospital; she was soon forced to withdraw under pressure from her male colleagues. In 1861 the Society of Apothecaries agreed to register her but, because no English university would accept her, she studied privately with some of the country's leading doctors, completing her training at the University of Paris, which awarded her a doctorate in medicine in 1870. In 1866 she opened St Mary's Dispensary for Women in north London, which in 1872 became the New Hospital for Women (renamed for its founder after her death). In 1871 she became the first woman elected to the London School Board, where she met her husband James Skelton Anderson (their daughter Louise trained as a surgeon), and for more than twenty years taught at the newly-opened

London School of Medicine for Women. Elizabeth Garrett Anderson was always vocal on the subject of women's rights, and from 1908 to 1911 was a member of the militant **Women's Social and Political Union**, though she later favoured constitutional suffrage as proposed by her sister Millicent. Most of the rest of her life was spent in Aldeburgh, where she followed her father and husband as mayor – the first woman in Britain to hold that office.

Jo Manton, *Elizabeth Garrett Anderson*, Methuen, 1965

Arahata Kanson [Arahata Katsuzō]
1887–1981
socialist journalist and activist

Arahata Kanson was one of the few Japanese radicals to experience both the early flowering of socialism before the first world war and the freedom of post-world war two democracy. He grew up in Yokohama and worked there in a naval arsenal until his reading of **Kōtoku Shūsui** and other leading socialists persuaded him to join the movement against the Russo-Japanese War of 1904–05. He established a branch of the socialist organisation Heiminsha in Yokohama and wrote many articles for its newspaper *Heimin Shimbun* and other socialist publications: his account of **Tanaka Shōzō**'s campaign to stop the pollution from the Ashio copper mine is considered a classic of Japanese journalism. His interest now turned to labour activism. He joined the young socialist workers' association **Yūaikai**, and in 1922 was one of the founders of the Japan Communist Party, but his efforts to build links between communism and Japanese mainstream politics earned him little reward from either: in 1927 he helped to establish the socialist Rōnōha (Labour-Farmer Faction), but put most of his effort into writing. He was jailed for two years in the 1937 government crackdown on its critics, and spent the war years under house arrest. In 1946 he helped to establish the Japan Socialist Party, joining its central committee and winning a seat in the Diet (Japanese parliament), but found the new party far too accommodating of capitalism and resigned in 1948. He spent the rest of his life writing, including a well-known autobiography and several important translations of English and Russian socialist works.

Charles M. Mergentime, 'Arahata Kanson', *Kodansha Encyclopedia of Japan*, 1983

Hannah Arendt
1906–1975
political philosopher and historian

Hannah Arendt's major achievement was to explore the evolution of political structures in the light of how those involved saw their roles and responsibilities; by extension she challenges each of us to think carefully about our own responsibilities. She was born in Hanover and grew up in a Jewish family in Königsberg, studying theology and philosophy at Marburg, Freiburg and Heidelberg. Her growing involvement with Zionism clashed with Third Reich antisemitism and in 1933 she was arrested and briefly detained; she and her husband Heinrich Blücher fled to France, where they worked with Jewish children. They were both imprisoned several times before escaping to the United States in 1941. For several years Hannah Arendt worked in publishing houses and Jewish organisations; in 1963 she secured her first academic post at Chicago University, and from 1967 until her death taught at the New School in New York. Her first book, *The Origins of Totalitarianism* (1951), established her as a major political writer. Describing the common features of Nazism and Stalinism, she showed how totalitarianism depends on the bureaucratisation of terror and the encouragement of mob psychology. *The Human Condition* (1958) stressed the importance of understanding politics as action and the purpose of politics as freedom: she explored how both have been negated by the modern emphasis on work. *On Revolution* (1963) examined the French and American Revolutions to demonstrate that longterm freedom can only be achieved by matching postrevolutionary organisation to revolutionary ideals. It warned Americans that they were in danger of losing their revolutionary tradition, a theme which made her popular with many 1960s radicals. The same year produced *Eichmann in Jerusalem*, where she showed the archetypal Jew-hater to be 'terribly and terrifyingly normal'. Many Jewish critics felt that, in portraying Eichmann as an ordinary man who had simply followed orders to the extreme, she was suggesting the complicity of the European Jews in their own destruction. In truth she was saying, as she always did, that true understanding must take into account the complexity of human motivation, and that we must remain vigilant in order to take timely and appropriate action in defence of freedom.

Hannah Arendt, *The Origins of Totalitarianism*, Meridian, 1951

Hannah Arendt, *The Human Condition*, University of Chicago Press, 1958

Hannah Arendt, *On Revolution*, Viking, 1963

Hannah Arendt, *Eichmann in Jerusalem: A Report on the Banality of Evil*, Viking, 1963

Elisabeth Young-Bruehl, *Hannah Arendt: For Love of the World*, Yale University Press, 1982

George Kateb, *Hannah Arendt: Politics, Conscience, Evil*, Rowman and Allanheld, 1984

Jean-Bertrand Aristide
1953–
priest, socialist politician

Haiti's record on human rights and democracy is a long and fascinating one, made all the more poignant by recent events in this Caribbean island nation. In 1697 Spain ceded Haiti to France, who exploited its rich agricultural potential using thousands of African slaves: by 1800 more than half a million slaves of African extraction lived in the country. Then in 1804, just six years after its French counterpart, a populist revolution led by former slave Toussaint l'Ouverture proclaimed the first black republic in the world, and the second American nation after the USA to become independent from European control. The fragile independence lasted until 1915, when economic crisis offered the excuse for a US-led invasion. The US military left only in 1934, leaving the wealthy Duvalier family as virtual dictators, and by the mid 1980s Haiti had fallen from being an important sugar and coffee producer to one of the world's poorest nations. When 'Baby Doc' Jean-Claude Duvalier took over from his father 'Papa Doc' François in 1971 the repression increased, the state police (the Tonton Macoutes) murdering more than 40,000 opponents between 1971 and 1985. Sham elections were held in 1984, and under growing international pressure 'Baby Doc' fled the country in 1986. Despite a new constitution and elections in 1988, military coups in 1989 and 1990 kept the Duvalier ghosts alive. Haiti's democratic front, however, had also had time to regroup: under the banner of the National Front for Change and Democracy it chose a 37-year-old priest, Father Jean-Bertrand Aristide, as its leader and spokesperson. Aristide had already gained a reputation for political activism: working with the slumdwellers of Port-au-Prince he had campaigned against Haiti's military élite, drug trafficking, and the complacency of Haiti's entrenched Roman Catholic hierarchy: the latter led to his banishment from the Silesian religious order in 1988. Aristide made the plight of Haiti's poor the basis of his campaign in the run-up to the December 1990 election, and largely as a result won 67% of the vote. Despite accusations that he supported human rights violations and mob violence, he was able within the first six months of his presidency to bring much-needed peace to Haiti, and was a truly popular and populist leader. In September 1991, however, a military coup installed the ruthless general Raoul Cedras, and Aristide spent the next two years in exile in the USA. In mid-1994 US president Bill Clinton sent a 20,000 strong peacekeeping force to Haiti: on October 10th Cedras left Haiti, and four days later Aristide returned to Port-au-Prince as president-elect, having agreed to step down in 1996 following free elections. As was clear from his tumultuous welcome, the majority of Haitians have great faith in Aristide's egalitarianism and his willingness to listen to the poor; for the small number of privileged, however, his name invokes fear and contempt, and he will have to work hard to involve all sections of Haitian society in their country's future.

Jean-Bertrand Aristide, *In the Parish of the Poor: Writings from Haiti*, Orbis, 1990
Jean-Bertrand Aristide, *Aristide: An Autobiography*, Orbis, 1993
Amy Wilentz, *The Rainy Season: Haiti Since Duvalier*, Simon and Schuster, 1989
James Ridgeway (ed.), *The Haiti Files*, Essential Books/Latin America Bureau, 1994

Raymond Aron
1905–1983
sociologist, journalist, political commentator

Clarity and truth were the watchwords of the French political sociologist Raymond Aron, and although his conclusions often went against the popular grain he was always ready to defend them with solid facts and lucid reasoning. He grew up in Paris and studied at the École Normale

Supérieure, where he was a close friend of **Jean-Paul Sartre**. From 1930 he spent two years in Germany, where he witnessed the rise of National Socialism and was impressed by the pioneering sociological methods of Max Weber. When France fell in 1940 the liberal Jewish Aron left for England to become editor and columnist for the Free French newspaper *La France libre*, which on his return to France launched him on a thirty-year career as a much-respected journalist, always prepared to set out political issues and their possible outcomes clearly and unflinchingly. From 1955 to 1968 Raymond Aron was professor of sociology at the Sorbonne, and in 1970 was appointed professor at the Collège de France. In the mid-1950s, seeing the repression of Stalinism, he was prepared to take an anti-Soviet stance, and attacked Sartre and other French intellectuals for their blind adherence to Soviet-style communism in *L'opium des intellectuels* (1955, 1957 in English). He was equally opposed to colonialism, and in the late 50s went against popular opinion to advocate French withdrawal from Algeria. Always preferring analysis to moralising and sloganising, he was critical of the 1968 student revolt, more for how it was organised than for what it hoped to achieve; this too set him apart from popular social commentators like Sartre and **Herbert Marcuse**. Virtually alone among French intellectuals of the 1970s, he was markedly pro-American, spending much time in the United States with politicians and diplomats. While this enabled him to take a global view on issues such as the cold war and nuclear strategy, it also tended to dilute and rigidify his later writing. Despite this tendency to misjudge and overgeneralise, analysis and popularisation were always Raymond Aron's strong points, his lifelong belief being that academics must always try to understand things as they really are and hold to their truth, however unpopular that may make them.

Raymond Aron, *Memoirs: Fifty Years of Political Reflection*, Holmes and Meier, 1991

Robert Colquhoun, *Raymond Aron: The Philosopher in History, 1905–1955*, Sage, 1986

Robert Colquhoun, *Raymond Aron: The Sociologist in History, 1955–1983*, Sage, 1986

Hanan [Daoud Mikhael] Ashrawi
1946–
teacher, human rights and peace campaigner

When she became a spokesperson for the Palestine Liberation Organisation (PLO) in 1988, Hanan Ashrawi played a major role in changing its public image from that of a terrorist organisation into one of a government in exile poised for political responsibility. The daughter of a wealthy Christian Palestinian doctor, Hanan Mikhael had her first taste of oppression as a child living under Jordanian occupation. In 1964 she went to the American University in Beirut and, after graduating in 1969 (the same year acting as a student representative for the Palestinian cause), spent four further years studying English literature at the University of Virginia. On her return she was offered the post of dean of the faculty of arts at Bir Zeit University on the West Bank, and a year later married Emil Ashrawi: they have two daughters. Throughout the 1970s and early 80s she was involved in student demonstrations and confrontations with the Israeli authorities, and the Ashrawi house in Ramallah frequently became a sanctuary for Palestinian families fleeing the violence of the Intifada. In December 1986 the Israeli army stormed Bir Zeit University, killing one student and injuring many others: Hanan narrowly escaped with her own life. Convinced that the PLO needed clarity and insight in its dealings with Israel and the wider world, Hanan Ashrawi persuaded the PLO leadership in 1988 to let her demonstrate a more humane, reasoned view of the Palestinian situation; her fluency and grasp of the complexity of the conflict, and her criticism of the shortcomings of both Israeli and Palestinian leaders, quickly made her a popular and respected spokesperson. In 1988 the Israeli government began to indicate a new willingness to talk to the previously-proscribed PLO, and at talks in 1991 in Madrid, in late 1992 in Washington, and in 1993 in Norway, Ashrawi was one of the PLO's leading negotiators, insisting on equal rights for all Palestinians and Israelis. On September 13th 1993 Israeli prime minister Yitzhak Rabin and PLO leader Yasser Arafat signed a peace accord, but a month earlier, unhappy with the way in which Arafat refused to delegate decision-making to the PLO negotiating team, Hanan Ashrawi had resigned as the organisation's official spokesperson. As a well-off intellectual leader in a predominantly poor country, and as a Christian woman in a male-dominated mainly Muslim society, Hanan Ashrawi is in many ways an anomaly amongst her own people, but her abhorrence of injustice and her reputation for integrity are unquestioned.

Barbara Victor, *Hanan Ashrawi: A Passion for Peace*, Fourth Estate, 1995

Sylvia Ashton-Warner
1905–1984
novelist, teacher

Sylvia Ashton-Warner was born in Stratford, New Zealand; her mother was an unconventional schoolteacher and her father often ill, so family battles marked her childhood. Sylvia trained as a teacher in Auckland and married Keith Henderson in 1931: they had three children and taught together in Maori schools. Always creative, chaotic and eccentric, she took a great interest in Maori culture, learning fluent Maori and producing hundreds of handmade reading books to teach children in words and stories that were relevant to their experience, though she often absented herself from the classroom for days at a time while she wrote, danced and painted in her private sanctuary. Her extraordinarily powerful and highly autobiographical first novel *Spinster* (1958) was about the creative but misunderstood teacher of a Maori infant class, a strong, frustrated passionate woman driven to drink and the edge of breakdown. Her other novels, so autobiographical and critical of her friends and colleagues that they were often published in the USA and not available in New Zealand, included *Incense to*

Idols (1960), *Bell Call* (1963), *Greenstone* (1967) and *Three* (1970). Her experiments in child-centred primary education, meanwhile, were documented in *Teacher* (1963), which rapidly became a bestseller and was read by many radical educators, especially in the USA where it was first published. In January 1969 Keith Henderson died after a long illness, and three months later Sylvia left New Zealand for Mauritius, Jerusalem, London and North America. In 1970 the pioneering Aspen Community School in Colorado asked her to be part of their inaugural team; she accepted the invitation and inspired many of her colleagues, but had little experience of organisation and cooperation: her frustration was again turned into another passionately critical book, *Spearpoint: Teacher in America* (1972). From 1971 to 1973 she lived in Vancouver, demonstrating to enthusiastic trainee teachers what the world of a five-year-old required from a schoolteacher, but even this failed to fulfil her, and for the last ten years of her life she returned to New Zealand. An angry, brilliant, self-destructive woman, Sylvia Ashton-Warner provided the inspiration for many of the child-centred educational reforms of the 1970s and 80s.

Sylvia Ashton-Warner, *Teacher*, Simon and Schuster, 1963
Sylvia Ashton-Warner, *Myself*, Simon and Schuster, 1967
Sylvia Ashton-Warner, *I Passed This Way*, Knopf, 1980
Lynley Hood, *Sylvia! The Biography of Sylvia Ashton-Warner*, Viking, 1988

Aung San Suu Kyi
1944–
social and political activist, politician

In 1886, following a series of British-led campaigns, Burma was annexed to India, but during the 1930s a growing tide of nationalism and discontent with colonial rule climaxed in the popular rebellions of 1938 and 1939. When war broke out, an influential group of anti-British nationalists known as 'The Thirty Comrades' supported the Japanese takeover of Burma, but when it became clear that Japan had no intention of honouring its promise of full independence, the Comrades, led by General Aung San, sided with the British to bring self-government to Burma. In May 1945 Aung San, who had recently fathered a daughter, started to organise a transition government, but in July 1947 was assassinated in a military coup. His daughter, Suu Kyi, was educated in England, where she met and married Oxford scholar Michael Aris and had two sons, but kept in close touch with events in Burma, hearing with growing concern about the excesses of the military dictatorship of Ne Win. In the three decades following his seizure of power in 1962 Ne Win's 'purification' tactics included rape, torture and slavery. Early in 1988, hearing that her mother was ill, Suu Kyi returned to Rangoon. At first she chose not to take part in the growing protest movement, but after a student massacre in August 1988 she felt she could not remain silent, and nearly half a million people attended the rally at which she first spoke, establishing her as the eloquent leader of Burma's struggle for human rights and democracy. As she travelled the country the military government

attempted to appease international concern by adopting a new constitution and announcing elections, at the same time renaming the country
Myanmar to reflect its multicultural heritage. Aung San Suu Kyi presented
an unacceptable threat to official platitudes, and in July 1989 she was
placed under armed house arrest in the family home. Her imprisonment
did not, however, prevent her National League for Democracy from winning a landslide election in May 1990, nor Suu Kyi from winning a Nobel
Peace Prize in 1991. The military government ignored the election results
and clamped down on known League supporters, but Suu Kyi remains
Myanmar's popular leader and the resumption of diplomatic relations
between Myanmar and the West hangs on Suu Kyi's release. In September
1994 her release was guaranteed if she would leave the country but, as so
often before, she reiterated that this was the last thing she was prepared
to do.

Aung San Suu Kyi, *Aung San*, Kiscadale Publications, 1990
Aung San Suu Kyi (ed. Michael Aris), *Freedom from Fear, and Other Writings*,
    Viking, 1991
Bertil Lintner, *Aung San Suu Kyi and Burma's Unfinished Renaissance*, Peacock, 1990

Uri Avnery
1923–
journalist, writer, politician, peace campaigner

Ever since the creation of the state of Israel in 1948 there have been
prominent Israelis insisting that Palestine must have the same right to
self-determination as does Israel, and notable among the voices promoting
dialogue and reconciliation is Uri Avnery. Avnery was born in 1923 in
Beckum, Germany; his family emigrated to Palestine in November 1933.
From 1938 until 1942 he was a member of the National Military Organization, an underground Jewish militia, and in 1947 he published his first
book, *Milhama Ve-shalom Ba-merkha Ha-shemi* (*War or Peace in the Semitic
Region*), a call for an alliance between the Hebrew and Arab national
movements. With the outbreak of war in 1948 Avnery joined the newly-
formed Israeli army, where he served in a commando unit and was
wounded in action. While a soldier he also acted as war correspondent for
Ha'aretz: his articles formed the basis of his bestselling *Be-sdot Pleshet 1948*
(*In the Fields of the Philistines*). However, his next book, exposing the ugly
side of the 1948 war, *Ha-tsad Ha-sheni shel Ha-matbe'a* (*The Other Side of the
Coin*, 1950) was boycotted by the authorities. In the same year he became
publisher and editor-in-chief of the news magazine *Haolam Hazeh*, a position which he held until 1990. Since 1948 Avnery has been an outspoken
advocate of the Israeli-Palestinian two-state solution: he propagated the
idea incessantly in *Haolam Hazeh*, and roundly criticised the military
adventures of the Ben Gurion regime, which branded him 'public enemy
number one'. In 1965 Avnery was one of the founders of the New Force
Party, the first Israeli party to advocate peace with a Palestinian state, and
was twice, in 1965 and 1969. elected as its representative in the Knesset

(Israeli parliament). The party's ideas were expounded in his book *Israel without Zionists* (1968). In 1975 Avnery was among the founders of the Israeli Council for Israeli-Palestinian Peace, an extraparliamentary organisation which established contact and dialogue with the Palestine Liberation Organisation (PLO) leadership. He also took part in the creation of the Shelli Peace Party in 1977, and as its representative again entered the Knesset. In July 1982, Avnery crossed the lines in besieged Beirut and met with Yasser Arafat, the first Israeli to do so: his meetings with Arafat and other PLO leaders were described in his 1988 book *My Friend the Enemy*. Avnery is at present among the leading activists of the Gush Shalom (Peace Bloc) movement, which in December 1992 grew out of the spontaneous protest against the Rabin government's decision to deport 415 Palestinian activists to Lebanon. He is a columnist for the daily newspaper *Ma'ariv* and a lecturer in journalism at Tel Aviv University.

Uri Avnery, *Israel without Zionists: A Plea for Peace in the Middle East*, Macmillan, 1968
Uri Avnery, *My Friend, The Enemy*, Zed, 1986

Nnamdi [Benjamin] Azikiwe
1904–
journalist, politician, political commentator

The obvious candidate for the presidency of the independent republic of Nigeria in 1963, Nnamdi Azikiwe has worked hard to understand the needs of his people and to balance the demands of tribal self-determination and intercultural reconciliation in West Africa. Born into an Ibo family from Onitsha, he was well-educated and worked as a clerk for four years. In 1925, determined to widen his horizons, he stowed away on a ship bound for the USA and worked hard to put himself through college, studying political science at Howard and Lincoln Universities. Later he studied journalism and taught at Lincoln. While in America he was much influenced by **Marcus Garvey's** black nationalism movement, and in 1934 returned to Africa to work as a journalist and freedom campaigner. For three years he was editor of the Accra-based *Africa Morning Post*, moving back to Nigeria to establish a chain of newspapers, among them the influential *West African Pilot*, and to become a leading voice for Ibo interests. His fierce yet reasoned editorials calling for an end to colonial rule paved the way for a Nigerian nationalist movement which coalesced in the mid-1940s under the banner of the Ibo-led National Council of Nigerian Citizens (NCNC). In 1951 Nigeria was granted internal self-rule, and in 1954 Nnamdi Azikiwe was elected prime minister of Eastern Nigeria, taking the NCNC into coalition with the Northern People's Congress after the 1959 elections to form the first government of a united Nigeria. Four years later he became president when independence was declared, but was ousted after three years in the first of many military coups. He returned to his home in Nsukka in Eastern Nigeria and worked hard to establish the University of Nigeria at Nsukka. Factional powermongering, especially between the Ibo of the south-east and the Yoruba of the south-west, led to the Biafran war of 1967–69, which Azikiwe counselled vehemently against. His ability to reconcile the different elements of Nigerian culture was rewarded in 1972 when he was appointed chancellor of Lagos University. He remained active in politics, working with the Nigeria People's Party until General Ibrahim Babangida's edict of 1986 banned political parties, but continues to write and speak about the importance of crosscultural cooperation.

> Nnamdi Azikiwe, *Zik: A Selection from the Speeches of Nnamdi Azikiwe*, Cambridge University Press, 1961
> Ronald Segal, *African Profiles*, Penguin, 1963

Mariama Bâ
1929–1981
novelist, teacher, feminist

Like the protagonist in her award-winning novel *Une si longue lettre* (*So Long a Letter*, 1979), Mariama Bâ knew exactly what Senegalese women were up against if they wanted their needs and aspirations to be taken seriously. How to balance the raising of a large family in a patriarchal culture against the liberation of her insight and creativity in writing became her lifelong struggle. She was born in Dakar, where her mother died young and her father, a high-ranking civil servant, insisted on his daughter having a full French education: characteristically she passed her entrance examination to the École Normale in 1943 with the highest mark of any candidate in French West Africa. Soon after finishing her education she married the Senegalese politician Obèye Diop and had nine children; they separated in the mid-1970s and he married a younger woman. Although she always stressed that *So Long a Letter* was not autobiographical, her experiences and feelings certainly informed her powerful writing: the novel won the prestigious Noma Award and was translated into more than a dozen languages. For several years Mariama Bâ had been working with Senegalese women's associations to raise awareness of issues such as women's education, polygamy and clitoridectomy, and she wanted her writing to arouse women to an awareness of their inferior status. She wrote one other novel, *Le chant écarlate* (*Scarlet Song*, 1981), about the tensions of racially-mixed marriage, but died shortly before it was published.

> Mariama Bâ (trans. Modupe Bode-Thomas), *So Long a Letter*, Heinemann, 1981 (repr. Virago, 1982)
> Mariama Bâ (trans. Dorothy Blair), *Scarlet Song*, Longman, 1986

Joan Baez
1941–
singer, peace activist

Perhaps the most famous of 1960s solo folk singers, Joan Baez has always believed that the folk tradition and concern for social justice go hand in hand, and has been actively involved in a wide range of peace and education programmes. She was born in New York and grew up in upstate New York,

California, Iraq, and Boston, where in the late 1950s she studied music (her particular interest being Anglo-American ballads and spirituals) and started singing in Harvard coffee houses. Her powerful yet sensitive voice and her wide repertoire soon came to the attention of folk artistes Theodore Bikel and Harry Belafonte, and at eighteen she was asked to sing at the Newport Folk Festival. Her singing career took off over the next twenty years, several of her albums becoming all-time bestsellers. She became friends with many older singers who were involved in movements for social change, including Odetta, The Weavers, and Peggy and **Pete Seeger**, and like her contemporaries Phil Ochs and Utah Phillips she too became involved in campaigning for civil and human rights. Her particular interest was the growing peace movement, and she worked hard to do what she could to bring an end to the **Vietnam War**. In 1968 she married draft resister David Harris, but after the three years he subsequently spent in prison they decided to separate in 1973. Joan herself was twice briefly imprisoned for her antiwar activities, and was in Hanoi during the ferocious Christmas 1972 bombing raids. Throughout the 1970s she actively supported nuclear disarmament and nonviolent social change, often arranging and appearing in benefit concerts. In 1965 she founded the Institute for the Study of Nonviolence in Carmel, California (now the Resource Center for Non-Violence in Santa Cruz), and in 1979 initiated Humanitas International, an organisation focusing on human rights and disarmament issues. She has continued to work for peace and reconciliation, being a longtime board member of **Amnesty International** and a frank and outspoken critic of human rights abuses wherever they are perpetrated.

Joan Baez, *Daybreak*, Dial Press, 1968
Joan Baez, *And a Voice to Sing With: A Memoir*, Summit, 1987
David Harris, *Goliath*, Avon Books, 1970

Rudolf Bahro
1935–
socialist and green activist and writer

Rudolf Bahro, as the title of his autobiographical *From Red to Green* (1984) would suggest, is the best-known of Europe's socialists-turned-greens, and has played a vital part in the building of the green movement in general and the German Green Party (**Die Grünen**) in particular. He was born in Bad Flinzberg in Silesia, and after a harrowing war became a committed Marxist and East German Communist Party member. As a journalist and union official he had access to worldwide information, and became increasingly critical of the Soviet Union's stance towards eastern Europe. Shortly after the invasion of Czechoslovakia in 1968 he started to write *The Alternative in Eastern Europe*, a survey of how its people could benefit from an emancipatory socialism which would liberate them from the alienation of both capitalism and centralised state bureaucracy; he completed the book in 1977 and it was published in West Germany. The East German authorities, who had been suspicious of his subversive thinking for some time, charged him with 'publishing state secrets' and gave him an eight-year prison sentence. Two years later, following international pressure for his release, he was allowed to settle in West Germany, where he quickly became involved in the rapidly-growing Die Grünen and sought to build bridges between the many West German socialist and Marxist factions. As his awareness of global ecological issues expanded during the 1980s he stressed the importance of questioning and ending the capitalist destruction of habitat and human spirit alike, and spoke and wrote passionately for a fundamental change in economic and political policies. His avowedly utopian vision, looking forward to a future of deindustrialised self-governing communes, put him firmly on the 'fundamentalist' wing of Die Grünen, and it was frustration with his party's mid-80s policy of pragmatic compromise that led to his dramatic resignation at its annual congress in June 1985. He has not given up his green idealism, however; since 1989 his main occupation has been the implementation of an Ecological Studies Programme at Humboldt University in (ex-East) Berlin, one of the few universities to offer every student a foundation course in ecological thinking.

Rudolf Bahro, *The Alternative in Eastern Europe*, Verso, 1978
Rudolf Bahro, *Socialism and Survival*, Heretic, 1982
Rudolf Bahro, *Building the Green Movement*, New Society, 1986
Rudolf Bahro, *Avoiding Social and Ecological Disaster: The Politics of World Transformation*, Gateway, 1994

Ella [Josephine] Baker
1903–1986
civil rights campaigner and activist

Although she is not as well known as other black American civil rights leaders, Ella Baker's high-level organising and bridge-building helped to shape much of the history of social protest for the half century from the mid-30s to her death. 'Strong people don't need strong leaders', she was fond of saying, and was critical of top-heavy structures and overly-important leaders – particularly male ones. She was born in Norfolk, Virginia and grew up in Littleton, North Carolina, where her parents encouraged her education, sending her to Shaw Academy and University in Raleigh. In 1928 she moved to New York, where the poverty and desperation of Depression Harlem had a tremendous impact on her. Her teaching job with the Workers Education Project brought her into contact with many leading radicals and organisations: the first of more than fifty political organisations she joined in her long activist career was a network of black consumer cooperatives, the Young Negroes Cooperative League, and she was soon busy with a range of community, educational and women's groups. In 1940 she became a field secretary of the National Association for the Advancement of Coloured People (NAACP), and three years later its director of branches, establishing a vast network of contacts throughout the southern states. In 1946, frustrated by its bureaucracy, she resigned from NAACP to campaign against segregation in New York schools, and in 1956 she joined with **Bayard Rustin** to establish In Friendship, a civil rights support network which foreshadowed her involvement with the influential Southern Christian Leadership Conference (SCLC), under the leadership of **Martin Luther King**. Again she soon found the top-heaviness oppressive and disempowering of ordinary people, so in 1960 called a conference at Shaw University which led to the establishment of the **Student Nonviolent Coordinating Committee** (SNCC). As mentor and inspiration to young radical students in SNCC, Ella Baker had a large hand in training many of the social protest leaders of the next three decades. Despite failing health she continued until her death to act as an adviser for a wide range of organisations, including antiwar groups and the **women's liberation movement**.

Ellen Cantarow, *Moving the Mountain: Women Working for Social Change*, Feminist Press, 1980

Charles Payne, 'Ella Baker and Models of Social Change', *Signs*, Summer 1989

Eve [Evelyn Barbara] Balfour
1898–1990
agriculturalist, writer, social and environmental activist

Eve Balfour, best known as the main inspiration behind the organic farming movement, herself grew in a rich and nurturing environment. The daughter of an aristocratic Scottish family, her relatives included a British prime minister, a viceroy of India and the first principal of Cambridge's all-women Newnham College, and when she became a vegetarian aged seven and decided to be a farmer at twelve her parents consented without demur. In 1918 she graduated from Reading University with a diploma in agriculture and was employed training Land Army girls; the following year Eve and her sister Mary rented a farm at Haughley in Suffolk. In the mid-1930s Eve Balfour fought for the abolition of tithes, an antiquated system of payments to the church which was depriving rural labourers of much of the fruits of their labour; the same period also saw the start of her lifelong companionship with fellow farmer Kathleen Carnley (usually known as 'KC'). In 1938, having read Lord Lymington's critique of orthodox farming methods, *Famine in England*, Eve Balfour and her neighbour Alice Debenham established the Haughley Research Trust to experiment with organic farming techniques. In 1943 she published her influential book *The Living Soil*, which aroused such a response from likeminded farmers and growers that in 1946 the Soil Association was formed, with Eve as its general secretary – within five years the organisation had more than three thousand members in 42 countries. As a result of the burgeoning interest in organic farming Eve and KC started to travel abroad, starting with a punishing American tour in 1951. Ten years later they moved from the farm to a nearby cottage, though Eve continued to lecture and write about organic farming until she suffered a stroke shortly before her death. At the age of ninety she was still growing her own vegetables and baking her own bread.

Eve Balfour, *The Living Soil*, Faber, 1943 (reissued as *The Living Soil and the Haughley Experiment* in 1975)

Eve Balfour, 'The Origins of the Soil Association', in Philip Conford (ed.), *The Organic Tradition*, Green Books, 1988

Michael Brander, *Eve Balfour, First of the Greens*, Faber, 1994

Henri Barbusse

1873–1935

novelist, journalist, pacifist

France's leading antiwar campaigner of the 1920s and 30s, Henri Barbusse was born on the outskirts of Paris and followed his father's profession as a journalist. He saw action as a soldier in 1914–15, and was so disturbed by what he experienced that in 1916 he published *Le feu* (*Under Fire*), a powerful condemnation of war and the class structure that sends its poorest men to die for a country's 'honour'. The book was a remarkable success in such a strongly patriotic era, and made Barbusse the natural leader of the nascent socialist pacifist youth movement in France. He joined the Socialist Party, and in May 1919 he and two of his colleagues launched the international organisation Clarté (Clarity), an attempt to rally intellectuals of all nations against imperialist wars. Clarté had considerable success in its early years, but by 1923 it had been virtually taken over by the French Communist Party, and Barbusse resigned from its governing council in protest against the move from humanistic pacifism to a narrow hardline political stance. He turned more to writing and journalism: in 1927 he published *Jésus*, a controversial novel portraying Jesus as an early communist, and the following year founded the weekly newspaper *Le monde*. In 1932 he organised the first World Conference of Intellectuals for Peace in Amsterdam and founded the Association of Revolutionary Writers with its journal *Commune*; two years later the second intellectuals' peace conference at the Salle Pleyel in Paris saw the launching of the influential leftwing Amsterdam-Pleyel Movement, which provided a platform for the launch of the French Popular Front in 1934. Sadly Barbusse died just before the triumph of the Popular Front, which embodied his twin ambitions of peace and mass mobilisation for social justice.

Henri Barbusse (trans. W. Fitzwater Wray, with an intro. by Brian Rhys), *Under Fire*, Dutton, 1926 (many reprints since)

Henri Barbusse (trans. Solon Librescot), *Jesus*, Dutton, 1928

Mary Ritter Beard

1876–1958

feminist, historian

The title of Mary Ritter Beard's best-known book, *Women as a Force in History* (1946), sums up both her approach and her personal contribution to feminism. Born and raised in Indianapolis, she studied at DePauw University in Asbury, where she met her future husband, Charles Austin Beard. They married in 1900 and spent two years in England, where Mary plunged herself into the women's suffrage movement. For the next two years she combined bringing up her daughter Miriam with studying sociology at

Columbia University, but found academia too limiting for her wideranging interests. Shortly after the birth of her second child, William, in 1907, she joined the National Women's Trade Union League, and for the next ten years was active in the suffrage and women's rights movements as an organiser, publicist and fundraiser. In 1917 Charles Beard resigned his Columbia professorship in protest against the firing of pacifist colleagues, and the family moved to Milford, Connecticut, where Mary studied and wrote the books with which she was to make her mark as a feminist historian. Starting in 1927 she and Charles collaborated in producing a famous series of histories of the United States, starting with *The Rise of American Civilization*; one of Mary's main concerns was to counter the false impression that 'all history is but the story of the man's world'. The 1930s saw the publication of several of Mary Ritter Beard's influential books including *On Understanding Women* (1931) and *America Through Women's Eyes* (1933); in 1942 she wrote a brilliant critique of the omissions and distortions concerning women presented in the *Encyclopedia Britannica*; and in 1946 she wrote *Women as a Force in History*, demonstrating how the women's rights movement too often concentrated on the oppression of women rather than on celebrating their manifold achievements. All her life Mary Ritter Beard refused to accept that equality meant women must conform to male standards, believing instead that they could most readily gain self-confidence and self-respect by understanding and publicising the many things that they and others had already achieved.

Mary Ritter Beard (ed. with an intro. by Nancy Cott), *A Woman Making History: Mary Ritter Beard through her Letters*, Yale University Press, 1991
Mary Ritter Beard (ed. Ann Lane), *Mary Ritter Beard: A Sourcebook*, Schocken, 1977

Simone [Lucie Ernestine] de Beauvoir
1908–1986
socialist-feminist writer and campaigner

Simone de Beauvoir was one of the most important postwar French writers and social critics, widely known for her contribution to existential philosophy, socialism and feminism, as well as for her acutely observed and often highly autobiographical novels. She was born into an upper middle class Parisian Catholic family, where she and her sister were expected to concentrate on their education. By the age of fourteen Simone had rejected religion and marriage, and had resolved to become a writer. While studying at the Sorbonne in 1929 she met **Jean-Paul Sartre**, who was to be her companion and collaborator until his death in 1979. Her first novel, *L'invitée* (*She Came To Stay*), was published in 1943 and several more followed, but it was with *Le deuxième sexe* (*The Second Sex*, 1949) that she first reached a broad audience. In a wideranging survey of biology, history and culture she showed how women are universally taught to be the 'other' to the dominant male sex. Her biological determinism was criticised by later feminists, but her analysis of oppression and the seeming intractability of women's predicament struck a chord with many thousands of readers. Her rejection of marriage and motherhood, in writing as well as in practice, gave both her and Jean-Paul explicit consent for other relationships, but in the circumstances she found it more demanding (and almost certainly less rewarding) than he did: by comparison with his many liaisons, only two men – the American socialist Nelson Algren and the writer Claude Lanzmann – became her intimates. For decades a convinced socialist who believed that socialism must come before women's emancipation, Simone de Beauvoir changed her priorities in the late 1960s, declaring in a 1972 interview that women's liberation 'could not wait for socialism and some male liberator'. Throughout her life she was a remarkably honest and insightful observer, both of social and political trends and of her own inner life, and both are interwoven in a series of four autobiographies of which the first, *Mémoires d'une jeune fille rangée*, appeared in 1958.

Simone de Beauvoir (trans. Howard Parshley), *The Second Sex*, Penguin, 1953
Simone de Beauvoir, *Memoirs of a Dutiful Daughter*, Penguin, 1963
Simone de Beauvoir, *The Prime of Life*, Penguin, 1965
Simone de Beauvoir, *Force of Circumstance*, Penguin, 1968
Simone de Beauvoir, *All Said and Done*, Penguin, 1977
Judith Okeley, *Simone de Beauvoir*, Virago, 1986

Carlos [Filipe Xiemenes] Belo
1948–
clergyman, human rights advocate

It is estimated that 200,000 East Timorese, or one third of its population, were massacred in the two decades after 1975, when Indonesian forces invaded the newly-independent state. As in many parts of the Third World, it is the local clergy who have taken a firm public stand against human rights abuse. In many ways East Timor-born but Madrid-educated Carlos Belo seemed an unlikely candidate to fight for his people's right to self-determination. When he became bishop of East Timor in 1983 after thirteen years in Portugal and only two in his home country, he was criticised as a moderate who had sold out to the Indonesian Suharto regime by taking Indonesian nationality. It very soon became clear, however, that he would take every opportunity to condemn the brutal violence of the Indonesian army in East Timor. In October 1983, soon after he was installed, he protested against arrests and violence in a sermon in Dili Cathedral, and a month later was rewarded by a letter of support from the Indonesian Bishops' Conference. As he continued to witness the atrocities perpetrated by the Indonesian authorities, from random torture and killing to enforced sterilisation, he became ever more vocal, and the first of two assassination attempts was made on him in 1989 after he had written to the United Nations appealing for international assistance. He was again ambushed in 1991, while visiting a mass grave near Viquique. In November 1991 hundreds of young people were massacred following a peaceful protest at Dili's Santa Cruz Cemetery, and Bishop Belo was placed under virtual house arrest 'in his own interests'. Indonesia continues to press forward with the 'integration' of East Timor into Indonesia, silencing domestic critics with draconian repression and the rest of the world with bland platitudes and promises of economic reward. In 1994, however, following pressure from governments such as New Zealand and Ireland, and the vivid portrayals of journalists like **John Pilger**, a United Nations human rights team started to document what Carlos Belo had been fighting against for more than a decade – nothing less than calculated and brutal mass genocide.

John Pilger, *Distant Voices*, Vintage, 1994

Tony [Anthony Neil Wedgwood] Benn
1925–
socialist politician

One of the few British politicians to hold a clear radical socialist line throughout the 60s and 70s, and even more firmly in the conservative climate of the 1980s, Tony Benn has added the adjective 'Bennite' to British politics. The son of a Labour member of parliament who became a peer, Viscount Stansgate, he grew up in London, attended Westminster School and New College, Oxford, and served in the RAF for three years in the second world war before returning to Oxford to complete his studies. In 1949 he married Caroline De Camp, who was to become a prominent educationalist; three of their four children have also become active in politics. He entered parliament in 1950 at the age of 25, but was forced to resign on his father's death in 1960; a three-year battle to disclaim his title and thus stand again for the House of Commons resulted in new legislation in 1963, and he re-entered parliament the following year, when the Labour Party won the general election. His rise in government was rapid, and he held important cabinet posts until Labour's defeat in 1979. Throughout the 1970s, and more markedly after 1979, Tony Benn's political stance became more radical, and he was soon a vocal supporter of a raft of imaginative socialist policies including unilateral nuclear disarmament, extended public ownership and sweeping constitutional reform. In 1981 he came very close to winning a ballot for the leadership of the Labour Party, but by 1983 the party's fortunes had slumped, and his Bristol seat was abolished in a boundary reorganisation. He re-entered the Commons the following year after a by-election victory and has remained a member of parliament ever since. His passionate yet reasoned oratory and writing, his support for human rights and civil rights issues, his honesty and enthusiasm, and his refusal to ignore difficult questions have endeared him to those who query many of the reactionary and opportunistic assumptions of contemporary politics. Six volumes of his carefully-recorded diaries have so far been published, providing much insight into British politics during the half century from 1940 to 1990.

Tony Benn, *Arguments for Socialism*, Cape, 1979

Tony Benn, *Arguments for Democracy*, Cape, 1981
Robert Jenkins, *Tony Benn: A Political Biography*, Writers and Readers, 1980
Sydney Higgins, *The Benn Inheritance: The Story of a Radical Family*, Weidenfeld
    and Nicholson, 1984

John [Peter] Berger
1926–
writer, art critic

In 1972 the British Broadcasting Corporation (BBC) screened a controversial series of programmes about classical art called 'Ways of Seeing'. The presenter was John Berger, an iconoclastic art critic and writer who upset much of the received wisdom of the art world by demonstrating that the context in which pictures are painted – who can afford to commission them; how artists and their patrons view women, children and property – is just as important to our understanding and appreciation of art as is the painting itself. John Berger grew up and trained as a painter in London, and then worked as a teacher, exhibiting in London galleries and helping to organise several early 1950s Artists for Peace exhibitions. His career as an art critic started with regular columns in the Labour Party newspaper *Tribune* and the socialist *New Statesman*, and throughout the 50s and 60s his writing became well known for its social and political insight as well as its artistic integrity. He firmly believed that good art is revolutionary, in that it encourages the viewer to think about the limits set by society and helps us to imagine a future in which human potential is set free. His *Success and Failure of Picasso* (1965) explored the problems of the artist in the modern world, and was matched four years later by a study of the Russian dissident artist Ernst Neizvestny, *Art and Revolution*, which showed how art must always achieve a balance between vision and practical limitation. It was the television series and book of 'Ways of Seeing' that brought John Berger's ideas to a wide audience: as a sequel and contrast to the BBC's earlier and conventionally patrician 'Civilisation' series by Sir Kenneth Clark, its socialist and feminist insights appealed enormously to a whole generation of radical teachers and students. In 1972 John Berger moved to Switzerland, and is now based in France's Haute Savoie, where for the last twenty years he has concentrated on creative writing and film-making; his particular interest has been the lives and achievements of Europe's 'outcasts' – its peasants, immigrants and exiles.

John Berger, *Success and Failure of Picasso*, Penguin, 1965
John Berger, *Art and Revolution*, Pantheon, 1969
John Berger, *Ways of Seeing*, Penguin, 1972
Peter Fuller, *Seeing Berger: A Revaluation of 'Ways of Seeing'*, Writers and Readers,
    1981

Alexander Berkman
1870–1936
anarchist, workers' rights activist

Alexander Berkman might have been just one of the many emigré Russians with revolutionary zeal burning in their blood who reached American shores in the 1880s and 90s only to be forgotten by subsequent generations, had he not on his first day ashore in New York met and fallen in love with the legendary anarchist **Emma Goldman**. That was August 15th 1889, and by 1892 the couple had established an ice cream parlour in New Haven to raise money to return to the Russian 'front'. In July of that year, however, there was a particularly vicious labour lockout at the Homestead Plant of the Carnegie Steel Company in Pennsylvania. A private army had been hired to murder dissident workers, and Berkman, outraged at the injustice, determined to assassinate the Carnegie chairman. The attempt failed miserably, and Alexander Berkman spent thirteen years in prison, reading and studying. When he and Emma Goldman were free to be together again it was more as friends and colleagues than as lovers: she offered him the editorship of her magazine *Mother Earth*, and from 1908 to 1915 he contributed substantially to its success. For the next two years he edited his own magazine, *The Blast*, but by now his interest in social and political change had narrowed to strikes and demonstrations. On December 21st 1919, following a series of 'red scares', Goldman and Berkman, together with 249 other 'alien radicals', were put on a ship for Russia. Although he was initially supportive of the Bolshevik Revolution, within a year he had disavowed it, arguing that the Bolsheviks were nothing less than a tyranny ruling in the name of the people. After a short stay in Germany he lived for a while in France, where he wrote his most important book, *The ABC's of Anarcho-Communism* (1927), arguing strongly for a society of free, independent, self-supporting communities. Another decade of statelessness and poverty proved too much for his morale and his health; though reconciled with Emma Goldman he killed himself after a second prostate operation in June 1936.

Alexander Berkman, *Now and After: The ABC's of Anarcho-Communism*, Vanguard Press, 1927

Alexander Berkman, *Prison Memoirs of an Anarchist*, Frontier Press, 1970

Richard Drinnon, *Rebel in Paradise: A Biography of Emma Goldman*, University of Chicago Press, 1961

Daniel Berrigan and Philip Berrigan
1921–   and 1923–
peace activists

The American peace campaigners Daniel and Philip Berrigan are the youngest of six sons of a loving but tough Catholic family. Daniel Berrigan became a Jesuit in 1939 and was ordained as a priest in 1942, teaching high school French and English until 1957, when he taught theology in a

Jesuit college. Returning to New York in 1965 after a sabbatical year in France, he became deeply involved in organising against the **Vietnam War**. When the church hierarchy sent him to South America as a disciplinary measure for his activism public reaction was strong; he returned after six weeks. Philip Berrigan, a US paratrooper in Europe during World War II, entered the Society of St. Joseph in 1950 after completing his interrupted studies. Serving as a parish priest and teacher in New Orleans, he was active in the civil rights movement until his superiors sent him north after refusing him permission to take part in the 1965 Selma march in Alabama. Assigned to an all-black parish in Baltimore, he immediately became involved in justice work again. In October 1967, protesting against the Vietnam War, Philip Berrigan was one of four people who destroyed military draft papers in Baltimore. The next May Philip and Daniel Berrigan took part in the Catonsville Nine action, burning 400 draft files with napalm that they had made following instructions in a US army manual. In 1973, Philip Berrigan and Elizabeth McAlister, who had left their religious orders and married several years earlier, established Jonah House in Baltimore as a centre for family life (they have three children) and a community of radical nonviolent activists. In September 1980 Daniel and Philip Berrigan participated in the first **Plowshares** action, and three years later Elizabeth McAlister Berrigan took part in another Plowshares action on an air force base in New York. Probably the best-known peace activists of the radical Catholic community in the USA, the Berrigans affirm that this community is a necessary source of inspiration, strength and support for lives committed to faith and social activism.

Charles DeBenedetti, *Peace Heroes in Twentieth-Century America*, Indiana University Press, 1986
Caroline Moorehead, *Troublesome People: The Warriors of Pacifism*, Adler and Adler, 1987
Michael True, *Justice Seekers, Peace Makers*, Twenty-Third Publications, 1985

Wendell Berry
1934–
writer, farmer, educator

Environmental writer and educator Wendell Berry was born and grew up in Henry County, Kentucky. After receiving his bachelor's and master's degrees from the University of Kentucky, he married Tanya Amyx in 1957. In 1965, by which time he had published his first novel and collection of poems and was teaching university English, he and Tanya and their two children moved to the farm in the Kentucky River Valley where the family has lived ever since. It is in his experience and reflections as a family farmer restoring and cultivating the land and learning the importance of traditional agricultural methods that his writing and social criticism is rooted. After a period of part-time teaching alongside his writing and farming, he returned to a post at the University of Kentucky in 1987, retiring in 1993. A prolific and incisive writer on cultural, agricultural and ecological issues, among his most influential works have been *The Unsettling of America* (1977) and *The Gift of Good Land* (1981). He argues for the spiritual and economic imperative of revitalising rural life, seeing a repopulated landscape of farmsteads and country towns in which people can thrive on a human scale, creating and exchanging both culture and the fruits of their labours as stewards of the land that sustains them. His writing and lecturing have been influential on both sides of the Atlantic, inspiring a generation of spiritually-inclined green activists.

Wendell Berry, *The Unsettling of America*, Sierra Club Books, 1977
Wendell Berry, *The Gift of Good Land*, North Point, 1981

Annie Besant [Annie Wood]
1847–1933
freethinker, feminist, social activist, occultist

Most renowned as the promoter, following the death of its founder Helena Blavatsky in 1891, of the religious philosophy known as Theosophy, Annie Besant had a long and controversial career which also included support for a wide range of radical causes, from freethinking and birth control to Indian independence and universal brotherhood. Born into a middle class London family, she was a devout Anglo-Catholic who married a priest when she was twenty. The marriage only lasted six years, and in revolt against her earlier beliefs Annie Besant plunged into the propagation of atheism, becoming in 1875 vice-president of the National Secular Society. In 1878 her estranged husband successfully sued for custody of their daughter Mabel on the grounds that Annie was an 'unfit mother'. Angry but un-daunted, Annie Besant threw herself into feminist and socialist activism, becoming an executive committee member of the **Fabian Society** in 1885, helping to organise a crucial matchgirls' strike in 1888, and enrolling at London University as one of its first woman students. Early in 1889 she met Helena Blavatsky: within six months she had become a member of the Esoteric Section of the Blavatsky Lodge, and when Blavatsky died Annie became Theosophy's natural leader. India was Theosophy's spiritual home, and in 1893 Annie Besant moved her base to Benares. In 1898 she was one of the founders of the Central Hindu College at Benares, by which time her romantic notions about Hindu culture had shifted to embrace the need for women's emancipation and a critical re-evaluation of Hinduism. In 1907 she was appointed president of the Theosophical Society, and the follow-ing year she and fellow Theosophist Charles Leadbeater adopted a twelve-year-old Brahmin boy, Jiddu Krishnamurti, as the next Hindu 'avatar' or messiah, a move which antagonised other Theosophist luminaries includ-ing Rudolf Steiner. By 1913 Annie Besant had become highly visible in Indian politics, writing and lecturing widely under the slogan 'Wake up, India!' In 1916 she formed the Home Rule for India League and was briefly imprisoned as a result; in 1917 she was a founder member of the Women's Indian Association and became president of the Indian National Congress, though her political influence soon began to be eclipsed by that of

Mohandas Gandhi. In her last years both her political and spiritual authority began to wane: in 1920 her long-time colleague Charles Leadbeater left Theosophy to form his own church, and in 1929 Krishnamurti publicly announced that he was not an avatar, but her ideas on social and spiritual reform have continued to have significant influence.

Annie Besant, *An Autobiography*, Theosophical Publishing House, various
    editions and dates
Arthur Hobart Nethercot, *The First Five Lives of Annie Besant*, University of
    Chicago Press, 1960
Arthur Hobart Nethercot, *The Last Four Lives of Annie Besant*, University of
    Chicago Press, 1963
Raj Kumar, *Annie Besant's Rise to Power in Indian Politics*, Concept, 1981
Anne Taylor, *Annie Besant: A Biography*, Oxford University Press, 1992

[Acharya] Vinoba Bhave
1895–1982
social activist and agrarian reformer

A Brahmin, Vinoba Bhave joined **Mohandas Gandhi** in 1916, and devoted the rest of his life to improving the lives of Indian villagers, especially the landless 'untouchables'. In 1948 several thousand members of the Gandhian Sarvodaya movement formed a loosely affiliated fellowship, and the following year Akhil Bharat Sarva Seva Sangh (All-India Association for the Service of All) was formed, with the primary purpose of transforming India into a society of self-governing villages: Vinoba Bhave soon emerged as its leader. From 1951 to 1956 he organised and publicised his Bhoodan Yajna (land gift) programme of land reform, whereby land was given by landowners to previously landless peasants; within five years 405,000 hectares had been thus redistributed. In the late 1950s the land gift programme was replaced by the more ambitious Gramdan campaign, which sought to assist the process of voluntary village communalism. By 1969 140,000 Indian villages had declared themselves in favour of Gramdan. Vinoba Bhave was more overtly anarchist than Gandhi, firmly believing that 'self-government means ruling your own self', and that government had no useful part to play however benevolent it might appear. He was, however, as firmly committed to nonviolence and popular politics as his mentor had been. By 1973 the Sarvodaya movement was split between the followers of Vinoba Bhave's 'gentle to gentler to gentlest' approach and **J.P. Narayan**'s more confrontative version of nonviolent struggle, which expressed itself in the student rebellions and mass demonstrations of 1974–75. Bhave showed his disapproval by taking a vow of silence for a year, but his silence was manipulated by the Indian government as a tacit sign of approval for the state of emergency established in mid-1975. Although Vinoba Bhave continued to work and teach anarchist nonviolence the cause was much weakened, and when he died in 1982 (three years after Narayan, who unlike Bhave was given the dubious honour of a state funeral) the Indian peasant movement lost one of its most influential advocates.

Vinoba Bhave, *Democratic Values*, Sarva Seva Sangh Prakashan, 1962
Vinoba Bhave, *Moved By Love: The Memoirs of Vinoba Bhave*, Green Books, 1994
Michael Sonnleitner, *Vinoba Bhave on Self-rule and Representative Democracy*,
    Promilla and Co., 1988

Steve [Bantu Stephen] Biko
1946–1977
black rights campaigner

Steve Biko's torture and brutal murder at the age of thirty by the South African security police transformed a young black radical overnight into a hero, martyr, and international voice for black consciousness. He showed millions, throughout South Africa and beyond, that a recognition of black identity could help the oppressed to break through the shackles of servitude. Steve Biko was born in King William's Town in the Eastern Cape, one of four children; his father died when he was four, but his mother worked hard for her children's welfare and education. In 1966 he went to the University of Natal to study medicine; here in July 1969 he was a cofounder of the black South African Students' Organisation (SASO). A year later he became editor of the SASO newsletter and started writing the regular column 'I Write What I Like'. In 1972, the year he helped to establish the Black People's Convention (BPC), he was dismissed from medical school for his activist work, and in March 1973 was banned and restricted to King William's Town. He continued to write for *Black Review* (which he helped to establish) and other publications; by 1974 his idea of black consciousness as an attitude of mind and a way of life was firmly rooted, and he was widely read and admired throughout black South Africa. In November 1974 SASO and BPC organised a series of pro-Mozambique-liberation rallies, following which, in April 1975, thirteen leaders (though not Biko) were charged under the Terrorism Act. Steve Biko was subpoenaed to appear at their trial in May 1976, using the public platform to give a detailed and lucid explanation of the goals of black consciousness. Following the 1976 Soweto uprising, repression by the security forces increased. Hemmed in by his banning order, his home under constant surveillance and his offices bugged, Steve Biko continued to use every possible avenue to stress the need for radical change in South Africa, but he knew that detention was inevitable. He was arrested in August 1977 while returning from Cape Town in contravention of his banning order, and subjected to weeks of questioning and torture. He died on September 12th, the 21st black person to die in a South African prison cell that year.

Steve Biko, *I Write What I Like: A Selection of Writings*, Heinemann, 1979
Donald Woods, *Biko*, Paddington Press, 1978
Barney Pityana *et al* (ed.), *Bounds of Possibility: The Legacy of Steve Biko and Black
    Consciousness*, Zed, 1992

Teresa Billington-Greig
1877–1964
suffragist, feminist activist

Although not often acknowledged as one of the more important British suffragists, Teresa Billington-Greig was for many years an active and original campaigner for women's rights, challenging the narrow 'votes for women' demand with a broad vision for the role of women which was in many ways decades ahead of her time. She grew up in a working-class family in Blackburn, and left home to live in Manchester at seventeen. She trained as a teacher, and became involved in the Ancoats University Settlement in the company of other progressive young intellectuals. In 1903 the suffragist **Emmeline Pankhurst**, who had recently founded the **Women's Social and Political Union** (WSPU), visited Manchester and immediately recognised Teresa Billington's speaking and organising skills: she arranged with **Keir Hardie** that Teresa should work as an organiser for the Independent Labour Party (ILP). The WSPU and the ILP took much up most of Teresa's energy for the next four years. In 1906 she was one of the first suffragists to be imprisoned in Holloway Prison, where her future husband, the socialist businessman Frederick Lewis Greig, was the only visitor allowed to see her. During 1907 her doubts about the WSPU's autocratic leadership and attention-grabbing militancy deepened; in October of that year she was one of the founders (with **Charlotte Despard**) of the breakaway **Women's Freedom League** (WFL), but by December 1910 there was little to choose between the tactics of the two organisations and she resigned from the WFL to write her critique of suffragism, *The Militant Suffrage Movement*. While she agreed that the suffragists were succeeding in gaining attention, she felt strongly that the women's movement would do better in the long term by means of 'reasoned revolt, working with clean hands, employing no aids of artifice and emotion to carry women beyond their depths'. Although her influence was most marked in the suffragist era, Teresa Billington-Greig continued to work for women's rights and equality for the rest of her long life – among other things she founded the Women's Billiards Association in 1923, and in 1937 returned to the WFL, concentrating on its Electoral Committee which after the war became the women in politics advocacy group Women for Westminster.

Teresa Billington-Greig (ed. Carol McPhee and Ann FitzGerald), *The Non-Violent Militant: Selected Writings of Teresa Billington-Greig*, Routledge and Kegan Paul, 1987

Ayse Bircan
1954–
journalist, human rights and women's rights activist

The daughter of working-class fourth-generation black Turks, Ayse Bircan grew up in Istanbul and was encouraged by her self-educated father to study. In 1975 she married a fellow activist with whom she had a son, and started a sociology course at Istanbul University, but had to leave again when rightwing students occupied the faculty. Almost immediately she became involved with grassroots political activism, editing a socialist youth newspaper, working as an area organiser for Ilerici Kadinlar Dernegi (the Turkish Progressive Women's Organisation), and cofounding the Turkish Peace Council. As a result of her activism she was taken to court and in 1979 was given a six-year prison sentence; together with other prominent activists she went into hiding. Following the military coup of 1980 she continued to work undercover, but three years later escaped to live with friends in London. At first the Turkish authorities refused to give her son a passport to join her in London, but relented five years later as a result of increasing political pressure. In London Ayse Bircan was one of the founders of the Turkish Community Centre, and in 1989 recommenced her university studies, still determined to fight for human rights in her home country.

Ayse Bircan, 'Black and Turkish', in Margaret Busby (ed.), *Daughters of Africa*, Jonathan Cape, 1992

Hugo Blanco [Galdos]
1935–
labour organiser, politician

In Peru's complex political history it is hard to unravel and judge the allegiances and integrity of individual players, yet Hugo Blanco's unswerving support for the deprived peasantry of his country has won him considerable admiration both at home and abroad. He grew up in a middle class family in Cuzco and studied agriculture in Argentina, where he was much influenced by the ideas of **Leon Trotsky**. Returning to Lima in 1956, he joined the Partido Obrero Revolucionario (Revolutionary Workers Party) and two years later started work as a tenant farmer in the valley of La Convención near Cuzco, where he saw at first hand how rich landowners maltreated their peasant tenants. Unlike many Latin American revolutionaries, Hugo Blanco stressed the need for disciplined community-based action, and was highly critical of those who thought that propaganda was any substitute for personal involvement in building an alternative economy. Within four years, largely due to his efforts, the number of peasant syndicates in La Convención had increased from six to 132, establishing schools, clinics and agricultural cooperatives. In November 1962 he organised a demonstration to protect a peasant being threatened by a landowner who had raped the peasant's daughter: the situation escalated rapidly and Blanco was imprisoned without trial for three years, at the end of which he was (almost certainly wrongly) convicted of killing two national guards and given a 25-year sentence in the island prison of El Frontón. Here he wrote *Tierra o muerte* (*Land or Death*), documenting the peasant struggle in Peru. He was freed in a 1970 amnesty, when General Juan Velasco Alvarado hoped that Blanco would add credibility to a nationwide land reform programme, but when Blanco advised peasants to take advantage of the reforms but distrust the regime he was deported. He spent most of the next six years in exile, but in 1978, running the election campaign from Argentina, his newly-formed FOCEP (Frente Obrero Campesino Estudiantil y Popular) received a large vote, making it (with Blanco as its leader) the third strongest group in the Peruvian National Assembly. FOCEP's platform, which was subsequently integrated with and diluted by that of the Izquierda Unida (an alliance of socialist groups), included self-determination by Peru's peasant farmers and a national programme of education and literacy. The economic plight of Peru in the 1980s put these aims low on the political agenda, but Hugo Blanco has continued to work both within and without the National Assembly for the rights of Peru's poorest citizens.

Hugo Blanco, *Land or Death: The Peasant Struggle in Peru*, Pathfinder Press, 1972
Nigel Haworth, 'Radicalization and the Left in Peru, 1976–1991', *The Latin American Left* (ed. Barry Carr and Steve Ellner), Westview Press/Latin America Bureau, 1993

Ernst Bloch
1885–1977
utopian/socialist philosopher

Philosophy, radical theology and Marxist political theory have all claimed Ernst's Bloch's ideas about hope, human nature and socialism as fascinating and disturbing grist to their particular mills. His particular skill was to humanise his lifelong faith in communism with a reasoned and reasonable optimism, demonstrating that true humanity must include a belief in the realisable though not-yet-realised fulfilment of human potential. Ernst Bloch grew up, steeped in German romantic literature, in the industrial German town of Ludwigshafen. He studied philosophy, physics and music at Munich, Würzburg and Berlin, and in 1918 started writing his acclaimed study *Geist der Utopie* (*The Spirit of Utopia*), where he argued for a dynamic view of nature as the setting for the fulfilment of yet-unrealised potential. Like many Jewish intellectuals he spent the war years in exile, first in Switzerland (where he met and married the imaginative socialist architect **Karola Piotrkowski**), and from 1938 to 1949 in the USA. These years were spent on his massive work *Das Prinzip Hoffnung* (*The Principle of Hope*), which was published after he returned to Germany to teach in Leipzig. Here he continued his exploration of literary, philosophical and practical utopias, tracing a path through 'the little waking dreams to the strong ones, via the wavering dreams that can be abused to the rigorous ones, via the shifting castles in the air to the one thing that is outstanding and needful'. The East German authorities were initially delighted to welcome an academic of Bloch's stature, but by the late 1950s his work was being discredited and his students harassed. In 1961, while on extended leave in West Germany, he and Karola were offered political asylum and he was given a professorship at Tübingen University. He spent his later years writing and lecturing, acclaimed as one of the great humanisers of the Marxist project.

Ernst Bloch, *A Philosophy of the Future*, Herder, 1970

Ernst Bloch (ed. Jack Zipes and Frank Mecklenbury), *The Principle of Hope*, Blackwell, 1986

Ruth Levitas, *The Concept of Utopia*, Philip Allan, 1990

Karola Bloch-Piotrkowski
1905–
architect, feminist, social activist

After the early 1930s Karola Bloch-Piotrkowski's career was closely allied with that of her philosopher husband **Ernst Bloch**, but she was an original thinker and activist in her own right, and after his death in 1977 remained involved in a range of feminist and green projects. She grew up in Lodz, Poland, and in Moscow, and studied politics and architecture in Berlin, Zürich and Vienna. In 1931 she joined Der Rote Student (The Red Student) in Berlin, an anti-Nazi discussion and awareness-raising group. As a Jewish Communist activist she fled Austria for Switzerland in 1933, where she met and married Ernst Bloch, and from 1938 to 1949 she worked as an architect (supporting her son and unemployed husband) and was an active member of the American Communist Party. Back in Germany she worked as an architect and engineer, and wrote widely on the role of architecture and interior design within the socialist vision; sadly the manuscript of her social history of the kitchen was lost when she and Ernst decided to stay in West Germany following the building of the Berlin Wall while they were on a lecture tour. In Tübingen, where Ernst was offered a guest professorship, Karola was the founder of the self-help organisation for young offenders Hilfe zur Selbsthilfe (From Help to Self-Help), and in 1980 she helped to organise and fund a shelter for battered women and their children. In the 1980s, especially following the television screening of a biographical documentary by Helga Reidemeister in 1981, she became a favourite guest speaker at socialist and **Die Grünen** meetings.

Magdalene Müller, 'Karola Bloch-Piotrkowski', *Biographical Dictionary of Neo-Marxism* (ed. Robert Gorman), Mansell, 1985

Augusto Boal
1931–
playwright, theatre director, politician

The Brazilian theatre director and politician Augusto Boal is one of the world's leading practitioners in the use of theatre to explore and find answers to complex social and political dilemmas. His pioneering techniques, including the 'theatre of the oppressed', 'forum theatre' and the 'cop in the head', are widely used to help people understand and experience the choices available to them, and Boal's recent move into electoral politics underlines his concern about real world issues. Augusto Boal grew up in Rio de Janeiro, and was educated there and at Columbia University. By 1955 he was directing his own one-act plays in New York, and in 1956 established the Teatro de Arena in São Paulo. The company travelled widely throughout Brazil, and Boal learned that it was not enough to use agitprop theatre to make people aware of oppression, especially if actors and directors were not willing to take the same personal risks as their audiences. In February 1971 Augusto Boal was arrested and imprisoned for three months by the oppressive Médici regime, and on his release he moved to Argentina, where for five years he directed the El Machette theatre company in Buenos Aires. In 1973 he took part in a literacy campaign in Peru, where he developed the idea of 'simultaneous dramaturgy', in which the audience participated in deciding the outcome of the theatrical action: from this developed the concept of 'forum theatre', in which members of the audience take the stage to enact solutions to their own dramatically portrayed dilemmas. In 1976 Boal moved to Lisbon, and two years later to Paris, where in 1979 he established the Centre du Théâtre de l'Opprimé (the Centre of the Theatre of the Oppressed). He found that although oppression manifested itself in more subtle ways in Europe than in Latin America, many of his techniques could be adapted and used to help people understand the interplay of power and powerlessness: he also developed new dramatic techniques, such as the 'cop in the head' and the 'rainbow of desires', in order to tackle internalised oppression. In 1989 the Theatre of the Oppressed was established in Rio de Janeiro, and in January 1993, using the slogan 'Corágem de ser feliz' ('Have the courage to be happy') he successfully stood as a PT (Partidos dos Trabalhadores; Workers Party) candidate for Rio city council.

Augusto Boal, *The Theatre of the Oppressed*, Pluto, 1988
Augusto Boal, *Games for Actors and Non-Actors*, Routledge, 1992
Augusto Boal, *The Rainbow of Desire*, Routledge, 1995
Mady Schutzman and Jan Cohen-Cruz, *Playing Boal*, Routledge, 1994

Heinrich [Theodor] Böll
1917–1985
novelist, libertarian, social critic

West Germany's leading chronicler and social critic grew up in Köln and started writing immediately after the second world war about his experiences as a disillusioned pacifist conscript. His 1950s novels portrayed the stresses of living in postwar Germany, with its problems of economic recovery and collective guilt, yet with little vision. A healthy Catholic faith and belief in family life (he married Annemarie Cech in 1942 and they had three sons) underlay his strong sense of the ethical responsibilities of being an author, and his novels exposed the hypocrisy of the power structures of church, state, military and media. Altogether he wrote nearly fifty novels and volumes of short stories, characterised by a sharpness of observation that matched his belief in the novelist's function to be a clear and unflinching social critic, and in 1972 he was awarded the Nobel Prize for Literature. His best-known book, translated into more than thirty languages, was *Die verlorene Ehre der Katharina Blum* (1974, 1975 in English), about the way that the media can distort the truth about an individual and infringe their most intimate privacy. From the mid-1970s on Heinrich Böll became a staunch supporter of **Die Grünen**, the German Green Party, and wrote increasingly about the dangers of the nuclear arms race and the undercover state security developed to 'protect' it – his support for fair hearings for leftwing terrorists made him a favourite scapegoat of the right, but he never let fame undermine his deeply-held egalitarian principles.

Heinrich Böll (trans. Leila Vennewitz), *The Lost Honour of Katherina Blum*, Penguin, 1978

Heinrich Böll (trans. Leila Vennewitz), *The Stories of Heinrich Böll*, Secker and Warburg, 1986

James Reid, *Heinrich Böll: A German of His Time*, Berg, 1987

Dietrich Bonhoeffer
1906–1945
theologian, social activist

On June 22nd 1939 pastor Dietrich Bonhoeffer wrote to his colleague Reinhold Niebuhr from the security of New York: 'I have made a mistake in coming to America. I must live through this difficult part of our national history with the Christian people of Germany. I will have no right to participate in the reconstruction of Christian life in Germany after the war if I do not share the trials of this time with my people.' Five years later the decision cost him his life, hanged in Buchenwald concentration camp for being implicated in the plot to assassinate Hitler, but his courage, integrity, and refusal to separate religion from politics inspired many socially-aware Christians in the decades after his death. He grew up in a religious middle class family in Breslau (now the Polish city of Wrocław), studied theology at Tübingen and Berlin, and became politicised during his time in Barcelona and New York in the late 1920s. He actively protested against the Nazi regime from its earliest days, becoming more vocal as its excesses grew. His skill lay in bringing together the teachings of Christianity and the realities of oppression, demonstrating clearly how responsible Christianity could not countenance random violence and blatant anti-Semitism. He attacked the moral laxity of 'cheap grace', his term for a blind forgiveness which allows antisocial acts if they are afterwards atoned for, and was an active ecumenist and internationalist. His church in Finkenwalde was closed by the Gestapo in 1937, and knowledge of his brother-in-law Hans von Dohnanyi's involvement in a plot to overthrow Hitler made him the more vulnerable. After short visits to Britain and the USA in mid-1939, when he seriously considered permanent exile, he returned to work underground in Germany, helping Jewish families and their allies and working within the resistance movement to overthrow the Nazi regime. He was arrested by the Gestapo in April 1943 and killed in April 1945, shortly before the liberation of Buchenwald by the American army. Much of his time in prison was spent writing what were subsequently published as *Letters and Papers from Prison*; these looked forward to a postwar amalgamation of church and world in a Christian 'coming of age', ideas that were eagerly embraced by a generation of liberal Christians in the 1950s and 60s.

Dietrich Bonhoeffer, *Letters and Papers from Prison*, Collins, 1953
Eberhard Bethge, *Dietrich Bonhoeffer: A Biography*, Collins, 1970

Yelena [Lusia Alikhanova] Bonner [Sakharov]
1923–
doctor, writer, human rights campaigner

Human rights campaigner Yelena Bonner is the daughter of an Armenian Bolshevik father and a Siberian Jewish mother, who as active Comintern officials were both arrested in 1937 when Yelena was fourteen: her father died in a prison camp and her mother was released in 1945. From 1941 to 1945 Yelena Bonner (in 1938 she took her mother's last name and called herself Yelena after a Turgenev heroine) worked as a nurse, often on the front line, and was seriously wounded in October 1938 when a bomb exploded near her train, causing her to lose much of her eyesight. Her disability did not, however, prevent her from becoming a doctor, her career from 1953 until she retired. From 1965 to 1972 she was a Communist Party member, but became increasingly concerned about the abuse of medicine and psychiatry under the Soviet regime. In 1970 she met and married the nuclear physicist and outspoken dissident **Andrey Sakharov** (she had been married before, from 1948 to 1965, and already had two children), and she and Andrey campaigned together for human rights in the Soviet Union, petitioning both at home and internationally on behalf of numerous dissidents. In 1976 Yelena Bonner was a founder and core member of the Moscow-based group established to monitor the 1975 Helsinki human rights accords. In January 1980 Sakharov was banished to Gorky, and for the next four years, alongside her own campaigning work, Yelena acted as messenger between Gorky and Moscow, keeping her husband informed of developments and his banishment in the public eye. In 1984, however, she too was exiled, to be released two years later, a few months before Sakharov received his own freedom following the personal intervention of Mikhail Gorbachev. Yelena Bonner spent her years in exile writing *Alone Together*, a personal account of her and Sakharov's relentless struggle for freedom and justice in the Soviet Union; after her husband's death in 1989 she turned to her childhood and wrote *Mothers and Daughters*, an account of the influences of her grandmother and mother on her early years.

Elena Bonner (trans. Alexander Cook), *Alone Together*, Knopf, 1986
Elena Bonner (trans. Antonina Bouis), *Mothers and Daughters*, Knopf, 1992
Andrei Sakharov (trans. Richard Lourie), *Memoirs*, Hutchinson, 1990

Murray Bookchin
1921–
libertarian teacher and writer, social ecologist

Murray Bookchin's formulation of 'social ecology', bringing together post-Marxist socialism, anarchism and ecological thinking, has had considerable influence over the thirty years during which his provocative writing has found an ever-widening audience. He grew up in a Russian immigrant family in New York, and as a young man immersed himself in labour activism, passing through Marxism and Communism to Trotskyism. In the 1960s and early 70s he edited the New York-based magazine *Anarchos*, and was involved in early protests against food additives and nuclear power. In 1975 he established the Institute for Social Ecology in Burlington, Vermont, where he has been based ever since. Murray Bookchin's first important collection of essays and articles, *Post-Scarcity Anarchism* (1971), showed him to be a widely-read and imaginative thinker, whose careful analysis was tempered (and sometimes marred) by scepticism and barbed vitriol. It included a 1964 essay, 'Ecology and Revolutionary Thought', in which he argued that a free society equates with an ecological society, a theme returned to in *Toward an Ecological Society* (1980), where he clarified the steps by which domination of people over each other inevitably leads to the human domination of nature. *The Ecology of Freedom* (1982) presented a mass of historical and anthropological evidence for the need to replace hierarchy with true freedom, while *Remaking Society* (1990) brought together the many strands of his thinking in a more readable synthesis. Murray Bookchin has consistently argued that only the creation of a free society will overcome the threat of widespread ecological disaster, to which end we must develop an 'ecological sensibility', based on reason and action, which integrates both the social and biological aspects of our nature. This must, he insists, involve a revolution whose aim is the dissolution rather than the redistribution of power. In the 1980s and 90s his surprisingly naive faith in technology and his refusal to endorse the 'biocentric' ethic (which argues that all living things have intrinsic worth) brought him into sharp conflict with other ecological thinkers, particularly 'deep ecologists', but his call for the integration of social and ecological renewal has provided direction and meaning for many green activists.

Murray Bookchin, *Post-Scarcity Anarchism*, Ramparts Press, 1971

Murray Bookchin, *Toward an Ecological Society*, Black Rose, 1980

Murray Bookchin, *The Ecology of Freedom*, Cheshire Books, 1982

Murray Bookchin, *Remaking Society: Pathways to a Green Future*, South End Press, 1990

Murray Bookchin, *Re-enchanting Humanity: A Defense of the Human Spirit against Antihumanism, Misanthropy, Mysticism and Primitivism*, Cassell, 1995

John Clark (ed.), *Renewing the Earth: The Promise of Social Ecology*, Green Print, 1990

Bertolt [Berthold Eugen Friedrich] Brecht
1898–1956
poet, dramatist, socialist

Bertolt Brecht is the twentieth century's best known radical playwright and theatre director, possessed of a unique ability to combine poetry, political insight and dramatic discipline to startling and influential effect. He grew up in the German city of Augsburg, and after an abortive medical training at Munich University turned to drama to express his politically-aware creativity. In 1922 he won the prestigious Kleist Prize for his *Trommeln in der Nacht* (*Trumpets in the Night*), and his highly successful collaborations with the composer Kurt Weill in *Dreigroschenoper* (*Threepenny Opera*, 1928) and *Mahagonny* (1930) secured his reputation. He joined the Communist Party in 1929, and during the 1930s produced some of his best work, including plays such as *Galileo* (1938), the long *Svendborg Poems*, and a series of essays on the purpose of theatre and the appropriate techniques for achieving dramatic effect. In 1933 he and his actress wife Helene Weigel (they were married in 1928 and she remained his collaborator until his death) were forced into exile, first in Denmark and from 1941 to 1947 in the USA, where his most famous play, *Der Kaukasische Kreidekreis* (*The Caucasian Chalk Circle*, 1944) was written. From 1949 until his death he and Helene lived in East Berlin, where he staged his epic war play *Mutter Courage* (*Mother Courage*, written in 1939) and founded the world-famous Berliner Ensemble, whose productions in the specially-designated Brecht Theatre brought his powerful plays to millions. His hardline (though not uncritical) support of communism and the East German regime, with his fervent belief in the economic exploitation and dehumanisation of capitalism, particularly endeared him to that country's authorities, but his themes of social concern and real-world dilemma are universal, appealing particularly to those who can identify with his political insights.

Bertolt Brecht (eds Ralph Mannheim and John Willett), *Collected Plays*, Random House, 1971

John Willett, *The Theatre of Bertolt Brecht*, New Directions, 1968

John Fuegi, *Bertolt Brecht: Chaos According to Plan*, Cambridge University Press, 1987

Vera [Mary] Brittain
1893–1970
writer, journalist, women's rights and peace activist

Vera Brittain was a strong, fluent and relentless voice for feminism and pacifism from the 1920s until her death; few British women possessed such a profound understanding of the dynamics of oppression or were so willing to put their beliefs into practice at every possible opportunity. She grew up in a middle class Staffordshire family, and while at boarding school read **Olive Schreiner**'s *Woman and Labour*, which resolved her to go to Oxford University. Her university education was interrupted by the war, when she worked as a nurse and was disgusted by the carnage that was wreaked by men doing their best to kill each other – she lost her fiancé, her brother and several other men friends in the European theatre. Back at Oxford she became firm friends with the essayist and novelist Winifred Holtby, a friendship which lasted until Winifred's death in 1935 and was celebrated in Vera's *Testament of Friendship* (1940). She married the philosopher George Catlin in 1925 and they moved to Canada, where he was lecturing and writing, but within a year she was back in England lodging with Winifred, having agreed a 'semi-detached marriage' with George. A 1928 essay, 'The Whole Duty of Woman', encapsulated her lifelong stance as a pragmatic feminist, showing that what women most lack is time to develop their creativity, intelligence and skills. Throughout her life she wrote and lectured endlessly on a wide range of radical platforms: as early as 1922 she was giving four speeches a week as a lecturer for the League of Nations, between 1934 and 1959 she undertook more than twelve extended lecture tours from Canada to India, and was still participating in peace demonstrations and sit-ins in her late seventies. Altogether she wrote 29 books, including novels, autobiography and political commentary. During the second world war she was vice-president of the **Women's International League for Peace and Freedom**, and was an early member of the **Peace Pledge Union**. She and George had two children: six years before her death her daughter Shirley (now Shirley Williams) became a Labour member of parliament.

Vera Brittain, *Testament of Youth: An Autobiographical Study of the Years 1900–1925*, Virago, 1978
Vera Brittain, *Testament of Experience, An Autobiographical Study of the Years 1925–1950*, Virago, 1979
Vera Brittain, *Testament of Friendship*, Virago, 1980
Dale Spender, *Women of Ideas*, Routledge and Kegan Paul, 1982

Bob Brown
1945–
environmental campaigner, doctor, green politician

Australia's most notorious green activist, Bob Brown became active in the environmental cause in 1976. Working at the time as a doctor, he spent a holiday rafting down the spectacular Franklin River in western Tasmania, only to discover when he reached the end of his trip that exploratory work had started on a massive dam project. He dropped his medical practice and became an early member and then director of the Tasmanian Wilderness Society (an organisation which had grown out of an unsuccessful campaign to prevent the obliteration of Lake Pedder by another large dam in 1972). During the seven-year battle to save the Franklin River basin, in one of the world's last remaining temperate rainforests and great wilderness areas, Bob Brown was mugged, attacked, and imprisoned along with 1,500 fellow protestors, but national and international pressure finally forced the Tasmanian government to drop the scheme in July 1983. Elected as a Green Independent to the Tasmanian government in 1983, he was for several years leader of the five Greens who hold the balance of power in Australia's smallest state. In 1987, during the battle to save the Farmhouse Creek forest, he was shot at; undeterred, however, the Greens were able to push through legislation to double the number of national parks in Tasmania. Bob Brown continues to use his position to speak out on environmental, peace and justice issues, and on **Earth Day** 1990 he was awarded a US Goldman Environmental Prize for his campaigning work.

Drew Hutton, *Green Politics in Australia*, Angus & Robertson, 1987

Rita Mae Brown
1944–
lesbian feminist activist and novelist

Rita Mae Brown began working to create a lesbian-feminist movement in the USA late in 1969. Having tried to introduce lesbianism as an issue within the **National Organization for Women** and lost her position as editor of its New York newsletter, she quickly moved to generate new structures. Through building coalitions with 'old' lesbians and systematically bringing up lesbianism as an issue at women's liberation meetings, she was at the forefront of lesbian consciousness-raising among feminists and the construction of lesbian feminist theory. The definition of lesbianism as a political choice in the affirmation of women was first presented in 'The Woman-identified Women', a position paper which she coauthored in May 1970. She left New York City for Washington DC in early 1971 and organised a consciousness-raising group for women who were just coming out as lesbians. This group established a collective household, named themselves The Furies after their newsletter of the same name, and during their tempestuous one-year lifespan made a significant and much-needed analysis of class dynamics within the American feminist movement. Over time Rita Mae Brown's identity as a lesbian separatist modulated to a 'pan-sexual' – though basically lesbian – sense of human relationship. She published a collection of essays and speeches, *A Plain Brown Rapper*, in 1976, but it is for her novels, especially her bestselling *Rubyfruit Jungle* (1973), that she is most widely known. In 1979 she started a much publicised two-year relationship with tennis star Martina Navratilova; when it ended she moved from New York to Los Angeles, where she founded the television and film option company American Artists and continues to write novels and screenplays.

Rita Mae Brown, *Rubyfruit Jungle*, Daughters Inc, 1973
Rita Mae Brown, *A Plain Brown Rapper*, Diana Press, 1976
Rita Mae Brown, *Starting from Scratch: A Different Kind of Writers' Manual*, Bantam, 1988
Alice Echols, *Daring to Be Bad: Radical Feminism in America 1967–1975*, University of Minnesota Press, 1989
Carol Ward, *Rita Mae Brown*, Twayne, 1993

Susan Brownmiller
1935–
journalist, writer, feminist

Susan Brownmiller, the author of the controversial and groundbreaking study of rape, *Against Our Will*, studied at Cornell University and has worked for more than thirty years as a journalist, news reporter and writer based in New York. In the early 1960s she was active in the civil rights movement, and in 1969 was a founder member of New York Radical Feminists. She published *Against Our Will* in 1975, and it received massive acclaim and criticism for daring to suggest that rape is 'nothing more or less than a conscious process of intimidation by which *all* men keep *all* women in a state of fear'. Criticism of her approach came from many quarters – from men who denied that rape featured in their relationship vocabulary, from black women who found her analysis racist, and from lesbians who felt that she denied the strength of women's solidarity against male violence – but *Against Our Will* succeeded in putting the issue of rape firmly on the political and social agenda. In 1984 came *Femininity*, a critique of prevailing cultural gender standards and the way they limit women. Two later books have continued her exploration of violence as a tool of social control: her 1989 fictional account, *Waverly Place*, of the notorious Steinberg case in which a Manhattan lawyer was convicted of brutalising his lover and killing his stepdaughter; and a 1994 account of her experiences in Vietnam.

Susan Brownmiller, *Against Our Will: Men, Women and Rape*, Simon and Schuster, 1975
Susan Brownmiller, *Femininity*, Simon and Schuster, 1984
Susan Brownmiller, *Waverly Place*, Grove, 1989
Susan Brownmiller, *Seeing Vietnam: Encounters of the Road and Heart*, Harper Collins, 1994
Alice Echols, *Daring to be Bad: Radical Feminism in America 1967–1975*, University of Minnesota Press, 1989

Gro Harlem Brundtland
1939–
politician, public health and equal rights campaigner

Gro Harlem Brundtland, Norway's first woman prime minister, is best known internationally as chair of the World Commission on Environment and Development, which in its groundbreaking 1987 report *Our Common Future* launched the concept of 'sustainable development'. Born in Oslo, where her father was a doctor and politician, she was educated at university there and at Harvard. In 1960 she married Arne Olav (now a leading figure in the opposition Conservative Party); they have four children. A qualified doctor with a particular interest in public health, she became a consultant to the ministry of health and social affairs in 1965, medical officer of Oslo City Health Department in 1968, and deputy director of the Oslo School Health Service in 1970. She had been a member of the Norwegian Labour Party since her student days, and her organisational talent gained her, at the age of 35, an appointment as minister for the environment, and two years later as vice-chair of the Labour Party. In 1977 she entered the Storting (Norwegian parliament) and took over as party leader and prime minister on the resignation of Odvar Nordli in 1981. Later that year the Labour Party was defeated, and she spent her five years in opposition concentrating on social, economic and environmental policy. During the early 1980s she was a member of the UN Commission on Disarmament and Security Issues, was chair of the World Commission on Environment and Development, and in 1985 joined the board of directors of the 'Better World Society'. She became prime minister for the second time in 1986, heading a cabinet of eight women and nine men – the most female cabinet in history. The Labour Party, with Brundtland as its leader, subsequently succeeded in heading a coalition government in the 1990 and 1994 elections. Europe's leading socialist woman political leader, Gro Harlem Brundtland has had to deal with some difficult compromises (such as backing Norway's right to continue whaling and ensuring that her country's interests can be protected within an expanding European Union), but she is generally considered to be a thoughtful if somewhat didactic politician.

> Gro Harlem Brundtland, *Our Common Future: World Commission on Environment and Development*, Oxford University Press, 1987

Martin Buber
1878–1965
spiritual philosopher

Martin Buber's important contribution to radical thought and action was his exploration of the relationship between human beings and their social, cultural and natural setting. Using his famous 'I-Thou' formulation, he made it clear that 'I' and 'you' have neither meaning nor independent existence apart from the relationship between them, a recognition of ecological interpedendence which contrasted with much prevailing scientific and political thinking and provided a framework for many new and exciting ideas in theology, education, psychotherapy, and the social and natural sciences. Martin Buber grew up in a Jewish family in Vienna, and studied philosophy at Vienna, Leipzig and Berlin. His early studies were concerned with the mystical tradition, particularly within the Hasidic Jewish tradition, but after the war he turned his attention to the nature of social reality, identifying his brand of political thinking as utopian socialism. His ideas were most fully explored in his *Ich und Du* (1923, 1937 in English), where he stressed the importance of the 'between' (*das Zwischen*) quality of relationships, distinguishing between the alienated 'I-It' relationship between people and the material, outside other, and the integrated 'I-Thou' relationship where the 'I' and the other are recognised as part of a whole, sharing responsibilities, concerns and potentialities. Buber saw God as the 'eternal Thou' glimpsed in daily experiences of the 'particular Thou', an idea which attracted many liberal theologians, both Jewish and Christian. During the 1940s and 50s, teaching at Frankfurt University, he became interested in the promise of socialism, which he saw primarily as a project of social and spiritual renewal rather than of political power. *Paths in Utopia* (1958) outlines his vision of a world where true community and a shared understanding of spiritual revelation, rather than state law and imposed morality, form the basis of society. An active Zionist all his life, he wrote extensively about the potential for creating such a 'non-state' for Jews and

Arabs in Palestine; he was excited about the potential of the kibbutz and other experiments in cooperation, but strongly opposed the creation of a Jewish state.

Martin Buber (trans. R.T. Smith), *I and Thou*, T. and T. Clark, 1937 (many editions since)
Martin Buber, *Paths in Utopia*, Beacon Press, 1958
Martin Buber, *Israel and the World: Essays in a Time of Crisis*, Schocken, 1963
Maurice Friedman, *Martin Buber: The Life of Dialogue*, University of Chicago Press, 1976
Maurice Friedman, *Encounter on the Narrow Ridge: The Life of Martin Buber*, Paragon House, 1991

Ormond [Edward] Burton
1893–1974
teacher, minister, antiwar activist

One of New Zealand's foremost antiwar campaigners, Ormond Burton grew up in Auckland and trained as a schoolteacher before volunteering for the Medical Corps in the first world war and serving in France and Gallipoli. On his return to New Zealand he trained for the Methodist ministry, and worked in Wellington for seven years from 1935, concentrating on the needs of the poor and the outcasts of society. Following his war experiences, Ormond Burton had become convinced of the need for active pacifism, and as the second world war loomed he became a leader of the newly-formed Christian Pacifist Society. On the first day of the war he spoke out against the conflict in front of the New Zealand parliament and was arrested: continued public protest resulted in his being imprisoned five times before the war ended. His uncompromising pacifism also brought him into conflict with his more conservative church seniors, and in 1942 he was dismissed from the ministry. He campaigned vigorously for the retrial of the seven hundred New Zealand conscientious objectors detained during the war, and as a result many of them were released. He also campaigned for prison reform, and his 1945 book *In Prison* eased conditions for many of those who remained in jail. In 1945 he returned to teaching at Wellington Technical College, and 1956 sought readmission to the Methodist ministry and was accepted. He retired in 1960, but continued to work for peace, protesting publicly against the Korean War and calling for civil disobedience to resist the nuclear arms race. He was a council member of the **Fellowship of Reconciliation** for many years, and continued to write and lecture until shortly before his death.

Ormond Burton, *A Testament of Peace*, New Zealand Christian Pacifist Society, 1940
Ormond Burton, *In Prison*, Reed, 1945
Ernest Crane, *I Can Do No Other: A Biography of the Reverend Ormond Burton*, Hodder and Stoughton, 1986
Elsie Locke, *Peace People: A History of Peace Activities in New Zealand*, Hazard Press, 1992

Amilcar Cabral
1924–1973
liberation theorist and activist

Amilcar Cabral was one of the foremost African radical theorists and activists of the twentieth century. Born in Bafata (then in Portuguese Guinea) to Cape Verde parents, he was educated in Bissau and at Lisbon University. Here, coming into contact with the antifascist movement, the Marxist underground and radical African nationalism, he gained a political awareness that was to shape his career. After working for the colonial civil service as an agricultural engineer, he directed the first agricultural census of Guinea in 1952–54: the insights and intimate knowledge he gained of African rural society were greatly to influence his political activities. He was forced to leave Guinea in 1955 as a result of his political beliefs, and in 1956 cofounded and took control of the Partido Africano da Independência da Guiné e Cabo Verde (PAIGC), quickly establishing himself as one of Africa's most dynamic revolutionary leaders. With fellow activists he planned and began a successful peasant-based liberation movement in 1964: within a year more than 40% of the countryside was in PAIGC hands, and communal food stores, cooperative agricultural projects and community schools had been established. Amilcar Cabral's considerable body of writing had much influence within his home country and throughout the Third World. He was a firm believer in the importance of grassroots organisation and was particularly concerned to involve women. He devoted much of his energy to educational programmes that would lead to popular participation in the nationalist movement. In 1970 the Portuguese military attempted a desperate invasion, with plans to kill Cabral and the Guinea president Sékou Touré, but the assassination plot failed and by 1972 it was clear that the Portuguese were no longer in control. Nonetheless Cabral was killed by Portuguese collaborators in January 1973, so he never saw the colonial regime fall in 1974 and Guinea-Bissau's first independent elected government take control the following year.

Amilcar Cabral, *Revolution in Guinea*, Stage One, 1969
Amilcar Cabral, *Unity and Struggle,* Heinemann, 1970
Patrick Chabal, *Amilcar Cabral: Revolutionary Leadership and People's War,*
    Cambridge University Press, 1983

Jim [James Ford] Cairns
1914–
socialist politician, antiwar campaigner

Australia's foremost radical socialist of the late 1960s and early 70s, Jim Cairns was born and grew up in Carlton, Victoria, and studied at the University of Melbourne. He worked as a clerk, a junior detective and an army education officer before returning to Melbourne University in 1946 to teach economic history. During and immediately after the second world war he became involved with the Communist Party of Australia, identifying himself as a socialist, pacifist and internationalist, and in 1955 was elected as a Labor Party member of the House of Representatives – he was to remain a parliamentarian for the next 22 years. By 1967 he had established himelf as the acknowledged leader of the left wing of the party, and in 1970, following the publication of his acclaimed historical survey of foreign involvement in Vietnam, *The Eagle and the Lotus*, emerged as the figurehead of Australian opposition to the **Vietnam War**. As instigator of the largest antiwar demonstrations in Australian history (those held in Melbourne in May and September 1970 and June 1971) he became both the most revered and the most hated of politicians, and a focus for a generation of disenchanted young Australians. In late 1972, when the war was nearly over, he became a minister in the first Labor government for 23 years, rising two years later to become deputy prime minister, symbolising the triumph of leftwing dissent over dominant conservatism. The triumph was shortlived: in 1975 he was dismissed by prime minister Gough Whitlam for his outspoken views on democracy and civil liberties, and two years later he decided not to stand for re-election to the House of Representatives. In the late 1970s he became prominent within the Down To Earth movement, promoting accountable community-based ecological politics, and has continued to be a staunch, if less public, critic of the competitiveness and acquisitiveness of contemporary Australian culture.

James Ford Cairns, *The Eagle and the Lotus: Western Intervention in Vietnam 1847–1968*, Lansdowne Press, 1969
James Ford Cairns, *The Quiet Revolution*, Widescope, 1975
Paul Ormonde, *A Foolish Passionate Man: A Biography of Jim Cairns*, Penguin (Melbourne), 1981

Helen Caldicott [Helen Broinowski]
1938–
paediatrician, antinuclear and environmental campaigner

Helen Caldicott's campaign against the nuclear threat was spurred by a girlhood reading of Nevil Shute's novel *On the Beach* (1957), a postholocaust tale with an Australian background which persuaded her that even Australians were not safe from the proliferation of nuclear weapons. She studied at the University of Adelaide Medical School, qualifying as a general practitioner, and for three years from 1966 held a fellowship at Harvard Medical School, after which she specialised in paediatrics. Her alarm at the threats to health posed by radioactivity led her to organise the successful campaign against atmospheric nuclear testing by the French in the South Pacific, and a subsequent campaign to stop Australian exports of uranium. In 1977 Helen Caldicott emigrated to the USA to work at Harvard Medical School and Boston Children's Hospital Medical Center. In 1978, the year in which she published her powerful book, *Nuclear Madness*, she founded and organised the reincarnation of Physicians for Social Responsibility and was its president until 1983, when she resigned over her opposition to all nuclear power and not just nuclear weapons. She was also founder of the influential Washington-based lobby group WAND (Women's Action for Nuclear Disarmament). In 1979 she visited the Soviet Union as part of a delegation invited by the Soviet Peace Committee and was shocked by the concerned attitude of officials and nuclear weapons scientists towards the possibility of nuclear war; when she returned to the USA to find a sense of total irresponsibility towards the nuclear threat she resolved to shelve her medical practice and campaign full-time against the folly of the nuclear mentality. In 1984 she published her second book, *Missile Envy*, which included a controversial and much-publicised interview with President Reagan. Helen Caldicott returned to Australia in 1987 and in 1990 stood for election to the House of Representatives, losing by only a small margin. For the last ten years she has been working on the global environmental threat, and in 1992 published *If You Love This Planet*. The distribution of her 1984 film of this title was restricted by the US Justice Department, who labelled it 'political propaganda'.

Helen Caldicott, *Nuclear Madness: What You Can Do*, Autumn Press, 1978
Helen Caldicott, *Missile Envy*, Morrow, 1984
Helen Caldicott, *If You Love This Planet: A Plan to Heal the Earth*, Norton, 1992

Ernest Callenbach
1929–
author, editor, environmental consultant

Although his main career has been in magazine and book editing, Ernest Callenbach's visionary novels *Ecotopia* (1975) and *Ecotopia Emerging* (1981) had a profound effect on the infant green movement both in North America and in Europe. Born in Pennsylvania and educated at the University of Chicago, he moved to California in 1954, and the ecotopian future he envisaged in his novels is firmly based in the US north-west. In the two novels green-minded Ecotopia declares independence from the rest of the USA to create an egalitarian pollution-free society based on appropriate technology, the first volume describing a visit by an outside visitor to the country and the second explaining (in a convincing fashion) how Ecotopia came to be. In 1985 Callenbach coauthored, with Michael Phillips, *A Citizen Legislature*, a fierce assault on the corruption of the US electoral process by campaign funders, arguing instead for a system of choosing political representatives in the same way as juries are chosen. Now retired from his editorial work at the University of California Press, Ernest Callenbach is scholar in residence at the Elmwood Institute, established to facilitate the appropriate dissemination of ecological innovation.

Ernest Callenbach, *Ecotopia: The Notebooks and Reports of William Weston*, Banyan Tree Books, 1975
Ernest Callenbach, *Ecotopia Emerging*, Banyan Tree Books, 1981
Ernest Callenbach and Michael Phillips, *A Citizen Legislature*, Banyan Tree Books, 1985

Helder [Pessõa] Câmara
1909–
clergyman, social justice activist

The twelfth of thirteen children born to a journalist father and a school-teacher mother in the Brazilian seaport city of Fortaleza, Helder Câmara was destined from an early age for the church. He was ordained in 1931, and in 1936 started to work in Rio de Janeiro among the *favelas*, the slums where the city's poorest inhabitants live. In 1952 he was named auxiliary bishop of Rio, and the same year established the National Conference of the Bishops of Brazil (CNBB), which soon became a leading force for social change in the country; he also helped to set up the Latin American Episcopal Conference (CELAM) in 1955. Much influenced in the late 1950s by educationalist **Paulo Freire**, the emphasis of his work shifted from pastoral aid to the self-empowerment or 'conscienticisation' of the poor, and in 1961 he founded the Movement for Grassroots Education (MEB). Within a year nearly 200,000 Brazilians were listening to its radio programmes, which taught political and social awareness as well as basic literacy skills. At the Second Vatican Council of 1962 Helder Câmara and other Third World bishops called for a worldwide 'church of the poor'; two years later, as a reaction against the liberalisation represented by programmes like MEB, a military coup ousted the Brazilian government. Ten days after the coup, on April 12th 1964, Helder Câmara was installed as archbishop of Recife and Olinda in north-eastern Brazil. He wasted no time in denouncing the excesses of the military rulers, holding a strong nonviolent stance against the tortures and disappearances of 'political dissidents'. In October 1968, with the backing of the CNBB and CELAM, he launched the movement Action, Justice and Peace; the Brazilian government responded by silencing him. For thirteen years he was banned from public speaking and newspapers could not mention his name. However, twenty-three years of military rule in Brazil failed to silence Helder Câmara, although he was several times the target of an assassination attempt; he continued to work for the poor of his country, using every opportunity to speak out against the excesses of militarism and the hypocrisy of much Western thinking about the Third World. He retired as archbishop in 1988, and now describes himself as 'an itinerant apostle of human rights, social justice and peace'.

Helder Câmara, *The Church and Colonialism: The Betrayal of the Third World*,
Dimension Books, 1969
José de Broucker, *Dom Helder Camara: The Violence of a Peacemaker*, Orbis,
1970

Beatrix Campbell
1947–
journalist, socialist, feminist

Born in Carlisle to active Communist parents, the radical British journalist Beatrix Campbell left school to seek her fortune in London, working from

1969 on the socialist newspaper *The Morning Star*. In 1970 she became active in the **women's movement**, and in 1972 cofounded *Red Rag*, a Marxist-feminist journal for which she wrote until it ceased publication in 1980. She had joined the magazine *Time Out* in 1979, but after a strike in 1981 over equal pay and worker consultation the majority of the staff left and set up the cooperatively-owned magazine *City Limits*. During the 1980s she was also a regular contributor to *Marxism Today*. In 1982 she coauthored, with journalist Anna Coote, an important history of women's liberation called *Sweet Freedom*, and in 1983 she travelled around Britain listening to working women and men, publishing their accounts and her responses in *Wigan Pier Revisited* (1984), an argument with **George Orwell**'s male-dominated depression journal *The Road to Wigan Pier*. In 1987, as the rightwing government of Margaret Thatcher was re-elected for a third term, Beatrix Campbell wrote *The Iron Ladies: Why Women Vote Tory*, and after the 1991 riots in Oxford, Cardiff and Tyneside she wrote *Goliath: Britain's Dangerous Places*, an analysis of crime and public order highlighting the diverse ways that women and men of different generations deal with economic crisis. Since 1993 she has written a column for *The Independent* newspaper, and continues to write in gay and radical journals.

Anna Coote and Beatrix Campbell, *Sweet Freedom: The Struggle for Women's Liberation*, Picador, 1982

Beatrix Campbell, *Wigan Pier Revisited: Poverty and Politics in the Eighties*, Virago, 1984

Beatrix Campbell, *Goliath: Britain's Dangerous Places*, Methuen, 1993,

Edward Carpenter
1844–1929
socialist, writer, homosexual rights advocate

Edward Carpenter was born into a well-off family in Brighton, England, and was destined by his family for the church. Though he studied theology at Cambridge and took orders, reading **Walt Whitman**'s *Leaves of Grass* in 1869 confirmed for him the importance of socialist comradeship and sexual freedom; in 1874 he began a long correspondence with Whitman and travelled to visit him in New Jersey in 1877. In the late 1870s and early 80s, working as a lecturer in the North of England, Carpenter was profoundly influenced by the women's movement, confiding to Whitman that 'the women will save us', and by the nascent Marxist movement in Britain. Edward Carpenter spent the early 1880s based in Sheffield amongst a group of radical socialist artisans, and in 1883 bought a house in Millthorpe near Chesterfield. He became a vegetarian and an overt homosexual, learned a variety of manual and gardening skills, and lectured widely in support of sexual reform, women's rights, industrial democracy and environmental issues including antivivisection and clean air legislation. In 1886 he helped to establish the Sheffield Socialist Society, a leading centre of socialist thinking which regularly invited speakers of the calibre of **Petr Kropotkin** and **Annie Besant**. He also wrote profusely, producing an influential long Whitmanesque poem, *Towards Democracy* (published in four parts, 1883–1902), and a series of essays, *Civilisation: Its Cause and Cure* (1889), which firmly equates the Victorian concept of progress and civilisation with a disease that stunts human potentialities. As the century closed Edward Carpenter turned increasingly to the theme of individual emancipation through personal spontaneity and mystical experience, being particularly influenced by Hinduism; at the same time his personal exploration of sexuality burgeoned, largely as a result of a long and deep relationship with George Merrill. Between 1894 and his death in 1929 he wrote widely on friendship, marriage, homosexuality and bisexuality, arguing strongly for the separation of sex and procreation and stressing the common, androgynous, 'Uranian' sexual needs of both women and men.

Edward Carpenter, *My Days and Dreams*, Scribner, 1916
Chushichi Tzuzuki, *Edward Carpenter: Prophet of Human Fellowship*, Cambridge
    University Press, 1980
Jeffrey Weeks, *Coming Out*, Quartet, 1987

Rachel Carson
1907–1964
biologist, environmental campaigner

The biologist Rachel Carson is best known as the author of *Silent Spring*, her detailed 1962 exposé of the harmful effects of chemical pesticides on human and environmental health and a book which many see as central to the birth of the modern green movement. The foundations of her knowledge and insight were laid early in her life, when her mother Maria encouraged Rachel's nature studies, first around their Springdale home in Pennsylvania and later in Maryland and Maine where Rachel lived with her mother and two orphaned nieces. She studied English and biology at college, receiving an MA in zoology from John Hopkins University in 1932. For the next twenty years she worked as a writer and editor for the US Fish and Wildlife Service, her engaging and informative wildlife books – *Under the Sea-Wind* (1941), *The Sea Around Us* (1951) and *The Edge of the Sea* (1955) – bringing a sense of the wonder in nature to thousands in North America and beyond. As early as 1945 Rrachel Carson had become concerned about the effects of DDT and other pesticides, but it was not until 1958, when her zoologist friend Olga Owens Huckins alerted her to the specific danger to birds and small mammals from aerial spraying, that she started researching in depth for *Silent Spring*. When her book appeared, with its reasoned attack on the use of pesticides and the powerful companies and politicians who benefited from the wholesale destruction of nature, she was systematically derided by establishment critics as 'hysterical', 'simplistic' and 'extremist'. Undaunted, she used her position and expertise as a respected scientist to create a network of concerned professional women to fight the use of harmful pesticides. By the end of 1963, her concerns had been validated by a Presidential Science Advisory Committee and a Senate Committee on Environmental Hazards, heralding an era of stricter controls on chemical pesticides. Rachel Carson died in April 1964, but not before she had seen many of her fears confirmed by independent and official studies, and action taken to stop the indiscriminate use of poisonous chemicals in the name of progress.

Rachel Carson, *Silent Spring*, Houghton Mifflin, 1962

Paul Brooks, *The House of Life: Rachel Carson at Work*, Houghton Mifflin, 1972

Vera Norwood, *Made From This Earth: American Women and Nature*, University of North Carolina Press, 1993

Adelaide Casely-Hayford [Adelaide Smith]
1868–1960
writer, teacher, black rights campaigner

The fact that Adelaide Casely-Hayford's biography, written by her granddaughter-in-law, is entitled *An African Victorian Feminist* immediately indicates that her contribution to African women's history is unique, for another candidate for that appellation has yet to emerge. Born of mixed Fanti and English ancestry in the British colony of Sierra Leone, she was educated in England and Germany before returning to Freetown in 1897 after her father's death. In 1903 she married the lawyer and writer John Casely-Hayford, and the following year their daughter Gladys May was born. After separating from her husband in the mid-1920s, Adelaide and her sister founded the Girls Vocational School in Freetown, and from 1926–28 they travelled and lectured in the USA to raise money for the project; during these years her awareness was heightened by exposure to the feminist and civil rights movements. She began her memoirs after her retirement from teaching in 1940, adding to them until her death at the age of 91. An accomplished writer, speaker and musician, she was clear and fearless in her advocacy of women's education and black pride. 'My Life and Times' (in *Memoirs and Poems*) ends with the memorable words 'If I have any advice worth giving to the rising generation of Africa it is this: *never* be ashamed of your colour. I have found from experience that this is the only way to happiness, the only way to retain one's self-respect, the only way to win the respect of other races, and the only way in which we can ever give a real contribution to the world.'

Adelaide Casely-Hayford and Gladys Casely-Hayford (ed. Lucilda Hunter), *Mother and Daughter: Memoirs and Poems*, Sierra Leone University Press, 1983

Adelaide M. Cromwell, *An African Victorian Feminist: The Life and Times of Adelaide Smith Casely Hayford*, Frank Cass, 1986

Chai Ling
1966–
pro-democracy advocate and activist

Chai Ling, one of the leaders of the Chinese pro-democracy demonstrations of 1989, was born and grew up in the Shandong province of northern China. In 1983 she moved to Beijing to study psychology and four years later was accepted by Beijing Normal University to further her studies in child psychology. Together with many of her teachers and contemporaries she became increasingly critical of the corrupt communist regime of Deng Xiaoping and Li Peng, but was also greatly influenced by the lives and works of **Gandhi** and **Martin Luther King**, so that in her public speaking and organising she constantly stressed the need for nonviolent direct action. In May 1989, following a month of growing student unease in Beijing, Chai Ling and her husband and fellow student Cheng Congde joined 3,000 other students in a hunger strike in Tiananmen Square to protest in support of open government and press freedom; during the course of the strike she adopted the role of 'commander-in-chief'. From mid-May until the Tiananmen Square massacre of June 3rd–4th she remained part of the strike and (together with her husband Cheng and student leaders Wuer Kaixi and Wang Dan) was one of the chief spokespeople for the need for a profound change in Chinese politics. One of the few radical women leaders in modern China, Chai Ling represents a new challenge to the dominance of male values within the Chinese pro-democracy movement, and has herself raised many questions about the place of women in a rapidly-Westernising China. Immediately after the massacre Chai and Cheng, together with many of their activist friends, escaped to the relative freedom of Hong Kong, whence they continue to work for the peaceful democratic reform of their home country.

Mok Chiu Yu and J. Frank Harrison (eds), *Voices from Tiananmen Square*, Black Rose, 1990
Jeffrey N. Wasserstrom and Elizabeth J. Perry (eds), *Popular Protest and Political Culture in Modern China: Learning from 1989*, Westview Press, 1992

Kamaladevi Chattopadhyay [Kamaladevi Ananthiah]
1903–1986
political activist, social reformer, crafts movement leader

The Indian reformer Kamaladevi Chattopadhyay was born in Mangalore and was educated in India and at Bedford College, London, and the London School of Economics; in 1919 she married the progressive poet and dramatist Harindranath Chattopadhyay, whom she divorced in 1964: they had one son. In 1927 she joined the Congress movement and was elected to the All India Congress, becoming organising secretary and president of the All India Women's Conference: from its inception she stressed the need for a strong women's movement throughout the subcontinent. She was also one of the few women interested in peasant organisations and the welfare of India's poorest workers; in 1935 she was a founder member of the All India Kisan (Peasants' Cooperatives) Congress, and throughout the 1930s and 40s Kamaladevi Chattopadhyay worked hard both for women's and peasant workers' rights – she was imprisoned four times for her active leadership. She was no supporter of **Mahatma Gandhi**, strongly denouncing what she saw as his sentimental and spiritual stance when what was needed was active militancy. In 1946 she was nominated to the Indian Constituent Assembly, but declined to accept as her interests remained primarily with the masses. After independence and partition in 1947 she founded the Indian Co-operative Union to help refugees, establishing a cooperative community at Faridabad near New Delhi for 300,000 refugees. Following the success of Faridabad she organised several more weaving and consumer cooperatives, and developed the highly successful Cottage Industries Emporium as an outlet for the goods produced. In 1952 she became chair of All India Handicrafts Limited, and helped to found the World Crafts Council of which she was senior vice-president; she was also president of the Theatre Centre of India. She received many national and international awards, and published books on Japanese, Chinese and American society, as well as on socialism and on Indian handicrafts.

Kamaladevi Chattopadhyay, *Indian Women's Battle for Freedom*, Abhinav, 1983
Jamila Brij Bhushan, *Kamaladevi Chattopadhyay: Portrait of a Rebel*, Abhinav
Publications, 1976

Judy Chicago [Judith Cohen]
1939–
artist, writer

The controversial American artist and writer Judy Chicago (she changed her name to that of her home city in 1970) is best known for the massive installation 'The Dinner Party', completed in 1979. She studied at the University of California at Los Angeles, where in 1961 she married Jerry Gerowitz, but he died two years later. In 1970 she married Lloyd Hamrol, and throughout the 1960s and 70s worked in California. She was one of the instigators of the feminist art movement: in 1973 she was one of the founders of the Feminist Studio Workshop in Los Angeles, and was influential in establishing the Women's Building which developed from the original Studio Workshop. She frequently attacked taboos about femininity and female sexuality, shocking her viewers with such works as 'Menstruation Bathroom' (1971); Joanna Demetrakis's 1972 film *Womanhouse* brought her work to a wider audience. The later 1970s were largely taken up with creating and mounting the extraordinary 'Dinner Party', which took the form of a triangular table fifteen metres across set with embroidered runners and ceramic plates, symbolising 39 guests representing different aspects of women's history, placed on a floor inscribed with the names of 999 women of achievement. Although the work involved dozens of crafts-people, it was accomplished largely through Chicago's vision and driving energy. The exhibition drew huge crowds in Los Angeles, Chicago, New York and London, and in 1990 was offered by the artist to the University of the District of Columbia for permanent exhibition; following reactionary criticism from politicians who called 'The Dinner Party' 'pornography' and 'weird sexual art', however, Judy Chicago pointedly withdrew her offer, and the exhibition remains in storage in northern California. 'The Dinner Party' was followed by other multimedia schemes including 'The Birth Project' (1985) and 'The Holocaust Project' (1993), the latter being a collaboration with her third husband, photographer Donald Woodman.

Judy Chicago now lives in Santa Fe, New Mexico, where her nonprofit organisation Through the Flower oversees the exhibition and care of her works.

Judy Chicago: *Through the Flower: My Struggle as a Woman Artist*, Doubleday, 1977
Judy Chicago, *The Dinner Party: A Symbol of Our Heritage*, Doubleday, 1979
Judy Chicago, *The Birth Project*, Doubleday, 1985
Judy Chicago, *Holocaust Project: From Darkness Into Light*, Penguin, 1993

[Avram] Noam Chomsky
1928–
linguist, political activist

Noam Chomsky, possibly the most vociferous contemporary critic of US foreign policy and the ideology that supports it, has the advantage of being a widely-admired scholar in a traditionally apolitical field, that of linguistics. Born in Philadelphia into a liberal Zionist family, he studied linguistics at Pennsylvania and Harvard. As a student he was interested in anarchism and Palestinian politics, and in 1953 he and his wife Carol visited Israel. By 1957, when he published his first major work in linguistics, *Syntactic Structures*, he had developed a theory of linguistic structure and language acquisition which was to revolutionise the subject, moving it wholesale from the classification of speech elements to a deep innate 'generative grammar' based on human biology and psychology. Noam Chomsky was drawn irrevocably into the political arena by the **Vietnam War**. His meticulously researched and highly readable *American Power and the New Mandarins* (1969) reached a wide audience, and he became a popular antiwar speaker, combining careful reason with an unshakable moral certainty which inspired sympathy in the blossoming antiwar lobby and hatred in President Nixon's supporters. In the 1970s and early 80s his political attention turned to the ways in which the West, and the USA in particular, was benefiting politically and economically from the Cold War, and from the mistaken assumption that its foreign policy was benign and responsible. His analyses of the way in which liberalism can uncritically support oppressive regimes such as Stalinism and blinkered Zionism have aroused anger on both left and right, but his ability to tread the radical road carefully yet unflinchingly has earned him much respect. While there are links between his political activism and his linguistic research – he wrote in *Language and Responsibility* (1979), for example, that they 'derive from certain common assumptions and attitudes' – he has often insisted that the two should be considered separately. Since 1955 Noam Chomsky has been based at Massachusetts Institute of Technology, where he is professor of linguistics, though much of his time is spent travelling and lecturing.

Noam Chomsky, *American Power and the New Mandarins*, Random House, 1969
Noam Chomsky, *The Chomsky Reader*, Pantheon, 1987
Noam Chomsky (ed. C.P. Otero), *Language and Politics*, Black Rose, 1989
Noam Chomsky, *World Orders, Old and New*, Columbia University Press, 1994

Justin Leiber, *Noam Chomsky: A Philosophic Overview*, St Martin's Press, 1975
Raphael Salkie, *The Chomsky Update: Linguistics and Politics*, Unwin Hyman, 1990

Daniel Cohn-Bendit
1945–
student leader, political and social activist

In 1968, when he was the most visible of the dissident French student leaders, he was called 'Danny the Red' – a tribute both to Daniel Cohn-Bendit's hair and to his ideology. Born in France of émigré German Jews, he was registered as stateless at birth, but adopted German citizenship in 1959 so as to avoid French military service. In 1967, at a time when feeling amongst French students was running high following proposals for the reorganisation of the university system, Daniel began his studies at Nanterre University, where he was a radical activist from the start, leading a group of fellow male students to 'sit in' at a 'forbidden' women's dormitory. On January 8th 1968 the French minister for youth, François Missoffe, made a reactionary speech suggesting that dissenting students needed nothing more than a cold swim: Daniel accused him of talking like a Nazi, and was threatened with deportation. Student reaction was swift: on January 26th forty students demonstrated, the university authorities called in the police and a thousand students gathered to repel them. The French student rebellion of **May 1968** was born. Two months later the 22 March Movement called for an outright rejection of capitalism, the division of labour and forced learning in universities, and Nanterre University embarked on disciplinary action against eight students including Cohn-Bendit. The attempted assassination of **Rudi Dutschke** on April 11th inflamed the situation, and following a number of outspoken speeches and pamphlets Daniel was arrested in Paris on May 3rd. Student protest quickly spread across France and beyond. Daniel spent the next few weeks on the road, speaking at demonstrations and sit-ins in Germany, Holland and England; while he was out of France he was banned from re-entering the country, and on May 24th riot police were waiting at the frontier as he arrived at the head of a thousand comrades. He complained that the press falsely made him into a 'leader', yet his cheeky return to Paris on May 29th, in defiance of his banning order, was followed by a major press conference in the Sorbonne. His audacious protests continued for several more months, but by early 1969 most students were back at their studies. Daniel Cohn-Bendit's short-lived influence as a fluent and resourceful social agitator affected a whole generation of radicals, and his subsequent career as a speaker, local government politician, writer and journalist (he joined the German Green Party (**Die Grünen**) in 1979 and has remained consistently active in radical journalism and campaigning) demonstrates that he is still convinced of the importance of grassroots political and social action.

Hervé Bourges (trans. B.R. Brewster), *The French Student Revolt: The Leaders Speak*, Hill and Wang, 1968
David Caute, *Sixty-Eight: The Year of the Barricades*, Hamish Hamilton, 1988

G.D.H. [George Douglas Howard] Cole
1889–1959
socialist, historian

G.D.H. Cole has been described as a 'socialist gadfly', a man whose imaginative ideas and prolific writings had a profound effect on every aspect of the interwar labour movement in Britain, even though he may have proved too much of an eclectic and propagandist for later generations within the labour movement. The son of an estate agent in west London, he encountered **William Morris** and then Fabianism while a student at Oxford University. From about 1914, Cole was a fluent and persuasive advocate of guild socialism, building on Morris's thinking about craft guilds to envisage industry based on cooperative guilds, rather than the alternative prevalent concept of socialist state ownership. His ideas were elaborated in a number of books including *Guild Socialism Re-stated* and *The Social Theory*, and had much influence on the reorganised Labour Party in the period immediately after the first world war. In 1925 he started to teach at Oxford, where a 'Cole Group' provided a focus for young leftwing intellectuals, and founded the Society for Socialist Enquiry and Propaganda (which soon became the Socialist League) and the New Fabian Research Bureau. At the end of the 1930s he and his wife Margaret resurrected the moribund **Fabian Society**, and in 1944 was appointed as professor of social and political theory at Oxford, a post he held until his retirement in 1957. A constant stream of books and pamphlets appeared throughout his career, including a multi-volume history of socialist thought and a number of important historical studies. There were few parts of the British labour movement in which G.D.H. Cole's influence was not felt, and although his firmly-held beliefs in decentralisation and pluralism were largely eclipsed by the postwar trend towards professionalisation and centralised control in academia and politics alike, his concerns and ideas have more recently become the subject of renewed interest.

G.D.H. Cole, *Guild Socialism Re-stated*, Parsons, 1920 (reprinted Transaction Books, 1980)

G.D.H. Cole, *The Social Theory*, Methuen, 1920 (selections reprinted in Paul Hirst (ed.) *The Pluralist Theory of the State*, Routledge, 1989)

Margaret Cole, *The Life of G.D.H. Cole*, Macmillan, 1971

Luther P. Carpenter, *G.D.H. Cole: An Intellectual Biography*, Cambridge University Press, 1973

Mairead Corrigan Maguire
1944–
peace campaigner

One of eight children born into a Catholic family in Belfast, the Irish peace campaigner Mairead Corrigan was educated at St Vincent's School and worked as a bookkeeper from the age of sixteen. She was also involved with voluntary Catholic clubs for teenagers and handicapped children. Early in 1976 three of her sister Anne's children were killed when a car driven by a suspected republican gunman careered out of control after he had been shot by the Northern Ireland security forces. Outraged by the British army's attitude and complacency following the children's deaths, she cofounded, with Betty Williams and Ciaran McKeaun, the Northern Irish Peace Movement – usually known as the Peace People. Together with Betty Williams, who left the movement in 1982 to settle in Florida, Mairead Corrigan was awarded the 1976 Nobel Peace Prize, and travelled abroad campaigning for the cause, meeting President Carter in 1978. Later that year she resigned from the Peace Movement's executive, but continued to work for it despite its apparently minimal impact on Northern Irish affairs. She became chair of the Peace Movement again in 1980, the year that her sister committed suicide; a year later Mairead married her brother-in-law Jackie Maguire. She has continued to work actively for peace, both in Ireland and internationally, travelling widely to lecture and monitor peace initiatives. In February 1994 she was part of a delegation of seven Nobel peace laureates who attempted to visit **Aung San Suu Kyi**, kept under house arrest by the illegal Myanmar government, and has clearly stated her conviction that Myanmar must become 'the world's new South Africa'. She is now certain that the Peace People have had a considerable influence in the developing peace negotiations in Northern Ireland, which in September 1994 led to a Sinn Fein ceasefire, followed two months later by a loyalist cessation of hostilities. 'We believe passionately', she said in a 1994 interview, ' that the only alternative to the gun is talking and more talking, including everyone and placing no conditions on those talks.'

Richard Deutsch, *Mairead Corrigan, Betty Williams*, Barron's, 1977

Herman Daly
1938–
economist

Herman Daly's chief contribution to radical thinking is the linking of economics with ecology in the model of the 'steady-state economy', which clearly distinguishes between finite and limiting resources like food, energy and human populations, and qualitative non-finite aspects of human experience such as wisdom and innovation. After studying economics at Rice and Vanderbilt Universities he taught economics at Yale and at Louisiana State University, and in Brazil as a Fulbright Scholar and Ford Foundation visiting professor; for 24 years from 1964 he was professor of economics at Louisiana State. His first major analysis of ecological economics came with the publication in 1977 of *Steady-State Economics*, and as a respected academic and economist he has been able to introduce his ideas into institutions like the World Bank, where he worked for six years from 1988 to 1994. He has also served as a consultant to the Ford Foundation, the World Council of Churches and the Joint Economic Committee of Congress. In the late 1980s he collaborated with John Cobb, professor of philosophy and theology at Claremont College, to produce *For the Common Good*, a 'steady-state' blueprint for America's alternative future economy and society. Since January 1994 Herman Daly has been senior research scholar at the University of Maryland's School of Public Affairs.

Herman Daly, *Steady-State Economics*, Freeman and Co, 1977 (2nd edn. 1991, Island Press)

Herman Daly, *Economics, Ecology, Ethics*, Freeman and Co, 1980

Herman Daly and John Cobb, *For the Common Good: Redirecting the Economy towards Community, the Environment and a Sustainable Future*, Beacon Press/Green Print, 1990

Mary Daly
1928–
radical feminist philosopher

The feminist writer Mary Daly was born in Schenectady, New York, studied at the College of St Rose, and since 1952 has taught philosophy and theology in the USA and Switzerland. The Jesuit administration fired Mary Daly from the Boston College theology department for her first book, *The Church and the Second Sex* (1968), which analysed Catholicism's history of mysogyny. Rehired with tenure after concerted student protest she continued teaching there, moving into a 'postchristian feminism' with *Beyond God the Father* (1973), exploring the feminist dimension of spirituality and the search for meaning in the **women's movement**. In *Gyn/Ecology* (1978), she examines how women, by listening to one another, find words for their experiences; thus they not only break out of the silence imposed and enforced by patriarchy, but out of its 'monodimensional reality' as well. From their new multidimensional reality, women generate new meanings, recycling old words and creating new ones. Naming and analysing a number of woman-hating practices across cultures, Mary Daly urges women to separate entirely from men to create a new, good universe. *Pure Lust* (1984) carries her philosophical explorations further in this direction, while *Webster's First New Intergalactic Wickedary of the English Language* (1987) provides a lexicon for some of her newly-articulated meanings. Mary Daly's questioning of the precepts behind the English language has contributed a powerful tool to radical feminism, but many readers find her method overly academic and almost inaccessible.

Mary Daly, *Beyond God the Father: Toward a Philosophy of Women's Liberation*, Beacon, 1973

Mary Daly, *Gyn/Ecology: The Metaethics of Radical Feminism*, Beacon, 1978

Mary Daly, *Pure Lust: Elemental Feminist Philosophy*, Beacon, 1984

Erik Dammann
1931–
environmentalist, internationalist

The Norwegian Erik Dammann is best known as the founder of Framtiden i Vore Hender (The Future in Our Hands, FIOH), an influential international organisation which at its height in the late 1970s had 25,000 active members. He began his professional life in design and advertising but, disillusioned with the consumerism his work required him to promote he and his family went to live in Polynesia, where they shared village life in a culture characterised by cooperation and sharing. He returned to Norway with the realisation that the West's emphasis on greed and competition had more to do with culture than with human nature, and in 1972 wrote *Framtiden i Vore Hender* (*The Future in Our Hands*, 1979), which quickly attracted much attention in Scandinavia and beyond. In 1974 Erik Dammann founded the FIOH movement, with affiliated organisations in more than a dozen countries, a development fund that has supported projects in more than twenty poor countries and an information centre in Norway. His 1979 book, *Revolusjon i Velstandssamfunnet* (*Revolution in the Affluent Society*, 1984) expanded his ideas about the role of personal, social and political change in the creation of a more caring and just society, and he has continued to work for grassroots empowerment, convinced that 'belief in the deeper values of the common people is our only hope'. In 1980 he initiated the Nordic research and information programme Alternative Future to promote investigation into and debate about a coherent and sustainable society, and in 1982 was awarded a Right Livelihood Award for his contribution towards creating a just world order.

Erik Dammann, *The Future in Our Hands*, Pergamon, 1979
Erik Dammann, *Revolution in the Affluent Society*, Heretic, 1984

Homa Darabi
1940–1994
teacher, feminist

Following a lifetime of struggling and campaigning against the repressive, misogynist regime of the Islamic government of Iran, Homa Darabi came to believe that the only way to impress upon the world the intractability of the situation of modern Iranian women was, in an act of public protest, to kill herself. Born into a liberal family in Tehran, she studied at Tehran University, where in 1960 she was imprisoned for organising an Iranian National Front demonstration demanding equal rights for women. After postgraduate study in the USA she returned to Tehran in 1976 and married another doctor, Manouchehre Kiyani; their two daughters both went on to study medicine. From then until 1991 Homa Darabi taught child psychiatry at Tehran University, a popular and respected teacher and researcher, but in that year she was dismissed for non-adherence to the Islamic dress code, which includes the wearing of a headscarf and long coat at all times in public. Her resistance to the draconian Iranian regime gathered momentum and she appealed against the decision: although an employment tribunal decided for her the university refused to reinstate her, instead issuing even stricter dress guidelines to women staff. On February 21st 1994, in a public square in the Tehran suburb of Shemiran, Homa Darabi tore off her headscarf and long coat, covered herself in petrol, and set herself on fire, proclaiming 'Down with tyranny, long live freedom, long live Iran!' More than 10,000 people attended her memorial service in

Tehran's Aliavad Mosque, and solidarity events were held throughout Europe and North America.

Angela [Yvonne] Davis
1944–
civil rights activist

From August 1970, when she was charged with kidnapping, conspiracy and murder, until February 1972, when she was released on bail and subsequently cleared, Angela Davis was a household name in the USA. 'Free Angela Davis' was a rallying call that united the civil rights movement, especially the black community. Angela Davis grew up in a middle class activist family in Birmingham, Alabama, surrounded by the segregation and disadvantage that fired her will to make things different for future generations of African Americans. She studied in New York, Brandeis University in Massachusetts, Paris, Frankfurt and the University of California at San Diego, being particularly influenced by **Herbert Marcuse** and his belief in the responsibility of the individual to rebel against injustice. By the end of 1967, following her return from Germany, she was actively involved in the **Student Nonviolent Coordinating Committee**, the Communist Party and the **Black Panther** movement. In 1969 she was offered a lectureship in philosophy at the University of California in Los Angeles; though she was a popular teacher the California authorities fired her because of her Communist Party membership. Her dismissal was overturned on appeal, but her ongoing support for imprisoned Black Panther members lost her her teaching post in mid-1970. Early 1970 had been largely taken up with her involvement with the 'Soledad Brothers', Black Panther members accused of murdering a prison guard, and she developed a deep emotional attachment with their leader, George Jackson. In August 1970 George's brother Jonathan tried to force his brother's release by taking hostages at the Marin County courthouse, but Jonathan, a judge and two other prisoners died in the resulting shootout. Angela Davis was immediately accused of involvement (the guns were hers, held legally following death threats), and went underground. Within days of her arrest in New York in October 1970 the entire civil rights movement had mobilised in her defence: when the case eventually went to trial two years later she was acquitted of all charges. After her release her defence committee was renamed the National Alliance Against Racist and Political Repression and, with Angela as its chair, defended many, mostly blacks and Hispanics, accused of political crimes. Alongside her teaching, Angela Davis remained politically active, running for the US vice-presidency on the Communist ticket in 1980 and 1984. In recent years she has become actively involved with the National Black Women's Health Project, and now lives in Oakland, where she teaches women's studies at San Francisco State University.

Angela Davis, *Women, Class, and Race*, Random House, 1981
Angela Davis, *Women, Culture, and Politics*, Random House, 1989
Angela Davis, *Angela Davis: An Autobiography*, Random House, 1988

Bettina Aptheker, *The Morning Breaks: The Trial of Angela Davis*, International
    Publishers, 1975

Dorothy Day
1897–1980
social reformer

Dorothy Day grew up in Brooklyn and Chicago, and at seventeen left home
for New York City to be a writer. Politically radical, she became part of a
circle of artists and activists, working as a journalist and writer. In 1924,
with money from an autobiographical novel, she bought a cottage in a
colony of radicals and artists just outside New York City and settled into a
common-law marriage. When she became pregnant her indistinct religious
faith blossomed into a commitment to Catholicism, and she left the
relationship. After five years of confusion, supporting herself and her
daughter with freelance writing, in December 1932 she met an itinerant
labourer and visionary, Peter Maurin. Her experience and skills, linked with
his passionate vision of communities of service based on a radical social
interpretation of Christian gospel, created the Catholic Worker Movement.
After establishing a newspaper, *The Catholic Worker*, which in two years
grew to a circulation of 150,000 and is still in existence, Dorothy Day went
on to organise the first 'hospitality house' for homeless people in New York
City. Within ten years thirty such Catholic Worker communities had sprung
up around the USA, and the number now stands at nearly a hundred.
Dorothy Day's pacifist neutrality during the **Spanish Civil War** drew outrage
from the church on the right and radicals on the left, and during the second
world war the Catholic Worker Movement split over the issue of pacifism.
Though she had been picketing the German embassy since Hitler came to
power, and had cofounded the Committee of Catholics to Fight Anti-
Semitism in 1939, Dorothy Day feared that using superior force to prevail
over fascism would create a new destructive power. She led Catholic
Workers in the vanguard of nonviolent direct actions against atomic
weapons and military bases, and so many people joined her resistance to
New York's civil defence exercises in the early 1950s that the programme
collapsed. For twenty more years she continued to travel and organise in
support of peace and justice; the last of her many arrests was in California
on a United Farm Workers picket line in 1973. After a heart attack in 1976
she led a contemplative life. Dorothy Day embraced voluntary poverty as
an affirmation of the abundance of life and spirit, love as the basis of
society, and service as a form of worship. Her legacy is a large body of
writing and a movement that has profoundly influenced Catholic radicalism
in the United States.

Robert Ellsberg, *By Little and By Little: The Selected Writings of Dorothy Day*,
    Knopf, 1983
William D. Miller, *A Harsh and Dreadful Love: Dorothy Day and the Catholic Worker
    Movement*, Image, 1974
Nancy L. Roberts, *Dorothy Day and the 'Catholic Worker'*, SUNY, 1984

[Jules] Régis Debray
1940–
socialist, teacher, writer

One of Europe's foremost writers about and critics of Latin American revolutionary politics in the 1960s and 70s, the French socialist Régis Debray has since become a fluent observer of the French cultural scene. Born into a comfortable middle class Parisian family, his entrance examination results for the École Normale Supérieure were the highest of his year. The same year, 1959, he returned from a holiday in the USA by way of Cuba, and was instantly infected by the optimism and energy of Fidel Castro's post-revolutionary regime. His lifetime passion and concern for political and social change in Latin America was fuelled by visits to every country on the continent (bar Paraguay) in 1963–67, meeting revolutionary leaders including **Salvador Allende** and the Venezuelan rebel leader Douglas Bravo, and mixing with peasant and workers' groups. In January 1966 he returned to Cuba to teach for six months at Havana University, and in late 1967 he was in Bolivia, accompanying **Che Guevara** on his fateful guerrilla struggle; as a result of his involvement Debray was sentenced to thirty years imprisonment. Three years of sometimes brutal incarceration ended with his pardon and return to France in 1970. His many books have stressed the need for any successful political and cultural revolution to be rooted firmly within the grasp of ordinary people, taking into account their everyday lives, expectations, hopes and fears. In 1981 the French president François Mitterand appointed Debray as special adviser on Latin American affairs. Since then he has been a fulltime writer and teacher, producing short stories and novels, the popular and caustic *Le pouvoir intellectuel en France* (1979, 1981 in English as *Teachers, Writers, Celebrities: Intellectuals of Modern France*) and an important biography of Charles de Gaulle (1994).

Régis Debray, *Revolution in the Revolution?*, Monthly Review Press, 1967
Régis Debray, *The Chilean Revolution: Conversations with Allende*, Pantheon, 1971
Régis Debray, *Critique of Political Reason*, Schocken, 1984
Leo Huberman and Paul Sweezy (eds), *Régis Debray and the Latin American Revolution*, Monthly Review Press, 1968

Eugene V. [Victor] Debs
1855–1926
labour activist and socialist leader

Born in Terre Haute, Indiana, to French immigrants who kept a grocery store and inculcated in their sons the values of the French enlightenment and the republican tradition, Eugene Debs was eager to engage in the American dream. He left school at fifteen for a railway job and studied business in the evenings. He joined the Brotherhood of Locomotive Firemen, became editor of its journal in 1880 and national secretary-treasurer five years later. Meanwhile he was active in civic organisations, and in 1884 was elected to the state legislature. In 1885 he married Katherine Metzel, daughter of a prosperous Terre Haute family. Though they soon ceased being lovers they remained married, and she worked with him through a lifetime of projects and campaigns. As a public figure – a powerful orator, local golden boy, and popular union leader who believed that workers and industrialists were partnered for mutual benefit – Eugene Debs was set for success by the time he was thirty. However, years of unsuccessful effort to create union solidarity strong enough to counter monopoly capitalism slowly changed his beliefs. He left the Brotherhood to help found the American Railway Union in 1893, and within a year had organised a nonviolent strike with such solid discipline and cross-trade support that the union won a court-arbitrated settlement. This victory swelled the membership, but the Union plunged almost at once into another industry-wide action, this time crushed violently. Eugene Debs spent six months in prison, and the union never recovered its strength. Nationally renowned by 1895, he became a socialist, and in 1900 ran the first of five campaigns as the Socialist Party's presidential candidate, leading the party for the next quarter century through the peak of its success, though he never held office. He took part in the 1905 founding convention of the **Industrial Workers of the World** (IWW) but did not seek leadership. Strongly opposed to IWW president 'Big Bill' Haywood's emphasis on sabotage and direct action, Eugene Debs voted to expel him from the Socialist Party's national committee; thousands of party members resigned in protest. This aspect of struggle was repugnant to Eugene Debs. His preferred way of participation was to advise on union actions, as he was often invited to do, and to raise public consciousness through his speeches and writing. The Socialist Party was severely repressed by the US government for opposing the first world war, and in 1918 Eugene Debs was arrested, convicted of sedition for his antiwar activity, and sentenced to ten years in prison. Conducting his final presidential campaign from prison, he received the largest vote ever cast for an American socialist. On Christmas Day 1921 he was pardoned by the president-elect and released. Though his health had deteriorated, he spent the years until his death in 1926 trying to rebuild the Socialist Party.

Ray Ginger, *The Bending Cross: A Biography of Eugene Victor Debs*, Rutgers
    University Press, 1949
Bernard Brommel, *Eugene V. Debs: Spokesman for Labor and Socialism*, Charles H.
    Kerr, 1978
Nick Salvatore, *Eugene V. Debs: Citizen and Socialist*, University of Illinois Press,
    1982

David Dellinger
1915–
civil rights and peace activist, writer

A middle-class Massachusetts upbringing may seem an unlikely beginning for one of America's most consistent and outspoken pacifist activists, but David Dellinger's radical career started early. After five years of university studies at Yale and New College, Oxford, his antiwar conviction put him in prison in 1940 for a year and a day for refusing to register for the newly-initiated draft; two years later he was given a further two-year sentence when he would not report for armed service induction or an assignment at a public service camp: he spent much of his time at Lewisberg Penitentiary protesting against the war and against racial segregation, which earned him several stretches of solitary confinement. For the next two decades David Dellinger and his family (he married Elizabeth Peterson in 1946) lived and worked communally in Newark and Glen Gardner, New Jersey, and he worked hard to convince others of the sense of nonviolent social change, editing and writing for magazines like *Direct Action* and *Liberation*, and working closely with the War Resisters League and the Committee for Nonviolent Action to organise demonstrations and meetings. With the advent of the **Vietnam War** he served as cochair of the New Mobilization Committee to End the War in Vietnam, visiting south-east Asia three times, and was one of the most influential figures within the antiwar movement. In 1968 he (along with **Abbie Hoffman** and others) was one of the 'Chicago Eight' indicted for conspiring to disrupt the 1968 Democratic National Convention. Following a series of colourful and often bizarre hearings most of the charges were dropped: public support rallied behind the defendants and the trial played a significant part in mobilising antiwar sentiment. After the end of the Vietnam War, David Dellinger continued to campaign on a broad front of civil rights and antimilitarism, setting out in a series of influential books his belief that it is crucial to campaign against the economic and social system that supports war and oppression, and not just against the inevitable results of that system.

David Dellinger, *Revolutionary Nonviolence*, Bobbs-Merrill, 1970
David Dellinger, *More Power Than We Know: The People's Movement Toward Democracy*, Anchor, 1975
David Dellinger, *Beyond Survival: New Directions for the Disarmament Movement*, South End, 1983
David Dellinger, *From Yale to Jail: The Life Story of a Moral Dissenter*, Pantheon, 1993

Barbara Deming
1917–1984
writer, pacifist, feminist

Barbara Deming's lifelong search for personal and cultural solutions to violence, oppression and limitation started early: she attended Quaker school in New City, New York, and entered the first of several significant lesbian relationships when she was sixteen. She studied drama at Bennington College and Western Reserve, and worked and taught in theatre and film studies until 1945, when she became a full-time writer. At about the same time she began a relationship with fellow Bennington graduate Vida Ginsberg, yet married Vida's brother Quentin in 1949; in 1954 she met artist Mary Meigs, and set up house with her at Wellfleet on Cape Cod, but it was not until the early 1970s that Barbara felt able to publicly declare herself a lesbian. In 1960 she travelled in Cuba and became interested in techniques of nonviolent resistance; by May 1961 she was participating in numerous peace and civil rights protests in the USA and the Middle East. The first of many prison sentences resulted from her involvement in a sit-in against nuclear testing in March 1962, and throughout the 1960s she campaigned consistently for civil rights and against the **Vietnam War**, making a point of criticising 'our' rather than 'the US' government. In the 1970s she turned her attention more towards the radical feminist cause: she and her new partner Jane Gapen Verlaine became active in Women Against Violence Against Women, and in 1976 established a feminist community at Sugarloaf Key, Florida. In 1979, with inherited money, Barbara Deming founded Money for Women (later the Barbara Deming Memorial Fund) to support feminist projects in art and education. Her last demonstration (with its inevitable prison sentence) was the 1983 Feminist Walk of the New York City Women's Pentagon Action. Many of the best known of her writings were collected together in *Remembering Who We Are*, published shortly before her death.

Barbara Deming, *We Cannot Live Without Our Lives*, Grossman, 1974
Barbara Deming, *Remembering Who We Are: A Barbara Deming Reader*, New
   Society, 1984
Barbara Deming, *Prisons That Could Not Hold*, Spinsters Ink, 1985

Charlotte Despard [Charlotte French]
1844–1939
social and political campaigner

The third daughter of a family of five girls and a youngest brother who was eventually to become Viceroy of Ireland, suffragist and civil rights campaigner Charlotte Despard wrote of herself that she 'must always have been more or less a rebel'. A fragmented home education and a three-year European Grand Tour was followed by her marriage in 1870 to Anglo-Irishman Maximilian Despard, and the next two decades saw the production of seven high-minded novels and a growing interest in Indian mysticism. Max died in 1890, and Charlotte now devoted herself to helping the poor, opening one of the first child welfare centres in London and becoming a popular speaker for the Independent Labour Party. She joined the **Women's Social and Political Union** and was made honorary secretary in 1906, but she disliked the autocratic rule of **Emmeline Pankhurst** and in 1907 was one of those who broke away to form the democratically-run **Women's Freedom League** (WFL), of which she was elected president. She was a striking figure, with white hair, upright bearing, and a costume which usually included a black lace mantilla and sandals: she was widely idolised, leading to accusations that she was steering the WFL towards her personal passions of communism and pacifism. In 1918 she left the WFL to devote herself to the Women's Peace Crusade. In 1918 she was one of the first eight women to stand for parliament, and in the same year her brother

Jack, now Field-Marshall Lord French, was sworn in as Viceroy of Ireland: he proceeded to rule the country, which was inexorably moving towards independence from Britain, with a rod of iron. Charlotte was already active in the London-based Irish Self Determination League, and from the spring of 1919 onwards spent more and more time in Ireland, supporting the home rule and suffragist movements and using her family connections to gain access and influence throughout the country. In January 1921 she moved to Ireland to work for Sinn Fein, and became president of the Women's Prisoners' Defence League; three months later her brother, now Lord Ypres, was retired from Ireland, and the country gained its long-awaited independence. Charlotte had always been an advocate of communism, and in 1930 visited the Soviet Union; three years later she was imprisoned for a month for defying an exclusion order and speaking in Newry, County Down, and in 1934, now ninety, she moved to Belfast to work for socialism amongst the workers of Northern Ireland. She died at the age of ninety-five, and was buried in Dublin's Glasnevin Cemetery near the grave of her mentor and ally, the Irish freedom campaigner Constance Markiewicz.

Margaret Mulvihill, *Charlotte Despard: A Biography*, Pandora, 1989

Ding Ling [Jian Bingzhi]
1902–1986
novelist, journalist, feminist

Ding Ling was one of the most important Chinese woman writers of the twentieth century, her sixty-year career spent exploring – both in personal experience and in fiction – the tensions between the idealistic individual and the revolutionary organisation. She was born into a gentry family with a tradition of public service, and was educated mostly by her liberal-minded mother. As a student in Taoynan she held strong views on liberty and the equality of women, and in 1919, after the events of the **May 4th Movement**, she ran away to join a coeducational school in Changsa, moving to Shanghai in 1921. From 1925 she lived with the poet Hu Yepin and made her name as a short story writer. She became active in **Lu Xun**'s League of Left-Wing Writers and by 1931 was editing one of its magazines, advising her writers not to become isolated from the masses. In 1931 Ding Ling and Hu Yepin joined the Communist Party; Hu was arrested and executed by the Nationalists, but Ding Ling escaped, eventually reaching the Communist-held north-west in 1936, where her fame warranted a personal reception by **Mao Zedong**. She soon became literary editor of *Liberation Daily*, where she wrote a regular column as well as short stories, frequently questioning women's role in the revolutionary struggle and giving space to a range of dissenting voices. Following Mao's 1944 edict that writers must depict life as the Party wanted it to be seen, Ding Ling complied by producing her best-known novel, *The Sun Shines on the Sanggan River* (1951), which won the Stalin Literary Prize and became a model for the modern Chinese novel. Though the plot conformed to the Party's wishes, Ding Ling added many subtle psychological insights to her novel, which gave it an enduring quality. During the 1950s Ding Ling, now married to Chen Ming, held several important literary posts and was a delegate to conferences in Budapest, Moscow and Paris, but during the purges of 1958 which followed the brief Hundred Flowers period she was expelled from the Writer's Union and the Party. She and Chen Ming were sent to remote Heilongjiang for 'reform through labour': her detention continued for 22 years, the last five in solitary confinement. They were released in 1975 and rehabilitated in 1978. Ding Ling spent the last years of her life working on a new edition of those of her works which had survived, and a sequel, *Days in the Cold*, to *The Sun Shines on the Sanggan River*.

Ding Ling, *The Sun Shines on the Sanggan River*, Foreign Languages Press, Beijing, 1953
John Beyer, 'Ding Ling', *Index on Censorship*, February 1980

Danilo Dolci
1924–
peace and social activist

Danilo Dolci grew up near Trieste, the son of an Italian stationmaster father and a Yugoslav mother. His love of music, literature and pacifism led him to question the fascist ideas that were rapidly gaining ground in prewar Italy; he resisted military service, and after the war worked in a Christian community and orphanage in the countryside south of Milan. Dolci had spent two months in Sicily as a child while his father was working in the small fishing village of Trappeto, and in February 1952 left a promising career as an architect in Milan to return to Sicily to help the poor – a 'calling of conscience' as he later described it. Appalled by the endemic poverty and hopelessness made worse by the grip of the mafia – 'one of the most miserable and blood-drenched areas in the world', he said – he spent much time listening to the local people, trying to understand their basic needs. Later that year he initiated a project to build a small infirmary for the village, helped by some of the many unemployed men. At the end of 1952, following the death of a child from starvation, Dolci's use of the Gandhian tactic of hunger striking forced the authorities to fund a much-needed irrigation scheme. Dolci's first books, *Act Quickly and Well, For Here They Are Dying* (1954) and *Bandits in Partinico* (1955), brought the plight of Sicily's rural poverty to a wider audience, and in June 1955, married to Trappeto widow Vincenzina Mangano, Dolci moved his base to Partinico. By now he had developed a model of community discussion and decision-making called *autoanalisi populari*, a pioneering model of community empowerment. Although much needed doing in Sicily – roads, schools and houses were all badly required – people were frightened of taking any action to help themselves. In 1956 Danilo Dolci organised a work party of unemployed men from Partinico to rebuild a road; though the action was peaceful many of the participants were arrested. Dolci was sentenced to four months' imprisonment, but used his court appearance to draw public attention to the inhumanity of allowing people to die of hunger when so many wanted to work for the improvement of their living conditions. His stance and methods earned him the sobriquet of 'the **Gandhi** of Sicily' and the support of many Italian intellectuals and activists. Though not a declared communist, in 1956 he was awarded the Lenin Peace Prize. News of his work spread throughout Italy and beyond, and with the foundation of the Centro Studi e Iniziative (Centre for Research and Initiative) in Partinico in May 1958 his work became more widely known. The centre's first major project was the construction of a new school and community centre, and within two years Dolci's organisation was working throughout western Sicily. Danilo Dolci consistently opposed the organised crime and graft associated with the mafia, and has fearlessly exposed mafia activity at every opportunity, always taking a strict nonviolent stance himself. For many years he has been active in **War Resisters International**, but his main focus has remained in Sicily, working with the underprivileged to help them build a better future for themselves.

Danilo Dolci, *A New World in the Making*, Greenwood, 1965
Danilo Dolci, *Sicilian Lives*, Writers and Readers, 1982
Jerre Mangioni, *A Passion for Sicilians: The World around Danilo Dolci*, Transaction Books, 1985
Michael Bess, *Realism, Utopia, and the Mushroom Cloud: Four Activist Intellectuals and their Strategies for Peace, 1945–1989*, University of Chicago Press, 1993.

Slavenka Drakulić
1950–
feminist, journalist, novelist

Born into an authoritarian Communist family in Rijeka, southern Croatia, Slavenka Drakulić left home at sixteen to live and work in Zagreb. After a short marriage which left her looking after her daughter Rujana, she went to the University of Zagreb to read literature and sociology. In 1979 she was cofounder of the first feminist group in Yugoslavia, and helped establish the first network of Eastern European women's groups. A widely read and respected journalist and novelist, her writing shows humanity, deep political and social insight into everyday life in Eastern Europe, and a wicked wit. In a writing and activist career straddling the breakup of communism in Yugoslavia and the war of 1992–94, she was one of the country's first feminist voices, her articles and essays reflecting her first-hand experience of official repression, and of the hypocrisy and hatred of civil war. In November 1992, together with four other feminist critics, Slavenka Drakulić was publicly denounced as a 'dangerous antigovernment feminist', and in 1993, following further official interference, she lost her job as a staff writer on the Croatian magazine *Newsweek*. Based still in Zagreb, she continues to travel and to write semi-autobiographical fiction and investigative journalism. Her novels include *Holograms of Fear* (1987, 1992 in English) and *Marble Skin* (1992, 1993 in English), while the collection of articles *How We Survived Communism and Even Laughed* (1992) demonstrates the range and wisdom of her journalism.

Slavenka Drakulić, *How We Survived Communism and Even Laughed*, Hutchinson, 1992

Alexander Dubček
1921–1992
communist politician, social and political activist

Alexander Dubček was the first communist leader in Eastern Europe to speak out against Soviet totalitarianism, his 'Prague Spring' of 1968 heralding the first signs of the breakup of the Soviet bloc. Born and brought up in Uhroveč in Slovakia, he took part in the Slovak resistance to the German occupation during the second world war. During the 1950s and early 60s his career as a Communist Party official was unremarkable: he studied in Moscow, in 1960 became secretary of the committee of the Slovakian Communist Party, and by 1967 was first secretary of the Party's central committee. For more than a decade there had been dissatisfaction with the centralised power of the Czechoslovak Communist Party, especially the way in which it eroded the rights of Slovaks, and during the mid-60s tentative attempts were made to introduce more freedom within the Soviet regime, moves which Dubček supported wholeheartedly. 'Socialism with a human face' took a major step forward with his election to the secretaryship of the Czechoslovak Communist Party in January 1968: almost immediately he implemented a wide range of policies including the lifting of censorship, more economic freedom, and a new form of Czech-Slovak federation. Although the Dubček regime carefully refrained from foreign policy initiatives that might infringe on Soviet bloc unity, the Prague reformers angered Leonid Brezhnev and the Soviet leadership. Several attempts at summit meeting reconciliation failed, and on August 21st 1968 Soviet tanks rolled into the streets of Prague. Czechoslovakia was quickly occupied by a combined miltary force from five Soviet bloc countries, and the reforms were systematically dismantled. After a short period when Dubček was reinstated subject to tight controls on his actions, he refused to submit to the required self-criticism and admit that the reforms had been misjudged and was exiled to Bratislava to work as a clerk. In 1989 the first postcommunist parliament under **Václav Havel** chose the hero of 1968 as its speaker, and following the division of Czechoslovakia in 1991 Slovakia's Social Democratic Party made him its leader. He died in November 1992 of injuries sustained in a car accident.

Alexander Dubček, *Dubček Speaks: Alexander Dubček with Andras Sugar*, Tauris, 1990
Alexander Dubček (ed. and trans. Jiri Hochman), *Hope Dies Last: The Autobiography of Alexander Dubček*, Kodansha, 1993
William Shawcross, *Dubček*, Simon and Schuster, 1990 (2nd revised ed.)
William Shawcross, *Dubček and Czechoslovakia 1968–1990*, Hogarth, 1990

W.E.B. [William Edward Burghardt] Du Bois
1868–1963
scholar, civil rights campaigner

The veteran civil rights campaigner W.E.B. Du Bois was born in Great Barrington, Massachusetts. His parents' marriage ended soon after he was born and he was raised in relative poverty by his mother, a domestic worker. The first African American to graduate from his high school, he continued his education with funds raised by people in his home town, Fisk in Tennessee. After two years he transferred to Harvard, where he remained – with time aside to study German philosophy in Berlin – until he received his PhD in 1895. Harvard inaugurated its *Historical Series* by publishing his dissertation on the suppression of the Atlantic slave trade, the first of the seventeen books he authored as a sociologist, historian, novelist and poet. At the turn of the century Du Bois articulated the concept of the 'double consciousness' of African Americans – reconciling their African identity with their assimilation into American society. This radical idea set him in opposition to the ruling paradigm of black accommodation to the white power structure, and made him a dynamic presence in African-American cultural and political life for decades. His twin careers as scholar and activist ran as mutually enriching themes through his long life. To the African-American community, which between 1890 and 1920 was facing intense racial violence and suppression, he brought the affirmation of historical analysis and cultural pride. He was a strong proponent of women's suffrage and an ally of black women as artists and activists. After organising several associations for black intellectuals, in 1910 he took the lead in founding the inter-racial National Association for the Advancement of Colored People (NAACP) to combat racist laws and practices through publicity and legislative pressure. As editor of NAACP's journal *The Crisis* for 24 years, he cultivated a vital interchange between culture and political thought. A fifty-year commitment to pan-Africanism created a context for his perspective on African-American issues, and by the end of his life it had become his central commitment. For most of his life an unaffiliated socialist, Du Bois spent several decades moving from an emphasis on enlightened leadership to an analysis that placed power within people and their experiences. In the 20s and early 30s he came under fire from various quarters – from black nationalist **Marcus Garvey** for being assimilationist, from the socialist labour organiser A. Philip Randolph for not being militant enough, from the NAACP for being too militant, and from mainstream labour unionists for not accommodating their racism. In 1934 he resigned from *The Crisis* to teach at Atlanta University, though he continued lecturing, founded a new journal (he edited four during the course of his life), travelled, studied Marxism, and wrote three books, including a striking application of original Marxist thought to the relationship between the collapse of slavery in the USA and the rise of European colonialism in Africa. Asked in 1944 to return to the NAACP as its executive secretary, he remained four years until he was dismissed. He turned fully to work on pan-Africanism and anti-imperialism, but in 1951 was indicted as a foreign agent. He was acquitted, but he and his wife, Shirley Graham, had their passports revoked until 1958. He wrote three more books and, once he was free to travel, undertook a world tour at the age of ninety. At the invitation of President **Kwame Nkrumah**, he moved to Ghana in 1961 to become a Ghanaian citizen and director of a long-dreamed-of project, *The Encyclopedia Africana*. He lived and worked in Africa until his death in August 1963.

W.E.B. Du Bois (ed. Herbert Aptheker), *The Correspondence of W.E.B. Du Bois*, University of Massachusetts Press, 1973–78

W.E.B. Du Bois, *The Autobiography of W.E.B. Du Bois: A Soliloquy on Viewing my Life from the Last Decade of its First Century*, International Publishers, 1968

John Henrik Clarke *et al*, *Black Titan: W.E.B. Du Bois; An Anthology by the Editors of Freedomways*, Beacon Press, 1970

Gerald Horne, *Black and Red: W.E.B. Du Bois and the Afro-American Response to the Cold War*, 1944–1963, State University of New York Press, 1986

Manning Marable, *W.E.B. Du Bois, Black Radical Democrat*, Twayne, 1986

Isadora [Dora Angela] Duncan
1877–1927
dancer, liberationist

While Isadora Duncan is primarily, and rightly, remembered as an experimental dancer who liberated the human body from the the constraints of the nineteenth century, her passionate belief in freedom extended far beyond the dance. She grew up in San Francisco, the daughter of a father who left his wife and family when Dora was still a baby, and a hardworking yet adventurous mother who encouraged her four children to explore their imaginations. At the age of ten Dora left school to teach dance, to satisfy her growing passion for the medium and to supplement the family's income, and within a few years was performing regularly. In 1895 she moved with her mother to Chicago and then to New York, where she quickly developed a reputation as a solo dancer, using minimal props and costumes to show how the unadorned body can speak of ultimate truths – she called it 'the highest intelligence in the freest body'. Her successes in Europe in the decade following her London debut in 1900 demonstrated that her freedom and harmony struck a chord with her rapturously appreciative audiences, though a less successful 1908 tour of the USA suggested that her home country was not yet ready for her. Isadora Duncan spurned marriage, and was happy that her many affairs and her three children by different fathers were public knowledge, proudly ignoring anyone who criticised her choices; tragically her first two children drowned in 1913 (aged eight and three) when their mother's car rolled into the River Seine, and her third died soon after birth. The outbreak of war in Europe persuaded her to return to America, but her final years, though punctuated by performance highlights in San Francisco, Moscow and Paris, were marked by disappointment and emotional stress. An invitation to open a school in Moscow was withdrawn after she had visited Russia in 1921–22, and her short-lived marriage to artist Sergei Yessenin ended with his suicide in 1925. Shortly after finishing her eloquently candid autobiography, *My Life* (1927), Isadora Duncan was killed in the French city of Nice when her shawl caught in the spokes of the wheel of a sports car.

Isadora Duncan (ed. Franklin Rosemont), *Isadora Speaks*, City Lights, 1981
Fredrika Blair, *Isadora: Portrait of the Artist as a Woman*, McGraw-Hill, 1986
Lillian Loewenthal, *The Search for Isadora: The Legend and Legacy of Isadora Duncan*, Princeton Book Co., 1993

Rudi Dutschke
1940–1979
student leader, political and social activist

'Red Rudi', as he was known by friends and enemies alike, was the most visible leader of the German student movement in the 1960s. He grew up in Luckenwalde in what was then the German Democratic Republic, but following a disagreement with the authorities over his university education he moved to West Berlin in August 1961, two days before the building of the Berlin Wall. As a student of sociology at the Free University and a founding member in 1962 of Subversive Aktion – which went on to become the majority grouping within the influential Sozialistischer Deutscher Studentenbund (German Socialist Student Organisation) – he was at the heart of German radical political activism throughout the volatile years leading up to 1968. By early 1968 he was regularly speaking at public meetings and demonstrations, often alongside established socialists like György Lukács, **Herbert Marcuse** and **Ernst Bloch**, and was arrested on several occasions. On April 11th 1968, six days after the assassination of **Martin Luther King**, Rudi Dutschke was shot several times while riding his bicycle by a lone gunman called Josef Bachmann: Dutschke survived, but suffered head injuries of which he died eleven years later. The assassination attempt sparked student riots throughout West Germany and played an important part in the **May 1968** student uprisings in Paris, and in December Dutschke was banned from West Germany, only to be expelled twice from England before he found a teaching post at Aarhus in Denmark. He returned to Germany in 1973 and immediately started campaigning against the **Vietnam War**, the 'Berufsverbot' (the exclusion of leftwing socialists from civil service employment) and the building of nuclear power stations. A growing concern about ecological issues led him to become an early member of **Die Grünen** (the German Green Party): he joined the Bremen Party in September 1979 but died just two months later.

David Caute, *Sixty-Eight: The Year of the Barricades*, Hamish Hamilton, 1988
Russell Berman, 'Rudi Dutschke', *Biographical Dictionary of Neo-Marxism* (ed. Robert Gorman), Mansell, 1986

Andrea Dworkin
1946–
feminist writer

Andrea Dworkin was born in Camden, New Jersey, and studied at Bennington College. She emerged as a powerful radical feminist voice with the publication of her first book, *Woman Hating* (1974). After the publication of her third, *Pornography: Men Possessing Women* (1981), she was invited by law professor Catharine MacKinnon to join her in teaching a seminar at the University of Minnesota. This concluded that the fundamental legal issue of pornography is not free speech, to be protected as a civil liberty, but the violation of women's civil rights. Andrea Dworkin and Catharine MacKinnon drafted an antipornography ordinance in 1983 at the request of the Minneapolis City Council, which held hearings on the links between pornography and sexual violence before passing the ordinance. The US Supreme Court declared the Minneapolis ordinance unconstitutional in 1985, but the campaign to get such legislation passed across the USA generated intense and often bitter debate among feminists, who remain split over the issue of whether granting the (male-defined and -dominated) legal system power to enforce legislated definitions of pornography would endanger women's – especially lesbian women's – choices of sexual expression. Andrea Dworkin continues to write and lecture widely on sexual politics, her recent books including two novels and a study of the power dynamics of sexual intercourse.

Andrea Dworkin, *Pornography: Men Possessing Women*, Perigee, 1981
Andrea Dworkin, *Right-Wing Women: The Politics of Domesticated Females*, Perigee, 1983
Andrea Dworkin, *Intercourse*, Secker & Warburg, 1987

[Catherine] Crystal Eastman
1881–1928
feminist, pacifist, social critic

A fluent and passionate feminist and civil rights campaigner, Crystal Eastman received her first and most formative teaching from her mother Annis, a progressive Congregationalist minister (as was her father). She grew up in Elmira, New York, with two brothers (the younger of whom, Max, was to become her colleague and a noted radical in his own right), and studied at Vassar College, Columbia University and New York University Law School. Her first fulltime work was as a researcher on the monumental 'Pittsburgh Survey', the first large-scale attempt to study the effects of industrialisation on urban workers. In 1911 she married an insurance agent, Wallace Benedict, but they were divorced five years later, Crystal pointedly refusing to claim alimony, declaring that 'No self-respecting feminist would claim alimony – it would be her own confession that she could not take care of herself.' By this time she was deeply involved in feminist campaigning, having been a founder member in 1913 of the Congressional Union for Woman Suffrage: for her the struggle was about freedom and total equality, and she was as opposed to laws favouring women as she was to those discriminating against them. During the first world war she assisted conscientious objectors, and in 1917 joined her brother Max on his radical journal *The Liberator*, for which she acted as editor and occasional columnist. The same year she married fellow pacifist Walter Fuller, and in 1921 they moved to London with their two children. Here she helped found a branch of the National Woman's Party and was active in the Conference of Labour Women. Crystal Eastman returned to the USA in 1927 and plunged straight into educational and childcare reform, but later that year she heard of Walter's death and her own health declined precipitously until she too died a year later.

Crystal Eastman, 'Mother-Worship' (1927), *The Nation 1865–1990: Selections from the Independent Magazine of Politics and Culture* (ed. Katrina Vauden Heuvel), Pluto, 1990

Crystal Eastman and Max Eastman (ed. Blanche Wiesen Cook), *Toward the Great Change: Crystal and Max Eastman on Feminism, Antimilitarism, and Revolution*, Garland, 1976

Crystal Eastman (ed. Blanche Wiesen Cook), *Crystal Eastman on Women and Revolution*, Oxford University Press, 1978

Max [Forrester] Eastman
1883–1969
socialist activist, writer and critic

Max Eastman's unfortunate rightward swing in the late 1940s, which allied him with the excesses of McCarthyism, put him beyond the pale for most postwar radicals, but his pacifism and anti-Stalinist Russophilia in the second quarter of the century marked him out as an original and fearless critic of mainstream hypocrisy. Growing up in the same fertile family setting as his feminist sister **Crystal**, he studied philosophy at Columbia University before establishing himself as a journalist and writer in New York's Greenwich Village. In 1912 he became editor of *Masses*, a socialist arts and criticism monthly, changing the title to *The Liberator* as its field of concern expanded, and he published the first of his fifteen books in 1915. Crystal joined him on *The Liberator* from 1917 to 1921, by which time he was in great demand as a socialist antiwar speaker and writer. The same year that she left for England he paid an extended visit to the Soviet Union, and for the next twenty years his mission became explaining communism to his fellow Americans. As **Trotsky**'s friend and literary agent, Max Eastman was one of the first Americans to take time to understand the intricacies of Soviet communism, which meant that he was also among the first to criticise the Stalin regime at a time when many American intellectuals were starting to embrace Soviet-style socialism. While his fellow liberals acclaimed Russia as a model of social and economic justice, he published detailed evidence to the contrary in *Stalin's Russia and the Crisis of Socialism* (1940). Lack of acknowledgement for his literary and critical skills caused a crisis of confidence in the mid-1940s: Max Eastman joined the staff of *Reader's Digest* and allied himself (though unconvincingly) with capitalist progress and nationalistic conservatism. He is best remembered as a fluent and perceptive writer, though his contribution to interwar socialist debate in America is now being rediscovered.

Max Eastman, *Love and Revolution: My Journey Through an Epoch*, Random House, 1964
Milton Cantor, *Max Eastman*, Twayne, 1970
William L. O'Neill, *The Last Romantic: A Life of Max Eastman*, Oxford University Press, 1978

Paul Ekins
1950–
environmental economist

Born in Indonesia and raised there and in Britain, the radical economist Paul Ekins was educated at London and Bradford Universities where important influences were **Theodore Roszak**, **Fritz Schumacher** and **Herman Daly**. In 1983 he cofounded The Other Economic Summit (TOES), an international network of economists working for the development of human potential, social justice and sustainable use of resources: starting with London in 1984 and Bonn in 1985, TOES has run an annual conference alongside the mainstream Economic Summits. In 1986 he caused much provocation within the UK Green Party when he and fellow member Jonathan Tyler, having attempted and failed to amend the constitution to regularise the structure of the party, outlined plans for a parallel organisation called Maingreen. Accused of attempting to subvert the party, he resigned after the 1987 elections. From 1987 to 1990 he was research director of the Right Livelihood Award (widely known as the alternative Nobel Prize), and remains an advisor. In 1988 he became coordinator of the Living Economy Network; together with his research at Birkbeck College, Cambridge University and the Schumacher College in Devon, these positions have enabled Paul Ekins to become a powerful and fluent exponent and populariser of current thought and practice in the field of appropriate economics.

Paul Ekins (ed.), *The Living Economy: A New Economics in the Making*, Routledge and Kegan Paul, 1986
Paul Ekins, *A New World Order: Grassroots Movements for Global Change*, Routledge, 1992
Paul Ekins and Manfred Max-Neef (eds), *Real-Life Economics: Understanding Wealth Creation*, Routledge, 1992

[Henry] Havelock Ellis
1859–1939
doctor, author, sexologist

Born to lower middle-class parents in Croydon, England, Havelock Ellis decided at the age of twenty, while teaching in Australia, to make the study of sex and morality his life's work. Returning to England to train as a doctor at St Thomas's Hospital in London, he also entered the growing circle of socialist thinkers and agitators which included **Karl Marx**'s daughter Eleanor, homosexual activist **Edward Carpenter** and South African feminist **Olive Schreiner**. In *The New Spirit* (1890) he set out his belief in social democracy and the emancipation of women, at the same time warning that the key problem facing the new century was sexual ignorance and bigotry. In 1891 he married Edith Lees, an open lesbian, and this and his growing friendships with homosexuals and endorsement by sex reform organisations helped him develop his ideas about the shortcomings and dangers of Victorian morality. A major 1894 study, *Man and Woman*, quietly and carefully established his views on the naturalness of homosexual desire, but a growing collaboration with the gay poet and critic John Addington Symonds led to the threat of legal action. Havelock Ellis's pioneering study of *Sexual Inversion* (1897) became the first of his seven-volume *Studies in the Psychology of Sex*, a work which in Great Britain was not considered suitable for readers other than medical professionals until 1935. *Sexual Inversion* made a clear distinction between 'homosexuality', any sexual relation between people of the same sex, and 'inversion', a congenital condition, though he was well aware in his later work of the problems this posed in practice. By subsequently concentrating his arguments on the importance of 'inversion' he placed himself in the mainstream of homosexual rights camapigners like Edward Carpenter and **Magnus Hirschfeld**, and always stressed the normality and 'respectability' of homosexuality. Because his ideas were based primarily on biology rather than socio-politics, however, he found it hard to integrate his ideas with wider radical issues. Thus although he supported women's and lesbian rights, and contributed a preface to **Radclyffe Hall**'s *The Well of Loneliness* in 1928, he saw women's sexuality as essentially passive. In 1938–39, just before he died in Suffolk, England, Havelock Ellis wrote an honest and engaging autobiography.

Havelock Ellis (new edn. with foreword by Françoise Delisle and intro. by Alan Hull Walton), *My Life*, Spearman, 1967
Sheila Rowbotham and Jeffrey Weeks, *Socialism and the New Life: The Personal and Sexual Politics of Edward Carpenter and Havelock Ellis*, Pluto, 1977
Phyllis Grosskurth, *Havelock Ellis: A Biography*, Knopf, 1980
Jeffrey Weeks, *Coming Out*, Quartet, 1987

Hans Magnus Enzenberger
1929–
writer, socialist, social critic

The German writer and critic Hans Magnus Enzenberger has been called 'the true heir to **Brecht**', and his imaginative writing and socialist-anarchist outlook have much in common with his fellow countryman. He grew up in the Bavarian town of Kaufbergen, being evacuated in 1942 to the Franconian countryside. He studied at Erlangen, Freiburg, Hamburg and Paris, and from the mid-1950s worked mostly in publishing and broadcasting.

He travelled extensively, including prolonged visits to Cuba and the Soviet Union in the 1960s, and in 1965 he founded the influential **new left** journal *Kursbuch*, which he edited until 1985. Since 1985 he has edited the Munich-based journal *Transatlantik*. In 1967 he married the Russian intellectual Maria Makarova, a radical thinker herself and the first woman to be elected a fellow of King's College, Cambridge; they separated in the early 1980s and in 1986 Enzenberger married his third wife, Katherina Bonitz. From the mid-60s onwards he was an important voice in West German leftwing culture, and in 1967–68 was a fluent supporter of radical social change, seeing the student-based revolution as a necessary departure from traditional German subservience. In several books and collections of essays he has explored the role of the media in setting the social and political agenda, and in recent years has written and spoken extensively on the links between politics, legislation and crime: his theory is that rules only work because people can bend them, and he has coined the neoanarchist dictum that 'anarchy prevents chaos'.

> Hans Magnus Enzenberger, *The Consciousness Industry: On Literature, Politics and the Media*, Seabury Press, 1974
> Hans Magnus Enzenberger, *Raids and Reconstructions: Essays on Politics, Crime and Culture*, Pluto, 1976

Vilma Espín [Guillois de Castro]
1930–
women's rights campaigner

Cuba's pioneering and controversial women's rights campaigner, Vilma Espín Guillois was born in Santiago to a Cuban father and French mother, and studied to be a chemical engineer. In 1952, during her fourth year at Oriente University, she became a political activist after Fulgencia Batista's pre-election coup which ended democratic government. She went to Massachusetts Institute of Technology as a postgraduate, returning to Cuba via Mexico, where she met the exiled Fidel Castro. She assisted in forming first aid brigades and women's units in preparation for the abortive revolution of November 1956, and afterwards liaised with the rebels in hiding. She worked alongside Raul Castro, Fidel's brother, who was to become chief of Cuba's armed forces: they married in January 1959 and had four children. After Castro came to power she led a delegation to the Congress of the International Federation of Democratic Women in Chile, and in 1960 helped to establish the Federación de Mujeres de Cuba (FMC, Federation of Cuban Women), to counter illiteracy, gain political participation, and organise workshops and employment. At Fidel's request Vilma Espín became the head of the FMC, and also became a member of the central committee of the Cuban Communist Party. She declared the FMC to be a feminine organisation rather than a feminist one, believing that the future of Cuban women would be best served by integration into the revolution rather than by the 'Western' route of individual fulfilment. In 1975 she was the chief architect of the radical Cuban Family Code, the key article of which reads 'Both partners must care for the family they have created, and each must cooperate with the other in the education, upbringing and guidance of the children.' The FMC, still led by Vilma Espín, claims a membership of about two million, or 80% of Cuban women and, acting as 'first lady' to her bachelor brother-in-law, she wields considerable power within Cuba. Her position as both member of the country's power élite and voice for women's rights has led to some difficult compromises and much criticism from human rights campaigners, but there is little doubt that the FMC has had considerable influence in improving the situation of women in Cuba.

Vilma Espín Guillois (ed. Deborah Shnookal), *Cuban Women Confront the Future: Three Decades after the Revolution*, Ocean, 1991

Elizabeth Stone (ed.), *Women and the Cuban Revolution*, Pathfinder Press, 1981

Alda do Espírito Santo
1926–
poet, teacher, political activist

Born in the Portuguese island colony of São Tomé e Principe and trained as a teacher, Alda do Espírito Santo developed a deep hatred for the virtual enslavement of her people that first found its voice in poetry. From 1953, when she penned her angry response to the massacre of Angolan Creoles by the Portuguese army in a poem entitled 'Onde estâo os homens cacados neste vente de lourura?' ('Where are the men swept by this wind of folly?'), her poems were included in several Portuguese and English anthologies of African writing. In the early 1960s she became active in the islands' growing liberation movement, and in 1965 was arrested and imprisoned for several months by the Portuguese authorities. Four years later she was active in the formation of the Movement for the Liberation of São Tomé e Principe, which in 1974 played the leading part in the transition to independence. She has since continued to work for human rights in her home country, and to write and teach.

Moore and Beier (eds), *Modern Poetry from Africa*, Penguin, 1968

Fang Lizhi
1936–
scientist, teacher, democracy campaigner

Fang Lizhi, an astrophysicist, cosmologist and author of fifteen books, who has in recent years consistently used his position to petition for human rights in China, has often been called 'China's **Sakharov**'. The son of a working class family (his father worked on the railways), he studied physics at Beijing University and became an assistant researcher at the Science Academy. He married fellow scientist Li Shuxian, and in 1957 both were labelled 'rightists' and expelled from the Communist Party. From 1957 to 1968 Fang Lizhi was a researcher at the Science and Technology University of Hefei in Anhui Province, where in 1968 he gained a professorship and finally became vice-chancellor. In 1986 he was an outspoken supporter of student demands for greater democracy and academic freedom, and as a result was expelled again from the Party in early 1987. In December 1988, disturbed by the intransigence of the Xiaoping government, Fang Lizhi took the unprecedented step of sending an open letter to Deng Xiaoping urging him to release all political prisoners and declare a general amnesty. Threatened with arrest, he and his family took refuge in the American Embassy in Beijing. In 1990 they were allowed to leave China: after a short stay in England Fang Lizhi took up a teaching post at the Institute for Advanced Study in Princeton, New Jersey, from which position he continues to write and petition for human rights in his native country. His under-standing of both Western and Chinese scientific and cultural traditions makes him a wise and thoughtful critic of both East and West, as shown in his 1991 collection of essays *Bringing Down the Great Wall*.

> Fang Lizhi (trans. and ed. James H. Williams), *Bringing Down the Great Wall: Writings on Science, Culture and Democracy in China*, Knopf, 1991

Frantz Fanon
1925–1961
psychiatrist, socialist writer and activist

Frantz Fanon, born in Martinique and trained in Paris, was one of the first black writer-activists to make it clear that racism benefited neither black nor white, and that the privileged native minority within the developing world, economically attached to capitalism and imperialism, could not be trusted to improve conditions for the poor majority. While studying medicine and psychiatry at Lyons University Fanon edited the black student journal *Tom-tom* and, after receiving his medical degree in 1951, was appointed head of the psychiatry department of Blida-Joinville Hospital in Algeria. A year later his first book was published: *Peau noire, masques blancs* (*Black Skin, White Masks*) drew on his own experience to show both the deliberate and the more subtle ways in which black people are taught to feel guilty about being black. In the mid-1950s he became an energetic supporter of the Algerian struggle for independence from France; in 1956 he became editor of the Algerian FLN (Front de Libération Nationale) newspaper and was a delegate at the First Congress of Black Writers and Artists in Paris. It was in late 1956 that he gave up medicine and became a fulltime writer and activist, but in 1959 he was seriously injured by a mine, and a year later, while Ghanaian ambassador of the Algerian provi-sional government, contracted the leukemia from which he died in a Washington hospital in December 1961. Frantz Fanon's reputation rests primarily on *Les damnés de la terre* (*The Wretched of the Earth*), written and published in the last year of his life, in which he condemned Africa's black bourgeoisie as a parasitic class, using nationalist rhetoric to maintain their own privilege: the real revolution in the developing world would come when the poor peasantry – 'the wretched of the earth' – rose to mass rebellion and refused to support oppression through their acquiescence.

Frantz Fanon (trans. Charles Lam Markmann), *Black Skin, White Masks*, Grove
  Press, 1952
Frantz Fanon (trans. Constance Farrington), *The Wretched of the Earth*, Grove
  Press, 1963
David Caute, *Fanon*, Fontana, 1970
Peter Geismar, *Fanon: The Revolutionary as Prophet*, Dial, 1971
Adele Jinadu, *Fanon: In Search of the African Revolution*, KPI, 1986

Shulamith Firestone
1945–
radical feminist activist

Shulamith Firestone was born in Ottawa, Canada, and grew up and was
educated in the US midwest. A political activist in Chicago, she attempted
to introduce women's issues to the new left, notably as an agenda item for
a 1967 National Conference for New Politics, where it was dismissed as
being beneath consideration. Soon afterwards she moved to New York City
to cofound New York Radical Women, the city's first women's liberation
group. She cofounded Redstockings in February 1969 as a militantly activist
radical feminist group, and the following autumn cofounded New York
Radical Feminists as a model for a grassroots feminist movement for radical
structural change. For two or three years Shulamith Firestone, sometimes
quoted as the founder of radical feminism, was highly visible, coediting
the important collections of articles on women's liberation *Notes from the
First Year* (1968) and *Notes from the Second Year* (1970). In 1970 her only
book was published, the influential *The Dialectic of Sex: The Case for Feminist
Revolution*. Applying Marx's historical-materialist dialectic to an analysis of
sex, class and culture, she saw the subordination of women as the first and
most fundamental form of oppression. She regarded women's reproductive function as the source of their vulnerability, and looked to technological advances to free them from the 'barbaric' processes of pregnancy and
lactation. She was, however, prepared to allow culture an important role
in male supremacy, and her definition of human culture as 'the attempt to
realise the conceivable in the possible' invites the exercise of imagination.
Ironically, by the time the book was published Shulamith Firestone had
become disillusioned with the response among feminists to her revolutionary position, and had dropped out of the **women's movement**.

Shulamith Firestone, *The Dialectic of Sex: The Case for Feminist Revolution*,
  Morrow, 1970
Alice Echols, *Daring to Be Bad: Radical Feminism in America, 1967–1975*,
  Minnesota University Press, 1989

Elizabeth Gurley Flynn
1890–1964
labour and civil liberties activist

Born in 1890 to Irish-American socialists, Elizabeth Gurley Flynn grew up
in New England mill towns and New York City. The vitality of her

impoverished family fostered the development of a lively sensibility and, with her first public speech at sixteen on the subject of women and socialism, her career was launched. Within a year Flynn was speaking for the **Industrial Workers of the World** (IWW); within two she had taken part in her first strike, dropped out of high school to go on a national speaking tour, and married another IWW organiser. Because she would not curtail her schedule, they separated in 1910 after the birth of their son, who was raised by her mother and sister. For a decade Flynn was an IWW organiser in the northeast USA, participating in the famous 1912 textile workers' strike in Lawrence, Massachusetts. She took an active part in many labour campaigns, often in the face of gruelling conditions and police violence, and organised worker support and defence committees. As government repression intensified she was instrumental in setting up the Workers Defense Union for immigrant activists facing deportation, and the **American Civil Liberties Union** (ACLU). In 1926 she suffered a collapse precipitated by the ending of her relationship with the anarchist Carlo Tresca, her lover since the 1912 Lawrence strike. For the next ten years she lived in Portland, Oregon, with her friend and colleague Marie Equie. Returning in 1936 to New York City, Flynn joined the Communist Party, resumed public speaking, and wrote a column for the *Daily Worker*. When in 1948 party members were indicted for conspiracy to advocate violent overthrow of the government, she headed their defence committee; in 1951 she was indicted and found guilty on the same charge. When she was released in 1957 after 28 months in prison, she continued organising for the Communist Party and became the first woman to head its national committee. After winning a case before the Supreme Court for the restoration of her passport, she made three trips to the Soviet Union. She died there during her final visit in 1964.

Elizabeth Gurley Flynn, *The Rebel Girl: An Autobiography, My First Life (1906–1926)*, International Publishers, 1955
Elizabeth Gurley Flynn, *The Alderson Story: My Life as a Political Prisoner*, International Publishers, 1963
Rosalyn Baxandall, *Words on Fire: The Life and Writings of Elizabeth Gurley Flynn*, Rutgers University Press, 1987

Michel Foucault
1926–1984
philosopher, social critic

The French philosopher and critic Michel Foucault has been an important influence for many leftwing intellectuals in the last quarter of the twentieth century, bringing together insights from history, psychology and philosophy in a wideranging exploration of the ways in which power can be used and abused. He grew up in Poitiers, and studied philosophy and psychology at the École Normale Supérieure in Paris before teaching in Sweden, Poland and Germany. In 1960 he returned to France to teach at the University of Clermont-Ferrand and to receive his master's degree: the following year saw the publication of his monumental history of madness, *Folie et déraison* (1965 in English). During the student revolt of **May 1968** he supported many of the demands of the protestors, often sharing a platform with **Jean-Paul Sartre**; this was also a personal turning point, and he thenceforward committed himself to the analysis of power structures and relationships in terms of practical problems and solutions. In 1970, four years after his history of ideas *Les mots et les choses* (1970 in English as *The Order of Things*) was published, he was appointed to the chair of 'history of systems of thought' at the Collège de France, but he also continued to work on power and madness – *Surveiller et punir* (*Discipline and Punish*, 1970) showed how disciplinary institutions are central nodes in the network of power relationships. Perhaps his best known work is in the field of power and sexuality: the first of six proposed volumes of *Histoire de la sexualité* (*The History of Sexuality*) appeared in 1976 (the second and third volumes were published after his death), again showing how the accepted standards of society provide the rationale for exercising power over those classified as 'deviant', and how these profound prejudices must be addressed if liberation is to be achieved.

Michel Foucault, *Madness and Civilisation: A History of Insanity in the Age of Reason*, Pantheon, 1965
Michel Foucault, *Discipline and Punish*, Pantheon, 1970
Michel Foucault, *The History of Sexuality*, Vol. 1, Pantheon, 1978
Alan Sheridan, *Michel Foucault: The Will to Truth*, Tavistock, 1980
Barry Smart, *Michel Foucault*, Tavistock, 1985

Matthew Fox
1940–
priest, social critic

Matthew Fox, the American priest who very publicly left the Roman Catholic Church in April 1994 in protest against the religious establishment's intransigence on political and ecological issues, is best known for his exploration of 'creation spirituality', which he defines as 'a joyful response to life itself, a deep ecumenism which draws on the wisdom of all religions to recover our inherent divinity and preserve the diversity of life on our planet'. Matthew Fox joined the Dominican Order in Chicago in 1960, and was ordained as a priest seven years later, completing his studies at the Aquinas Institute, the Institut Catholique in Paris, and the University of Münster in Germany. In the early 1970s, influenced equally by Christian mysticism and social activism, he started to write books about creative, socially-aware spirituality, including *On Becoming a Musical, Mystical Bear* (1972) and *Whee! We, Wee All The Way Home* (1976). In 1977 he established the Institute in Culture and Creation Spirituality at Mundelein College in Chicago, which six years later moved to Oakland, California, as an affiliate of Holy Names College. 1983 saw the publication of *Original Blessing*, a primer in creation spirituality which called for compassion and justice in linking human experience and the lessons of the natural world. In 1984 his criticism of religious dogma, his sanctioning of homosexuality, and an invitation to the feminist activist **Starhawk** to teach at Holy Names brought him to the attention of the Vatican hierarchy: despite widespread support he was banned from teaching for a year in May 1988. As soon as he was able to speak publicly again he continued to criticise the oppressive practices of the church, drawing on feminist and socialist sources to demonstrate the true role of spirituality in a rapidly-changing world. Inevitably, in March 1993 Matthew Fox was expelled from the Dominican Order, and a year later decided to leave the Roman Catholic Church, his spiritual home for twenty-seven years, for the relative freedom of the Episcopalian Church. The combination of joy and responsibility embraced by Matthew Fox's creation spirituality has provided inspiration and hope for many thousands of Christians, and he continues to be a popular speaker throughout the English-speaking world, and increasingly in Germany and Switzerland.

> Matthew Fox, *The Coming of the Cosmic Christ: The Healing of Mother Earth and the Birth of a Global Renaissance*, Harper and Row, 1988
> Matthew Fox, *Creation Spirituality: Liberating Gifts for the Peoples of the Earth*, Harper San Francisco, 1991
> Matthew Fox, *The Reinvention of Work: A New Vision of Livelihood for Our Time*, Harper San Francisco, 1994

Paulo Freire
1921–
educator

Paulo Freire was born and grew up in the north-eastern Brazilian city of Recife. He trained as a teacher and specialised in the planning and implementation of literacy programmes, soon recognising that, though political and social empowerment cannot be achieved without the freedom and understanding offered by literacy, illiteracy does not mean ignorance of ways of 'reading' the world. As coordinator of Brazil's National Plan of Adult Literacy in the 1950s he developed an approach to education which combines learning with the mobilisation and organisation of the under-privileged, a process he calls 'conscienticisation'. By the mid-1960s versions of his method were being used in literacy campaigns throughout Latin America. With the Brazilian military coup of May 1964 Paulo Freire was forced into exile, working first in Chile and later in the USA and Guinea-Bissau; 1970 saw the publication of his best-known book, *Pedagogy of the Oppressed*, which was quickly translated into several languages. From 1974 to 1981 he was based in Geneva as a consultant with the World Council of Churches; he returned to Brazil in 1981 to become professor of education at the Catholic University of São Paulo, and in 1991 was appointed secretary of education for the city. Freire's intellectual sources are diverse, from the neo-Marxist philosophy of Althusser to the revolutionary methods of **Che Guevara** and **Mao Zedong,** and they have inevitably mellowed over the years. What Paulo Freire has succeeded in doing, however, is emphasising that the world's oppressed millions have a right to an appropriate type of education that they choose and help to organise themselves, an education which springs from their particular needs and situations and is not dictated by privileged outsiders. He has clarified the links between power and knowledge in a very practical way, and provided an educational model of political empowerment for many of the social movements of the 1970s and beyond.

Paulo Freire (trans. Myra Ramos), *Pedagogy of the Oppressed*, Herder and Herder, 1970

Paulo Freire (trans. Donaldo Macedo), *The Politics of Education: Culture, Power and Liberation*, Bergin and Garvey, 1985

Peter McLaren and Peter Leonard (eds), *Paulo Freire: A Critical Encounter*, Routledge, 1992

Betty Friedan [Betty Naomi Goldstein]
1921–
feminist writer and organiser

Born in Peoria, Illinois, the feminist Betty Friedan has spent most of her adult life living and working in New York City. She received a degree in psychology from Smith College in 1947, and later studied at the University of California at Berkeley and at the Esalen Institute. In 1947 she married Carl Friedan; they had three children, and were divorced in 1969. Her first book, *The Feminine Mystique* (1963), was groundbreaking in its time because it addressed the pain of middle-class women submerged in the domestic sphere and raised issues at the heart of the feminist struggles of earlier generations. It had an enormous impact and is widely regarded as the book which launched modern feminism in the USA. Betty Friedan was the founder and first president (1966–1970) of the **National Organization for Women** (NOW). Operating from the premise that 'the gut issues of this revolution involve employment and education and new social institutions', she came into direct conflict with the more hardline aspects of the burgeoning **women's movement**. She saw radical feminism's politicisation of personal life as a diversion from the real struggle of integrating women into the public sphere, criticised cultural feminism as a retreat from the movement's real necessities and possibilities, and called lesbianism 'the lavender menace', fearing that it would undermine the movement's public credibility. In 1976 she published a collection of essays, *It Changed My Life*, and in 1981, while she was at Columbia University researching changing sex roles and the ageing process, she wrote the 'sequel' to *The Feminine Mystique*, *The Second Stage*. Here she argues against a '*feminist* mystique' that would deny motherhood and nurturing as part of women's person-hood. In recent years Betty Friedan's time has been divided between teaching at a number of US universities, writing and campaigning, focusing on furthering women's integration into the public sphere and lobbying for reforms in divorce, abortion law, employment, housing and education.

Betty Friedan, *The Feminine Mystique*, Norton, 1963

Betty Friedan, *The Second Stage*, Summit, 1981
Alice Echols, *Daring to be Bad: Radical Feminism in America 1967–1975*, University
of Minnesota Press, 1989

Erich Fromm
1900–1980
psychoanalyst, teacher, writer

Born in Frankfurt-am-Rhein, the only child of Jewish parents, Erich Fromm
studied at Frankfurt and Heidelberg and then trained in psychoanalysis at
the Berlin Psychoanalytical Institute. From 1928 to 1938 he was associated
with the Institute for Social Research, and after he fled Nazi Germany for
the USA in 1933 he worked and taught in New York alongside other
neo-Freudians including **Karen Horney**, Harry Sullivan, and Frieda Reich-
mann, whom he married but later divorced. Though his training was in
classical Freudian analysis, his interest in political, cultural and economic
influences made him a learned and fluent critic of control-based regimes.
His deep knowledge of both Freud and **Marx** enabled him to comprehend
and develop their common approaches, whilst remaining convinced that
both oversimplified the human condition, with potentially destructive
consequences. His first book, *Escape from Freedom*, published in 1941
shortly after he broke with the Institute for Social Research, described how
the transition from feudalism to capitalism alienated people from land and
community, increasing their insecurity and their dependence on external
power systems such as fascism. In *Man for Himself* (1947) and *The Sane Society*
(1951) he expanded these themes in a contemporary context. In 1943 Erich
Fromm had left the American Institute of Psychoanalysis because of what
he saw as a growing over-professionalisation of the discipline, and from
1949 to 1971 he lived in Mexico, where in 1951 he became a professor at
the National University of Mexico and shortly afterwards set up the Mexican
Institute of Psychoanalysis. He continued to travel widely, especially in the
USA, where he was active in SANE (National Committee for a Sane Nuclear
Policy – he provided the acronym). The 1955–1974 period also saw a lively
debate between Fromm and **Herbert Marcuse**, who criticised the former
for unwittingly siding with capitalism and concentrating on personal needs
at the expense of practical and political action. Erich Fromm's best known
books, *The Art of Loving* (1956), *The Crisis of Psychoanalysis* (1970), *The
Anatomy of Human Destructiveness* (1973) and *To Have or To Be?* (1976),
nevertheless show him to be a prolific, sensitive and fearless critic of
capitalism, consumerism, violence and imposed authority. In the face of
widespread disempowerment he remained an optimist, believing that
humanistic socialism could be achieved. Fromm moved to Switzerland in
1971, where he continued to write and research, and died in Muralto in
March 1980.

Erich Fromm, *Escape from Freedom*, Rinehart and Winston, 1941
Erich Fromm, *To Have or To Be?*, Harper, 1976

John Schaar, *Escape from Authority: The Perspectives of Erich Fromm*, Basic Books, 1961

David Burston, *The Legacy of Erich Fromm*, Harvard, 1991

Mahatma [Mohandas Karamchand] Gandhi
1869–1948
social and political campaigner

Mohandas Gandhi's achievement in guiding India through the turbulent decades prior to independence was considerable, as was his commitment to nonviolence, self-knowledge and spiritual mastery, but his influence quickly spread far beyond his home country to provide an inspiration rarely matched in the twentieth century. Born into a politically active family in Porbander, he trained in London as a lawyer, and in 1893 was offered a post as legal adviser to an Indian firm in Pretoria, South Africa. During his twenty years in South Africa he worked diligently to protest against racist laws, developing his philosophy and practice of nonviolent resistance or 'satyagraha'. Within a few years of returning to India in 1915 he had become the acknowledged leader of the independence movement, urging the transformation of the Indian National Congress into a powerful nationwide organisation and the inclusion in political decision-making of all sections of the population, including women, landless peasants and the traditional 'untouchables'. He both stressed and modelled the need for courage, self-respect, justice, compassion, and inner and outer peace, and was prepared to experiment and take risks, though his personal relationships, especially with his wife Kasturbai whom he married when he was thirteen, were often less than respectful. The basis of Gandhi's conviction was his belief in a higher intelligence or 'satya', embodied in all living things. This required people to care for one another and to embrace 'ahimsa' or nonviolence to achieve cooperation and avoid coercion. He saw the strength of the state as violence in a concentrated form, and urged the use of nonviolent civil disobedience against arbitrary official power, often joining such demonstrations of noncooperation to underline his solidarity with the oppressed majority. He rejected Western-style industrialisation, insisting that the future of India lay with small-scale agriculture and manufacturing: to prove his point he refused to wear factory-made clothes, and most often wore nothing more than a loincloth, the uniform of India's poorest. Four times – in 1922, 1930, 1933 and 1942 – he was arrested and jailed by the British authorities, to which he replied by undertaking hunger strikes. In the late 1940s, with violence growing between Hindus and Moslems, Gandhi became convinced that Indian independence could only be achieved at the cost of partitioning the country and, when it appeared that an independent Indian government would renege on its promise to transfer Pakistan's assets to the newly-independent Moslem state, he successfully fasted in order to force India to honour its promises. His insistence upon justice cost him his life, for he was assassinated by a fervent Hindu nationalist at a prayer meeting in January 1948. For thirty years he had been hailed as the 'mahatma' or 'great soul' of India, and his ideas and practices have inspired many of the great pacifists and human rights activists of the last half century.

Mahatma Gandhi (ed. Raghavan Iyer), *The Moral and Political Thought of Mahatma Gandhi*, Oxford University Press, 1973
Mahatma Gandhi (ed. Raghavan Iyer), *The Essential Writings of Mahatma Gandhi*, Oxford University Press, 1991
George Woodcock, *Gandhi*, Fontana, 1972
Ved Mehta, *Mahatma Gandhi and his Apostles*, Viking, 1977

Marianella García-Villas
1948–1983
lawyer, journalist, human rights campaigner

In 1978, even before the military coup of October 1979 heralded wide-spread torture and bloodshed, Salvadoran lawyer and congress member Marianella García-Villas first brought the world's attention to the massive human rights violations that were taking place in her country. When she was 26 she was elected on the Christian Democratic ticket as the youngest congressional deputy in the El Salvador government, but resigned shortly before the coup because her fellow politicians refused to take seriously the escalating number of civilians being killed by the armed forces. In 1978 she initiated the Commission for Human Rights of El Salvador (CDHES); within weeks she was detained and tortured, her parents' home was destroyed, and her family was forced into exile. In 1981 the CDHES offices in San Salvador were twice raided and bombed, and three of her coworkers were detained and 'disappeared', but still Marianella continued to collect detailed evidence of killings and other human rights abuses, though she decided to move the main office of CDHES to Mexico City. In January 1983 she returned to El Salvador to collect evidence on the use of chemical weapons by the Salvadoran army for a United Nations report; on March 14th she was captured, tortured, raped and murdered. When the war in El Salvador finally ended in 1990, largely as a result of world pressure based on information supplied by organisations like CDHES, more than 70,000 Salvadorans were dead and more than a million had fled their country.

Marilyn Thomson, *Women of El Salvador: The Price of Freedom*, Zed, 1986

Marcus [Mosiah] Garvey
1887–1940
civil rights campaigner, pan-Africanism advocate

In the anti-black decades of the 1910s and 1920s, Jamaica-born Marcus Garvey provided hundreds of thousands of African Americans with a renewed pride and inspiration. In 1912–14 he spent two years in London, where he was influenced by ideas about Pan-Africanism, and on his return to Kingston he established, with Amy Ashwood, the Universal Negro Improvement Association (UNIA), a forum for black culture and educational initiatives. In 1916 Marcus Garvey travelled to New York to raise funds for the UNIA: he decided to stay and turn the Association into a political liberation movement. Although black education remained a key element of what became known as 'Garveyism', its main thrust quickly became black nationalism and the establishment of an African homeland for African Americans. By 1921 Marcus Garvey's passionate rhetoric had attracted a million adherents, while his newspaper *Negro World*, though banned in several Caribbean and African countries, carried his appeals far and wide. The UNIA also established a shipping company, the Black Star Line, initially designed to develop commerce between black producers in the Caribbean and US consumers, but with plans to offer passenger services between the Americas and Africa. The Black Star Line served as a powerful aid to black solidarity, but official opposition found an easy target in the UNIA and its growing empire. Marcus Garvey and his organisation came under the scrutiny of Edgar Hoover's infant Federal Bureau of Investigation, which tried unsuccessfully to keep Garvey out of the country following a Caribbean tour in 1921, finally succeeding in convicting him two years later of fraud. By this time he had developed a decidedly patriotic and capitalist stance; since many of his followers were idealistic socialists his shift caused considerable friction within the UNIA. When he chose to meet with Ku Klux Klan leaders in June 1922, on the premise that the UNIA and KKK had similar separatist aims, the more radical members of the UNIA were appalled, and were relieved when in 1925 he was given a five-year prison sentence. He served two years before being pardoned and deported to Jamaica. Although the UNIA was now a divided and splintered organisation, Garvey remained its *de facto* leader until the late 1930s. In the late 1920s his People's Political Party had a shortlived success in Jamaica, but from 1935 he based himself in England. Despite his rightward shift, his message of black consciousness, pan-African unity and cultural resistance caught the imagination of many black activists, and 'Garveyism' continued to inform black nationalism and anti-imperialism for many decades after his death.

Marcus Garvey (ed. Amy Jacques Garvey), *Philosophy and Opinions of Marcus Garvey, or, Africa for the Africans*, Atheneum Press, 1969
David Cronon, *Black Moses: The Story of Marcus Garvey and the Universal Negro Improvement Association*, University of Wisconsin Press, 1955
Amy Jacques Garvey, *Garvey and Garveyism*, Octagon, 1968
Elton Fax, *Garvey: The Story of a Black Pioneer Nationalist*, Dodd, Mead, 1972

[Sri] Aurobindo Ghose
1872–1950
poet, philosopher, political activist

One of India's foremost twentieth-century philosopher-poets and the founder of the renowned ashram at Pondicherry in southern India, Aurobindo Ghose ('Sri' is a Hindu title prefixed to the names of deities and distinguished persons) was also an outspoken critic of British rule in his country. He was born into a well-off family in Konnagar, West Bengal, and for fourteen years from the age of seven lived and was educated in England.

In 1890 he received a scholarship to Kings College, Cambridge, where in 1892 he first publicly advocated Indian freedom in student speeches. Returning to India in 1893, he joined the Baroda State Service, quickly rising to become principal of the State College. To his Hindi and European languages he added Sanskrit, Marathi, Gujurati and Bengali; meanwhile he wrote radical articles for Bombay newspapers and helped to establish a network of revolutionary groups. Aurobindo Ghose married Mrinalini Devi in 1901, but within a few years the political and educational work which took him away from Bengal left both of them to their own personal and spiritual devices. The 1905 partition of Bengal brought his leadership qualities to the fore, and the following year he was the first to declare the need for complete autonomy from British control. He was arrested several times, and following his detention in May 1908 spent a year in prison. In February 1910, on the eve of yet another British search of his offices, he escaped to the French enclave of Pondicherry and withdrew himself from overt political activity. He combined his interest in poetry and yoga with a practical philosophy of individual and collective evolution towards truth and full consciousness. With the assistance of the French couple Paul and Mira Richard, his ashram in Pondicherry grew as disciples came to study his 'integral yoga', taking a more permanent form in 1926 when Aurobindo went into complete seclusion and Mira Richard ('the Mother') became its figurehead until her death in 1974. The ashram's most ambitious project was the establishment of the new city of Auroville to strengthen the educational and community-building aspects of Aurobindo's teaching: by 1970 it had several thousand inhabitants, and despite legal disputes about ownership and land rights the Pondicherry ashram continues to thrive.

Aurobindo Ghose (ed. Robert A. McDermott), *The Essential Aurobindo*, Schocken,1973

Karan Singh, *Prophet of Indian Nationalism: A Study of the Political Thought of Sri Aurobindo Ghosh*, Allen and Unwin, 1963

K.R. Srinivasa Iyengar, *Sri Aurobindo: A Biography and a History*, Sri Aurobindo International Centre, 1985

Charlotte Perkins [Stetson] Gilman [Charlotte Anna Perkins]
1860–1935
writer, feminist

From her earliest years, when her father left the family and her mother, bringing up Charlotte and her brother Thomas in poverty, withheld her affection 'to spare her children disillusionment', Charlotte Perkins knew that the oppression of women could not go unchallenged. She was born in Hartford, Connecticut, but the family moved nineteen times in the first eighteen years of her life, making education and friendships hard to sustain. Working as a governess and art teacher in her late teens and early twenties, she devoted herself to reading, exercise and periods of self-denial. In May 1884 she married Providence artist Charles Stetson, and their daughter Katharine was born the following year. Marriage and childbirth precipitated an illness which rapidly worsened into almost complete breakdown (graphically described in her 1892 story 'The Yellow Wall-Paper'), but the remission resulting from a visit to California on her own in 1885 convinced her that her sanity lay in detachment from Charles: they separated three years later and were divorced in 1894, but when Charles married Charlotte's closest friend, author Grace Ellery Channing, Charlotte remained friends with both and sent Katharine to live with the couple. Still in financial straits, Charlotte travelled, lectured and wrote profusely, becoming much influenced by the ideas of **Edward Bellamy** and the British **Fabians**. In 1898 her acclaimed feminist manifesto *Women and Economics* was published, a passionate and detailed argument for women's economic independence, and the next 25 years saw a constant stream of articles, essays and novels on the theme of equality and emancipation including the feminist utopian novel *Herland* (1915). In 1900 she married her first cousin, the lawyer George Gilman, but settling down was not Charlotte's style, and in addition to her writing and lecturing she became involved in the women's suffrage movement, attending the 1913 International Suffrage Convention in Budapest and cofounding in 1915 (with **Jane Addams** and others) the Woman's Peace Party. She continued to hold a strong feminist line through the 1920s and 30s, insisting that what appeared to be growing sexual freedom was largely at the cost of women's independence. Diagnosed as having breast cancer in 1932 and following George's sudden death two years later, Charlotte Perkins Gilman took her own life in August 1935.

Charlotte Perkins Gilman (ed. Ann Lane), *The Charlotte Perkins Gilman Reader*, Pantheon, 1980

Charlotte Perkins Gilman (ed. Ann Lane), *Herland*, Pantheon, 1979

Charlotte Perkins Gilman, *The Living of Charlotte Perkins Gilman: An Autobiography*, Appleton-Century, 1935 (repr. University of Wisconsin Press, 1991)

Mary Hill, *Charlotte Perkins Gilman: The Making of a Radical Feminist 1860–96*, Temple University Press, 1980

Ann Lane, *To Herland and Beyond: The Life and Work of Charlotte Perkins Gilman*, Pantheon, 1990

Emma Goldman
1869–1940
anarchist, political activist

'Born to ride whirlwinds', wrote an admirer of hers in 1914, and the breadth and passion of Emma Goldman's radical interests are without compare in early twentieth-century anarchism. She was born into an orthodox Jewish family in Kovno, now the Lithuanian city of Kaunas. Unloved by her family (her father was interested only in sons), she found solace in schoolwork and reading, and it was not until she emigrated with her sister Helena to New York in 1885 that she began to feel alive. Her 1887 marriage to fellow factory worker Jacob Kershner failed within months, and she soon became involved in the anarchist movement, being particularly influenced by the ideas of **Petr Kropotkin**. In August 1889 she met two men who were to change her life: Johann Most, editor of the inflammatory newspaper *Freiheit* (*Freedom*), and **Alexander Berkman**, who was to become her lifelong intimate and colleague-in-arms. During the 1892 Homestead dispute she helped Berkman prepare for an unsuccessful assassination attempt on the Carnegie chairman (as a result of which Berkman spent thirteen years in jail), and she went to prison for a year in 1893–94 on a charge of incitement to violence. A magnetic speaker, tireless organiser and copious writer, she crisscrossed America lecturing on anarchism, trade unionism, free love, the new drama and women's autonomy. Subjected to frequent and brutal attacks by police and vigilantes, she waged countless battles for free speech and inspired thousands with her refusal to be cowed into submission. From 1906 to 1917 she edited (latterly with Berkman) the influential radical monthly *Mother Earth*, and published numerous books and pamphlets including *Anarchism and Other Essays* (1911). The US government had long sought a way to rid the country of 'Red Emma': in 1908 they withdrew her US citizenship, sentenced her in June 1917 to two years imprisonment for her involvement in the anticonscription campaign, and in December 1919 deported her (with Berkman and 249 other 'alien radicals') to Russia. She quickly recognised the intolerable oppression of the Bolsheviks and left Russia again in 1921, writing *My Disillusionment in Russia* (1923) in exile in Sweden and Germany. In 1925 she married James Colton to obtain British citizenship and a degree of security, but, ever fearful of economic and emotional dependence, spent the rest of her life travelling, lecturing and campaigning. Following Berkman's suicide in 1936 Emma threw herself into support for the anti-Franco forces in the **Spanish Civil War**, and it was while in Toronto raising funds in February 1940 that she suffered a fatal stroke: the US government relented sufficiently to allow her body to be buried near the Haymarket anarchist martyrs in Chicago's Waldheim Cemetery.

Emma Goldman (ed. Alix Kates Shulman), *Red Emma Speaks: An Emma Goldman Reader*, Schocken, 1982
Emma Goldman, *Living My Life*, Da Capo Press, 1970 (repr. of 1931 ed.)
Richard Drinnon, *Rebel in Paradise*, Bantam, 1961
Alice Wexler, *Emma Goldman in America*, Beacon, 1984
Alice Wexler, *Emma Goldman in Exile*, Bantam, 1989

Vida Goldstein
1869–1949
feminist, pacifist

The pioneering Australian feminist Vida Goldstein was born in Portland, Victoria, and educated at the Presbyterian Ladies College in Melbourne and Melbourne University. In 1900 she became the editor of the feminist journal *The Women's Sphere*, and in 1903, standing as a candidate for the Australian Senate the year after women won the vote, she was the first woman in the English-speaking world to stand for a national legislature.

The following year she was in Europe for the first **International Woman Suffrage Alliance** congress in Berlin, where she was appointed recording secretary. Her interests went far beyond rights for women, and she actively supported a range of social and political isues including the abolition of sweated workshops, widely available birth control, and fair wages legislation. In 1907 she wrote an important article entitled 'Socialism of Today: An Australian View', which attacked free market capitalism and traced the links between poverty, crime and ill health. With the advent of war in 1914, Vida Goldstein directed her energies towards peace campaigning. She was elected chair of the Australian Peace Alliance, and in 1915 founded the Women's Peace Army (WPA). *The Woman Voter*, which Goldstein had edited in 1905, became the unofficial voice of the WPA, focusing on the publication of antiwar material. The most significant contribution of Goldstein and the WPA was a highly successful campaign against Australia's conscription referendums in 1916 and 1917. It was not surprising that the activities of the WPA became targets of attack by established authority – the press, police, and the military. Meetings were often violently disrupted, threats were made to remove their printing press, and WPA mail was subject to government censorship. With the rejection of conscription in the second referendum, Goldstein made her fifth and final attempt to enter the Senate, but her advocacy of peace had lost her considerable support. In 1919 she was invited to attend the International Congress of Women in Zürich as one of the three Australian delegates: the WPA dissolved itself on her departure and *The Woman Voter* ceased publication. Vida Goldstein did not return to Australia for three years, and when she did it was as a practitioner and advocate of the Christian Science Church. She thereafter passed into political obscurity, her only public political act after 1922 being a statement of support sent to a Melbourne antinuclear meeting in 1946.

Norman MacKenzie, 'Vida Goldstein: The Australian Suffragette', *The Australian Journal of Politics and History*, 6, November 1960
Janine Haines, *Suffrage to Sufferance: A Hundred Years of Women in Politics*, Allen and Unwin (Australia), 1992

Paul Goodman
1911–1972
writer, anarchist

In many ways Paul Goodman could be described as an anarchist dilettante with one foot in conventional America and the other firmly in its developing counterculture, a stance guaranteed to ensure conflict and controversy. Born into poverty in Manhattan, he graduated from City College in the early years of the depression. For several years his elder sister supported him while he wrote, studied and taught, and in 1936 he was offered a postgraduate place at the University of Chicago, where he met his first wife and was dismissed because he refused to be discreet about his bisexuality. Returning to New York with a wife and baby, he became film critic for *Partisan Review* and wrote articles and poems, but a shortlived teaching post in a progressive school ended when he was accused of seducing his students. As an anarchist, pacifist, draft-dodger and sexual experimenter it was hard for him to find work or publishers, but 1947 saw the publication of *Communitas*, an important critique of town planning written with his brother Percival, and four years later he collaborated with Frederick Perls and Ralph Hefferline on *Gestalt Therapy*, the cornerstone of an influential new technique in psychotherapy. Now remarried and with a second child to support, he turned to offering psychotherapy for a living, though never stopped writing for the anarchist and pacifist press. His best-known book, *Growing Up Absurd*, appeared at just the right moment to inspire and shape the nascent thrust of political activism: its mix of American liberal heritage and idealism, exhorting the country's youth to complete a range of 'unfinished revolutions', brought Paul Goodman's name to the forefront of radical thinking. For the next decade he travelled widely, lecturing and writing, but by the late 1960s, following a heart attack and the death of his son in a hiking accident, he had turned to more personal themes, writing in *New Reformation* (1970) that 'I want only that the children have bright eyes, the river be clean, food and sex be available, and nobody be pushed around.'

Paul Goodman, *Growing Up Absurd*, Random House, 1960
Paul Goodman, *Utopian Essays and Practical Proposals*, Random House, 1962
Paul Goodman, *People or Personnel*, Random House, 1965
Peter Parisi (ed.), *Artist of the Actual: Essays on Paul Goodman*, Scarecrow, 1986
Kingsley Widmer, *Paul Goodman*, Twayne, 1980

Natalya [Yevgenevna] Gorbanevskaya
1936–
poet, editor, human rights activist

The Russian poet Natalya Gorbanevskaya is best known for her human rights campaigning in the 1960s, and particularly for her part in the August 1968 Red Square demonstration against the Soviet invasion of Czechoslovakia. Already an established writer and poet in her early twenties, she had been publishing in *samizdat* from 1961, and a few of her poems had appeared in official journals in 1966. In April 1968 she was a founding editor of the human rights movement's journal, *A Chronicle of Current Events*, and was briefly detained; four months later she and seven colleagues staged a public demonstration against the Czech invasion in Moscow's Red Square. Following this and more than a year of other outspoken public protests, Natalya Gorbanevskaya was arrested and imprisoned in December 1969, first in Butyrki Prison and then in a psychiatric hospital in Kazan, experiences described vividly in *Red Square at Noon* (1972). She was released in February 1972 and continued to write steadily, including fiction, poetry and social and political criticism. In 1975, fearing further reprisals, she emigrated to France, where since 1983 she has been working in Paris as an editor for the important emigré journal *Kontinent*, publishing and reviewing new writing from Russia and Eastern Europe.

Natalia Gorbanevskaya (trans. Alexander Lieven), *Red Square at Noon*, Deutsch, 1972

Natalya Gorbanevskaya (ed. Daniel Weissbort), *Selected Poems: with a Transcript of her Trial and Papers relating to her Detention in a Prison Psychiatric Hospital*, Carcanet, 1972

Catriona Kelly, 'Natalya Gorbanevskaya', *An Encyclopedia of Continental Women Writers*, St James Press, 1991

André Gorz
1924–
philosopher, social critic

The innovative socialist writer and critic André Gorz was born into a middle class family in Vienna, his father a Jew and his mother Christian. As a schoolboy he watched the growing Nazi threat take over his country until, in July 1939, the family left Austria for Switzerland. At the age of sixteen he decided to 'become French' to avoid the pain of choosing between his different Germanic roots: **Jean-Paul Sartre** became his mentor, and in 1948 Gorz moved to Paris, where he and Sartre became close colleagues. The formative experiences of his early life are described in his philosophical autobiography, *Le traître* (1958, 1989 in English), written a few years after he moved to Paris, which was his home until he 'retired' to write and garden in a village in northern Burgundy in 1987. The existential philosophy and social criticism of Sartre and his circle inspired Gorz to write about the links between the philosophy of autonomy and freedom and real-world politics. In 1950 he was one of the founders of the influential journal *Le nouvel observateur*, for which he wrote under the pseudonym Michel Bosquet for nearly twenty years, and for many years he edited its sister journal *Les temps modernes*. His early writings offered robust support for working class struggle, and his 1964 book *Stratégie ouvrière et néocapitalisme* (1967 in English) was one of the few to anticipate the links between workers and students which developed from the events of **May 1968**. An early interest in the developing ecology movement resulted in *Ecologie et politique* (1975, 1980 in English), raising a series of linked environmental and development issues which helped shape green-tinted socialist thinking. Ever abreast of current developments, he foresaw in *Adieu au prolétariat* (1980, 1982 in English) and *Les chemins du paradis* (1983, 1985 in English) how work-related class divisions would break down with the advent of new technology that allowed a redefinition of work as both liberating and empowering self-exploration. For many, however, Gorz's most important book is his *Métamorphoses du travail* (1988, 1989 in English as *Critique of Economic Reason*), in which he forcefully questions the colonisation of daily life by the demonstrably false logic of conventional economics.

André Gorz, *The Traitor*, Verso, 1989

André Gorz, *Strategy for Labour: A Radical Proposal*, Beacon, 1967

André Gorz, *Ecology as Politics*, South End Press, 1980

André Gorz, *Paths to Paradise: On the Liberation from Work*, Pluto, 1985

André Gorz, *Critique of Economic Reason*, Verso, 1989

Judy Grahn
1940–
lesbian poet, publisher, cultural historian

Born in Chicago to working class parents and growing up in New Mexico, the radical feminist poet Judy Grahn began writing as a child, but stopped once she left home. A possible career in the US Air Force ended when she was expelled at 21 for being a lesbian, but her true vocation re-emerged when she began writing again at 26 after a serious illness. She attended six colleges, ultimately receiving a degree from San Francisco State University in 1984. Long before then, however, she had emerged as a powerfully creative and nurturing force in the community of women's and lesbian-feminist culture. In 1969 she cofounded the Women's Press Collective, one of the earliest feminist presses enabling 'unpublishable' women to reach their audience, and published her first book, *Edward the Dyke and Other Poems*, in 1971. The renaissance of women's literature which she led on the US west coast together with (among others) **Susan Griffin**, Pat Parker and Alta was very much of the voice as well as the printed page; poetry readings have always had a special place in American lesbian culture, and Judy Grahn is one of the most respected poets on the circuit. In the mid-1980s she published two cultural studies, *Another Mother Tongue: Gay Words, Gay Worlds* (1984) and *The Highest Apple: Sappho and the Lesbian Poetic Tradition* (1985). She has also published fiction and several collections of poetry, including a series in progress named for the queens of the four tarot suits.

Judy Grahn, *The Work of a Common Woman*, St Martin's Press, 1978
Judy Grahn, *Another Mother Tongue: Gay Words, Gay Worlds*, Beacon, 1984
Judy Grahn, *Blood, Bread, and Roses: How Menstruation Created the World*, Beacon, 1993
Margaret Cruikshank, *The Gay and Lesbian Liberation Movement*, Routledge, 1992

Antonio Gramsci
1891–1937
socialist leader and writer

One of the most influential and innovative Marxist theoreticians and activists of the early twentieth century, Antonio Gramsci was born into a lower middle class family in the impoverished Sardinian town of Ales. In 1911 he won a scholarship to Turin University, where he was much influenced by the idealist philosopher Benedetto Croce and became involved in the Turin working class movement. His experience of both peasant culture and an industrialised city convinced him of the complexity of political structures and organisations, and of ordinary people's need to understand the benefits of socialism rather than having it thrust upon them. In 1919 Gramsci helped to found the socialist weekly *L'ordine nuovo* (*The New Order*) to bring Marxism in line with Italian experience, and to be a mouthpiece for the rapidly developing factory council movement; two years later he was one of the first members of the Italian Communist Party, leading it during the difficult years following Mussolini's march on Rome and the fascist seizure of power. His health, which had never been good, began to decline through the 1920s (he spent much of his visit to the 1922 Third **International** congress in a Russian sanatorium), and his arrest and imprisonment in November 1926 exacerbated his discomfort. He nevertheless used his years of confinement to think carefully and write lucidly about the nature of politics and the role of the revolutionary; much of this writing was collected in his widely-read *Prison Notebooks*. It was his ability to see the wider picture and his refusal to simplify and dogmatise that have kept his ideas relevant while those of many of his contemporary Marxist thinkers have been forgotten. He foresaw the widening of 'the political' to include many aspects of everyday life, thought carefully about the purpose of the state, and analysed the need for eclectic alliances in order to offer a way forward for socialism. Recognising that class analysis and simplistic economics alone could not explain the changes necessary for true democracy, he paved the way for much modern political and economic thinking. In the mid-1930s Antonio Gramsci became seriously ill and was moved to a clinic in Formia and then to Quisisana near Rome, where he died shortly before he was due to be released.

Antonio Gramsci (ed. David Forgacs), *A Gramsci Reader: Selected Writings 1916–1935*, Lawrence and Wishart, 1985
Antonio Gramsci (ed. and trans. Quintin Hoare and Geoffrey Nowell Smith), *Selections from the Prison Notebooks*, Lawrence and Wishart, 1971
Guiseppe Fiori, *Antonio Gramsci: Life of a Revolutionary*, New Left Books, 1970
Joseph Femia, *Gramsci's Political Thought*, Clarendon Press, 1981

Germaine Greer
1939–
feminist writer and critic

From her publishing debut with *The Female Eunuch* in 1970, Germaine Greer has built a reputation as a lively and combative feminist writer and broadcaster. Born in Melbourne, Australia, she was educated at convent school and Melbourne University before teaching English at Sydney University. She moved to England in 1964, completed a PhD on Shakespeare's early comedies in 1967, and went on to teach drama at the University of Warwick, where she started writing regular articles for alternative magazines including *Screw* and *Private Eye*. Her first and only experience of marriage was a three-week liaison with journalist Paul de Feu in 1968; the absence of children in her life is mentioned wistfully in her later writing. The runaway success of *The Female Eunuch*, a powerful personal statement about women's subordination, was widely discussed, though her ideas about the 'castration of women' alienated her from many radical feminists. Her later books cover a wide variety of subjects, from women artists (*The Obstacle Race*, 1979) and fertility (*Sex and Destiny*, 1984) to Shakespeare

(*Shakespeare*, 1985) and ageing (*The Change*, 1992), while she was for several years a columnist for *The Sunday Times* and continues to air her often controversial ideas in numerous articles and radio and television programmes. In 1979 Germaine Greer became a director of the Tulsa Centre for the Study of Women's Literature in Oklahoma, and for several years spent much time in the USA as well as in her English and Italian homes. Critics and readers have often found her writing and ideas self-centred and inconsistent, yet her use of personal experience (particularly in *The Female Eunuch*, *The Change*, and the autobiographical exploration *Daddy, We Hardly Knew You*) makes her an engaging and honest if sometimes a frustrating writer.

Germaine Greer, *The Female Eunuch*, MacGibbon and Kee, 1970
Germaine Greer, *Sex and Destiny: The Politics of Human Fertility*, Secker and Warburg, 1984
Germaine Greer, *Daddy, We Hardly Knew You*, Viking, 1989
Germaine Greer, *The Change: Women, Ageing, and the Menopause*, Knopf, 1992

Susan Griffin
1943–
feminist philosopher and poet

The feminist writer Susan Griffin was born in Los Angeles and studied at San Francisco State University. She has a daughter with John Levy, to whom she was married from 1966 to 1970. With the establishment of women's presses, she was able to publish her first collection of poetry, *Dear Sky* (1971), which has been followed by several others, the most recent being *Unremembered Country* (1987). Considering herself primarily a poet, she has brought her poetic sensibility to her powerful and influential studies of culture, creating works that are subtle, lucid and eloquent. The first of these, *Woman and Nature: The Roaring Inside Her* (1978), contrasts patriarchal judgements on nature and women with the liberation of women's vision and voices. *Rape: the Power of Consciousness* (1979), revised as *Rape: the Politics of Consciousness* (1986), examines physical and psychological control in a sexually schizophrenic male culture. In *Pornography and Silence: Culture's Revenge Against Nature* (1981), she studies the 'pornographic mind of our culture'. In her most recent prose work, *A Chorus of Stones: The Private Life of War* (1992), she meditatively explores the workings of secrets and denial in her own life and family history, in the lives of other people, and in military policy and war. Listening for resonances among aspects of life that we are taught to regard as separate and unrelated, Susan Griffin weaves together personal memory and experience, interviews, creative imagination, and historical research in a way that characterises her genius and its power to illuminate human experience.

Susan Griffin, *Woman and Nature: The Roaring Inside Her*, Harper and Row, 1978
Susan Griffin, *Pornography and Silence: Culture's Revenge Against Nature*, Harper and Row, 1981
Susan Griffin, *A Chorus of Stones: The Private Life of War*, Doubleday, 1992

Jerzy Grotowski
1933–
theatre director and teacher

Jerzy Grotowski was born and grew up in the south-east Polish city of Rzeszów, and studied acting in Cracow and Moscow. After directing a travelling theatre in Soviet Central Asia he was appointed artistic director of the municipal theatre in the small Polish town of Opole, where he created his first permanent 'theatre laboratory' company. In 1965 his company moved to Wrocław, where he continued to explore experimental theatre methods. Both his teaching and his influential book *Towards a Poor Theatre* (1968 in Polish and Danish; 1969 in English) stress that theatre, unlike the passive artforms of film and television, must build on the unique communion between actor and audience rather than depending on expensive and complex technology. His acclaimed 1960s productions of classics like Christopher Marlowe's *Dr Faustus* involved gesture, experimental vocal techniques and creative cutting of the texts to make them more immediate to the audience; tours of Europe and America spread his ideas among a new generation of directors and actors including Julian Beck of the New York-based Living Theatre and the British director Peter Brook. In the early 1970s Jerzy Grotowski moved away from the role of theatre producer towards the creation of rural paratheatrical 'happenings' which include spiritual retreat, strenuous gymnastics and spontaneous staged events. His influence at the forefront of experimental theatre has waned and he has become more of a spiritual guru than an avant-garde practitioner, but his concept of theatre as involvement in real-world drama has since developed into important areas like **Augusto Boal**'s 'Theatre of the Oppressed'.

Jerzy Grotowski, *Towards a Poor Theatre*, Eyre Methuen, 1969 (new edn 1976)
Jennifer Kumiega, *The Theatre of Grotowski*, Methuen, 1985
Zbigniew Osinski (ed. Lillian Vallee and Robert Findlay), *Grotowski and his Laboratory*, PAJ Publications, 1987

Che Guevara [Ernesto Guevara de la Serna]
1928–1967
revolutionary activist and writer

'Born in Argentina, fought in Cuba, and started to be a revolutionary in Guatamala' was Che Guevara's own summary of his life shortly before he was killed by a CIA-sponsored Bolivian army squad at the age of 39, but it does not adequately explain how he came to be a universal icon of revolutionary struggle in the 1960s and early 70s. Born in Rosario into a middle class Argentine family of Spanish-Irish descent, he qualified as a doctor in 1953, but his travels throughout Latin America and his reading of **Gramsci**, **Fanon** and **Mariátegui** convinced him that armed revolution was the only way to bring about the radical changes necessary for the emancipation of the poverty-stricken masses. The Castro campaign in Cuba was where he cut his activist teeth, and he soon became one of Fidel

Castro's principal lieutenants: after the overthrow of the Batista government in January 1959 Che (a nickname derived from his constant use of the interjection 'che') Guevara held a series of key posts in the Cuban government, using every opportunity to speak out against imperialism and neocolonialism. His manual on guerrilla tactics, *Guerra de guerrillas* (1960, 1961 in English) was widely translated, and by the mid-1960s Che Guevara was a legend: a middle-class intellectual who sacrificed his career to fight for the world's oppressed. In April 1965 he dropped out of public life and returned to the front, first in the civil war in Congo and then in Bolivia, where he trained and led a guerrilla troop in the Santa Cruz region. His early – perhaps inevitable – violent death won him further admiration among the millions clamouring for the overthrow of repressive capitalism, and coincided with the massive rise of unrest that culminated in the events of May 1968. His ideas, however, lived on: many, such as the need for a non-materialistic socialism for the poor, diversity and flexibility of response to oppression, and the role of small groups in organising revolutionary activity, have echoes in contemporary development theory.

Che Guevara, *Che Guevara Speaks: Selected Speeches and Writings*, Grove Press, 1968
Che Guevara (ed. Rolando Bonachea and Nelson Valdes), *Che: Selected Works of Ernesto Guevara*, MIT Press, 1969
Che Guevara (ed. Robert Scheer), *Diary of Che Guevara*, Bantam, 1968
Jay Mallin (ed.), *Che Guevara in Revolution: A Documentary Overview*, University of Miami Press, 1969
Michael Lowy, *The Marxism of Che Guevara*, Monthly Review Press, 1973

Gustavo Gutiérrez
1928–
clergyman, liberation theologist

The Peruvian priest and teacher Gustavo Gutiérrez is the main instigator and best known advocate of the principles and practice of liberation theology, a political-religious movement which has had much influence throughout the poorer countries of the world in the decades since the early 1970s. Despite his Spanish name, Gustavo Gutiérrez is of Indian origin, and grew up in Lima, becoming a Catholic priest in 1959. As early as 1964 he was advocating a conception of theology based directly on experience or praxis, and a more developed version entitled 'Towards a Theology of Liberation' was presented at the important Medellín Conference of Latin American Bishops in 1968. It was with the publication of his first book, *Teologia de la liberación* (1971, 1973 in English), that he became widely known as an advocate of a theology that would address the real concerns of the people of Latin America, rather than simply being an inappropriate derivative of European interpretations and opinions. Gutiérrez argued that social and political context is crucial to theological debate, mediating the symbols, myths and practices that give meaning to religious experience. Furthermore, the church cannot ignore the circumstances that have led to inequality and poverty, and must develop an understanding of the economic, social and political roots of oppression in order to suggest and implement useful social change. He has since written several further books to clarify how theology and political and social activism can work together to improve the position of the poor majority in Latin America, arguing in favour of participatory democracy and socialist economics. He successfully uses Marxist class analysis alongside the church's commitment to the poor to justify engagement in a variety of reformist and revolutionary causes. Despite the range and depth of his writing and teaching, Gustavo Gutiérrez has always stressed daily lived experience as the basis for a truly liberatory theology, and as the founder of the Bartolomé de las Casas Centre in Rimac, where he lives and works, he has demonstrated that his pastoral duty to the poor is what matters most, not scholarly works for the delectation of the rich.

Gustavo Gutiérrez, *A Theology of Liberation*, Orbis, 1973
Gustavo Gutiérrez, *The Power of the Poor in History*, Orbis, 1983
Ruth Martin Brown, *Gustavo Gutiérrez*, John Knox Press, 1980
Paul A. Sigmund, *Liberation Theology at the Crossroads*, Oxford University Press, 1990

Jürgen Habermas
1929–
philosopher and social theorist

Together with **Theodor Adorno** and **Max Horkheimer**, Jürgen Habermas is one of the best known social philosophers of the later German 'Frankfurt School', whose main thrust is a 'critical theory' which questions the role and authority of 'reason' in modern society. Brought up in Düsseldorf and educated at Göttingen, Zürich and Bonn Universities, he studied Adorno, **Marx** and Freud during the 1950s and quickly recognised the links between philosophy, politics and psychology. In 1955 he married Ute Wesselhöft (they have three children), and from 1961 to 1964 taught at the University of Heidelberg before becoming director of the Max Planck Institute at Starnberg, Munich, in 1971 and professor of philosophy at Frankfurt University in 1982. His early books, *Theorie und Praxis* (1963, 1974 in English) and *Erkenntnis und Interesse* (1968, 1971 in English) link philosophy and science in a critique which demonstrates that all knowledge derives from assumptions about the world and human nature which are not, as is often claimed, value-free, and which must be questioned. It is crucial that the interests inherent in 'reasoned debate' are identified and analysed, thus restoring the appropriate links between theory and practice. During the 1970s Habermas worked intensively on the philosophical foundations of democracy, seeking to show that truth and sincerity are integral to human nature, and how the supposed reasonableness of capitalism and bureaucracy create crises of rationality and legitimation, an exploration which culminated in *Theorie des Kommunikativen Handelns* (1981, 1984 and 1987 in English) and *Faktizität und Geltung* (1992, 1995 in English). Jürgen

Habermas's range of interests is immense, his learning prodigious: he is equally at home in philosophy, sociology, political theory and jurisprudence, and his voice is listened to respectfully throughout the academic and politically literate world.

Jürgen Habermas, *Theory and Practice*, Heinemann, 1974

Jürgen Habermas, *Knowledge and Human Interests*, Beacon, 1971

Jürgen Habermas, *The Theory of Communicative Action*, Polity Press, 1984 (Vol. I) and 1987 (Vol. II)

Jürgen Habermas, *Between Norms and Facts*, MIT Press, 1995

Jürgen Habermas (ed Steven Siedman), *Jürgen Habermas on Society and Politics: A Reader*, Beacon, 1989

William Outhwaite, *Habermas: A Critical Introduction*, Polity, 1994

[Margeurite] Radclyffe Hall
1880–1943
poet and novelist

A widely-read poet and novelist in the interwar period, Radclyffe Hall was born in Hampshire, England, and grew up in London. Her writing career started with several volumes of poetry, and her first two novels met with much literary acclaim. She is best known, however, for her open lesbianism – her longterm lovers included the soprano Mabel Batten and Una, the wife of Admiral (later Sir) Ernest Troubridge, and her attempt in her tract-cum-novel *The Well of Loneliness* (1928) to engage public sympathy for lesbian relationships. During the 1920s, however, public opinion had hardened against homosexuality, and the British parliament had debated extending the law to criminalise lesbianism; against this background *The Well of Loneliness*, written from a deep sense of duty and sadness, inevitably became the subject of legal action. Despite a protest letter to *The Times* signed by forty literary figures including Vita Sackville-West, Leonard and **Virginia Woolf** and E.M. Forster, the novel was banned as 'obscene libel', and Radclyffe Hall herself was deeply upset that the book achieved salacious notoriety rather than being read as an important moral text. It was not reissued in Britain until 1949, though it was widely read in the American edition. As well as publicising the hardline stance of 1920s censors, *The Well of Loneliness* had a profound influence on the course of social attitudes, providing lesbian activism with an important touchstone. Radclyffe Hall maintained her relationship with Una Troubridge, also her biographer, and continued to write until her death.

Radclyffe Hall, *The Well of Loneliness*, 1928 (many recent editions)

Una Troubridge, *The Life and Death of Radclyffe Hall*, Hammond and Hammond, 1961

Vera Brittain, *Radclyffe Hall: A Case of Obscenity?*, Femina, 1968

Stuart [McPhail] Hall
1932–
sociologist, social activist, peace campaigner

Few social scientists have explored the contemporary scene as widely and deeply as Stuart Hall, or become so actively involved in the causes closest to their heart. Born into an upwardly-mobile middle class black family in Kingston, Jamaica, he won a Rhodes Scholarship to Merton College, Cambridge, in 1951, where he studied literature and became actively involved in West Indian and socialist politics, being a founding member of the New Left Club and its journal *Universities and Left Review*. When in 1959 this publication merged with **E.P. Thompson**'s *The New Reasoner* to become the *New Left Review*, Stuart Hall was its first editor. In 1964 he was appointed assistant director of the Centre for Contemporary Cultural Studies at the University of Birmingham, becoming its director in 1974. He left Birmingham in 1979 to become professor of sociology at the Open University, a post he still holds. During the late 1970s and 80s he became active in the **Campaign for Nuclear Disarmament**, and has helped to establish a number of groups to combat racism, emerging as one of the left's most articulate voices in the struggle against the reactionary right. To a large extent his formulation of 'Marxism without guarantees' has succeeded in creating a political and intellectual alliance among the farflung remnants of the new left. Stuart Hall has worked with his colleagues at the Centre for Contemporary Cultural Studies and the Open University on a range of important and controversial topics, including working class culture, violence and policing, youth subcultures, racism, gender politics, the influence of the mass media, and effective responses to the rise of the new right. His willingness to engage with the complexities and contradictions of the real world, and to recognise the need for and become involved in the struggle for change, have inspired many of his students and readers to think carefully and deeply about the wider implications of sociological exploration.

Stuart Hall *et al*, *Policing the Crisis: Mugging, The State, and Law and Order*, Macmillan, 1978
Stuart Hall, Dorothy Hobson, Andrew Lowe and Paul Willis (eds), *Culture, Media, Language*, Hutchinson, 1980
Stuart Hall, *The Hard Road to Renewal: Thatcherism and the Crisis of the Left*, Verso, 1988
Stuart Hall and Martin Jacques (eds), *New Times: The Changing Face of Politics in the 1990s*, Laurence and Wishart/Marxism Today, 1989

Fannie Lou Hamer [Fannie Lou Townsend]
1917–1977
civil rights campaigner

Raised as the youngest of a family of twenty children on a cotton plantation in Montgomery County, Mississippi, Fannie Lou Hamer worked all her life for equal rights, her dignified persistence and eloquence coming to represent the qualities required for an effective civil rights movement. From the age of six she worked in the cotton fields, using her spare time to learn reading and writing; in 1944 the plantation owner, recognising her literacy, made her the plantation's record keeper, and a year later she married tractor driver Perry Hamer. For the next eighteen years they worked as sharecroppers, but her life changed in 1962 when she attempted unsuccessfully to register to vote. Surviving verbal abuse and a murder attempt, she became a field officer for the **Student Nonviolent Coordinating Committee** (SNCC) in 1963, and the following year was one of the founders of Mississippi Freedom Democratic Party (MFDP). As the MFDP's vice-chair she worked hard to gain a Democratic Party pledge not to recognise all-white delegations at its 1968 congress, having been present in 1965 when the US Congress refused to condone Mississippi's all-white delegation. Understanding that lack of access to the political process went hand-in-hand with poverty, she campaigned relentlessly for voter registration, giving talks and helping to organise local campaigns across the country. In 1969 Fanny Lou Hamer established the Freedom Farms Corporation to help poor families grow food, and when the following year the National Council of Negro Women set up the Fanny Lou Hamer Day Care Centre in 1970 she became the board's first chair. Diagnosed with cancer in the early 1970s, she continued to campaign until the end of her life, determined to do all she could to transform the South. Her best-remembered words are 'I'm sick and tired of being sick and tired', and she was fond of pointing out to whites with little patience for the process of change that the black population of the South had been tired and impatient for generations, yet was still prepared to work hard for justice and equality.

Kay Mills, *This Little Light of Mine: The Life of Fannie Lou Hamer*, Dutton, 1993
Penny Colman, *Fannie Lou Hamer and the Fight for the Vote*, Millbrook, 1993
Vicki Crawford, Jacqueline Anne Rouse and Barbara Woods (eds), *Women in the Civil Rights Movement: Trailblazers and Torchbearers*, 1941–1965, Carlson, 1990

[James] Keir Hardie
1856–1915
socialist politician, workers' rights campaigner

Keir Hardie was born into a Scottish mining family, where poverty, workers' struggles and his stepfather's heavy drinking soon propelled him into trade unionism, temperance and religion. From the age of ten he worked in a coal mine, later making up his education at night school. The failure of the Scottish miners' strike of 1887 fuelled his antagonism towards the Liberal-dominated Trades Union Council, and the following year he became secretary of the newly-established Scottish Labour Party. He entered the British parliament as a Labour candidate in 1892 and soon won the epithet 'member for the unemployed', though his unorthodox approach to parliamentary procedure sometimes infuriated other Labour politicians. In 1893 he succeeded in his main ambition, to form a national, independent, working-class political party: the Independent Labour Party. He lost his parliamentary seat in 1895, but re-entered the House of Commons in 1900. Following the Labour Party's major electoral success in 1906 he was elected the first chairman of the parliamentary Labour Party, though ill health, extraparliamentary activism, a world tour in the summer of 1907, and domestic issues (including an extramarital affair with suffragist **Sylvia Pankhurst**) meant frequent absences from the House. In addition to his passionate advocacy of workers' rights he was vigorous in his support of women's suffrage, and when the threat of war loomed in 1914 his fervent pacifism and internationalism in the face of rampant patriotism required enormous courage. Pressure of work contributed to a mild stroke in January 1915, and he died eight months later from pneumonia. Organisation and cooperation were never Keir Hardie's strong points, but throughout his life he remained remarkably consistent in his support of Christian pacifism, the needs of the unemployed, and women's rights. His writings and speeches inspired the growing labour movement, and did much to articulate the aspirations of the British working class.

Kenneth Morgan, *Keir Hardie: Radical and Socialist*, Weidenfeld and Nicolson, 1975
Caroline Benn, *Keir Hardie*, Hutchinson, 1992

[Edward] Michael Harrington
1928–1989
social activist, democratic socialist

The American socialist writer and activist Michael Harrington is best known for *The Other America* (1962), the influential book which helped persuade the Johnson administration to launch its 'war on poverty'. Harrington grew up in a devout Catholic family in St Louis, Missouri, and studied at Holy Cross College, Yale and Chicago before moving to New York in 1949 to become involved in the Catholic Worker movement, editing the group's newsletter and organising peace marches. In 1953 he left both the Catholic church and the Catholic Worker movement for the more secular radicalism of the Young People's Socialist League and a year later the even more radical Young Socialist League. During the 1950s he became a keen observer of American social and political life, writing numerous articles for *Partisan Review*, *Dissent* and *Commonweal*, and giving lectures on behalf of the League and the Socialist Party. The publication of *The Other America*, arguing that poverty was far more widespread than was commonly assumed, brought him to the attention of a wider audience, and for the next quarter century he remained a prominent and influential commentator on US social policy. He was present at the founding convention of **Students for a Democratic Society** in 1962, but alienated himself by refusing to call for unconditional withdrawal from Vietnam and denouncing its leadership for insufficient anticommunism, both of which positions he quickly regretted. In 1972 he was appointed to the chair of political science at Queen's University, and the following year founded the Democratic Socialist Organizing Committee in an attempt to remind the Democatic Party of its liberal ideals. In 1983 the Committee merged with the New American Movement, and Michael Harrington served as cochair of the resulting organisation, Democratic Socialists of America. He also continued to write: an important survey of socialist theory and history, *Socialism*, appeared in 1972, and his last books, an autobiography and an exploration of the socialist vision for the twenty-first century, were published shortly before his death from cancer in July 1989.

Michael Harrington, *The Other America: Poverty in the United States*, Macmillan, 1962
Michael Harrington, *Socialism*, Saturday Review Press, 1972
Michael Harrington, *The Long-Distance Runner: An Autobiography*, Holt, 1988
Michael Harrington, *Socialism: Past and Future*, Arcade, 1989

Václav Havel
1936–
dramatist, civil rights campaigner, politician

Eastern Europe's best known civil rights activist turned politician is the Czech president Václav Havel. He was born into a prosperous business family in Prague, but was debarred by the communist authorities from receiving a university education because of his privileged origins. He found work as a laboratory technician, at the same time studying literature and drama in evening classes. In 1959 he was given a job as a stagehand at Prague's Theatre on the Balustrade, and gradually took on more and more responsibility at the theatre. He began to establish a reputation as a playwright with his first play, *Zahradni slavnost* (1963, 1969 in English as *The Garden Party*), and won his first international award in 1969. In 1968 he was a leading voice for democratic change, and was banned from public life soon after the Soviet invasion of Czechoslovakia: he was forced out of the theatre, and found work as a taxi driver and brewer. In 1977 he was one of the founders and chief speakers of the civil rights group **Charter 77**, and in 1978 he helped set up the Committee for the Defence of the Unjustly Persecuted. Detained without trial from January to May 1977, he was sentenced in October to fourteen months imprisonment, suspended for three years, for 'anti-state activities'. In 1979, shortly after his marriage to Olga Šplíchalová, he was jailed for four years for sedition, and was again detained in February 1989, but his detention attracted international outrage and he was released in May. In November 1989 he helped to establish the democratic political party Civic Forum, swiftly emerging as its undeclared leader and, for all his expressions of reluctance about political involvement, was the prime mover in the 'velvet revolution' which brought down the communist regime. Elected president of the republic in December 1989 for an interim six-month period, he was the only person considered to have the moral stature to lead the country into the first free elections since 1946. In July 1990 Václav Havel was re-elected with an overwhelming majority, and when the newly-formed Czech Republic held its first elections in June 1992 he became the leader of a coalition government dominated by political groupings based on the original Civic Forum. A fluent, witty, observant and much-admired politician, Václav Havel has combined modesty and courage to lead his country towards true democracy.

Václav Havel (trans. Paul Wilson), *Letters to Olga: June 1979–September 1982*, Knopf, 1988

Václav Havel (trans. Paul Wilson), *Disturbing the Peace: A Conversation with Karel Hvizdala*, Faber, 1990

Michael Simmons, *The Reluctant President: A Political Life of Václav Havel*, Methuen, 1991

Eda Kriseova (trans. Caleb Crain), *Václav Havel: The Authorized Biography*, St. Martin's Press, 1993

Hazel Henderson
1933–
economist, futurist, public service activist

The influential economist and futurist Hazel Henderson was born in Britain, moving to the USA via the Caribbean in the late 1950s and becoming a US citizen in 1961. Self-trained as an economist and environmentalist, her first articles were published in business magazines in the early 1970s. From 1974 to 1980 she served as a member of the US Congress Office of Technology Assessment Advisory Council, and on other official advisory councils. In 1974 she established the Princeton Center for Alternative Futures, a select network of academics and activists exploring creative human-scale organisations and the transitions of industrial societies. She helped found a number of public interest groups, including the New York-based Council on Economic Priorities, Environmentalists for Full Employment, and the Worldwatch Institute; she also helped to establish and wrote regularly for *Futures Research Quarterly* and *New Options Newsletter*. In 1986 she moved to St Augustine, Florida, where she continues to work as an independent futurist, maintaining the Alternatives Future network, lecturing at the University of Florida, and travelling widely to lecture and run workshops and seminars. Of her three major books on the relevance of economics to the real world, the first two, *Creating Alternative Futures* (1978) and *The Politics of the Solar Age* (1981), collect some of the most important of the many articles she wrote between 1973 and 1981. Her *Paradigms in Progress* (1991) offers a more rounded and tightly-argued case for abandoning many of the economic assumptions that are destroying the planet and stunting human potential. She makes it clear that any sustainable world order must include security from pollution, poverty and hunger.

Hazel Henderson, *Creating Alternative Futures: The End of Economics*, Putnam, 1978

Hazel Henderson, *The Politics of the Solar Age: Alternatives to Economics*, Doubleday, 1981

Hazel Henderson, *Paradigms in Progress: Life Beyond Economics*, Knowledge Systems, 1991

Hiratsuka Raichō [Hiratsuka Haruko]
1886–1971
feminist, women's rights activist, peace campaigner

Japan's leading early feminist, Hiratsuka Raichō grew up in Tokyo, the daughter of a government official who had studied law in Europe. She was much influenced by her reading in Western philosophy, but was also a Zen Buddhist and practised meditation throughout her life. In 1911 she formed the feminist literary and debating society **Seitōsha**, together with its women-only magazine *Seitō*, introducing the first issue with her women's manifesto entitled 'Genshi josei wa taiyō de atta' ('In the Beginning Woman was the Sun'), which was to remain her slogan throughout her long career. In 1914 Raichō left home to live with the artist Okumura Hiroshi, with whom she had two children, and in 1918 she and the poet **Yosano Akiko** published an important debate about the nature of motherhood. In 1920 Hiratsuka Raichō and **Ichikawa Fusae** formed Shin Fujin Kyōkai (New Women's Association) to press for women's political rights. Within three years a small but important achievement was the amendment of the Public Order and Police Law, which gave women the right to attend political meetings (though they were still not allowed to form or join a political party). In the 1930s Raichō worked with women's consumer organisations and continued to write, and after the war became involved in peace campaigning. She strongly opposed the 1951 San Francisco Peace Treaty, which gave the United States the right to station military forces in Japan, and was president of the Nihon Fujin Dantai Rengōkai (Federation of Japanese Women's Societies), which campaigned energetically for pacifism, until shortly before her death. In 1954 her Japanese Women's Appeal, a call to the women of the world to help ban the hydrogen bomb, led to the holding of a World Mothers' Convention in Tokyo.

Susan Pharr, *Political Women in Japan*, University of California Press, 1981
Margret Neuss, 'Hiratsuka Raichō', *Kodansha Encyclopedia of Japan*, 1983

Magnus Hirschfeld
1868–1935
doctor, gay rights advocate, sexologist

'Per scientiam ad justitiam' ('through knowledge to justice') was the motto of the pioneering German sexologist and sexual freedom campaigner Magnus Hirschfeld. The son of a doctor in the Baltic town of Kolberg, he studied philology and philosophy before turning to medicine in 1893, practising in Magdeburg and then Charlottenberg until 1909. In 1897 he had founded the first homosexual reform society in Germany, and two years later established the *Jahrbuch für Sexuelle Zwischenstufen* (*Yearbook for Sexual Intermediacy*), which appeared annually until the early 1920s. His study of transvestites (he coined the word) was published in 1910, and a weighty and widely-researched study of homosexuality, offering what for many years was the definitive statement on its biological roots, came out four years later. Hirschfeld found research and writing easier than campaigning, but nonetheless made time to organise the Scientific Humanitarian Society, which petitioned for the decriminalisation of homosexuality and succeeded in obtaining support from many public figures including Albert Einstein, Herman Hesse and Thomas Mann. By 1912, following correspondence with **Havelock Ellis** and **Edward Carpenter**, a British branch of the Society had been established, and Hirschfeld was the main speaker at the 1913 International Medical Congress in London. In 1919 he opened the Institute for Sexual Science in Berlin, which soon housed a mass of international data and a library of more than 20,000 books: three years later he convened the World League for Sexual Reform, with representatives from America, Europe and Russia (**Aleksandra Kollontai** attended congresses from Russia and **Dora Russell** was secretary of the British branch). By 1930 the League had a membership of 130,000, but on May 6th 1933 (while Hirschfeld was abroad) Nazi stormtroopers raided the Institute and burnt most of its archives and library. He died two years later, while trying to reestablish the Institute in France.

Magnus Hirschfeld, *Men and Women: The World Journey of a Sexologist*, Putnam, 1935

Magnus Hirschfeld (trans. Michael Lombardi-Nash), *Transvestites: The Erotic Drive to Cross-dress*, Prometheus, 1991

Jeffrey Weeks, *Coming Out*, Quartet, 1977

Charlotte Wolff, *Magnus Hirschfeld: A Portrait of a Pioneer in Sexology*, Quartet, 1986

Eric [John Ernest] Hobsbawm
1917–
Marxist socialist, social historian

A courageous social historian, Eric Hobsbawm explored and documented the early labour movement, then went on to write a monumental four-volume social history of the world from a socialist perspective. Born in Alexandria to a British father and an Austrian mother, he grew up in Vienna before being sent at the age of fourteen to study in Berlin. As the Nazi threat intensified he enrolled in the Young Communist League and was active in producing and disseminating anti-Nazi literature. In 1935 the family returned to London, and three years later he started to study history at King's College, Cambridge. His communist politics kept Eric Hobsbawm out of active service, and he spent much of the war in the Army Education Corps. In 1949 he was appointed a fellow of King's College, and three years later founded (with **E.P. Thompson** and others) the influential historical journal *Past and Present*, one of the few to take labour history seriously. His first book, *Labour's Turning Point* (1948), documented the diversity and dynamism of the early labour movement, a subject he returned to in many articles and essays, while *Primitive Rebels* (1959) explored the links betwen revolution, rebellion and social change. In 1959 he moved to Birkbeck College, London, where in 1970 he became professor of history. 1962 saw the publication of the first of four massive historical surveys (*The Age of Revolution*; *The Age of Capital* (1975); *The Age of Empire* (1987) and *The Age of Extremes* (1994)) spanning two and a half centuries of capitalism and its discontents. The last volume concludes that 'the structures of human societies themselves, including even some of the social foundations of the capitalist economy, are on the point of being destroyed by the erosion of what we have inherited from the past. Our world risks both explosion and implosion. It must change.' In 1982 Eric Hobsbawm retired as professor at Birkbeck, and now teaches at the New School of Social Research in New York.

Eric Hobsbawm, *Primitive Rebels: Studies in the Archaic Forms of Social Movement in the Nineteenth and Twentieth Centuries*, Praeger, 1959
Eric Hobsbawm, *The Forward March of Labour Halted?*, New Left Books, 1981
Eric Hobsbawm, *The Age of Extremes: The Short 20th Century, 1914–1991*, Michael Joseph, 1994

Abbie [Abbott Howard] Hoffman
1936–1989
social, political and environmental activist

Writing of his approach to activism in his autobiography *Soon to be a Major Motion Picture*, Abbie Hoffman declared that 'all you need is a little nerve and a willingness to be considered an embarrassment'. He grew up in a Jewish family in Worcester, Massachusetts, and studied psychology at Brandeis and Berkeley before returning to Worcester in 1960 to work as a hospital psychologist and organise civil rights and peace demonstrations. At Brandeis he was impressed by the pioneering humanistic psychologist **Abraham Maslow**, who taught that rebellion was a healthier route to self-actualisation than conformity: throughout his life Abbie Hoffman reiterated the importance of hope and optimism in the struggle for human dignity. His major civil rights involvement was with Friends of SNCC, the northern support group of the **Student Nonviolent Coordinating Committee**, and in 1965 he was engaged to establish retail outlets for southern craft products. A year later, while he was establishing a major outlet in New York, SNCC abandoned its integrationist goals and purged the organisation of white members. Abbie Hoffman now became involved with the emerging counterculture, organising New York hippies in a series of theatrical antiwar actions: his best known piece of street theatre was when in 1967 a group of hippies threw banknotes onto the floor of the New York Stock Exchange: many newspapers carried telling pictures of stockbrokers fighting for their share. In 1968 he and Jerry Rubin formed the loosely-structured Youth International Party or '**Yippies**', which in August of that year held a street demonstration outside the Democratic National Convention in Chicago which was broken up by violent police action. Hoffman and seven others were charged with conspiring to commit violence, and proceeded to turn the trial into a showcase for hip culture and antiwar politics: Hoffman was sentenced to five years imprisonment, but both conviction and contempt citations were overturned on appeal. He was now a sought-after speaker and performance artist, but in 1973 he was arrested for selling cocaine to undercover police: faced with a ten-year sentence he went underground and changed his name to Barry Freed. As Freed he organised in 1978 the successful 'Save the River' campaign to prevent the Hudson River being dredged, coming out of 'hiding' when his autobiography was published in 1980. He went on to organise another successful campaign, against the building of the Point Pleasant power station on the Delaware River, but severe depression drove him to attempt suicide in 1984; four years later, after a serious road accident, he killed himself. Always positive on behalf of others despite his own inner turmoil, Abbie Hoffman convinced thousands of activists that the struggle was worthwhile, and could even be fun on the way.

Abbie Hoffman, *Soon to be a Major Motion Picture*, Putnam, 1980
Abbie Hoffman, *The Best of Abbie Hoffman*, Four Walls Eight Windows, 1990
Marty Jezer, *Abbie Hoffman: American Rebel*, Rutgers University Press, 1992

bell hooks [Gloria Watkins]
1952–
feminist writer and cultural critic

The black feminist writer and teacher bell hooks grew up in the small town of Hopkinsville, Kentucky. As a child in a community of caring black people she benefited from the relaxed intermingling of private and public life despite having to struggle with violence in her own family. Though her writing began with (and still includes) poetry and plays, in her mid-twenties she was moved to challenge feminism's then-prevailing construct of a universalised 'woman' by raising questions about class and racial differences between women. In *Feminist Theory: From Margin to Center* (1984) she sought to place sexism in context alongside other forms of oppression based on race, class and age, all being manifestations of domination. For bell hooks, resistance to oppression must go beyond reacting to the forces of oppression; it must include being able to imagine other ways of living in the world, forming relationships and conducting our lives on the basis of new consciousness, creating 'communities of resistance'. **Thich Nhat Hanh**, whose community in France provides such a model, is one of her primary teachers in her life-work of 'decolonising the mind', and spiritual practice one of the resources she brings to her cultural and political insight. An essayist and lecturer whose analysis is both incisive and accessible, bell hooks puts theory to the test of human experiences in daily life. She teaches at Oberlin College in Ohio.

bell hooks, *Ain't I a Woman: Black Women and Feminism*, South End, 1981
bell hooks, *Yearning: Race, Gender and Cultural Politics*, South End,
Andrea Juno and V. Vale (eds), *Angry Women*, Re/Search No. 13, 1991

Max Horkheimer
1895–1973
philosopher, social theorist

One of the most influential social philosophers of the later 'Frankfurt School', Max Horkheimer's chief contribution to radicalism is his formulation of a holistic and ethical 'critical theory' to set against the scientism and materialism of 'traditional theory'. Born into a wealthy Jewish family in Stuttgart, he studied philosophy at Munich, Freiburg and Frankfurt am Main Universities. In 1923 his friend Felix Weil established the Institute for Social Research at Frankfurt, and in 1930 Max Horkheimer took over as its director; three years later, however, Hitler's rise to power forced the exile of many of the Institute's staff to the USA. Having with his colleague **Theodor Adorno** rehoused the Institute at Columbia University, he spent most of the war in California, working with Jewish support groups and, as director of the research division of the American Jewish Committee, commissioning the influential series 'Studies in Prejudice'. While in California he also wrote, with Adorno, *Dialektik der Aufklärung* (1947; *Dialectic of Enlightenment*, 1972), a pessimistic study showing how 'the curse of irresistible progress is irresistible repression'. By now Max Horkheimer had, in a series of widely-read essays, formulated his concept of critical theory (a term he first used in 1937), in an attempt to understand why the promise of 'progress' had failed in its liberatory role. He returned to Frankfurt to teach in the restored Institute for Social Research in 1949, and by the mid-1950s had become a major intellectual influence within radical philosophy. His later rejection of reason, idealism, Marxism, and ultimately of almost any certainty at all, however, left him in his later writings with no more than a religious faith in which at least God knew the difference between good and evil, together with an uneasy blend of utopianism and profound doubt. Whatever the contradictions and difficulties inherent in Horkheimer's critical theory, he undoubtedly succeeded in demonstrating how most existing theory, and particularly theory which leaves out the dimension of human consciousness and motivation, is inadequate in explaining the twentieth-century predicament.

Max Horkheimer and Theodor Adorno, *Dialectic of Enlightenment*, Herder, 1972
Peter Stirk, *Max Horkheimer: A New Interpretation*, Barnes and Noble, 1992
Seyla Benhabib, Wolfgang Bonss and John McCole (eds), *On Max Horkheimer: New Perspectives*, MIT Press, 1993

Karen Horney [Karen Danielsen]
1885–1953
psychoanalyst, feminist, teacher

Karen Horney, the psychoanalyst who in the 1930s pointed out to Sigmund Freud how male-centred and anti-woman much of his thinking was, is now recognised as one of the most important psychotherapists of the first half of the century. She grew up in Hamburg and studied medicine at the

University of Berlin. From 1920 to 1932 she taught at the Berlin Psycho-analytic Institute, during which time she married Oskar Horney and had three daughters. In 1932 she emigrated to the USA and taught psychoanalysis in Chicago and New York, but was becoming increasingly critical of Freudian theory and practice, particularly the way in which it makes limiting assumptions about women and female sexuality. To counter what she felt was an overemphasis on biological explanations for human behaviour she started to develop her own theory, stressing cultural and social influences on the development of personality. When she published her ideas in *New Waves in Psychoanalysis* (1939), opposition to her radical ideas grew rapidly within the analytic establishment and she was prevented from continuing her training; she responded by establishing in 1941 the American Association for the Advancement of Psychoanalysis, which she directed until her death. Of her later writings *Neurosis and Human Growth* (1951) provides the most complete overview of her thinking: she downplayed Freud's emphasis on libido in favour of 'a healthy striving towards self-actualisation', and wrote of a 'central inner force, common to all human beings and yet unique in each, which is the deep source of growth'. In many ways she laid the foundations for the important insights of **Abraham Maslow** and **Carl Rogers** a decade later, and her integrative and feminist insights have had a considerable impact on the subsequent development of the psychoanalytic approach, influencing such practitioners as **Erich Fromm** and **Juliet Mitchell**.

Karen Horney, *New Ways in Psychoanalysis*, Norton, 1980 (rev. ver. of 1939 ed.)
Karen Horney, *Neurosis and Human Growth: The Struggle toward Self-Realisation*, Norton, 1991 (repr. of 1951 ed.)
Marcia Westcott, *The Feminist Legacy of Karen Horney*, Yale University Press, 1986
Susan Quinn, *A Mind of Her Own: The Life and Times of Karen Horney*, Macmillan, 1988

Ebenezer Howard
1850–1928
town planner, social reformer

Ebenezer Howard, pioneer town planner and instigator of the 'garden city movement', grew up in Victorian London, where he experienced at first hand the overcrowding and pollution which accompanied rapid urban growth with little thought for the city-dwellers' needs for fresh air and greenery. He trained as a stenographer and worked in the City of London, but in the late 1880s went to work as a homesteader in Nebraska. Here he encountered the writings of **Ralph Waldo Emerson** and **Walt Whitman**, which nurtured his ideas about the advantages of rural living. His experiment in farming ended in dismal failure in 1893, but on his way home he visited the Columbian Exhibition in Chicago where he was much impressed with the City Beautiful Movement exhibit designed by Frederick Law Olmsted and Daniel Burnham. Back in Britain, and further encouraged by his reading of the utopian works of **Edward Bellamy**, he wrote the book upon which his reputation and influence are based: *To-morrow: A Peaceful Path to Real Reform*. It criticised the social and environmental problems associated with the uncontrolled growth of large cities and the concomitant decline of the countryside, and made detailed proposals for the establishment and maintenance of 'garden cities', in which the various uses of the land were municipally controlled for the public good and all land was held in public ownership. The book's impact was swift and powerful: the Garden City Association was founded by Howard and eleven colleagues in 1899, and by 1902 a company had been formed to build the first garden city at Letchworth in Hertfordshire, north of London, which took much of its creative inspiration from **William Morris**'s arts and crafts movement. The second, Welwyn Garden City, was started in 1920; many more followed both in Britain and in other countries including the USA and Russia. Ebenezer Howard continued to promote the garden city movement until his death, and his ideas had considerable influence for several more decades: he often commands the epithet 'the father of modern town planning'.

Ebenezer Howard, *Garden Cities of Tomorrow* (rev. ed. of *To-morrow: A Peaceful Path to Real Reform*), Attic Books, 1985 (repr. of 1902 ed.)

Dugald MacFadyen, *Sir Ebenezer Howard and the Town Planning Movement*, MIT Press, 1970 (rep. of 1933 ed.)

Robert Beavers, *The Garden City Utopia: A Critical Biography of Ebenezer Howard*, Macmillan, 1988

Hu Feng [Chang Ku-Fei]
1903–1985
writer, poet, social critic

The Chinese writer and critic Hu Feng is best known for supporting the creative endeavours of ordinary people, and for speaking out in the 1940s and 50s against the mechanistic uniformity of communist propaganda paraded as literature. He grew up in a peasant family in Hupeh, but did well at school, and while studying in Nanking in 1923 joined the Communist Youth League and began to write. He went to Japan in 1928, but was expelled five years later for participating in a socialist demonstration. From 1933 onwards he lived and worked as a writer and editor in Shanghai, where he joined **Lu Xun**'s League of Left-Wing Writers – Lu was to be his friend, colleague and mentor for much of his life. **Mao Zedong**'s 1942 Yenan proclamation of 1942 that 'literature must be an instrument of political utility' aroused Hu Feng and his supporters to a concerted campaign of opposition, though by the late 1940s he was reconciled to praising Mao and his programme in order to continue writing. Because of his independent approach to Marxism and his affirmation that the artist is entitled to an individual vision of truth, he was singled out for attack in the 1955 campaign for 'ideological purity' led by Chou Yang, but following Mao Zedong's 'Hundred Flowers' declaration of 1956 he was openly supported by a growing number of intellectuals, and opinions which had been denounced as heresy were now publicly debated: his ideas about 'mechanised literature' were used by many communist leaders, and his name became a symbol of protest against state control of intellectual and artistic activity. When the party launched its 'anti-rightist drive' of 1957, however, discussion of Hu's ideas and praise for his courage were silenced: he was arrested and spent the next 22 years in prisons and 'reform through labour' farms. He was eventually released in January 1979, when he was 'rehabilitated' and elected as a member of the Chinese People's Consultative Conference for Sichuan Province. In 1981 he regained his membership of the Chinese Writers' Association, and continued to write until his death from cancer in June 1985.

'Hu Feng', *Biographical Dictionary of Republican China* (Howard L. Boorman (ed.)), Columbia University Press, 1969

Dolores Ibárruri
1895–1989
antifascist journalist, communist politician

Dolores Ibárruri was born into a mining family in Gallarta in the Basque north of Spain; after she left school she worked in a dress shop, marrying at twenty and having five children, of whom only two survived. In 1918 she started writing articles for the workers' newspaper *El minero vizcaine* (*The Basque Miner*) under her lifelong pseudonym 'Pasionaria' (passion flower), and in 1920 was elected to the provincial committee of the Spanish Communist Party (Partido Comunisto de España, PCE). By 1930 she was working as an editor on the party's official newspaper, and two years later she was appointed to the PCE's central committee. In November 1933 La Pasionaria founded the Group of Antifascist Women, and she took a leading part in igniting the **Spanish Civil War** of 1936–39, stirring the massed forces of antifascism with her slogan of 'no pasaran' ('they shall not pass'). Pass they did, however, over the River Ebro and into communist-held Catalonia. In 1942 Dolores Ibárruri fled to France and thence to Moscow, where she spent most of the next 33 years. Although she remained a highranking official in the PCE (now in exile in Paris), the death of her hero Iosif Stalin, the admission of Spain to the United Nations, and distance from her home country all conspired to isolate her from her grassroots support. When she eventually returned to Spain after Franco's death in 1975 she won election to the Spanish upper house, the Cortés, but the gesture was more in remembrance of what she had been rather than the hardline, narrow-minded and outdated communist she had become.

Dolores Ibárruri, *They Shall Not Pass: The Autobiography of La Pasionaria*, International Publishers, 1991

Ichikawa Fusae
1893–1981
politician, women's rights activist

Born into a farming family in the Aichi region of central Japan, Ichikawa Fusae later claimed that she determined to improve women's lot in Japan when she saw how cruelly her father treated her mother. She trained as a teacher in Nagoya, and worked for several years as a teacher and the first women reporter for the liberal newspaper *Nagoya Shimbun*. In 1918 she visited Tokyo, where she joined the feminist activist **Hiratsuka Raichō** to form Shin Fujin Kyōkai (The New Women's Association) to press for women's political rights. From 1920 to 1924 she studied in the USA, where she met many leading suffragists including Carrie Chapman Catt, the founder of the League of Women Voters, and Alice Paul of the National Women's Party. A tall woman who smoked and wore her hair short, she was ridiculed by the Japanese press, but her steadfastness was for several years able to hold together a movement that was always in danger of fragmentation. In 1928 the Seiyūkai, one of Japan's two main political parties, took up the issue of women's suffrage, and in early 1931, following intense pressure from Ichikawa and her fellow activists, was able to push a bill giving women the vote through the lower house of the Diet (Japanese parliament). By this time, however, both the Japanese left and the suffrage movement were experiencing turbulent infighting: a public pro-suffrage rally in February 1931 erupted into bitter ideological argument, and violence broke out when a man attempted to drag Ichikawa from the speaker's podium. The following month the suffrage bill was heavily defeated in the House of Peers. The Japanese women's movement took many years to recover, and it was not until 1946 that women were given the vote. After two decades of lonely campaigning against a background of Japanese expansionism and political repression, Ichikawa Fusae returned to public political life in the late 1940s, founding the Women's Suffrage Centre and becoming head of the New Japan Women's League. In 1953 she was elected to the Diet, where she served for eighteen years. In 1974 she returned with the support of a strong women's alliance, and in 1980, a year before she died, was re-elected with more votes than any other candidate.

Susan Pharr, *Political Women in Japan*, University of California Press, 1981
Dee Ann Vavich, 'Ichikawa Fusae: A Pioneer in Women's Suffrage', *Monumenta Nipponica* 22 (1967)

Ivan Illich
1926–
writer, social and political commentator

There are few key areas of radical concern in the 1970s and 80s in which Ivan Illich has not made a major contribution: from education and health to employment and gender issues he has broken new ground. He grew up in Vienna, and was ordained as a Catholic priest in 1951. His studies took him to Florence, Rome, Munich and Salzburg before he was appointed vice-rector of the Catholic University of Ponce in Puerto Rico in 1956; in 1960, however, he was forced to resign after questioning church intervention in national politics, and moved to Mexico, where he set up the Centro Intercultural de Documentación in Cuernavaca. Illich left the priesthood in 1969, a natural consequence of his damning critique of the churches' missionary activity in Latin America, but is still based in Cuernavaca though he spends much of his time teaching in the USA and Germany. In 1970 his first book, *Celebration of Awareness*, matched the mood of the times with its bold critique of bureaucratic institutions and its call for personal freedom, but it was *Deschooling Society* (1972) which made him a household name. Its common sense argument that programmed schooling is at best incidental – and at its worst antipathetic – to a child's most important learning experiences was seized upon by radical teachers and students alike. Subsequent books applied the same detailed research and incisive reasoning to ideas about community (*Tools for Conviviality*, 1973), energy (*Energy and Equity*, 1974), medicine and healthcare (*Medical Nemesis*, 1976), modernity and progress (*Toward a History of Needs*, 1978) and work (*Shadow Work*, 1981). He was frequently criticised for not acknowledging the benefits of technological innovation and improving standards, yet many of his concerns were, within a decade of his analyses, to become major debates among forward-looking policy-makers. In 1982 he turned his attention to the limitations imposed by sex roles in *Gender*, and in *H(2)0 and the Waters of Forgetfulness* (1986) explored the problems inherent in the concept of liberation. Ivan Illich's early work may appear dated in the light of social and institutional changes during the 1980s and 90s, yet his role in bringing about those very changes has been crucial.

Ivan Illich, *Celebration of Awareness: A Call for Institutional Awareness*, Doubleday, 1970
Ivan Illich, *Deschooling Society*, Harper, 1971
Ivan Illich, *Medical Nemesis: The Expropriation of Health*, Calder and Boyars, 1975
Ivan Illich, *Shadow Work*, Boyars, 1981
Ivan Illich, *Gender*, Pantheon, 1983
Ivan Illich, *H(2)0 and the Waters of Forgetfulness*, Heyday, 1987
Edward Pease, *Encountering Ivan Illich*, Hertzberg, 1974

Ishikawa Sanshirō
1876–1956
anarchist, writer and labour organiser

Born early enough to witness the rigged trial and execution of Japan's early anarchist leaders, and living to see the beginnings of student unrest in the 1950s, Ishikawa Sanshirō's tireless campaigning and visionary writing mirrored in Japan many of the West's radical trends. As a young man Ishikawa was heavily influenced by Kōtoku Shūsui, whose execution in 1911 created an early martyr to the radical cause. From 1903 to 1907 he was a member of the socialist group **Heiminsha**, and was imprisoned for violating the press laws when he became publisher of its relaunched newspaper in 1907. He was also involved with socialist feminist Fukuda Hideko and her journal *Sekai Fujin*. From 1913 to 1920 Ishikawa lived in exile in Europe, mostly with the anarchist Reclus family in Brussels, but he returned to Japan to help found Zenkoku Jiren (All-Japan Libertarian Federation of Labour Unions) in 1926; by 1931 Zenkoku Jiren achieved a membership of 16,000, mostly of workers in small firms, but its antifascist stance attracted the attention of the authorities and it was banned in 1935. Ishikawa Sanshirō continued to campaign for workers' rights and democracy, writing many pamphlets and addressing meetings, and in 1946 was cofounder of Nihon Anākisuto Dōmei (Anarchist League of Japan). After the second world war he produced an anarchist vision of a bright new society in *Japan Fifty Years Later* (1950), which is still widely read, and in 1956 published an autobiography.

Peter Marshall, *Demanding the Impossible*, Harper Collins, 1992

Itō Noe
1895–1923
feminist, anarchist

The joint translator into Japanese of **Emma Goldman** and **Petr Kropotkin**, Itō Noe was raised in a village in the Fukuoka region of southern Japan and educated at Ueno Girls' High School near Tokyo. In 1913 she was forced into an arranged marriage in her home village, but soon escaped back to Tokyo, where she joined the feminist group Seitōsha, editing its magazine *Seitō* from 1915 to 1916. In 1916, after leaving her second husband, she started living with the anarchist **Ōsugi Sakae** and worked with him to develop the Japanese anarchist movement. As well as translating anarchist classics into Japanese she wrote several autobiographical novels and numerous articles on feminism and anarchism, at the same time as bringing up a large family. In 1921 she was one of the founders of Sekirankai, a socialist women's organisation. Two years later, shortly after the birth of her seventh child, she and Ōsugi were killed by military police in Tokyo during the purge of leftwing activists following the Great Kantō Earthquake of September 1923.

Nancy Andrew, 'Itō Noe', *Kodansha Encyclopedia of Japan*, 1983

C.L.R. [Cyril Lionel Robert] James
1901–1989
historian, writer

The Trinidadian writer and activist C.L.R. James was a careful and thorough analyst and explorer of Marxist theory and practice, and his emphasis on the latter is what marks him out from many others of his generation. Born and raised in Chaguanas, he studied at Royal College in Port of Spain before emigrating to England in 1932. His original intention was to become a novelist, but he soon became involved in Trotskyist politics and black history: his most important books date from his six years in London. *The Black Jacobins* (1938) showed how the slave revolt which created the first independent black nation in Haiti was related to and inspired by the French Revolution, while *A History of Negro Revolt* (1939) provided a much-needed overview of black protest. In 1938 James went to the USA, where he stayed until McCarthyism forced his expulsion in 1953. Here he helped form the Trotskyist Workers Party and its faction known as the Johnson-Forest Tendency, which operated on the understanding that workers were able to organise themselves rather than needing to be organised from above. After a short stay in Britain C.L.R. James returned to Trinidad, where he worked for a while with the ruling People's National Movement (arguing that in the absence of a revolutionary movement the first priority was independence from colonial rule), before forming the revolutionary Workers and Farmers Party in 1966: the party had little success, and in 1973 James returned to London, where he lived in London's working class borough of Brixton until his death. James' ability to listen to and articulate the black experience of imperialism and neocolonialism inspired many who came into contact with him, and his refusal to accept the simplistic solutions of mainstream Marxism ensured that his reasoning was always fresh and incisive.

C.L.R. James, *The Black Jacobins: Toussaint l'Ouverture and the San Domingo Revolution*, Random House, 1938

C.L.R. James, *A History of Negro Revolt*, Fact Books, 1939

C.L.R. James, *The Future in the Present* and *Spheres of Existence* (selected writings), Lawrence Hill, 1977 and 1980

Paul Buhle, *C.L.R. James: The Artisan Revolutionary*, Verso, 1988

Victor Jara
1938–1973
singer, civil rights campaigner

The Chilean singer-songwriter Victor Jara received international acclaim following his death at the hands of the military junta which overthrew the socialist regime of his friend **Salvador Allende**, but he had for many years been using the immediacy and passion of popular art to empower the ordinary people of Chile. Victor Jara grew up in a labouring family in Lonquen, a mountain village south-west of Santiago, but the family moved to Santiago after his mother spent a year in hospital. Victor went to a Catholic school and in 1950 entered a seminary in San Bernardo; he then spent a year in compulsory military service. An accomplished guitarist and singer, he started to work in plays, mimes and choral performances in Santiago theatres, rising to work as a theatre director and becoming increasingly interested in traditional Chilean folk songs and dances. In 1960 he met and married the English dancer Joan Turner Roberts, with whom he had two daughters, and continued to work as a theatre director and performer, working for nine years from 1961 with the Theatre Institute of the University of Chile. During his travels around Chile, much influenced by the rising tide of populist socialism, Victor collected, wrote and sang a growing and varied repertoire of songs, releasing his first hit record in 1964. As well as performing, Victor and Joan continued to work for socialist reform, using theatre, music and dance to convey the message of hope and change: in 1967 Victor dedicated one of his most popular songs, 'El Aparecido' ('The One Who Has Appeared') to **Che Guevara**, and started singing regularly at demonstrations and student protest meetings. In 1969 he organised the first Festival of New Chilean Song in Santiago and, while Chile moved towards the elections that would bring Allende to power in September 1970, the right wing press started to use Victor Jara as a target of ridicule and hatred. For the time being, however, the left had succeeded, and Victor was in demand all over Latin America and in Europe as a performer and ambassador for Allende's Chile. In March 1973 the Allende government was re-elected, but on September 11th a military coup led by Augusto Pinochet overthrew Chile's fragile democracy. Allende was murdered in the presidential palace, and Victor, who had been engaged to sing that day at Santiago Technical University, was arrested and taken with hundreds of others to a nearby stadium, where he was killed five days later. Victor Jara's moving songs were subsequently performed by many folk singers, and Joan Jara has continued to work hard for human rights in Latin America and beyond.

Victor Jara (foreword by Pete Seeger), *Victor Jara: His Life and Songs*, Elm Tree
    Books, 1976
Joan Jara, *Victor, An Unfinished Song*, Cape, 1983
Patrick White, *Homage to Victor Jara*, Steel Rail, 1985

Derek Jarman
1942–1994
film-maker, artist, writer, gay rights advocate

An outrageous and inspired artist, Derek Jarman's career was established during the 60s in London, where both his creativity and his homosexuality were able to flourish in fertile soil. He was born and brought up in suburban North London, and was often to return to his roots in an attempt to understand and describe the shared experiences of his generation. He studied at King's College and the Slade Institute's Department of Theatre Design; by the late 1960s he was already established as an inventive opera set designer, and in 1970 cut his film teeth as the set designer for Ken Russell's *The Devils*. Through the early 70s he experimented with film, but it was with *Sebastiane* (1976) that he first made his mark as a film-maker, aided by the denunciation of its nudity by the puritanical Mary Whitehouse. *Jubilee* (1978), *The Tempest* (1979), and most notably *Caravaggio* (1986) enhanced his reputation, all using Jarman's vivid imagination rather than expensive effects to achieve often breathtaking sequences. As well as making films he achieved considerable success both as an artist and as a writer, the latter starting with his autobiographical *Dancing Ledge* in 1984.

Throughout his career he wore his gayness ('queer' was his preferred word) with pride, convincing many of his radical contemporaries of the need to celebrate the variety of artistic traditions even when the mainstream seems dedicated to cultural mediocrity. In December 1986 he was diagnosed HIV-positive, but this seemed only to strengthen his fighting spirit. 'Finding I was body positive,' he wrote in 1991, 'I set myself a target: I would disclose my secret and survive Margaret Thatcher. I did.' His *Last of England* (a book and a film produced in 1987) was a ferocious attack on the moral and spiritual poverty of 1980s Britain, though by the early nineties films like *The Garden* (1990), *Wittgenstein* (1992) and *Blue* (1993) had become more personal and contemplative. He also continued to paint and write, finishing his last book, *Chroma*, only months before he finally succumbed to the AIDS virus. He had fought for dignity, friendship, understanding and the vital importance of creativity to the end.

Derek Jarman, *Dancing Ledge*, Quartet, 1984 (rev. edn 1991)
Derek Jarman, *At Your Own Risk: A Saint's Testament*, Hutchinson, 1992

Carolina Maria de Jesús
1913–1977
diarist

Carolina Maria de Jesús grew up in a poor family in the town of Sacramento in the Brazilian state of Minas Gerais. Educated to second grade, she started working as soon as she left school and had three children by a husband who left her. Like many impoverished Brazilians, she ended up in a slum *favela* in São Paulo, selling scrap paper and foraging for food for herself and her children. She had always liked books and writing for, as she explained, 'when I was writing I was in a golden palace, with crystal windows and silver chandeliers'. Starting in 1955 she kept a detailed and graphic diary of her life in the city slums, and with the help of journalist Audalio Dantas found a publisher for it. When *Casa de alvenaria* was published in 1961 it became an instant bestseller, selling out of its first edition of 10,000 in three days. Two years later it was still on the bestseller list, having sold more copies than any other Brazilian book in history, and the English translation, *Child of the Dark*, was also widely read. Carolina Maria de Jesús and her children were able to move into a comfortable house and help many of their *favela* neighbours; she continued to write until her death.

Carolina Maria de Jesús (trans. David St Clair), *Child of the Dark: The Diary of Carolina Maria de Jesús*, New American Library, 1963

Jiu Jin
1875–1907
revolutionary feminist, poet

Jiu Jin was the most remarkable of the feminists of China's early revolutionary period. She was given a broad education by her liberal parents and, living in a period of corruption, decadence and foreign domination, committed herself in her early twenties to the struggle for nationalism and reform. As her father was a Manchu official she had travelled widely within China, and after marrying a merchant's son in 1899 went to live in cosmopolitan Beijing. In 1904 she decided that marriage and material advantage were not conducive to her own emancipation: leaving her husband and son and selling her jewellery to provide herself with an income, she sailed for Japan where she studied for two years, writing poetry and articles for revolutionary journals and learning riding and self-defence. In her writing she constantly stressed the theme of heroic women who could rid their country of slavery and oppression. Her semi-autobiographical prose-poem, *Stones of the Jing-Wei Bird* (1905), was an early Chinese feminist classic, following the lives of five women as they threw off the constraints of traditional society and immersed themselves in revolutionary politics. Returning to China in 1906, she became a teacher in a girls' school in Chekiang, and was appointed as a representative of **Sun Yat-Sen**'s Revolutionary Alliance. She transformed the school into a centre for revolutionary activity and started publication of *The Chinese Women's Journal*. In 1907, however, she was implicated in a plot to overthrow the government, and was arrested and summarily executed. She soon became a legendary heroine and a model for generations of revolutionary Chinese women: women's armies invoked her spirit during the 1911 revolution and Sun Yat-Sen attended a memorial service to her in 1912.

Jonathan D. Spence, *The Gate of Heavenly Peace: The Chinese and their Reveloution 1895–1980*, Penguin, 1982

Kumari Jayawarden, *Feminism and Nationalism in the Third World*, Zed, 1986

Mother Jones [Mary Harris]
1830–1930
labour organiser

Mother Jones, the legendary American labour organiser, was born Mary Harris in Cork, Ireland. In her self-created role as mother to the family of working people, she would give her date of birth as May Day 1830, but may have been ten years younger. Her parents, who came from a tradition of active resistance to British rule, emigrated to North America when she was a child. She went to school in Toronto, taught at a convent in Michigan, worked as a seamstress in Chicago, and then moved to Memphis, Tennessee, to teach. There she married George Jones, an iron worker and union man, in 1861; six years later, he and their four children died in a yellow fever epidemic. Mary Jones returned to Chicago to set up a seamstress shop, which burned down in the Chicago fire of 1871. As she continued dressmaking for wealthy people, she became involved in union organising, and by 1880 she no longer had a permanent home, moving from place to place educating and organising workers, mostly coal miners, and their families. She had no use for the women's suffrage movement, regarding it as a bourgeois diversion from the class struggle. She helped organise the Socialist Party and later took part in the inception of the **Industrial Workers**

of the World, but her strengths did not lie in developing organisations, nor did she maintain a coherent political perspective. With her fighting spirit she had an extraordinary ability to rally exhausted people, and when she emerged at the turn of the century as 'Mother' to a loving family of working people, her authority as the voice of American radical conscious-ness was based on her own energy and courage. Mother Jones organised miners' wives to beat off strikebreakers with mops and brooms, and led children working in textile mills on a march from Pennsylvania to the home of President Theodore Roosevelt in New York. When a military court charged her with conspiracy to commit murder after a strike in West Virginia became violent, the governor of the state pardoned her. She headed at once to Colorado to support miners striking at a Rockefeller company, was jailed and thrown out of the state three times. When hired thugs machine-gunned and torched the tents of miners' families she toured the country and testified to the brutality in Congress. Mother Jones went on working into the 1920s, and enjoyed a gala celebration of her hundredth (or was it merely her ninetieth?) birthday. She died later that year and was buried, as she wished, in a union miners' cemetery.

Mother Jones, *The Autobiography of Mother Jones* (ed. Mary Field Parton), Charles H. Kerr, 1990.

Philip S. Foner, ed., *Mother Jones Speaks*, Monad, 1983.

Dale Fetherling, *Mother Jones: The Miners' Angel*, Southern Illinois University Press, 1974.

Priscilla Long, *Mother Jones: Woman Organizer, and Her Relations with Miners' Wives, Working Women, and the Suffrage Movement*, Red Sun Press, 1976.

Helen Joseph [Helen Beatrice May Fenell]
1905–1992
civil rights campaigner

One of South Africa's most persistent and actively subversive opponents of apartheid in South Africa, Helen Joseph overcame prison, house arrest, banning and severe illness to continue the fight for freedom and equality. She was born in southern England and spent three years in India before arriving in South Africa in 1931. She married Michael Joseph in 1932 (they divorced in 1948) and became a social worker, and after the war (when she worked as an army information officer) she started to involve herself in union work. She soon became aware that even the most 'progressive' of unions and political parties were not particularly interested in a universal franchise, so in 1952 she helped to establish the Congress of Democrats, in 1954 the Federation of South African Women (FedSAW), and in 1955 the Congress of the People. In August 1956 she helped to organise the historic FedSAW march on Pretoria, when 20,000 women from all over South Africa marched to protest against the pass laws which restricted black workers' freedom of movement. She was banned (restricted in her movements and prevented from working and publishing in South Africa) for the first time in 1957, and detained for five months in 1960. After her ban expired in 1962, she undertook a 7,000-mile journey throughout the country seeking out banished people, and was then served with South Africa's first house arrest order. During this time she became a close friend and ally of **Winnie Mandela**, whom she often referred to as her 'adopted daughter'. The arrest order was lifted in 1971 when she was suffering from cancer, but was reimposed from 1980 to 1982. In 1983 she was elected a patron of the United Democratic Front, a nonracial alliance of community, labour, church and women's groups, and spoke as passionately as ever at its launch. By the late 1980s the movement for democracy in South Africa was growing stronger by the day, and despite failing health Helen Joseph continued to impart in her speeches and writing the dignity, modesty, bluntness and humour that had always been her hallmarks. She died on Christmas Day, 1992.

Helen Joseph, *If This Be Treason*, Deutsch, 1963
Helen Joseph, *Tomorrow's Sun*, Hutchinson, 1966
Helen Joseph, *Side By Side*, Zed, 1986
Beata Lipman, *We Make Freedom: Women in South Africa*, Pandora, 1984

Kagawa Toyohiko
1888–1960
preacher, social reformer, labour leader, peace campaigner

Kagawa Toyohiko, sometimes referred to as 'Japan's **Gandhi**', is that country's best-known social activist and pacifist, especially in the English-speaking world, for during his many visits to North America between 1914 and 1941 he worked hard to build bridges between the two countries. Kagawa was born in Kōbe and orphaned at an early age; he was baptised a Christian while at middle school in Tokushima and went on to study at Kōbe Theological School and Princeton Theological Seminary in the USA. Returning to Japan in 1917, he devoted himself to helping the poor of Kōbe. In 1919 he joined the socialist organisation **Yūaikai** and led an unsuccessful 1921 strike by workers at the Mitsui and Kawasaki shipyards; he then moved to the Tōhoku region and helped to establish Japan's first nation-wide farmers' union. The enormous success of his first book, the strongly autobiographical *Shisen o Koete* (1920, *Beyond the Line of Death*, translated into English as *Before the Dawn*), provided him with funding to continue his proselytising work. As well as the powerful social gospel which he took every opportunity to preach, Kagawa Toyohiko also stressed the international pacifist cause. He was one of the founders of the National Anti-War League in 1928, and during his visits to the USA in 1931, 1935 and 1941 argued for the imperative of mutual understanding and cooperation. Recognising the impossibility of a peaceful solution to the Pacific War in the short term, Kagawa renounced his absolute pacifism in 1943, but resumed his pacifist activities with great vigour as soon as the war had ended. In 1946 he became a member of the upper house of the Diet (Japanese parliament) and, until it was discovered that he had been critical of both sides during the war, was considered by the leaders of the occupation forces as a possible prime minister. In his later years he was an enthusiastic supporter of the World Federation movement as a channel for ensuring world peace.

Kagawa Toyohiko (trans. I. Fukumoto and T. Satchell), *Before the Dawn*, George Doran, 1924

Kagawa Toyohiko (trans. Marion Draper), *Brotherhood Economics*, Harper and Bros., 1936

Jessie M. Trout, *Kagawa, Japanese Prophet: Witness in Life and Word*, Association Press, 1959

George Brown Bikle, *The New Jerusalem: Aspects of Utopianism in the Thought of Kagawa Toyohiko*, University of Arizona Press, 1976

Kang Yuwei
1859–1927
scholar, writer, reformer

One of China's leading intellectuals and reformers of the late nineteenth and early twentieth centuries, Kang Yuwei voiced calls for change that were marked by his insistence on equality and compassion. Born into a landlord-bureaucrat family, he travelled widely in Europe and North America, and in 1891 established the Wanmu Academy, which quickly developed into a centre for ideas about political reform. In 1895 he started a reformist newspaper, and wrote a book (which was banned) on the need to reinterpret Confucian texts so as to advocate a structural reform of Chinese society, while still respecting its ancient traditions. Kang Yuwei's major work was *The Book of the Great Community* (1903), a utopian vision in which he recognised that both rich and poor suffer from oppression, and envisioned a future without states and monarchs where men and women can be friendly and equal. He described women's oppression in China with great eloquence and indignation, and imagined a country in which the traditional family system had been abolished, where marriage was a renewable contract, and where women and men dressed the same. His ideas had considerable effect amongst the more radical intellectuals, with men cutting off their pigtails and women wearing their hair short and dressing in Western-style clothes as a symbol of emancipation. Kang Yuwei matched words with action, and was active in many early campaigns to ban the binding of women's feet.

Compilation Group for the History of Modern China Series, *The Reform Movement of 1898*, Foreign Languages Press, Beijing, 1976

Jonathan D. Spence, *The Gate of Heavenly Peace: The Chinese and their Reveloution 1895–1980*, Penguin, 1982

Kumari Jayawarden, *Feminism and Nationalism in the Third World*, Zed, 1986

Raden Ajeng Kartini
1879–1904
feminist, educationalist

The Javanese feminist Raden Ajeng Kartini was born in the northern town of Mayong, the daughter of a regional administrator. From an early age she set herself against the traditional seclusion and passivity of Javanese women. In 1898 she was one of the first Indonesian women to attend a European-style school, where she learned fluent Dutch as well as being introduced to the ideas being discussed by the Dutch colonialists: she was particularly inspired by the ideas of the Indian feminist **Pandita Ramabai**. With her newfound insight into both Javanese and European culture she started to write letters to correspondents in both Indonesia and Europe, discussing a wide range of subjects from the social segregation of women and the need for health education to the changing relationships between Indonesians and their colonial overlords. Kartini and two of her sisters, Kardinah and Roekmini, decided not to marry until they chose (a course then unheard of in traditional Javanese society). In 1900 Kartini started an important correspondence with a young Dutch socialist feminist, Estelle Zeehandelaar, and also met the newly-appointed Dutch director of education for the Netherlands East Indies, J.H. Abendanon, who after her death was instrumental in publishing her letters. In 1903, after two years of frustration and family disapproval, Kartini and Roekmini opened a girls' school in Mayong; the same year she wrote a memorandum to the colonial government called *Educate the Javanese!* which, thanks to Abendanon's interest, had a considerable effect on official policy. In November 1903, with a written promise from her future husband that she could continue her educational work, Kartini agreed to marry local administrator Raden Adipati Djojo Adiningrat. She refused to let her pregnancy halt the progress of the school, and continued to write on a variety of subjects including poverty and official corruption. In September 1904 her son was born, but four days after the birth Kartini was dead. Her collected letters were published in Dutch in 1911 and in English in 1920, and her aims were kept alive in a growing number of 'Kartini Schools' in Holland and Indonesia. Her sisters Roekmini, Kardinah and Soematri ran girls' school for many years, and in 1963 her birthday was declared an Indonesian public holiday.

Raden Adjeng Kartini (trans. Agnes Louise Symmers; foreword by Louis Couperus and intro. by Sartono Kartodirdjo), *Letters of a Javanese Princess*, Oxford University Press (Kuala Lumpur), 1976

Raden Adjeng Kartini (trans. Joost Cote), *Letters from Kartini: An Indonesian Feminist, 1900–1904*, Hyland House, 1992

Ailsa Thomson Zainu'ddin *et al*, *Kartini Centenary : Indonesian Women Then and Now*, Monash University, 1980

Jean Stewart Taylor, 'Raden Ajeng Kartini', *Signs: Journal of Women in Culture and Society*, Spring 1976

Petra Kelly [Petra Karin Lehmann]
1947–1992
green activist and politician

The death in October 1992 of Petra Kelly, best known of the leaders of **Die Grünen** (the German Green Party) in the 1980s, at the hand of her ex-military lover Gert Bastian, shocked the world. She was born in Günzberg, Bavaria, but when her mother remarried a US army officer in 1958 the family moved, first to a US base near Stuttgart and a year later to Fort Benning in Georgia, USA. In 1966 Petra Kelly enrolled in the American University in Washington to study politics and international relations. While she was at university her ten-year-old sister Grace developed cancer, from which she died three years later: thereafter Petra campaigned consistently for a better understanding of the causes and treatments of childhood cancer. In 1970 she returned to Europe to study at the Europa Institute in Amsterdam, and in 1971 started working in Brussels for the European Economic Community (EEC): her work with the EEC Economic and Social Committee concentrated on environmental and health policy. In 1972 she joined the Association of Environmental Protection Action Groups, a West German umbrella organisation, and the Social Democratic Party, from which she resigned in 1979 in protest against its apparent inaction on issues such as nuclear defence and equal opportunities. An innately political animal, she moved directly into the upper echelons of Die Grünen, becoming one of its three speakers in March 1980. She quickly became the international voice of the burgeoning German green movement, being awarded the Right Livelihood Award in 1982 and the Peace Woman of the Year Award in 1983, the year she was elected as one of seventeen Green members of the West German Bundestag. For the next decade she campaigned hard for the issues closest to her heart – nuclear disarmament, human rights, Tibet, and women's issues. Her pragmatic stance, however, annoyed and alienated more fundamentalist green activists, and Die Grünen's failure to win any seats in the December 1990 German elections was blamed partly on infighting between the Kellyite 'realos' and the 'fundis': the following year Die Grünen voted against her candidacy for party speaker. Petra Kelly had met Gert Bastian in 1980, and by the end of the decade they were rarely seen apart. Although she was still much in demand as a speaker and writer, when on October 1st 1992 Bastian shot first Petra and then himself their bodies were not discovered in their Bonn apartment for nearly three weeks – his motive appears to have been to save them both from the pain of future rejection and shame. Petra Kelly's legacy inspired many thousands of green activists, and her death reminded the movement of the costs of singlemindedness and dedication.

Petra Kelly, *Fighting for Hope*, Chatto and Windus, 1984
Petra Kelly (ed. Glenn Paige and Sarah Gilliatt), *Petra Kelly: Nonviolence Speaks to Power*, Center for Global Nonviolence, 1992

Petra Kelly (ed. Arnold Kotler), *Thinking Green! Essays on Environmentalism, Feminism and Nonviolence*, Parallax, 1994

Sara Parkin, *The Life and Death of Petra Kelly*, Pandora, 1994

Jomo Kenyatta [Johnstone Kamaua Ngengi]
*c.*1894–1978
writer, teacher, freedom campaigner, politician

Jomo Kenyatta was the most controversial black African of the 1950s. Denounced by the colonial administration of Kenya as 'the leader to darkness and death', he nevertheless led his people to independence and earned the respect and affection of both black and white, and of the world community. He was born at Ichaweri in the Kikuyu area of what was then British East Africa, and attended mission school before becoming a clerk in Nairobi and joining the Kikuyu Central Association (KCA) in 1924. During his first visit to Britain in 1929 he successfully lobbied for the introduction of independent Kikuyu schools; he returned to London in 1931 to petition for land rights, and stayed for fifteen years, studying and campaigning; while in Britain he married Edna Clarke, by whom he had a son (he already had two Kikuyu wives in Kenya), and met several other influential black nationalists including **Kwame Nkrumah** and **W.E.B. Du Bois**. On his return to Kenya in 1946 he worked as a teacher and political activist; he also married again, and with his fourth wife Ngina (another Kikuyu) had four more children. As the president of the Kenya African National Union (KANU) he was accused of incitement when racial tension broke out in violence in 1952: a state of emergency was declared and Kenyatta was arrested on suspicion of managing Mau Mau, an organisation formed to oppose colonial policies, though he always denied any personal connection. By the time he was released seven years later the 'emergency' was over: 199 whites and 12,500 blacks were dead. Independence was now inevitable, and Jomo Kenyatta became president on December 12th 1963. He showed considerable skill in bringing together his country's mixed peoples in a policy called 'harambee' (Swahili for 'pulling together'), developing grass-roots health and education systems and refusing to align Kenya with East or West, but his brand of African socialism was not as pure as that of his neighbour **Julius Nyerere**. He amassed considerable personal wealth, in-sisted on one-party rule (which persists under his protégé Daniel arap Moi), and his rival Tom Mboya was killed in suspicious circumstances, but at his death he was much mourned, and Kenya has avoided much of the blood-shed which has accompanied the independence of many African states.

Jomo Kenyatta, *Suffering without Bitterness: The Founding of the Kenya Nation*, East Africa Publishing House, 1968

Jeremy Murray-Brown, *Kenyatta*, Allen and Unwin, 1979

Dennis Wepman, *Jomo Kenyatta*, Burke, 1988

Martin Luther King, Jr
1929–1968
Baptist minister, civil rights activist

Martin Luther King, Jr, was born in Atlanta, Georgia. The child of a prominent clergy family active in the National Association for the Advancement of Colored People, he developed a solid sense of social responsibility and justice nurtured by African-American community life in the racially-segregated US South. He attended Morehouse College, Crozer Theological Seminary, and Boston University, studying sociology and philosophy and receiving a PhD in systematic theology. In 1954 he took his first church in Montgomery, Alabama, and within a few months was leading a boycott, organised by professional black women, against racially-segregated seating on buses. This sustained and successful nonviolent action provided a powerful model of an African-American community directly confronting oppressive power. In the following decade, as the black freedom struggle challenged and disrupted the social order of the South through sit-ins, freedom rides, marches and voter registration campaigns, Martin Luther King was, and was widely perceived as, the most influential leader in the movement. He organised and applied pressure through Gandhian nonviolent direct action infused with the spiritual power of black churches – an African-American satyagraha or 'soul force'. He was able to convince people, through their shared belief in and experience of their power, to confront and prevail over injustice. He also appealed to white liberals to bring social reality into accord with the professed ideals of American society. Martin Luther King's famous 'I have a dream' speech at the August 1963 march on Washington articulated his faith that the transformation of social relationships will follow when people's moral core is touched. The award of the Nobel Peace Prize in 1964 marked the apotheosis of Martin Luther King as a black leader recognised as the conscience of his society. Even as civil rights legislation was finally being enacted, however, riots in northern cities drew his attention to the despair and anger of northern blacks. Now he was confronting the most deeply entrenched capitalist interests in America. As he moved to link racism and poverty, he encountered strong opposition from southern civil rights colleagues as well as losing most of his support from the northern liberal establishment. When in 1967 he emerged publicly as an antiwar activist, it was in the face of even stronger opposition from his old allies, but he insisted that the link between peace and justice is unbreakable. In 1968, in the midst of organising the Poor People's Campaign in Washington DC, Martin Luther King travelled to Memphis, Tennessee to support striking sanitation workers. On April 4th he was shot and killed as he stood on the balcony of his motel room. The courage with which he sustained not only his work, but also his development as an organiser and activist, testify to the moral power on which he based his faith and work. His creative genius lay in melding Gandhian principles with an African-American idiom; the blend was enormously eloquent, and maintains a power that continues to inspire liberation movements in their own struggles all over the world.

James H. Cone, *Martin & Malcolm & America: A Dream or a Nightmare*, Orbis, 1991
David G. Garrow, *Bearing the Cross: Martin Luther King, Jr., and the Southern Christian Leadership Conference*, Morrow, 1986

Kiryū Yūyū
1873–1941
journalist, pacifist

Kiryū Yūyū grew up in Kanazawa in central Japan and studied at Tokyo University. Even as a student he was a prolific writer, publishing essays and a novel while still at university, and when he became a journalist in 1899 he used the newspapers he worked for as a channel for his spirited antimilitarism. For thirty years, many of them as editor-in-chief of the influential *Shinano Mainichi Shimbun*, he wrote outspoken editorials, many of them critical of Japan's militaristic government. Articles like 'The Ominous Cloud of the Japan-America War' and 'A Look at the Coming Difficulties for Japan' aroused the ire of the authorities, and when in 1933 he wrote an editorial headlined 'Laughing at the Kantō Air Defence Exercises' he was removed from his post. He continued to write his pacifist articles in his own publication, *Tazan no Ishi*, of which he published 176 issues in the eight years before he died of pneumonia in September 1941. Two months later Japanese forces attacked Pearl Harbor.

William D. Hoover, 'Kiryū Yūyū', *Biographical Dictionary of Modern Peace Leaders* (ed. Harold Josephson), Greenwood, 1985

Leopold Kohr
1909–1994
economist, writer, political commentator

Fritz Schumacher popularised the phrase 'small is beautiful', but it was the Austrian economist Leopold Kohr (in whose house in Puerto Rico Schumacher wrote his famous book) who most fully developed the idea of appropriate-scale political economy. Kohr was born and grew up in the small town of Oberndorf near Salzburg, and was fond of saying 'Everything I have learned worth knowing I learned in that small town'. He studied law and politics at Innsbruck and Vienna Universities, travelled in Spain during the Spanish Civil War as a freelance journalist, and had to leave Austria in a hurry and without papers in 1938 after writing an article critical of Hitler's regime. He ended up in Canada doing research work, and for the rest of his working life taught university-level economics, first at Toronto and Rutgers, then in Puerto Rico (1955–73), and latterly at the University of Aberystwyth in Wales (1973–78). All his books centred on the problems created by overgrown political, economic and social systems. *The Breakdown of Nations* (1957) provided detailed evidence of the efficiency and stability of small autonomous states, *Development Without Aid* (1973) argued that Third World countries could provide more for their people through self-sufficiency projects than through integration with the world economy, and *The Overdeveloped Nations* (1977) showed clearly how 'the larger the state, the worse off is the citizen'. He turned many of his ideas into specific proposals, and some were acted on. In 1969 he advised the leaders of the small Caribbean island of Anguilla to secede from St Kitts-Nevis; it promptly declared itself a republic and, although the rebellion was quickly quelled, the island became autonomous eleven years later. Having settled in Wales in 1973 he quickly adopted the cause of Welsh autonomy, and wrote an influential pamphlet entitled *Is Wales Viable?* In 1983 he was awarded a Right Livelihood Award, and in 1985 became president of the Salzburg-based Leopold Kohr Academy, which teaches a range of practical and political skills.

Leopold Kohr, *The Breakdown of Nations*, Routledge, 1957
Leopold Kohr, *Development Without Aid*, Davies, 1973
Leopold Kohr, *The Overdeveloped Nations: The Diseconomies of Scale*, Davies, 1977

Aleksandra Kollontai [Aleksandra Mikhaylovna Domontovich]
1872–1952
political activist, women's rights campaigner

Aleksandra Kollontai is generally considered to be Russia's most important pioneer feminist, though in her own country she is remembered more as a revolutionary and diplomat. She was born into an aristocratic family in St Petersburg, married her cousin Vladimir Kollontai in 1893, and had a son with him before they separated in 1898. Already well-versed in the writings of **Marx** and **Engels**, she studied for a year in Switzerland before returning to St Petersburg, joining the illegal Social Democratic Labour Party and starting to write about Marxist theory and practice. By 1905 she had become immersed in women's rights, though during the 1905 revolution she opposed the prevailing middle class version of feminism, being more interested in organising with working class women. In 1908 she fled Russia to avoid arrest, and it was during her ten-year exile that she wrote much of her most original work, exploring women's dependency and how it might be overcome following the abolition of private property, which she saw as the basis of and model for male power over women. In 1915 Kollontai joined the Bolsheviks, returning to Russia after the revolution of February 1917. She served briefly as commissar for social welfare, helping to draft the marriage laws and protective legislation for women workers; she also married her lover, commissar for the navy Pavel Dybenko, but this marriage too was short-lived. Her opposition to the Treaty of Brest-Litovsk led to her resignation from the Council of Commissars; she remained deeply concerned with women's issues, however, in 1918 helping to organise the first Congress of Russian Women and a year later the women's department of the Communist Party (Zhenotdel), which she headed from 1920 to 1922, when she was removed and given a diplomatic post in Norway. She spent the next 23 years in the diplomatic service, during which time she wrote several novels about women and their political struggle; in

1944 she negotiated the Soviet-Finnish armistice and, returning to the Soviet Union, served briefly as an adviser on foreign affairs before retiring due to ill health. Despite her later exile and relative obscurity, her work on behalf of working women during and after the Bolshevik Revolution remains Aleksandra Kollontai's abiding legacy.

Alexandra Kollontai, *The Autobiography of a Sexually Emancipated Women*, Herder, 1971

Alexandra Kollontai (ed. Alix Holt), *Selected Writings*, Hill, 1978

Barbara Evans Clements, *Bolshevik Feminist: The Life of Aleksandra Kollontai*, Indiana University Press, 1979

Beatrice Farnsworth, *Alexandra Kollontai*, Stanford University Press, 1980

Kōtoku Shūsui [Kōtoku Denjirō]
1871–1911
socialist activist and journalist, anarchist

For more than three decades, from his execution to the defeat of Japan in 1945, the name of Kōtoku Shūsui spelled 'dangerous traitor' to the Japanese authorities, while for radicals, both of his own era and of half a century later, he was the perfect symbol of a visionary willing to die for the populist cause. Born in Nakamura, a small town on the island of Shikoku, Kōtoku was a bright child and, although poverty prevented him from finishing school, studied and worked in Ōsaka with the eccentric scholar-journalist Nakae Chōmin, who introduced him to the works of **Rousseau** and **Petr Kropotkin**. Kōtoku started work as a journalist in 1893; by the late 1890s his dissatisfaction with the repressive militaristic policies of the Meiji regime had been voiced in his best-known book, *Nijisseiki no Kaibutsu Teikoku Shugi* (*Imperialism: The Spectre of the Twentieth Century*, 1901). In 1903, as war between Japan and Russia loomed, Kōtoku Shūsui and his journalist colleague Sakai Toshihiko resigned from the newspaper *Yorozu Chōzō* in protest at its militarist stance: they established the socialist-pacifist group **Heiminsha** and its newspaper *Heimin Shimbun*, which in 1904, just before it was closed down by the authorities and Kōtoku imprisoned for five months, carried the first Japanese translation of the *Communist Manifesto*. He now committed himself to the advocacy of direct action against the repressive government and inspired many leftwing activists, but in 1910, together with his common-law wife Kanno Suga, he was implicated in a plot to murder the Meiji emperor. Although he was almost certainly innocent of direct involvement, he was sentenced to death and hanged in January 1911. An outspoken and prescient critic of his times, Kōtoku was resurrected in the 1960s as a symbol of unflinching opposition to a dictatorial and inhumane government.

F.G. Notehelfer, *Kōtoku Shūsui: Portrait of a Japanese Radical*, Cambridge University Press, 1971

Larry Kramer
1935–
writer and AIDS activist

American writer and public health activist Larry Kramer was born in Bridgeport, Connecticut, graduating from Yale University in 1957. He worked in London as a production executive for Columbia Pictures from 1961 to 1965 and then moved to New York to work for United Artists. His 1970 screenplay of *Women in Love*, based on the novel by D.H. Lawrence, was nominated for an Oscar; his novel, *Faggots* (1978), however, met with a hostile reception from gay critics for its gritty depiction of the gay subculture's promiscuity and destructive effect of this on intimacy between gay partners. By the late 1970s nagging health problems were beginning to trouble men in New York's gay community. Alert to the appearance and spread of these strange symptoms, and to the first deaths, Larry Kramer cofounded Gay Men's Health Crisis in 1981. In the gay community he was charged with gay homophobia and anti-eroticism for suggesting that the spread of this unknown epidemic was linked with 'something we are doing'; officials, meanwhile, were doing nothing. By 1983, having succeeded in politicising the AIDS issue within the gay community, he withdrew from organising in order to write *The Normal Heart*. The play was premiered on April 21st 1985 and hailed as a masterpiece of political theatre, receiving the Best Play of the Year award in both London and Chicago; it at last won official recognition for AIDS as a civic crisis. Both in his creative work and in his campaigning Larry Kramer framed the gay movement as an issue not of sexual but of human liberation. He saw the promiscuity of the US gay subculture in which AIDS first spread as a distorted and inadequate response to the homophobia that denies gays the freedom of open partnership and the right to legal marriage. He also recognised the inaction of the governmental and medical establishments in the face of the AIDS epidemic as virulent homophobia. He was named Man of the Year for AIDS in Los Angeles in 1986, and in 1987 received the Arts and Communication award from the Human Rights Campaign Fund. In 1988, still seeking an effective means of mobilising direct action, he founded the influential campaigning network ACT-UP (**AIDS Coalition to Unleash Power**). He has continued to spearhead the organised militant response to AIDS; his *Reports from the Holocaust* (1990) vividly described his experiences as an AIDS activist.

Larry Kramer, *Faggots*, Random House, 1978

Larry Kramer, *Reports from the Holocaust: The Making of an AIDS Activist*, Penguin, 1990

Randy Shilts, *And the Band Played On*, Penguin, 1987

Petr [Alekseevich] Kropotkin
1842–1921
geographer, social anarchist, writer

The 'anarchist prince' Petr Kropotkin can justly be considered the main source of modern anarchist thinking, his ideas about the ills of imposed authority and centralised bureaucracy inspiring generations of radical activists right through to the 1970s and 80s, when many rediscovered his forward-looking ideas. He was born into a noble Moscow family and served in the Imperial Army from 1862 to 1867, spending several years in Siberia where he studied the landscape and enjoyed sharing the company of the peasantry; he also read **Tolstoy** and learned to distrust centralised authority. He then returned to St Petersburg to continue his scientific studies, at the same time becoming more involved with radicalism, including the revolutionary Chaikovsky Circle. His subversive activities were halted by his arrest and imprisonment in March 1874, but three years later he escaped and fled to England. The next forty years were spent in exile in Britain, France and Switzerland, where he wrote his most important anarchist tracts including *Fields, Factories and Workshops* (1898) and *Mutual Aid* (1902), as well as continuing to produce pioneering works in geography and geology. Anticipating later green thinking, Kropotkin recognised the social and environmental limits to growth and progress, and criticised authoritarian regimes for stifling innate human inventiveness and cooperation. He saw a future in which people participated directly in decisions affecting their lives, and redefined 'political economy' to mean the best and most energy-efficient way of fulfilling people's true needs. He fervently believed that such a revolution was not only possible, but inevitable, and his unshakeable faith in an anarchist future successfully combined hope with vision, qualities which have ensured his enduring popularity. Petr Kropotkin became less involved in the day-to-day organisation of the European anarchist movement after 1890, and was quick to distance himself from the growing number of terrorist atrocities perpetrated in the name of anarchism: his purpose was to show that true anarchism was rooted in science and ethics, not in mindless violence. After the Bolshevik Revolution in February 1917 he returned to Moscow, where he died four years later.

Peter Kropotkin, *Fields, Factories and Workshops*, Harper and Row, 1974 (repr. of 1898 ed.)

Peter Kropotkin, *Mutual Aid: A Factor of Evolution*, Freedom Press, 1987 (repr. of 1917 ed.)

George Woodcock and Ivan Avakumovič, *The Anarchist Prince: A Biographical Study of Peter Kropotkin*, Schocken, 1950

Martin Miller, *Kropotkin*, University of Chicago Press, 1976

Kuroda Joichi
1951–
environmental campaigner and activist

A graduate in rural sociology, Kuroda Joichi has quickly become one of Japan's leading green campaigners. As the coordinator of the Japan Tropical Forest Action Network (JATAN), set up in 1987 by **Friends of the Earth** Japan, his inventive and persistent probing of Japan's wasteful 'scrap and rebuild' economy quickly brought tangible results. Japan's taste for exotic natural resources is well-researched by environmentalists, and its seemingly insatiable appetite for tropical hardwoods is voracious – in 1990 it imported 20 million cubic metres, more than a third of the world total. Kuroda Joichi's researches into the tropical timber trade made him the obvious candidate to spearhead JATAN, and within weeks of the organisation's launch he publicised his discovery that large sums of foreign aid were funding massively destructive deforestation in Sarawak on land part-owned by one of Japan's biggest companies. The resulting scandal did much to publicise the green cause, and Kuroda capitalised on the new awareness by producing, with French activist François Nectoux, a detailed study of Japan's timber trade, *Timber from the South Seas* (1989). In March 1989 JATAN, with Kuroda at the helm, organised a massive rainforest demonstration in the heart of Tokyo's business district, and later that year it organised the first of several 'Rock for the Rainforests' concerts. Kuroda Joichi's work has inspired several similar Japanese environmental campaigns, notably against whaling and indiscriminate tuna fishing.

Fred Pearce, *Green Warriors*, Bodley Head, 1991

Ellen Kuzwayo
1918–
educator, women's rights activist

Ellen Kuzwayo has been called 'The Mother of Soweto', acknowledging her tireless work for more than thirty years to organise and improve the status of black women in the South African region of the Transvaal. Born in Thaba Nchu into an extended family with a strong grandmother and an enlightened grandfather, she trained as a teacher and then, having married and had three children, as a social worker. From 1964 to 1976 she was secretary of the Young Women's Christian Association in the Transvaal, helping women in a variety of health, education, agriculture and small-scale technology projects. In 1976, during the period of the Soweto student uprising and the imposition of martial law, she was the only woman on the 'Committee of Ten' elected to represent the local community. Since then she has worked mostly in Soweto, founding the Soweto Zomani Sisters as a network of women's self-help economic and discussion groups, and bringing together church groups, trade unions and other organisations to work for women's rights. A vociferous and fluent speaker, she is clear that unless women's contribution to the freedom struggle is fully acknowledged, much of South Africa's newly-found liberation is threatened.

Ellen Kuzwayo, *Call Me Woman*, Womens Press, 1985
Beata Lipman, *We Make Freedom: Women in South Africa*, Pandora, 1984

Selma [Ottiliana Lovisa] Lagerlöf
1858–1940
writer, teacher, women's rights advocate

Considered by many Swedes to be their country's greatest early twentieth-century writer, Selma Lagerlöf captured the imagination of her many readers with the freshness of her insight and creativity. By the time she was awarded the Nobel Prize for Literature in 1909, the first women to receive it, she was already well-known throughout Europe and beyond and, as Vita Sackville-West commented in her preface to a 1931 biography, 'She writes always as a woman: not one of her books could have been written by a man.' Selma Lagerlöf grew up in Mårbacka in rural Värmland, and local traditions and legends became an important source of her inspiration; she suffered from poor health, which forced her to spend much time in quiet introspection. She went to teacher training college in Stockholm, and her first novella, *Gösta Berling's Saga*, was published in 1891 to much critical acclaim; she continued to write bestselling novels and autobiography for the rest of her life. From 1895 to 1912 she spent much of her time travelling throughout Europe and the Middle East, accompanied by her close friend the writer Sophie Elkan and using her experiences as the basis for her writing. In 1911 she became active in the suffrage movement, delivering an important speech at the sixth convention of the **International Woman Suffrage Alliance** in Stockholm. During the 1914–18 war she was involved in Polish relief work, and two postwar collections of short stories express her horror of the violence and inhumanity she witnessed during those years. One of the joys of her life was the opportunity to buy back her family's farm when it came on the market in 1908; she died in the house where she was born.

Selma Edström, *Selma Lagerlöf*, Twayne, 1985
Rose Collis, *Portraits to the Wall: Historic Lesbian Lives Unveiled*, Cassell, 1994

R.D. [Ronald David] Laing
1927–1989
psychiatrist, writer

R.D. Laing was a straight-talking Glasgow-born doctor and psychiatrist who in the 1960s and 70s questioned many conventional wisdoms about psychiatry and family life. He studied at Glasgow University and the Tavistock Institute for Human Relations in London, practising as a psychiatrist with a special interest in schizophrenia and dysfunctional families. His public career began in 1959 with the publication of *The Divided Self*, which showed how what might seem abnormal about a schizophrenic to most people often makes total sense from within that schizophrenic's own worldview. His popular and accessible writing style, and his willingness to share his outspoken yet keenly-observed insights into human nature, had much popular appeal, and his subsequent books, including *The Self and Others* (1962), *Sanity, Madness and the Family* (in collaboration with Aaron Esterson, 1964), *The Politics of Experience* and *The Bird of Paradise* (1967), *The Politics of the Family* (1969) and *Knots* (1970), all became bestsellers. In April 1965 Laing and some of his likeminded colleagues founded the Philadelphia Association to provide housing and treatment for mentally disordered patients, particularly people suffering from schizophrenia: the first of its centres, Kingsley Hall in East London, achieved both success and widespread public interest. Throughout his career R.D. Laing consistently opposed the unnecessary confinement of mental patients; as a political libertarian he believed that everyone, including psychotics, had the right to choose how and where to spend their time. He doubted whether schizophrenia is a real illness, and always strove to find meaning – and thus potential healing – in bizarre behaviour. He held strong but well-argued views on child-rearing, education, religion, sex and drugs, and his willingness to criticise authoritarian regimes found a ready audience within radical circles. His ideas were frequently distorted and taken to extremes by well-meaning disciples (for whom he had little patience), yet his insights and techniques have had a lasting impact on psychiatry and psychotherapy, particularly in the way that schizophrenia and family issues are handled.

R.D. Laing, *The Divided Self*, Penguin, 1962
R.D. Laing, *The Politics of Experience* and *The Bird of Paradise*, Penguin, 1967
R.D. Laing, *Madness and Folly: The Making of a Psychiatrist*, Macmillan, 1985
    (reissued the following year as *Wisdom, Madness and Folly*)
Roy Coad, *Laing*, Hodder, 1979

George Lansbury
1859–1940
socialist politician, journalist and peace campaigner

Britain's most consistent antiwar and populist politician of the early twentieth century, George Lansbury was born into a working class family in Lowestoft, Suffolk, and grew up in the East End of London. In 1884, married and with three small children, he emigrated to Australia, but after a disastrous year in Queensland returned to agitate against the misleading propaganda that had tempted so many to leave home: the outcome was the establishment in 1886 of the Emigration Information Department. George Lansbury now became actively involved in a range of political action on behalf of the poor of East London, joining the Social Democratic Federation and subsequently the Independent Labour Party and the Labour Party. In the 'khaki election' during the Boer War in 1900 he courageously stood as an antiwar socialist candidate, but only in 1910 was he elected to parliament. Already well-known for favouring direct action (in 1892 he forced a workhouse inspector to taste institutional porridge for himself, and in 1905 led a large deputation of destitute women to Prime Minister Balfour's private office), he continued to fight for the underprivileged: while stoutly defending women's rights in 1913 he was expelled from the House of Commons and briefly imprisoned in Pentonville, where he promptly went on hunger strike. He now became editor of the *Daily Herald* in time to publish the headline 'War is Hell' at the outbreak of hostilities; he held this influential position until 1924. In 1919 he was also appointed mayor of the London borough of Poplar, where he led a campaign to ensure that the city's poorest districts were not expected to pay for their services at the same rate as richer boroughs. Poplar Council's refusal to levy rates on the poor led to Lansbury's second short term in prison, this time in Brixton. He was returned to parliament in 1922, and for four years from 1931 led the Labour Party in opposition: by 1935, however, his convinced pacifism was hard to sustain amid the preparations for a seemingly inevitable war in Europe, and he was again forced to leave national politics. During the late 1930s George Lansbury served as chair of the No More War Movement and as president of **War Resisters International**; at the time of his death he was also president of the **Peace Pledge Union** (PPU). His last message to the PPU concluded: 'So, comrades, with confidence hold on to the truth your conscience reveals to you, and honour and respect those whose conscience leads them along the opposite road.'

George Lansbury, *My Life*, Constable, 1928
Raymond Postgate, *The Life of George Lansbury*, Longmans, 1951
Jonathan Schneer, *George Lansbury*, Manchester University Press, 1990

Frances Moore Lappé
1944–
writer, educator and social activist

Frances Moore was born in 1944 in Pendleton, Oregon, and graduated from Earlham College in 1966. She had two children with her first husband, Marc Lappé, whom she married in 1967. The striking success of her first book, *Diet for a Small Planet* (1971), testified to the power of what was to be the basic characteristic of her work: radical analysis framed so that ordinary people can act upon it. After showing how it is gross inequalities in buying power that are at the root of hunger, *Diet* offered recipes using high-yield grains and beans, rather than meat, as protein sources. With Joseph Collins, Frances Moore Lappé founded the Institute for Food and Development Policy (IFDP), also known as Food First, in 1975 as a centre of education for action, conducting research and analysis to provide organisers and movements with effective tools for social change. During her fifteen years with IFDP she coauthored many publications, demonstrating that it is antidemocratic power structures, nor primarily scarcity or overpopulation, that create hunger. She and Joseph Collins argue in *Aid as Obstacle* (1980) that the most effective response that people in industrialised nations can make to the hunger of people in the Third World is to remove the obstacles that deny people the ability to feed themselves. This means cutting the military aid that keeps élitist antidemocratic governments in control, for, as she has observed, 'It takes violence to keep people hungry'. Her work has won her a number of awards, including the Right Livelihood Award in 1987 'for revealing the economic and political causes of world hunger and how citizens can help remedy them'. She left San Francisco in 1990 for Brattleboro, Vermont, to found and direct with her second husband Paul Martin Du Bois the Center for Living Democracy, an organisation working to encourage the creation of a truly participatory democracy in the USA.

Frances Moore Lappé and Joseph Collins, *World Hunger: Twelve Myths*, Food First, 1986

Frances Moore Lappé and Rachel Schurman, *Taking Population Seriously*, Food First, 1990

Frances Moore Lappé and Paul Martin Du Bois, *Rebuilding Our Nation, Remaking Our Lives*, Jossey-Bass, 1994

Christopher Lasch
historian, social critic
1932–1994

A penetrating critic of materialistic progress and corporate capitalism, Christopher Lasch's detailed and disturbing surveys of American life demonstrate the progressive use of historical study in social criticism and contemporary decision-making. Lasch grew up in Omaha, Nebraska, and studied at Harvard and Columbia. He considered becoming a journalist like his father, but chose university teaching instead, lecturing at Williams College, the University of Iowa and Northwestern University before joining the history faculty at the University of Rochester in 1970. In 1979 he was appointed Rochester's Don Alonzo Watson Professor of History, a post he held until his death. Christopher Lasch had always been interested in the history of radicalism in the USA, and his early books, *The American Liberals and the Russian Revolution* (1962) and *The New Radicalism in America* (1965), explored the tensions between liberal reform and political activism. *The Agony of the American Left* (1969) came out of Lasch's concern that affluence was in danger of snuffing out America's awareness of alternatives to capitalism, and called for a new, mature radical programme for the USA. It was his bestselling *Culture of Narcissism* (1979) that brought Christopher Lasch's fluent and incisive analysis to a wider audience: here he showed how the rugged individualism upon which America had flourished for decades was turning into a shallow consumption-led narcissism in which corporations and bureaucratic government feed false needs at the cost of individual integrity. In this and subsequent books Lasch was especially interested in the notion that each generation should be better off than its predecessor: he was convinced that, because people's true needs for community and involvement were not being met, this would always lead to a yearning for the relative simplicity and meaningfulness of bygone eras. During the 1980s and 90s Christopher Lasch was a regular contributor to national magazines and newspapers, and an adviser to the Center for the

Study of Commercialism. Married (to fellow historian Nell Commager) and with four grown children, he died of cancer in February 1994.

Christopher Lasch, *The New Radicalism in America*, Vintage, 1965
Christopher Lasch, *The Agony of the American Left*, Knopf, 1969
Christopher Lasch, *The Culture of Narcissism: America in an Age of Diminishing Expectations*, Norton, 1979
Christopher Lasch, *The Minimal Self*, Norton, 1984

Vladimir Ilich Lenin [Vladimir Ilich Ulyanov]
1870–1924
revolutionary, politician

Lenin's achievement in masterminding the establishment of state communism throughout eastern Europe and northern Asia makes him one of the key political figures of the early twentieth century. He was born in Simbirsk (renamed Ulyanovsk after his death) and raised in an intellectual middle class family. In 1887 his oldest brother Aleksandr, who had joined an underground circle while studying at St Petersburg University, was implicated in a plot to murder the Emperor, arrested and hanged. Lenin inherited his brother's books (which included works by **Marx**, **Engels**, and the Russian Marxist Plekhanov), and was himself involved with revolutionary organisations while studying at Kazan and St Petersburg Universities. From 1893 to 1895 he developed links with other Marxists, both at home and in exile, but in December 1895 he was arrested, spending two years in prison and three in Siberian exile, where he met and married fellow revolutionary Nadezhda Krupskaya. After his release in 1900 he went to Switzerland to make contact with Plekhanov: they took effective control of the nascent Russian Democratic Labour Party and founded the important journal *Iskra* (*The Spark*). Seeking a method for speeding up the revolutionary process without abandoning the Marxist belief in inevitable proletarian success, Lenin evolved the idea of the Party, a dedicated group of professional revolutionaries who would act as the 'vanguard of the proletariat' – widespread class consciousness could come later. There was much criticism of Lenin's centralist and disciplinarian approach, and at the 1903 Democratic Labour Party Congress the issue split the party between Lenin's followers (the 'Bolsheviks' or 'majoritarians') and his opponents (the 'Mensheviks' or 'minoritarians'). This would have had little impact within Russia if revolutionary pressure had not erupted, first in 1905 and again in 1917. After the 1905 revolution Lenin spent two years in Russia, but found little support for Bolshevism; in 1917, however, he was much better prepared, having in 1912 set up the Party's Central Committee and established himself through his writings and organising ability as the Bolsheviks' natural leader. Although the February 1917 revolution took Lenin by surprise, he quickly established the Bolshevik Central Committee in St Petersburg: in October the Provisional Government was overthrown and, following a Red Guard coup, a Lenin-led Council of People's Commissars took its place – the Soviet Union was born. Decrees concerning land reform and the need for peace were quickly passed, but civil unrest grew and Lenin was only able to maintain control by exerting ever more centralised power. Unrest turned into civil war, yet his leadership (and **Leon Trotsky**'s role as military commander) succeeded in overcoming opposition; towards the end of the war in 1919 Lenin showed that he was capable of flexibility, promising autonomy to the country's non-Russian nationalities and widespread land reform to give peasants land of their own. By now, however, he was very ill: weakened by an assassination attempt in 1918, he had a stroke in 1921 and spent much of his last two years scarcely able to speak or move. His death left a dangerous power vacuum, to be filled by Iosif Stalin with disastrous results. After Lenin's death both he and his writings were canonised, the latter as the key texts of Marxism-Leninism and the basis of communist thought. Throughout his life and thought, however, ran the contradiction of using centralised control to effect populist revolution: his 1917 prediction that 'dictatorship will eventually wither away into a noncoercive, classless and stateless society' was doomed – largely by his own actions – never to materialise.

V.I. Lenin, *Selected Works*, Lawrence and Wishart, 1969
Herman Weber, *Lenin: His Life and Works*, Macmillan, 1980
Robert Service, *Lenin: A Political Life*, Macmillan, 1985 (Vol. 1) and 1991 (Vol 2)
Ronald Clark, *Lenin: The Man Behind The Mask*, Faber, 1988

Sidney Lens [Sidney Okun]
1912–1986
labour organiser, peace activist, writer

The influential American labour organiser and peace campaigner Sidney Lens (he changed his name in 1934 when blacklisted for union activity) was born in Newark, New Jersey; his father died when he was three years old and his mother supported the family by working in a New York sweatshop. His first experience of the dangers of labour organising came when he was working as a waiter in an Adirondack resort in 1930: he led a strike for better working conditions and, as a result, was dragged from his bed one night, beaten by the local police and abandoned in the forest. He now threw himself into labour organising, helping to mobilise journalists in New York, auto workers in Detroit and cab drivers in Washington. In 1941 he successfully formed a Chicago branch of the United Services Employees Union, ridding the union of mob influence and providing himself with a base of operations for most of his career. Sidney Lens vigorously opposed America's entry into the second world war, and for the rest of his life worked to combine labour organising with peace campaigning. In 1960 he was a cofounder of the Fair Play for Cuba Committee and became a leader in the anti-**Vietnam War** campaign; in 1976 he helped to establish the antinuclear peace organisation Mobilization for Survival, and in 1985 was one of the organisers of the Conference on Socialism and Activism in New York. He was also a fervent believer in broadly-based socialist political movements, becoming active in the People's Party in the early 1970s and the Citizens' Party in the early 80s. The author of numerous books and articles, he also wrote a compelling autobiography, *Unrepetant Radical*.

Sidney Lens, *Radicalism in America*, Crowell, 1966 (rev. ed. Schenkman, 1982)
Sidney Lens, *The Promise and Pitfalls of Revolution*, United Church Press, 1974
Sidney Lens, *Unrepentant Radical*, Beacon, 1980

Li Fei-Kan (Pa Chin)
1904–
novelist, anarchist and cultural critic

The Chinese anarchist Li Fei-Kan was born in Chengtu, the capital of Sichuan province, where his father was magistrate from 1906 to 1911. His mother died when he was ten and his father two years later; he then went to live with his despotic grandfather, which instilled in him an intense hatred for the traditional Chinese family system. As a teenager in 1919 he read an article by **Emma Goldman** and resolved to become an anarchist, an ambition he was able to develop when in 1927 he went to study in Paris for two years. While in Paris he translated **Petr Kropotkin**'s *Ethics* into Chinese, and adopted the *nom-de-plume* 'Pa Chin', a contraction of the names of his mentors **Bakunin** and Kropotkin. He was particularly shocked by the execution of the American anarchists **Sacco and Vanzetti** in August 1927, and he wrote many articles about them and other revolutionaries. Pa Chin's best-known work is the still-popular trilogy *Torrent* (*Family, 1933; Spring,1938; Autumn*,1940), a vivid family saga later made into a film and translated into English. In the mid-1940s Li Fei-Kan, a trenchant critic of centralised political power, turned to journalism and public speaking. Although imprisoned on several occasions (the latest in 1987 when he spoke in support of protesting students), he has always re-emerged to resume his role as one of China's leading writers and critics, his loyal public following ensuring that his voice has not been stifled. Even during the growth and tribulations of China's democracy movement in the late 1980s Pa Chin, still as vociferous as ever, remained for many young writers and activists a symbol of steadfastness in the radical cause.

Pa Chin, *Family*, Anchor, 1972
Olga Lang, *Pa Chin and His Writings: Chinese Youth between the Two Revolutions*, Harvard University Press, 1967
Helmut Martin and Jeffrey Kinkley (eds), *Modern Chinese Writers: Self-Portrayals*, Sharpe, 1992

Vicente Lombardo Toledano
1894–1968
labour organiser

By the late 1940s many Mexican activists felt that the social and political goals of the 1911 revolution had been forgotten, and it was clear that political corruption and complacency had allowed large landowners to maintain control over the country's predominantly agricultural economy. Vicente Lombardo Toledano was a writer and journalist who had as a young man written about and been inspired by **Emiliano Zapata**'s attempts to bring about agrarian reform, only to see these policies thwarted when in 1916 President Venustiano Carranza engaged the support of the anarcho-syndicalist Casa del Obrero Mundial (World Workers' Federation) against Zapata, before banning the Casa and reversing the agrarians' achievements. In 1948, having written for many years about the need to reempower Mexico's working class, Lombardo established the Partido Popular (PP) to unify the demands of intellectuals and manual workers within a nationalist socialist framework. He recognised that the key to self-determination for Mexico's rural poor was reform of land tenure, combined with freedom from the imposition of Spanish as a dominant language and the use of threat and violence to ensure compliance with centralist policies. The PP and its successor, the Partido Popular Socialista (PPS), both headed by Lombardo, worked hard for social and economic justice by peaceful means, and the PPS remains an important force in leftwing Mexican politics. Lombardo was also a fervent believer in the need for workers to organise internationally, and was the founder of the Confederación de Trabajadores de America Latina (Confederation of Latin American Workers).

Vicente Lombardo Toledano, *Fifth Column in Mexico*, Council for Pan-American Democracy, 1942

Vicente Lombardo Toledano, *The United States and Mexico: Two Nations, One Ideal*, Council for Pan-American Democracy, 1942

Robert P. Milton, *Mexican Marxist: Vicente Lombardo Toledano*, University of North Carolina Press, 1966

Audre Lorde
1934–1992
poet, essayist, political activist

A year before she died the black poet and activist Audre Lorde was appointed New York State's Walt Whitman Poet Laureate: Governor Mario Cuomo spoke for many when he described her as 'a voice of eloquent courage and unflinching honesty'. She was born to a Grenadian mother and a Barbadian father in the poor New York district of Harlem: Audre grew up poor, almost blind (until thick glasses were prescribed), and frequently punished, yet a streak of rebellion already existed when, at the age of thirteen, she wrote to President Truman to protest against racial discrimination in ice cream shops. By the early 1950s she was involved in political activism, taking part in the 1953 Washington demonstration to free the **Rosenbergs** and joining the Labor Youth League and the Harlem Writers' Guild; she also started experimenting with lesbian relationships, and became an outspoken advocate of gay rights. The 1960s and 70s, though often exhilarating, continued to be precarious both economically and emotionally as she fearlessly exposed the unacknowledged racism within radical circles, especially among feminists: in a much-debated open letter to **Mary Daly** in 1979 she wrote 'To imply that all women suffer the same oppression is to lose sight of the many varied tools of patriarchy. The oppression of women knows no ethnic or racial boundaries, but that does not mean it is identical within those boundaries.' Another favourite theme was demolishing ideas about what is 'normal', arguing for a 'mythical norm' which almost everybody recognises as 'not me'. Audre Lorde's influence grew rapidly through the 1980s, and in 1981 she was a cofounder of the publishing house Kitchen Table which made the writings of women of colour more widely available. During most of the 1980s she taught at New York's Hunter College, continuing to write poetry, essays and articles and helping to found Sisterhood in Support of Sisters in South Africa and the National Coalition of Black Lesbians and Gays. She was diagnosed as having breast cancer in 1978, and published *The Cancer Journals* in an attempt to examine the political context of her disease. In 1989 she moved with her partner Gloria Joseph to the Virgin Islands, where she died three years later.

Audre Lorde, *The Cancer Journals*, Spinsters Ink, 1980
Audre Lorde, *Zami: A New Spelling of My Name*, Persephone, 1982
Audre Lorde, *A Burst of Light*, Firebrand, 1988
Cherrie Moraga and Gloria Anzaldua (eds), *This Bridge Called My Back: Writings by Radical Women of Color*, Kitchen Table, 1983
Lisa Duggan, 'Audre Lorde', *The American Radical* (ed. Mari Jo Buhle, Paul Buhle and Harvey J. Kaye), Routledge, 1993

Lu Xun [Zhou Shuren]
1881–1936
writer, poet and social critic

'Lies written in ink can never disguise facts written in blood' wrote the Chinese critic Lu Xun in 1926, just after police in Beijing shot into a crowd of students, killing forty of them. It is hardly surprising that Lu Xun's warning was vividly remembered 63 years later by the students of the 1989 hunger strike in Tiananmen Square. Born to an educated family in Shaoxing, south of Shanghai, Lu Xun studied to be a doctor at Nanjing and in Japan, but in his early twenties he resolved to devote his life to literature and the documentation of oppression in his home country, especially of the Chinese by the Japanese, of the ordinary people by a cruel administration, and of women under a feudal patriarchy. Already a prolific translator of European and Russian literature, he started writing fiction and poetry in 1918, coming to public notice with a story called 'The Diary of a Madman' about the endemic self-destructive aspect of Chinese culture. By 1926, when he settled permanently in Shanghai, he was regarded as one of the best storytellers of his age. Following the 1927 *volte-face* by the nationalist Kuomintang government of Chiang Kai-Shek, when more than 40,000 communists were massacred, Lu Xun became an increasingly outspoken critic of state repression and violence. The latter years of his life were spent in hiding in the Japanese enclave of Shanghai. Admired by **Mao Zedong** and with his reputation reinstated after the Communist victory of 1949, Lu Xun is considered one of China's great literary radicals. Contemporary social activists, however, point out that he would have been as critical of the repressions of the late 1980s as he was of the injustices he witnessed in his lifetime, and mention of Lu Xun still arouses suspicion amongst Chinese authorities.

Lu Hsun: Collected Works (4 volumes, ed. Yang Hsianyi and Gladys Yang), Foreign Languages Press, Beijing, 1956
Michael True, *To Construct Peace*, Twenty-Third Publications, 1992

Albert [John] Luthuli
1898–1967
teacher, civil rights campaigner

The first African to receive a Nobel Peace Prize, Albert Luthuli was president of the **African National Congress** (ANC) from 1952 until his death. He was born near Bulawayo in Southern Rhodesia (now Zimbabwe) and educated at a Methodist mission school, where he continued to teach for fifteen years until 1936, when he was elected chief of the Zulu Abasemakholweni tribe. In 1945 he joined the ANC and quickly rose within the organisation, becoming president of the Natal branch in 1951 and president-general the following year. Albert Luthuli was strongly influenced by his Christian convictions and by the American civil rights struggle; he was insistent that white and black, women and men, were equal. He refused to endorse armed insurrection, putting his faith in Gandhian passive resistance. In the late 1950s he was repeatedly arrested for 'provoking hostilities'; in December 1956 he was charged (along with **Nelson Mandela**, **Oliver Tambo** and **Walter Sisulu**) with high treason under the Suppression of Communism Act, but the charges were dropped the following year. In 1959 he was banished to a remote farm in western Natal and his freedom of movement severely restricted. In 1960 he was allowed to travel to Stockholm to receive the Nobel Prize, but on his return to South Africa was subjected to even stricter restrictions: the ANC was banned and the South African media were forbidden to publish Albert Luthuli's words. He was killed when he fell under a train at Stanger in Natal in September 1967 (many believe that the 'accident' was planned), but remained an inspiration to the liberation struggle in South Africa through its most difficult years.

Albert Luthuli, *Let My People Go*, McGraw Hill, 1962
Mary Benson, *Chief Albert Luthuli of South Africa*, Oxford University Press, 1963

José Lutzenberger
1927–
environmental activist

Born into a German-Brazilian family in the southern Brazilian state of Rio Grande do Sul, José Lutzenberger studied at the University of Rio Grande do Sul and Louisiana State University before working as a technical adviser for Brazilian fertiliser companies from 1952 to 1957. From 1957 to 1970 he worked as an international consultant for the chemical multinational BASF, but became increasingly concerned about the use of agrichemicals and left BASF in 1971. He set up a vigorous and successful campaign against conventional chemical methods of farming, promoting instead regenerative, organic agriculture. This campaign, which included the requirement for licences for the sale of agripoisons, was very successful and caused a pronounced reduction in agricide use in Brazil. In 1972 José Lutzenberger was instrumental in founding AGAPAN, Brazil's first grassroots environmental organisation, and by the mid-1980s was lecturing internationally, his favourite and fluent themes (in the five languages he speaks) being the uselessness and perniciousness of Western models of development, and the importance of self-reliance. José Lutzenberger has long been a trenchant critic of large-scale World Bank projects, and in the late 1980s was influential in introducing environmental awareness to the Bank. He was awarded a Right Livelihood Award in 1988, and in March 1990 was unexpectedly invited to serve in the newly-created post of special environmental secretary to Fernando Collor de Mello's National Renovation Government, where he continued to work both nationally and internationally for the sensitive implementation of community-based environmental policies. After two years as a government minister he resigned in protest at the slow progress being made in environmental issues, and returned to writing, lecturing and grassroots activism, as well as running his two small appropriate technology companies. He also presides over the Fundaçao GAIA, a foundation for the promotion of sustainable development which runs a farm and a cultural centre for organic farming and environmental awareness.

Jeremy Seabrook, *Pioneers of Change*, Zed, 1993

Rosa Luxemburg
1870–1919
socialist activist, pacifist, writer

Had Rosa Luxemburg's model of communist revolution triumphed over that of her erstwhile friend and colleague **Lenin**, the social and economic disruption created by the first world war might have resulted in a more populist and humane version of Marxist communism. Luxemburg was born into a Jewish merchant's family in the Polish town of Zamosc, from her earliest years displaying a love of learning and of asking difficult questions. In 1886 she graduated at the top of her class from the Warsaw girls' gymnasium, and three years later fled to Switzerland to avoid arrest for involvement in underground political circles. While in Zürich studying for doctorates in law and philosophy she worked with Russian communist exiles including Plekhanov and **Lenin**, and started a lifelong relationship with fellow Polish exile Leo Jogiches. Already a leader of the nascent Polish Communist Party, in 1898 she moved to Berlin and took German citizenship (by means of a marriage of convenience to Gustav Lübeck). Here she taught, wrote, and rose rapidly within German communist circles, using every opportunity to promote Marxist ideas and to develop her own views on revolutionary consciousness. Rosa Luxemburg maintained that the communist movement already had enough theory: what was now required was grassroots awareness of the need to organise against capitalism. Her historical studies convinced her that mass actions, such as strikes and boycotts, were the most effective revolutionary activities, and that the role of the party was educational and supportive rather than dogmatic and dictatorial. Such ideas inevitably deepened the rift between Luxemburg and centralists within communist ranks, and her later writings express her anger about events in the post-revolutionary Soviet Union. A convinced pacifist, Luxemburg steadfastly opposed German entry into the first world war, and for this and her involvement with the communist movement spent a year in prison in 1915–16. Her 1916 letters from prison, known as the *Spartakusbriefe*, led to the formation of the Spartakusbund, which in 1918 she and Karl Liebknecht regrouped as the German Communist Party. Outvoted by her party, she reluctantly supported the doomed 'Spartacus Uprising' of January 1919: she and Liebknecht were promptly arrested and beaten to death by Prussian Freikorps officers.

Rosa Luxemburg (ed. Dick Howard), *Selected Writings*, Monthly Review Press, 1971

Rosa Luxemburg, *The Russian Revolution* and *Leninism or Marxism?* University of Michigan Press, 1976

John Peter Nettl, *Rosa Luxemburg*, Oxford University Press, 1966

Elzbieta Ettinger, *Rosa Luxemburg: A Life*, Harrap, 1987

Wangari Maathai
1940–
environmental and community activist

Born into a privileged Kenyan family, Wangari Maathai trained in the USA and at the University of Nairobi, receiving her doctorate in veterinerary anatomy in 1971. She married a Kenyan politician and in 1974 they established an environmental services company called Envirocare, employing poor people to plant trees and tend gardens. She and her husband separated in 1977, at a time when the company was struggling, but she was invited to attend the Vancouver UN Conference on Human Settlement Habitat, which gave her the confidence and contacts to restart the tree planting programme for which she is best known. On her return from Vancouver she was offered the post of associate professor of anatomy at Nairobi University, and became very active in the Kenyan National Council of Women, of which she has been chair since 1980. The Green Belt Movement, a nationwide community-based tree planting programme which Wangari Maathai initiated in 1977 and which gained rapid momentum in the mid-1980s, has succeeded in involving more than half a million schoolchildren and 15,000 farmers in planting tree belts in a country that would otherwise have suffered increasing desertification; by 1993 the Green Belt idea had spread to twelve other African countries. Wangari Maathai stresses the importance of women's involvement and of native agricultural traditions. Her community-based activism and her outspoken criticism of the reactionary Kenyan administration of Daniel arap Moi has made her the subject of continual official harassment. In early 1992 she was arrested and detained several times by riot police, on one occasion being beaten unconscious, and in March 1993 was prohibited from holding a seminar on ethnic violence. In the face of this opposition she has continued to travel and lecture on community development issues, and the Kenyan National Council of Women has coordinated numerous actions and boycotts against the Moi regime.

Fred Pearce, *Green Warriors: The People and the Politics behind the Environmental Revolution*, Bodley Head, 1991

Samora [Moïsés] Machel
1933–1986
civil rights campaigner, soldier, socialist politician

In the 1890s the Mozambiquan village where Samora Machel grew up, Xilembene in Gaza Province, was the scene of a bitter struggle between the Portuguese army and local warriors. The well-armed Portuguese inevitably won this and many similar battles, but the spirit of resistance to the foreign occupation never died, and when he heard Eduardo Mondlane, the founder of FRELIMO (Front for the Liberation of Mozambique), speak in Maputo in 1961, Samora Machel quickly made arrangements to join the organisation in Tanzania. By 1964 he was leading undercover FRELIMO missions into Mozambique, and following the assassination of Mondlane in 1969, actively supported by **Julius Nyerere** of Tanzania, Machel became FRELIMO's president-in-exile. His first wife and fellow activist Josina died in 1971, which affected him deeply, but FRELIMO was now growing rapidly in its influence, and when the Portuguese dictatorship was overthrown in 1974 the path for independence negotiations was wide open. On June 25th 1975 Mozambique declared independence, with Samora Machel as its president. Confronted by economic devastation, disease and illiteracy his socialist government nationalised land and key industries but, quickly recognising that hardline measures were not helping the people, Machel softened his approach, emphasising the need for community initiatives, education and healthcare; he particularly stressed the importance of the liberation of women, and placed many women in leadership positions. In 1976 the nationalist struggle against the Ian Smith regime in Rhodesia closed the border between the two countries, causing economic hardship, and in the early 1980s the South African-backed reactionary forces of RENAMO (Movement of National Resistance) became a constant irritation; widespread drought made the situation even worse. Samora Machel attempted to negotiate peace with South Africa and a non-aggression pact was signed in 1984, but RENAMO continued its covert actions despite international denunciation. As he was returning from a conference of South African frontline states in Zambia in October 1986 Samora Machel's aircraft crashed close to the South African border and all aboard were killed; there were indications that the instrument panel had been tampered with.

Samora Machel (ed. Barry Munslow, trans. Michael Wolfers), *Samora Machel: An African Revolutionary: Selected Speeches and Writings*, Zed, 1985
Ian Christie, *Samora Machel: A Biography*, Panaf Books, 1989

John Maclean
1879–1923
socialist educator and campaigner, pacifist

Scotland's best known early twentieth-century radical socialist, John Maclean grew up in Glasgow, one of a family of seven children of parents who had been evicted from the Scottish Highlands during the clearances of the 1840s. His father died when he was eight and his mother returned to work as a weaver in order to see her children properly cared for and educated. John Maclean started to train as a Presbyterian minister, but his reading of **Marx** and other socialist texts converted him to socialist communism and he finished his education in political science and classics at Glasgow University, graduating in 1903. Throughout his life he saw his main purpose as educating Scots in the political and economic advantages to be gained from socialism, the main planks of his campaigning being independence from England for Scotland and Ireland, redistribution of land and resources, and a fervent antimilitarism. In 1916 he helped to establish the Scottish Labour College, and after the 1917 Russian Revolution devoted much time and effort (though by no means uncritically) to gathering public support for the Bolshevik regime. The first world war propelled John Maclean into national and international prominence, and the growing influence of radical socialism in west central Scotland ('Red Clydeside' as it came to be known) was largely a result of his promotion of Marxist-Leninist socialism; in 1918 **Lenin** officially appointed Maclean as Glasgow's Bolshevik consul. John Maclean's antiwar campaigning resulted in four separate prison sentences between 1918 and his death. His compassion and selflessness, recalled in several songs and poems, have remained an example to the Scottish labour movement.

John Maclean (ed. Nan Milton), *In the Rapids of Revolution: Essays, Articles and Letters 1902–23*, Allison and Busby, 1978
Iain McLean, *The Legend of Red Clydeside*, John Donald, 1983

Joanna [Rogers] Macy
1929–
philosopher and activist

Joanna Rogers grew up in New York City, vividly affected by the poverty around her home and her father's tyranny within it. In adolescence she had a profound Christian conversion experience, and built on the sense of grace she felt by preparing for a church vocation. Her theological studies at university proved stifling, and she turned her attention to the study of social justice issues, researching Third World nationalism with a Fulbright grant. When she returned she married Frances Macy and they raised three children. In the 1960s her husband's job took the family to India to work with Tibetan refugees; here Joanna Macy encountered Buddhism and started practising meditation. Back in California she took a doctorate in early Buddhism, and in 1979, wanting to see how Buddhist teachings were being applied in a movement for social change, went to Sri Lanka to study the **Sarvodaya Shramadana** self-help movement: she wrote of her experiences in *Dharma and Development* (1983). Concerned about the apparent inability of so many Westerners to act in the face of catastrophic planetary crisis, she drew upon her work in Buddhism and social and systems theory to trace this inaction to a sense of powerlessness rooted in the belief that each person exists in isolation. In the late 1970s she began conducting workshops in 'despair and empowerment', and was a founder of the international Interhelp network – her ideas about powerlessness and empowerment are presented in the 1983 book *Despair and Personal Power in the Nuclear Age*. Five years later she coauthored *Thinking Like A Mountain*, a collection of writing by leading deep ecologists which underlines the importance of human beings' ecological sense of self. A professor of philosophy and religion at the California Institute of Integral Studies, Joanna Macy travels widely, lecturing and conducting workshops.

Joanna Macy, *Despair and Personal Power in the Nuclear Age*, New Society, 1983
Joanna Macy, John Seed, Pat Fleming and Arne Naess, *Thinking Like a Mountain: Toward a Council of All Beings*, Heretic/New Society, 1988
Anne Bancroft, *Weavers of Wisdom*, Arkana, 1989

Lina Magaia
1945–
writer, journalist, women's rights activist

Lina Magaia's experiences as a woman in wartorn Mozambique reflect those of many whose courage has brought that country painfully from colonialism, poverty and oppression into an era of fragile but growing hope for the future. Her mixed-race father insisted on his three children having a good education, and when he was reclassified as a *assimilado* ('similar to white') in 1957 Lina was able to transfer to a Portuguese school, where she was the only black; she learned very early how to stand up for her rights. She started writing newspaper articles when she was sixteen, and four years later determined to join FRELIMO (Front for the Liberation of Mozambique) in Tanzania, but was arrested at the border and imprisoned for three months. In 1967 she won a scholarship to Lisbon University, and was in Portugal with her young son during the overthrow of the Salazar dictatorship in April 1974; after a short period of violence the Portuguese government ended half a century of colonial rule in Mozambique. Lina Magaia returned to join FRELIMO in Tanzania, where her son died of dysentery shortly before FRELIMO finally liberated the Mozambiquan capital Maputo. She married shortly after independence, had three more children of her own and adopted two war orphans. In the late 1970s, at the request of the new president **Samora Machel**, she helped to establish an educational system in Mozambique, and in 1980 became head of the state sugar cooperative at Manhiça. She started to write again: her many articles and her 1988 book of stories, *Dumba nenque* (*Trust Your Feet*), chronicle her people's struggle through the decade of violence and poverty which dogged Mozambique's efforts at self-determination. As well as denouncing Western governments for systematically undermining Mozambique's stability, she is outspoken about the patriarchal nature of traditional Mozambiquan society, where bride-buying (*lobolo*) and polygamy are still widespread.

Lina Magaia (trans. Michael Wolfers), *Dumba Nenque: Peasant Tales of Tragedy in Mozambique*, Africa World Press, 1988
Stephanie Urdang, *And Still They Dance: Women, War and the Struggle for Change in Mozambique*, Earthscan, 1989

Ricardo Flóres Magón
1874–1922
anarchist and land rights campaigner

As a boy in the southern Mexican region of Oaxaca, Ricardo Magón observed at first hand how an anarchist peasant community worked the land and sharing its produce communally; he could also see that the harsh military regime of Porfirio Díaz, with large private armies belonging to rich landowners, threatened the mass of poor Mexicans. An avid reader of **Kropotkin**, **Bakunin** and **Malatesta**, he founded with his brothers Jesús and Enrique the anarchist journal *Regeneración* in Mexico City in 1900; within three years it reached a circulation of nearly thirty thousand. This was too much of a threat to the Díaz regime, and in 1904 Ricardo and Enrique were expelled to the USA; Ricardo never returned to Mexico, and spent more than half of the rest of his life in prison. *Regeneración* was quickly relaunched in San Antonio, and in 1905 Ricardo Magón founded the Partido Liberal Mexicano (PLM) in St Louis. In 1908 the PLM initiated a series of border raids in the El Paso area, and in January 1911 more than five hundred Liberales briefly succeeded in establishing themselves in Baja California. In September 1911 Ricardo Magón wrote a new PLM manifesto, upon which **Emiliano Zapata** based his *Plan de Ayala*, an appeal for human and land rights to the shortlived liberal government of Francisco Madero. The Liberales (also known as Magonistas) continued to work for their idea of an anarchist utopia based on traditional Mexican land tenure, organising Mexican workers into trade unions affiliated with **Industrial Workers of the World**, and issuing provocative anti-authoritarian statements. In another PLM manifesto of 1918, addressed to 'the anarchists of the world', Ricardo Magón again stressed 'the tyranny of government in all its forms'; in the narrow-minded patriotic climate of wartime this earned him arrest and twenty years in Leavenworth Penitentiary in Kansas, where he died (or many say was murdered) four years later. Ironically, after his death the Mexican government honoured Ricardo Flóres Magón as 'a great precursor of the Mexican Revolution' and buried him in Mexico City's Rotunda of Illustrious Men.

Ricardo Flóres Magón, *Prison Letters of Ricardo Flóres Magón to Lilly Sarnoff*, International Review of Social History, 1977

Ward S. Albro, *Always a Rebel: Ricardo Flóres Magón and the Mexican Revolution*, Texan Christian University Press, 1992

David Poole (ed.), *Land and Liberty: Anarchist Influences in the Mexican Revolution*, Cienfuegos Press, 1977

Errico Malatesta
1853–1932
anarchist activist and organiser

Together with **Mikhail Bakunin** and **Petr Kropotkin**, Errico Malatesta ranks as one of the most important anarchist thinkers and activists of the late nineteenth and early twentieth centuries. Uniting theory, experience and action with a consistency rare among his colleagues, his independence and modesty contrasted sharply with the picture of the wild revolutionary agitator painted by many of his contemporary critics. Malatesta grew up in a liberal landowning family near Naples in southern Italy, and was first arrested when at the age of fourteen he wrote to King Victor Emmanuel II complaining about a local injustice. He discovered the writings of Bakunin while at university in Naples, and in 1872 met his new mentor in Switzerland. By 1876 he favoured Kropotkin's ideas about communism over Bakunin's collectivism, but by the mid-1880s had rejected both as too deterministic, formulating instead his own version of anarchism, best outlined in his 1891 pamphlet *Anarchy*. He starts from the premise that human beings naturally develop voluntary systems of solidarity and mutual aid in the struggle against arbitrarily imposed authority. Matching actions with words, he was involved in numerous uprisings and campaigns, mostly in Italy but also in other parts of Europe and in North and South America (he spent nearly half his long life in exile, and more than ten years in prison). His most successful years, 1919–21, were spent based in Milan, where he started the anarchist daily *Umanità nova* and organised the revolutionary workers' group Unione Sindicale, which at its height had more than 400,000 members; the movement collapsed, however, with Malatesta's arrest and Mussolini's rise to power. An anarchist attempt to assassinate Mussolini in 1926 was used as an excuse to silence all opposition, and for the last five years of his life Errico Malatesta was held under house arrest, too influential to be hanged or imprisoned. Ever realistic, humane and optimistic, Malatesta's anarchist vision has continued to inspire the anarchist movement both in Italy and further afield.

Errico Malatesta (trans. V. Richards), *Anarchy*, Freedom Press, 1974

Vernon Richards (ed.) *Errico Malatesta: His Life and Ideas*, Freedom Press, 1965

Peter Marshall, *Demanding the Impossible: A History of Anarchism*, Harper Collins, 1992

Nelson [Rolihlala] Mandela
1918–
civil rights campaigner, lawyer, politician

When he became South Africa's first black president in May 1994, Nelson Mandela proclaimed that 'years of imprisonment could not stamp out our determination to be free; years of intimidation and violence could not stop us – and we will not be stopped now.' The world's most famous political prisoner for most of the 27 years he spent in prison, he was born into a noble Xhosa family in Umtata in the Transkei. A graduate of Fort Hare College and Witwatersrand University, he trained and worked as a lawyer, sharing his Johannesburg practice from 1952 with **Oliver Tambo**, at the same time involving himself in the work of the **African National Congress** (ANC) and becoming a national organiser. Together with ANC leader **Albert Luthuli**, Oliver Tambo and **Walter Sisulu**, he was first arrested in 1956 and charged with treason under the Suppression of Communism Act. He was eventually acquitted on this charge and released in 1961, the year in which the ANC abandoned nonviolence. While in prison he married **Winnie Nomzano**, his second wife, who was to work tirelessly for his release and for the ANC cause; their formal separation in 1992 is generally believed to have been for pragmatic as much as for personal reasons. Nelson Mandela was arrested again in 1962 and sentenced to five years imprisonment, then faced fresh treason charges after the authorities uncovered the 'high command' of the ANC's military wing Umkhonto we Sizwe (Spear of the Nation) at Rivonia, Johannesburg, in July 1963. His powerful speech from the dock in April 1964 confirmed his status as the most influential of the ANC political prisoners; it included the denial that he was a Communist, the admission that he had helped form Umkhonto, and the affirmation that he was prepared to die for the ending of white supremacy. Sentenced to life imprisonment, he was sent to Robben Island (later being transferred to Pollsmoor and Victor Vester prison near Paarl), maintaining his dignity even with his jailers and urging his fellow prisoners to educate themselves and retain their high ideals. In 1986 he surprised the visiting Commonwealth Eminent Persons Group by his grip on rapidly-changing political developments. By now he was revered in black communities throughout South Africa and beyond, and during the 1980s 'Free Nelson Mandela' became an international rallying-call. Following a bout of tuberculosis in 1988 his imprisonment became more akin to house arrest, and on February 11th 1990, a week after the ANC and other 'illegal' organisations were unbanned, he was released to universal acclamation. He quickly held strategy talks with other ANC leaders in Zambia, preparatory to the re-establishment of a full ANC presence in South Africa. Later in the year he travelled to the Middle East (where he endorsed the goals of the Palestine Liberation Organisation), Europe and North America, addressing the United Nations and a joint session of the US Congress. In 1993 Nelson Mandela and then president F.W. de Klerk were jointly awarded the Nobel

Peace Prize for their uneasy partnership in negotiating South Africa's transition to a nonracial democracy. South Africa's first all-race elections were set for April 1994; the ANC and its president Nelson Mandela achieved the expected victory, winning a small but decisive majority.

Nelson Mandela, *No Easy Walk to Freedom*, Heinemann, 1965

Nelson Mandela, *Struggle is my Life*, Pathfinder, 1991

Nelson Mandela, *Long Walk to Freedom: The Autobiography of Nelson Mandela*, Little, Brown, 1994

Fatima Meer, *Higher than Hope: The Authorised Biography of Nelson Mandela*, Hamish Hamilton, 1990

Winnie [Nomzano] Mandela
1936–
civil rights and women's rights campaigner

'Mother of the Nation', wife of the world's most famous political prisoner, still popular among black South Africans despite allegations of assault and corruption, Winnie Mandela has always been a force to reckon with. Born in north-east Transkei, Winnie Nomzano was training as a social worker when **Oliver Tambo**'s wife Adelaide introduced her to **Nelson Mandela** in 1957. They were married in June 1958, when Winnie was pregnant with their first daughter; their second daughter was born in 1960 while Nelson was in prison awaiting trial. When her husband was jailed for life in 1964, she quickly had to find her own political feet as well as raising two young children. She continued defiantly to wear the colours of the banned **African National Congress** (ANC), and in 1977 she was banished to the small town of Brandfort in the Orange Free State, 200 miles from her home in Johannesburg. To the ANC she became a symbol of patient solidarity, but her home life, hemmed in by petty officialdom and violence (her house was bombed three times), tested that patience beyond its limit. In August 1985 Winnie Mandela returned to Soweto in contravention of her banning order. Uncompromising as ever, she quickly adapted to the politics of the black township. While the ANC attempted to distance itself from the killing of black government-paid informers, Winnie Mandela supported limited violence as justified and necessary. Late in 1989 she became embroiled in another aspect of township violence when a fourteen-year-old boy, a member of the football club which used her house as a base, was allegedly sexually abused by a local white minister and then assaulted and murdered by blacks who accused him of treachery. Whatever the facts (she was ultimately acquitted on an assault charge, though fined for the lesser charge of kidnapping), the ANC leadership increasingly felt that she was harming its cause and attempted to reduce her profile within the organisation. When Nelson Mandela was freed in February 1990, Winnie was once again cast in the role of loyal wife. She was genuinely delighted by his release, but ANC and media allegations about her private life and political instability (she was accused of infidelity and embezzlement of ANC funds, both of which she strenuously denied) made her life difficult, especially when the Mandelas' separation was announced in April 1992. Though many had written her off as a political force by the end of 1992, she returned to head the influential ANC Women's League in December 1993. Despite her strong and continuing influence on the activist wing of the ANC, allegations of financial irregularity continue to surround her: in January 1995 eleven of the League's executive, including Adelaide Tambo, resigned in protest over what they saw as Winnie Mandela's high-handed conduct in organising sponsorship without due consultation.

Winnie Mandela, *Part of My Soul*, Penguin, 1985
Sharon Goulds, *Winnie Mandela: In Her Own Time*, Hamish Hamilton, 1988
Nokwanda Sithole, 'Winnie Mandela: Her Story', *Essence*, April 1994

Mao Zedong
1893–1976
revolutionary, politician

Mao Zedong, the archetypal revolutionary who overcame seemingly impossible odds to become leader of the People's Republic of China in 1949, went on to become one of the most blinkered tyrants the world has known, responsible for mass repression and genocide in the name of class struggle and socialist democracy. He was born into a peasant family in Hunan, became a convinced Marxist in 1919, and participated in the First Congress of the Chinese Communist Party (CCP) in 1921. His experiences of peasant demonstrations against repression persuaded him of the revolutionary potential of the Chinese peasantry, and he rose to power after communism was driven into the countryside by the Kuomintang nationalists after 1927. In November 1931 a Soviet republic was declared in Kiangsi province with Mao as chairman, but in 1934 Kuomintang troops forced Mao's People's Liberation ('Red') Army to abandon Kiangsi and undertake the famous Long March to northern China. Over the next fifteen years the communists consolidated their position, using guerrilla tactics to control large areas of the country; many of Mao's best-known writings date from this period, as does his leadership of the CCP and his 1939 marriage (his third) to actress-revolutionary Jiang Qing. After a number of unsuccessful attempts to ally the Kuomintang and the CCP in a common cause, Mao chose the route of civil war: the now-powerful People's Liberation Army easily won and the republic was declared in Beijing on October 1st 1949. Little was heard or seen from the new leader for several years, but in 1956 he promoted a policy called 'Let a Hundred Flowers Bloom', intended to demonstrate that the CCP could listen and respond to criticism from China's intellectuals. When he discovered widespread disquiet about the party's leadership, he turned instead to the masses for support, initiating the 'Great Leap Forward' of 1958, reorganising the country into 'people's communes' and marking the end of China's reliance on the Soviet model. This caused massive economic disruption and, rather than listening to his colleagues and learning from his mistakes, Mao pushed through even more far-reaching policies in the Great Proletarian Cultural Revolution of

1966–69. To widespread repression and famine the Red Army now added cultural destruction and extensive social disclocation, but the cult of Mao allowed for little dissent within China and the Cultural Revolution sounded a positive note with many Western radicals, Mao's *Little Red Book* being much read and discussed following the events following May 1968. China was still suffering from the aftermath of the Cultural Revolution when Mao died in September 1976, leaving a power vacuum which was only partially resolved by the imprisonment of his widow Jiang Qing (one of the so-called 'Gang of Four') and the victory of the reactionary pragmatist Deng Xiao-ping. The young Mao's contribution to Marxist-Leninist activism is un-doubted, and the CCP's emphasis on rural solidarity and guerrilla tactics inspired many revolutionaries in the 1950s and 60s, but his inability and unwillingness to transcend his later cult status undermined much of what he had set out to achieve.

Mao Tse-tung, *Selected Works of Mao Tse-tung*, Foreign Languages Press, Beijing, 1967–77
Stuart Schram, *Mao Tse-tung*, Penguin, 1967
Dick Wilson (ed.), *Mao Tse-tung in the Scales of History: A Preliminary Assessment*, Cambridge University Press, 1977
Stuart Schram, *The Thought of Mao Zedong*, Cambridge University Press, 1989

Manning Marable
1950–
Marxist historian, black rights campaigner

For two decades the black American historian and activist Manning Marable has endeavoured to document and analyse his people's recent past in order to inform and educate the post-**Martin Luther King** generation about the achievements and potential pitfalls of the 1960s civil rights movement. His stance, which is avowedly Marxist and transformationist, starts from the premise that the key issue for African Americans is not race itself, but widespread inequalities between social groups: his many books and arti-cles thus avoid both the separatist and integrationist schools of thought among black American leaders of the 1980s and 90s. Manning Marable grew up in Cincinatti and studied history at Earlham College in Richmond, Indiana, Nairobi University in Kenya, and the Universities of Wisconsin and Maryland, where he was active in the black student movement in the late 1960s and early 70s. He subsequently taught at Smith College and Tuska-gee Institute, and in 1983 was appointed professor of sociology at Colgate University at Hamilton, New York. Professorships at Ohio State University and the University of Colorado followed, and he is currently professor of history at Columbia University. During the early 1980s he was a leading voice for the Democratic Socialists of America (DSA), and initiated DSA's National and Racial Minorities Coordinating Committee. Manning Marable published his first collection of essays, *Blackwater: Essays on Black and Southern History*, in 1978, and several subsequent collections of essays and articles continue his exploration of black history from a Marxist perspective.

Most influential, however, have been his modern histories of black politics in the USA, Africa and the Caribbean (*Black American Politics*, 1985, and *African and Caribbean Politics*, 1987), works of detailed and authoritative scholarship which conclude that 'at the heart of Black politics is a series of crimes' perpetrated by the white power élite (and their black agents) against individuals and organisations involved in black empowerment. He also writes the monthly 'Along the Color Line' column which appears in a number of progressive publications. Despite apparent setbacks to the cause of equal rights in recent years, Marable remains optimistic, concerned in his writing and teaching to help oppressed groups to understand that the power to transform society lies within their grasp.

Manning Marable, *From the Grassroots: Essays Toward Afro-American Liberation*, South End, 1980

Manning Marable, *Black American Politics: From the Washington Marches to Jesse Jackson*, Verso, 1985

Manning Marable, *African and Caribbean Politics: From Kwame Nkrumah to the Grenada Revolution*, Verso, 1987

Manning Marable, *The Crisis of Color and Democracy: Essays on Race, Class and Power*, Common Courage, 1992

Herbert Marcuse
1898–1979
social philosopher, new left critic and activist

By the mid-1960s the German-born philosopher-guru Herbert Marcuse was widely read and debated in activist circles worldwide. His early career had paralleled that of his Frankfurt School colleagues **Adorno** and **Horkheimer** and, were it not for his shift towards popular cultural criticism following his 1953 decision to remain in the USA, a shift which coincided precisely with the radical trends of the time, he may well have shared their relative obscurity. Marcuse grew up in prewar Berlin, and after military service in 1916–18 studied literature, philosophy and political economy at Berlin and Freiburg Universities. His promotion to a university professorship was blocked by the rise of Nazism, so in 1933 he worked with the Institute for Social Research's Geneva branch, the following year moving with the Institute to the USA. From the late 1920s until the early 50s his writing concentrated on the historical roots of Marxism and Nazism: his first work to appear in English translation, *Reason and Revolution* (1941), traced the links between Hegel and the dialectical approach of Marxism. *Eros and Civilisation* (1955) was his first widely read book, drawing on **Marx** and Freud to envision a free society which would fulfil people's need for purpose, play and creative expression. Marcuse's analysis generated a protracted debate with psychologist **Erich Fromm**, who accused Marcuse of irresponsible hedonism; Marcuse countered with charges of collaboration with the capitalist status quo. Anticipating the values of the 1960s counterculture, *Eros and Civilisation* remained a bestseller for several years, as did *One-Dimensional Man* (1964), a warning that both capitalism and communism alike were creating a deadening uniformity in which critical thinking and protest were in danger of withering away. By now Marcuse was an important figurehead of the **new left**, and his damning criticism in books such as *An Essay on Liberation* (1969) of those who refused to take an active stand in the controversies of the late 1960s won him a reputation as a radical who matched word with action. Marcuse was now a favourite on the US lecture circuit, and 1972 saw the publication of his *Counterrevolution and Revolt*, expressing fears that many of the liberties fought for in the 1960s were being eroded in a rightward political trend. Often criticised for being a bandwagon philosopher and critic, Marcuse's Marxist libertarianism and faith in cultural revolution were in truth remarkably consistent, and his writings and involvement in the turbulent politics of the 60s and 70s played an important part in the development of radical theory and practice.

Herbert Marcuse, *Eros and Civilization*, Beacon, 1955
Herbert Marcuse, *One-Dimensional Man*, Beacon, 1964
Herbert Marcuse, *An Essay on Liberation*, Beacon, 1969
Herbert Marcuse, *Counterrevolution and Revolt*, Beacon, 1972
Barry Katz, *Herbert Marcuse*, Verso, 1982

José Carlos Mariátegui
1894–1930
Marxist activist, teacher and writer

José Carlos Mariátegui, an innovative and successful early twentieth-century Latin American Marxist activist, was born in the southern Peruvian town of Moquegua. He was crippled in one leg from birth, but neither this nor his lack of formal education prevented him from becoming a successful journalist with a Lima daily paper. Forced into exile in 1919 by the repressive regime of Bernardino Leguía, he travelled to Europe, where he met **Lenin**, **Trotsky** and **Gramsci** (and where, in Italy, he married). When he returned to Peru in 1923 he immediately set about creating a Peruvian Marxism which used the insights of Marxist analysis yet took full account of the circumstances prevailing in his home country. Despite losing his good leg the following year and having to spend the rest of his life in a wheelchair, he devoted the next seven years to organising a working class movement which culminated in the formation of the Partido Socialista de Perú (Peruvian Socialist Party) in 1928 and the Confederación General de Trabajadores de Perú (General Confederation of Peruvian Workers) in 1929. He also wrote a large number of essays and articles, and edited the important magazine *Amauta* from 1924 until his death. His flexible adaptation of Marxist principles to accommodate and learn from local conditions marks Mariátegui out from most early Latin American socialist reformers, and many of his ideas about development and dependency broke new ground. Always concerned that the socialist revolution should benefit everyone, he put considerable effort into listening to – and sharing his insights with – Peru's varied communities. By the late 1920s José Carlos

Mariátegui was regularly subjected to police searches and questioning, and was briefly imprisoned in 1929: this and ever-increasing pressure of work brought about his premature death in April 1930.

José Carlos Mariátegui, *Seven Interpretative Essays on Peruvian Reality*, University of Texas Press, 1972

Jesús Chavarría, *José Carlos Mariátegui and the Rise of Modern Peru*, University of New Mexico Press, 1979

Harry Vanden, *National Marxism in Latin America: José Carlos Mariátegui's Thought and Politics*, Lynne Rienner, 1986

Munsif Marzuqi
1945–
doctor, teacher, writer, human rights campaigner

Tunisia's leading social critic and human rights activist Munsif Marzuqi grew up in Tunis and trained as a doctor. He came to prominence in 1986 with the publication of *Da' Watani Yastayqiz Fi al-Siyasah al-Ukhra* (*Let My Country Wake Up*), a collection of essays on development, democracy, Islam, identity and freedom of information. This represented an appeal to President Bourguiba to allow the Tunisian people to 'wake up' and share the task of finding solutions to the country's social, economic and political problems, and criticised in particular the widespread lack of understanding and discussion of Tunisian history: 'We are almost completely ignorant,' Marzuqi wrote, 'about those who were oppressed, crucified and murdered to keep the face of truth from being revealed.' As soon as the book was published, however, it caused an uproar and Marzuqi was arrested and tried – he was released, but the book remains banned. Munsif Marzuqi is now professor of medicine at Tunis University and continues to write and campaign for human rights, leading the struggle in Tunisia against censorship and arbitrary justice.

'Moncef al-Marzouki', *Index on Censorship*, 1, 1989

Abraham [Harold] Maslow
1908–1970
psychologist, therapist, writer

Abraham Maslow was one of the most influential voices for holistic client-centred psychotherapy in the 1960s and 70s, a movement which became known as humanistic psychotherapy or the 'third force' in psychology (alongside psychoanalysis and behaviourist psychology). The eldest of seven children of a Jewish family, he grew up in New York, a shy and retiring child. He studied psychology at the University of Wisconsin, receiving his PhD in 1934, and went on to teach at Brooklyn College, working mainly with underprivileged young people. Here he met and worked with other psychologists who were questioning the social and political role of psychotherapy, including **Karen Horney** and **Erich Fromm**. The suffering and horror of the second world war had a profound influence on him, and he started to work out a theory of human motivation which emphasised the intrinsic normality of human growth and interaction, explored in a series of books starting with *Motivation and Personality* (1954). He took the idea of 'self-actualisation', originated by the psychotherapist Kurt Goldstein, and developed it to describe how the realisation of a person's full potential is the most important of human needs; Maslow also placed great reliance on the ability of his clients to understand and heal themselves with a minimal need for therapeutic direction. He coined the term 'peak experience', much overused in the hippy era, to describe the high points in a person's life, when their experience of beauty and love becomes immediate and tangible. In 1951 he became professor of psychology at Brandeis University, where he taught until shortly before his death. In the early 1960s he was one of the founders of the Esalen Institute at Big Sur in California, the birthplace of the human potential movement.

Abraham Maslow, *Motivation and Personality*, Van Nostrand Reinhold, 1954
Abraham Maslow, *Toward a Psychology of Being*, Van Nostrand Reinhold, 1962
Abraham Maslow, *The Farther Reaches of Human Nature*, Van Nostrand Reinhold, 1971

H.J. [Harold John] Massingham
1888–1952
writer, agriculturalist, social critic

The English writer, naturalist and pioneering conservationist H.J. Massingham had radical blood in him: his father, Henry Massingham, was a well-known radical journalist who edited the influential liberal weekly *The Nation* from 1907 to 1923. Harold grew up in London and was educated at Westminster School and Queen's College, Oxford before embarking in his father's footsteps on a journalistic career. A passionate amateur birdwatcher, he was a cofounder in 1919 of the Plumage Group, a campaign to ban the use of wild birds' feathers in the millinery trade. Though he was arrested and briefly held for accosting upper class women in London's Piccadilly, the campaign was successful, and showed Massingham that campaigning for conservation causes was worth the effort. During the next decade he divided his time between London and the English countryside, writing for magazines and producing a number of popular nature titles. In 1930, shortly after he had married for the second time, he was able to move to Chipping Campden in the Cotswold Hills, where his views on ecology and conservation began to flow into a series of thoughtful and poetic books about rural England, including *Country* (1934), *Genius of England* (1937) and *The Wisdom of the Fields* (1945). His thinking, though out of line with the majority in prewar Britain, foreshadowed many of the green ideas which resurfaced in the 1970s: concern about the loss of hedgerows, the dangers of chemicals and the adulteration of food. He consistently argued for a holistic, ecological (both words that he often used) approach to livelihood and political and economic organisation, and was utterly opposed to the empty nihilism of fascism. Following an accident in 1937 Massingham contracted blood poisoning, which required the amputation of a leg, but he continued to travel, write and, using organic principles, till his garden at Long Crendon in the Chiltern Hills. At his death his extensive library and collection of traditional farm tools was donated to the Museum of Country Life in Reading.

H. J. Massingham, *A Mirror of England: An Anthology of the Writings of H.J. Massingham*, Green Books, 1990

H. J. Massingham, *Remembrance: An Autobiography*, Batsford, 1942

Matsumoto Jiichirō
1887–1966
civil rights campaigner, politician

Born into an outcast Japanese *buraku* family in Kyoto, Matsumoto Jiichirō experienced much injustice and discrimination at school and at work, and determined that he would do whatever he could to work for equal rights and opportunities for his fellow *burakumin*. In 1911, after several years in the Japanese-occupied town of Dalien (now Luta) on the Chinese mainland, he returned to Fukuoka in southern Japan to establish a successful building company. In 1922 he helped to found Suiheisha (the Levelling Movement), but missed its first meeting in Kyushu because he was arrested on a sham charge three days beforehand. He formulated much of Suiheisha's policy and provided most of its funding. Between 1925 and 1928 he was arrested and imprisoned several times on conspiracy charges. In 1936 he stood as a parliamentary candidate for the Social Masses Party and was elected to the Japanese Diet (parliament), where with a short break at the end of the second world war he served until his death. In 1946 he established the National Committee for Buraku Emancipation, which quickly grew into a mass movement, and oversaw its development into the **Buraku Kaihō Undō** (Buraku Emancipation Movement) in 1955.

George De Vos and Hiroshi Wagatsuma, *Japan's Invisible Race*, University of California Press, 1966

Ian Neary, *Political Protest and Social Control in Pre-war Japan: The Origins of Buraku Liberation*, Manchester University Press, 1989

Manfred Max-Neef
1932–
economist

Born into a family of German origin and brought up in Chile, the radical economist Manfred Max-Neef studied economics at the University of Chile and Chile's Graduate School for Latin American Economic Studies. In the early 1960s he taught at the University of California in Berkeley, and between 1965 and 1973 worked with several international agencies including the Pan American Union, the Food and Agriculture Organisation and the International Labour Organisation (ILO). In 1972, as head of an ILO mission to Ecuador, he developed a large-scale programme for peasant involvement in local affairs, but an army coup made him *persona non grata*, and Max-Neef returned to Chile. After the overthrow of the socialist

Allende government by the violent Pinochet regime Manfred Max-Neef left his home country and spent ten years travelling throughout Latin America, developing the theory and practice of 'barefoot economics': this was to become the basis of his ideas about 'human scale development', whose final elaboration he completed with the cooperation of a group of likeminded Latin American economists and sponsorship from the Dag Hammarskjöld Foundation. In 1983 he was awarded a Right Livelihood Award for his contribution to a more humane economy. Returning to Santiago, he used the prize money to establish CEPAUR, the Centre for Development Alternatives, which acts as an information network for local communities in South America, enabling them to learn appropriate strategies and skills from one another. Manfred Max-Neef's main contribution to radical thought is the idea of 'human scale development', building on **Kirkpatrick Sale**'s emphasis of the importance of 'human scale'. In *Human Scale Development* (1987 in Spanish; 1989 in English) he clearly distinguishes between wants and needs that enhance the true development of human potential and those that violate it. In 1993 Manfred Max-Neef ran as a presidential candidate in Chile's national elections, gaining wide support from young people and groups supporting radical change. In July 1994 he was appointed rector of the Austral University of Chile.

> Manfred Max-Neef, *Human Scale Development: Conception, Application and Further Reflections*, Dag Hammarskjöld Foundation, 1989
> Paul Ekins and Manfred Max-Neef (eds), *Real Life Economics: Understanding Wealth Creation*, Routledge, 1992

Roy [Aleksandrovich] Medvedev
1925–
historian, social and cultural critic

The historian Roy Medvedev was born to Russian parents living in Georgia, grew up in Tbilisi, and studied philosophy and education at Leningrad University. His interest in Soviet history was stimulated by Khrushchev's 1956 revelations about the Stalin regime, and in the early 1960s he started researching his first – and arguably his most important – book, *Let History Judge*, a detailed history and indictment of Stalinism. His efforts to publish the book through official Soviet channels resulted in his expulsion from the Communist Party in 1969, and it was first published in 1972 in English, together with *A Question of Madness* (coauthored with his twin brother Zhores, a geneticist who has lived in London since 1973). Unlike many Soviet dissidents, Roy Medvedev never turned his back on **Marx** and **Lenin**, seeing the Stalinist era as an unfortunate and distorting interval on the path to real socialism, and the many books written (and published in the West) during his twenty years as an academic outcast underline his faith in the potential for democratic reform. In the climate of *glasnost* during the Gorbachev era many of Medvedev's ideas were reinstated as acceptable radical criticism of Soviet communism, and in 1988 he was readmitted to the Communist Party. His works began to be widely read in the Soviet

Union, and in 1989 he was elected to the congress of people's deputies, the next year being appointed to the party's central committee. In December 1989 the Communist Party newspaper *Pravda* published a 1974 Medvedev article that mentioned **Aleksandr Solzhenitsyn**'s criticism of Lenin, the first such criticism to be published in the official Soviet press. Following the abortive coup of August 1991, the outlawing of the Communist Party and the collapse of the Soviet Union, Roy Medvedev was one of the founders of the Socialist Party of Working People, the largest leftwing grouping on the Russian political spectrum. He is now a cochair of the party and editor of its newspaper, though he still finds time to write and to pursue his historical researches.

Roy Medvedev (trans. Colleen Taylor), *Let History Judge: The Origins and Consequences of Stalinism*, Knopf, 1971 (rev. ed. 1989)

Roy Medvedev, (trans. Ellen DeKadt), *On Socialist Democracy*, Knopf, 1975

Roy Medvedev (trans. and ed. William Packer), *On Soviet Dissent*, Columbia University Press, 1980

Roy Medvedev and Giulietto Chiesa (trans. Michael Moore), *Time of Change: An Insider's View of Russia's Transformation*, Pantheon, 1989

Ulrike [Marie] Meinhof
1934–1976
antifascist activist and writer

Ulrike Meinhof is usually portrayed as a coldhearted terrorist, lending her name to a gang totally committed to violence in order to overthrow German authority. The truth, unsurprisingly, is rather different. She was born in Oldenberg and moved to Jena when she was two; both her parents died before she was fifteen, and she was fostered by Renate Riemeck, a history professor and one of the founders of the Deutsches Friedensunion (German Peace Union). Ulrike studied at Marburg, Munster and Hamburg universities, and was active in the early ban-the-bomb movement. From 1959 to 1968 she was a regular contributor to the radical journal *Konkret*, and in 1961 married fellow journalist Klaus Rainer Rohl; the following year they had twin daughters. In 1968 they were divorced, and Ulrike moved from Hamburg to Berlin to work as a freelance journalist, where she also became active in the anti-**Vietnam War** campaign and the student protests that were shaking German universities at the time. Her writing stressed the dangers to modern Germany of nuclear rearmament and the extension of police powers, and raised many of the issues still faced by German radicals. She was angered by the attempt on the life of student leader **Rudi Dutschke** in April 1968 and was persuaded by fellow radicals Andreas Baader and Gudrun Ensllin to join their Rote Armee Fraktion (Red Army Faction). Late in 1968 Baader and Ensllin were jailed for an arson attack on a Frankfurt department store; they were released on bail a year later, but Baader (now a student hero) was promptly rearrested. On May 14th 1970 Ulrike Meinhof was present when Andreas Baader was 'liberated' from his Berlin prison and, though her role in the escape was marginal, she was forced, with Baader and Ensllin (now widely known as the 'Baader-Meinhof Group'), to live underground. She spent some time in Jordan (where the popular press had her 'training with Palestinian guerrillas') before returning to Germany. In June 1972 she was arrested and sentenced to eight years imprisonment for her part in freeing Baader; she was kept in solitary confinement, first in Köln-Ossendorf and then in Stammheim near Stuttgart, a recently-opened high security prison for political criminals. She died on May 6th 1976: the official cause of death was suicide by hanging (as was the verdict on Andreas Baader's 'suicide' a year later), though many were convinced that her death was officially-sanctioned murder.

Tineke Ritmeester, 'Ulrike Meinhof', *Biographical Dictionary of Neo-Marxism* (ed. Robert Gorman), Mansell, 1985

David Kramer, 'Ulrike Meinhof: An Emancipated Terrorist?', *European Women on the Left* (ed. Jane Slaughter and Robert Kern), Greenwood, 1981

Jillian Becker, *Hitler's Children: The Story of the Baader-Meinhof Terrorist Group*, Lippincott, 1977

Stefan Aust (trans. A. Bell), *The Baader-Meinhof Group: The Inside Story of a Phenomenon*, Bodley Head, 1987

Freda Meissner-Blau
1927–
environmental and human rights campaigner, politician

The Austrian green activist and politician Freda Meissner-Blau has become one of the clearest and most experienced voices of the the new European 'rainbow politics'. She was born in Dresden and grew up in Linz and Vienna, returning to Dresden at the end of the war in time to witness the firebombing of the city in February 1945. In 1949 she married a French businessman, and they and their young son lived in the Belgian Congo (now Zaire) for several years before returning to Paris, where Freda worked as a translator with UNESCO. In 1962 they moved to Vienna, where Freda studied psychology and sociology at Vienna University and had twins, and in 1968, living again in Paris, she was much affected by the May uprisings. By now Freda was determined to find her own path, insisting in 1972 that the family return to Vienna, where she became actively involved in the peace movement and the growing Austrian women's movement: she soon became leader of Frauen gegen Atomenergie (Women Against Atomic Energy) and took part in many demonstrations and petitions. In 1984, when the Austrian government announced their plan to dam the Danube for a huge power station at Au, an unspoilt forest area rich in wildlife, Austrian conservationists united in opposition, and the veteran campaigner Freda Meissner-Blau was an obvious spokeswoman. The Au campaign quickly became the 'Au War', with thousands of protestors using nonviolent tactics to prevent construction proceeding. The decision to build the dam was overturned in October 1985, and in 1986 Freda was persuaded to stand as an Alternative List candidate for the Austrian government. Winning 5.5% of the vote, she was inaugurated in January 1987, and has since continued to use her position to stress the importance of the green perspective and of the involvement of women in political and economic decision-making.

Rigoberta Menchú
1960–
campaigner for minority and women's rights

In September 1979, when she was nineteen, Rigoberta Menchú's younger brother was kidnapped by the Guatemalan army, accused of helping his fellow Mayan peasants fight for land rights, tortured and burnt to death in front of his family. A few months later her father led a peaceful protest; he too was burnt to death, and her mother was raped, tortured and killed. They were just a handful of the estimated 150,000 Indians murdered by the Guatemalan military since the military coup of 1954. As a young girl Rigoberta Menchú vowed that she would do whatever was necessary to tell the world about what was happening to her people; by day she worked on the plantations, by night she studied Spanish; after she moved to Guatemala City to work as a maid in 1976 she started to make contact with the international women's and civil rights movements. In 1980, following the worsening of the genocide and the murder of so many of her family, she fled to Mexico, where she lived in a refugee camp with thousands of other exiled Mayans. She continued to work with international human rights groups, and became a frequent visitor to the United Nations; in 1984 her powerful and widely-praised autobiography was published. The awarding of the 1992 Nobel Peace Prize to Rigoberta Menchú provided an excellent chance for the world to ask 'Where are the women?', but few took advantage of that opportunity, preferring to treat her as an ungendered Indian rights advocate. Rigoberta herself stressed that the award was a condemnation of the repression in her home county, and in particular the suffering of women, rather than a personal accolade. Following the award of the Nobel Prize, and despite death threats, Rigoberta Menchú returned to Guatemala City, to be greeted by thousands of supporters cheering and shouting 'Viva Rigoberta!' In June 1993 Guatemala held free elections, resulting in the election to the presidency of Ramiro de Leon Carpio, a human rights leader. Rigoberta Menchú continues to be an outspoken proponent of minority and women's rights worldwide, though much of her effort goes into working face-to-face with the Indian population of Guatemala.

> Rigoberta Menchú (ed. Elisabeth Burgos-Debray), *I, Rigoberta: An Indian Woman in Guatemala*, Verso, 1984

Chico Mendes
1944–1988
union organiser and rainforest activist

Raised in poverty as a second generation settler in Acre, the westernmost state of Brazil, Chico Mendes became a rubber tapper at the age of twelve. His education, received in his late teens mostly from the ex-revolutionary organiser Euclides Távora, helped him to become a union organiser. Like many of his fellow rubber tappers, Chico Mendes recognised the value of maintaining the integrity of the rainforest and its peoples against the pervasive threat of clearcutting for extensive cattle ranching, a trend which began in the mid-1960s. In 1976 he and his coworkers organised the first of many *empates*, mass actions to prevent chainsaw gangs from cutting the forest; of the 45 or so *empates* that took place in Xapua and Brasiléia between 1976 and 1987 about a third were successful, saving some three million acres of forest from destruction. In 1985 the National Rubber Tappers' Union was formed, and attempted to persuade the ranchers and the powerful Ranchers' League of the economic importance of the rain-forest. In 1987 the United Nations honoured Chico Mendes with a Global 500 award, and in 1988 the Brazilian government created a pilot 'extractive reserve' in Acre. Landowners in the vicinity of Xapuri, the headquarters of the Tappers' Union, were becoming increasingly and openly hostile to the threats to their dominance, and in December 1988 Chico Mendes was killed outside his home by agents of the clearcutters. Shortly before he was assassinated he wrote that his dream was to see all of the Amazon forest conserved, and that he did not want flowers at his funeral because he knew that they, like everything else, would be taken from the forest and nothing given back in exchange.

Susanna Hecht and Alexander Cockburn, *The Fate of the Forest*, Verso, 1989
Chico Mendes and Tony Gross, *Fight for the Forest: Chico Mendes in His Own Words*, Latin America Bureau, 1989

Fatima Mernissi
1940–
feminist activist and academic

Fatima Mernissi is one of the most courageous and eloquent feminist voices in North Africa today. She grew up in a traditional household in the Moroccan city of Fez, and studied politics at the Muhammed V University in Rabat and at the Sorbonne in Paris; she then went to the USA to study for her PhD at Brandeis University, returning to Morocco in 1974. Her chosen PhD subject was 'Male-Female Dynamics in a Modern Muslim Society', published in 1975 as *Beyond the Veil*, and as a university teacher at Muhammed V University and the Institut Universitaire de la Recherche Scientifique in Rabat she has continued to explore sex roles and politics in the Arab world. Of her many books, the first to receive widespread Arab attention was *The Veil and the Male Élite* (1991), which was banned in Morocco immediately after it was published in France, though it has since been published in Arabic and Turkish. In it she criticises contemporary Moslem conservatives for upholding male privilege under the pretence of maintaining the purity of Islam, arguing that there is no historical or philosophical basis for women's subjugation within the Islamic tradition. Her 1992 book, *Islam and Democracy*, goes even further, accusing modern

Arab leaders of 'gutting one of the most promising religions in human history of its substance'.

Fatima Mernissi (trans. Mary Jo Lakeland), *The Veil and the Male Élite: A Feminist Interpretation of Women's Rights in Islam*, Addison-Wesley, 1991

Fatima Mernissi (trans. Mary Jo Lakeland), *Islam and Democracy: Fear of the Modern World*, Addison-Wesley, 1992

Margot Badran and Miriam Cooke (ed.), *Opening the Gates: A Century of Arab Feminist Writing*, Virago, 1990

Thomas [Feverel] Merton
1915–1968
monk, mystic, peace activist

The son of a New Zealand painter father and an American dancer mother, Thomas Merton was born in south-eastern France and grew up in Europe and the USA. He studied at Cambridge and Columbia Universities; his first poems and reviews were published in the late 1930s. While at Columbia he converted to Roman Catholicism for reasons explained cogently and passionately in his biography *The Seven Storey Mountain*, which favourable critics including Evelyn Waugh and Graham Greene helped to make a bestseller. In 1949 he was ordained as a Trappist monk and from then on made Gethsemani Monastery in rural Kentucky his home. He wrote profusely on spiritual and social issues, maintaining a lively correspondence with many leading social activists. It was his solid grasp of the links between simple spirituality and the social tensions of the material world that made his writings accessible to so many; he did not shy away from an engagement in the most important issues of the day – the nuclear threat, cold warmongering and the **Vietnam War** in particular. His outspoken fluency brought him into conflict with his superiors: from around 1960 his writings were increasingly censored, and in 1962 he was silenced for more than a year until a papal encyclical, *Pacem in Terris*, declared that 'just war' was an outdated concept. Thomas Merton saw no contradiction between a monastic life and involvement in political struggle. 'I make monastic silence a protest against the lies of politicians, propagandists and agitators,' he wrote in 1963, 'and when I speak it is to deny that my faith and my church can ever seriously be aligned with the forces of injustice and destruction.' Though he occasionally visited friends in New York, most of his campaigning was in the form of letters and articles, so a decision to visit south-east Asia in 1968 to meet Buddhist monks and **Tenzin Gyatso** (the Fourteenth Dalai Lama) was a major, and ultimately fateful, one – as the result of an accident while visiting Thailand he died in a Bangkok hospital. His power, passion and simplicity have lived on in his writings, however, and he remains one of the most important spiritually-aware activists of the century.

Thomas Merton, *The Seven Storey Mountain*, SPCK, 1990 (new printing of 1948 edn)

Monica Furlong, *Merton: A Biography*, Harper and Row, 1980

M. Basil Pennington, *Thomas Merton, Brother Monk: The Quest for True Freedom*, Harper and Row, 1990

Harvey [Bernard] Milk
1928–1978
politician, gay rights campaigner

'Let the bullet that rips my brain open every closet door in America,' said Harvey Milk to his tape recorder in October 1978, knowing that his overtly pro-gay stance in San Francisco's city government might well cost him his life. Harvey, who grew up in a Jewish New York family, came out as a homosexual in his late teens. In 1972, with his partner Scott Smith, he opened a photographic shop in San Francisco's Castro Street, which quickly became a centre for neighbourhood and gay activism. Within a year he had become the *de facto* 'Mayor of Castro Street', organising a neighbourhood business association, running a boycott against beer companies who refused to employ gay drivers, and standing (unsuccessfully, though with widespread support) in the 1973 San Francisco city elections. The election of pro-gay mayor George Moscone in 1975 encouraged Harvey to stand for office again, and in November 1977 he ran and won in the election for city supervisor for San Francisco's District 5. He proved a capable and innovative administrator, and within a year had become one of the most popular of city politicians. While gay rights rose rapidly up the political agenda, the backlash was also gaining force. The summer of 1978 in California saw a concerted attempt to keep gay teachers out of the classroom – the Briggs initiative or Proposition 6; although it was overwhelmingly defeated in the November elections the campaign left gays exhausted and their enemies enraged. Violence against gay and lesbian premises and individuals intensified, and on November 27th a former police chief and supervisor, Dan White, smuggled a gun through the basement of City Hall and assassinated both Harvey Milk and George Moscone. The city was stunned by the deaths, and even more so by the manslaughter verdict given out on May 21st 1979; six months of frustration spilled out in city-wide riots. Though the anti-gay faction, aided by the city police, continued to harass the gay community, the achievements of Harvey Milk and his colleagues had changed the face of San Francisco politics for good, and the strength of the gay community and its allies in the 1980s owed much to his work and to his sacrifice.

Randy Shilts, *The Mayor of Castro Street: The Life and Times of Harvey Milk*, St Martins Press, 1982

John D'Emilio, 'Gay Politics and Community in San Francisco since World War II', in Martin Bauml Duberman, Martha Vicinus and George Chauncey (eds), *Hidden From History: Reclaiming the Gay and Lesbian Past*, New American Library, 1989

Kate [Katherine Murray] Millett
1934–
feminist activist, writer, sculptor and artist

Kate Millett was born in St Paul, Minnesota, graduated from the University of Minnesota in 1956, and read literature at St. Hilda's College, Oxford, from 1956 to 1958. After teaching English at the University of North Carolina and working at a kindergarten in New York City, she went to Japan, where from 1961 to 1963 she worked as a sculptor; here she met her future husband, Fumio Yoshimura, and they married in 1965. She returned to New York, teaching in the English Department at Barnard College and studying at Columbia University. Active in the civil rights movement, she was a founding member in 1966 of the **National Organization for Women**, chairing its education committee, and joined New York Radical Women at its inception in 1967. In 1968 a paper she wrote for a campaign to organise a women's liberation group at Columbia was banned by the university authorities. It argued that the relationship between men and women, being based on power and maintained by ideology, is political. Censorship failed dismally: the idea was developed and elaborated in her book, *Sexual Politics* (1970), which is still studied as the first significant statement of radical feminist theory. Kate Millett remained active in the **women's movement** through the 1970s and was expelled from Iran for her work with women there (*Going to Iran*, 1982). Though her work as an artist went into abeyance during the early 70s, since 1976 she has generally mounted a one-woman show every two years. She divides her time between New York City and Women's Art Colony Farm, which she founded in upstate New York. She has written many books, including the autobiographical *Flying* (1974) and *The Loony Bin Trip* (1990). Her most recent, *The Politics of Cruelty* (1994), is a study of political detention and torture.

Kate Millett, *Sexual Politics*, Doubleday, 1970
Kate Millett, *Flying*, Knopf, 1974
Kate Millett, *The Politics of Cruelty: An Essay on the Literature of Political Imprisonment*, Norton, 1994

C. [Charles] Wright Mills
1916–1962
sociologist, social critic

C. Wright Mills, the labour researcher turned social critic who provided a radical sociological rationale for the postwar **new left**, grew up in Waco, Texas, and studied philosophy at the University of Texas at Austin. While working for his doctorate in sociology at the University of Wisconsin he came into contact with the Marxist ideas of the Frankfurt School and, by the time of his 1945 move to New York, where he worked first in the Bureau of Applied Social Research and then in Columbia's Department of Sociology (home to the Frankfurt School in wartime exile), he had already developed the framework of power élites and the need for consensus which characterised much of his mature work. His first major book, *The New Men of Power* (1948), examined the role of American labour leaders, to be followed in 1951 with a historical survey of America's middle class in *White Collar*. The book that brought him to wider attention was *The Power Élite* (1956), showing how postwar America was under the control of a small number of powerful men whose monopoly of decision-making threatened democracy. Mills' committed pacifism dated from angry opposition to the second world war, and his concern that postwar detente was creating a world under the constant threat of war led him to write books like *The Causes of World War Three* (1958), a fluent attack on American foreign policy, and *Listen, Yankee* (1960), defending the Cuban revolution against its American critics. He also wrote a widely read primer on radical sociology, *The Sociological Imagination* (1959), and at the time of his early death was working on a five-volume survey of twentieth-century sociology. Increasingly influential within radical circles, Mills took the opportunity of circulating in early 1960 a fiery and widely-read manifesto, 'Letter to the New Left', in which he announced the end of ideological orthodoxy and the dawn of a new radicalism; his letter provided the framework for numerous radical statements, including the 1962 Port Huron Statement of **Students for a Democratic Society**. In December 1960 Mills suffered a stroke while preparing for a television debate about Cuba, and died fourteen months later.

C. Wright Mills, *The New Men of Power: America's Labor Leaders*, Harcourt Brace, 1948

C. Wright Mills, *The Power Élite*, Oxford University Press, 1956

C. Wright Mills, *The Sociological Imagination*, Oxford University Press, 1959

Rick Tilman, *C. Wright Mills: A Native Radical and his American Intellectual Roots*, Pennsylvania State University Press, 1984

Juliet Mitchell
1940–
teacher, writer, feminist and psychoanalyst

Juliet Mitchell's considerable contributions to the theory, practice and interplay of feminism, Marxism and psychoanalysis have allowed many bridges to be built between these three often disparate disciplines. She was born in New Zealand but moved to England when she was three years old. She studied English at Oxford, graduating in 1962, and then taught at Leeds and Reading Universities. For several years she was on the editorial board of *New Left Review*, an important British neo-Marxist journal, and in the late 1960s was one of the founders of the **women's movement** in Britain. She wrote an influential article about women's struggle, 'The Longest Revolution', in *New Left Review* in 1966 (the negative response from several male colleagues persuaded her to leave the magazine), helped to organise the first British Women's Liberation Conference in 1970, and was an active member of the London Women's Liberation Workshop. In 1970 she gave up teaching to concentrate on writing and lecturing, and the first of her several books, *Woman's Estate*, was published in 1972. In *Woman's Estate* she made it clear that women are oppressed in several interacting spheres – work, reproduction, sexuality and socialisation – and that radical change must take place in each area before women are truly free. Because oppression occurs across the range of women's interactions in the world, she argued, there is no simple 'magic pill' for liberation. Her interest in the family and its role in social control led her to question the assumptions of Freudian psychoanalysis, but unlike **Betty Friedan** and **Kate Millett**, who dismissed Freud as beyond the patriarchal pale, she argued in *Psychoanalysis and Feminism* (1974) that Freud's work and some recent trends in psycho-analysis, specifically the ideas of the French psychoanalyst Jacques Lacan, do have important insights for feminist belief and practice. After the publication of *Psychoanalysis and Feminism* Juliet Mitchell trained as an analyst at the Institute of Psychoanalysis, and continues to write, lecture, and be a parent alongside her analytic practice. While many of her ideas about the integration of Freud, **Marx** and feminism are still hotly debated, her important contribution to all three is undeniable.

Juliet Mitchell, *Woman's Estate*, Penguin, 1972
Juliet Mitchell, *Psychoanalysis and Feminism*, Allen Lane, 1974
Juliet Mitchell, *Women: The Longest Revolution*, Virago, 1984

Bill Mollison
1928–
environmental activist and writer

The Australian scientist and environmentalist Bill Mollison is best known as the developer of the concept of permaculture, a system of perennial agriculture designed to fulfil the needs of both human beings and their local environment in an integrated, self-sustaining ecosystem. Though the ideas behind permaculture had been long in gestation, Bill Mollison only settled to explore them in practice in 1974, having tried his hand at a variety of skills. He grew up in the Tasmanian fishing village of Stanley, and left school at fifteen. Several years of working as a fisherman, forester, trapper and millworker were followed in 1954 by a spell working as a biologist with Australia's Wildlife Survey. By the mid-60s he was back in Tasmania, teaching at the University of Tasmania, where he established a pioneering environmental psychology unit. While at the university he learned that the Tasmanian government was refusing to give school grants to Aboriginal children because they could not prove their Aboriginal lineage, so he spent several years helping to compile the three-volume *Genealogies of Tasmanian Aborigines*, which forced the government to issue grants to the children of many needy families. In the mid-1970s Mollison shifted his emphasis from protest to the exploration of positive solutions, and set up the Perma-culture Institute at Tyalgum in New South Wales to experiment with practical ways of improving ecological design for both rural and urban areas. The aim of permaculture is to revive the crucial relationship between land and people, and Bill Mollison's innovative and eminently practical ideas about companion crops, crop rotations, edible gardening and the importance of biodiversity spread rapidly. Since the publication of *Permaculture One* in 1978 the Institute's teachers have trained more than 10,000 people all over the world in the principles of sustainable agriculture, reforestation, and the need for environmental education. In 1981 Bill Mollison was awarded the Right Livelihood Award for his work.

Bill Mollison and David Holmgren, *Permaculture One: A Perennial Agriculture for Human Settlements*, Tagari, 1978

Bill Mollison, *Permaculture Two: Practical Design for Town and Country in Permanent Agriculture*, Tagari, 1979

Bill Mollison with Reny Mia Slay, *Introduction to Permaculture*, Tagari, 1991

Bill Mollison, *The Permaculture Book of Ferment and Human Nutrition*, Tagari, 1993

Maria Montessori
1870–1952
psychiatrist, educator

The innovative Italian educator Maria Montessori was born at Chiaraville and studied medicine at Rome University, graduating in 1894 to become Italy's first medically-qualified woman doctor. For several years she taught in the university's psychiatric unit, where she took a particular interest in the education of backward children. As director of the Scuola Ortofrenetica in Rome, in 1899 she entered some of her eight-year-old 'idiots' for the standard state examinations and achieved superb results. In the late 1890s Maria Montessori also became actively involved in championing women's rights, representing Italian women at international women's congresses in Berlin and London. From 1896 to 1906 she was professor of hygiene at the Magistero Femminile, one of Italy's two women's colleges, and in 1904 she was also appointed professor of anthropology at Rome University. It was her work with children in the slum district of San Lorenzo in 1907–08, however, that persuaded her to devote the rest of her life primarily to education. Taking charge of the Casa dei Bambini in San Lorenzo, she and her helpers developed an education method based on developing children's spontaneous interest in their world without the need for formal rewards and punishments. By encouraging children's innate need for stimulation, order, concentration and creativity, she demonstrated that they can largely be responsible for their own learning and self-discipline. She particularly stressed the need for children to have spaces – 'children's houses' – which they can claim as their own. The 'Montessori Method', as it came to be known, was outlined in a series of books starting with *Il metodo della pedagogia scientifica* (1909) and *Autoeducazione* (1912). Her ideas took root remarkably quickly, and by the mid-1920s there were Montessori Schools and Children's Houses in more than a dozen countries, the movement being particularly strong in Italy, Germany, Austria, Britain, India and the USA. Throughout the 1920s and 30s Maria Montessori travelled widely, lecturing and organising training courses: 1925 saw the inauguration of a series of International Montessori Congresses. She was teaching in India when war broke out in 1939: though she was technically an 'enemy alien' she was given special dispensation to stay until 1946. After the war she based herself at Noordwijk in the Netherlands, and was still actively teaching and organising until she died at the age of 81.

Maria Montessori (trans. Anne George), *The Montessori Method*, Schocken, 1964

E. Mortimer Standing, *Maria Montessori: Her Life and Work*, Hollis and Carter, 1957

Rita Kramer, *Maria Montessori: A Biography*, Putnam, 1976

Robin [Evonne] Morgan
1941–
feminist writer, editor and activist

Born in Lake Worth, Florida, Robin Morgan's first career was as a child actor in the television series 'I remember Mama'. Living in New York City in the 1960s, where she was working as a book editor, she came to the **women's movement** from activism in the antiwar movement and the **Yippies**. She was a member of the city's first women's liberation group, New York Radical Women, and did most of the organising for the group's 1968 Miss America Pageant protest, a landmark event in publicising the notion of women's liberation. She was an active and vocal participant in the development of feminist theory, compiling the important anthology *Sisterhood Is Powerful* (1970). A proponent of what came to be called cultural feminism, she encouraged women to put energy into creating alternative institutions as a concrete move towards self-determination and power, rather than trying to confront oppressive institutions directly. In the decades since, Robin Morgan has played a sustained role in encouraging the development of the women's movement. Her work within the international women's movement has included eight years as the 'World' columnist for *Ms.* magazine, advising the UN General Assembly Conference on Gender in 1985–86 and the UN Convention to End All Forms of Discrimination Against Women in 1987, and serving on the advisory board of ISIS, an international network for crosscultural exchange among women. She was an editor for *Ms.* from 1974 to 1987 and editor-in-chief from 1990 to 1993, and has twice been visiting professor at US universities. Of her many books, which include anthologies, fiction and poetry, the most revealing of her own activism are *Going Too Far* (1978) and *The Anatomy of Freedom* (1982), which include honest and poignant portrayals of the challenges and the pain of her relationships with her husband, the poet Kenneth Pitchford, and her son Blake.

Robin Morgan, *Sisterhood is Powerful: An Anthology of Writings from the Women's Liberation Movement*, Vintage, 1970

Robin Morgan, *Going Too Far: The Personal Chronicle of a Feminist*, Random House, 1978

Robin Morgan, *The Anatomy of Freedom*, Doubleday, 1982

Alice Echols, *Daring to be Bad: Radical Feminism in America 1967–1975*, University of Minnesota Press, 1989

Toni Morrison [Chloe Anthony Wofford]
1931–
feminist writer and activist

'I think long and hard about what my novels should do,' said black American author Toni Morrison in a 1981 interview. 'They should clarify the roles that have become obscured, they ought to identify those things in the past that are useful and those things that are not, and they ought to give nourishment.' She grew up in Lorain, Ohio, the daughter of parents who had migrated from Alabama to escape poverty and debt and who were determined to offer their four children a better life. After studying English at Howard University and Cornell, she taught briefly at Texas Southern University before returning to Howard in 1957, where she joined a writers' group and met and married Jamaican architect Harold Morrison: they moved to Washington and had two sons, but the marriage ended in 1964. With two young children to support, Toni Morrison worked as a textbook editor, but also found time to write, and her first novel, *The Bluest Eye*, was published in 1970. Over the next fifteen years she rose rapidly within the publishing company Random House, and by the time she could afford to support herself by writing in 1984 was a senior editor, the only black women in such a powerful position. Her novel *Sula* (1973) broke new ground with its strong and poetic portrayal of women's friendship and solidarity, while *Song of Solomon* (1977) and *Tar Baby* (1981) contined to demonstrate the range and versatility of Morrison's sensitivity and insight. During the 1970s she also worked, as in-house editor, on *The Black Book*, an important pictorial history of African-American life in America. *Beloved* (1987) is Toni Morrison's best known novel, the story of a mother who decides to kill her children rather than having them returned to slavery, and of the dead daughter who returns to haunt her. It was *Beloved*, with its beauty, passion, psychological complexity and political depth, that won Morrison the Pulitzer Prize. In 1989 she was appointed professor of humanities at Princeton University, continuing to write about the black American experience in *Jazz* (1992), the second of a planned trilogy that started with *Beloved*. In 1993 Toni Morrison was awarded the Nobel Prize for Literature: characteristically she took a large party of friends and colleagues to the Stockholm presentation to share her good fortune, afterwards declaring that she found most Swedes 'spontaneity-impaired'.

Toni Morrison, *Sula*, Knopf, 1973
Toni Morrison, *Beloved*, Knopf, 1987
Carolyn Denard, 'Toni Morrison', *Black Women in America: An Historical Encyclopedia* (ed. Darlene Clark Hine), Carlson, 1993
Middleton Harris et al, *The Black Book*, Random House, 1974

Bill [William Robert] Morrow
1888–1980
labour activist, politician, pacifist

The Australian labour and peace activist Bill Morrow grew up in Rockhampton, Queensland, and left school at ten to work on the railways. He soon became involved in union organisation in Queensland and Tasmania, and in 1936 became secretary of the Tasmanian branch of the Australian Railways Union, rising by 1946 to become president of the Tasmanian Trades Union Council. He had joined the Australian Labor Party (ALP) in 1908, but his association with the ALP was a rocky one: he took an active part in the party's internal struggle over the issue of conscription during the first world war, and in 1938 was expelled for refusing to endorse universal military training. His time in the Australian Senate between 1946 and 1953 was marked by extreme controversy: during a period of rabid anticommunism he called for friendly relations with the revolutionary communist government of China, support for the communist-led New South Wales miners' strike of 1949, opposition to the Communist Party Dissolution Bill even when it was officially endorsed by his own party, rejection of the 1951 bill for compulsory national service, and backing for the communist-supported Australian Peace Council. He felt that the struggle of the Australian working class was constantly being thwarted by the narrowness of his country's partisan politics, particularly the careerism and religious sectarianism of the ALP and the authoritarian rigidity of the Australian Communist Party. After he left the ALP in 1953, Bill Morrow attended the World Peace Council conference in Budapest, the first of many overseas travels in the cause of peace. He then dedicated himself to working with the Australian peace movement. In 1954 he became secretary of the New South Wales Peace Council, a position he held until 1963 when he was eased out by younger activists whose peace politics were not informed by the style of the 'old left'. As if to confirm their decision, he became Australia's first and only recipient of the Lenin Peace Prize. Ironically, though, his allegiance was turning to China, and for the rest of his life one of his main concerns was the improvement of Australia's relations with China, mainly through the Australia-China Society. Bill Morrow spent a lifetime working for a peacful, egalitarian, socialist Australia, and is remembered as a political activist of conviction and integrity.

Audrey Johnson, *Fly a Rebel Flag: Bill Morrow 1988–1980*, Penguin (Australia), 1986

Robert [Gabriel] Mugabe
1924–
teacher, campaigner for self-determination, politician

One of the more consistent, loyal and thoughtful of southern Africa's nationalist-leaders-turned-politician, Robert Mugabe's post-independence career as president of Zimbabwe has nevertheless been marred by inaction in the face of growing corruption and economic hardship. Raised in Kutama in Southern Rhodesia (later Zimbabwe), he went to university in South Africa and London before becoming a college teacher; for two years from 1958 he taught in Ghana, where he met his wife Sally. On his return to Rhodesia he became involved in nationalist politics, first with the National Democratic Party, then with Joshua Nkomo's ZAPU (Zimbabwe African Peoples Union), and from August 1963 (following Nkomo's flight to Tanzania to establish a government in exile, a tactic which Mugabe saw as unnecessary since internal pressure on Ian Smith's regime in Rhodesia was already growing rapidly) as cofounder of ZANU (Zimbabwe African National Union). In 1964 he was arrested and imprisoned for ten years, together with many of his present cabinet members to whom he remains remarkably loyal, but in 1975 he escaped to Mozambique. In 1979 Mugabe and Nkomo negotiated Zimbabwe's independence at the Lancaster House Conference, and with massive support from the country's black majority Robert Mugabe became Zimbabwe's first black prime minister. He confounded his critics by adhering strictly to the terms of Lancaster House, stressing equality, integration and continuity rather than choosing the route of state socialism; initially his policies won widespread grassroots support, especially the promise to return most of the land expropriated by white farmers. The ZAPU/ZANU rift was not healed until 1987, by which time it had become clear that reform was being stifled by widespread official corruption. By 1994 half the country's arable land was still in large white-owned holdings, and much of the land which had been distributed was in the hands of politicians and government officials; Robert Mugabe belatedly ordered a public enquiry, but it is possible that a general election in 1995 will see the end of his political career.

Lorraine Eide, *Robert Mugabe*, Chelsea House, 1989

Lewis Mumford
1895–1990
historian, architect, social critic

One of the most influential critics of the modern metropolis and the blind technology that goes with it, Lewis Mumford grew up in Flushing, New York, and studied engineering at Stuyvesant High School. An early and abiding mentor was Patrick Geddes, from whom he borrowed and adapted the ecological concept of the urban region to demonstrate how culture and the physical environment must take account of each other if we are to understand human potential and how it can be fulfilled. In 1923 he was one of the founder members of the Regional Planning Association of America, and his early books, for example *Sticks and Stones* (1924) and *The Brown Decades* (1931), argued from the lessons of American architectural history for a more humane and relevant urban environment. Throughout his long career he stressed how the reckless drive for profit and expansion in the modern city was destroying the vital connections that made it possible for people to live in cities. He welcomed much modern architecture, and was a fluent champion of architects like Frank Lloyd Wright, but saw the blind use of large-scale building technology as numbing and destructive of the human spirit. His critics saw him as anti-progress and anti-technology, and his voluminous writings sometimes tended towards the moralistic, but he always extolled the virtues of what he called 'polytechnics', the range of skills available to free people living in communities not dominated by external states and multinational companies. It was his 1938 study, *The Culture of Cities*, that firmly established Lewis Mumford's international reputation as an urban historian and critic, a reputation that was consolidated by a string of books about culture and history culminating in *The City in History* (1961), which won the 1962 National Book Award. After the second world war he became involved in the antinuclear debate, publishing *In The Name of Sanity* in 1954, and was encouraged by the rise of the environmental movement of the 1970s and 80s as a vindication of many of the ideas he had propounded decades earlier.

Lewis Mumford, *Findings and Keepings: Analects for an Autobiography*, Harcourt Brace Jovanovich, 1975
Lewis Mumford, *My Works and Days*, Harcourt Brace Jovanovich, 1979
Donald Miller, *Lewis Mumford: A Life*, Weidenfeld and Nicholson, 1989
Thomas Parke Hughes, *Lewis Mumford: Public Intellectual*, Oxford University Press, 1990

Emily Murphy [Emily Gowan Ferguson]
1868–1933
feminist, lawyer, writer

Born in Cooksville, Ontario, the Canadian feminist writer and lawyer Emily Ferguson was educated at Bishop Strachan School, Toronto. In 1887 she married Arthur Murphy, a travelling missionary and rector of Chatham, Ontario, and they had two daughters. In 1904 they moved to Swan River, Manitoba, and three years later to Edmonton, Alberta, where Emily became a leading social reformer, campaigning against drunkenness and rural poverty, and working for the suffrage movement, especially for the legal rights of women and for the establishment of a special court to hear women's evidence in 'difficult' cases such as divorce or sexual assault. In 1916 the Women's Court was established in Edmonton, and Emily became the first woman magistrate in the British Empire, attached to the juvenile court. When she came to pass sentence on her first case the defence lawyer challenged her authority, claiming 'you are not even a person', since under a British act of 1876 women were vulnerable to legal penalties but did not have legal rights or privileges. Her position was however upheld by the Supreme Court of Alberta in 1916, and she then campaigned for women to be admitted to the Senate. After long deliberation the Supreme Court finally decided in 1928 that 'women, children, criminals and idiots are not legally persons', but an appeal to the British Privy Council resulted in the ruling that 'persons' covered both sexes and that women were eligible for seats in the senate – the successful appeal became widely known as 'The Persons Case'. In 1931 Emily Murphy resigned her judicial post, but remained a supervisor of Alberta's prisons and asylums. Emily was also a writer, keeping a diary on which she based *Janey Canuck Abroad* (1901), a satirical account of the splendours of England and Germany, detailing slum conditions and exploitations as well as European affectations, and in 1922 she wrote a study of drug addiction, *The Black Candle*.

Byrne Hope Sanders, *Emily Murphy: Crusader*, Macmillan (Canada), 1945
Christine Mander, *Emily Murphy: Rebel*, Simon and Pierre, 1985

Nabawiya Musa
1890–1951
feminist, educator, writer

Nabawiya Musa, one of Egypt's foremost campaigners for women's rights and women's access to education, was born into a middle-class family in a village near Zigazig in the Eastern Delta. She attended the Saniyya School, Egypt's first teacher training college for women, and in 1907 was the first – and last – woman to sit the secondary school teaching certificate examination until after Egyptian independence in 1924. She became a teacher and then principal in a girls' school, and was the first woman to be made a schools inspector. When she criticised the lack of choice in girls' education she was fired, but set up her own school, Madrasat Banat al-Ashraf, with campuses in Cairo and Alexandria. Her best-known book, *Al-Mara wa al-Amal* (*Woman and Work*) was published in 1920, offering a broadranging critique of traditional patriarchal Arab culture and the limitations it places on women. In 1922 Nabawiya Musa founded the Association for the Progress of Women; she was a founding member of the Egyptian Feminist Union and one of Egypt's first delegates to the **International Woman Suffrage Alliance** when it met in Rome in 1923. She also wrote widely on women's education, and founded a journal called *Al-Fatah* (*The Girl*). She never married, determined to live her life on her own terms and devote it to providing education that would give Egyptian women the necessary respect and confidence to play a full part in their country's future.

Margot Badran and Miriam Cooke (ed.), *Opening the Gates: A Century of Arab Feminist Writing*, Virago, 1990
Leila Ahmed, *Women and Gender in Islam*, Yale University Press, 1992

A.J. [Abraham Johannes] Muste
1885–1967
labour and peace campaigner

The career of the veteran US labour and peace campaigner A.J. Muste spanned decades of leftwing intrigue and infighting, yet his reputation as a thoughtful and caring organiser and arbitrator ensured that he was highly regarded by almost every section of the radical left. He was born at Zierikzee in the Netherlands, but when he was six the family emigrated to Grand Rapids, Michigan. From an early age he was expected to become a

Dutch Reformed Church minister: he graduated from a New Jersey Seminary in 1909, married minister's daughter Anna Huizenga, and started his ministry in New York's Lower East Side. As the first world war loomed Muste, a convinced pacifist, felt that he could not support the churches' stance on violence and conscription, and from then on he and Anna found their spiritual home within the Society of Friends; they also gained purpose and inspiration from involvement with the **Fellowship of Reconciliation** (FOR). Early in 1919 an impending textile strike at Lawrence, Massachusetts, involved Muste and his colleagues in organising and negotiating between the various nationalities and factions; by the end of the first week he was executive secretary of the strike committee, and when strike ended with success for the workers Muste's reputation was assured. In 1921 he was one of the founders of the Brookwood Labor College at Katonah, New York, which in its heyday in the late 20s and early 30s produced many labour and peace organisers; the College also provided a focus for links between the various factions within the labour and communist movements. Between 1932 and 1936 Muste moved towards Trotskyite communism as a basis for his activism, and met **Trotsky** during a visit to Norway in 1936. While in Paris with Anna for the Trotskyists' Fourth **International**, however, he stepped into St Sulpice Church and experienced a reconversion to Christian pacifism which did not waver for the rest of his life. He now became one of America's leading voices in opposition to war, institutionalised violence, and the nuclear arms race. As an executive director of FOR in the 1940s he defended conscientious objectors, and sponsored the early work of the **Congress of Racial Equality** (CORE). After his 'retirement' from FOR in 1953 he threw himself into wider organisation and activism, becoming involved in a broad range of antiwar and antinuclear actions and alliances. In 1956 he cofounded the important antiwar monthly *Liberation*, and in 1966, at the age of 81, travelled to Vietnam 'to convey the spirit of peace to its stricken people': he died in February 1967, two weeks after his return to the USA.

A.J. Muste, *Not By Might*, Garland Library, 1971 (repr. of 1947 ed.)

Nat Hentoff, *Peace Agitator: The Story of A.J. Muste*, Macmillan, 1963

Jo Ann Ooiman Robinson, *Abraham Went Out: A Biography of A.J. Muste*, Temple University Press, 1981

Saiza Nabarawi [Zainab Murad]
1897–1985
feminist, journalist

Saiza Nabarawi, one of Egypt's leading campaigners for women's rights, had an uncertain childhood. She was born at the Minshawi Palace outside Cairo, but as an infant was adopted and taken to live in Paris, where she went to convent school and then the Saint Germain des Près Institute. When she was thirteen she was sent back to Egypt and, when her foster mother committed suicide a year later, her natural parents, poor people who spoke only Arabic, came to her French school to claim her. Saiza

Nabarawi rejected them, however, and went to live with her maternal grandparents in Cairo, where she met the women's rights campaigner **Huda Shaarawi**. In 1923, on their return from the **International Woman Suffrage Alliance** conference in Rome, Nabarawi and Shaarawi publicly removed their veils on Cairo railway station as an act of public defiance against the veiling laws. From then until her death Saiza Nabarawi spent her life campaigning for women's liberation, national liberation and peace. From 1925 to 1940 she edited *L'Égyptienne*, the newspaper of the Egyptian Feminist Union, and as its editor was the first woman delegate to attend the Egyptian parliament as an official observer; she was not, however, allowed entry to the main chamber, and protested about the double standards in Egyptian public life in one of many outspoken *L'Égyptienne* editorials.

Margot Badran and Miriam Cooke (ed.), *Opening the Gates: A Century of Arab Feminist Writing*, Virago, 1990
Leila Ahmed, *Women and Gender in Islam*, Yale University Press, 1992

Sarojini Naidu [Sarojini Chattopadhyay]
1879–1949
poet, independence and human rights campaigner

The poet-politician Sarojini Naidu stands alongside her friend and mentor **Gandhi** as one of India's great reforming orators and organisers. Born in Hyderabad (now in Pakistan) into a Brahmin family noted for its learning, she passed the matriculation examination for the University of Madras at the age of twelve. She was sent to England at sixteen and studied at King's College, London, and Girton College, Cambridge. The rigour of her education, combined with falling in love with her future husband, Govindarajulu Naidu, led to a breakdown in 1895 (thereafter her health was never good), but she returned to India in 1898 and, against her family's wishes, married Naidu: between 1899 and 1903 they had four children. Three collections of poems published between 1912 and 1917 established her reputation as a poet; the same period saw her organising flood relief in Hyderabad and speaking at women's conferences. Between 1903 and 1917 she became friends with many of the leaders of the growing Indian home rule movement, including Gopal Krishna Gokhale, Rabindranath Tagore, **Annie Besant** and Mahatma Gandhi. By 1919 Sarojini Naidu had emerged as a political leader in her own right, and worked closely with Gandhi to launch the Civil Disobedience Movement in April 1919. In 1924 she investigated the condition of Indians working in East and South Africa, and in 1925 was the second woman (after Annie Besant) to become president of the Indian National Congress. In 1928 she visited Britain and the USA, where she spoke on behalf of the nationalist campaign. The same year she chaired the All India Conference for Educational Reform. In 1930 she took over the Anti-Salt Law campaign when Gandhi was imprisoned, and was arrested after leading a raid on a salt depot on the Gujerat coast; she was imprisoned again in 1932 and 1942. At Indian independence in 1947 she became governor of Uttar Pradesh, India's largest state, and presided over the important Asia Relations Conference. She died in office in Lucknow in March 1949, shortly after her seventieth birthday.

Sarojini Naidu, *Speeches and Writings*, G.A. Nateson and Co., Madras, 1919

Padmini Sathianadhan Sengupta, *Sarojini Naidu: A Biography*, Asia Publishing House, 1966

Tara Ali Baig, *Sarojini Naidu*, Government of India Ministry of Information and Broadcasting, 1974

J.P. [Jayaprakash] Narayan
1902–1979
socialist politician, social and political activist and critic

During the early years of his career Jayaprakash Narayan was a competent Indian leftwing politician, working like many for a socialist state in India, but it was his transition to asceticism and social activism that made him unique within the Indian radical tradition. After studying in the USA he returned to India a dedicated socialist, and was soon one of the leaders of a leftwing democratic grouping within the Indian National Congress. In the mid-1930s he was a founding member of the Congress Socialist Party of India, which played an important role in the country's struggle for self-determination: from 1942 to 1946 he led an armed revolt against the British administration, and was the last political prisoner to be released prior to independence in 1947. Within a decade Narayan had become disillusioned with the way in which the Nehru government was ignoring the real needs of Indians: in 1954 he renounced politics and joined **Vinoba Bhave's** sarvodaya movement. In his writings and actions of the next two decades he stressed the importance of community initiative and grassroots power, since central government could not be relied on – as he said of himself, 'I provide the meeting ground between **Lenin** and **Gandhi**.' He was particularly critical of the repressive regime of Indira Gandhi (Nehru's daughter), which in 1975 declared a state of emergency and imposed press censorship. Stressing the need for the Sarvodaya movement to embrace nonviolent direct action and Gandhian civil disobedience, he called for and took part in mass demonstrations against government repression, calling for 'total revolution'. Here he parted company with Bhave, whose disapproval of the Narayan campaign was expressed by taking a vow of silence: in June 1975 Jayaprakash Narayan was arrested and placed in solitary confinement for five months. His health suffered considerably during his detention, though in prison he wrote a moving account of his exploration of effective ways of fostering social and political change. In 1976–77 Narayan was active in the formation of the Janata People's Party which defeated Indira Gandhi in the March 1977 elections, holding true to his vision of a truly participatory politics, but the shortlived Janata government failed to change India's deeprooted power structure, and a year after Narayan's death in 1979 Indira Gandhi was back in power and India had drifted even further into authoritarian rule.

Jayaprakash Narayan, *Socialism, Sarvadaya, and Democracy*, Asia Publishing House, 1964

Jai Prakash Narain (Jayaprakash Narayan), *Prison Diary*, University of Washington Press, 1977

Ajit Bhattacharjea, *Jayaprakash Narayan: A Political Biography*, Vikas, 1975

Lakshmi Narain Lal, *Jayaprakash: Rebel Extraordinary*, Indian Book Company, 1975

Taslima Nasrin

1962–

feminist poet and novelist

Bangladeshi writer and poet Taslima Nasrin shot to prominence in 1993 with the publication of her second novel, *Lajja* (*Shame*), which vividly portrays the sufferings of Bangladesh's Hindu minority and the efforts of human rights campaigners to counter the growing tide of sectarian violence and sexual abuse. Taslima Nasrin was born and grew up in Mymensingh, where she studied medicine at Mymensingh Medical School and practised for several years as a gynaecologist. She published her first book of poetry in 1989 and has since published nine books; she also wrote a widely-read syndicated newspaper column, in which she regularly highlighted sectarian atrocities. Published simultaneously in Bangladesh and India, *Lajja* became an immediate bestseller, but provoked a violent and widespread backlash from Islamic fundamentalists. In May 1994 Nasrin was reported in a Calcutta newspaper as suggesting that the *Koran* should be amended to reflect contemporary social values; though she denied it, saying that she had been referring not to the *Koran* but to traditional Islamic sharia law, the fundamentalist Jamaat-e-Islami party called for her arrest on charges of 'injuring Moslem sentiments', while populist Islamic groups called for the death penalty or *fatwa*. Under such pressure she was forced into hiding while death threats and attacks on individuals, newspapers and institutions continued: these came to a head on June 30th, with a national strike called by Islamic fundamentalists pressing for Taslima Nasrin's death and secularists protesting against rising fundamentalism. The Swedish government, with official Bangladeshi agreement, offered her asylum until the situation in Bangladesh improved; this was timed to coincide with her receipt in August 1994 of an international PEN Club award. Interviewed shortly after her arrival in Sweden Taslima Nasrin said that she would continue her fight against fundamentalism, 'which is spreading darkness in many parts of the world'.

Taslima Nasrin, *Shame*, Penguin India, 1994

'Fatwas for a Feminist', *The Economist*, 18 June 1994

'Exiled Writer Vows to Fight Extremism', *The Guardian*, 19 August 1994

Holly Near
1949–
singer, songwriter and activist

Holly Near, one of America's best-known contemporary singer-songwriters, grew up on a farm in California, and though she began her performance career as an actor, appearing in the Broadway production of *Hair* and in several films, her direction changed after she joined the 'Free the Army' tour protesting against US involvement in the **Vietnam War**. Singing at innumerable concerts, benefits and marches, she has made a powerful, sustained contribution with her voice and songs to the peace and justice, antinuclear, **women's**, and **gay and lesbian pride movements** in the USA. In 1973 she founded Redwood Records to produce her first album, *Hang in There*, and has made over fifteen more albums in the last twenty years. Since the late 1970s, after making her relationship with singer-songwriter Meg Christian public and releasing *Imagine My Surprise*, her work has concentrated on women's issues, actively fostering the development and distribution of women's music.

Holly Near, *Fire in the Rain – Singer in the Storm: An Autobiography*, Morrow, 1990

Scott Nearing
1883–1983
political and environmental activist

'The majority will always be for caution, hesitation and the status quo, and against creativity and innovation,' wrote Scott Nearing in 1922. 'The innovator must therefore always be a minoritarian, an object of opposition, scorn, hatred.' He was all too aware of that opposition, for at an early age he had rejected the material comfort which accompanied his family's privileged status. His family had ruled and owned much of the mining town of Morris Run, Pennsylvania, for half a century, but the exploitation of labour (particularly of child labour) disgusted Scott. Having studied economics at the Wharton School of the University of Pennsylvania, he vowed to use his best efforts to promote equality and the improvement of working conditions. He soon paid the price for his outspoken views, being sacked from his teaching post at Wharton in 1915 for speaking out against child labour. On the brink of war in 1917 he was fired from another teaching post at the University of Toledo for writing that 'war is nothing more than organised destruction and mass murder': this low point in his life also saw the end of his first marriage, to Nellie Seeds. The following year, following the publication of the pacifist tract *The Great Madness*, Nearing was indicted for treason by the US government, but escaped imprisonment by delivering an eloquent defence at his trial in February 1919. From 1917 to 1922 he was a member of the Socialist Party and from 1927 to 1929 of the Communist Party, succeeding in being expelled from both for his criticism of state socialism. In 1928 he started living with the activist and musician Helen Knothe (they married in 1947), and in 1932 they bought a farm in

Jamaica, Vermont, where they established an organic smallholding and maple sugar orchard, practising and writing about the voluntary simplicity that Scott (and now Helen) Nearing had always advocated. As well as working the land, first at the Jamaica farm and from 1951 at Harbourside, Maine, the Nearings continued to write profusely, producing the best-selling *Living The Good Life* in 1954 as well as a stream of other books and articles. By the 1970s they had become icons of social and environmental activism, and until his death two weeks after his hundredth birthday Scott Nearing continued to work actively for the causes dearest to his heart: vegetarianism, organic growing, federalism, compassion and peace.

Scott Nearing (ed. Steve Sherman), *A Scott Nearing Reader*, Scarecrow, 1989
Scott Nearing, *The Conscience of a Radical*, Social Science Institute, 1965
Scott Nearing, *The Making of a Radical: A Political Biography*, Harper and Row, 1972
Helen Nearing, *Loving and Leaving the Good Life*, Chelsea Green, 1992

A.S. [Alexander Sutherland] Neill
1883–1973
educator

The progressive educationalist and founder of Summerhill, one of the best known experiments in radical education, A.S. Neill grew up in the Scottish town of Forfar and studied English at Edinburgh University. He then taught in Scottish state schools, becoming increasingly disillusioned with conventional educational practice: his experiences both of teaching and of expressing his dissatisfaction are amusingly described in *A Dominie's Log* (1915) and *A Dominie Dismissed* (1916), which together with *A Dominie Abroad* (1923) were reissued as *The Dominie Books* in 1975. In 1921 Neill was joint founder of a progressive international school in Hellerau near Dresden, which moved three years later to Sonntagberg in Austria. He returned to England in 1924 to set up the progressive school for which he became famous, Summerhill, located first on a hill of that name near Lyme Regis in Dorset and later at Leiston in Suffolk, where it still operates. Summerhill began as an experimental school, taking forty children aged between five and sixteen, and from its inception its key principle was freedom. Thus all lessons were optional, school rules were established by a school parliament where teachers and pupils had equal rights, there was no religious instruction, and close friendships, intimacy and sexual experimentation were all accepted as part of children's growth experience. Neill's approach to education inevitably aroused both admiration and hostility, both of which he countered with plain speaking and a wealth of firsthand experience. Though he kept in close touch with similar educational experiments, he always maintained that his inspiration came more from psychologists than from educationalists. He was a close personal friend of **Wilhelm Reich**, with whom he conducted a lengthy correspondence, and modelled Summerhill's self-government on Homer Lane's *Little Commonwealth*. Neill's first wife, Lilian Richardson, died in 1944 (they had married in 1927), and a year later he married Ena Wood. Alexander and Ena's daughter, Zoë, became very involved with the running of Summerhill.

A.S. Neill, *Summerhill: A Radical Approach to Child Rearing*, Gollancz, 1961

A.S. Neill, *Talking of Summerhill*, Gollancz, 1967

A.S. Neill, *Neill! Neill! Orange Peel! A Personal View of Ninety Years*, Weidenfeld and Nicolson, 1973

Jonathan Croall, *Neill of Summerhill: The Permanent Rebel*, Routledge and Kegan Paul, 1983

Pablo Neruda [Ricardo Eliezer Neftali Reyes y Basoalto]
1904–1973
poet, diplomat, liberationist

Although best known as a poet, the Chilean Pablo Neruda (he changed his name while still at high school in memory of the anarchist Czech poet Jan Neruda, 1834–91) was very much a political and social activist, embracing socialist anarchism and communism and in his last years becoming a friend and active supporter of **Salvador Allende**. The son of a railway worker, Neruda grew up in Temuco in southern Chile before moving to Santiago in 1921 to enrol at the University of Chile. Though he never finished his studies, his first published poems were well-received and he won first prize in a national literary competition. He was rewarded with consular positions, first in south-east Asia and later in Spain, where he was the Chilean consul in Madrid when civil war broke out in 1936. He sided actively with the Republicans against the Fascists, becoming (as he described it) 'the accessible poet of enslaved humanity': his poetry of the late 1930s and 1940s, often considered to be his most powerful, reflected his socialist concerns. After three years in Mexico Neruda returned to Chile in 1943 and successfully stood as a Communist candidate for the Senate in 1945. Three years later the Communist Party was banned and he was forced into hiding, first in Chile and then in exile in Mexico, where he published one of his longest and most overtly political poem cycles, *Canto General* (1950). He returned to Chile after the populist defeat of 1952, turning his attention and his poetry towards simplicity, lyricism and touching self-criticism. In 1967 his health started to deteriorate and he moved to the seaside town of Isla Negra, where he continued to write poetry and to speak out against fascism. The winner of many awards, Pablo Neruda was particularly honoured by the Lenin Peace Prize in 1953 and the Nobel Literature Prize in 1971. When Allende came to power in 1970, the mutual respect between him and Neruda was much enhanced, only to be shattered by the 1973 military coup which destroyed Allende and signalled widespread violence and destruction throughout Chile. Two weeks after the coup Pablo Neruda died in a Santiago clinic – many said of shock and despair.

Pablo Neruda (ed. Rene de Costa), *The Poetry of Pablo Neruda*, Harvard University Press, 1979

Pablo Neruda (trans. Hardie St Martin), *Memoirs*, Farrar, Straus and Giroux, 1977

Frank Riess, *The Word and The Stone*, Oxford University Press, 1972

Harrison Ngau
1960–
environmental activist

One of Malaysia's leading rainforest activists, Harrison Ngau has experienced at first hand the destruction of both his environment and his culture by the government-encouraged logging companies which moved wholesale into Sarawak (the Malaysian part of Borneo) in the late 1970s. A member of the Kayan tribe, he grew up in a traditional longhouse on the River Baram, where the cultivation of small fields, forest farming and hunting had been the way of living for generations. He went to school in Marudi, and then worked for an oil prospecting company in the coastal town of Miri. Between 1977 and 1979 the timber companies which had already devastated the coastal forests started to move inland, and Harrison Ngau joined with other young villagers to resist their underhand tactics, which included bribing village elders with money and alcohol. In 1982 he was invited by Sahabat Alam Malaysia (SAM; Malaysian **Friends of the Earth**) to establish a Sarawak branch in Marudi, and has since worked tirelessly for the Borneo rainforest and its inhabitants. One of the first conservationists to stress that the key to the future of the rainforests is the security of its traditional peoples, he helped to establish a network of information and joint action between widely scattered tribal communities. By 1986 SAM had succeeded in establishing the first legally binding contract between a tribal community and a timber company, but demand for timber was growing, especially from Japan, and logging was reaching deep into central Borneo. The biggest battle for Harrison Ngau and SAM began in 1987, when Penan tribespeople barricaded logging roads in south-eastern Sarawak: the timber traders publicly attacked Ngau, and in October 1987 he was arrested and detained under Malaysia's Internal Security Act. The battle of the barricades raged through 1988 and 1989, with many Penan being arrested: the timber companies increased their operations, often working day and night, but in late 1989 the legal battle started to go the way of the rainforest campaigners. In 1990 the Sarawak state government, faced with growing grassroots and international pressure, opened a dialogue with the Penan, and in November 1993 Sarawak became the first Malaysian state to recognise the primacy of tribal land rights over logging interests in law, though in many areas the logging – and the protest – continue apace.

Fred Pearce, *Green Warriors: The People and the Politics behind the Environmental Revolution*, Bodley Head, 1991

Kwame [Francis Nwia Kofie] Nkrumah
1909–1972
writer, politician

Kwame Nkrumah's most noteworthy achievement, one of many, was to lead Ghana in 1957 to become the first black African country to win independence after decades of colonial rule. Although the power this bestowed on him went to his head later on, when he instituted repressive legislation and spent large sums of money on lavish state projects, he was for many years an inspiring symbol of African self-determination. Kwame Nkrumah was born at Nkroful in the western Gold Coast (now the area of Ghana near the border with Côte d'Ivoire), and studied in Accra before leaving for America in 1935. He studied political science at Lincoln University and the University of Pennsylvania, where his thinking was much influenced by the black nationalist **Marcus Garvey**, followed by two years at London University, where he met **W.E.B. Du Bois**. In 1947 he was asked to return to the Gold Coast to lead a newly-formed nationalist party, but it proved much too moderate for his aspirations for liberation, and he formed his own Convention People's Party (CPP), which in January 1950 launched a **Gandhi**-style campaign of nonviolent action. He was promptly imprisoned, but a year later the CPP won a landslide election victory and Nkrumah was freed and made prime minister: he immediately called for independence, a demand which won unanimous support in the national assembly. His ability to work more or less harmoniously with the outgoing colonial administration enabled the CPP to secure a smooth transition to independence, and on March 6th 1957 the Gold Coast became Ghana, a traditional name of Nkrumah's choosing. He continued to work for the pan-African cause, and in 1963 was instrumental in establishing the Organisation of African Unity, but under his increasingly demagogic rule Ghana faced a political and economic crisis. In 1966, while he was on a state visit to Beijing, an army coup (the first of many) established military rule, and Nkrumah spent the last years of his life as a political exile in nearby Guinea. He died in Romania while undergoing treatment for cancer. Despite his ultimate failure, Kwame Nkrumah was the first black African leader to be taken seriously by the major world powers, and he gave many Africans genuine hope and confidence in a postcolonial future for their continent.

Kwame Nkrumah, *Ghana: The Autobiography of Kwame Nkrumah*, Nelson, 1957
Basil Davidson, *Black Star: A View of the Life and Times of Kwame Nkrumah*,
    Westview Press, 1989
David Birmingham, *Kwame Nkrumah*, Cardinal, 1990

Sam [Shafilshuna Samuel] Nujoma
1929–
civil rights campaigner, politician

Sam Nujoma is one of the few African nationalist-freedom-fighters-turned-politician to have survived both internal factionalism and external assassination threats and become a respected and thoughtful leader of his people. His task has not been an easy one, for Namibia (previously South West Africa) has a tragic history of colonial violence. When Nujoma was born in Ongandjera in northern Namibia his country was a German colony; its indigenous Herero and Ovambo peoples had been decimated and much of its agricultural and mineral wealth appropriated. South Africa annexed the territory in 1947 and, despite international opposition which in 1968 forced the United Nations to declare the occupation illegal, only finally ceded control of Namibia to the Namibians in 1989, after decades of bloodshed and economic coercion. Sam Nujoma worked for many years as a railwayman and clerk, becoming actively involved in trade unionism and populist politics in the late 1950s. In 1959 he was one of the founders of SWAPO (South West Africa People's Organisation), and in 1960, after being arrested and detained, left the country in fear of his life. The following year he established SWAPO's provisional headquarters in Dar es Salaam; when he returned to Namibia in 1966 he was again detained and ordered out of the country. He spent most of the next thirty years in exile, devoting himself to leading the campaign to win international recognition for his people's right to self-determination. In 1988, after fifteen years of escalating warfare in which SWAPO forces (with military and economic help from Angola and Cuba) fought the South African army, a ceasefire was negotiated and free elections called: Sam Nujoma was asked by SWAPO to return to Namibia to lead its campaign. The following year SWAPO won a resounding electoral victory and, as Namibia's president, Sam Nujoma has proved to be an able and evenhanded politician, committing his country to multiparty politics, a democratic constitution and a declaration of human rights.

Richard Gibson, *African Liberation Movements: Contemporary Struggles Against White Minority Rule*, Oxford University Press, 1972
Donald Sparks and December Green, *Namibia: The Nation after Independence*, Westview Press, 1992

Flora [Florence Nwanzuruaha] Nwapa
1931–
novelist, teacher, publisher

In 1966 Flora Nwapa was the first Nigerian woman ever to have a novel published: *Efuru*, like much of her subsequent writing, drew on her experience of Nigerian life to show how a woman must balance her personal needs with community and family demands. The eldest of six children, Flora Nwapa was raised in the Eastern Nigerian town of Oguta, studying in Nigeria and at Edinburgh University before returning home in 1958. In the early 60s she married and held a series of administrative and teaching posts; returning to Eastern Nigeria in 1966 she experienced the Biafran war at first hand, and afterwards worked for five years in the ministry of health and social welfare where one of her chief responsibilities was the care of the children orphaned as a result of the war. For several years she had been concerned that one of the main problems for Nigerian writers, especially women, was the lack of publishing outlets, so in 1978 she retired from government work and established her own printing press, Tana Press, and a publishing company, the Flora Nwapa Company. One of her main objectives, she explained in a 1981 interview, 'is to inform and educate women all over the world, especially feminists, about the role of women in Nigeria, their economic independence, their relationship with their husbands and children, their traditional beliefs and their status in the community as a whole.' Her work has inspired a new generation of Nigerian feminist writers, including Buchi Emecheta, Ifeoma Okoye and Zaynab Alkali.

Flora Nwapa, *Efuru*, Heinemann, 1966
Flora Nwapa, *Idu*, Heinemann, 1970
Flora Nwapa, *Women are Different*, Tana Press, 1986

[Mwalimu] Julius [Kambarage] Nyerere
1922–
socialist politician and educator

Julius Nyerere of Tanzania represents the clearsighted and humane face of postcolonial African leadership. To a remarkable extent transcending tribal divisions and opportunities for personal material advancement, he has largely succeeded in leading his country from colonialism to peaceful independence. The son of a tribal chief, he was born and raised in the Zanaki village of Butiama near the shore of Lake Victoria. He received an excellent education for the time, studying in Uganda and at Edinburgh University, where he read history, politics and economics. Returning to Tanganyika in 1952, he married Maria Magige who soon bore the first of their eight children; his rise in national politics led him smoothly from president of the Tanganyika Africa Association in 1953 to prime minister of the newly-independent Tanganyika in December 1961. In 1964, after a popular revolt overthrew the Zanzibar government, Tanganyika and Zanzibar united to form the United Republic of Tanzania: the union is often upheld as an example of what could be achieved in other parts of Africa. A self-proclaimed socialist, Julius Nyerere clarified his doctrine in an early-60s pamphlet, *Ujamaa: The Basis of African Socialism* ('ujamaa' is Swahili for 'family cooperation'), and in 1967 his TANU (Tanzania African National Union) party adopted the Arusha Declaration which emphasised egalitarianism, self-reliance, and the importance of rural development. 1977 saw a concerted move against growing official corruption, and TANU and the Zanzibar Afro-Shiraz Party combined to form a new ruling party, Chama Cha Mapinduzi (CCM). In 1980 Nyerere announced that he would be standing down at the 1985 elections, although he retained the chairmanship of CCM until 1990. His personal life has always mirrored his political thinking: he continues to live austerely, and takes a modest pension; his example has earned him great respect both at home and abroad. His career is not entirely without criticism from some quarters – for many years Tanzania has been a one-party state, for example, though this is now changing – but his championing of grassroots politics and Africa-wide issues like the campaign against apartheid have ensured that Tanzania is one of the few African countries not to have endured bloody coups and civil wars since independence.

Julius Nyerere, *Freedom and Unity: Essays on Socialism*, Oxford University Press, 1966
Julius Nyerere, *Freedom and Socialism*, Oxford University Press, 1968
Julius Nyerere, *On Socialism*, Oxford University Press, 1970

Cranford Pratt, *The Critical Phase in Tanzania 1945–68: Nyerere and the Emergence of a Socialist Strategy*, Oxford University Press, 1980

Ann Oakley [Ann Titmuss]
1944–
feminist, sociologist, writer

Ann Oakley, British sociologist, feminist and more recently novelist, grew up in a radical middle class family in London (her father was the pioneering administrator Richard Titmuss) and studied at Chiswick Polytechnic and Somerville College, Oxford, where in 1964 she married fellow student Robin Oakley. Two children, a period of severe depression, and a feminist reawakening later, she enrolled at London University, where her doctoral dissertation explored women's attitudes to housework. In 1972, while working as a researcher, she published *Sex, Gender and Society*, a pioneering and influential study of the role of myth and reality in defining gender. Drawing on human biology and the anthropological work of Margaret Mead as well as the growing field of radical sociology, she showed how gender is a continuum which defies classification, thus laying the foundations of the social feminist position within the British **women's movement**. Her next two books, *Housewife* and *The Sociology of Housework* (both 1974), built on her longstanding interest in housework as a socio-political issue. In 1974 she was appointed as Research Officer at Bedford College, and in 1976, with **Juliet Mitchell**, edited the important collection of feminist essays *The Rights and Wrongs of Women*. Having had another child, two miscarriages and a cancer diagnosis, Ann Oakley now became very interested in the social and psychological aspects of childbirth and motherhood. In 1979 she started working as a consultant to the National Perinatal Epidemiology Unit at Churchill Hospital, Oxford, and wrote two books – *Becoming a Mother* (1979) and *Women Confined* (1980) – linking her own experiences with the theory and practice of childbirth. In 1983 she returned to London University, where she is now professor of sociology and social policy and directs an education and health research unit; she has also continued to write, publishing the frank autobiography *Taking It Like a Woman* (1984) and a volume of essays and poetry, *Telling the Truth about Jerusalem* (1986), as well as a number of bestselling novels.

Ann Oakley, *Sex, Gender and Society*, Maurice Temple Smith, 1972
Ann Oakley, *The Sociology of Housework*, Robertson, 1974
Ann Oakley, *Taking It Like a Woman*, Cape, 1984
Ann Oakley, *Telling the Truth about Jerusalem*, Blackwell, 1986
Ann Oakley, *Essays on Women, Medicine and Health*, Edinburgh University Press, 1993

Molara Ogundipe-Leslie
1949–
poet, literary critic, women's rights campaigner

Molara Ogundipe-Leslie is one of Nigeria's leading literary critics and women's rights activists: in a 1986 interview she made it clear that for African women 'the kernel of self-determination and dignity lies in self-reliance, ensuring that no one exploits their labour'. She was born in Lagos into a Yoruba family in which education was considered vitally important, and in 1977 graduated from Ibadan University with a first class honours degree in English. Married with children, she has taught at universities in Nigeria and the USA, including Columbia, Berkeley and Harvard. For several years in the mid-1980s she was a member of the editorial board of the Lagos-based newspaper *The Guardian*, which gave her real insight into the plight of a country suffering extreme economic mismanagement and political powermongering. She has also been active in the nascent women's movement in Nigeria, and is a government adviser on the mobilisation of women within Nigerian society, though she is best known as a champion of African literature as a vehicle for understanding the development of modern African society. She is currently professor of English at Ogun State University at Ago-Iwoye.

Molara Ogundipe-Leslie, *Sew the Old Days*, Evans Brothers, 1985
Margaret Busby (ed.), *Daughters of Africa*, Jonathan Cape, 1992

Daniel Ortega [Saavedra]
1945–
political and social activist, politician

Since the mid-nineteenth century Nicaragua, lying strategically between Caribbean and Pacific, North and South America, has been subject to regular US-supported invasions, occupations and coups. In 1912 and again in 1926 US marines were sent in force to support puppet governments, the second time facing strong resistance from a well-organised popular army under the command of Augusto Sandino. For more than six years his 3,000 men held out against 12,000 marines, and when the US left in 1933 Sandino kept his word that he would lay down his arms as soon as the last marine had left. He was betrayed, however, and within a year had been murdered by Anastasio Somoza García: first Somoza and then his sons Luis and Anastasio proceeded to rule Nicaragua with ever-increasing force and repression for the next 45 years, their National Guard relying on US military and economic support. Around 1960, however, the Frente Sandinista de Liberación Nacional (FSLN: Sandinista National Liberation Front) was founded, and in 1962 the young student Daniel Ortega, who was studying law at the Central American University in Managua, took charge of the FSLN Student Movement. Though arrested, imprisoned and tortured several times during the 1960s and 70s he quickly moved into the national leadership of the FSLN, and when popular unrest at last boiled over, following the assassination of the opposition leader in January 1978, Ortega was the obvious candidate to lead the Frente Sandinista to victory, which he did in July 1979. After six long years of civil war and more than 50,000 deaths at the hands of the Somoza 'Contras', Daniel Ortega was formally inaugurated as Nicaragua's president in January 1985. Sandinista social and economic policy had its roots firmly in homegrown Marxist socialism, and Ortega has consistently stressed the importance of an independent, nonaligned Nicaragua run along socialist lines. To this end he negotiated a 1989 accord to dismantle the Contra army, in return promising free elections in 1990. Although he lost the presidential election to his anti-Somoza ally Violeta Chamorro, largely as a result of Sandinista infighting and nepotism, he retains considerable influence within Nicaragua as a semi-official diplomat and spokesman.

Marcus Bruce (ed.), *Sandinistas Speak: Speeches, Writings and Interviews with Leaders of Nicaragua's Revolution*, Pathfinder, 1982
Thomas W. Walker (ed.), *Nicaragua in Revolution*, Praeger, 1982
Lou Dematteis and Chris Vail, *Nicaragua: A Decade of Revolution*, Norton, 1991
Roger Miranda, *The Civil War in Nicaragua: Inside the Sandinistas*, Transaction, 1993

George Orwell [Eric Arthur Blair]
1903–1950
writer, journalist, social critic

Best known for his incisive socio-political novels *Animal Farm* and *1984*, George Orwell's soul-searching refusal to indulge in political cant frequently left him with few supporters and many false allies. Eric Blair/George Orwell (he changed his name in 1933 at his publishers' suggestion) was born in India to a civil service family, and after studying at Eton (where his marks were so poor that plans for taking Oxford entrance exams were dropped) returned to Asia, where from 1922 to 1927 he worked for the Indian Imperial Police in Burma. Influenced by the rising tide of nationalism in Burma and the draconian measures introduced to quell it, Blair resigned and returned to Europe. He spent the next decade identifying with the underclasses, living for some time as a tramp and earning a living as a manual labourer, experiences which were graphically portrayed in *Down and Out in Paris and London*, published in 1933 by the leftwing publishers Gollancz. In 1936, the year Orwell married Eileen O'Shaughnessy, Victor Gollancz suggested that he spend several months in the north of England, experiencing working conditions at first hand: the resulting book, *The Road to Wigan Pier*, became a bestseller, stirring the consciences of many of its middle-class readers. By the end of 1936 Orwell was in Spain, fighting against Franco's forces and experiencing both the promise and the pain of an idealistic yet fatally divided resistance: the resultant *Homage to Catalonia* (1938) annoyed many socialists with its criticism of hardline Stalinism and its support for communist heterodoxy. During the second world war George Orwell worked as a radio journalist with the BBC, at the same time writing *Animal Farm*, a fable of the dangers of authoritarian communism. Having been turned down by several major publishers, *Animal Farm* was eventually published in 1945 to widespread critical acclaim. Orwell's refusal to condone Stalinism brought him much admiration from rightwing readers of *Animal Farm*, who failed to notice that its socialist author had made it clear that the ruling pigs' decision to join the farmers at the end of the story constituted a betrayal of the revolution, rather than support for authoritarianism. Eileen's sudden death in 1945 and Orwell's own ill health took him to the Scottish island of Jura, where he wrote *1984*, his nightmare vision of a totalitarian Britain. Again the right ironically saw his work as a definitive exposure of Soviet-style communism, but Orwell was always clear that 'democratic' Britain held the seeds of a totalitarianism all the more dangerous for its apparent gentility. A year after the publication of *1984* Orwell's tuberculosis proved fatal. His insistence on the dignity and courage of ordinary people has ensured his continuing reputation and readership.

George Orwell, *The Road to Wigan Pier*, 1937 (many editions since)
George Orwell, *Homage to Catalonia*, 1938 (many editions since)
George Orwell, *Animal Farm*, 1945 (many editions since)
George Orwell, *1984*, 1949 (many editions since)
Raymond Williams, *Orwell*, Fontana, 1971
Bernard Crick, *George Orwell: A Life*, Secker and Warburg, 1980

Ōsugi Sakae
1885–1923
anarchist and socialist

Ōsugi Sakae continued into the 1920s the Japanese anarchist-socialist tradition cut short by the execution in 1911 of his mentor **Kōtoku Shūsui**. Ōsugi was born into a military family on the island of Shikoku, and was himself destined for a military career; while at college in Tokyo, however, he read Kōtoku, and in 1906 took part in the first of many protests – against increasing trolleybus fares in Tokyo. He spent much of the next four years in prison, reading **Bakunin** and **Kropotkin**, and thus avoided being implicated in the 1910 treason trial in which Kōtoku was sentenced to death. In 1912, impatient with the caution of other radicals in the wake of the trial, Ōsugi and his friend **Arahata Kanson** started to publish the anarchist journal *Kindai Shisō* (*Modern Thought*), one of seven that he was involved with until his death. In 1916, although he was already married and having another affair, he started to live with fellow anarchist **Itō Noe**; together they translated **Emma Goldman** and Petr Kropotkin, and had five children. After the 1917 Russian Revolution Ōsugi began to be very active in the labour movement, growing critical of Soviet communism as it moved rapidly to infringe civil liberties. In September 1923, during the confused aftermath of the Great Kantō Earthquake, Ōsugi and Itō were beaten to death by military police as part of a concerted campaign against leftwing activists.

Thomas Stanley, Ōsugi Sakae, Anarchist in Taishō Japan: The Creativity of the Ego, Council on East Asian Studies, 1982

Thomas Stanley, A Japanese Anarchist's Rejection of Marxism-Leninism: Ōsugi Sakae and the Russian Revolution, Western Conference of the Association for Asian Studies, 1978

Ōyama Ikuo
1880–1955
educator, writer, social activist

An energetic campaigner for true democracy, Japanese academic and author Ōyama Ikuo grew up in the Hyōgo region of central Japan, and studied sociology and politics at Waseda University in Japan and the Universities of Chicago and Munich. Returning to Japan in 1914 he became a professor at Waseda, and almost immediately started to campaign for the establishment of accountable government at every level of Japanese life. In 1917 he resigned his professorship in support of a colleague who had been dismissed on political grounds, and worked for three years as a journalist on the Ōsaka Asahi Shimbun: he used the opportunity to protest against the sending of Japanese troops to Siberia and was forced to leave his job. He was then asked to return to Waseda University, where he quickly became popular with radical students, helping them to organise protests and study groups, but in 1927 he was forced to resign from his teaching post. He spent the next three years rescuing the Rōnōto (Labour-Farmer Party) after it has been disbanded by the government, and stood successfully for a seat in the House of Representatives in the 1930 elections. He had always taken a pacifist stance against growing Japanese military expansionism, and in 1933, fearing for his life, he and his wife travelled to the United States, where he taught at Northwestern University until 1947. Finally he rejoined the faculty at Waseda and in 1950 was elected to the House of Councillors, continuing until his death to promote the cause of peace and democratic reform.

Peter Duus, 'Ōyama Ikuo and the Search for Democracy', Dilemmas of Growth in Prewar Japan (ed. James Morley), Princeton University Press, 1971

Paulinho Paiakan
1954–
native rights and rainforest activist

Paiakan is one of several members of Brazil's indigenous peoples to have spoken out against dam-building, deforestation and mining in the Indians' traditional territories during the late 1980s and early 90s. The Kayapó live in the Altamira region of the Amazon rainforest, and over many centuries have learned to manage the forest for food and sustenance through a sophisticated system of seed selection, soil enrichment and crop rotation. In the mid-1980s the Brazilian government announced plans to build, with World Bank assistance, a series of dams on the Xingu River in Altamira, which would flood 97,000 square miles and displace nearly half a million people, including most of the Kayapó. Early in 1988 Paiakan and another Kayapó chief, Kuben-i, attended a conference on tropical deforestation in Florida, speaking about their concerns regarding the building of the Xingu dam complex with the help of their ally and interpreter, anthropologist Darrell Posey. Paiakan often referred to the rainforest as 'our university', explaining 'I am trying to save the knowledge that the forests and this planet are alive, to give it back to you who have lost the understanding.' With the assistance of environmental and human rights groups he travelled widely during 1988 and 1989, meeting campaigners, politicians and World Bank officials in an attempt to stop the project. In February 1989, at the site of the proposed dam, the Kayapó convened an international symposium: a month later the World Bank announced that it would no longer fund the Xingu dam project, but would instead support the development of small-scale electricity production and distribution. The Kayapó campaign has since been emulated by several indigenous Amazon peoples, notably by the Yanomami against illegal gold mining. The Yanomami had not made contact with 'whiteman' until the 1950s, and in succeeding decades had been decimated by western diseases. Following an intensive campaign by their leaders (notably Davi Kopenawa Yanomami) and **Survival International** in 1989, they were in 1992 allocated large protected reserves by both the Brazilian and Venezuelan governments.

Susanna Hecht and Alexander Cockburn, *The Fate of the Forest: Developers, Destroyers and Defenders of the Amazon*, Verso, 1989

Christabel Pankhurst
1880–1958
women's rights campaigner

Emmeline Pankhurst's oldest daughter grew up in Manchester and was educated there and in Switzerland. Following her father's death she worked as a registrar with her mother and then studied law at Manchester University, at the same time becoming involved in trade unionism and the labour movement. In 1903, growing impatient with the Independent Labour Party's unwillingness to stress women's rights, Christabel and Emmeline founded the **Women's Social and Political Union** (WSPU). With its 'Votes for Women' slogan the WSPU quickly gained support and momentum, and once the *Daily Mail*, following Christabel's and her colleague Annie Kenny's first arrest in Manchester in 1905, had coined the term 'suffragette', her reputation as a fiery orator and activist was assured. Her militancy was further inflamed by the refusal of Lincoln's Inn to accept her as a barrister. In 1907 she moved to London and spent the next six years as one of the WSPU's best known organisers and speakers, being arrested and imprisoned several times. Threatened with a conspiracy charge in 1912, she fled to Paris to join a lesbian feminist group for several months before returning to England to edit *The Suffragette*, for which she wrote long articles on subjects such as prostitution and venereal disease, taking a strong separatist line. After 1914, when she joined her mother in the wartime recruitment drive, she turned away from the suffrage issue. In 1918 she stood for parliament on a collectivist ticket and was narrowly defeated; after 1920 she became a second adventist Christian and wrote a series of bestselling tracts. Christabel moved to California in 1940, completing her autobiographical history of women's suffrage, *Unshackled*, shortly before her death.

Christabel Pankhurst, *Unshackled: The Story of How We Won the Vote*, Hutchinson, 1959
David Mitchell, *Queen Christabel*, Macdonald and Janes, 1977
Barbara Castle, *Sylvia and Christabel Pankhurst*, Penguin, 1987

Emmeline Pankhurst [Emmeline Goulden]
1858–1928
women's rights campaigner

By the outbreak of the first world war in 1914, the Pankhurst family – Emmeline and her three daughters, **Christabel**, **Sylvia** and Adela – were virtually synonymous with the struggle for women's enfranchisment in Britain. Although they each went their own way after the war, their joint efforts were instrumental in bringing the vote to British women in 1928, and though many women (and men) played an important part in the campaign the Pankhursts achieved an almost mythical status. Emmeline grew up in a radical merchant's family in Manchester, attending her first suffrage meeting with her mother when she was just fourteen. She was educated in Manchester and Paris, and at 21 married the progressive barrister Richard Pankhurst: together they worked for the Married Women's Property Committee and the Manchester Women's Suffrage Committee and, after moving to London in 1885, joined the **Fabian Society** and the Independent Labour Party in 1893. After Richard died in 1898 Emmeline and her five children moved back to Manchester, where she worked as a registrar. In 1903 she and her eldest daughter Christabel formed the influential **Women's Social and Political Union** (WSPU): when the WSPU adopted a militant policy of civil disobedience in 1905 Emmeline went to live with Sylvia in London and took part in a series of actions and demonstrations organised by the rapidly-growing Union. The first arrest of many, in 1908, was followed by four years of feverish lecturing, fundraising, activism, arrests and hunger strikes: in 1913 she was arrested twelve times, once appearing at the speaker's podium on a stretcher. As war loomed, Emmeline and Christabel threw themselves into the recruitment drive, which led to a irreparable rift between them and Emmeline's pacifist daughters Sylvia and Adela. After the war Emmeline Pankhurst lectured for the National Council for Combating Venereal Disease in Canada before returning exhausted to contest the Whitechapel seat for the Conservative Party in the 1928 election. Though she died shortly before the election, she did live just long enough to witness full suffrage for British women.

Emmeline Pankhurst, *My Own Story*, Kraus, 1971 (repr. of 1914 edn)
E. Sylvia Pankhurst, *The Life of Emmeline Pankhurst*, Laurie, 1935

Andrew Rosen, *Rise Up, Women: The Militant Campaign of the Women's Social and Political Union 1903–1914*, Routledge, 1974

David Mitchell, *The Fighting Pankhursts: A Study in Tenacity*, Macmillan, 1967

[Estelle] Sylvia Pankhurst
1882–1960
women's rights campaigner, artist, pacifist, socialist activist

Emmeline Pankhurst's two younger daughters, Sylvia and Adela (1885–1961), shared many of the concerns of their mother and older sister, but when with the threat of war in 1914 Emmeline and **Christabel** threw themselves wholeheartedly into the recruitment drive the ardently pacifist younger sisters were shocked to such an extent that they both made an almost complete break with their erstwhile allies. Sylvia went to art college in Manchester and won a scholarship to Venice before studying art at the Royal Academy. She joined the **Women's Social and Political Union** (WSPU) in its earliest days and helped found several branches in London's East End. Sylvia used her artistic talents to produce banners, posters, murals, jewellery and household goods proclaiming the suffragette message, and at the height of the WSPU's militancy was imprisoned thirteen times, being force-fed while on hunger strike on several occasions. After Sylvia's break with her mother in 1914, at which time Adela emigrated to Australia to become involved with the peace and trade union movements there, Sylvia founded the pacifist socialist journal *Worker's Dreadnought*, and worked as a nurse, a teacher and an organiser of cooperatives. In 1920 she stowed away on a Finnish ship and visited the USSR, where she met **Lenin**. On her return she published *Soviet Russia As I Saw It* (1921) and became a prominent member of the British Communist Party, until it expelled her for refusing to hand over control of the *Worker's Dreadnought*. In 1928 she had a son by the Italian socialist Silvio Orto, but declined to name the father in protest against the persecution of unmarried mothers. During the 1930s she spent much of her time campaigning against the rise of fascism in Italy, and became deeply involved with the Abyssinian struggle. From 1936 to 1956 she edited the *Ethiopian News*, and in 1956 moved to live in Ethiopia, where she edited the *Ethiopian Observer* until her death.

E. Sylvia Pankhurst, (ed. Kathryn Dodd), *A Sylvia Pankhurst Reader*, Manchester University Press, 1993

Barbara Castle, *Sylvia and Christabel Pankhurst*, Penguin, 1987

Patricia W. Romero, *E. Sylvia Pankhurst: Portrait of a Radical*, Yale University Press, 1987

Ian Bullock, *Sylvia Pankhurst: From Artist to Anti-fascist*, Macmillan, 1992

Sara Parkin [Sara Lamb McEwan]
1946–
environmental campaigner and activist

The environmental campaigner Sara Parkin trained as a nurse, working in Scotland and the north of England and specialising in sex education. In

1977 she joined the fledgling Ecology Party (renamed the Green Party in 1985), and in the 1979 general election stood against the ultra-rightwing Conservative Keith Joseph. In 1980 she moved with her family (she has two sons) to Lyon in France, where her husband Donald Maxwell Parkin (Max) is employed by the World Health Organisation, but continued to work actively with the UK Green Party, being appointed international liaison secretary from 1983 to 1990, speaker on international affairs from 1989 to 1991, and elected chair of the executive in 1992. Throughout the 1980s she worked with greens in other countries to build the Coordination of European Greens, of which she was secretary from 1985 to 1990. After the unexpectedly good performance of the UK Green Party in the 1989 European elections, she shot to prominence as a passionate yet level-headed exponent of green ideas and policies. Like **Petra Kelly**, whose biography she wrote in 1994, Sara Parkin's pragmatism and celebrity status have been criticised by the more anarchist and decentralist elements of the green movement in Britain. At the end of 1992 she stepped down from Green Party activity, her vision of a credible green politics for Britain at odds with the party's increasing fragmentation and factionalism. She continues to lecture, advise and campaign on green issues to audiences as diverse as schoolchildren and senior NATO officers, and in September 1994 was a cofounder, together with **Jonathon Porritt**, of Forum For The Future, a partnership of independent consultants committed to environmental sustainability.

Sara Parkin, *Green Parties: An International Guide*, Heretic, 1989
Sara Parkin, *Green Futures*, Fount, 1990

Fran [Frances] Peavey
1941–
social change catalyst

Born and raised in Idaho, Fran Peavey's family and community life fostered integrity, critical thinking and a strong sense of place. She left it in 1961 for the political and social ferment of San Francisco. Teaching science, and finding she had much to learn about the lives of her young black students, she contacted the local chapter of the National Association for the Advancement of Colored People and arranged weekly 'lessons' for herself. In the late 1960s, while pursuing doctoral studies in innovation theory and technological forecasting, she realised she was far more interested in learning how people and societies change, and how different it is to work for change from the heart rather than from abstract principles. Particularly striking in Fran Peavey's multifaceted career is her 'American Willing to Listen' project, which began in 1980 and has continued during her many world travels since: she goes to a public place, spreads a large sign saying 'American Willing to Listen', and spends many hours listening to the people who come to talk to her about their concerns. In 1980 in India she helped to inaugurate an ongoing strategy to clean the sacred Ganges River. In the early 1980s she was a member of an antinuclear group in San Francisco;

out of this evolved her career as an Atomic Comic, and her cofounding of the Interhelp network. In 1986 she published *Heart Politics*, and began keeping a journal about the AIDS epidemic. Early in 1988 she learned that she was HIV-positive and, when friends with whom she had shared the journal urged her to publish it, did so as *A Shallow Pool of Time* (1990).

Fran Peavey, *Heart Politics*, New Society, 1986
Fran Peavey, *A Shallow Pool of Time: An HIV+ Woman Grapples with the AIDS Epidemic*, New Society, 1990

Matti [Mattityahu] Peled
1923–
teacher, politician, peace campaigner

The veteran Israeli peace campaigner Matti Peled grew up in British-ruled Palestine, and in 1938 joined the Hagana (Jewish Militia), serving in its élite unit, the Palmach, which became part of the Israeli Defence Forces in 1948. He was the military governor of the Gaza Strip during its first occupation by Israel in 1956–1957, reaching the rank of major general in 1964: in 1967 he was a member of the general staff, and played an active part in the deliberations preceding the Six-Day War. Peled resigned from the army in 1969 to study Arab literature at the University of California in Los Angeles, where he gained his doctorate in 1971. He started to teach at Tel Aviv University, and between 1974 and 1978 headed the department of Arab language and literature, where he taught until 1990. In 1975 Matti Peled helped to establish the Israeli Council for Israeli-Palestinian Peace, and was elected its first president. Over the next eight years he participated in numerous meetings (first secret and later open) with Palestinian leaders, culminating in a much-publicised 1983 meeting with Yasser Arafat in Tunis. In 1984 Peled was elected to the Knesset (Israeli parliament) and was a member until 1988, representing the Jewish-Arab Progressive List for Peace. Matti Peled is a frequent participant in conferences both in Israel and abroad, speaking on subjects ranging from pre-Islamic Arabic poetry to regional and global nuclear disarmament. In January 1995 he won critical acclaim for his translation into Hebrew of *Sages of Darkness* by the Kurdish-Syrian exiled writer Salim Barakat.

Uri Avnery, *My Friend, The Enemy*, Zed, 1986

[Anne-]Madeleine Pelletier
1874–1939
doctor, writer, feminist, pacifist

The French doctor, writer and feminist Madeleine Pelletier grew up in Paris and trained as a doctor at the University of Paris, from which she graduated in 1899. In 1903 she became the first woman in France to qualify to work in mental hospitals. She joined the women's suffrage movement in the 1890s and, influenced by the **Women's Social and Political Union**, adopted outspoken and militant tactics, one of the few early French feminists to do so. She often wore male clothing to symbolise her demand for equality. In 1906 she was a cofounder of La Solidarité des Femmes, the radical wing of the French women's movement, and edited the feminist journal *La suffragiste* from 1907 to 1914, during which period she wrote several books about feminism and sexual freedom. She worked for women's suffrage and equal rights from within the socialist movement until 1913, when she joined the anarchist movement, finding their policies more egalitarian. As war approached in 1914 Madeleine Pelletier expressed her disgust of war in a series of pamphlets, explaining how war was both anti-women and anti-working class, yet her first priority was always women's suffrage, and she felt it important that women should have an equal right to conscription. In 1915, having attempted and failed to join the medical corps, she volunteered to work with the Red Cross, where to the dismay of her socialist allies she insisted on treating the wounded of both sides. After the war she turned her attention to campaigning for women's rights to birth control and legal abortions, and worked among the poorer women of Paris, often performing illegal terminations herself. In 1939 she was charged with this 'crime' and confined to an asylum, where she died six months later.

Marilyn Boxer and Jean Quataert, *Socialist Women: European Socialist Feminism in the Nineteenth and Early Twentieth Centuries*, Elsevier, 1978
Felicia Gordon, *The Integral Feminist: Madeleine Pelletier 1874–1939*, Polity, 1990

Marge Piercy
1936–
novelist, poet, political activist

One of the most imaginative and politically aware American poets and novelists of recent decades, Marge Piercy grew up in a Jewish family in a working class section of Detroit, before scholarships and fellowships took her to Michigan and Northwestern Universities. Leaving university in 1958, she spent several years living in New York City and Chicago, travelling in Europe, and writing poetry and fiction (mostly unpublished because, in her own words, both were 'too feminist and too political'). In the mid-1960s she became actively involved in the civil rights movement and **Students for a Democratic Society**: being gassed and beaten during demonstrations affected her health, an important factor in her decision to move in 1971 to Cape Cod, where she now lives with her third husband, the writer and playwright Ira Wood. By 1969 she was involved in the **women's movement** in New York, where she was a staff member on the journal *Leviathan* and wrote a widely-read article about sexual politics, 'The Grand Coolie Damn', for the anthology *Sisterhood is Powerful*. Of her many innovative and often overtly political novels, *Vida* (1979) explored the psychology of a women involved in activism bordering on terrorism and *Fly Away Home* (1984) looked at the politics of urban development, while the acclaimed *Woman on the Edge of Time* (1976) told of a Chicana women locked up in a mental hospital who is taken by a time-traveller to visit a future world in which a down-to-earth utopia is pitted against the worst of sexist and racist oppression. More than a dozen volumes of poetry, particularly those written since *Stone, Paper, Knife* (1983), show Marge Piercy to be a fluent, accessible and many-faceted poet who weaves personal experience, political insight and naturalistic imagery into compulsive and memorable lines.

Marge Piercy, *Woman on the Edge of Time*, Knopf, 1976
Marge Piercy, *Stone, Paper, Knife*, Knopf, 1983
Margarete Keulen, *Radical Imagination: Feminist Conceptions of the Future in Ursula le Guin, Marge Piercy and Sally Miller Gearhart*, Lang, 1991
Sue Walker (ed.), *Ways of Knowing: Essays on Marge Piercy*, Negative Capability Press, 1991
Kerstin Shands, *The Repair of the World: The Novels of Marge Piercy*, Greenwood, 1994

John [Richard] Pilger
1939–
investigative journalist, author and film-maker

Born in Sydney, Australia, John Pilger started working as a journalist for the Sydney *Daily Telegraph* in 1958. In 1962 he based himself in London, where he worked first for Reuter, then for the *Daily Mirror*, quickly rising to become a feature writer and the newspaper's chief foreign correspondent, a post which he held until 1986. From 1966 to 1975 he covered the **Vietnam War** as a newspaper and television journalist, winning numerous international awards for his incisive, courageous and honest reporting. In the 70s he also established himself as an influential film-maker: his 36 documentary films include 'The Quiet Mutiny' (1970) about the incipient revolt of US troops in Vietnam, 'A Faraway Country' (1977) filmed secretly in Czechoslovakia, and 'Year Zero: The Silent Death of Cambodia' (1979). 'Year Zero' is credited with alerting the world to the horrors of the Pol Pot terror, and was the first of six Pilger films about Cambodia. The 1970s also saw the birth of his two children, Sam and Zoë. As well as Vietnam, Eastern Europe and Cambodia, John Pilger's films and journalism cover Biafra, the India-Pakistan conflict, Palestine, Nicaragua, El Salvador and Northern Ireland, and he continues to travel the world, interviewing, reporting and writing about repression and injustice wherever it is to be found. His themes are the cruelty and the lies and platitudes of governments and their agents. His method is to report as honestly as is possible, using the words of firsthand witnesses wherever he can, and to ask difficult questions of those in power: one of his early achievements was to elicit from a US military media officer in Vietnam that 'collateral damage' meant 'civilian deaths'. In 1993 he travelled secretly to East Timor, writing numerous articles and producing a television film to demonstrate the involvement of Western governments in selling arms to the repressive Suharto regime in Indonesia. In 1994 he turned his main attention to the international arms trade, showing how the threat of violence had grown rather than diminished with the end of the Cold War. Still based in London he continues, through his journalism, to call to account those in power. He is, in his colleague Martha Gellhorn's words, 'a brave and invaluable witness to his time'.

John Pilger, *The Struggle for Cambodia and Vietnam*, New Statesman, 1982
John Pilger, *Heroes*, Cape, 1986
John Pilger, *A Secret Country*, Cape, 1989
John Pilger, *Distant Voices*, Vintage, 1992 (rev. edn 1994)

Adelheid Popp [Adelheid Dworak]
1869–1939
socialist activist, feminist

The Austrian activist Adelheid Popp is best known in the German-speaking world for her two eloquent and powerful volumes of working class auto-biography published in 1910 and 1915, *Die Jugendgeschichte einer Arbeiterin* (*Autobiography of a Working Woman*) and *Erinnerungen aus meinen Kindheits-und Mädchenjahren* (*Memoirs of Childhood and Womanhood*). Adelheid grew up in a village outside Vienna, the fifteenth child of an alcoholic weaver who frequently abused his wife and children and who died when she was six. After three years of school she started working as a cleaner, factory worker and seamstress, and by the age of thirteen was so exhausted and debilitated that she spent several months in hospital. In her later teens she became involved in the developing socialist movement in Austria, and from then on devoted her life to campaigning for workers' and womens' rights, even though she had to continue working to help support two children of her own. By 1892 she had become a spokesperson for the Austrian socialist women's movement, and in 1893 led a first women's strike for better pay and conditions in a clothing factory near Vienna. She also founded a group called Libertas to provide women with a grounding in political debate. Adelheid Popp consistently fought male trade unionists' resistance to women's interests, and in 1896 failed by one vote to persuade the Austrian Trade Union Congress to back an official women's organisation. She continued to fight for equal rights for women (including the right to equal pay, divorce reform, and the provision of childcare) until the rise of Nazism in the 1930s, when she worked with the Austrian resistance up to her death.

Angelika Bammer, 'Adelheid Popp', *An Encyclopedia of Continental Women Writers* (ed. Katherina Wilson), St James's Press, 1991

Jonathon [Espie] Porritt
1950–
environmental campaigner

The eldest son of a privileged family (his father was governor general of New Zealand and surgeon to the British royal family), the environmental campaigner Jonathon Porritt studied at Eton College and Oxford University. Shortly after graduating, while he was working as a teacher in London, he joined the nascent Ecology Party (in 1985 renamed the Green Party) and stood as a candidate in the 1977 and 1978 local elections. Between 1979 and 1984 he contested two general and two European elections, his eloquence on environmental concerns receiving considerable attention. Already an Ecology Party council member, he was elected joint chair in 1979, a position he held with a short break until 1984, when he was offered the directorship of **Friends of the Earth** (UK). At FoE he continued to be an ardent, influential (and, because of his background, officially acceptable) voice for environmentalism, and FoE's growing membership and campaigning power owed a great deal to his insight and tenacity. In 1990 Jonathon Porritt left FoE to concentrate on journalism, lecturing and coordinating broadly based environmental pressure networks; a widely rumoured return to mainstream politics has not yet materialised, though his friendship-cum-environmental-consultancy with the British heir to the throne Prince Charles has kept him in the eye of the media. In 1986 he married Sarah Staniforth, with whom he has two daughters, and in 1992 he moved his base from London to the Gloucestershire town of Cheltenham. In 1993 he was appointed chair of the United Nations Environment and Development Committee for the UK, and in December 1994, with **Sara Parkin**, was a cofounder of Forum For The Future, a partnership of independent consultants committed to environmental sustainability.

Jonathon Porritt, *Seeing Green: The Politics of Ecology*, Blackwell, 1984

Seksan Prasotkun (or Prasertkul)
1952–
writer, historian, social activist

The Thai political activist and historian Seksan Prasotkun was one of the student leaders at Bangkok University in October 1973, when condemnation of the longstanding military dictatorship (protests supported by the young monarch Rama IX and sections of the army) forced rapid political and social change, leading to the elections of 1975. An active member of the Communist Party of Thailand (CPT), Prasotkun trained briefly in Vietnam and Laos, returning to Thailand shortly before another military coup plunged it back into civil war in October 1976. Like many young CPT members, he was convinced that the Party had been crippled by its identification with Chinese Maoism, and had unthinkingly – and fatally – allowed the country to become ruled by a reactionary alliance of religion, military and monarchy. In the late 1970s he was a leader in the armed guerrilla struggle against a succession of military rulers, and when the CPT split in 1981 over support for China, Seksan Prasotkun was one of the leaders of the anti-Chinese grouping. Free elections were again held in 1983, and since 1984 Prasotkun has been teaching history at the University of Bangkok. In an important series of historical studies he has explored the interplay of colonial and native interests in the politics and economy of Thailand, demonstrating how complex these interactions have been and how dangerous it is to praise 'traditional' Thai values without analysing whose values it is that are being upheld. In particular he has criticised the failure of the CPT to learn from Thai history and their excessive enthusiasm for the adoption of Maoist platitudes at the expense of the needs of the Thai people.

Benedict Anderson, 'Radicalism and Communism in Thailand and Indonesia', *New Left Review*, December 1993

Pandita Ramabai [Sarasvati]
1858–1922
writer, women's rights campaigner

A pioneering Indian feminist, Pandita Ramabai was an active campaigner for improvements in the status of women. She was born in the state of Maharashtra to a Sanskrit scholar father who believed that women are as entitled to education as men, and who therefore ensured that his wife and daughters became Sanskrit scholars in their own right. Because of his unorthodox views the family was hounded from place to place, and when he, his wife and another daughter all died during the famine of 1874 Ramabai steeled herself to fight the Hindu traditions which forbade women a full part in society alone. In 1878 she and her surviving brother went to Calcutta, where her critique of Hinduism made her popular in Bengali reformist circles and her knowledge of Sanskrit earned her the title 'Pandita' ('Learned One'). In 1882 she was widowed with a newborn daughter, and faced growing pressure to conform to the 'proper' deportment of a widow. Already well known for her lectures on social reform, she now threw herself into a life of travel and agitation, starting a series of women's organisations in Bombay state, campaigning for women's medical training and education, and writing an influential tract on women's emancipation, *Sthri Dharma Neeti* (*Women's Religious Law*, 1882). She travelled to England in 1883 and the United States and Canada in 1886 to lecture on the condition of women in India, and wrote books on the same subject, *The High Caste Hindu Woman* (1887) being well received and leading to the formation of the Ramabai Association to collect funds for women's activities in India. Pandita Ramabai was also politically active, being one of the few women delegates to attend the Indian National Congress sessions in 1889. In the last twenty years of her life she converted to Christianity, and established a series of women's projects including girls' schools, orphanages, and widows' homes.

Pandita Ramabai Sarasvati, *The Letters and Correspondence of Pandita Ramabai Sarasvati*, Maharashtra State Board for Literature and Culture, 1977
Padmini Sathianadhan Sengupta, *Pandita Ramabai Sarasvati: Her Life and Work*, Asia Publishing House, 1970
Kumari Jayawarden, *Feminism and Nationalism in the Third World*, Zed, 1986

Irina [Borisovna] Ratushinskaya
1954–
poet, political activist

A descendant of Russianised Polish nobility, by training a physicist and mathematician, Irina Ratushinskaya fled her home country in 1986 and became a symbol of fluent and passionate Russian protest. She had been writing poetry since her childhood in Odessa, and realised in her early twenties, when she was working as a teacher, that she could use it to protest against Soviet repression of human rights. Her courageous poetic attacks on injustice circulated widely in *samizdat* within the Soviet Union in the early 1980s, and three volumes of poetry appeared in English in 1984 (*No, I'm Not Afraid*) and 1986 (*Pencil Letter* and *Beyond The Limit*). In 1979 she married Igor Geraschenko, a friend she had known since her childhood, at a time when they were both exploring the relevance of Christianity to their human rights campaigning. In September 1982 Irina Ratushinskaya was arrested, and on her twenty-ninth birthday sentenced to seven years hard labour and five years internal exile. After three and a half years, in October 1986, she was released and allowed to leave the Soviet Union with her husband, who needed medical treatment in London. During her time in prison she had composed more than two hundred poems, committing each to memory to avoid additional punishment. Her two eloquent volumes of memoirs, *Grey is the Colour of Hope* (1988) and *In the Beginning* (1990), have been widely translated, and in 1989, following *perestroika*, her work began to be published in Russia. Though she still lives and writes in London, Irina Ratushinskaya spends much of her time travelling, lecturing, and continuing to campaign for human rights.

Irina Ratushinskaya (trans. Alyona Kojevnikov), *Grey is the Colour of Hope*, Hodder and Stoughton, 1988
Irina Ratushinskaya (trans. Alyona Kojevnikov), *In the Beginning*, Hodder and Stoughton, 1990
Dick Rogers, *Irina*, Lion, 1987

Bernice Johnson Reagon
1942–
singer, cultural worker and activist

Bernice Johnson Reagon grew up in rural Georgia singing sacred African-American music in the choir of her father's Baptist church. In the early 1960s, while she was taking part in the **Student Nonviolent Coordinating Committee** voter registration campaign in Mississippi, she sang with the Freedom Singers. In Washington DC a decade later, raising two children, studying for a PhD in history, and working as vocal director of the DC Repertory Company, she founded Sweet Honey in the Rock. This *a cappella* sextet of women singers has created a repertoire remarkable for the vividness of its musical range – embracing hymns, blues, African chants, jazz and rap – and its political eloquence, touring widely and recording twenty albums in as many years. Bernice Johnson Reagon also serves as curator of the division of community life in the Smithsonian Institution's National Museum of American History. In 1987 she was awarded a prestigious MacArthur Foundation grant.

Bernice Johnson Reagon (ed.), *We Who Believe in Freedom: Sweet Honey in the Rock . . . Still on the Journey*, Doubleday, 1993

John Reed
1887–1920
labour organiser, journalist, writer

John Reed, the 'romantic revolutionary' whose short but passionate life embraced civil war in Mexico, the first world war and the Bolshevik Revolution, was the son of a prosperous family from Portland, Oregon. After leaving Harvard, he spent much of 1910 travelling in Europe before settling in New York's Greenwich Village in 1911 to begin work as a journalist. Like many of his Harvard-educated colleagues he developed a reputation as a bohemian and playboy, but at the end of 1912 he read **Max Eastman**'s new socialist journal *Masses* and put his energy into writing for it. In 1913 Reed helped to organise a 'strike pageant' in Madison Square Gardens for striking silk workers in Paterson, New Jersey, and in 1914 travelled with the guerrilla forces of Pancho Villa during the Mexican civil war: the resulting account of his experiences, *Insurgent Mexico* (1914), was patchy but vivid, and became popular among leftwing Americans. In late 1914 he was sent to Europe to report for the *Metropolitan*, and in 1917 arrived in Petrograd just in time to witness the Bolshevik seizure of power. Though he spoke little Russian he followed the events of the October Revolution closely, and quickly wrote *Ten Days That Shook The World* (1919), the first detailed account of the revolution to be published in the West. His espousal of Bolshevism made him popular in the Soviet Union, though he fared less well in US communist circles. Following his expulsion from the Socialist Party in August 1919, Reed formed the Communist Labor Party, which spent the next year fighting the US Communist Party for Soviet approval. By this time John Reed had returned to Russia for the Second Congress of the Communist International, where he argued passionately that the industrial unionism of the **Industrial Workers of the World** was the only viable model for revolution in America. While in Russia he contracted typhus and died in October 1917: he is buried in the wall of the Kremlin in Moscow.

John Reed, *Ten Days That Shook The World*, 1919 (many editions since)
Robert Rosenstone, *Romantic Revolutionary: A Biography of John Reed*, Knopf, 1975
Eric Homberger, *John Reed*, St Martin's Press, 1990

Wilhelm Reich
1897–1957
psychoanalyst, sexologist, antifascist activist

One of the most original social thinkers and activists of the century, Wilhelm Reich's troubled career embraced psychotherapy, sex, cosmology and Marxism in a mixture that could hardly have been more threatening to the authoritarian status quo. Born in Dobrzynica in Austrian Galicia, he moved to Vienna after the first world war to study medicine and psychoanalysis; by 1924 he was director of the Viennese Psychoanalytic Society. In 1927 he published *Die Funktion des Orgasmus* (1942 in English), stressing the need for sexual fulfilment in order to achieve personal integration; as a result of this and Reich's criticism of Freud's underemphasis of social factors such as poverty and lack of education, Freud distanced himself from the Austrian school. In 1930 Wilhelm Reich moved to Berlin and joined the Kommunistische Partie Deutschlands (KPD); during the 1930s, drawing heavily on Marxist theory and his own personal and professional experience, he wrote a string of important books including *Der Einbruch der Sexualmoral* (1932, 1971 in English), *Massenpsychologie des Faschismus* (1933, 1946 in English) and *Die Sexuelle Revolution* (1936, 1945 in English). Neither the KPD nor the psychoanalytic establishment appreciated his frank treatment of sex and power: in 1933 he was expelled from the Party and the following year from the International Psychoanalytic Association. He moved to Norway to concentrate on his studies into sexuality, vegetotherapy (an early form of muscle-based emotional release therapy) and cosmic or 'orgone' energy, and in 1939 emigrated to the USA, where he felt he would have more freedom to experiment. In 1940 he established an institute in Maine called Organon, where he and a few colleagues developed the orgone concept, which involved the building of an insulated box or 'orgone accumulator' in which a person could sit and be healed by 'orgone particles'. In the late 1940s, with the beginnings of the 'red scare', Reich with his communist background was targeted for official attention. In 1954 the Food and Drug Administration charged him with selling accumulators in defance of an injunction; he died of a heart attack in Lewisburg Prison, Pennsylvania. Ten years after his death his ideas were rediscovered by the radical movement of the 1960s, who found his combination of sex and radical politics a powerful inspiration; his contribution to psychotherapy has since been considerable, with many varieties of 'neo-Reichian therapy' being taught and practised.

Wilhelm Reich, *The Function of the Orgasm*, Farrar, Strauss and Giroux, 1961 (many recent reprints)

Wilhelm Reich, *The Mass Psychology of Fascism*, Orgone University Press, 1946 (many recent reprints)

W. Edward Mann, *Wilhelm Reich: The Man Who Dreamed of Tomorrow*, Crucible, 1990

Adrienne [Cecile] Rich
1929–
poet, essayist, feminist

The powerful feminist voice of Adrienne Rich has produced a flood of important poems and essays in the twenty years since the mid-1970s, when she started, as she says of herself, 'to write directly and overtly as a woman'. She was born into an educated Baltimore family and studied at Radcliffe, where she won the Yale Younger Poets Award in 1951. Two years later she married Harvard professor Alfred Conrad and had three sons; she and Conrad separated in 1966, and since then she has taught English (and latterly feminist studies) at New York, Brandeis, Bryn Mawr, Rutgers, Cornell, California and Stanford Universities. She had been publishing poetry since 1955, but it was her first nonfiction book, *Of Woman Born* (1976), which established her as an important feminist author. *Of Woman Born* exposed the supposedly 'natural' phenomenon of childbirth as being constructed largely by ideology and patriarchy. The same fluent semipoetic style was used to great effect in *On Lies, Secrets, and Silence* (1979), which showed how these three predominantly male tactics keep both women and men in constant fear and mistrust. Adrienne Rich's late 1970s poetry traced the acknowledgement of her lesbianism, and from 1981 to 1983 she coedited the influential lesbian feminist journal *Sinister Wisdom*. Adrienne Rich's major contribution to contemporary feminism is due in no small part to her unique ability to weave personal experience and political insight into immediate and compelling verse and prose.

Adrienne Rich, *Of Mother Born: Motherhood as Experience and Institution*, Norton, 1976
Adrienne Rich, *On Lies, Secrets, and Silence*, Norton, 1979
Adrienne Rich, *Blood, Bread and Poetry*, Norton, 1986
Claire Keyes, *The Aesthetics of Power: The Poetry of Adrienne Rich*, University of Georgia Press, 1986

Paul [Leroy] Robeson
1898–1976
actor, singer, civil rights activist

Famous worldwide as a performer yet revered equally for his courage and outspokenness, Paul Robeson's long and many-faceted career demonstrated an unquenchable passion for justice, integrity and international understanding. He was the youngest of six children born into a radical New Jersey family; his mother died when he was six years old, and his father, an ex-slave and a minister, moved with the children to Somerville. Reverend Robeson was determined that his children would do the best they could; Paul excelled at school and earned a scholarship to Rutgers University, where from 1915 to 1919 he was the only African-American student. Here he achieved very good academic grades, played twice for the All-America baseball team, and won many elocution prizes. From Rutgers he went straight to Columbia University's law school, where he married Eslanda

Cordozo (their son Paul was born in 1927), but by the time he graduated in 1923 his lifelong stage career had already begun. From his New York debut to outstanding performances on Broadway and at London's Savoy Theatre, Paul Robeson rapidly became the world's leading black actor, drawing huge audiences to award-winning performances of classical and contemporary theatre. He augmented his acting by singing a wide repertoire of international songs, including many from minority cultures; he learned languages such as Chinese, Yiddish and Russian in order to bring this multicultural heritage to his Western audiences. During the 1930s Robeson spent much time in London, where his circle of friends included **Kwame Nkrumah**, **Jomo Kenyatta** and Jawaharlal Nehru; in 1934 he paid the first of several visits to the Soviet Union at the invitation of the film-maker Sergei Eisenstein, and in 1938 he demonstrated his commitment to the fight against fascism by visiting Spain and speaking and singing in support of the nationalists. He raised money to fight the Italian invasion of Abyssinia, cofounded the Council of African Affairs in 1937, and, back in the USA after 1939, threatened black armed struggle if antilynching legislation were not enacted. After the war, Paul Robeson's civil rights activities and anticolonialism brought him into fierce conflict with the US government. His refusal to condemn communism led to a virulent CIA witchhunt, official blacklisting and intimidation, and in 1950 to the withdrawal of his passport. Exiled in his own country, he continued to speak out from whatever platform was available, including the influential journal *Freedom* (later *Freedomways*). After his passport was restored following a Supreme Court decision in 1958 (the year in which he published his autobiography *Here I Stand*), he travelled widely in Europe and Australia, performing to large sympathetic audiences, but his health was now deteriorating. He officially retired in 1963, but could still write ten years later 'You can be sure that in my heart I go on singing.' A relentless and versatile fighter for civil liberties, Paul Robeson provided a model and an inspiration for minority groups worldwide during some of the darkest days of the twentieth century.

Paul Robeson (ed. Philip Foner), *Paul Robeson Speaks: Writings, Speeches, Interviews, 1918–1974*, Brunner/Mazel, 1978
Paul Robeson, *Here I Stand*, Beacon, 1988 (rep. of 1958 edn)
Charles Wright, *Robeson: Labor's Forgotten Champion*, Balamp, 1975
Susan Robeson, *The Whole World In His Hands*, Citadel, 1981
Martin Duberman, *Paul Robeson*, Knopf, 1988

Walter [Anthony] Rodney
1942–1980
historian, political activist

When Walter Rodney was assassinated on June 13th 1980 by a bomb placed by agents of the reactionary Guyanan regime of Forbes Burnham, the Caribbean lost one of its greatest historians and most popular political figures. Rodney was born into a politically aware working class family in

Georgetown and read history at the University of the West Indies at Mano, Jamaica (then an external college of London University) before receiving a scholarship in 1963 to study at the London School of Oriental Studies. While researching the history of the Guinea Coast he was much influenced by **C.L.R. James** and the work of **Amilcar Cabral**. In 1966, newly married to his wife Patricia, he started to teach at the University College of Dar es Salaam in Tanzania, returning to Mona two years later to establish a course in African history. Alongside his university lecturing he taught enormously popular courses in history and black power in downtown Kingston; as a result his return to Jamaica from a 1968 congress of black writers in Canada was banned by the Jamaican government, sparking massive popular demonstrations. He and his family returned to Dar es Salaam for six years: there were now three children to support, and while Walter looked after them so that Patricia could complete her studies in public health and social work, he worked on *The Groundings With My Brothers* (1969), about his Jamaican experiences, and the influential *How Europe Underdeveloped Africa* (1972). In 1974 Walter Rodney was asked to head the history department at the new University of Guyana, but arrived home to find the appointment withdrawn by the Burnham government. He continued to teach, however, and was a cofounder in 1975 of the Working People's Alliance, a populist multiracial grouping which posed a significant threat to the incumbent regime. His courageous decision to remain in Guyana resulted in his violent murder; though the people of Georgetown were instructed not to mark his funeral, many thousands of ordinary Guyanese people walked alongside his coffin to the graveyard.

Walter Rodney, *The Groundings With My Brothers*, Bogle L'Ouverture, 1969
Walter Rodney, *How Europe Underdeveloped Africa*, Bogle L'Ouverture, 1972
Walter Rodney, *A History of the Guyanese Working People 1881–1905*, Heinemann, 1981
Edward Alpers and Pierre-Michel Fontaine (eds), *Walter Rodney, Revolutionary and Scholar: A Tribute*, Centre for Afro-American Studies, 1982

Carl [Ranson] Rogers
1902–1987
psychologist, therapist, writer

Carl Rogers, the American psychologist who pioneered the 'client-centred' approach to psychotherapy, was born and grew up in Oak Ridge, Illinois. Having toyed briefly with the idea of entering the church, he studied psychology at Union Theological Seminary in New York and Columbia University, where he met his wife and lifetime companion Helen. He worked for several years in a community guidance clinic in Rochester, New York, where he came to realise that the majority of therapists attempted to guide their patients far more than was necessary, often disempowering them in the process. In 1957 he went to teach at the University of Wisconsin, continuing to work therapeutically with groups and individuals until shortly before his death. Over the years he developed what he called his 'nondirective' or 'client-centred' approach to psychotherapy, believing that therapists can best help their patients (he preferred to call them 'clients') not so much by doing a great deal as by paying them total attention and offering a minimal amount of appropriate and supportive feedback (a technique he called 'unconditional positive regard'). In this way the low self-esteem displayed by many people seeking therapeutic help can be replaced with a sense of real self-worth. Like fellow psychotherapist **Abraham Maslow**, Rogers firmly believed that every human being has a right and a need to grow towards their full potential, an idea explored in depth in his influential book *On Becoming a Person* (1961). He was particularly concerned that psychotherapy should not become an élitist tool, available only to the better off, and was entirely aware that the empowerment of the individual constitutes a political act which presents a massive threat to the professional establishment. His sensitive client-centred approach to psychotherapy is often called 'Rogerian', and his ideas helped to create widespread interest in personal growth in the 1960s and 70s, especially in the USA. *A Way of Being* (1980), published towards the end of his life, provides a candid view of Carl Rogers' own experiences in relation to his work, including his thoughts on old age and the development of the client-centred approach over the previous two decades.

Carl Rogers, *On Becoming a Person*, Houghton Mifflin, 1961
Carl Rogers, *A Way of Being*, Houghton Mifflin, 1980
Brian Thorne, *Carl Rogers*, Sage, 1992

Oscar [Arnulfo] Romero
1917–1980
clergyman, human rights activist

Six weeks before he was murdered while saying mass in San Salvador Cathedral, Archbishop Romero wrote to US president Jimmy Carter begging him to halt military assistance to the military junta which went on to kill more than 70,000 El Salvadorans. Carter did not listen, nor did Reagan and Bush, and the USA did not stop its massive aid to the repressive military regime until the murder in late 1989 of six Jesuit priests (including the rector of the University of Central America, Ignacio Ellacuria) provoked an international outcry. Born near the Honduras border in eastern El Salvador, Oscar Romero trained for the ministry and became a priest while working in Rome in 1942. In 1945 he returned to his home country, becoming an auxiliary bishop in 1967 and archbishop of El Salvador in 1977. Only weeks after his ordination, he officiated at the funeral of Rutilio Grande, a popular priest committed to peaceful activism who had been murdered while helping landless peasants. Oscar Romero now began to speak more forcefully against the suffering of El Salvador, using his weekly sermons to demand an end to police abuse and official oppression. He refused government protection, explaining to President Napoleón Duarte that 'a shepherd seeks no security as long as the flock is threatened'. In a sermon in February 1980 Oscar Romero made it clear that, in the real world of guns and repression, religious faith and political choice are inseparable: 'The church, like every individual, is faced with the most basic option for its faith, being for life or for death – on this point there is no possible neutrality. Either we serve the life of Salvadorans, or we are accomplices in their death.' On March 24th, while officiating at holy mass, he was shot dead by a gunman.

Oscar Romero, *Voice of the Voiceless*, Orbis, 1985
Jon Sobrino, *Archbishop Romero: Memories and Reflections*, Orbis, 1990

Theodore Roszak
1933–
historian, novelist, social critic

The American historian and social critic Theodore Roszak was born and grew up in Chicago, and studied history and philosophy at the University of California at Los Angeles (UCLA) and Princeton. From 1959 to 1962 he taught at Stanford University, and during the 1960s spent several long periods in London, editing *Peace News* in 1964–65 and helping to found the Campaign Against Racial Discrimination and the Anti-University of London. At UCLA he met his wife, the poet Betty Greenwald, with whom he compiled the pioneering feminist anthology *Masculine/Feminine* (1970). As a young academic Theodore Roszak wrote about the emerging youthful 'counter culture' for *The Nation* magazine, and came to widespread public attention with *The Making of a Counter Culture* (1969), which quickly became a textbook for thousands of dissenting students and leftwingers by virtue of its systematic critique of the experts and technocrats who are destroying the ancient covenant between nature and humans and cutting the vital link between knowledge and wisdom. *Where The Wasteland Ends* (1972) continued the same theme, calling for a regeneration of religious sensibility, a communitarian approach to work, and a truly participatory democracy. In 1973 Theodore Roszak was appointed professor of history and chair of general studies at California State University, Hayward, where he still teaches. As well as writing successful novels, he has continued to produce articles, essays and books examing the developing links between personal self-exploration and the understanding of ecological principles, including *Person/Planet* (1978), *Unfinished Animal* (1979), *The Cult of Information* (1986) and *The Voice of the Earth* (1992). In 1994 he cofounded the Ecopsychology Institute at California State University, of which he is director.

Theodore Roszak, *The Making of a Counter Culture: Reflections on the Technocratic Society and its Youthful Opposition*, Doubleday, 1969
Theodore Roszak, *Where the Wasteland Ends: Politics and Transcendence in Postindustrial Society*, Doubleday, 1972
Theodore Roszak, *Person/Planet: The Creative Disintegration of Industrial Society*, Doubleday, 1978
Theodore Roszak, *The Voice of the Earth: An Exploration of Ecopsychology*, Simon and Schuster, 1992

Sheila Rowbotham
1943–
feminist writer and activist, historian

Sheila Rowbotham was one of the earliest organisers and chroniclers of the British **women's liberation movement** of the 1970s, and has continued in that important role to the present. She grew up in a middle-class Tory family in Leeds and was educated at a Methodist boarding school and St Hilda's College, Oxford, graduating with a history degree in 1964. Moving to London, she became involved in leftwing politics. By 1966 she was involved with the Vietnam solidarity movement, and in 1968 was one of the founders of the socialist newspaper *Black Dwarf*. Recognising by this time that feminism and socialism were uneasy companions, in 1969 she helped to organise Britain's first Women's Liberation Conference, held at Ruskin College, Oxford, in Febuary 1970. The next few years were taken up with a frenzy of organising and writing: as well as helping to maintain the momentum of the new movement Sheila Rowbotham wrote three groundbreaking books. *Women, Resistance and Revolution* (1972) and *Hidden From History* (1973) linked the new feminism with women's historical struggle, establishing the foundations for much later feminist history, while *Women's Consciousness, Man's World* (1973) brought together feminism, socialism and personal experience in a telling integration of domestic issues and political analysis. Sheila's son Will was born in 1977, at a time when she was moving back towards mainstream socialism and becoming uneasy with the radical feminist dogma of women who had little historical insight or political experience; in 1979 she was coauthor and organiser of a book and conference called 'Beyond The Fragments', designed to help foster a more humane socialism in Britain. Since the early 1980s Sheila Rowbotham has continued to teach and to write on the growth of the women's movement both in Britain and worldwide. As well as writing two plays, she has produced two important surveys of the late twentieth-century women's movement, and worked for several years in the Popular Planning Unit of the Greater London Council. She is currently a research fellow at Birkbeck College, London, where she is working on emerging forms of women's economic organisation in the West and in the Third World. Since 1988, in close collaboration with development economist Swasti Mitter, she has been studying the ways in which women in both rich and poor countries are affected by – and develop their own – economic organisations and technological strategies.

Sheila Rowbotham, *Women, Resistance and Revolution*, Penguin, 1972
Sheila Rowbotham, *Women's Consciousness, Man's World*, Penguin, 1973
Sheila Rowbotham, *Hidden from History*, Pluto, 1973
Sheila Rowbotham, *The Past is Before Us: Feminism in Action since the 1960s*, Pandora, 1989
Sheila Rowbotham, *Women in Movement: Feminism and Social Action*, Routledge, 1992

Sheila Rowbotham and Swasti Mitter (eds), *Dignity and Daily Bread: New Forms of Economic Organisation Among Poor Women in the Third World and the First*, Routledge, 1994

Manabendra Nath Roy [Narendra Nath Bhattacharya]
1887–1954
communist, humanist, social reformer

Manabendra Nath Roy's political development from militant nationalist to communist and finally to liberal humanist mirrored the journey of many Indian intellectuals of his generation, yet his determination and achievement at each stage singles him out as a remarkable and influential individual. He grew up in Arabalia in West Bengal, the son of a Brahmin schoolteacher, joining the militant nationalists under Jatin Mukherji in 1905: he was arrested three times and spent twenty months in prison for his involvement in terrorist activities against the British. In 1915 he left India for Java, China and Japan, ending up in New York, where he read **Karl Marx** in a public library. The main aim of his travels had been to secure German arms for the Indian struggle, and when the USA joined the war in 1916 Roy escaped to Mexico to avoid arrest; here, impressed by the achievement of the Bolshevik Revolution, he embraced Marxism wholeheartedly and formed the Mexican Socialist Party, which in 1919 became the first communist party outside Soviet Russia. At **Lenin's** invitation, Roy attended the Second Congress of the Communist **International** in Moscow, where he became a trusted adviser to Lenin on communist policy in colonial countries such as India; by 1924 he was a full member of the Comintern. After Lenin's death, however, his views on China and post-Lenin developments in Russia angered Stalin: in 1930 Roy flew secretly back to India, where he was promptly jailed for six years, during which period he wrote his extensive prison notebooks. Concerned about what was happening in the communist world, he now turned to what he called 'radical humanism', whose crucial features were social justice, self-government, and a cooperative economy. Setting his ideas against **Gandhi's** nationalism and spirituality, he formed first a League of Radical Congressmen within the Indian National Congress and then, in 1940, his own Radical Democratic Party. Its emphasis on local politics at a time when nationwide parties were gathering momentum meant that it had little impact, and in 1948 Manabendra Nath Roy disbanded it and concentrated all his efforts on the recently-established Indian Renaissance Institute, a think tank which offered training courses and led to the founding of Renaissance Clubs in several Indian cities. In the aftermath of Indian independence Roy's contribution to his country's political evolution became overshadowed, but his fervent belief in human goodness and morality, given the lifetime's experience and thought which led to his conclusions, have inspired many Indians in the decades since his death.

Manabendra Rath Noy, *Politics, Power and Parties*, Renaissance, 1960
Manabendra Rath Noy, *Memoirs*, Allen and Unwin, 1964

Samaren Roy, *The Restless Brahmin: The Early Life of M.N. Roy*, Allied Publishers, 1970

Samaren Roy, *India's First Communist*, Minerva, 1988

Bertrand [Arthur William] Russell
1872–1970
philosopher, peace activist

A brilliant intellectual from a background of title and privilege, Bertrand Russell maintained a remarkably consistent stand on moral and political issues throughout his long life, though regularly insisting that his politics were quite unconnected with his philosophical enquiries. His parents died when he was very young and, until he entered Trinity College, Cambridge, at the age of eighteen, he was brought up by his grandmother, the widow of the Liberal prime minister John Russell, and taught by private tutors. In 1895, shortly after marrying Alys Pearsall Smith, Bertrand was appointed lecturer in philosophy at Trinity, and the next twenty years saw the publication of a series of original studies in logic and epistemology. His radical proclivities became apparent when he stood (unsuccessfully) for parliament on a Liberal suffragist ticket in the 1907 general election, and in his determined opposition to the first world war, which cost him first a fine, then dismissal from Trinity, and finally a six-month prison sentence. After the war he continued his philosophical studies and married his second wife, **Dora** Black, in 1921. While they were together he wrote the popular *Marriage and Morals* (1929) and *The Pursuit of Happiness* (1930), provoking much critical comment from those who knew about his increasingly complex marital and extramarital relationships, and *On Education* (1926) and *Education and the Social Order* (1932), based on the beliefs that also led to the founding by Dora and Bertrand of the progressive Beacon Hill School. By the summer of 1928, however, Bertrand had moved on to the woman who was to become his third wife, Patricia Spence, leaving Dora to look after Beacon Hill and their two children. In 1931, when his older brother died, Bertrand succeeded to the family title, but refused to use it. In the 1920s he had been highly critical of authoritarian developments in the Soviet Union, and during the 1930s warned of the implications of fascism in books like *Freedom and Organisation* (1934) and *Power* (1938). The outbreak of the second world war found him in the USA, where his radical ideas initially barred him from teaching, so he turned his efforts to writing his bestselling *History of Western Philosophy* (1945). Still a convinced pacifist and a sponsor of the **Peace Pledge Union**, he foresaw the dangers of nuclear confrontation, and warned in a typically haughty and unsolicited series of letters to world leaders that nuclear arms threatened all of civilisation, and must therefore be phased out and banned. In 1958 he became the first president of the **Campaign for Nuclear Disarmament**, two years later resigning to form the Committee of 100 to pursue the same ends by acts of public civil disobedience: the following year Bertrand (now in his ninetieth year) and his fourth wife, Edith Finch, were imprisoned for taking part in a sit-down demonstration in London's Whitehall. In 1963 he moved to Penrhyndeudraeth in mid-Wales and concentrated his energies on the new Bertrand Russell Peace Foundation, which continued to sue for nuclear disarmament as well as sponsoring an international tribunal which found the US army guilty of war crimes in Vietnam. Despite his human failings as a man born to material and patriarchal privilege, Bertrand Russell is remembered as one of the twentieth century's greatest philosophers and antimilitarists.

Bertrand Russell, *The Autobiography of Bertrand Russell* (3 vols), Unwin, 1967–1969 (new edn Routledge, 1991)
Alan Ryan, *Bertrand Russell: A Political Life*, Hill and Wang, 1988
Caroline Moorehead, *Bertrand Russell*, Sinclair-Stevenson, 1992

Dora Russell [Dora Black]
1894–1986
writer, women's rights and peace activist

An influential and radical British feminist of the mid-century, Dora Russell fought for justice and equal rights until the end of her long life. As a 22-year-old student at Girton College, Cambridge, Dora Black met the philosopher **Bertrand Russell**, then married to his first wife Alys. In 1917 Russell invited Dora to travel with him to Russia but then changed his mind; she went anyway, travelling on a forged passport and sharing a platform at the 1917 Women's Congress with **Aleksandra Kollontai**. After a tour of China with Russell in 1920, they were married in 1921. Their son John was born in November of that year and their daughter Kate in December 1923. In 1924 Dora Russell published the first of three important books, an assessment of sexual politics called *Hypatia: or Women and Knowledge*. This was followed by *The Right to be Happy* (1927), a passionate plea for sexual freedom partly inspired by **Margaret Sanger**'s sex education campaign. In 1927 the Russells founded a progressive school called Beacon Hill; Dora Russell's radical ideas about education were outlined in her 1932 book *In Defence of Children*. While Dora was lecturing in the USA in the summer of 1928 Bertrand started a relationship with an Oxford undergraduate, Patricia Spence, who was to become his third wife; he left Dora to look after children and school virtually singlehanded, and after they were divorced in 1932 they never spoke to each other again. Meanwhile Dora Russell met and married an American journalist, Griffin Barry, and had two more children. When war broke out the school was requisitioned and she worked for the ministry of information until 1945. After the war she became active in the civil rights and peace movements, being a founding member of both the National Council for Civil Liberties (now **Liberty**) and the **Campaign for Nuclear Disarmament**. In 1958 she organised and led the Women's Peace Caravan, a group of women who travelled to Moscow to protest against nuclear proliferation, and continued to work actively in the peace movement until her death, being an avid supporter of the

Greenham Common Peace Women and attending her last demonstration, at the St Mawgan RAF base in Cornwall, at the age of 91.

Dora Russell, *Hypatia, or Women and Knowledge*, Kegan Paul, Trench Trubner, 1926
Dora Russell, *The Tamarisk Tree* (3 volumes), Virago, 1977–85
Dale Spender, *Women of Ideas*, Routledge and Kegan Paul, 1982

Bayard Rustin
1910–1987
civil rights campaigner, pacifist

The American civil rights leader Bayard Rustin grew up in West Chester, Pennsylvania. and in the 30s moved to New York, where he sang in cafes with Leadbelly and Josh White. He became an organiser with the Young Communist League in 1938, but when it shifted its pacifist stance he joined the **Fellowship of Reconciliation** (FOR). In 1941 he was asked by the civil rights activist (and thenceforth lifelong colleague) A. Philip Randolph to help organise a March on Washington by 100,000 black people, and was severely critical when Randolph chose to cancel the march following Franklin Roosevelt's order banning racial discrimination in war production. Rustin felt that the issue of discrimination was far from settled, not to mention the implied support for US involvement in the build-up to war. In 1942 Rustin was arrested in Tennessee for refusing to move to the back of a bus, and in 1943 received a 28-month prison sentence for non-cooperation with the draft. After his release in 1945 he led the Free India Committee, and was repeatedly arrested for demonstrating outside the British Embassy; in 1948 he spent six months in newly-independent India. In 1947 he organised the FOR Journey of Reconciliation, the first of many 'Freedom Rides'. Late in 1948 he joined Randolph to form the League of Nonviolent Civil Disobedience, and from 1953 to 1964 served as executive secretary to the War Resisters League (WRL). In 1955 **Martin Luther King** invited Bayard Rustin to organise the Montgomery bus boycott, and Rustin served as King's adviser and assistant for the next seven years, bringing the civil rights struggle to the attention of a wide cross-section of Americans. Rustin masterminded the massive August 28th 1963 March on Washington, when a quarter of a million people assembled around the Lincoln Memorial, though some critics felt he had been coopted by the previously hostile US administration in order to gain official permission for the march. When in 1964 he left the WRL to become director of the A. Philip Randolph Institute, his closer involvement with mainstream politics and unions alienated many of his erstwhile colleagues, and by the mid-1970s he had become distinctly conservative, refusing to condemn the **Vietnam War** and Israel's treatment of Palestinians. By the time of his death many political activists saw Bayard Rustin as a liability, though few denied that his influence and organisational skills had been crucial to the success of the civil rights movement.

Bayard Rustin, *Down the Line: The Collected Writings of Bayard Rustin*, Quadrangle, 1971
Bayard Rustin, *Strategies for Freedom*, Columbia University Press, 1976
Max Green, 'An Interview with Bayard Rustin', *New Perspectives,* Winter 1985

Nawal el Sa'dawi
1930–
doctor, novelist, women's rights activist

Born in the northern Egyptian village of Dafr Tahla, Nawal el Sa'dawi trained as a doctor and rose to become, in 1972, Egypt's director general of health education, a remarkable achievement for an Arab woman. By this time she had also achieved considerable success as a writer, having published her first novel and collection of short stories while still in her twenties. In 1969 her landmark study of Arab women and their struggle for liberation, *Women and Sex*, was published (1972 in English); it was banned by the Egyptian censors and she was forced to find publishers for her work outside Egypt, the Arab editions being produced in Beirut. In 1972 her outspoken opinions on the need for sweeping social and political change in Egypt became too much for the Sadat regime, and she was dismissed from her post in the ministry of health. She continued to write and work for women's rights, both in Egypt and abroad, and in the late 1970s produced several more controversial books, including the novel *Woman at Point Zero* (1974, 1978 in English), about a condemned woman imprisoned in the notorious Qanatir Prison for killing a pimp, and *The Hidden Face of Eve: Women in the Arab World* (1980). In September 1981 Nawal el Sa'dawi was herself charged with 'crimes against the state' and imprisoned in Qanatir; fortunately for her, Anwar al Sadat was assassinated two months later and she was freed – her prison experience is told in *Memoirs from the Women's Prison* (1983). In 1982 she founded the Pan-Arab Women's Rights Organisation. From her family base in Cairo (she is married with two children) she has continued writing novels, of which more than fifteen have been published, and working internationally for freedom and justice; many of her travels and campaigns are described in her autobiography *My Travels Around the World* (1991). Her name still appears on the 'death lists' of some fanatical terrorist organisations, but her books have had a profound effect on successive generations of young Egyptians.

Nawal el Sa'dawi, *The Hidden Face of Eve: Women in the Arab World*, Zed, 1980
Nawal el Sa'dawi, *My Travels Around the World*, Methuen, 1991

Amina Said
1914–
women's rights campaigner, journalist, writer

Amina Said, Egypt's pioneering woman journalist, was born in Asyut, and was educated at the Shubra Girls' Secondary School in Cairo, the first state school to give girls an education equivalent to boys. Here she met **Huda Shaarawi**, who encouraged her to join the youth group of Shaqiqat, the

Egyptian Feminist Union. In 1931, two years after women were first admitted, she enrolled at Cairo University, and then made her career as a journalist, the first Egyptian woman to do so. In 1954 she founded a mass-circulation magazine for women, *Hawa*, for which she continued to write until her retirement in 1981. Her provocative and carefully reasoned *Hawa* editorials inevitably antagonised the authorities and many Moslem fundamentalists, but they also reached many thousands of sympathetic readers. Amina Said has held many senior positions in publishing, including vice-president of the Egyptian Press Syndicate and president of the administrative council of Dar al-Hilal, one of Egypt's largest publishing houses.

Margot Badran and Miriam Cooke (ed.), *Opening the Gates: A Century of Arab Feminist Writing*, Virago, 1990

Edward W. [Wadie] Said
1935–
educator, writer, literary and political critic

In recent years the Palestinian-born American teacher and critic Edward Said has become one of the most eloquent and learned of those voices promoting a deeper understanding of Western perceptions of and attitudes towards Asian – and more specifically Middle Eastern – history and culture. Born into an educated Christian family in Jerusalem, his family fled Palestine when Israel gained its independence in 1948; he did his schooling in Egypt and the USA and then studied English and history at Princeton, followed by comparative literature at Harvard. He started to teach at Columbia University in 1963, where he was appointed professor in 1970, the year he married Mariam Cortas; they have two children. Early studies in literary criticism were followed in 1978 by *Orientalism*, a groundbreaking enquiry demonstrating how the nineteenth-century scholarly concept of 'orientalism' created fundamental misperceptions about the East, which in turn were used to develop an ethnocentric rationale for oppressive imperialism. From the mid-1970s, in an effort to help Westerners see beyond the clichés and stereotypes of terrorism and barbarism, Edward Said had been writing about Palestine's plight; on the practical level he became an active supporter of the Palestine Liberation Organisation and a member of the Palestine National Council. In his books *The Question of Palestine* (1980) and *After the Last Sky* (1986) he traced the dilemma of the Palestinians in responding to Israeli rule and Western prejudices. In the months leading up to the Gulf War of 1991, Edward Said consistently presented a reasoned opposition to the anti-Arab consensus of media and politicians, and has continued to work for a peaceful political solution to Middle Eastern conflicts which can embrace the cultural homogeneity of the region. His acclaimed 1993 book, *Culture and Imperialism*, expanded on many of the themes of *Orientalism*, showing how many of the myths of colonialism inevitably met with resistance in the occupied territories, and explored the possibilities for a postcolonial world order. A cosmopolitan, cultured and fluent scholar, Edward Said has been a major contributor to the ongoing debate about crosscultural relations in the modern world.

Edward W. Said, *Orientalism*, Pantheon, 1978
Edward W. Said, *After the Last Sky: Palestinian Lives*, Pantheon, 1986
Edward W. Said, *Culture and Imperialism*, Knopf, 1993
Michael Sprinker (ed.), *Edward Said: A Critical Reader*, Blackwell, 1992

Andrey [Dmitrievich] Sakharov
1921–1989
physicist, political and social critic, writer

The Russian nuclear physicist Andrey Sakharov played a crucial role in the Soviet nuclear weapons programme, until, recognising the threat of nuclear proliferation to international cooperation and human rights, he eventually became one of his country's leading dissidents. The son of a physics teacher, he too studied physics at Moscow University before starting work as a research engineer. Believing that the Soviet Union must have nuclear weapons to maintain the international balance of power, he worked towards the testing of the first Soviet hydrogen bomb in 1953, for which he was elected a member of the Academy of Sciences and received many state honours. In the late 1950s he became concerned about the effects of radioactive fallout and called for an end to nuclear testing, which brought him into conflict with Khrushchev, and by the late 1960s was using his influence to protest about such issues as the use of 'psychiatric hospitals' to contain dissidents, the pollution of Lake Baikal, and Soviet hostility towards the West. In 1968 he published an article entitled 'Progress, Peaceful Coexistence and Intellectual Freedom', calling for Soviet-American friendship and understanding; when it was published in the West he was deprived of many of his privileges and barred from secret government work. In 1970 he met and married the doctor and fellow activist **Yelena Bonner**, and they campaigned together for human rights in the Soviet Union, petitioning both at home and internationally. In 1975 Sakharov was awarded the Nobel Peace Prize for his human rights work, but in January 1980 Brezhnev banished him to the 'closed city' of Gorky; he continued to work for human rights, with Yelena acting as a messenger between Moscow and Gorky until she too was exiled in 1984. In December 1986 Gorbachev allowed them to return to Moscow, where Sakharov threw himself into renewed campaigning for freedom and democratisation. Enjoying immense moral authority and popular support, he was elected to the Congress of People's Deputies in 1989, where he immediately became a prominent member of the new legislature. He died suddenly in December 1989 during the Second Congress of People's Deputies, having shortly beforehand completed his widely read and typically modest *Memoirs*.

Andrei Sakharov (trans. Richard Lourie), *Memoirs*, Knopf, 1990
Andrei Sakharov, *Moscow and Beyond, 1986–1989* (trans. Antonina Bouis),
    Knopf, 1991
George Bailey, *The Making of Andrei Sakharov*, Allen Lane, 1989

[John] Kirkpatrick Sale
1937–
writer, journalist, social commentator

The American writer Kirkpatrick Sale was born and brought up in Ithaca, New York State, and studied history at Cornell University before marrying Faith Apfelbaum in 1962 and teaching at the University of Ghana for two years from 1963. His subsequent career has been in New York-based journalism (he was editor of the *New York Times Magazine* in 1965–66 and of *The Nation* in 1981–82) and environmental activism, where his ability to encapsulate and popularise issues within the developing green movement has inspired readers and colleagues alike. In 1973 he wrote a useful history of **Students for a Democratic Society**, but it is for his later books that he is best known. *Human Scale* (1980) drew on the ideas of **Fritz Schumacher** and **Leopold Kohr** to demonstrate how 'growthmania' ignores the critical importance of human-scale environments and institutions, while *Dwellers in the Land* (1985) explained the importance of living consciously within the possibilities and the limitations of the natural environment of our home region. Sale was a cofounder and since 1980 has been a board member of the E.F. Schumacher Society of America, established to promote Schumacher's ideas and keep alive the scholarship of decentralism. He was also a cofounder of the North American Bioregional Congress and of the New York Greens, and is an active member of the Hudson Bioregional Council. Kirkpatrick Sale's most recent books, *The Conquest of Paradise* (1991) and *The Green Revolution* (1993), continued his exploration of the way in which 'Western civilisation', particularly in its industrial phase, has distanced itself from nature so completely that it is now hellbent on a path of global destruction, from which we can rescue ourselves only by a return to the vision and wisdom of nature-based tribal cultures.

Kirkpatrick Sale, *SDS: The Rise of the Students for a Democratic Society*, Random House, 1973

Kirkpatrick Sale, *Human Scale*, Secker and Warburg, 1980

Kirkpatrick Sale, *Dwellers in the Land: The Bioregional Vision*, Sierra Club Books, 1985

Kirkpatrick Sale, *The Conquest of Paradise: Christopher Columbus and the Columbian Legacy*, Hodder and Stoughton, 1991

Kirkpatrick Sale, *The Green Revolution*, Hill and Wang, 1993

Margaret Sanger [Margaret Louise Higgins]
1879–1966
feminist, birth control campaigner

The American birth control pioneer Margaret Sanger's achievement was to give women real choices over their fertility and reproduction. The sixth of eleven children whose mother died of exhaustion and tuberculosis when Margaret was a teenager yet whose radical father lived well into his eighties, she took heed of the contrast in her parents' fates when formulating her own feminist outlook. She became a schoolteacher in New Jersey, then trained as a nurse, and in 1902 married the architect William Sanger, going to live in New York's Westchester County. The following year she delivered – with great difficulty – the first of her three children, and in 1910, convinced that there was more to life than suburban childraising, moved into Manhattan. She enlisted in the radical labour movement, and learned alongside **Elizabeth Gurley Flynn** and **Emma Goldman** that women could be excellent organisers and persuasive speakers. Seeing at first hand the suffering of poor city women, she started speaking out on sexual reform, venereal disease and birth control. A 1913 Sanger article about syphilis caused the socialist weekly *The Call* to be banned, and in March 1914 she started a militant feminist journal *The Woman Rebel*. By now living apart from William, she travelled to Europe, meeting **Havelock Ellis**, **Marie Stopes**, and the Dutch birth control pioneer Aletta Jacobs. She arrived home to find her husband arrested and her sister jailed for their involvement in disseminating information, and her daughter dying of pneumonia, but the resulting public sympathy and Margaret's own determination combined to ensure that birth control was firmly placed on the political agenda. In October 1916 she opened a birth control clinic in Brooklyn which treated 488 women in the nine days before it was closed by the police. Her arrest made her a national figure, and by 1921 the law had been changed to allow the circulation of birth control information (though only to doctors). Margaret, now divorced from William, organised the American Birth Control League in 1921. Playing down her radical past, she sought financial support from socialites and philanthropists, and in 1922 married oil millionaire J. Noah Slee, which ensured that her work would not founder for want of money. In 1923 she opened the influential Birth Control Clinic Research Bureau, which became a model for more than 300 clinics established throughout the USA by 1938. Though less active after 1930, Margaret Sanger played an important part in the setting up in 1952 of the International Planned Parenthood Foundation, and during the mid-1950s championed research into the contraceptive pill.

Margaret Sanger, *My Fight for Birth Control*, Maxwell Reprint Co., 1969 (repr. of 1931 ed.)
Margaret Sanger, *Margaret Sanger: An Autobiography*, Maxwell Reprint Co, 1970 (repr. of 1938 ed.)
David Kennedy, *Birth Control in America: The Career of Margaret Sanger*, Yale University Press, 1970
Madeleine Gray, *Margaret Sanger: A Biography of the Champion of Birth Control*, R. Marek, 1979

Thomas Sankara
1949–1987
army officer, socialist politician

On October 15th 1987 Thomas Sankara, the innovative socialist president of the West African state of Burkina Faso, was assassinated together with twelve of his aides. It was the end of a five-year experiment in more-or-less peaceful grassroots socialist revolution, led by a man of austere habits who shunned personal wealth and worked hard both for his own people and for oppressed minorities worldwide. Thomas Sankara was born in Yako in the north of what was then the French colony of Upper Volta; the country officially gained its independence in 1960. After four years of military preparatory school in Ouagadougou he left in 1970 for military college in Madagascar; two years later, while he was studying in Antsirabe, thousands of demonstrating students and workers toppled the Madagascan government and installed a shortlived socialist regime. During the 1970s Upper Volta experienced intense drought and a series of military coups; Sankara, returning home in 1976 as an army captain, was deeply disturbed by what he found. A popular commander with both the army and the people of Upper Volta, he was nominated as president in 1982 following yet another coup. His revolutionary government quickly established programmes for primary health care, immunisation, literacy in the three main indigenous languages, school building, reforestation and food subsidies; some of his policies, such as nominating a day when men did food shopping so that they would know how hard women worked, and renaming his country Burkina Faso – 'land of worthy men', were unconventional and inventive. He was also a conspicuous supporter of others suffering oppression at the hands of neocolonialist powers, and spoke at international meetings in support of Nicaraguan self-determination and the **African National Congress**. It was perhaps inevitable that his progressive regime threatened those in his country who thirsted for power and wealth: he was murdered in a coup led by his second-in-command Blaise Compaoré, who promptly ordered the building of a presidential palace and a personal aircraft, and announced that private enterprise and foreign capital would from now on be welcome in Burkina Faso.

Thomas Sankara (ed. Doug Cooper), *Thomas Sankara Speaks: The Burkino Faso Revolution 1983–87*, Pathfinder, 1988

Issam Sartawi
1934–1983
human rights activist, peace campaigner

Long before the Israeli government decided in 1993 that it must recognise and negotiate peacefully with the Palestinians, some Palestinian freedom fighters had already come to realise that, despite the oppression of Israeli rule in the occupied territories, it was better to wage peace than armed struggle. It was out of his involvement in those freedom organisations that advocated a violent response, including Fatah, the Action Organisation for the Liberation of Palestine, and the Palestine Liberation Organisation (PLO), that Issam Sartawi came to understand how Jew and Arab had in fact a long and cooperative history which had only become disrupted in the mid-twentieth century. From this understanding came his fervent belief in the possibility for friendly Jewish and Arab cooperation that would once again lead to peaceful coexistence. He grew up in Acre and Haifa, but after Israeli independence in 1948 his family fled to Iraq, where he studied medicine at Baghdad University and married an Iraqi wife; in 1959 they moved to the USA, where Issam finished his medical studies and became a heart surgeon. The 1967 Six Day War persuaded him that his duty lay in his occupied homeland: he returned to the Middle East, and by 1970 had become a senior member of the PLO Executive Committee. During the early 1970s his researches into Arab-Jewish history demonstrated the involvement of Zionists and the British government in inciting inter-racial violence during the 1940s and 50s, violence which led to the forced exile of thousands of Jews from Israel's Arab neighbours. Realising that both Arab and Jewish communities had suffered from the postwar partition of the region, Issam Sartawi worked hard, with some success, to convince Arab governments to rescind anti-Jewish legislation. By 1976 he was convinced that a Palestinian state could only be established with full Israeli agreement, and that to achieve this Israeli public opinion had to change. Working with Palestinian and Israeli colleagues (notably **Uri Avnery** and **Matti Peled**), and speaking on platforms throughout Europe, the USA and the Middle East he passionately argued the case for Israeli-Palestinian dialogue. Given the suspicion and hatred generated between Israel and its Arab neighbours it was hardly surprising that Issam Sartawi should be maligned by Israeli hardliners who wanted to rid the world of 'Palestinian terrorists', but it was not only the Israeli government and its allies who found war more to their liking than peace. Although the majority of the PLO, including its leader Yasser Arafat, publicly backed Sartawi's dialogue with pro-Palestinian Israelis, a growing number of militant extremists within the Palestine National Council (PNC), headed by the Abu Nidal faction of Fatah, denounced him as a traitor. Shouted down at the fifteenth conference of the PNC in Damascus in April 1981, Sartawi pointedly resigned from the Council. The June 1982 war in Lebanon, initiated by an increasingly aggressive Israeli administration, hardened the PNC's anti-Israeli stance. At a packed meeting in London addressed by Sartawi and Avnery in February 1983 (and where both were heckled by extremist Zionists and Abu Nidal supporters), Sartawi yet again made it clear that there was little chance for peace in the Middle East while the fanatics on both sides effectively collaborated to prolong the bloodshed. Two months later in Albufeira, Portugal, while attending yet another international meeting to stress the need for dialogue between Arab and Israeli, Issam Sartawi was shot dead by an Abu Nidal gunman: an Abu Nidal communiqué announced its pleasure in 'executing the death sentence passed on the criminal traitor Sartawi, agent of the Israeli, British and US intelligence services.'

Uri Avnery, *My Friend, The Enemy*, Zed, 1986

Jean-Paul Sartre
1905–1980
philosopher, writer, political and social critic

The founder of an influential school of philosophy and an active supporter of a wide range of radical causes, Jean-Paul Sartre is, by virtue of his consistent efforts to link belief and action, one of the most important twentieth-century thinker-activists. He was born into a prominent Parisian family, where his sense of childhood rejection led to an abiding distaste for bourgeois standards. He graduated in 1929 from the École Normale Supérieure (where he met **Simone de Beauvoir**, who was to become his lifelong companion), and from 1931 taught philosophy. Two books brought him to public notice: the philosophical and semi-autobiographical novel *La nausée* (1938, 1948 in English), and *L'être et le néant* (1943, 1956 in English), which advocated a philosophy of ultimate freedom based on choice, responsibility and authenticity, an approach called 'existentialism' which quickly captured the mood of change and dissatisfaction that characterised postwar Europe. The war, and a period as a prisoner in 1940, convinced Sartre that freedom must be matched with purpose, and he increasingly became involved in social and political action. An established novelist and playwright, his work explored the ethical dilemmas of freedom, and in *Qu'est-ce que la littérature?* (1947, 1950 in English) he made clear his belief that literature must serve the same struggle against evil as does the politically aware author. In 1945 he was the cofounder with **Raymond Aron**, Simone de Beauvoir and Maurice Merleau-Ponty of the influential radical journal *Les temps modernes*, which for more than two decades provided a forum for his developing ideas. Believing that authenticity demanded that he should be as free as possible from authoritarian compromises, he consistently refused all official honours, from membership of the Académie Française to the Nobel Prize, yet throughout the 1960s and 70s he commanded a unique position in French public affairs. He also believed that the ideal form of political organisation was the small, shortlived 'rassemblement' and, though he maintained a good working relationship with the French Communist Party, was critical of any sign of rigidity in ideas or organisation. As the Cold War deepened in the 1950s Sartre's political activity intensified, as did his exploration of the links between existentialism and Marxism: the former led to confrontations with authority (*Paris-Match* once called him a 'civil war machine' and the Vatican banned his books, though his status ensured that he was never arrested), the latter to his 1960 *Critique de la raison dialectique* (1976 in English). In **May 1968** Sartre declared himself for small Maoist student-style 'groupuscules' and became editor of the journal *La cause du peuple*, in open defiance of its being banned by the French government. Tireless in his support for total freedom and full personal responsibility in all areas of life, even when these result in pain and acute moral dilemma, Jean-Paul Sartre courageously modelled the ideals he strove to elucidate.

Jean-Paul Sartre, *What is Literature?*, Methuen, 1950
Jean-Paul Sartre, *Being and Nothingness*, Methuen, 1958
Jean-Paul Sartre, *Critique of Dialectical Reason*, New Left Books, 1976
Jean-Paul Sartre, *Sartre in the Seventies: Interviews and Political Essays*, Deutsch, 1978
Ronald Aronson, *Jean-Paul Sartre: Philosophy in the World*, New Left Books, 1980

Olive [Emilie Albertina] Schreiner
1855–1920
novelist, feminist, pacifist

Feminist and novelist Olive Schreiner was born into a large missionary family on a farm on the South Africa/Basutoland (now Lesotho) border. She was educated at home until at the age of fifteen she became a governess. It was also in her teens that she began to write, though her progressive (and at the time extremely controversial) novel *The Story of an African Farm*, in which a woman chooses to have a child on her own, rejects marriage and dies in childbirth, was not published until 1883. In 1881 Olive Schreiner had moved to England in search of a publisher; here she met **Havelock Ellis** and **Edward Carpenter**, both of whom became firm friends. While in England she immersed herself in radical political circles, debating and corresponding at length about women's sexual, spiritual and political needs. In 1894 she returned to South Africa to marry farmer-politician Samuel Cronwright; their only child died shortly after being born. The two now immersed themselves in political activism, condemning the aggressive imperialist policies of both adversaries in the Boer War; Olive Schreiner also worked with suffrage organisations and women's trade unions. She wrote several more books after her return to South Africa, including two volumes of essays, *Women and Labour* (1911) and *Thoughts on South Africa* (1923), and travelled widely, both in Africa and on several occasions to England, where her failing health required specialist treatment. She died, as she wished it, in her native country.

Olive Schreiner, *The Story of an African Farm*, 1883 (many editions since)
Olive Schreiner, *Women and Labour*, Virago, 1978
Ruth First and Ann Scott, *Olive Schreiner*, Women's Press, 1989

Fritz [Ernst Friedrich] Schumacher
1911–1977
economist, environmentalist

Fritz Schumacher's contribution to radical economic thinking has been profound and pervasive, yet the implications of his seemingly simple ideas so threaten the basic assumptions of economic life that he is still often thought of as a crank (though he was fond of pointing out that a crank is an excellent and appropriate tool with which to make revolutions). He grew up in Bonn, where his father was a professor of economics, and almost inevitably became an economist himself, studying in Berlin, Bonn, Oxford, Cambridge and Columbia. While in Berlin in the mid-1930s he met and married Anna Maria ('Muschi') Petersen, with whom he had four children. Unable to complete a degree course, he tried his hand at international trading and investment counselling in Germany before spending the war as an 'enemy alien' working on farms in rural England. In 1949 Fritz Schumacher joined the British National Coal Board (NCB) as an economic adviser, a post which he held for twenty years, but his was no conventional career. When in 1955 he was seconded as a United Nations adviser to Burma he realised that the last thing that country needed was Western-style development; from this experience he developed his concept of 'Buddhist economics', stressing renewable resources, native wisdom and minimal interference. As well as becoming a Buddhist and Gandhian pacifist, he also took up organic gardening (he was later appointed president of the Soil Association) and was a keen proponent of self-sufficiency. Within the NCB he offered advice on energy efficiency, decentralisation and the risks of nuclear power. Muschi died of cancer in 1960, and Fritz married his Swiss *au pair*, Vreni Rosenberger, by whom he had four more children. In 1962 he was invited to India, again to advise on economic development: on his return he developed the idea of an 'intermediate technology' which combined Western research with Third World production and labour to produce appropriate tools and machinery for the needs of poorer countries. Three years later he founded the London-based Intermediate Technology Development Group. Schumacher exploded on the world scene in 1970 with his alternative economics manifesto *Small is Beautiful*, which by the end of the decade had been translated into fifteen languages and sold half a million copies. Its lucid explanation of why growth and development were simply not delivering their promised salvation appealed both to the growing counterculture and to many disillusioned economists and entrepreneurs. The last years of Schumacher's life were spent lecturing and writing for an ever-growing audience: during his 1976 tour of America he spoke to more than 60,000 people. His passionate belief in a humane alternative to mainstream economics inspired a number of Schumacher Societies and the annual Schumacher Lectures, which continue his call for appropriate, human-scale technology and organisation.

E.F, Schumacher, *Small is Beautiful*, Blond and Briggs, 1967
E.F. Schumacher, *A Guide for the Perplexed*, Cape, 1977
E.F. Schumacher, *Good Work*, Cape, 1979
Barbara Wood, *Alias Papa: A Life of Fritz Schumacher*, Harper and Row, 1984

Rosika Schwimmer
1877–1948
women's rights campaigner, pacifist

Feminist, pacifist, internationalist – in all these areas the Hungarian activist Rosika Schwimmer broke new ground and tested the limits of political and social transformation. After training as a musician, Budapest-born Rosika played a prominent part in mobilising Hungarian women to claim their rights. In 1904 she founded the Hungarian Feminist Association (open to women and men), and from 1907 to 1928 edited the feminist journal *A Nö és a Társadalom* (*Woman and Society*, later called simply *A Nö* or *Woman*). Her tireless campaigning both at home and internationally (she spent several months each year travelling and lecturing) played a vital part in winning the vote for Hungarian women in 1920, one of the shortest and most successful suffrage campaigns in the history of the movement. In 1914 Rosika Schwimmer was working as a journalist in London, and became deeply involved in the peace movement, lecturing throughout Europe and North America on the need for mediation and international understanding. Her appeals galvanised several American peace groups into action, including the Emergency Federation of Peace Forces and the Women's Peace Party, and in December 1915 she was able to persuade the automobile magnate Henry Ford to sponsor a 'Peace Ship' to visit countries on both sides of the conflict. Although a combination of impracticability and opposition meant that the ship only reached Christiania (now Oslo), the follow-up conference in Stockholm in February 1916 played an important part in breaking the worldwide censorship of war news and came close to winning Swedish and Danish support for a conference of neutral governments. When Hungary became a democratic republic in 1918, Rosika Schwimmer was appointed as the country's representative in Switzerland, the world's first woman ambassador. A year later the democratic Károlyi regime was overthrown by the communist dictatorship of Béla Kún: Rosika Schwimmer immediately resigned in protest and spent two dangerous years in Hungary before being smuggled down the Danube to Vienna and thence to the USA. Unaware of reactionary sentiment in postwar America, she was shocked to find herself slandered for her peace efforts and refused US citizenship. Stateless for the rest of her life, she launched a campaign for stateless people in 1933. In 1935 she proposed, with **Mary Ritter Beard**, setting up a World Centre for Women's Archives, and in 1937 she established a Campaign for World Government. For the last decade of her life she lived with her sister in New York, and in 1948, shortly before her death, was nominated for the Nobel Peace Prize.

> Rosika Schwimmer and Lola Maverick Lloyd, *Chaos, War or a New World Order? What We Must Do to Establish the All-Inclusive, Non-Military, Democratic Federation of Nations*, Campaign for World Government, 1937
> Edith Wynner, *Rosika Schwimmer: World Patriot*, Dutton, 1947

Rose Scott
1847–1925
social reformer, women's rights campaigner, pacifist

The pioneering Australian feminist Rose Scott, best known for her advocacy of women's and children's rights, grew up on a cattle station in New South Wales and later in Newcastle and Sydney, taught by her mother and looking after her sister's orphaned son (Rose herself never married, explaining that 'life is too short to waste on the admiration of one man'). Her father died in 1879, leaving Rose sufficient means to live the rest of her life in relative comfort. Her campaigning work for women's rights started in 1891, when she was appointed secretary of the newly-formed Womanhood Suffrage League, and by the time her mother died in 1896 Rose had become an accomplished public speaker. She took up the cause of young women working excessive hours, which led to the passing of an early closing act in 1899, and was also instrumental in the appointment of women within the police force and the factories inspectorate, and the improvement of conditions for women prisoners. The vote was granted to Australian women in 1902 and the Suffrage League was disbanded, but in its place Rose Scott organised the League for Political Education, becoming its president in 1910. In 1907 she turned her attention to the pacifist cause, launching the New South Wales Peace Society as a branch of the London Peace Society: she remained its president until almost the end of the first world war. She was still campaigning for social justice not long before her death, her later victories including the establishment of separate children's courts with specially-trained staff and the right of Australian women to equal legal status with men.

Judith Allen, *Rose Scott: Vision and Revision in Feminism*, Oxford University Press, 1994

Marian Sawyer and Marian Simms, *A Woman's Place: Women and Politics in Australia*, Allen and Unwin, 1984

Pete Seeger
1919–
singer, songwriter, pacifist, environmental campaigner

The three Seeger children – Pete, his brother Mike (born 1933) and his sister Peggy (born 1935) – could hardly have had a better background for becoming politically-aware musicians. Their father, Charles Seeger (1886–1979), was a talented composer and ethnomusicologist who stressed the role of song in political resistance; their mother Constance was also a powerful radicalising influence. All the Seeger children became important singer-songwriters, Peggy marrying and collaborating with the English political singer and playwright Ewan MacColl in many concerts and recordings. Pete Seeger, however, is the best known of the three. He grew up in New York and planned to become a journalist, but hearing the five-string banjo at a music festival in Asheville, North Carolina, in 1936 set him firmly on the road to becoming a musician. In March 1940 he met Woody Guthrie at a benefit concert, and they became founder members of the radical musical collective the Almanac Singers, specialising in labour and peace songs. In 1942, the year he married fellow singer Tashi Ohta, he also joined the Communist Party. One of his best known songs, 'If I Had a Hammer' (written with Lee Hays), came out of the depths of the McCarthy era, to be followed in the 50s by such classics as 'Where Have All the Flowers Gone?' and 'We Shall Overcome', the latter becoming the *de facto* anthem of the American civil rights crusade of the 1960s. Pete Seeger, now singing with The Weavers, inevitably came to the attention of the authorities for his 'subversive activities': in 1955 he was subpoenaed by the House Un-American Activities Committee, and in 1961 was found guilty of contempt and sentenced to ten years imprisonment, but his case was dismissed on a technicality. A deeply committed pacifist, he was hurt and offended by US involvement in the **Vietnam War**, and used every opportunity to condemn government policy. Throughout the late 60s and early 70s Pete Seeger continued to record and to perform numerous benefits for a variety of radical causes, but increasingly his attention became focused on environmental issues: the sailing ship *Clearwater*, which he built and launched on New York's Hudson River in 1969, became the symbol of his concern about growing pollution. The Clearwater Campaign, with an annual festival to raise funds to clean up the Hudson River, continues to involve thousands of young people in learning about and working for a cleaner environment; Pete and Toshi Seeger are still involved in the organisation of Clearwater, and new Seeger songs are still being written.

Pete Seeger, *The Incompleat Folksinger*, Simon and Schuster, 1972
David King Dunaway, *How Can I Keep from Singing? Pete Seeger*, McGraw-Hill, 1983

Léopold [Sédar] Senghor
1906–
poet, teacher, politician

For many black francophone Africans Léopold Senghor is a model of the way in which African consciousness and European artistic traditions can fuse to produce exciting new forms of expression, and he is doubly admired for successfully embracing both literary creativity and practical politics. He was raised in the Serer village of Joal on the Senegalese coast and educated in a Catholic mission school. In 1928 he received a scholarship to study in France, and became the first black African to receive a degree from a French university, the Sorbonne. He spent most of the next thirty years teaching and writing in France, using his native artistic forms and traditions to develop poetry characterised by African rhythms, words and images – in the introduction to Senghor's 1948 anthology of black African poetry, *Anthologie de la nouvelle poésie nègre et malgache*, **Jean-Paul Sartre** wrote that 'this is the most powerful revolutionary verse currently being written'. Together with the Martiniquan poet and dramatist Aimé Césaire, whom he met in Paris in the early 1930s, Senghor developed the idea of 'négritude', which he defined as 'the sum total of the values of the civilisation of the African world'. In 1945 his political career began with his election to the French Constituent Assembly as a Senegal deputy; in 1948 he established an independent Senegal-based socialist party, remaining an elected representative to the French government; and in 1960 he was the natural choice to be first president of an independent Senegal. He now had the opportunity to promote his version of 'African socialism', a reformist collectivism that Senghor believes is inherent in traditional African economies, rather than the revolutionary overthrow of capitalism. His approach did little to redistribute his country's wealth, the majority of which is still French-owned, and he was often accused of aligning himself too much with French interests; a widespread drought in the mid-1970s also created economic problems. When Léopold Senghor stepped down from the presidency in January 1981, however, he received wide praise for his gradual and largely peaceful approach to the political and economic transition of Senegal from colonialism to self-determination.

Léopold Sédar Senghor (ed. John Reed and Clive Wake), *Prose and Poetry*, Heinemann, 1976

Léopold Sédar Senghor, *African Sojourn*, Arpel Graphics, 1989

Janet G. Vaillant, *Black, French and African: The Life of Léopold Sédar Senghor*, Harvard University Press, 1990

Huda Shaarawi
1879–1947
feminist activist

Huda Shaarawi, the daughter of an Egyptian sultan and a harem wife, led the early struggle for women's rights in the Middle East. She grew up in a large and wealthy family at Minya in Upper Egypt, and was married to a much older cousin, but received a good private education and read widely. By 1910 she was active in women's organisations, and in 1919 led the first Egyptian women's nationalist demonstration against British rule. In 1923, together with **Saiza Nabarawi** and **Nabawiya Musa**, she attended the **International Woman Suffrage Alliance** conference in Rome, and on their return Nabarawi and Shaarawi publicly removed their veils at Cairo railway station in a symbolic act of emancipation. The same year she founded the Egyptian Feminist Union, acting as its president until 1947. On the international front she was for many years a member of the International Alliance of Women for Suffrage and Equal Citizenship, and became a vice-president in 1935, speaking and taking part in demonstrations throughout the Arab Middle East, Turkey and Europe. In 1938 she called a conference in Cairo to address and defend the Palestinian cause, which was attended by delegates from seven Arab countries; at a follow-up conference in 1944 the Arab Feminist Union was founded, with its news-letter, *al-Mara al-Arabiyya*: for the two years before her death Huda Shaarawi was its president. Her memoirs, which offer fascinating insights into her early years as well as into the strains and achievements of her public life as a feminist activist, were published nearly forty years after her death.

Huda Shaarawi (ed. Margot Badran), *Harem Years: The Memoirs of an Egyptian Feminist, 1879–1924*, Virago, 1986

Leila Ahmed, *Women and Gender in Islam*, Yale University Press, 1992

Margot Badran and Miriam Cooke (ed.), *Opening the Gates: A Century of Arab Feminist Writing*, Virago, 1990

Ali Shari'ati
1933–1977
Islamic liberationist

Iran's turbulent modern history reached a climax with the overthrow in January 1979 of Shah Pahlavi in the so-called Islamic Revolution, led by the exiled Islamic fundamentalist Ayatollah Khomeini. Many Iranian radicals of a variety of persuasions had looked forward to far-reaching social and political change which would accurately reflect the country's cultural and religious heritage, but those who shared the late Ali Shari'ati's liberationist philosophy were to be disappointed by the new government's narrow-minded power struggle which led to another ten years of internecine bloodshed and economic and social hardship. Shari'ati was born in Khorasan (where his father was a socialist-inclined cleric who supported Mohammed Mossadeq's National Front), and went on to study at Meshed University. In 1959 he won a government scholarship to study at the Sorbonne in Paris, arriving at the height of student protest over the Algerian and Congo revolutions. He joined the National Front in exile and the newly-formed Liberation Movement, read and translated **Sartre**, **Guevara** and **Fanon**, and organised numerous demonstrations in support of Third World liberation movements. In 1965, having received his doctorate, Shari'ati returned to Iran, only to be arrested at the border and jailed for six months. On his release he taught in Meshed and published a series of influential lectures entitled *Islamshenasi* (*Islamology*), on the strength of which he was offered in 1969 a teaching post at the prestigious Hosayneih-e Ershad in Tehran. For the three years until the secret police closed the Hosayneih, Shari'ati was its most popular teacher, his lectures on Islamic Marxism being widely reproduced and distributed in print and on tape. He believed that the true message of Islam was liberation, equality and community, which had become subverted to narrow political ends: his ideas appealed to a broad cross-section of Iranian intelligentsia. Soon after the Hosayneih was closed down Shari'ati was arrested and imprisoned. Unable to publish or lecture, in 1977 he was given a passport to leave for England. A month after arriving in London he was dead, according to the authorities of a massive heart attack, though his supporters have always suspected the involvement of the Iranian secret police. Ali Shari'ati's gospel of Islamic liberation was sometimes crude and convoluted, and has frequently been contorted to partisan ends, but his ideas undoubtedly played an important part in the evolution of radical Iranian politics.

Ali Shari'ati (trans. Hamid Algar), *On the Sociology of Islam*, Mizan Press, 1979
Nikki Keddie, *Roots of Revolution*, Yale University Press, 1981
Ervand Abrahamian, *Radical Islam: The Iranian Mojahedin*, Tauris, 1989

Kate Wilson Sheppard [Katherine Malcolm]
1848–1934
social reformer, feminist

In 1893 New Zealand was the first country in the world to grant women the vote on equal terms with men, a fact which is due in no small measure to the efforts of Kate Wilson Sheppard. She was born in Glasgow and raised on the Scottish island of Islay until in 1869, following her father's death, she and her sisters emigrated to Christchurch. Two years later Kate Malcolm married Christchurch city councillor Walter Sheppard, and was soon involved in the suffrage campaign, spearheaded by the Women's Christian Temperance Union of which she became franchise department superintendent in 1885. For the next six years Kate Wilson Sheppard led the New Zealand suffrage campaign, writings leaflets, visiting and corresponding with feminists abroad, and speaking on numerous platforms. Her main achievement was a series of national petitions, the first in 1888, which by 1893 bore more than 30,000 signatures, nearly a third of the adult female population. That and the efforts of a network of Franchise Leagues ensured the successful passage of the 1893 electoral act: New Zealand women voted for the first time in elections later the same year. In 1896 Kate Sheppard organised a conference in Christchurch at which the National Council of Women was founded with her as its president; with breaks from 1899–1905, when she travelled widely in Europe, and from 1907–14 after the organisation hit financial and organisational problems, she remained its president until 1918. In 1909 she was appointed honorary vice-president of the International Council of Women. Walter Sheppard died in 1915 and in 1925 Kate married William Sidney Lovell-Smith, who in 1905 had written a history of the franchise movement in New Zealand; he died in 1929 and she lived for another six years, just long enough to see Elizabeth McCombs elected as New Zealand's first woman member of parliament.

> *The Suffragists: Women Who Worked for the Vote: Essays from the Dictionary of New Zealand Biography* (intro. by Dorothy Page), Bridget Williams Books/Dictionary of New Zealand Biography, 1993

Vandana Shiva
1952–
scientist, environmentalist and ecofeminist

Born in Dehra Dun in the northern Indian state of Uttar Pradesh, the daughter of a Himalayan forester, Vandana Shiva trained as a physicist in India and Canada, but in 1979 decided instead to devote herself to radical environmentalism, feminism and community action. In the late 1970s she was briefly married to biologist Jayanto Bandyopadhyay, with whom she had a son, Kartikeya; her bitter experience of the inequality of opportunity that existed between Indian men and women, and the custody battle after the separation, gave her firsthand experience of the widespread oppression of Indian women and helped form her feminist outlook. Teaching herself forestry, agroscience and biotechnology, she became a learned and determined critic and opponent of Western-style agriculture and development. In 1987 she published a detailed critique of the Tropical Forestry Action Plan, and spent much time in the late 80s travelling throughout rural India talking to and learning from women's experience of practical environmental action. She has been particularly influenced by the **Chipko** 'embrace-the-trees' campaigns in Uttar Pradesh, and in 1990 established the Research Foundation for Science, Technology and Natural Resource Policy, which operates from her home in Dehra Dun. Vandana Shiva forcefully combines feminist analysis with a deep understanding of Indian spiritual and nonviolent traditions, exposing the biased and patriarchal nature of modern science and politics. Throughout the early 90s she travelled widely, becoming well known as a proponent of the radical insights of ecofeminism. Her fluent and passionate 1989 book *Staying Alive: Women, Ecology and Development*, rapidly became a rallying point for ecofeminist ideas, while her 1993 survey, *Ecofeminism* (written with Dutch sociologist Maria Mies), showed clearly how a wide range of issues, from biogenetic diversity to reproductive rights, can be brought together in a common analysis. She is currently a leader in the movement to conserve native seeds and to prevent the patenting of genetic processes. Vandana Shiva was awarded the Right Livelihood Award in 1993 for her contribution to ecofeminism and sustainable development.

Vandana Shiva, *Staying Alive: Women, Ecology and Development*, Zed, 1989
Maria Mies and Vandana Shiva, *Ecofeminism*, Fernwood/Zed, 1993

Upton [Beall] Sinclair
1878–1968
socialist journalist and novelist

Generally considered the greatest socialist writer of his era, Upton Sinclair's novels, plays and essays encapsulated the social and economic concerns of America and turned them into compelling and widely read human dramas. He was born in Baltimore, educated at New York's City College, and spent the first years of his working life as a hack journalist, writing anything that would earn him a little money. It was this exploitative work that gave him an insight into the poverty trap in which so many were incarcerated. A supportive clergyman, George Heron, provided him with the space and income to write his first serious novel, *Manassas*, in 1902. Upton Sinclair joined the Socialist Party in 1904, and remained a convinced but pragmatic socialist all his life, a stance which alienated some of his more radical colleagues. In 1904 he spent seven weeks in the stockyards of Chicago researching conditions in the meat-packing industry. The resulting novel, *The Jungle* (1906), graphically portrayed the appalling working conditions in the meat trade: it quickly became a bestseller and firmly established Sinclair as the best known of the so-called 'muckraking' writers. One of the results of the publication of *The Jungle* was a campaign to regulate the sanitary conditions of the meat industry: because his primary interest had been the poor state of workers' rights, a disappointed Sinclair remarked that he had 'aimed at the public heart, but had by accident hit the stomach'. His novels of the 1910s and 20s, such as *King Coal* (1917) and *Oil* (1927), demonstrated how a combination of careful observation and exciting plot could bring complex social and economic issues vividly to life, while his more polemical works like *The Goose Step* (1923) and *Mammonart* (1925) infuriated the establishment with their critique of capitalism and militarism. In 1934 Sinclair's pragmatic socialist style collided with that of the growing communist movement; when he stood for the governorship of California on a broad socialist coalition ticket (under the banner of End Poverty In California or EPIC) he was only narrowly defeated. His literary output continued unabated, and 1939 saw the first of eleven 'Lanny Budd' novels, describing twentieth-century American history through the eyes of their eponymous protagonist: the third Lanny Budd novel, *From Dragon's Teeth* (1943), won him a Pulitzer Prize, while the action of the last, *The Return of Lanny Budd* (1953), took place against a background of worldwide democratic revolt against state communism. Ever a visionary socialist, Upton Sinclair's prodigious literary output did much to popularise the issues and arguments of the American left.

Upton Sinclair, *The Jungle*, 1906 (many editions)
Leon Harris, *Upton Sinclair: American Rebel*, Crowell, 1975
Eric Homberger, *American Writers and Radical Politics 1900–1939: Equivocal Commitments*, Macmillan, 1986

Walter Sisulu
1912–
freedom campaigner, politician

The influential **African National Congress** (ANC) leader Walter Sisulu grew up in Johannesburg, and joined the ANC's Youth League in 1940 while living in Soweto. In 1948 he married fellow activist, nurse and midwife Albertina Totiwe, with whom he had five children. The ANC's secretary-general in the period after the second world war, he was a close friend and mentor to **Nelson Mandela**, whose first wife, Evelyn Mase, was Sisulu's cousin. Arrested on treason charges in November 1963, he was sentenced with Mandela to life imprisonment at the 1964 Rivonia treason trial and held with him in the prison on Robben Island. Here Walter Sisulu gained a reputation among his fellow prisoners and their guards for dignity and perseverance, urging the inmates to educate themselves and prepare for eventual liberation. Released with a group of longterm political prisoners in October 1989, and reunited with Albertina, he was a dignified spokesman in the continuing campaign to free Nelson Mandela. In March 1990 he was re-elected to the ANC's national executive, and in May joined the negotiating team for the first talks with the government in Cape Town. At the ANC's July 1991 conference he was elected deputy president, a position he still holds. During Walter Sisulu's years in prison, Albertina Sisulu continued to work relentlessly for the freedom struggle. She was first banned for five years in 1964, followed by ten years of house arrest and a further two years of banning. She was also imprisoned several times between 1963 and 1985. In 1983 she was named as one of the three presidents of the broadly-based United Democratic Front. Three of her five children spent years in exile, returning to South Africa in 1990. Her eldest son Max (born in 1945 and first detained with his mother in 1963) studied in the Soviet Union and founded the exiled ANC's department of economic planning in Lusaka, Zambia; another son, Zwelakhe (born 1950), made his mark as a journalist, editing the radical *New Nation* and becoming the focus of human rights campaign efforts when he was imprisoned for two years from 1986 to 1988.

> Walter Sisulu, *The Road to Liberation*, University of Cape Town, 1990
> Fatima Meer, *Higher than Hope: The Authorised Biography of Nelson Mandela*,
>   Hamish Hamilton, 1990

Joe Slovo
1926–1995
lawyer, freedom campaigner

When **Nelson Mandela** was freed from prison in February 1990, his first public speech included a glowing appreciation of Joe Slovo's pivotal role within the **African National Congress** (ANC). Joe Slovo was born into a poor Jewish family in Lithuania, and was ten when he moved to South Africa. His first job was in a warehouse, where he became union shop steward and led his first – successful – strike when he was seventeen. He joined the army in 1944; when he returned he studied law at Witwatersrand University and was called to the Johannesburg bar in 1951. He joined the South African Communist Party (SACP) in 1940, becoming active in 1953 when the party reorganised itself as an underground movement following its banning in 1950. In 1959 he married fellow activist Ruth First, and their home became a meeting place for radicals of all races. In 1961 he was one of the founders of Umkhonto we Sizwe (Spear of the Nation), then an independent organisation which was later to become the ANC's military wing. When most of the top ANC leadership were arrested at Rivonia in 1963 Joe Slovo was abroad; 27 years of exile were to follow. Convinced that the violence of apartheid had to be met with appropriate violence until it was overcome, he spent much of his time in exile as ANC chief of staff (in 1985 he became the first white person on the ANC executive), organising a highly visible militant resistance movement. Based in London and Maputo in Mozambique, he travelled widely to gain support and requisition weaponry; his links with the USSR were strong – and strongly criticised. In August 1982 a parcel bomb sent by the South African police killed Ruth First at Maputo University. In 1987 Joe Slovo became SACP president, relinquishing his Umkhonto role, and by 1990, when he wrote the widely read pamphlet *Has Socialism Failed?*, was moving from a strict Marxist-Leninist stance to a more accommodating – though still unashamedly socialist – line. With the unbanning of the ANC and the SACP in 1990, Joe Slovo was as relieved as anyone to abandon the armed struggle; he continued to work closely with the ANC leadership, and was rewarded in May 1994 with the government post of minister of housing. He quickly came to terms with the practical and political issues surrounding the provision of decent houses for more than half a million poor black families, his reasoned arguments and clear strategies winning the confidence of bankers and homeless alike. He was already suffering from leukemia when elected to the government, and died in January 1995: more than 100,000 people attended his funeral.

Joe Slovo, Basil Davidson and Anthony Wilkinson, *Southern Africa: The New Politics of Revolution*, Penguin, 1976
Joe Slovo, *Has Socialism Failed?*, Inkululeko Publications, 1990

Agnes Smedley
1892–1950
journalist, novelist, feminist

From her birth in rural Missouri into a family of 'poor white scum' (her own words), to her death in exile under suspicion as a spy, Agnes Smedley worked tirelessly to waken the world to the horrors of poverty, ignorance and violence. Her refusal to toe any party line, especially one dictated by wealth and privilege, earned her **Emma Goldman**'s praise as 'an earnest and true rebel'. Her mother died when Agnes was eighteen and her labouring father was often absent, so her education was patchy until at nineteen she enrolled at an Arizona high school. A year later she was married, but in 1916 divorced and moved to New York. Here, working as a secretary, she became involved with **Margaret Sanger**'s birth control movement and also with the Indian nationalist movement: in 1918 she was arrested and imprisoned for espionage. While in jail she wrote short stories, and continued to write when she was released, including articles for *The Call* and Sanger's *Birth Control Review*. In 1920 she went to Germany to live with the exiled Indian revolutionary Virendranath Chattopadhyaya, and helped to set up Berlin's first birth control clinic; when the relationship ended she went into psychoanalysis and wrote *Daughter of Earth* (1929), hailed as the first proletarian feminist autobiography. In 1928 Agnes Smedley made the momentous decision to work as a journalist in China, where she spent most of the next thirteen years, travelling with the Red Army as it fought the Kuomintang. As well as writing five books and more than 300 articles about China, she helped to organise a number of relief organisations and projects and became a personal friend of many Chinese radicals, including the intellectuals Lao She and Liu Liangmo and revolutionaries like Chen Hansheng and **Ding Ling**. Her writings about China made her the best known Western populariser of the Chinese revolution, and it is with justification and understatement that she is sometimes referred to as 'China's **John Reed**'. In 1941 Agnes Smedley returned to the USA, primarily because of ill health, only to find that her links with the communist struggle in China made her a public enemy in her home country. Knowing that she could save herself if she denounced the Soviet Union and the American Communist Party, she refused to do so even though she hated much of what both stood for: always her own woman, she chose carefully whom and what to support or criticise. McCarthyism and accusations of espionage eventually drove her from America: following the communist victory she planned to return to China, stopping first in England. Here, in an Oxford hospital following an unsuccessful operation, she died in May 1950. Even in death she remained controversial, with the FBI and the Chinese government each accusing the other of having murdered her. She was buried in Beijing's Cemetery for Revolutionaries.

Agnes Smedley, *Daughter of Earth*, Virago, 1977 (reissue of 1928 edn)
Agnes Smedley, *Battle Hymn of China*, Feminist Press, 1973 (reissue of 1944 edn)
Agnes Smedley (ed. Janice R. MacKinnon and Stephen R. MacKinnon), *Portraits of Chinese Women in Revolution*, Feminist Press, 1976
Janice R. MacKinnon and Stephen R. MacKinnon, *Agnes Smedley: The Life and Times of an American Radical*, Virago, 1988

Ethel [Mary] Smyth
1858–1944
composer, writer, women's rights campaigner

Although it tends to belittle Ethel Smyth's stature as a composer and campaigner, the best-known episode of her long life – conducting her *March of the Women* with a toothbrush from the window of her Holloway Prison cell following a 1911 suffragette demonstration – is also very characteristic. Had she been a man her musical career would have been much easier, and had she not been a far-from-closet lesbian her 'respectable' colleagues would have found her company and achievements more comfortable, but she was determined to carve herself a highly visible niche on both counts. The daughter of a military family, she grew up in Kent and studied music at the Leipzig Conservatory, where Brahms and Tchaikovsky were important influences. Although she produced a considerable output of excellent music it was hard to persuade concert organisers to perform it and even harder to find a recording company willing to take her seriously: her *Serenade in D* was performed at the Crystal Palace in 1891, followed by her *Mass in D* at the Albert Hall in 1893, yet despite favourable reviews there were only nineteen performances of her major choral works between 1893 and 1933, and only one recording (of her *Wreckers* overture). In 1910 she was introduced to **Emmeline Pankhurst** and devoted much of the next two years to the suffragist cause; she also fell deeply in love with her feminist mentor, and for many years provided a retreat for her at her Sussex cottage. During the 1914–18 war she lived in France and began to write travel books, and also her autobiography, in which she consistently berated the patriarchal British music establishment for its antediluvian attitude towards women. In the latter part of her life she was a close friend of **Virginia Woolf**, whom she met in 1930, and became very deaf, needing an ear trumpet to hear the Sadler's Wells concert held to celebrate her 75th birthday. It is only very recently, with the growing concern that women composers are still virtually invisible, that Ethel Smyth's powerful music has been revived with any sort of regularity.

Ethel Smyth, *Impressions that Remained*, Da Capo Press, 1981 (repr. of 1919 edn)
Christopher St John, *Ethel Smyth: A Biography*, Longman, 1959

Gary Snyder
1930–
poet, essayist, social and environmental campaigner

Best known as a spiritually and environmentally aware poet, Gary Snyder was brought up on his parents' farm north of Seattle, Washington. He attended Reed College, where he refined his interest in radical politics, a process which led him to nonviolent anarchist ideas and a passion for Zen Buddhism. After graduating Snyder became a seaman, worked for the forest service, and did graduate work in linguistics at Indiana University. While studying Chinese and Japanese at Berkeley between 1953 and 1956 he met Allen Ginsberg, Jack Kerouac, Lawrence Ferlinghetti, Tuli Kupferberg and other members of the **Beats**: Kerouac later immortalised Snyder as 'Jaffy Ryder' in *The Dharma Bums*. Gary Snyder spent most of the period between 1956 and 1968 learning the strenuous discipline of Zen in Daitoku-ji, a Buddhist monastery in Kyoto, Japan. His rich yet approachable poems and essays celebrate community, appropriateness, the variety of nature and the importance of recognising and working with its rhythms: they have been collected in a series of volumes including *The Back Country* (1967), *Earth House Hold* (1969), *Turtle Island* (1974), *Axe Handles* (1983) and *No Nature* (1992). Gary Snyder was awarded the Pulitzer Prize for his poetry in 1975. His prose, such as *The Practice of the Wild* (1990), presents a combination of ecological, anarchist, decentralist, bioregional and Buddhist perspectives. He still lives in the mountains of northern California, working with local environmental groups and contributing poems and articles to a wide range of newspapers and magazines.

Gary Snyder, *Earth House Hold: Technical Notes and Queries to Fellow Dharma Revolutionaries*, New Directions, 1969
Gary Snyder, *The Real Work: Talks and Interviews 1964–1979*, New Directions, 1980
David Kherdian, *A Biographical Sketch and Descriptive Checklist of Gary Snyder*, Oyez, 1965
Bob Steuding, *Gary Snyder*, Twayne, 1976
Patrick Murphy, *Understanding Gary Snyder*, University of South Carolina Press, 1992

Aleksandr [Isaevich] Solzhenitsyn
1918–
novelist, political and social critic

Russia's best known twentieth-century novelist, Aleksandr Solzhenitsyn was awarded the 1970 Nobel Prize for Literature 'for the ethical force with which he has pursued the indispensable traditions of Russian literature'.

He grew up in Rostov, looked after by his mother (his father, an artillery officer, died in a shooting accident before Aleksandr was born). He studied mathematics and physics at Rostov University, at the same time pursuing an external literature course with Moscow University and coming increasingly under the influence of Marxist-Leninist orthodoxy. In 1940 he married fellow student Natalya Reshetovskaya, but the outbreak of war the following year parted them. For the next four years he served in the Soviet army, but in February 1945 was arrested for writing critical remarks about Stalin. He was sentenced without trial to eight years hard labour, spent partly in the Marfino special scientific prison (the setting for *The First Circle*), partly at Ekibastuz Prison in Kazakhstan, where he developed skin cancer in 1952 and was transferred to a hospital in Tashkent (the setting for *Cancer Ward*). Pronounced cured, he completed his sentence a year later and moved to Miltsevo in central Russia. Here, reunited with his wife, he wrote *One Day in the Life of Ivan Denisovich* (1962), a description of camp life which brought him immediate recognition, including the approval of Nikita Khrushchev. After Khrushchev's downfall in 1964, however, the KGB began investigations which led to the confiscation of many of Solzhenitsyn's papers and manuscripts (including that of *The First Circle*), and in May 1967 open conflict erupted following his letter to the Fourth National Congress of Soviet Writers, demanding the abolition of censorship, the rehabilitation of writers killed during the purges, and the restoration of his personal papers. The confrontation grew more intense with the publication abroad of *The First Circle* (1968) and *Cancer Ward* (1969), and particularly after the Nobel award. Solzhenitsyn steadfastly continued to write, finishing *The Gulag Archipelago* (a vast survey of the labour camp system based on personal testimony, published in 1974–78) and the first volume, *August 1914* (1971), of the epic historical cycle *The Red Wheel*. His expulsion from the Writer's Union in 1969 was followed by an acrimonious end to his first marriage, a charge of treason, deprivation of his citizenship, and, in February 1974, forcible expulsion. With his new wife Natalya Svetlova (by whom he has had three sons) he settled in Vermont after a short sojourn in Germany and Switzerland, continuing to work on *The Red Wheel* and addressing audiences on the dangers of Soviet communism and Western complacency. Even as Western interest in Solzhenitsyn was declining towards the end of the 1980s, pressure was mounting within Russia for his rehabilitation. In 1989, more than a quarter of a century after *Ivan Denisovich*, his stories and novels were once again beginning to be published in his home country, but it was not until 1994 that he and Natalya returned to Russia. Still able to annoy a wide spectrum of critics who find his ideas too traditional, too radical or too self-centred, his powerful novels and considerable personal influence nevertheless continue to play an important part in Russia's cultural regeneration.

Alexander Solzhenitsyn (trans. Max Hayward and Ronald Hingley), *One Day in the Life of Ivan Denisovich*, Praeger, 1963

Alexander Solzhenitsyn (trans. Thomas Whitney), *The Gulag Archipelago*, Harper and Row, 1974–1978

Leopold Labedz (ed.), *Solzhenitsyn: A Documentary Record*, Penguin, 1970

Stephen Carter, *The Politics of Solzhenitsyn*, Harper and Row, 1977

Michael Scammell, *Solzhenitsyn: A Biography*, Norton, 1984

Wole Soyinka

1934–

playwright, poet, novelist

One of Nigeria's leading writers and an influential critic of official abuse in West Africa, Wole Soyinka was born and grew up in Abeokuta in south-western Nigeria, a childhood vividly portrayed in his *Ake: The Year of Childhood* (1983). He studied at Ibadan and at Leeds University in England, and began his theatre career at the Royal Court in London; his first play was published in 1959. He returned to Nigeria in 1960 and in 1965 was unsuccessfully charged with allegedly forcing Radio Nigeria to broadcast antigovernment propaganda, but increasing harassment as a result of his outspoken criticism of the military regime of General Yacuba Gowon led to his detention in 1967–69. His experience of these years is recorded in *The Man Died* (1972), a classic of prison literature. Since 1970 Wole Soyinka has spent his time writing innovative and acclaimed novels, plays and poetry (he was awarded the Nobel Prize for Literature in 1986), and teaching. From 1976 to 1985 he was professor of comparative literature, and thereafter head of the dramatic arts department at Ife University, and has also been visiting lecturer at other universities in West Africa (Ibadan and Accra), England (Cambridge) and the USA (Yale). During the mid-1980s, following the military coups of Generals Muhammed Buhari in 1984 and Ibrahim Babangida in 1985, Wole Soyinka was once more active in the struggle against dictatorship, which led to the banning of his film *Blues for a Prodigal* (1985). As well as speaking out against arbitrary military power, he has always made it clear that the chief threats to freedom are cultural and religious fanaticism, whether in Nigeria, other parts of Africa, or further afield. A first volume of memoirs, *The Penkelemes Years: 1946–1965* ('penkelemes' is a Yoruba corruption of 'peculiar mess'), was written as a result of his outrage at the annulment of the 1993 presidential elections and his disbelief at the apparently short memories of so many Nigerians.

Wole Soyinka, *The Man Died: The Prison Notes of Wole Soyinka*, Harper and Row, 1972

Wole Soyinka, *The Penkelemes Years: A Memoir 1946–1965*, Methuen, 1994

Wole Soyinka, *Art, Dialogue and Outrage*, Methuen, 1993

Dale Spender

1943–

feminist, teacher, writer

The energetic and prolific Australian feminist writer and editor Dale Spender was born in Newcastle, New South Wales, grew up in Sydney, and taught high school English for nine years before taking a post at James Cook University in 1974. The following year she moved to London, where she started lecturing at London University's Institute of Education. Her growing interest in and involvement with the **women's movement**, and particularly her interest in language and sex, burst into print in the early 1980s with a string of influential books and Spender-edited collections. *Man Made Language* (1980) explored the deepseated reasons for women's apparent silence within male-dominated society; *Invisible Women* (1982) showed how boys almost invariably received privileged attention in the classroom, while girls' needs and interests were systematically undervalued. Her research into the history of the modern women's movement, and interviews and friendships with many older feminists who were active earlier in the century, led to the influential studies *Women of Ideas* (1982) and *There's Always Been a Women's Movement This Century* (1983). Dale Spender's interest in feminist history led to her involvement with the Fawcett Library and several editorships of feminist journals and reference projects, including *Women's Studies International Forum* and the *International Encyclopedia of Women's Studies*. In the late 1980s, following her study of early women novelists, *Mothers of the Novel* (1986), she turned her attention to anthologising and introducing the work of British and Australian women writers, producing such collections as *Writing a New World: Two Hundred Years of Australian Women Writers* (1988), *The Anthology of British Women Writers* (with Janet Todd, 1988), and *The Penguin Anthology of Australian Women's Writing* (1988). Her work in Australia has meant that since 1987 she has spent more time in Sydney than in London, but she still travels widely, and is currently working on the relationship between women, literature and information technology. Dale Spender's fluent, honest and often witty insights have done much to provide the contemporary women's movement with a living history and the intellectual foundations for its further development.

Dale Spender, *Man Made Language*, Routledge and Kegan Paul, 1980
Dale Spender, *Invisible Women: The Schooling Scandal*, Writers and Readers, 1982
Dale Spender, *Women of Ideas, and What Men Have Done to Them*, Routledge and Kegan Paul, 1982
Dale Spender, *There's Always Been a Women's Movement This Century*, Routledge and Kegan Paul, 1983

Starhawk [Miriam Simos]
1951–
author, teacher, political activist

Born and raised in a radical Jewish family in St Paul, Minnesota, Miriam Simos's father died when she was five and the family moved to California when she was ten. She studied at the University of California in Los Angeles, and first met feminist wiccan witches while studying anthropology in the late 1960s. She began practising pagan craft ritual herself, a journey described in the introduction to her first book, *The Spiral Dance* (1979), which established her (and her wicca name of Starhawk) as a lucid and powerful exponent of the contemporary relevance of traditional feminine/ pagan spirituality. It was with *Dreaming the Dark* (1982; new edition 1988) that Starhawk became widely known in radical circles. During the early 80s, together with other pagan activists, she was involved in a series of actions, notably the blockade of the Diablo Canyon nuclear plant in California. In 1981 she was one of the founders of Matrix, a modern coven established at the time of Diablo to introduce the ideas and ceremonies of spiritual empowerment into contemporary social activism, and *Dreaming the Dark* drew on this experience to explore the various strands of power, sex, magic and ritual. Perhaps the most influential of her ideas has been the clear distinction between 'power-from-within' (courage), 'power-over' (control) and 'power-with' (solidarity). In 1986 she cofounded Reclaiming, a pioneering San Francisco-based centre for feminist spirituality and counselling. *Truth or Dare* (1987) built on her previous work to explore the psychological and practical implications of endemic disempowerment, and how it can be countered. Starhawk lives in San Francisco, travelling widely to work on personal empowerment with political and environmental action groups. She is currently writing a second novel, and a resource book for children which draws on the goddess tradition.

Starhawk, *The Spiral Dance: A Rebirth of the Ancient Religion of the Great Goddess*, Harper and Row, 1979

Starhawk, *Dreaming the Dark: Magic, Sex and Politics*, Harper and Row, 1981

Starhawk, *Truth or Dare: Encounters with Power, Authority and Mystery*, Harper and Row, 1987

Gloria Steinem
1934–
feminist writer, editor, lecturer and activist

The American feminist Gloria Steinem was born in Toledo, Ohio, and graduated from Smith College in 1956. After a year of further studies in India, where she was inspired by the Gandhian tradition, she became executive director of the Independent Research Service in Cambridge, Massachusetts, before embarking on a career as a freelance journalist in New York City in 1960. She cofounded *New York Magazine* in 1968, and in 1971 was a founding editor of *Ms.* magazine. It is for her work as a *Ms.* editor and contributor, and as a veteran campaigner for women's rights, that she is best known. During the first half of the 1970s, continuing with her activism in various civil rights, peace and justice, and election campaigns, and earning a doctorate in human justice from Simmons College, she cofounded the Women's Action Alliance, the National Women's Political Caucus, the Ms. Foundation for Women, and the Coalition of Labor Union Women. In 1979 she cofounded Voters for Choice, a nonpartisan political action committee supporting women's right to legal abortion and other areas of reproductive freedom; she currently serves as its president. As a writer and lecturer she has maintained a longterm presence as a radical feminist, not only addressing women's political issues but aiming to empower women in practical ways. Her writing appears in many feminist anthologies and she has published several books, including a collection of articles and essays, *Outrageous Acts and Everyday Rebellions* (1983), and *Revolution from Within: A Book of Self-Esteem* (1992) and *Moving Beyond Words* (1994).

Gloria Steinem, *Outrageous Acts and Everyday Rebellions*, Holt Rinehart and
  Winston, 1983
Gloria Steinem, *Revolution from Within: A Book of Self-Esteem*, Little Brown, 1992
Gloria Steinem, *Moving Beyond Words*, Simon & Schuster, 1994

Marie Stopes
1880–1958
scientist, birth control campaigner

Unlike the birth control pioneers **Margaret Sanger** and Aletta Jacobs, who were mainly interested in the health and economic aspects of excessive childbearing, Marie Stopes' chief concern was that fear of pregnancy should not spoil the enjoyment of sex, a view which put her many decades ahead of her time. She was born in Edinburgh, the daughter of architect Henry Stopes and his feminist wife Charlotte Carmichael Stopes, and was educated at home in London until she was twelve. She went to St George's High School in Edinburgh and then to the North London Collegiate School before gaining a degree in botany and geology from University College London in 1902. She then went to Munich, obtaining her PhD in 1904; the same year, as lecturer in botany, she became the first woman to join the science faculty at Manchester University. She rapidly became an expert on fossil plants, spending 1907–08 researching in Japan and publishing *Ancient Plants* (1910) and a two-volume *Cretaceous Flora* (1913–15). In 1911, while recovering from an attachment to a Japanese professor, she married Canadian botanist Reginald Ruggles Gates in Montreal: the inadequacy of their sex life caused her to read widely on the subject. In 1915 she met Margaret Sanger in London, and agreed to help organise a birth control petition to President Woodrow Wilson. After her marriage was annulled in 1916 on the grounds of non-consummation, she started to campaign and write on birth control and sex education. In 1918 she married the air pilot Humphrey Verdon Roe. Their first child was stillborn, but a second baby, a boy, was born in 1924. Marie Stopes' 1918 books *Married Love* and *Wise Parenthood* caused an uproar, sold millions of copies, and were translated into thirteen languages. Her other books, including *Radiant Motherhood* (1920), *Contraception: its History, Theory and Practice* (1923) and *Enduring Passion* (1928), were also bestsellers. In 1921 she and Humphrey opened Britain's first free birth control clinic in Islington, against intense opposition from the medical establishment and the Catholic Church. Her many legal battles, one of which went to the House of Lords, brought her cause to widespread public attention. In the mid-1930s her second marriage began to deteriorate, and in July 1938 Humphrey agreed to a written statement giving her back her full sexual freedom: several passionate affairs followed between 1939 and 1952. After the second world war she campaigned for birth control in the Far East, and became interested in mysticism, writing several volumes of poetry on the subject. She had for several years maintained that she would live to be a hundred, but in 1957 was diagnosed with cancer and flew to Germany for a 'secret cure': she died a year later. Marie Stopes' fearless and fluent arguments for the availability of sex education and birth control laid the foundations for such organisations as the Family Planning Association, and hastened the widespread availability of birth control advice and assistance in the 1950s and 60s.

Keith Briant, *Passionate Paradox: The Life of Marie Stopes*, Norton, 1962
Ruth Hall, *Marie Stopes: A Biography*, Deutsch, 1977
June Rose, *Marie Stopes and the Sexual Revolution*, Faber and Faber, 1992

Jessie [Mary Grey Lillingstone] Street
1889–1970
feminist, social reformer

Born into an upper class Sydney family, Jessie Street first became interested in women's rights during a visit to England when, at the age of 22, she witnessed the largest suffrage march ever held in that country. Five years later she met the feminist Annie Golding, who was to become a lifelong friend, and she became increasingly involved in women's rights and socialism. In 1938, with her younger sister Phillipa, Jessie visited the Soviet Union, where she saw a degree of women's involvement in politics and the economy which strengthened her resolve to change the role of Australian women. She joined the Labor Party in 1939, and was a founding member of the United Associations of Women – though she never joined the Communist Party she had soon earned herself the title 'Red Jessie'. In July 1941 she was instrumental in establishing the Russian Medical Aid and Comforts Committee, which collected medicines and clothing for the beleaguered Red Army. In the early 1940s she was also one of the leaders of the Australian Women's Charter Movement, campaigning for a strong postwar role for Australian women. Next to women's rights the most important agenda item for Jessie Street was world peace. She was the Australian Peace Council delegate to the 1950 World Peace Congress in Warsaw, and was active in the Australian peace movement throughout the 1950s and 60s. Towards the end of her life she turned her attention to Aboriginal rights, and campaigned passionately in the 1967 referendum which started the slow climb by Australian Aborigines towards the reclamation of their traditional lands.

Jessie Street, *Truth or Repose*, Australasian Book Society, 1966
Peter Sekuless, *Jessie Street: A Rewarding but Unrewarded Life*, Queensland University Press, 1978

Sun Yat-Sen [Sun Wen]
1866–1925
democratic revolutionary campaigner and politician

When Sun Wen was born in Hsiang-Shan in China's Kwangtung province, the ruling Manchu (Qing) dynasty was already tottering under the joint pressures of Western expansionism and internal dissent. The former had led to the capture of Beijing in 1860 and the arrival of the first European missionaries in China, the latter to the Taiping rebellion of 1853. The young Sun, inspired by hearing about the exploits of Kwangtung-born Taiping leader Hung Hsiu-Chuan, resolved to continue the fight against the all-powerful Manchu rulers. After three years at a Christian school in Hawaii he studied medicine in Guangzhou (Canton) and Hong Kong, graduating in 1892. While a student he helped to establish the Hsing Chung Hui (Revive China Society), but was forced to flee China for the USA and Europe when his active involvement was discovered in 1895. In 1896, while in London, he was kidnapped by Chinese diplomats but was able to escape: the episode brought him to the attention of the overseas Chinese community, who began to rally round him as a potential nationalist leader. In 1905 he founded the Tong-Meng Hui (Allied League), and two years later issued the first version of his famous manifesto, *The Three Principles of the People*, the three being nationalism, democracy, and the redistribution of land. By 1911 the strength of feeling against the Manchu regime and its foreign collaborators was ready to erupt in revolution, and Sun Yat-Sen was its obvious leader. One of his main strengths was his ability to understand and embrace the diversity of China's population and aspirations; his integrity and firm belief in equality ensured that his ideas and policies received widespread support, both within China and from neighbouring countries, especially from the postrevolutionary Soviet Union. In 1912 he resigned the presidency in favour of Yuan Shih-Kai, but as Yuan's imperial ambitions became clearer Sun Yat-Sen and his colleagues organised the Kuomintang (National People's Party) to further the egalitarian nationalistic ends of the 1911 revolution. In 1917 and again in 1921 the Kuomintang established a rival government, with Sun Yat-Sen acting as a respected elder statesman until his death in March 1925.

Sun Yat-Sen (ed. F.W. Vrio), *The Three Principles of the People*, China Publishing House, 1981

Paul Myron Linebarger, *Sun Yat-Sen and the Chinese Republic*, AMS, 1969 (repr. of 1937 ed.)

Harold Schiffrin, *Sun Yat-Sen and the Origins of the Chinese Revolution*, University of California Press, 1968

Lyon Sharman, *Sun Yat-Sen: His Life and Its Meaning*, Stanford University Press, 1984

Efua Sutherland [Efua Theodora Morgue]
1924–
playwright, poet, teacher

Efua Sutherland, one of West Africa's best known playwrights, grew up in a Christian family at Cape Coast in what was then the British Gold Coast and is now Ghana. She studied in Ghana and in England, at the universities of Cambridge and London, and in 1951 returned to the Gold Coast to teach. She married her American teacher husband William Sutherland in 1954, and they have three children. For several years she had wanted to establish community and children's theatre in her native land, and in 1958, a year after her country gained its independence, she founded the Ghana Drama Studio in Accra. For more than thirty years Efua Sutherland has worked with communities throughout Ghana to establish village theatres where both new and traditional dramatic forms can flourish: she has always stressed the role of traditional culture and the importance of creative self-reliance, and sees theatre as an important medium for social and political self-reflection. Her blending of community theatre and experimental drama have found expression in a number of plays, the best known of which are *Edufa* (first performed in 1962) and *The Marriage of Anansewaa* (1971).

Efua Theodora Sutherland, *Edufa*, Longman, 1967
Efua Theodora Sutherland, *The Marriage of Anansewaa*, Longman, 1975 (repr. 1987)

Helen Suzman [Helen Gavronsky]
1917–
economist, politician

South Africa's foremost liberal politician was born at Germiston in the Transvaal, the daughter of a Lithuanian Jewish emigrant father and a mother who died when Helen was born. After a convent schooling and an economics degree from Witwatersrand University she worked during the war as a statistician and then returned to Witwatersrand to teach economics. In 1937 she married Moses Suzman, and had two daughters. She entered the South African parliament as a United Party (UP) candidate in 1953, and during her 36 years as an MP (eight as a UP member and then, after the breakaway from the UP in 1961, as a Progressive), she consistently argued the case for liberal reform. For thirteen of those years she was the sole liberal voice in a solidly apartheid government, surviving five prime ministers and six general elections. As well as using her rhetoric and barbed humour to good effect in parliamentary debate, she also worked relentlessly at the grassroots. She visited prisoners and detainees, spent much time in black townships and squatter camps, and consistently confronted ministers, officials and police officers. As she explained in her autobiography, 'I took advantage of my status as an MP to gain access to many places out of bounds to the general public. I put into practice my conviction that, to speak with authority, one must see for oneself.' As a result of her persistent activism Helen Suzman endured hate mail, abuse, threats, telephone tapping and antisemitism, yet she was much admired even by her political opponents. She bowed out of parliamentary politics in 1989, her achievements having been acknowledged and appreciated at the highest level both inside and outside South Africa.

Helen Suzman, *In No Uncertain Terms*, Sinclair Stevenson, 1993

Thomas [Stephen] Szasz
1920–
psychiatrist, teacher, writer

The pioneering psychiatrist Thomas Szasz was born in Budapest in Hungary, emigrating to the USA when he was eighteen. He studied physics and medicine at Cincinatti University, then trained as a psychiatrist and psychoanalyst in Chicago. In the 1960s his name became associated with what he called, in a 1960 article and in his best known book a year later, 'the myth of mental illness'. Based on nearly twenty years of experience as a medic and psychiatrist he asserted that, since psychiatrists cannot agree about the causes and best treatments for schizophrenia, there is every possibility that it is a bogus illness being treated by bogus doctors. He accused psychiatrists of taking on the role of witch-hunters, keeping those who do not fit into society drugged and locked up where they cannot upset the status quo. In a continuous stream of well researched and popularly written books, notably *Law, Liberty and Psychiatry* (1963), *Psychiatric Injustice* (1965), *The Manufacture of Madness* (1970), *Psychiatric Slavery* (1977), *Insanity: The Idea and its Consequences* (1987) and *Cruel Compassion* (1994), Thomas Szasz has continued to question mainstream models of insanity, pinpointing many examples of the use of the 'mad' label to control dissidents and other 'undesirables', and demonstrating how thousands of people are detained against their will on the unsatisfactory grounds that they have a psychiatric illness. He has always argued that people with psychiatric problems must have their needs and actions taken seriously: this means that the most effective treatment will take place only where someone asks for help of their own free will. It also, he argues, implies that 'diminished responsibility' due to insanity is no defence for antisocial and criminal behaviour. Since 1956 Thomas Szasz has been working and teaching at the SUNY Health Centre in Syracuse, New York, where he is professor of psychiatry.

Thomas Szasz, *The Myth of Mental Illness*, Secker and Warburg, 1962
Thomas Szasz, *Insanity: The Idea and its Consequences*, Wiley, 1987
Thomas Szasz, *Cruel Compassion: Psychiatric Control of Society's Unwanted*, Wiley, 1994

Oliver [Reginald] Tambo
1917–1993
lawyer, civil rights campaigner

If there was one individual responsible for successfully shepherding the **African National Congress** (ANC) through the dark period when it was banned by the South African government from 1960 to 1990, it was Oliver Tambo. Born in Cape Province, he became a teacher and then a solicitor, sharing a Johannesburg practice with **Nelson Mandela** from 1951 to 1960. In 1956 he was arrested and charged with treason, together with Mandela, under the Suppression of Communism Act. He became ANC deputy president in 1958, and when the ANC was banned he escaped to London. Over the next thirty years, before he finally returned to South Africa to attend the ANC's December 1990 conference, Oliver Tambo achieved the complex and often depressing task of holding a movement together when it had little more than its own rhetoric to feed on. He spent years travelling around the world encouraging ANC exiles and drumming up support for what must often have felt like a lost cause, an achievement to which Nelson Mandela gave instant recognition when he left prison in 1990 and met his old colleague in Stockholm, insisting that he remain president of the ANC. In the late 1980s, when the ANC's demands were at last being taken seriously by the South African government, Oliver Tambo was central in the drafting of the Harare Declaration, though a stroke in 1989 sapped much of his energy. From then on he played no direct role in formulating policy within the movement, though he remained chairman until his much mourned death in April 1993.

Oliver Tambo, *Oliver Tambo Speaks: Preparing for Power*, Heinemann, 1987
E.S. Reddy (ed.), *Oliver Tambo and the Struggle Against Apartheid*, Sterling, 1987

Tanaka Shōzō
1841–1913
social reformer, environmentalist

Tanaka Shōzō, Japan's pioneer 'green activist', was the son of the headman (*shōya*) of a village in Tochigi prefecture, north of Tokyo. He succeeded his father in his twenties, and for the next twenty-five years entered what he later called his 'university period'. On three separate occasions he found himself pitted against local official corruption, was wrongly convicted, jailed and tortured – and was later proved innocent. His experiences of attempting to work as a just administrator within a dishonest regime made him determined to fight for the rights of relatively powerless individuals and communities. During the 1870s he helped to launch one of Japan's first liberal newspapers, *Tochigi Shimbun*, in 1886 he was asked to become chairman of the Tochigi prefectural assembly, and in 1890 he was elected by a large majority as a member of Japan's first Diet (the parliament inaugurated by the Meiji Constitution of 1889). Almost immediately he was thrown into the first of several anti-pollution battles. A large area of the

Kantō Plain to the north-east of Tokyo was being poisoned by effluent from the massive copper mine at Ashio. Tanaka called for the government to close down the mine, but little notice was taken. As the years went by more and more peasants suffered from the effluent; even though he was able in 1897 to persuade the government to impose stringent pollution control measures these had little effect, and in 1901 he resigned in disgust. Two years later the Japanese government unveiled plans to build a huge dam project on the Watarasegawa River above the Kantō Plain; this involved the destruction of the ancient village of Yanaka. Tanaka Shōzō led the campaign against the building of the dam, living for three years with the Yanaka villagers; in 1907, however, the last houses were pulled down. The final years of his life were spent attempting to persuade whoever would listen that lasting solutions arise from a loving understanding of the natural environment and the people who have lived in it all their lives. He walked hundreds of miles studying the Japanese landscape, and died in a peasant's hut. Although the government in Tokyo had forgotten about the 'mad river man', more than 50,000 people gathered for his funeral.

Kenneth Strong, *Ox Against the Storm: A Biography of Tanaka Shozo, Japan's Conservationist Pioneer*, University of British Columbia Press, 1977

Peter Tatchell
1952–
gay rights activist

The influential gay rights activist Peter Tatchell was born in Melbourne, Australia: inspired by press reports of the first gay liberation protests in New York, he came out as gay in 1969. Two years later he moved to England and immediately became involved in the Gay Liberation Front. In 1972 he led a campaign to interrupt lectures by the psychiatrist Hans Eysenck, who endorsed the use of electric shock aversion therapy for homosexuals, and the following year spoke at the World Youth Festival in East Berlin, the first time anyone had publicly advocated the ideas of lesbian and gay liberation in a communist country. When in 1983 Peter Tatchell stood as a Labour candidate in the Bermondsey by-election in south London he was vilified for advocating lesbian and gay rights and subjected to media smears and violent attacks, an experience described in his book *The Battle for Bermondsey*. In 1987 his lobbying of the **African National Congress** resulted in that organisation officially renouncing homophobia, making its first public commitment to homosexual equality, and accepting constitutional proposals which resulted in the post-apartheid constitution explicitly guaranteeing nondiscrimination on the grounds of sexual orientation. The same year he founded the UK AIDS Vigil Organisation and drafted the world's first comprehensive 'AIDS and Human Rights Charter'. In 1989 he was a founding member of London ACT-UP (**AIDS Coalition To Unleash Power**), and in 1990 of the lesbian and gay direct action group OutRage. In 1991 Peter Tatchell lodged a formal complaint against the European Community (EC), arguing that by failing to include lesbian and gay people in its antidiscrimination initiatives the EC was violating its obligations to ensure equality and human rights. Following this complaint, the EC conceded its legal competence to enact policies protecting lesbians and gay men against discrimination, and introduced its first initiatives to tackle homophobia in the workplace. Based in London, Peter Tatchell remains a high-profile lecturer, author, broadcaster, journalist, researcher and activist on issues of concern to the lesbian and gay community.

Peter Tatchell, *The Battle for Bermondsey*, Heretic/GMP, 1983
Peter Tatchell, *Europe in the Pink: Lesbian and Gay Equality in the New Europe*, GMP, 1992

Tenzin Gyatso [Dalai Lama]
1935–
spiritual leader and peace and civil rights advocate

The unbroken line of Dalai Lamas, Tibetan heads of state and religious leaders, dates back to Gedun Truppa (1391–1475), though the title itself (meaning 'ocean of wisdom') was first used in the sixteenth century. Each is believed to be a reincarnation of the previous Dalai Lama, and the succession is chosen by oracle and testing following the death of the previous holder of the title. Tenzin Gyatso, then a boy of two living in the remote village of Takster, was thus selected as Tibet's fourteenth spiritual and temporal leader, and taken at the age of four to live in the royal palaces of Potala and Norbulingka in Lhasa. In 1949 the Chinese army invaded and occupied Tibet, and started to dismantle Tibetan culture in the name of 'progress'. Though only sixteen, two years younger than is customary, Tenzin Gyatso became the country's head of state. He travelled widely in China and India, visiting **Mao Zedong** and the site of **Gandhi**'s cremation (where he vowed to devote his life to nonviolence), but the situation in Tibet deteriorated rapidly. In 1959, fearing for his life, he was forced to leave Lhasa, and was offered sanctuary by the Indian government. At Dharamsala in the Himalayan foothills of Himachal Pradesh the Tibetan community established a government in exile (the Kashag), and a small town complete with schools, libraries and colleges. Charged with preserving Tibetan life and culture against the tyranny of Chinese hegemony, the Dalai Lama has travelled widely, taking every opportunity to advance the Tibetan cause. He has consistently refused Chinese offers to allow him to return from exile on the condition that he stays in Beijing; in return the Chinese government pointedly rejected a five-point peace plan he presented to the US Congress in September 1987 and to the European parliament in March 1988. In 1989 he was awarded a Nobel Peace Prize. He continues to work untiringly for the liberation of Tibet. In the early summer of 1993 a world tour included meetings with US president Bill Clinton and Polish leader Lech Wałęsa; a second meeting with the US president and vice-president in April 1994 led to renewed US demands on China to open realistic negotiations about the future of Tibet.

Dalai Lama, *My Land and My People*, Potala, 1983
Dalai Lama, *Freedom in Exile*, Hodder, 1990
Whitney Stewart, *To the Lion Throne: The Story of the Fourteenth Dalai Lama*,
   Snow Lion, 1991

Thich Nhat Hanh
1926–
spiritual teacher, poet, peace activist

Thich Nhat Hanh was born in a village in central Vietnam, becoming a Buddhist monk when he was sixteen. He soon found the traditional monastic training limited and stifling, and together with a few friends he moved to Saigon, where they lived in an abandoned temple and edited Buddhist books and newsletters; he had published four books before he was twenty years old. In 1952 he founded the first Buddhist high school in Vietnam, and in 1959 was one of the founders of Van Hanh Buddhist University in Saigon. For two years from 1961 he studied comparative religion at Princeton and Columbia Universities in the USA, returning in 1963 to a wartorn Vietnam. His important book *Engaged Buddhism*, published in 1963, exhorted Buddhists to work actively but nonviolently for peace and social justice. In 1966 Thich Nhat Hanh toured Europe and the USA in an effort to educate and explain the need for peace in Vietnam; among others he met and impressed **Martin Luther King**, Jr. His frankness and evenhanded condemnation during this extended tour made it impossible for him to return to Vietnam, and he was granted asylum by the French government; a hermitage in south-western France has been his home in exile ever since. Following the end of the war in 1975, Thich Nhat Hanh helped to organise an underground network of engaged Buddhists who distributed aid and assisted refugees; his French home has since become a centre for a growing number of peace activists and initiatives. In 1977 he entered a five-year period of retreat, which provoked the Vietnamese government twice to announce that he had died. He continued to be an influential advocate for human rights, and in 1982 started to travel again, teaching the techniques of conscious engagement to a growing number of students. It is largely due to him that Buddhism, as a socially engaged and politically aware spiritual movement, has influenced many thousands of social activists, especially in the USA, where he now spends much of his time.

Thich Nhat Hanh, *Being Peace*, Parallax, 1987
Thich Nhat Hanh, *Be Still and Know: Meditation for Peacemakers*, Pax Christi, 1987
Catherine Ingram, *In the Footsteps of Gandhi: Conversations with Spiritual Social
   Activists*, Parallax, 1990

Ngugi wa Thiong'o [James Ngugi]
1938–
writer, teacher, political activist

Kenya's foremost modern novelist, playwright and political commentator, Ngugi wa Thiong'o was born and grew up in Limuru near Nairobi, and studied at Makarere University in Uganda and Leeds University in England. His first novel was published in 1964: *Weep Not, Child* is the harrowing story of a Kenyan family caught in the grip of the 1950s Mau Mau emergency, and was an immediate success; many of his later novels and plays examine how Kenyan politics have affected the lives of ordinary people. In 1967 he started teaching literature at Nairobi University, where he was appointed professor in 1971. His outspoken political views, and particularly his criticism of official corruption and the random infringement of civil rights, inevitably brought him into conflict with the authorities, and he was imprisoned for a year from January 1978, over the period of Kenyatta's death and Daniel arap Moi's takeover: his journal of that time, *Detained*, was published in 1981. Ngugi wa Thiong'o had long emphasised the importance of using African traditions and languages in the expression of African culture, and in 1980–81 he worked with the villagers of Kamiriithu in central Kenya to produce a musical drama in Kikuyu and other tribal languages. *Maitu Njugira (Mother, Sing for Me)* was due to open at the National Theatre in Nairobi in February 1981, but at the last minute the police and theatre management were instructed to prevent the production from taking place. Fearing for his life, Ngugi wa Thiong'o left Kenya for England, and has been an exile ever since, writing and teaching at universities in Europe and North America. In 1986, having made the decision to write fiction only in his native Kikuyu, he set out his concerns about the disappearing culture of Africa in *Decolonising the Mind*, a theme taken up in *Moving the Centre: The Struggle for Cultural Freedoms* (1993). In a recent novel, *Matigari* (published in 1989 and immediately banned in Kenya), he wrote about an African rebel leader working to overthrow a capitalist system that is even worse than colonialism; in the early 1990s the Kenyan socialist underground movement Mwakenya named Ngugi wa Thiong'o as one of its inspirations.

Ngugi wa Thiong'o, *Detained: A Writer's Prison Diary*, Heinemann, 1981
Ngugi wa Thiong'o, *Decolonising the Mind*, Currey, 1986
Ngugi wa Thiong'o, *Moving the Centre: The Struggle for Cultural Freedoms*, Currey, 1993
Biodun Jeyifo: *Ngugi wa Thiong'o: Literature for the Revolution*, Pluto, 1993

E.P. [Edward Palmer] Thompson
1924–1993
historian, socialist and peace campaigner

The younger of two sons of a progressive missionary family recently returned from India, Edward Thompson grew up in Oxford, England, where

Mohandas Gandhi and Jawaharlal Nehru were amongst the steady flow of Indian visitors. He went to Cambridge University, where he (like his brother Frank at Oxford) joined the Communist Party. While Edward was serving in North Africa and Italy as a tank commander, Frank was captured and executed for supporting the anti-Nazi partisans in Bulgaria. In 1946 Edward returned to Cambridge to finish his history degree, and in the summer of 1947, after a visit to Bulgaria with his mother, spent several weeks working with young socialists from all over Europe on the Great Yugoslav Youth Railway Project. In 1948 he moved to Leeds to work as a tutor in history and literature. Here he married another social historian, Dorothy Towers, who was to be his lifelong intellectual and activist collaborator; they and their three children remained in Yorkshire until 1965. This did not, however, prevent him from taking a full part in the movement that became the British **new left**. In 1956, disgusted by Khrushchev's attitudes and policies, he resigned from the Communist Party, and founded *The Reasoner*, the first of several important publications he helped to establish. 1964 saw the publication of his best known book, *The Making of the English Working Class*, with its vivid portrayal of generations of workers locked into the industrial machine. The success of the book helped to secure him the Directorship of the Centre for Social History at the newly-established Warwick University in 1965, but his growing criticism of the business ethos of the university forced his resignation in 1971. Through the 1970s he continued to write social history, and became increasingly associated with the humane, pragmatic face of neo-Marxism, passionately criticising in numerous articles and in his book *The Poverty of Theory* (1978) what he saw as the sterility of verbose theorising. During this period his attention also turned to the growing threat of nuclear war. As well as *Writing by Candlelight*, a powerful exposé of the rhetoric of nuclear politics, 1980 saw the publication of *Protest and Survive*, a response (coauthored with Dan Smith) to the official whitewash guide to nuclear war, *Protect and Survive*. E.P. Thompson went on to become a vice-president of the **Campaign for Nuclear Disarmament** and to devote much of his time to the European peace movement. In his collected essays, *Customs in Common* (1991), he wrote of the importance of the movement in dispersing the 'polluting cloud' of the Cold War. After a long illness, exacerbated no doubt by overwork, he died in August 1993.

E.P. Thompson, *The Making of the English Working Class*, Gollancz, 1964

E.P. Thompson, *The Poverty of Theory*, Merlin, 1978

E.P. Thompson, *Writing by Candlelight*, Merlin, 1980

E.P. Thompson, *Customs in Common*, Merlin, 1991

Bryan Palmer, *The Making of E.P. Thompson: Marxism, Humanism and History*, New Hogtown Press, 1981

Pramoedya Ananta Toer
1926–
novelist, political commentator

Pramoedya Ananta Toer is Indonesia's best-known writer and social critic, though his books have been banned by the repressive Suharto dictatorship and he has spent most of the last thirty years in prison or else in severely restricted confinement. His experience under Suharto, however, was by no means his first taste of official displeasure: he also has the unique distinction of having been imprisoned by the Dutch in 1947–49 as a nationalist revolutionary and by the Sukarno regime in 1961 for publicly defending the Chinese minority in Indonesia. Pramoedya Ananta Toer (generally known as 'Pram') grew up in Blora on the north coast of East Java, where his schoolteacher father and devoutly Islamic mother instilled in him the importance of community responsibility. After school he trained as a radio operator, and during the Japanese occupation of 1942–45 worked for the Japanese news agency Domei. In August 1945 he joined the nationalist army, and in 1947 was appointed head of the publications section of the Voice of Free Indonesia. His nationalist views led to his arrest and imprisonment: he was released when Indonesian independence was finally granted in December 1949, spending his time in prison writing *The Fugitive*, a novel about the ongoing struggle for freedom in Indonesia. During the 1950s Pram ran his own news agency in Jakarta and, although never officially a communist, became a member and leading spokesman for the party's cultural wing Lembaga Kebudayaan Rakyat (LEKRA). His growing support for leftwing causes, and particularly his enthusiasm for Chinese-style communism, brought him into conflict with the Sukarno government in 1961, when he spent another period in prison, but in general he was passionately supportive of the socialist government's policies. In September 1965 a military coup led to massive bloodshed and the imprisonment of thousands suspected of having communist sympathies: Pramoedya's house in Jakarta was burnt down and he was imprisoned on the remote Moluccan island of Buru. For eight years he was denied writing materials, but instead created oral novels that were passed around the camp. In 1980 *This Earth of Mankind* and *A Child of All Nations* were published from smuggled manuscripts: they both became bestsellers, but were quickly banned, as were the other two volumes of the 'Buru Tetralogy'. In 1980 the final Buru prisoners was released, but ever since then Pramoedya Ananta Toer has remained under virtual house arrest in East Jakarta with his wife and three children.

Pramoedya Ananta Toer (trans. Harry Aveling), *The Fugitive*, Heinemann, 1975
Pramoedya Ananta Toer (trans. Max Lane), *This Earth of Mankind*, Penguin, 1981
Swami Anand Haridas, 'Pramoedya Ananta Toer', *Index on Censorship*, 5/1978
Suzanne Charlé, 'Prisoner Without a Cell', *The Nation*, 3 February, 1992

Camilo Torres [Restrepo]
1929–1966
priest, social reformer, revolutionary

Many Latin American clergy have stressed that religious duty and social responsibility go hand in hand, even to the extent of direct confrontation with the power élite: few have been prepared to stand by their principles to the extent of Colombian priest Camilo Torres. He was born into a privileged Bogotá family (his father a pediatrician, his mother a campaigner for women's rights); in 1947 he entered the Seminario Concilar de Bogotá to study for the priesthood, and in 1954 transferred to the Catholic University of Louvain in Belgium. His early religious studies had convinced him of the importance of true neighbourly love, and while at Louvain he was much influenced by the French worker-priest movement; he also read widely in Marxism and sociology. Returning to Colombia in 1958, he was appointed lecturer and chaplain at the National University in Bogotá, the following year helping to establish the country's first sociology department. It was a student strike at the University in the wake of the **Cuban Revolution** that radicalised the already-popular Camilo Torres. In June 1962 he publicly objected to the dismissal of ten student leaders, immediately becoming a hero of the struggle against authority: he was forced to resign, but was at once offered a teaching post at the Higher School of Public Education, where he threw himself into the establishment of co-operatives and grassroots training projects. By 1964 he saw his task as uniting Colombia's political opposition into the Frente Unido (United Front), and in May 1965 became *de facto* leader of the populist front. His ostracism from the church was now inevitable, and he was laicised the following month. Camilo Torres now worked hard to build up the Frente Unido, travelling the country to lecture, organise and write in favour of a broad-based revolution. Although support from workers and students was widespread, the sect-ridden Frente Unido began to collapse, and Torres was offered government bribes to leave the country. He felt that the only choice remaining to him was to join Fabio Castaño's ELN (Ejército de Liberación Nacional; National Liberation Army), explaining in a January 1966 'Message from the Mountains' his belief that armed struggle was now the only way to liberation. He was killed in a raid in Santander province a month later. Throughout Colombia's subsequent history of repression and violence, Camilo Torres's faith in the social gospel has remained a beacon of hope to those who would build true democracy in Colombia.

Camilo Torres (ed. John Grassi), *Revolutionary Priest: The Complete Writings and Messages of Camilo Torres*, Random House, 1971

Camilo Torres, *Revolutionary Writings*, Harper and Row, 1972

German Guzman, *Camilo Torres*, Sheed and Ward, 1969

Walter J. Broderick, *Camilo Torres: A Biography of the Priest-Guerillero*, Doubleday, 1975

Robert Tressell [Robert Phillipe Noonan]
1870–1911
signwriter and housepainter, socialist campaigner, writer

Robert Tressell's only novel *The Ragged Trousered Philanthropists*, published three years after his death, was the first important work to give an authentic account of the nascent class struggle in Edwardian Britain. Tressell, whose real name was Noonan, grew up in Ireland; when his family fell on hard times after his policemen father died, Robert emigrated to South Africa in 1890, where he married and started working as a builder and housepainter. In 1902 he returned to the British Isles and settled in the English south coast town of Hastings with his sister Adelaide and daughter Kathleen, working as a signwriter for several local building firms. He joined the Social-Democratic Federation (a forerunner of the Labour Party), and played an active part in local politics. His experiences in the building trade and his understanding of the socialist dream provided the material for *The Ragged Trousered Philanthropists*, in which Hastings was transformed into Mugborough and the action described a year in the lives of a group of working men and their families. Debates on socialism, employment and capitalism were skilfully interwoven with a sympathetic yet unromantic portrayal of the decorating and undertaking business, the chief protagonist being the journeyman-visionary Frank Owen. The 'philanthropists' of the title were the workers who toiled for pitiful wages at their 'noble and unselfish task' of making money for their employers, yet made no effort to understand or better their situation. Despite the later success and influence of his novel, Robert Noonan found it impossible to interest a publisher in his book: disillusioned, he decided in 1910 to emigrate to Canada. His health, which had never been good, deteriorated *en route*, and he died of tuberculosis in a Liverpool workhouse hospital the following February. An abridged version of *The Ragged Trousered Philanthropists* was published in 1914, and over the next forty years it became a classic text of the Labour movement. In 1946 the original handwritten manuscript was rediscovered, showing that the first published version had been much altered and given a pessimistic ending: the new edition – as written by Noonan – appeared in 1955, and has continued to inspire those who believe in a more just and socially aware society.

Robert Tressell, *The Ragged Trousered Philanthropists*, 1914 (revised edition 1955; many editions since)

Frank Swinnerton, *The Adventures of a Manuscript, Being the Story of The Ragged Trousered Philanthropists*, Richards, 1956

Jack Mitchell, *Robert Tressell and The Ragged Trousered Philanthropists*, Lawrence and Wishart, 1969

Frederick Cyril Ball, *One of the Damned: The Life and Times of Robert Tressell, Author of The Ragged Trousered Philanthropists*, Weidenfeld and Nicolson, 1973

Leon Trotsky [Lev Davidovich Bronshtein]
1879–1940
Marxist activist and writer, politician

Leon Trotsky is one of the most important revolutionary socialists of the twentieth century, his ideas presaging and helping to explain the course of the international radical left. He grew up in a well-off Jewish farming family in the Ukraine, graduating from agrarian socialism to Marxism and becoming a cofounder of the South Russian Workers Union in the late 1890s. In 1898 he was arrested, and in 1902 fled for England to join **Lenin** on the staff of the émigré journal *Iskra (The Spark)*. Early in 1905 he returned to Russia and became the chairman of the first St Petersburg Soviet, but was arrested again and spent two years in prison. Here he wrote *Results and Propositions* (1906), in which he originally propounded the idea of 'permanent revolution'. Until this time the followers of Marx had assumed that revolution would erupt in countries where capitalism was the most advanced; Trotsky presciently suggested that it was more likely to occur in a country like Russia, where a peasant society would be led by a highly concentrated industrial working class. He also made clear his belief that such a revolution would have to occur in more than one country for change to be viable and permanent, an idea which was to bring him into direct conflict with Stalin's 'socialism in one country'. Trotsky again escaped from Russia in 1907 and settled in Vienna, writing anti-imperialist and antiwar articles and organising the 1915 Zimmerwald Conference of European antiwar socialists. He returned to St Petersburg (now renamed Petrograd) after the February 1917 revolution and quickly aligned himself with Lenin's Bolsheviks. Harnessing his considerable organisational and oratorical skills, Leon Trotsky become the chief architect of the October 1917 revolution, and was rewarded with the post of commissar of foreign affairs in the first Lenin cabinet. Soon the erstwhile antiwar socialist was in charge of organising a new 'Red Army', first to fight a civil war and then, in 1921, to attempt an invasion of Poland. Ever a resourceful pragmatist, Trotsky used the Red Army's defeat and the resultant economic and social turmoil to propose a radical new economic policy which would combine elements of state planning and small-scale capitalism. Were it not for Lenin's death in 1924 Trotsky might have succeeded in his reforms, but Stalin's ascendance ensured otherwise. Leon Trotsky was exiled to Alma-Ata in 1927 and deported the following year, travelling via Turkey and Norway to Mexico. Though it took him some time to understand the implications of the Stalinist regime, by the mid-1930s Trotsky had become fluently vocal in his denunciation of what he saw as the betrayal of the 1917 revolution, and in 1938 was the main organiser of the Fourth **International** in opposition to the Moscow-based Third **International**. Still optimistic that socialist revolution was possible and that a genuine Soviet workers' state could survive Stalin, Leon Trotsky was assassinated by one of Stalin's hitmen at his Mexican home in Coyoacan in August 1940. Trotsky's name is still anathema to many Russians today, and his ideas have suffered with the general demise of Marxism, yet he is widely acknowledged as one of the most consistent of Marxist-Leninist practitioners and as a highly talented and influential writer and polemicist.

Leon Trotsky, *The History of the Russian Revolution* (many editions)

Leon Trotsky, *My Life*, Grosset and Dunlap, 1960

Isaac Deutscher, *The Prophet Armed*; *The Prophet Unarmed*; *The Prophet Outcast*, Oxford University Press, 1954, 1959, 1963

B. Knei-Paz, *The Social and Political Thought of Leon Trotsky*, Oxford University Press, 1978

Tsuda Umeko
progressive educator
1865–1929

Japan's foremost pioneer of women's education was born and grew up in Tokyo, the daughter of a *samurai* father who became an expert in Western agricultural techniques. In 1871, at the age of six, Tsuda Umeko was one of five girls among a group of 54 students to be offered an education in the United States, and lived with a family in Washington DC. She returned to Japan in 1882, becoming a private tutor and then a teacher in a newly-opened school for the daughters of the nobility. Determined that further education should be more widely available for Japanese women, she went back to the United States in 1889 for three years to study education at Bryn Mawr College in Pennsylvania. By 1900 she had sufficient resources to establish her own Women's English School (Joshi Eigaku Juku). Although it began with only ten students, it grew quickly and made an important contribution to providing women with acceptable and stimulating careers as secondary level English teachers. When Tsuda Umeko died her college was renamed the Tsuda English School (Tsuda Eigo Juku) and moved to a new site in Kodaira, to the east of Tokyo. Tsuda College (Tsuda Juku Daigaku), as it was renamed in 1949, is now a leading women's university, with an internationally-known Research Institute of Language.

Desmond [Mpilo] Tutu
1931–
clergyman, civil rights campaigner

Grinning and whooping as he cast his vote in South Africa's first free election in April 1994, Archbishop Desmond Tutu's years of campaigning against apartheid at last appeared vindicated. Born in Klerksdorp in the southern Transvaal, Desmond Tutu was educated in South Africa and England before becoming an Anglican parish priest in the Transvaal in 1960. His quiet but stubborn advocacy of nonviolent protest, together with his obvious concern for the plight of South Africa's black majority, gained him widespread popularity as he rose to become dean of Johannesburg in 1975 and bishop of Lesotho in 1976. He went on to become South Africa's first black general secretary of the South African Council of Churches in

1979, the first black bishop of Johannesburg in 1984 (also the year he was awarded a Nobel Peace Prize), and the first black Anglican archbishop of Capetown in 1986 – his increasing authority making it ever harder for the government to stifle his calls for an end to white domination. He roundly condemned President P.W. Botha's state of emergency in April 1987 and advocated a boycott of the 1988 segregated-race municipal elections; in early 1988 he was briefly held in detention. Following the succession of Botha by F.W. de Klerk in February 1989, Desmond Tutu took the opportunity to speak out more forcefully for the abolition of apartheid, and in September of that year he led the 'March for Peace' through Cape Town. Following **Nelson Mandela's** release from prison in February 1990 Archbishop Tutu ceded some of the limelight to Mandela and de Klerk, but has continued to work and pray for peace and justice in South Africa, particularly stressing the need for forgiveness and reconciliation.

> Desmond Tutu, *Hope and Suffering: Sermons and Speeches* (Mothobi Mutloatse and John Webster ed.), Fount, 1984
> Desmond Tutu, *Crying in the Wilderness: The Struggle for Justice in South Africa*, Mowbray, 1990
> Desmond Tutu, *The Rainbow People of God: South Africa's Victory over Apartheid*, Doubleday, 1994
> Shirley du Boulay, *Tutu: Voice of the Voiceless*, Hodder, 1988

U Thant
1909–1974
educationalist, United Nations official

The United Nations' third Secretary General, the Buddhist Burmese diplomat U Thant, was elected in 1962 at a time when the nature of the UN's leadership was being deeply questioned. The Soviet Union had withdrawn its support from the Swede Dag Hammarsköld, who was killed in a plane crash in the Congo during a peace mission, and had it not been for U Thant's international reputation for integrity and impartiality the UN might well have been led by a triumvirate from that period onwards. U Thant grew up in Pantanaw and was educated at Rangoon University before becoming a teacher in his home town. On Burmese independence in 1948 he was appointed to a ministry post in the department of education, and in 1957 he became Burma's permanent representative at the United Nations. As a Buddhist, he was trained to be modest and to cherish compassion and evenhandedness, qualities which would serve him well as United Nations leader. He had the foresight to recognise, even in the 1960s, that the main barriers to international peace and cooperation were wealth and military power, rather than the conflict between communism and democracy, and used his position to encourage dialogue, mutual respect and absolute discretion. He played an important part in the resolution of the Cuban missile crisis in 1962 and in the ending of the 1964 war in Cyprus, and in the late 1960s he made several personal attempts to bring the factions involved in the Vietnam War to the negotiating table. Perhaps his most remarkable success was the 1965 ceasefire following the war between India and Pakistan, and the successful UN presence along the border while the area was demilitarised. He was not so fortunate during the Middle East 'Six-Day War' of May 1967, when Egypt insisted on the removal of the UN Emergency Force along the Egypt-Israel border and Israel refused to have the force stationed on its territory: U Thant was widely blamed for having escalated the war, though most historians now believe that he had little choice. His term as UN secretary general ended in 1971, when the Austrian Kurt Waldheim took over the office, and U Thant died in New York three years later.

U Thant, *View from the UN*, Doubleday, 1978
June Bingham, *U Thant of Burma*, Gollancz, 1966

János Vargha
1950–
environmentalist and social activist

János Vargha was only six years old when Soviet tanks rolled into Budapest, the Hungarian capital, but in 1981, by now a biologist and journalist, he was one of the first Hungarians to openly criticise the pro-Soviet government, thus playing a small but crucial part in the overthrow of Stalinist regimes from Berlin to Bucharest. In 1977 the Hungarian and Czech governments signed an agreement to build a series of dams along the River Danube (their shared border) to generate hydroelectricity, including one at Nagymaros on the scenic Danube Bend. In 1980 János Vargha joined the staff of the environmental magazine *Buvar* to work alongside his respected environmentalist colleague Anna Varkonyi; one of his first articles, a detailed criticism of the dam project, was banned. In 1981 he started to edit *Tudomany*, the Hungarian edition of *Scientific American*, where he printed the article in full, and in August of that year was one of the founders of the influential environmental pressure group Duna Kör (Danube Circle); in the face of government opposition the group organised petitions, marches and press conferences. As criticism of the project increased, official displeasure mounted: in June 1985 János Vargha published a detailed environmental impact study of the Nagymaros dam and later that year Duna Kör was awarded a Right Livelihood Award; Vargha was harassed by the secret police, censured for 'green anarchism', and fired from his job, though he continued to work with even greater vigour against the dam project. In mid-1988 the appointment of pro-glasnost (but still pro-dam) Károlyi Grosz as Hungarian Communist Party secretary allowed Duna Kör to emerge from its underground existence, and when contractors started to excavate at Nagymaros in September 50,000 people marched through the streets of Budapest. In May 1989 the Hungarian government cancelled work on their part of the project, and began negotiations with their Czech counterparts to cancel the scheme altogether. In 1989 János Vargha was one of the founders of the SzDSz (Alliance of Free Democrats), now Hungary's leading opposition party, but he has consistently declined to accept political office, preferring to stay firmly in the field of environmental research and informed activism.

Fred Pearce, *Green Warriors: The People and the Politics behind the Environmental Revolution*, Bodley Head, 1991

Bertha von Suttner [Bertha Freiin Kinsky von Wchinitz und Tettau]
1843–1914
novelist, pacifist

In the development of pacifist thinking in the late nineteenth and early twentieth centuries, no other book had as much influence as did Bertha von Suttner's novel *Die Waffen Nieder!* (*Lay Down Your Arms!*), which by 1914 had reached its 210 thousandth copy in German and had been translated into almost every European language including Esperanto. Yet Bertha von Suttner was an unlikely candidate for activism: she was born into the Austrian nobility and, when her father died and her mother gambled away the family fortune, she became a governess and wrote light fiction for a living. In 1876 she answered an advertisement for a governess to the Paris household of the Swedish inventor Alfred Nobel, but after only a week the Nobels were recalled to Sweden and her brief employment was terminated. Returning to Vienna, she eloped with the youngest son of her previous employers' family, Arthur von Suttner, to Tiflis in the Caucasus, where they both became writers of short stories and topical novels. They returned to Austria in May 1885, and in 1886 visited the Nobels in Paris, where Bertha was first introduced to the work of Hodgson Pratt's International Arbitration and Peace Association. Resolving to 'do some service for peace', she immediately set to writing *Lay Down Your Arms! The Autobiography of Martha von Tilling*, relating the story of an Austrian woman who loses her first husband on the Magenta battlefield in 1859 and whose second husband, having fought against the Danes in 1864, is reported missing after the Austro-Prussian Battle of Königgräz, where she seeks him out among the carnage and suffering. The Tillings, now aware of the peace movement, are caught in Paris at the outbreak of war in 1870, where the husband is falsely accused of spying and shot by a patriotic firing squad. *Lay Down Your Arms!*, at first rejected by several publishers, quickly became a bestseller, and the von Suttners used the impetus to organise a series of interparliamentary conferences on peace, starting in 1888 and reaching a climax at the 1899 Hague Peace Conference, attended by representatives from 26 governments. Arthur died in 1902, but Bertha continued campaigning despite having to deal with the ailing Suttner family business fortunes. After Alfred Nobel's death in 1896 she became heavily involved in the work of the Nobel Foundation, and was awarded the Peace Prize herself in 1905. She continued to write and lecture energetically, in 1912 visiting the USA, where she spoke to nearly half a million people. Ironically she died just seven days before the outbreak of the first world war, the conflict she had worked so hard to avert.

Bertha von Suttner, *Lay Down Your Arms!*, Garland, 1972 (repr. of 1892 edn)
Beatrix Kempf, *Suffragette for Peace: The Life of Bertha von Suttner*, Wolff, 1972

Lech Wałęsa
1943–
labour organiser, politician

Hero and figurehead of the Polish transition from communism to democracy during the 1980s, Lech Wałęsa's sturdy hands-on political style won him much admiration among those who in 1990 elected him president, at the same time highlighting the problems facing a grassroots organiser elevated to unaccustomed statesmanship. Lech Wałęsa was born into a Catholic peasant family in Popowo in Włocławek province; his father died in a German prison camp when Lech was eighteen months old. Hating both his stepfather and rural life, he escaped as soon as possible, first to do his military service and then to work as an electrician in the Lenin Shipyard at Gdańsk. In 1969 he married Danuta Mirosława (they have seven children), whose courage and determination have played a crucial part in his achievement. When workers' protests erupted in the Baltic ports in December 1970 Lech Wałęsa headed a strike committee, and in 1976 his complaints about conditions in the shipyard cost him his job. He found work in a machine repair shop, but in 1979 was sacked for participating in anniversary celebrations of the 1970 protests. When a strike was called in the Lenin Shipyard in August 1980 he became head of the interfactory committee which at the end of August signed the Gdańsk Accords with government leaders, allowing free trade unions and the right to strike. The trade union **Solidarność** (Solidarity) was created the following month, with Wałęsa as leader. By the time of the union's first conference in September 1981 the tensions, both within Solidarność and in its relations with the government, were severe; when in December a referendum was proposed for ending communist rule, the authorities declared martial law. Lech Wałęsa was detained for eleven months, the government explaining to foreign journalists that he was simply a figment of the radical imagination. Early in 1983 he returned to work at the shipyard, and in October 1983 was awarded the Nobel Peace Prize, though he was denied an exit visa to receive it. He had remained the *de facto* leader of Solidarność, and in October 1987 he was appointed chair of the national executive. When industrial unrest in 1988 forced the government to seek accommodation with its opposition Wałęsa negotiated talks, which early in 1989 resulted in democratic reforms and Solidarność's re-legalisation. After elections in June 1989 he persuaded parties previously allied to the communist Polish United Workers' Party to defect to a Solidarność-led coalition government, thus ending communist rule in Poland. He sponsored Tadeusz Mazowiecki for prime minister, but by mid-1990 he was at odds with Mazowiecki's government over economic policy, and his presidential ambitions drove other Solidarność leaders to accuse him of behaving dictatorially. He nevertheless gained a landslide victory in the presidential elections in

December 1990 (whereupon he resigned as chair of Solidarność), and continued to press for widespread social and economic reform in Poland. As new presidential elections loomed in 1995, however, criticism of his authoritarianism grew among both politicians and electorate, and his chances of winning a second term as president seemed increasingly slim.

Lech Walesa, *A Path of Hope*, Collins Harvill, 1987
Lech Walesa, *The Struggle and The Triumph*, Arcade, 1992
Michael Dobbs, *Poland, Solidarity, Walesa*, McGraw-Hill, 1981
Jarosław Kurski, *Lech Walesa: Democrat or Dictator?*, Westview, 1993
Roger Boyes, *The Naked President: A Political Life of Lech Walesa*, Secker and Warburg, 1994

Alice [Malsenior] Walker
1944–
novelist, feminist

Alice Walker has probably done more than any other contemporary black American writer to chronicle the complexities of poor black women's experience, constantly reminding her readers of the importance of indomitable spirit. The youngest of eight children born into a Georgia sharecropping family, she learnt early on to defend herself in a white male-dominated world, and the loss of an eye to a brother's carelessness with a shotgun had some positive results, in that her mother attempted to make amends by allowing Alice to read rather than do housework, and she was given, presciently, a sewing machine, a suitcase and a typewriter. A small scholarship took her to Spelman College in Atlanta in 1961 and she transferred to New York's Sarah Lawrence College two years later, where she wrote her first published book of poetry, *Once* (1968). After graduating in 1965, Alice Walker returned to Georgia to work in the civil rights movement: here she met and married civil rights lawyer Melvyn Rosenman Leventhal, and completed her first novel, *The Third Life of Grange Copeland* (1970) only days before the birth of their daughter Rebecca. After teaching at Jackson State University and Tougaloo College, she moved north in 1971, teaching at Wellesley College and the University of Massachusetts and continuing to write novels, essays and poetry. *Meridian* (1976) was a vivid semi-autobiographical novel about a woman's experience of the hopes and disappointments of the 1960s civil rights movement, while *The Color Purple* (1982) brought her work to international attention, winning the 1983 Pulitzer and American Book Awards and being made two years later into a major film. Its portrayal of black male violence towards black women provoked controversy, but *The Color Purple*'s honest and heartfelt acknowledgement of black women's courage and solidarity won widespread acclaim. Alice Walker's exploration of black women's heritage led to the 1983 publication of *In Search of Our Mothers' Gardens*, in which she coined the term 'womanist' to acknowledge black women's immediate experience of oppression ('womanist is to feminist as purple is to lavender'). In 1979, by now divorced, she moved from New York to California, where she continues to write about freedom, nature, endurance, and the impact of subtle and not-so-subtle oppression within black relationships. Her most recent books include *Living By The Word, Selected Writings 1973–1987* (1988) and the mystical and dreamlike *The Temple of My Familiar* (1990).

Alice Walker, *Meridian*, Harcourt Brace Jovanovich, 1976

Alice Walker, *The Color Purple*, Harcourt Brace Jovanovich, 1982

Alice Walker, *In Search of Our Mothers' Gardens: Womanist Prose*, Harcourt Brace Jovanovich, 1983

Donna Haisty Winchell, *Alice Walker*, Twayne, 1992

Marilyn Waring

1952–
politician, economist, farmer

Born and bred a rural New Zealander, Marilyn Waring studied politics and economics in her home country and at Harvard and Rutgers universities in the USA. In 1975 she was elected to the New Zealand parliament, where she served until 1984, when she crossed the floor and made a crucial antinuclear speech; she then withdrew from the government, causing a snap election which brought down the Muldoon administration and set New Zealand on the non-nuclear path espoused by the Lange administration (for which, ironically, David Lange rather than Marilyn Waring received a Nobel Peace Prize). During her time as a politician she was appointed to, and then chaired, the Public Expenditure Select Committee, an experience which helped her to understand the inequity of international accounting procedures, particularly the complete invisibility of women's contribution and of environmental factors. Her first book, *Women, Politics and Power* (1985) showed how little women's contribution to society is valued, and in 1988 her landmark study of feminist and environmental economics, *If Women Counted*, was published. For several years until 1993 she was executive director of the Sisterhood is Global Institute. Marilyn Waring now runs an angora goat farm in New Zealand's North Island, teaches law, government and policy at the Albany Campus of Massey University, and continues to write and lecture.

Marilyn Waring, *Women, Politics and Power*, Allen and Unwin/Port Nicholson Press, 1985

Marilyn Waring, *If Women Counted: A New Feminist Economics*, Harper and Row, 1988

Helen Forsey, 'Back into the Quagmire: Linking Patriarchy and Planetary Destruction', *Alternatives*, May/June 1993

Beatrice Webb [Martha Beatrice Potter]

1858–1943
social reformer, historian

Long before she met and married **Sidney Webb** in 1892, Beatrice Potter had devoted her life to the fight for the rights of 'the people of the abyss'. The seventh of eight children born to Gloucestershire railway and timber magnate Richard Potter and his weary wife Lawrencina, she rejected what 'high society' had to offer (including the option of marrying the Liberal leader Joseph Chamberlain), and set out to educate herself in the ways of the 'real world'. In 1883 she started working in London's East End for Octavia Hill's Charity Organisation Society, experiencing at first hand the squalor and hopelessness of the city's working classes. In 1888 she gave evidence to a House of Lords Select Committee on sweated labour and wrote a popular account of the cooperative movement: by 1890, the year she met Sidney, she was a convinced socialist. Beatrice found it hard to give up the desire for intimacy and children, as demanded by the practical nature of her marriage to Sidney, but despite her doubts and recurrent illnesses threw herself into the collaboration. Her private means allowed Sidney to engage in fulltime research, and financed one of their first joint projects, the establishment in 1894 of the London School of Economics as an independent college for the social sciences. Between 1894 and 1929 the Webbs collaborated on a wide range of sociohistorical studies, Beatrice's investigative skills complementing Sidney's grasp of theory and attention to detail. Their pioneering *History of Trade Unionism* (1894) was followed by *Industrial Democracy* (1897), and between 1903 and 1929 they produced the eleven-volume definitive study of *English Local Government*, firmly establishing labour and local government history as part of Britain's socioeconomic heritage. In 1909 Beatrice was a member of the important Royal Commission on the archaic Poor Laws and with **George Lansbury** and two others produced a minority report proposing their total abolition. In 1913 the Webbs successfully launched the radical socialist journal *New Statesman*, but the war left Beatrice exhausted, though she continued to write and served on a number of committees. In 1922 they bought a house at Passfield Corner in east Hampshire, and Sidney's final exit from government following the ignominious fall of Labour in 1931 allowed them a new degree of freedom. In 1932 they visited the Soviet Union, Beatrice being taken with the promise of communism to the extent of writing the eulogistic *Soviet Communism: A New Civilisation* (1935). She spent the last years of her eventful life entertaining at Passfield Corner and writing the story of her half-century-long partnership with Sidney.

Beatrice Webb, *Our Partnership*, Longman, 1948
Lisanne Radice, *Beatrice and Sidney Webb*, Macmillan, 1984
Carol Seymour-Jones, *Beatrice Webb: Woman of Conflict*, Alison and Busby, 1992

Sidney [James] Webb
1859–1947
social reformer, historian, politician

The crucially important intellectual and organisational partnership built up by Sidney Webb and **Beatrice** Potter over fifty years of married life nearly came to grief in its early stages, for though their ideals had much in common their background could hardly have been more different. While Beatrice was an upper middle class woman of wealth and beauty, Sidney's father was a struggling London hairdresser, and what Sidney lacked in looks and assurance was only slowly built up through faith, ambition and a powerful intellectual appetite. At the age of seventeen Sidney became a clerk and two years later a civil servant, studying for a degree at evening classes. In 1885 he joined the recently-formed **Fabian Society**, quickly helping to build it into an influential socialist research and discussion forum, and in 1887 wrote a bestselling Fabian pamphlet called *Facts for Socialists*, which so impressed Beatrice Potter that in January 1890 she sought him out to ask about research sources in the British Museum. Here started an uneven two-year courtship which resulted in their marriage in July 1892, coinciding with Sidney's landslide election to the Greater London Council. Their joint achievements – learned and popular histories of trade unionism, industrial democracy and local government; the growth of the Fabian Society with its vision of collectivism rooted in fair government; the founding of the London School of Economics in 1894 and the *New Statesman* in 1913 – are covered in more detail in Beatrice Webb's entry. In all these endeavours Beatrice's fluency and social skills were balanced with Sidney's patient, often pedantic, attention to detail. After the first world war, Sidney Webb's impatience with the slow reformism of the Liberal Party drove him into the rapidly-growing Labour Party, of which by 1916 he was a member of the executive and in 1918 drafted much of the constitution, establishing the party as a credible political force with coherent socialist goals. His election as a Labour member of parliament in 1920 was something of an anticlimax, since he was by nature better at steering from behind the scenes than at dealing with the broad issues of everyday politics: in 1929 he was made a peer, serving until 1931 as colonial secretary. In their last years the Webbs' house at Passfield Corner in Hampshire became a mecca for the intellectual élite, with Beatrice converted to Soviet-style communism, but Sidney characteristically continuing to campaign for a specifically British form of pragmatic socialism.

Margaret Cole, *The Webbs and Their Work*, Muller, 1949
Norman and Jeanne Mackenzie, *The First Fabians*, Simon and Schuster, 1977
Lisanne Radice, *Beatrice and Sidney Webb: Fabian Socialists*, Macmillan, 1984

Wei Jingsheng
1950–
civil rights activist, writer

For the fifteen years between 1979 and his release in September 1993, Wei Jinsheng was China's best-known political prisoner. Insisting that the only way forward for China is true democracy achieved by peaceful grassroots activism, he set himself on an inevitable collision course with the authoritarianism of the Xiaoping regime. He grew up in Beijing, where his father was a minor party bureaucrat, and was sixteen, just about to start senior school, when the Cultural Revolution began in 1966. Already an ardent Maoist, he at once became a Red Guard, and the following year joined the 'Action Group' of Guards opposed to Mao's wife Jiang Qing and her political faction. The group was soon banned, and Wei Jingsheng spent more than a year in self-imposed exile in the countryside of Anhui Province. He trained as an electrician, and during the 'Peking Spring' of 1978–79 edited the unofficial but influential magazine *Tansuo* (*Exploration*), in which he wrote editorials highly critical of Deng Xiaoping's dictatorial regime and calling for democracy to accompany China's economic reform programme. He was arrested in March 1979, convicted eight months later of 'passing military secrets to foreign journalists and conducting counter-revolutionary propaganda and agitation', and sentenced to fifteen years imprisonment. Shortly before his arrest Wei Jingsheng had completed an account of his experiences of the Cultural Revolution, *Searching for the Truth*, which circulated widely in China and, in extracts, abroad. The Xiaoping government finally released Wei Jingsheng in September 1993, ten days before the International Olympic Committee was due to announce the venue for the 2000 Olympic Games, an honour for which China's leaders were prepared to ease their iron grip and be seen as addressing their human rights record, in order that Beijing might be selected as host city. The attempt was, not surprisingly, unsuccessful, and Wei Jingsheng was detained again in April 1994 for speaking his mind to foreign journalists and for openly criticising the Chinese government's record on human rights.

Wei Jingsheng, 'Searching for the Truth', *Index on Censorship*, March 1981

Louise Weiss
1893–1983
writer, feminist, pacifist, politician

The French journalist and writer Louise Weiss was born in Arras in northern France, and studied at Oxford University and the Paris Sorbonne. During the first world war she ran a small field hospital in Brittany, and in 1918 she started to work for *L'Europe nouvelle*, one of the most influential political weeklies in France during the 1920s. In the autumn of 1921 she travelled to Moscow to interview Bolshevik leaders including **Trotsky**, and by 1923 was *L'Europe nouvelle*'s editor-in-chief. When the newspaper closed in 1930 Louise Weiss organised the École de la Paix (Peace Academy) at the Sorbonne, a weekly forum where leading figures from politics and the arts could discuss the 'science of peace' on a neutral platform. As peace in Europe became an ever more elusive goal, in October 1934 she formed the feminist group La Femme Nouvelle, establishing an office on the Champs Élysées and causing a national stir in 1936 when, wearing a Molyneux evening gown, she chained herself with other women across the rue Royale. She declined the bait of a cabinet post, continuing to fight for the vote (eventually obtained in 1944) and for other causes, such as the elimination of 'obey' from the French marriage vows. As a member of the resistance during the second world war, Louise Weiss ran the illicit newspaper *La nouvelle république*. From 1945 until her old age she travelled widely, directing films and documentaries for French television. She also achieved fame as a writer. Her novel *La Marseillaise* won the Literature Prize of the French Academy in 1947, and her series of travel books from 1948 to 1960 was widely acclaimed, though her defence of colonialism and strong moral leadership increasingly smacked of authoritarianism. In 1974 Louise Weiss caused more outrage to the establishment by proposing herself as a member of the French Academy in protest against its exclusion of women. In 1971 she founded the Institute for the Science of Peace in Strasbourg, at the age of 83 was a delegate to UNESCO, and in 1979 became the oldest member of the European parliament, remaining fiercely energetic until her death at the age of ninety. Her memoirs include *Tempête sur l'Occident, 1945–1975* (1976), and the six volumes of *Mémoires d'une Européenne* (1968–76).

Michael Bess, *Realism, Utopia, and the Mushroom Cloud: Four Activist Intellectuals and their Strategies for Peace, 1945–1989*, University of Chicago Press, 1993

Rebecca West [Cicely Isabel Fairfield]
1892–1983
feminist, journalist, novelist

One of the most consistently outspoken radical feminists of the century, Rebecca West's long writing and activist career was notable for its precise and uncompromising analysis of what she had no hesitation in calling the 'sex war'. She was born in London into an independently-minded Anglo-Irish family and educated in Edinburgh (where she, her mother and two sisters lived after her father's death) and at the Royal Academy of Dramatic Art in London. It was here, after playing the strongwilled **Ibsen** heroine of *Rosmersholm* in 1910, that she changed her name. The same year she started writing for the feminist journal *The Freewoman*, moving on to *The Clarion* in 1912. Her informed, witty articles, often laced with cutting sarcasm, played a major part in spreading the feminist message – a typical and often-quoted sentence, from a November 1914 *Clarion* piece, runs 'I myself have never been able to find out exactly what feminism is: I only know that people call me a feminist whenever I express sentiments that differentiate me from a doormat'. Throughout the period of prewar militant suffragism Rebecca West reported on the violence being meted out to women who were merely demanding justice, and in 1918 her analysis of freedom and equity found a new medium in *The Return of the Soldier*, the first of more than a dozen powerful novels. Although she was highly critical of male privilege, she also insisted on women's right to love as they choose. From 1913 to 1923 she had a much-publicised affair with the novelist H.G. Wells, with whom she had a son, and in 1930 married the banker Henry Maxwell Andrews, who died in 1968. Of her interwar novels, *The Judge* (1922) explores the challenges involved in unmarried motherhood, while *Harriet Hume* (1929) looks at the interplay of passion and political ambition. In the late 1930s Rebecca and her husband travelled extensively in Yugoslavia, an experience described with brilliance and accuracy in *Black Lamb and Grey*

Falcon (1941), considered by many to be her best book. She attended the Nuremberg trials of 1945–46: *The Meaning of Treason* (1949) was based on articles about Nuremberg commissioned by *New Yorker* magazine. Almost inevitably her reputation and the quality and passion of her writing have tended to be eclipsed by charges of extremism and aggression, but feminist reassessment of her work in the 1980s led to the republication of many of her works, and she is now recognised as one of the main torchbearers of twentieth-century British feminism.

Rebecca West, *The Judge*, 1922 (many editions since)
Rebecca West, *Black Lamb and Grey Falcon*, 1941 (many editions since)
Dale Spender, *There's Always Been a Women's Movement This Century*, Pandora, 1983
Victoria Glendinning, *Rebecca West: A Life*, Macmillan, 1987

Raymond [Henry] Williams
1921–1988
cultural historian, critic and writer

Perhaps the most important British socialist intellectual of the late twentieth century, Raymond Williams grew up in the Welsh borders. He was a working class boy (his father was a signalman and a staunch trade unionist), but his academic ability easily achieved for him a place at Abergavenny Grammar School and a scholarship to Cambridge University. The second world war delayed his studies, but he graduated in 1946, and for fifteen years worked in adult education with Oxford University's extramural department. He married his wife Joyce in 1942, and they had three children. In 1961 he was appointed lecturer in English at Cambridge University, and in 1974 professor of drama. His first book is his most important: when *Culture and Society* was published in 1958 it fluently encapsulated the Left's newfound interest in its roots and its historical purpose. He demonstrated that literary criticism must take account of the relationship of writers to their cultural background, and that literature is a 'social construct' rather than an immediate response to social conditions. *The Long Revolution* (1961) went on to insist that any generation's values must come from an engagement with contemporary social change, rather than from any fixed set of inherited values. In the 1970s his writing – fiction (*The Fight for Manod*, 1979) as well as analysis (*The Country and the City*, 1973) – concentrated on the balance between tradition (community, family, land) and technological progress; he was also working on *Keywords* (1976, new expanded edition 1983), which traces the historical development of many of the ideas used in cultural and political debate. In the 1980s he turned to reanalysing 'the project of the left', and *Towards 2000* (1983) is an ambitious attempt to rethink many fundamental socialist questions. Though his reputation and influence rests primarily on his writing and teaching, he was also active against the invasions of Suez and Hungary in the 1950s, in the **Campaign for Nuclear Disarmament** actions of the 60s, and during the British miners' strike of 1984–85. He was one of the instigators of the **new left**, editing the influential *May Day Manifesto* of 1968 and contributing regularly to *New Left Review*. His ability to bring together both a rootedness in real community and a considered and intelligent socialist optimism inspired a generation of leftwing radicals in Britain and beyond.

Raymond Williams, *Culture and Society*, Chatto and Windus, 1958
Raymond Williams, *Towards 2000*, Chatto and Windus, 1983
Stephen Regan, *Raymond Williams*, Harvester Wheatsheaf, 1993

Virginia Woolf [Adeline Virginia Stephen]
1882–1941
novelist, feminist, pacifist

Virginia Woolf's reputation as one of the most innovative, honest and courageous novelists and essayists of the century is justifiably founded on her ability to explore and analyse the minutiae of human emotions, behaviour and motivation, and not to flinch when the implications of that exploration became horrifyingly apparent. Virginia was born into an upper middle class London family: both her parents had been married before, so as well as three (soon to be four) children born to Leslie and Julia Stephen there were also three children from Julia's first marriage and a daughter from Leslie's. Though often portrayed as a lively literary household (her father was a critic and cofounder of the *Dictionary of National Biography*), its patriarchal structure encouraged abusive behaviour, and Virginia (like her sister Vanessa) was regularly sexually abused by her two half-brothers George and Gerald Duckworth: the abuse went on until she was in her early twenties. Julia Stephen died of influenza in 1895 – 'the greatest disaster that could happen' wrote Virginia – and in 1904 Leslie died too. Virginia and her siblings now began their 'voyage out' from their Victorian family background, a journey which began with Virginia, Vanessa, and their younger brother Adrian's association with older brother Thoby's Cambridge student set, known as 'The Apostles'. Based first at the Stephen home in Gordon Square and then in another Bloomsbury house rented by Virginia and Adrian, the 'Bloomsbury Group' developed to become a highly creative and avant garde literary circle. Virginia Stephen started writing her first novel in 1907; it was published, shortly after her marriage in 1912 to fellow Bloomsburyite Leonard Woolf, as *The Voyage Out*. Six months later Virginia had a serious breakdown and tried to overdose on sleeping pills, all the time recording her thoughts and feelings meticulously in the diary she kept from 1897 to her death. For the next thirty years, always fighting the spectres of violence and despair, she wrote a series of powerful, personal novels, each breaking new ground in the detailed portrayal of internal process played out against the background of social and political change. She also wrote extended essays, two of which, *A Room of One's Own* (1929) and *Three Guineas* (1938) stand out as beacons of radical feminism and antimilitarism. *A Room of One's Own* explained how women's histories and lives are devalued because they are not recorded, and they are not recorded because, unlike men, women do not have access to space and financial resources of their own. *Three Guineas*, written as war in Europe threatened, demonstrated the links between patriarchy, militarism and fascism and made it clear that it was men who wage war, not women: Virginia proposed a 'Society of Outsiders', pacifists educated and active in international affairs, who could reject militarism and provide hope for the world. As the war deepened, however, together with her own personal battle against 'the waves' of self-exploration and self-knowledge, she chose in March 1941 to end her life, by drowning herself in a river near to their Sussex home.

Virginia Woolf, *A Room of One's Own*, 1929 (many editions since)
Virginia Woolf, *Three Guineas*, 1938 (many editions since)
Phyllis Rose, *Woman of Letters: A Life of Virginia Woolf*, Oxford University Press, 1978
Alex Zwerdling, *Virginia Woolf and the Real World*, University of California Press, 1986
Louise DeSalvo, *Virginia Woolf: The Impact of Childhood Sexual Abuse on her Life and Work*, Beacon, 1989
James King, *Virginia Woolf*, Hamish Hamilton, 1994

Malcolm X [Malcolm Little; Al Hajj Malik al-Shabazz]
1925–1964
black nationalist leader

Malcolm X (a name he adopted in 1953 as a Black Muslim to stress his status as an ex-slave rather than keeping his family's white slaveowner's name) was born Malcolm Little in Omaha, Nebraska. His parents were active in the black nationalist United Negro Improvement Association. His family moved twice because of racist threats, and when he was four their home in Lansing, Michigan, was burned to the ground. Two years later his father was run over by a streetcar; his mother broke down trying to raise eight children in extreme poverty, and they were scattered to foster homes. Dropping out of school after eighth grade, he went to live with a half sister in Boston. He embarked upon a criminal career, and in 1946 was imprisoned for burglary. In prison he educated himself through a voracious programme of reading, and at the suggestion of an older brother began studying the teachings of the Nation of Islam (Black Muslims), with its affirmation of black culture and belief that all whites are devils. After his parole in 1952 he devoted himself to the Nation of Islam and its leader, Elijah Muhammad, who became his spiritual father. In less than a year he was a minister with the Nation, and through his unstinting work and charismatic presence was soon its national spokesman. Addressing himself to poor northern urban blacks, sharing and articulating their anger, Malcolm X brilliantly modelled the black pride, self-realisation and militancy that he preached. The eloquence with which he forged the Nation's doctrines into a devastating critique of American society, and asserted the right of blacks to defend themselves against racial violence, drew the hostility of the government and liberal social commentators. Malcolm X scorned **Martin Luther King**'s concept of an integrated society whose creation was spearheaded by the redemptive power of black people's suffering. His activist nature, however, was frustrated by the Nation's lack of political engagement. Early in 1964, deeply estranged from Elijah Muhammad, he left the organisation. On pilgrimage to Mecca shortly afterwards, he encountered the heart of Islamic religious teachings for the first time, and was received by white Muslims with a graciousness that transformed his fundamentalist racial judgements. His political analysis of racism, however, did not slip. He returned to New York and founded the Organization of Afro-American Unity (OAAU) to participate fully in the wider civil rights movement. A longer trip through the Middle East and Africa later in the year developed his international contacts and strengthened his sense of the links between African-American and other liberation struggles. In January 1965 his home was firebombed. He, his wife Betty Shabazz, who was pregnant, and their three young daughters escaped injury. On February 21st, as he stood to address an OAAU assembly in New York City, Malcolm X was gunned down, apparently by members of the Nation of Islam, the usual police shadow contingent being nowhere in evidence. An exploratory meeting between Malcolm X and Martin Luther King had been arranged for the following week.

Malcolm X and Alex Haley, *The Autobiography of Malcolm X*, Grove, 1964
James H. Cone, *Martin & Malcolm & America: A Dream or a Nightmare*, Orbis, 1991

Xiang Jingyu
1895–1928
teacher, feminist, women's rights activist

Xiang Jingyu, one of China's pioneer feminist revolutionaries, was born into a prosperous liberal family in Hunan province. As a student at Zhangsha in 1915, she was a friend of **Mao Zedong** and other radicals. After graduating in 1916 Xiang opened a girls' school, campaigned against footbinding and traditional feudal marriage, and in 1919 led student demonstrations as part of the **May 4th Movement**, a nationwide demonstration aimed at modernising Chinese society. She cut her hair short to symbolise her refusal to follow a traditional women's role, and the fashion soon became widespread amongst Chinese feminists and intellectuals. In 1920 she spent some time in France, working in a textile mill and meeting French Marxists. On her return she married fellow communist Kai Hseng and had a baby, brought up jointly with her sister. At the Chinese Communist Party's Second National Congress in 1922 Xiang was elected to the Central Committee, where she established and became head of the Women's Department. The author of many articles on the position of women in China, including the important *Thesis on the Emancipation and Transformation of Women*, she believed passionately that only radical social change would offer women the voice they deserved, and that women's emancipation was crucial to the establishment of socialism. After the

Kuomintang rout of the Communist Party in 1927 Xiang Jingyu was arrested for political subversion, and was executed in May 1928.

Agnes Smedley (ed. Jan MacKinnon and Steve MacKinnon), *Portraits of Chinese Women in Revolution*, The Feminist Press, 1976

Yosano Akiko [Hō Shō]
1878–1942
poet, educationalist, women's rights campaigner

The Japanese poet Yosano Akiko is best known today for her lyrical translations of the classic *Tale of Genji*, but in the 1920s and 30s she was also an ardent campaigner for women's suffrage and free coeducational schools. She grew up in the city of Sakai near Ōsaka, and when she was 22 met and married the poet Yosano Tekkan; she had herself been writing poetry since she was a child, and in 1901 published a remarkable collection of nearly four hundred love poems called *Midaregami* (*Tangled Hair*). During the next forty years, as well as raising eleven children, Yosano Akiko wrote another twenty volumes of poetry and a large amount of social commentary in books and articles. She was particularly critical of Japan's aggressive foreign policy and the refusal to give women the vote, and as her children grew up she became involved in the campaign for universal schools for both girls and boys: in 1921 she became dean and lecturer at Bunka Gakuin, a newly-established free school near Tokyo. In her later years Yosano Akiko kept an open house for struggling young writers, although by now she wrote little poetry she produced a constant stream of newspaper and magazine articles on social and political issues, and was one of the compilers of a comprehensive anthology of modern Japanese poetry.

Yosano Akiko (trans. Dennis Maloney and Hide Oshiro), *Tangled Hair: Love Poems of Yosano Akiko*, White Pine, 1987
Amy T. Matsumoto, 'Yosano Akiko', *Kodansha Encyclopedia of Japan*, 1983

Emiliano Zapata
1879–1919
peasants' rights and land reform campaigner

The son of a prosperous farming family in the southern Mexican sugar-producing region of Morelos, Emiliano Zapata spent his early years as a cowboy, horse trainer and sharecropper. In 1909 a hacienda owner claimed village land and water supplies; Zapata joined the campaign to reclaim the land and was condemned to forced labour. With the outbreak of the Mexican Revolution the following year the community elected Zapata to lead the land rights struggle; nearby villages joined the cause, and he soon found himself the leader of a growing land rights movement. When a government force was sent to crush the 'bandit uprising' in Morelos, it was met by Emiliano Zapata's well-organised 'agrarians'; in the following year many haciendas were 'liberated' for the use of evicted peasant farmers and, as well as fighting government forces, Zapata's followers often helped with ploughing and harvesting. In 1911 the liberal Francisco Madero became president of a regime which overthrew the long-lived military dictatorship of Porfirio Díaz; although Zapata initially supported Madero, he grew impatient when it became clear that peasant land rights were not a priority. In October 1911 Emiliano Zapata published the *Plan de Ayala*, based on **Ricardo Flóres Magón**'s earlier anarchist-communist manifesto, in which he called for 'the land free, free for all, without overseers or masters'. In the confusion which followed Madero's assassination in 1913, Zapata's agrarian forces linked with those of the more aggressive Pancho Villa to resist the centralist US-backed regime of Venustiano Carranza; when in 1916 Carranza managed to enlist the support of the anarcho-syndicalist Casa del Obrero Mundial (World Workers' Federation) he cleverly succeeded in setting revolutionary against revolutionary. Within a year Carranza had driven Emiliano Zapata's forces back to Morelos, banned the Casa, and reversed all of the agrarians' achievements. Zapata continued to campaign from his mountain stronghold, still arguing for a free and equal society for all Mexicans; all such hopes were dashed, however, when he was murdered in an ambush in April 1919. Today he is considered a Mexican hero, many of his land reform demands having been enacted by later governments. In 1979 his son Mateo (born 1918) launched a new peasants' rights group named after his father's *Plan de Ayala*; the CNPA (Coordinadora Nacional Plan de Ayala) became an important part of the growing Mexican grassroots reform movement of the 1980s. More recently the early 1990s liberation movement for the southern Mexican state of Chiapas named itself the Ejército Zapatista de Liberación Nacional in memory of Emiliano Zapata.

Roger Parkinson, *Zapata: A Biography*, Stein and Day, 1975
John Womack, *Zapata and the Mexican Revolution*, Thames and Hudson, 1972

Clara Zetkin [Clara Eissner]
1857–1933
socialist, feminist

The German socialist and feminist leader Clara Zetkin was one of the few early communists to successfully embrace feminism, socialism and pacifism within a consistent framework of theory and action. She grew up in Wiederau in Saxony, where her feminist mother was a strong influence, as was Auguste Schmidt, the socialist-feminist principal of the Steyber Institute where Clara prepared for a teaching career, graduating in 1878. In 1881 she joined the new Sozialdemokratische Partie Deutschlands (SPD) and, having met the Russian revolutionary exile Ossip Zetkin in Leipzig, went to live with him in Paris when he was expelled from Germany in 1882. They had two sons and lived together until his death in 1889, but never married because Clara did not want to lose her German citizenship. In 1890 she returned to Germany, basing herself in Stuttgart and rising quickly within the SPD leadership. By 1891 she was editor of the socialist women's journal *Die Arbeiterin*, which she transformed into the influential *Die Gleichheit* (Equality). Clara Zetkin rejected many of the aims of the middle class suffrage movement, believing that it was the needs of working women (and she included mothers) that must be socialism's main concern. In 1907 she was one of the founders of the International Socialist Women's Congress, and at its second congress in Stockholm in 1910 successfully proposed that an annual Women's Day be made an international event. Her radical position on women's full participation in the running of society and, as war loomed, her increasingly exposed pacifism (shared by only a few allies including **Rosa Luxemburg** and Karl Liebknecht) made her position within the SPD vulnerable, and after she had helped to organise the 1915 Berne Peace Conference she was expelled from the party. In 1918 she was one of the founders of the Kommunistische Partie Deutschlands (KPD), becoming an executive committee member of the Communist **International**, heading the International Women's Secretariat, and editing the women's journal *Die Kommunistin*. She served as a communist member of the German Reichstag from 1920 to 1932, and presided over the last session before it was burned down in February 1933. She spent much time in the Soviet Union during her last years and was a close friend of **Lenin**; she died in a Russian clinic.

Karen Honeycutt, 'Clara Zetkin: A Socialist Approach to the Problem of
    Women's Oppression', *European Women on the Left* (ed. Jane Slaughter and
    Robert Kern), Greenwood, 1981
Dorothea Reetz, *Clara Zetkin as a Socialist Speaker*, International Publishers, 1987

GROUPS AND MOVEMENTS

Abalone Alliance
1976–1981
antinuclear protest

The Abalone Alliance was formed in 1976 with the aim of shutting down the Diablo Canyon nuclear plant on the central California coast. For several years the plant had been the target of legal actions by a local women's antinuclear group. Some of these women, wanting to engage in civil disobedience, found common cause with peace activists interested in a mass antinuclear movement based on nonviolent direct action. At its first organising conference, the Abalone adopted the structural principles of the **Clamshell Alliance**, basing action on affinity groups and making decisions through consensus. Members organised into local groups, and small monthly regional conferences created solidarity. A strong anarcha-feminist presence fostered the linking of revolutionary vision with the exercise of respect. The Abalone's first two actions were intended to publicise the dangers of the plant (in addition to the usual dangers, Diablo was built on an earthquake fault line). At the first, on August 7th 1977, 1,500 people demonstrated at the gate and 47, mostly local residents, occupied the site and were arrested; a year later, 5,000 rallied and 487 were arrested. Having decided after much debate not to stage a massive occupation until the granting of the plant's licence was imminent, the Abalone had three years to wait. During the summer of 1981 5,000 people took part in nonviolence trainings, a prerequisite for participation, and on September 15th the occupation began. As the action was ending after two weeks and 1,900 arrests, a plant supervisor announced that in studying the plans he had discovered a dangerous flaw requiring major and expensive repairs, thus indefinitely postponing the plant's operation. The Abalone did not continue as an organisation beyond this blockade.

> Barbara Epstein, *Political Protest and Cultural Revolution: Nonviolent Direct Action in the 1970s and 1980s*, University of California Press, 1991

African National Congress [ANC]
1912–
liberation and self-determination movement

Founded in January 1912 as the South African Native National Congress, the ANC is Africa's longest-lived liberation movement. It was established by a group of intellectuals who sought to unite the people of South Africa across tribal lines. In its early years the ANC stressed dialogue, education and democratic representation, but by the 1940s had become little more than a debating society. In the late 1940s, however, a new generation of impatient young members (including **Nelson Mandela, Oliver Tambo, Walter Sisulu** and Anton Lembede) galvanised the organisation into action, arranging marches, boycotts and strikes. Membership soared as the ANC, led by **Albert Luthuli**, promoted a series of passive resistance campaigns against white minority rule, and in 1956 the Congress joined forces with other radical organisations to endorse the Freedom Charter, calling for a nonracial democracy in South Africa. In 1959 a large section of the ANC, led by Robert Sobukwe, broke away to create the African-only Pan-African Congress (PAC). After the 1960 massacre of people protesting against pass laws at Sharpeville, government repression became ever harsher through the 1960s and 70s: the ANC and PAC were banned in 1960, and Mandela, Sisulu and many other ANC leaders were imprisoned. Oliver Tambo led the organisation into exile first in London, then in Lusaka, his careful patience being rewarded with a massive influx of membership following the 1976 Soweto uprising. Many young ANC recruits were trained in Mozambique, Lesotho and Angola, returning to sabotage and disrupt the white war machine; the imposition in 1986 of a state of emergency only served to increase the organisation's determination to overcome apartheid. By the time the white South African government moved to negotiate with the ANC in the late 1980s, the Congress had become a well-organised and respected political movement: in 1989 its blueprint for change in South Africa, the Harare Declaration, was accepted by a number of governments and international organisations. After thirty long years the ANC was unbanned on February 2nd 1990 and immediately opened a Johannesburg office; Nelson Mandela was released from prison nine days later and became the ANC's official leader on March 2nd. With South Africa's first nonracial elections set for April 1994 the ANC quickly built up a formidable national organisation, with hundreds of local branches, led by a national executive committee and a range of research and policy departments. It surprised nobody that the African National Congress won a clear majority in the constituent assembly and, despite the enormity of the task of rebuilding South Africa as a democratic, egalitarian society, Nelson Mandela's moderate yet decisive leadership of the ANC's broad-based membership has largely succeeded in bringing South Africa calmly through the early days of its new order.

Mary Benson, *The African Patriots: The Story of the African National Congress of South Africa*, Faber and Faber, 1963

Francis Meli, *South Africa Belongs To Us: A History of the ANC*, Zimbabwe Publishing House, 1988

Willie Esterhuyse and Philip Nel (eds), *The ANC and its Leaders*, Tafelberg, 1990

Heidi Holland, *The Struggle: A History of the African National Congress*, Braziller, 1990

AIDS Coalition to Unleash Power [ACT-UP]
1987–
health campaigning network

The AIDS Coalition to Unleash Power began in March 1987, after the gay health activist and playwright **Larry Kramer** told an audience of gay men in San Francisco that two thirds of them might well be dead within five years. Concern quickly turned into action, and a growing network of AIDS activists, angry about the US government's unwillingness to devote time and resources to AIDS research and treatment, has become increasingly vocal about its determination to understand the condition and to find ways of offering cheap and available therapy for AIDS sufferers. ACT-UP activists are convinced that the government and the medical establishment have consistently blocked the development of a cure for AIDS, and have artificially inflated the cost of available treatments. ACT-UP now has chapters and affiliated organisations worldwide, and works to exchange ideas related to AIDS activism and to maintain a lively debate about the politics of AIDS and public health care. ACT-UP's demands include free medical care for all infected with HIV, affordable treatment on demand, and access to clean syringes and needles for addicted drug users. Its actions have included petitions, marches, interruptions of public events, silent stand-up protests during church services, members chaining themselves to a balcony in the New York Stock Exchange, covering official buildings with red tape to symbolise government delays, spraying outlines of bodies on the street to represent those who have died, and traffic-stopping 'die-ins'. From its inception women have been conspicuously active within ACT-UP. During a conference on Women and HIV Infection in Washington in December 1990, for example, women from ACT-UP interrupted speakers from the US Centers for Disease Control and the National Institutes of Health (the chief funders of AIDS research in the USA), demanding that largescale studies on women at risk of infection should be carried out, and that the official definition of AIDS should be widened to include manifestations of the virus particular to women. The demand for equal access to testing and information for women continues: in 1994 an ACT-UP affiliate, the New York-based HIV Law Project, filed a Citizen's Petition against the Food and Drug Administration demanding equal access for women living with HIV.

Margaret Cruikshank, *The Gay and Lesbian Liberation Movement*, Routledge, 1992

American Civil Liberties Union [ACLU]
1920–
civil rights organisation

When the American Civil Liberties Union was formed in 1920 the freedoms promised by the US constitution were being denied on almost every front: attorney general A. Mitchell Palmer was waging war against the **Industrial Workers of the World** (IWW), many first world war conscientious objectors were still in prison, racial segregation was considered the law of the land,

and sex discrimination was firmly institutionalised. The ACLU was founded by a group of likeminded libertarians including **Jane Addams**, **Elizabeth Gurley Flynn**, Helen Keller, Norman Thomas, Morris Hillquit and Roger Baldwin. Baldwin, a draft refuser during the first world war who had with **Crystal Eastman** established a civil liberties bureau within the American Union Against Militarism in 1917, served as the ACLU's executive director for thirty years. In its first year the ACLU worked to prevent the deportation of aliens for their radical beliefs, opposed attacks on the rights of the IWW and trade unions to hold meetings and organise, and secured the release of hundreds imprisoned for expressing antiwar opinions. In March 1925 Tennessee passed a law forbidding the teaching of Darwinian evolution, and the ACLU at once sought to test this infringement of free speech, securing John Scopes, a young science teacher, as a plaintiff. The veteran radical lawyer Clarence Darrow headed the ACLU's volunteer defence team, and although Scopes was convicted on a technicality the $100 fine was later waived. In 1939, when Jersey City mayor Frank Hague claimed the right to deny free speech to anyone he thought radical, the ACLU successfully prosecuted him in the Supreme Court; in 1940, however, many radicals felt that the ACLU had itself become a tool of the establishment when it ousted Elizabeth Gurley Flynn for being an active member of the Communist Party. Two and a half months after the Japanese attack on Pearl Harbor in 1942, 110,000 Japanese Americans were sent to concentration camps, an episode described by the ACLU as 'the worst single wholesale violation of civil rights of American citizens in our history': the Union did much to publicise their case. Throughout the 1950s the ACLU fought the McCarthyite witch-hunt of supposed 'subversives', and in 1954 played a major part in the successful battle to make the racial segregation of schools illegal. In 1973 the ACLU was the first major national organisation to call for the impeachment of president Richard Nixon for using illegal methods of surveillance, and in the same year it played an important role in decriminalising abortion. In defending the universal right to free speech, the ACLU has several times been accused of inciting hatred, the best known case being its 1977 defence of a group of American Nazis wanting to demonstrate in the streets of Skokie, a predominantly Jewish suburb of Chicago, yet during the 1980s and 90s the ACLU has continued to fight for civil rights on a wide range of radical fronts, including gay rights, reproductive freedom, action against censorship and religious tolerance. With a membership in excess of a quarter of a million, three hundred chapters throughout the USA, and sixty staff attorneys handling more than six thousand cases each year, the ACLU continues to prove that, in Roger Baldwin's words, 'Eternal vigilance is the price of liberty'.

Peggy Lamson, *Roger Baldwin, Founder of the American Civil Liberties Union: A Portrait*, Houghton Mifflin, 1976

Donald Oscar Johnson, *The Challenge to American Freedoms: World War I and the Rise of the American Civil Liberties Union*, University of Kentucky Press, 1963

Samuel Walker, *In Defense of American Liberties: A History of the ACLU*, Oxford University Press, 1990

William A. Donohue, *Twilight of Liberty: The Legacy of the ACLU*, Transaction Publishers, 1994

American Friends Service Committee [AFSC]
1917–
peace campaigning organisation

From its establishment in the seventeenth century, members of the Society of Friends (also known as Quakers) have refused to participate in war, believing that violence suppresses love, truth and freedom, and breeds fear, hatred and prejudice. Three weeks after the USA entered the first world war in 1917, fourteen members of the American Society of Friends met to discuss what Quakers might do to alleviate the agony of wartorn Europe, explaining in founder member Rufus Jones's words that 'The alternative to war is not inactivity and cowardice. It is the irresistible and constructive power of goodwill.' Within six months, 116 men and women were trained and sent to France to do civilian relief work. After the war AFSC greatly expanded its research and relief work, and in 1924 became a permanent organisation. Under Clarence Pickett, executive secretary from 1929 until 1950, AFSC extended its activities throughout the world, sending relief aid to both loyalists and nationalists during the **Spanish Civil War**, and sending $7 million worth of relief aid to battle-scarred Europe and Japan. In 1947 AFSC and its British counterpart the Friends Service Council were awarded the Nobel Peace Prize. Though AFSC has earned worldwide respect for its relief work, it sees its primary purpose as promoting peace and reconciliation. During the 1930s it organised work-camps and peace caravans, publications and a large network of speakers, and after the second world war spoke out strongly for unilateral disarmament and arranged numerous seminars and conferences. In 1955 AFSC published the forward-looking and influential report *Speak Truth to Power*, laying out the prerequisites for world peace as full disarmament and an end to poverty and colonialism. During the **Vietnam War**, AFSC peace workers demonstrated publicly against American involvement, counselled men about the draft, and organised direct action projects against the war. In 1966 a group of activists led by Lawrence Scott founded A Quaker Action Group (AQAG), which achieved much publicity when it attempted to ship medical supplies into Vietnam, and led a nonviolent action to demilitarise the Puerto Rican island of Culebra where the US Navy carried out target practice. The Movement for a New Society (MNS) grew out of AQAG in 1971, setting up a range of projects to encourage a simple lifestyle and create a source of sustained fellowship and moral support. MNS encourages community involvement, collective work, and a broad concept of nonviolence which unites political action with responsible and joyful living.

Clarence Pickett, *For More Than Bread, An Autobiographical Account of Twenty-Two Years' Work with the American Friends Service Committee*, Little Brown, 1953

Marvin Ross Weisbord, *Some Form of Peace: True Stories of the American Friends Service Committee at Home and Abroad*, Viking, 1968

Robert Cooney and Helen Michalowski (eds), *The Power of the People: Active Nonviolence in the United States*, New Society, 1987

American Indian Movement [AIM]
1968–
self-determination movement

The American Indian Movement, an activist Indian group concerned with the civil rights of American Indians, was formed in 1968 in Minneapolis and was initially created to oppose the discriminatory practices of the police in the arrest of Indians in Minneapolis and St. Paul. The appeal of the social movement quickly spread to other urban areas in the United States and Canada, where chapters of AIM were formed. In November 1972, AIM was instrumental in the week-long occupation by Indians of the Bureau of Indian Affairs building in Washington DC, and early in 1973 the group's ten-week takeover of Wounded Knee, an Oglala Sioux hamlet on the Pine Ridge reservation in South Dakota, attracted worldwide attention, largely because of the US government's violent response: calling the AIM 'the shock troops of Indian sovereignty', the Bureau of Indian Affairs murdered several AIM leaders including Pedro Bissonette of the Oglala Sioux. By the time the government-requisitioned section of Pine Ridge was returned to the Oglala in 1976, 69 Indians had died and 350 had been seriously wounded. In 1974 AIM created the International Indian Treaty Council, which in 1977 was given official nongovernmental organisation status with the United Nations, the first indigenous group in the world to be so recognised. In 1981 AIM leader Russell Means led a group to a traditional Indian site in the Black Hills near Rapid City, land claimed by the US Forest Service; this time a restraining order on the federal authorities prevented a repeat of Pine Ridge, and the 'Yellow Thunder Camp' occupation lasted until 1986, spawning several similar actions. Although largely an urban phenomenon that arose in response to racist attitudes in American cities, AIM has also become involved in tribal affairs on Indian reservations, though some tribal peoples disclaim affiliation with the movement, accusing it of provoking confrontation. In addition to being a social activist movement, the group is firmly oriented toward native spirituality and, based still in Minneapolis, continues to work for American Indian rights.

Rex Weyler, *Blood of the Land: The Government and Corporate War against the American Indian Movement*, Everest House, 1982

Ward Churchill and Jim Vander Wall, *Agents of Repression: The FBI's Secret Wars against the Black Panther Party and the American Indian Movement*, South End Press, 1988

Kenneth Stern, *Loud Hawk: The United States versus the American Indian Movement*, University of Oklahoma Press, 1994

Amnesty International
1961–
human rights organisation

Amnesty International originated in a newspaper article, 'The Forgotten Prisoners', written by English lawyer Peter Benenson and published in the newspaper *The Observer* in May 1961. At that time student protestors in Portugal and trade unionists in Spain were being arrested, dissenters faced long prison terms in East Germany, detainees in South Africa were being brutally ill-treated, civil rights workers in the USA were being persecuted, political trials were taking place in the Soviet Union, and in many other countries people were being imprisoned, tortured or executed because their opinions were unacceptable to the ruling authorities. Benenson called for an 'Appeal for Amnesty' to free men and women held in prison because of their religious and political beliefs, for the first time calling them 'prisoners of conscience', though he made it clear that Amnesty would not support prisoners who had used or advocated violence. Within a month more than a thousand people had offered to help, and six months later a permanent international movement had been established. One of Amnesty's first prisoners of conscience was **Nelson Mandela**, but when in 1964 he was convicted of sabotage by the South African government his Amnesty support group, in strict accordance with Amnesty guidelines on the use of violence even in difficult cases like Mandela's, ended its campaign on his behalf. Following an internal controversy in 1966 centering on the investigation of torture allegations by the British authorities in Aden, Peter Benenson was replaced by an elected director general. Nevertheless, Amnesty's activities grew rapidly, and by the mid-1980s the organisation had national sections in forty-four countries, local groups in sixty countries, and a worldwide membership of more than half a million. In 1977 Amnesty International was awarded the Nobel Peace Prize for its contribution to 'securing the ground for freedom, for justice, and thereby also for peace in the world.' Amnesty International opposes the use of torture and the death penalty, and issues regular reports on human rights conditions throughout the world. It calls for observance of the United Nations Universal Declaration of Human Rights, the International Covenant on Civil and Political Rights, and other international human rights agreements. One of its most important contributions to human rights observance is its willingness to maintain dialogue with governments of every political complexion, thus ensuring its complete neutrality; it is for this reason that it has never accepted government funding. At its 1991 international meeting in Yokohama, Japan, Amnesty adopted a pioneering resolution recognising as prisoners of conscience gay men and lesbians who are imprisoned for their choice of sexuality. London-based Amnesty now has 47 national sections and members in 150 countries.

Egon Larsen, *A Flame in Barbed Wire: The Story of Amnesty International*, Muller, 1978

Cosmas Desmond, *Persecution East and West: Human Rights, Political Prisoners, and Amnesty*, Penguin, 1983

Amnesty International, *Voices for Freedom*, Amnesty International Publications, 1986

Marie Staunton and Sally Fenn (eds), *The Amnesty International Handbook*, Optima, 1990

Animal Rights Movement
c.1820–
liberation movement

The prevention of cruelty to animals became an important movement in early nineteenth-century England, where it developed alongside the anti-slavery movement. The first anticruelty bill was introduced in parliament in 1800, and in 1824 Richard Martin, who two years earlier had succeeded in establishing legislation to prevent cruelty to domestic animals, founded the Society for the Prevention of Cruelty to Animals (SPCA) to help enforce the law: Queen Victoria added the prefix 'Royal' in 1840. Henry Bergh established the American SPCA in New York in 1866; he hoped it would become a national organisation, but the ASPCA remained primarily a local animal shelter programme. The American Humane Association (AHA), with divisions for children and animals, was founded in 1877, and became the leading national advocate for animal protection and child protection services. The antivivisection movement was strong in Britain and the USA in the 1890s, but by the early twentieth century had been overwhelmed by the prestige of scientific medicine. Led by organisations like the Humanitarian League and the powerful voices of **Leo Tolstoy** and Émile Zola, **Percy Bysshe Shelley** and George Bernard Shaw, the European animal rights movement worked hard to stop animal cruelty and promote compassion and vegetarianism. By the mid-twentieth century national associations for the protection of animals had been established in most Western countries, while in north America a growing network of humane groups flourished on an expanding base of pet lovers. During the mid-1950s increasing pressure to widen animal protection into active advocacy created divisions within the movement, particularly in the USA, where in 1954 the more activist Humane Society of the United States split from the American Humane Association, which in turn engendered further internal dissent. Still in the USA, the Society for Animal Protective Legislation was established in 1955 to lobby for the Humane Slaughter Act, which was passed in 1958. The 1960s and 70s saw the launch of a number of important national and international animal welfare organisations, including the International Primate Protection League, launched in 1973 following public concern stimulated by Jane Goodall and Dian Fossey's work with chimpanzees and gorillas. In the 1970s the animal rights movement began to find respectable intellectual and ethical underpinning in the work of academics like Peter Singer and Tom Regan, Richard Ryder and Stephen Clark, who popularised the concept of 'speciesism' as an equally oppressive parallel to racism and sexism. Animal rights activists, of whom it is estimated that three-quarters are women, were now able to ask – with feminist biologists like Caroline Merchant – questions such as 'Can all living things suffer? Do trees have standing? Do rocks have rights?' During the 1970s campaigners also began to use direct action tactics to oppose laboratory experimentation on animals, factory farming, hunting and the wearing of fur. Animal rights organisations proliferated in the early 1980s, from the militant Animal Liberation Front to wildlife rescue networks, and a new tactical and political sophistication led to some high-profile successes, such as US government support to phase out the infamous Draize Eye Irritancy Test and the LD 50 Test (which establishes the dose of a toxic substance that will kill half of a group of test animals). As the issues around animal rights have expanded and become more complex, questions of 'purity' have sometimes divided the movement. On one hand the philosopher Tom Regan believes in 'animal rights fundamentalism', a compete abolition of all exploitation of animals for human purposes; on the other the founder of People for the Ethical Treatment of Animals, Ingrid Newkirk, argues that cooperation with all allies, issue by issue, is the only way to achieve lasting success. At a more everyday level, there is much lively discussion about whether a vegan who eats no animal products is a better animal rights advocate than a vegetarian who eats cheese and milk, or an organic farmer who rears and eats humanely-produced meat. There is no doubt, however, that the animal rights movement has achieved a great deal of support and maturity during the 1980s and 90s, and animal rights are now firmly on the political agenda.

Peter Singer, *Animal Liberation*, Avon, 1977
Tom Regan, *The Case for Animal Rights*, University of California Press, 1983
Jon Wynne-Tyson (ed.), *The Extended Circle: A Dictionary of Humane Thought*, Centaur, 1985

Association of Community Organizations for Reform Now [ACORN]
1970–
community action network

Although by the mid 1960s the civil rights movement had achieved the legal ratification of many of the constitutional rights of poor Americans, the pervasive paradox of 'poverty amidst plenty' was all too evident. Welfare agencies now had an obligation to inform the poor of their rights, but only a minority understood the system well enough to use it to their best advantage. A number of welfare rights organisations sprang up across the country and in June 1966, following a national Walk for Adequate Welfare, a group of concerned activists including academics Richard Cloward and Frances Fox Piven, and Campaign for Racial Equality director George Wiley, established the National Welfare Rights Organization (NWRO). Soon the NWRO had 170 active groups in sixty cities, and the organisation successfully coordinated many 'basic needs' campaigns to ensure that poor people had adequate clothing and furniture. After 1969 the NWRO concentrated more on national lobbying to ensure nationally guaranteed levels of welfare support, and at the 1972 Democratic Convention presented a 'Poor People's Platform' which received widespread support. After Wiley's sudden death in 1973, however, the NWRO quickly fell apart. Meanwhile in Arkansas the seeds had been sown for what was to become America's largest community action network of the 1970s. When George Wiley sent NWRO organiser Wade Rathke to Little Rock in June 1970 they shared a vision of a multiracial, state-wide, neighbourhood-based operation which would address the whole range of issues facing low-and moderate-income Arkansans. In the midst of their first successful campaign, a redistribution of used furniture and appliances to a thousand poor families, Rathke gave his new organisation the name ACORN: Arkansas Community Organizations for Reform Now. As welfare reform dropped down the political agenda with nationwide reforms in place, ACORN rapidly expanded its membership by stressing community solidarity in the face of official compacency. By 1974, with a network of offices and a membership of more than 50,000, ACORN was using vigils, petitions and sit-ins to force power companies to reduce charges for poorer families and to offer compensation to pollution-affected farmers. By 1980, renamed the Association of Community Organizations for Reform Now, ACORN's activities covered more than a dozen states. During the presidential campaign of 1980 ACORN again set out a 'People's Platform', and in Philadelphia in 1981 initiated a large-scale programme of squatting empty city houses to protest against homelessness. The campaign soon spread to a dozen other cities, culminating in the erection of a 'tent city' alongside the White House in June 1982: a year later Congress enacted important new low-income housing legislation. ACORN membership contracted in the mid-1980s, but the organisation, now based in Washington DC, continues to work at grassroots and national levels for the rights of America's poorer citizens, particularly in the areas of housing and access to financial services. In 1989 ACORN was one of the instigators of the Financial Democracy Campaign, an alliance of more than four hundred groups working for a safe and democratic financial system for ordinary Americans; in 1990 it presented a revised fourteen-point People's Platform to Congress; and in 1993 initiated a campaign to provide fair and affordable insurance for low-income black households. More than 75,000 families currently belong to the organisation, a majority being women-headed black and Latino households.

Madeleine Adamson and Seth Borgos, *This Mighty Dream: Social Protest Movements in the United States*, Routledge and Kegan Paul, 1985

Gary Delgado, *Organizing the Movement: The Roots and Growth of ACORN*, Temple University Press, 1986

Daniel Russell, *Political Organizing in Grassroots Politics*, University Press of America, 1990

David Walls, *The Activist's Almanac: The Concerned Citizen's Guide to the Leading Advocacy Organizations in America*, Simon and Schuster, 1993

Bangladesh Rural Advancement Committee [BRAC]
1972–
rural development organisation

Following the Bangladesh War of Liberation against Pakistan in 1970–71, many thousands of poor Bangladeshi refugees returned from India, and in 1972 relief official F.H. Abed set up BRAC to improve the plight of the rural poor by developing their ability to mobilise and manage their own resources. The organisation's growth was phenomenal, and by 1990 it was the largest development organisation in Bangladesh, employing more than 4,000 staff and with a membership of 350,000, 60% of them women, in 3,200 villages. BRAC focuses on the landless and operates on the principle of cooperative self-help, covering a wide range of linked areas including education, training, health, legal advice, credit support and small-scale agricultural and economic development. Continuing to expand its activities in the early 1990s, recent successes have included the establishment of a community bank, the production of a citizens' report on the Bangladeshi environment, and the transfer of production from tobacco (increasingly being recognised in Bangladesh as a serious health hazard) to silk for use in community workshops.

BRAC, *A Brief on BRAC*, BRAC, Dhaka, 1988
Paul Ekins, *A New World Order*, Routledge, 1992

Beat Generation
1949–*c*.1967
cultural protest movement

The grouping of protest artists to which author Jack Kerouac gave the name 'the beat generation' came together in San Francisco in the early 1950s. Although it was a cultural movement rather than an overtly political one, and was generally more interested in drugs, mysticism and sexual experimentation than in social activism, Beat opposition to racism, militarism and capitalism was passionate and consistent. The Beats (the name neatly linked the ideas of weariness with the old order and the beatification of the new) provided a nurturing environment for the counterculture of the 1960s with which the **new left** was inextricably linked. Kerouac and his friends Neil Cassady, Gregory Corso, Lawrence Ferlinghetti, Allen Ginsberg and **Gary Snyder** formed the core of the Beats, whose chief contributions to the rapidly-expanding counterculture were small press publishing and performance poetry, both of which became an essential part of the alternative politics of the 1960s and beyond. In 1953 Lawrence Ferlinghetti opened the pioneering City Lights bookstore in San Francisco, and Allen Ginsberg's 1956 collection of protest poems, *Howl*, sold nearly half a million copies, proving it possible to bypass mainstream publishing houses and still reach a mass audience. It was during a public reading of *Howl* in a San

Francisco coffee-house that Ginsberg was arrested and charged with obscenity, an action guaranteed to achieve national attention and widespread admiration. Some of the Beats had a more or less clear political mission: Gary Snyder to understand the importance of nature and the active spiritual life; William Everson (alias Brother Antoninus) to reconcile Roman Catholicism and social activism; Allen Ginsberg to work for peace (during a 1967 Pentagon action he led a group which attempted to levitate the building by sounding a Buddhist OM). Others, like Jack Kerouac and William Burroughs, sank deeply into drugs and reactionary nihilism. By the late 1960s many new left activists had taken on board the spirit of the Beats, including **Abbie Hoffman** with books like *Woodstock Nation* (1969) and its printed exhortation to 'Steal This Book', and **Yippie** Jerry Rubin: the Beats had entered the annals of American cultural history.

> Roger Lewis, *Outlaws of America: The Underground Press and Its Context: Notes on a Cultural Revolution*, Penguin, 1972
> Paul Buhle, Jayne Cortez, Philip Lamantia, Franklin Rosemont, Penelope Rosemont, and Nancy Joyce Peters (eds), *Free Spirits: Annals of the Insurgent Imagination*, City Lights Books, 1982
> Barry Miles, *Ginsberg: A Biography*, Simon and Schuster, 1989

Beheiren [Betonamu ni Heiwa o Shimin Rengō, People's Organisation for Peace in Vietnam]
1965–1974
peace organisation

When American forces started bombing North Vietnam in 1965, a number of Japanese peace activists joined forces to establish Beheiren, a broadly-based antiwar group. The organisers of the group included novelists Oda Makoto and Kaitō Ken, and sociologist Tsurumi Shunsuke. Beheiren held a number of teach-ins about the American involvement in Vietnam, published a weekly magazine, and in 1966 ran a full-page 'Stop the Bombing' advertisement in the *New York Times*, offering refuge in Japan to American soldiers who deserted on conscientious grounds. The organisation was disbanded in January 1974 on the first anniversary of the Paris Peace Treaty.

> Thomas Havens, *Fire Across the Sea: The Vietnam War and Japan 1965–1975*, Princeton University Press, 1987

Black Panther Party [BPP]
1966–1975
black liberation movement

Though the Black Panther Party's espousal of militancy puts it on the edge of the civil rights movement, it was the best known black activist organisation of the late 1960s, and had the express and considered political goal of black self-determination. For several years the BPP provided young urban American black people with a model of reasoned resistance against arbitrary police power and widespread discrimination. The Black Panther Party for Self-Defense ('for Self-Defense' was dropped in 1967) was founded by Huey Newton and Bobby Seale, who had been students together at Oakland's Merritt College. Inspired by the ideas of **Frantz Fanon** and **Malcolm X**, they saw the BPP's chief role as monitoring police activities in black communities in order to ensure that civil rights were being respected, and soon many young urban blacks were seen wearing the BPP's distinctive black berets and leather jackets. The BPP's hardline stance on black self-determination inevitably led the organisation into regular conflict with the police, and in October 1967 Huey Newton was arrested on a murder charge after an altercation with Oakland police which left one policeman dead and another injured. With the Party's leader in jail, prison activist and Malcolm X follower Eldridge Cleaver became the Panthers' minister of information: a powerful speaker, he called for oppressed blacks to liberate themselves – by force if necessary. Early in 1968 Stokely Carmichael, looking for a new cause following the demise of the **Student National Coordinating Committee** (with which the BPP had a short alliance), challenged Cleaver's leadership, but the internal struggle was overshadowed by a determined FBI campaign to destroy the organisation. On April 6th 1968 police raided a house where several Panthers were living, killing the seventeen-year-old treasurer and wounding Cleaver. By the end of the decade 28 Panthers had been killed. After Huey Newton was released from prison in 1970 he stressed the need for the BPP to involve itself in community service and to take part in electoral politics, but by 1975, faced with further criminal charges, he had fled to Cuba and the BPP was all but extinct.

Bobby Seale, *Seize the Time: The Story of the Black Panther Party and Huey P. Newton*, Random House, 1970
Philip Foner, *The Black Panthers Speak*, Lippincott, 1970
Huey Newton, *Revolutionary Suicide*, Harcourt Brace Jovanovich, 1973

Buraku Kaihō Undō [Buraku Emancipation Movement; formerly Suiheisha, Levelling Movement]
1922–
civil rights organisation

Japan's outcast class, or *burakumin*, traces its origins to ancient times. There are some 100,000 people of *burakumin* origin in Japan: despite the legal equality granted them in 1871, widespread discrimination against them persists to this day. The first *burakumin* rights associations were established in the early 1900s, advocating education and self-help as the main ways of overcoming discrimination, but it was not until the formation of the national organisation Suiheisha in March 1922 that *buraku* liberation achieved a unified voice and direction. Suiheisha, under the leadership of **Matsumoto Jiichirō**, condemned all discrimination and called for political, economic and social reform; by the late 1920s the organisation, now dominated by Bolshevik ideas of proletarian revolution, was a major player in Japan's grassroots socialist movement. Its influence started to wane again in the 1930s and during the war it became almost completely dormant, but the *buraku* cause was kept alive by Matsumoto Jiichirō throughout his long service in the Diet (Japanese parliament), from his election in 1936 to his death thirty years later. Between 1946 and 1950 he helped to resuscitate the popular movement as Buraku Kaihō Undō, which again became a broadly-based leftwing movement which received widespread support. In 1955 it was renamed the Buraku Kaihō Dōmei (Buraku Emancipation League), which represents a large number of *burakumin* communities. Its strong leftwing tendencies have, however, discouraged others from joining; several more moderate communities have formed their own federation, the Dōwakai, and rivalry between the two organisations has impeded progress towards *buraku* emancipation.

George De Vos and Hiroshi Wagatsuma, *Japan's Invisible Race*, University of California Press, 1966

Theodore Brameld, *Japan: Culture, Education and Change in Two Communities*, Holt, Rinehart and Winston, 1968

Ian Neary, *Political Protest and Social Control in Pre-war Japan: The Origins of Buraku Liberation*, Manchester University Press, 1989

Campaign for Nuclear Disarmament [CND]
1958–
peace organisation

The world's first atomic bomb test took place in the New Mexico desert in July 1945, and a month later Hiroshima and Nagasaki lay in ruins, the only cities ever to be deliberately destroyed by these frighteningly powerful new weapons. Thenceforth, however, the world lay under the perpetual threat that the proliferating nuclear stockpiles would one day be used: as the threat grew, so did the voices of concern and protest. In Britain, where much of the early nuclear research had been done, a hundred Cambridge scientists petitioned the government to stop working on the bomb in 1950, but the country's leaders were determined to remain runners in the nuclear race and the first British atomic warhead was tested in October 1952. Over the next few years antinuclear initiatives multiplied, involving a growing number of well-known peace and human rights campaigners including veteran pacifist churchman John Collins, pacifist Labour politician Fenner Brockway, women's suffrage campaigner Gertrude Fishwick and peace campaigners Pat Arrowsmith and Peggy Duff. During the summer of 1957 antinuclear activists within the Labour Party formed the Labour H-bomb Campaign Committee and organised a four thousand-strong unilateral nuclear disarmament rally in London's Trafalgar Square: it was to be the first of many. At the end of that year Kingsley Martin, editor of the leftwing *New Statesman*, convened a meeting to launch a nationwide mass movement against nuclear weapons, and CND held its first meeting in January 1958, with **Bertrand Russell** (the initiator in 1955 of the Pugwash conference for scientists working for peace) as president and John Collins as chairman. The first of many Easter marches from the atomic weapons research laboratory at Aldermaston to central London took place three months later, with banners carrying the circular symbol, designed by Gerald Holtom, which was to become synonymous with the antinuclear campaign worldwide. Late in 1960 an internal CND disagreement became public when John Collins criticised Bertrand Russell's involvement with a militant splinter group, the Committee of 100 (descendants of the Direct Action Group which had attempted to disrupt British tests in the Pacific in 1958). Russell resigned from the presidency and CND was further debilitated by internal debates about democracy and civil disobedience, yet the Committee of 100's newsworthy 1961 campaign of sit-downs in London streets kept the antinuclear issue alive. From 1962 to 1980, though the nuclear disarmament debate continued, CND was more or less dormant, but **E.P. Thompson** and Dan Smith's powerful 1980 rebuttal of the official 'nuclear protection' argument, *Protest and Survive*, attracted many new members both to CND and to the new European campaign END (European Nuclear Disarmament). Eighty thousand people attended a rally in London the following October to protest against the deployment of US cruise missiles at **Greenham Common** in Berkshire, where in mid-1981 a **Women's Peace Camp** was established which was to become a potent symbol of pacifist concern and inspire similar actions in several other countries. In October 1983 nearly half a million CND demonstrators filled Trafalgar Square, and in 1984 a growing number of 'peace camps' were established alongside nuclear bases, most notably the Rainbow Fields Village at Molesworth in Cambridgeshire: the destruction of the Molesworth camp by troops and police the following February increased public sympathy. By the end of the 1980s CND, END and the worldwide nuclear disarmament movement had played an important part in breaking the international deadlock which had powered the nuclear arms race for thirty years. While it was most immediately Mikhail Gorbachev's historic 1987 decision to remove intermediate-range nuclear weapons from Europe that led to the first major reductions in the world's nuclear arsenals, the nuclear disarmament campaign had brought the issue to the attention of many millions, of whom hundreds of thousands had taken personal action against weapons of mass destruction. Though CND in the mid-1990s no longer has the widespread appeal of the 1960s and 80s, it continues to campaign for the complete elimination of all nuclear weapons, particularly Britain's own nuclear arsenal which that country has so far refused to decommission.

John Minnion and Philip Bolsover (eds), *The CND Story*, Allison and Busby, 1983
Joan Ruddock, *CND Scrapbook*, Optima, 1987
James Hinton, *Protests and Visions: Peace Politics in Twentieth Century Britain*, Hutchinson, 1989

Charter 77
1977–1989
human rights movement

At the beginning of 1968 progressive Czechoslovak communist leaders decided that widespread political reform was needed. **Alexander Dubček** was elected to replace Antonía Novotný as first secretary of the Communist party, and began a wideranging programme entitled 'socialism with a human face' aimed at the democratisation of the Communist Party and growing independence from Moscow. A period of openness and cultural freedom, the 'Prague Spring', followed as the nation gave Dubček its support. Despite Dubček's assurances that Czechoslovakia would not abandon communism and leave the Soviet bloc the Soviet Union was uneasy, and when demands for a halt to liberalisation went unheeded Soviet forces invaded on August 21st 1968 and occupied the country. International condemnation forced the Soviet leaders to retain Dubček and his associates, but in April 1969 he was replaced by the hardline Gustav Husák. Dubček, now in forced isolation, became one symbol of the Prague Spring: a less ambiguous martyr was Jan Palach, a Prague student who in January 1969 immolated himself in protest at the Soviet invasion. Among the young Czechoslovak intellectuals determined not to let democracy die was playwright **Václav Havel**, who in April 1975 wrote an open letter to Husák expressing his concern about the longterm effects of fear and repression: Husák did not reply, and official intimidation continued. In 1977 Havel was one of the chief instigators of Charter 77, a group of 242 academics, intellectuals and churchmen who presented the Czech government with a signed charter demanding that it comply with the Universal Declaration of Human Rights. Many more signatories followed, as did official harassment, interrogation and imprisonment. The main Charter spokespeople – Havel, Jirí Hajek, and philosophy professor Jan Patočka – were treated particularly harshly, and Patočka died in March 1977 following a gruelling interrogation lasting many days. Despite official denunciation of Charter 77 as 'antipopulist libel' produced by a 'bankrupt reactionary bourgeoisie', the movement flowered during the 1980s. By the end of 1988, following Ivan Jirous's August article 'Enough is Enough' and the publication in October of the Movement for Civil Liberties' manifesto 'Democracy For All', the Czechoslovak people were hungry for democratic change. In January 1989, the twentieth anniversary of Jan Palach's death, a massive illegal demonstration was held in Prague's Wenceslas Square: the police cracked down and jailed many of the leaders, including Václav Havel, but international pressure and massive demonstrations secured his early release. On November 18th Havel declared the formation of the democratic political party Civic Forum; six days later the entire politburo of the Communist Party resigned and Husák's reign of fear ended. The 'Velvet Revolution', as it came to be known, demonstrated the power of a courageous, determined and sensitive civil rights movement and ensured that, despite political differences and economic problems, the Czech and Slovak republics (Czechoslovakia divided into its constituent parts in January 1993 following a peaceful referendum) have been remarkably successful in making the transition from state communism to popular democracy.

Hans-Peter Riese (ed.) (trans. Eugen Loebl), *Since the Prague Spring: The Continuing Struggle for Human Rights in Czechoslovakia*, Random House, 1979
Gordon Skilling, *Charter 77 and Human Rights in Czechoslovakia*, Allen and Unwin, 1981
Janusz Bugajski, *Czechoslovakia: Charter 77's Decade of Dissent*, Praeger, 1987
Gordon Skilling and Paul Wilson (eds), *Civic Freedom in Central Europe: Voices from Czechoslovakia*, St. Martin's Press, 1991

Chipko Movement
1973–
environmental protest movement

Among **Gandhi**'s many disciples were two English women, Madeleine Slade and Catherine Heilman, better known by their Indian names of Mirabehn and Saralabehn. After Indian independence Mirabehn established an ashram in the Himalayas above Tehri, and Saralabehn ran a girls' school. Both loved the Himalayan forests, and became increasingly concerned about the state forestry department's policy of licensing tracts of forest, which for generations had provided sustainable crops for local villagers, to private companies interested only in rapid and indiscriminate felling. One of Saralabehn's disciples married a young politician, Sunderlal Bahaguna, who under Mirabehn's influence renounced politics to work with the rural poor: during the 1960s they worked with the villagers of Tehri to establish a network of forest-based craft cooperatives. Their activities were increasingly threatened by commercial forestry, however, and villagers became angry about the destruction of the forest they had looked after for so many centuries. Early in 1970, when loggers with guns threatened a group of women and children in the forest above Reni, Gawra Devi bared her breasts in an act of defiance, declaring that 'the forest is our mother' and challenging them to kill her along with her trees. Numerous similar protests came to a head in 1973, when the concession to log part of the Mandal Forest in the Akananda Valley was given to a company from Allahabad, five hundred miles away, in preference to the local village cooperative. Remembering a two-hundred-year-old story about the willingness of members of the nature-worshipping Bishnois sect to die hugging their sacred trees rather than allow them to be felled, Mandal villagers protected their trees by hugging them. They used the Gharwali word for 'hugging' – chipko – to describe their action, and the Chipko Movement was born. Though this protest was ultimately successful there were many similar threats, and for the next ten years Bahaguna and his Chipko colleagues walked the length and breadth of northern India, helping to build Chipko into a powerful movement able to influence national forestry policy. Under the guidance of Chipko leader Chadi Prasad Bhatt, a tree planting campaign involved the planting of more than a million trees between 1973 and 1989, and by the end of the 1980s more than three hundred villages were actively supporting Chipko. In 1987 the Chipko Movement was awarded a Right Livelihood Award. Chipko has increasingly expanded its concerns to embrace other environmental threats: its members have led opposition to plans for quarrying and dam building, and the organisation has spawned several similar initiatives in other parts of India, such as the Appiko Movement in the southern state of Karnataka. Sunderlal Bahaguna's ideas about sustainable, locally based conservation now have widespread support both throughout India and internationally, one of his leading supporters being the environmental campaigner **Vandana Shiva**, who is herself based at Dehra Dun near the Chipko heartland.

Sunderlal Bahaguna, 'Chipko: From Saving the Forests to the Reconstruction of Society', *Replenishing the Earth: The Right Livelihood Awards 1986–89* (ed. Tom Woodhouse), Green Books, 1990

Thomas Weber, *Hugging the Trees: The Story of the Chipko Movement*, Viking, 1988

Fred Pearce, *Green Warriors: The People and the Politics behind the Environmental Revolution*, Bodley Head, 1991

Clamshell Alliance
1976–1978
antinuclear protest

The Clamshell Alliance was organised in 1976 in response to the planned construction of the Seabrook nuclear power plant on the coast of New Hampshire in the northeastern USA. Inspired by the year-long occupation which had just succeeded in cancelling construction of a nuclear plant in Wyhl, Germany, the Clamshell was conceived as a mass movement based on nonviolent direct action. After the civil rights movement it was only the second such attempt in US history, and the first to adopt affinity groups as its structural basis and consensus as its decision-making procedure. Clamshell actions followed a sequence designed to build a sense of community while at the same time drawing public attention to Seabrook and the issues of nuclear power. On August 1st 1976 eighteen local people walked onto the site and were arrested; they were followed three weeks later by 180 protestors, who were also arrested. At the end of April 1977, 2,400 from the New England region occupied the site; 1,400 who disregarded orders to leave were arrested and held for two weeks in seven armouries around the state. This action attracted many more people to the Clamshell, and intensive preparations, including nonviolence trainings, were made for another mass occupation in June 1978. When disagreement over whether to cut the chain link fence around the site could not be resolved, however, the informal leadership called off the occupation. A legal demonstration of 20,000 people on June 28th was Clamshell's largest, but the breakdown of its internal procedures resulted in the breakup of the alliance. Though its lifespan was short, the Clamshell served as an inspiration and model for other nonviolent direct action campaigns.

Barbara Epstein, *Political Protest and Cultural Revolution: Nonviolent Direct Action in the 1970s and 1980s*, University of California, 1991

Communes Movement
*c.*1825–
social and economic reform movement

The 'communes movement', also known as the 'communities movement' or the 'intentional community movement', covers a wide range of utopian and communal ideas and experiments. Its roots can be traced to tribal, village and monastic origins which are centuries old, but the modern movement is generally seen as having two main periods of growth and development: the first in the late nineteenth and early twentieth centuries, and the second starting in the mid-1970s. The first period of development had at its centre the utopian ideas of **Robert Owen** and **Charles Fourier**, and a number of model communities of which the best known were Owen's New Lanark (in Scotland) and New Harmony (in Indiana), and the Fourier-inspired Brook Farm near Boston, Massachusetts. Other nineteenth-century utopian communes in the USA included Étienne Cabet's experiments at Nauvoo, Illinois and St Louis, Iowa, Eric Jansen's Bishop's Hill in Illinois, and John Humphrey Noyes' Oneida in New York State: most suffered from the imposed extremist views of their founders. In Europe **Tolstoy**'s ideas inspired a number of communal projects such as the Whiteway Community in Gloucestershire, England. Other resource-sharing communes were inspired by simple Christianity, most notably the anabaptist Bruderhof ('brotherhood') community, which established its first communal house at Sannerz in Germany in 1922. In 1928 the Bruderhof made contact with the likeminded Hutterites in the USA, and by 1950 there were Bruderhof communes in Germany, Britain, Paraguay and the USA. By the early 1960s, however, the movement was in rapid decline; today the Bruderhof is active mostly in the USA, with smaller communities in Britain, Germany and Canada. The urge to get 'back to the land' and the communitarian ideas of **Petr Kropotkin** and **William Morris** led both to small-scale communal experiments and to wider social movements such as **Ebenezer Howard**'s 'garden cities movement', and the 'plotlands' and 'land settlement' movements in Britain. Between the two world wars a number of rural communes were established in Europe, America and Australia, but from the early 1930s onwards it was the Israeli 'kibbutz' which most fully developed the collective model, being owned communally by its members and organised on cooperative principles. During the second world war a number of conscientious objectors, particularly in Britain, established pacifist agricultural communes, usually known as 'colonies', but most of these experiments were wound up at the end of the war. The second major outburst of the communes movement, which started in the late 1960s and reached its peak in the late 1970s, was very much a concomitant of the growing counterculture of the period, inspired by a concern for equality, environmental responsibility, freedom and cooperation. Inspiration came from a range of sources, including psychologist B.F. Skinner's semi-utopian novel *Walden II* (1948), **Ernest Callenbach's** novel *Ecotopia* (1975), **Theodore Roszak's** *Person/Planet* (1979), spiritual leaders both Eastern and Western, the squatter movement, **Scott Nearing's** back-to-the-land philosophy, the need for spiritual and therapeutic retreat, and newly-published classics including the works of **Gerard Winstanley** and Petr Kropotkin. In north America four early 70s communities – Twin Oaks, Dandelion, East Wind and Sandhill – were founder members of the Federation of Egalitarian Communities, and by the late 1970s the commune movement in north America was expanding rapidly, with its own magazine, *Communities*, and an annual *Directory of Intentional Communities*: there are currently just over three hundred communal projects listed in the directory. In Britain the Communes Movement was started in 1968: among its early (and still active) members were Crabapple, Laurieston Hall, Redfield and Old Hall. The umbrella organisation in Britain is now called the Communes Network, which publishes the bi-annual *Diggers and Dreamers* directory listing more than eighty communal projects. Many other countries have active commune networks, including Germany, France, Spain, Holland, Italy, Denmark, Belgium, Austria, Australia and New Zealand.

John Mercer, *Communes: A Social History and Guide*, Prism, 1984
Corinne McLaughlin and Gordon Davidson, *Builders of the Dawn*, Sirius, 1985
David Pepper, *Communes and the Green Vision*, Green Print, 1991

Congress of Racial Equality [CORE]
1943–1968
civil rights organisation

On June 28th 1917, two days after American troops landed in France, eight thousand silent black people marched down New York's Fifth Avenue bearing banners saying 'Make America Safe for Democracy'. Among the march's leaders were **W.E.B. Du Bois** and James Wendell Thompson, who eight years earlier had founded the National Association for the Advancement of Colored People (NAACP) to fight for the freedom promised by the Thirteenth Amendment of 1865 but as yet almost entirely ignored. In the 1920s frustrated blacks began to read about **Gandhi's** successful direct action campaigns in India, and A. Philip Randolph (1889–1979), president of the influential Brotherhood of Sleeping Car Porters, organised a series of actions, culminating in a massive 1941 'March on Washington'. Randolph won his objective, a presidential order banning job discrimination, without the march taking place, but as yet there was still no national organisation for the promotion of civil rights through the use of nonviolent direct action. Into this gap emerged, early in 1943, the Chicago-based Congress of Racial Equality. During its early months CORE organised increasingly successful sit-ins in segregated restaurants and public facilities. James Farmer, one of CORE's founders who had served as race relations secretary for the

Fellowship of Reconciliation (FOR), then under the leadership of A.J. Muste, spread the word about what was happening in Chicago, and CORE groups were formed in Detroit, Syracuse and New York. By 1948 CORE had integrated many previously white-only establishments, including the Palisades Park in New Jersey, theatres in Denver, restaurants in Detroit, and swimming pools in Cleveland and Los Angeles, training hundreds of people in the techniques of nonviolent action. CORE's first major national demonstration was a Journey of Reconciliation, organised with the FOR, in the spring of 1947. An interracial group travelled by bus throughout the South, meeting with little harassment but with some arrests: **Bayard Rustin**, Joe Felmet and Igal Roodenko served thirty-day sentences on segregated North Carolina chaingangs for sitting together at the front of a bus. The Journey of Reconciliation gave national publicity to CORE and its use of nonviolent direct action to fight racial discrimination, but by the end of the decade CORE's influence had waned. The lessons of nonviolent resistance were, however, to prove crucial when in 1955 the black people of Montgomery, Alabama, refused (following Rosa Parks' courageous lead and strengthened by **Martin Luther King**'s organisational skills) to travel on segregated buses. The Montgomery bus boycott, which led to the historic 1956 supreme court decision that racial segregation was unconstitutional, vindicated the nonviolent methods pioneered by Gandhi and developed by CORE. When in early 1960 black college students in the South spontaneously generated a massive wave of lunch-counter sit-ins, CORE reactivated its network and organised solidarity picket lines in the north. In May 1961 CORE organised a series of Freedom Rides in the South, this time encountering severe violence. CORE was the most racially integrated of the civil rights groups, but many black activists now began calling for a black nationalist approach to justice. In 1964 James Farmer, wanting CORE to remain racially integrated, asked white members to withdraw from prominent roles. Under new leadership in 1967 CORE became an all-black organisation, and then a much-diminished black nationalist group which had virtually petered out by 1969.

Inge Powell Bell, *CORE and the Strategy of Nonviolence*, Random House, 1968
August Meier and Elliott Rudwick, *CORE: A Study in the Civil Rights Movement, 1942–1968*, University of Illinois Press, 1975

Cuban Revolution
1956–1961
democracy struggle

From Christopher Columbus's arrival in 1492 to the socialist revolution of 1959, the Caribbean island of Cuba rarely knew freedom. By the mid-sixteenth century the native population had been wiped out, to be replaced by African slave workers, and independence won in 1895 was quickly overturned by a US invasion in 1899. American forces occupied Cuba until 1902, and continued to have a strong hold over this island which the USA considered to be within its 'natural sphere of influence': the air and naval base at Guantánamo remains an important US 'possession'. A series of cruel and bloody dictatorships, latterly that of Fulgencia Batista, came to an end in 1958 when guerrilla columns led by Fidel Castro's Mexican-trained generals **Che Guevara** and Camilo Cienfuegos closed in on Havana: at the end of December Batista fled to the USA. Castro, who had arrived in Cuba in December 1956, was interviewed early in 1957 by senior *New York Times* reporter Herbert Matthews: he gave the man and his campaign an image of courageous and righteous struggle against tyranny which struck a strong chord with many on the left. Early in 1959 Fidel Castro's Rebel Army quickly established a radical socialist government in Havana which, much to the surprise and annoyance of the US government, won massive popular support. The new Cuban regime implemented a far-reaching programme of agrarian reform and nationalised several US-owned companies. Castro's success inspired many American radicals. James Baldwin, **C. Wright Mills** and **Jean-Paul Sartre** all visited Cuba and wrote in support of its brave socialist experiment, while thousands of students, many of whom visited Cuba in 1959–60, formed the Fair Play for Cuba Committee with its 'Hands Off Cuba' slogan. By the time US forces staged the abortive April 1961 Bay of Pigs invasion, the first military defeat of US troops in Latin America, the American left was divided over Cuba: pro-Soviet traditionalists were delighted by Soviet involvement in the Caribbean, while the **new left** regretted the swing towards hardline communism. Despite its sometimes repressive and aggressive tactics, the Castro regime brought many important benefits to ordinary Cubans: its education and health care programmes became models for many other developing countries. On the broader canvas, support for the Cuban revolution provided many American radicals with organisational experience which would prove invaluable when the US government turned its sights towards Vietnam.

Lee Locoweed, *Castro's Cuba: Cuba's Fidel*, Vintage, 1969
James O'Connor, *The Origins of Socialism in Cuba*, Cornell University Press, 1970
Wayne Smith, *The Closest of Enemies*, Norton, 1987
Philip Brenner, *From Confrontation to Negotiations: US-Cuban Relations*, Westview Press, 1988
Philip Brenner *et al*, *Cuba Reader*, Grove, 1989

Daughters of Bilitis [DOB]
1955–c.1971
lesbian liberation organisation

In 1894 the French poet Pierre Louys published an expurgated edition of *Les chansons de Bilitis*, supposedly translated from the Greek, about the adventures of Bilitis, one of the circle of women who assembled around the lesbian poetess Sappho in the sixth century BC. It was only after Louys' death, in the late 1920s, that unedited editions of *Chansons de Bilitis* appeared, including several explicitly lesbian passages. When the world's first politically-oriented lesbian organisation was established in San Francisco in October 1955 it drew on the legend of Bilitis for its name, nonsensical to most observers but full of meaning to lesbians. DOB's founders, Del Martin and Phyllis Lyon, had settled in San Francisco as lovers in 1953, and with six other women established the organisation along the lines of the male gay **Mattachine Society** to attempt to change public attitudes towards lesbianism. In April 1956 DOB joined forces with the Mattachine Society to sponsor a conference on strategies for changing public opinion, and in October 1956 started to produce the monthly magazine *The Ladder*, an important publication which for sixteen years was to air a wide range of lesbian issues and help break down the isolation of lesbian women. As well as countering misinformation and prejudice about lesbian women, DOB also provided self-help and a sense of belonging in a society largely hostile towards same-sex relationships. Although DOB never attracted many working class women, nor professional women who felt they had already achieved recognition, for more than a decade it was the main rallying point for lesbians in the USA.

Del Martin and Phyllis Lyon, *Lesbian/Woman* (rev. ed., first pub. 1972), Bantam, 1983

Evelyn Gettone, 'Bilitis', *Encyclopedia of Homosexuality* (ed. Wayne Dynes), Garland, 1990

Democracy Movement
1989–
civil rights movement

Following the death of **Mao Zedong** in 1976 the efficient but ruthless economic reformer Deng Xiaoping eventually emerged triumphant. From 1979 onwards he set out to dismantle Mao's bureaucratic collective regime to create a market-led economy which, over the next ten years, was to create rampant inflation, officially-sanctioned profiteering and widespread misuse of public funds. University students were seen as the money-earning potential of China's rosy future, yet many were uneasy with the appalling quality of life of most Chinese, and felt alienated both from their own cultural roots and from students in other countries. In December 1986 there were student demonstrations in several Chinese cities, the largest in Shanghai, demanding democracy, honest elections and press freedom. The 1987 Student Movement was officially labelled 'bourgeois liberalisation', arising from the 'lack of a resolute attitude by certain leading comrades' in the Chinese Communist Party (CCP), particularly general secretary Hu Yaobang. Hu was considered by many Chinese liberals to be one of the few officials open to demands for democratisation and untainted by corruption, and following his death on April 15th 1989 three thousand Beijing students marched to Tiananmen Square to submit a petition demanding, among other things, the officially-sanctioned right to hold protest demonstrations. By April 18th 30,000 students had gathered in the square, rising to 200,000 by the evening of the 21st. Forty-seven academics presented a petition requesting government recognition of the student's Democracy Movement, but the document was rejected. On April 22nd, the date set for

Hu Yaobang's funeral, an action committee formed by students from nineteen Beijing universities organised a march to Tiananmen Square to take part in the funeral. On April 26th an official statement claimed that the Movement was a 'planned conspiracy by a handful of troublemakers in illegal organisations', and a 20,000-strong élite battalion of the Chinese army was ordered into Beijing. Further large-scale demonstrations took place at the beginning of May, organised by the newly-formed Autonomous Students' Union of Beijing Universities (ASUBU), and in the face of official inaction three thousand students started a hunger strike in Tiananmen Square on May 13th. On May 18th student leader Wuer Kaixi appeared in a televised dialogue with CCP Premier Li Peng, but the Chinese government line hardened, and on May 20th martial law was declared. The scene was now set for a showdown. Demonstrations and marches in support of the Beijing students were held across the country and in neighbouring Hong Kong, and the students continued their protest in Tiananmen Square, on May 30th installing a Goddess of Democracy statue. On the evening of June 3rd the government's patience snapped: with more than 100,000 people in the square soldiers and tanks moved in, ruthlessly mowing down anything in their path. By the following day more than five thousand people had died or 'gone missing', and 30,000 were injured. The ASUBU was declared illegal, and on June 9th Deng Xiaoping appeared on television to congratulate the troops. Thousands of students, including the Movement's leaders **Chai Ling**, Li Lu, Wuer Kaixi and Wang Dan left China for the safety of Hong Kong and the West. The 1989 Democracy Movement, also known as the 'Beijing Spring', was not an isolated incident on China's road to modern communism. It demonstrated a widespread dislike and mistrust of a corrupt authoritarian state willing to use any weapon to control dissenters. By early 1995 it was clear that an elderly and ailing Deng Xiaoping was losing his hold on power at the head of the CCP, and once Deng is no more the issue of democracy in China will resurface with renewed urgency.

Mok Chiu Yu and J. Frank Harrison, *Voices from Tiananmen Square: Beijing Spring and the Democracy Movement*, Black Rose, 1990

Ruth Cherrington, *China's Students: The Struggle for Democracy*, Routledge, 1991

Jeffrey N. Wasserstrom and Elizabeth J. Perry (eds), *Popular Protest and Political Culture in Modern China: Learning from 1989*, Westview, 1992

Earth Day
1970–
environmental action event

The first Earth Day was celebrated across the USA on April 22nd 1970, and for many chroniclers of the environmental movement marked the point at which environmental concern came of age and the modern green movement was born. The original idea for an Earth Day came from a Wisconsin senator, Gaylord Nelson, but it was a 25-year-old Stanford law student, Denis Hayes, who coordinated the national network of lectures, teach-ins, workshops and rallies which involved more than twenty million Americans, the country's largest mass demonstration since the victory celebrations at the end of the second world war. Environmental Action (EA), a Hayes-inspired outgrowth of Earth Day, began to coordinate local ecology groups and actions throughout the country, organisations like the Environmental Defense Fund, the Sierra Club and the Wilderness Society adopted a more activist stance, and within months of Earth Day 1970 the US government established the Environmental Protection Agency. In 1976 Denis Hayes was appointed head of the newly-established government-funded Solar Energy Research Institute in Golden, Colorado, but when environmentally-aware Jimmy Carter handed the presidency to arch-Republican Ronald Reagan the door slammed on the environment movement. Hayes finished the law degree he had interrupted to organise the 1970 event, raised a family, and continued to be involved in a scaled-down EA. By 1990, however, Reagan had given way to Bush, and Denis Hayes was again at the heart of a massive organisation to celebrate the twentieth anniversary of the original Earth Day. April 22nd 1990 saw an estimated two hundred million people in 137 countries involved in Earth Day events. The hype and commercialism of the event, together with its lack of deep understanding and of emphasis on longterm solutions, were criticised by some ecologists (notably **Kirkpatrick Sale**), but there is no doubt that Earth Day 1990, and the similar events that have been held each April since then, have involved many thousands of people in environmental actions which have led to marked changes in longterm environmental awareness. Whether such a shift is sufficient to fulfil Denis Hayes' original vision of a green planet without first having to experience the pain of major ecocatastrophe remains to be seen.

Kirkpatrick Sale, 'The Trouble with Earth Day', *The Nation*, April 30th 1990.

Earth First! [EF!]
1980–
environmental campaigning network

Foremost among the enviroactivist networks of the 1980s and 90s, Earth First! was founded by disaffected Wilderness Society staff member and lobbyist Dave Foreman. Tired of the compromises being made by leading US environmental organisations, especially over the use of wilderness areas for logging, roads, power lines, waste dumping and dams, he and a few colleagues started organising and advocating nonviolent actions to prevent such destruction. Many early EF! activists, inspired by Edward Abbey's 1975 novel *The Monkey Wrench Gang*, defended the use of 'ecotage' – spiking trees to make their felling hazardous, disabling heavy equipment, cutting down fences and billboards. EF! thus developed an undeserved reputation as a terrorist group, but in the event such tactics were rarely used, and though hundreds of its members have been arrested during nonviolent actions few have ever been charged with sabotage. From its inception Dave Foreman saw EF! as grounded in 'deep ecology', a term coined by the

Norwegian philosopher Arne Naess in 1973 to emphasise the nature-centredness of ecology. Many deep ecologists argue that all lifeforms have equal value and equal rights, and by extension that nature will inevitably use disease, starvation and 'natural disasters' to stem human excesses. By 1987 critics of what was described as the antihumanity of deep ecology, most notably social ecologist **Murray Bookchin**, were attacking EF! and Foreman as 'eco-brutalists': for some years the debate divided both EF! and the wider green movement. In 1990 the monkeywrenching question came to the fore during the 'Redwood Summer' action to prevent the clearcutting of northern Californian old-growth forests. EF! leaders Judi Bari and Mike Roselle publicly denounced the use of tree spiking following an incident two years earlier when a sawmill worker had been injured when a blade shattered on a spiked tree: an angry Foreman saw their statement as a betrayal of the organisation's role in saving the forest, and shortly afterwards resigned from EF!. In late May 1990 Redwood Summer organiser Judi Bari and her colleague Darryl Cherney were seriously injured when a bomb, probably placed by pro-forestry interests, exploded in their car in Oakland. EF! has now developed a network throughout North America, and the first European branches have been established. Whereas in the USA EF!'s major campaign has been to save wilderness areas, in Britain the main focus has been protest against destructive road schemes.

Edward Abbey, *The Monkey Wrench Gang*, Lippincott, 1975
Judi Bari, *Timber Wars*, Common Courage Press, 1994
David Walls, *The Activist's Almanac: The Concerned Citizen's Guide to the Leading Advocacy Organizations in America*, Simon and Schuster, 1993

Equal Rights Amendment [ERA]
1923–1982
equal rights campaign

To a large extent the history of the US Equal Rights Amendment is also that of the veteran suffrage campaigner Alice Paul, who had the foresight to recognise that the granting of the vote to US women in 1921 was only the first step on the path to full equal rights legislation. Drafted by Paul and introduced into Congress in 1923, her proposed amendment to the US constitution was designed to make any discrimination on grounds of sex unconstitutional. All legislation pertaining to employment, marriage, conscription and admission to publicly funded schools or programmes would be required to apply equally to men and women. Between the early 1920s and the emergence of 'second wave feminism' in the 1960s the ERA was kept alive by the National Women's Party (NWP), which had been established by Alice Paul in 1916. The NWP kept the ERA alive by persistently lobbying both political parties, but its narrow focus and sometimes blatantly racist sentiments drove an enduring wedge between it and other civil rights organisations. Early in 1972, with the emergence of the **women's movement** and pressure from the **National Organization for Women** (NOW), the ERA finally made it to the floor of Congress, and in

March 1972 it was sent to the states for ratification: Hawaii was the first
to ratify, followed closely by Nebraska. By the end of 1973 thirty states had
passed the amendment, and only five more were required to make it part
of the constitution. At this point a highly-organised and well-financed
opposition, representing some of the most conservative forces in America,
halted its progress. Playing on sexual conservatism and fears of homosexuality, the opposition persuaded several state legislatures to withdraw their
original ratification. The NOW concentrated its energies on achieving
passage of the ERA: the amendment became the unifying issue for many
American feminists and, as more Americans became determined to have
the principle of equal rights enshrined in the constitution, so the backlash
grew stronger. Although the Republican Party had been in favour of the
ERA, in 1980 Ronald Reagan declared himself and his party to be opposed
to it: the period for ratification expired on June 30th 1982 and the
opportunity for an equal rights amendment died. Perhaps it was fortunate
that Alice Paul had herself died five years earlier, at a time when it was
expected that her long-fought-for amendment would at last be adopted.

Susan Becker, *Origins of the Equal Rights Amendment: American Feminism Between
the Wars*, Greenwood, 1981
Sarah Slavin (ed.), *The Equal Rights Amendment: The Politics and Process of
Ratification of the 27th Amendment to the US Constitution*, Haworth, 1982
Jane Mansbridge, *Why We Lost the ERA*, University of Chicago Press, 1986
Christine Lunardini, *From Equal Suffrage to Equal Rights: Alice Paul and the
National Woman's Party, 1910–1928*, New York University Press, 1986

Fabian Society
1884–
socialist research and educational organisation

The politically pragmatic but consistently radical Fabian Society is the
oldest socialist organisation in Britain, and the longest-lived political
research organisation in the world. For more than a century its 'Fabian
Tracts', now numbering some five hundred, have informed politicians and
policy makers about a wide range of social and economic issues, and its
members have included many of the best-known British radicals. The
as-yet-unnamed society started life as a discussion group in 1883, meeting
in disillusioned stockbroker Edward Pease's house in London. Many of its
early members were also adherents of the Fellowship of New Life, a utopian
group established by charismatic Scottish shepherd Thomas Davidson. At
its January 1884 meeting Frank Podmore suggested that the new group,
'whose ultimate aim should be the reconstruction of society in accordance
with the highest moral possibilities', should be named after the third
century BC Roman general Quintus Fabius Cunctator, who chose to deploy
a series of small-scale guerrilla skirmishes rather than a single all-out attack
in order to defeat Hannibal's army. During its long life the Society has,
whatever other disagreements have threatened its integrity, consistently
held that gradual radical reform is preferable to immediate revolutionary

action. Fabians have thus aimed to influence government and affect policy by permeation rather than by direct power, and to provide the research and analysis to support their views. One of their chief methods was the publishing of booklets or tracts: the first two Fabian Tracts were *Why are the Many Poor?* (1884) by W.L. Phillips, a housepainter and one of the few working-class members, and *A Manifesto* (1884) by George Bernard Shaw. Shaw wrote many other important tracts, as did **Sidney Webb**: *Fabian Essays in Socialism* (1889), edited by Shaw with contributions by Webb and **Annie Besant** sold well and attracted much attention. Other notable early Fabians were **William Morris**, **Beatrice** Potter (who married **Webb** in 1892), H.G. Wells, Leonard Woolf (later married to **Virginia Woolf**) and **Havelock Ellis**. By 1890 the Fabian Society was well established, both in London and in several other cities including Edinburgh and Sheffield. Rapidly developing socialist ideas spread quickly through Fabian talks and literature, and the Society was a key constituent of the Labour Representation Committee, founded in 1900, which in 1905 became the Labour Party: the Committee's leading spokesman was Fabian socialist politician Ramsay Macdonald. With the establishment of the Labour Party the Fabian Society became *de facto* the party's research agency, continuing to 'educate, agitate, organise' as its founders had wished. By 1930, however, it was all but moribund, and survived the decade largely through the efforts of Oxford academic **G.D.H. Cole** and his wife Margaret Cole, who resurrected it in 1939. The Fabian Society was particularly active in the 1950s and 60s, with Shirley Williams (daughter of **Vera Brittain** and soon to become an important radical voice as a Labour member of parliament) as its general secretary from 1960 to 1964. By the late 1970s, however, the Society was in severe financial and organisational straits, yet as its centenary approached it was again re-launched at a House of Commons meeting in July 1983, where more formal links with the Labour Party were established.

Margaret Cole, *The Story of Fabian Socialism*, Heinemann, 1961
Norman and Jeanne MacKenzie, *The First Fabians*, Weidenfeld and Nicolson, 1977
Patricia Pugh, *Educate, Agitate, Organise: 100 Years of Fabian Socialism*, Methuen, 1984

Fellowship of Reconciliation [FOR]
1915–
peace organisation

The Fellowship of Reconciliation was founded in Cambridge, England, by pacifists Henry Hodgkin and Richard Roberts, to serve as a support community for conscientious objectors during the first world war. In 1915 Hodgkin visited New York, where a group of 68 men and women established FOR in the USA as the country's leading voice for protestant religious pacifism. Hodgkin and Roberts envisaged an international religious community of different faiths committed to nonviolence as a principle of life, and after the war, in October 1919, they invited fifty pacifists from ten countries to meet at Bilthoven in The Netherlands to create an International FOR. Travelling secretaries were appointed to travel around Europe on goodwill tours talking about Christianity and peace, and although such tours were often met with indifference and lack of interest, FOR's unmistakable commitment inspired a number of practical actions. At Verdun, where some of the bitterest fighting had taken place, Swiss FOR member Pierre Ceresole led an international team to rebuild the area; in Germany, Latvia and Estonia FOR members brought together cross-community teams to rebuild and to form new bonds of friendship. It was within US FOR that the beginnings of a distinctive American approach to nonviolent direct action were forged in the 1940s, and **A.J. Muste**, its president for many years, who gave the peace movement the memorable slogan 'There is no way to peace; peace is the way'. FOR members were active in the formation of a number of important civil rights organisations and alliances, including the **Congress of Racial Equality**. After the second world war FOR again did much to rebuild shattered communities and international alliances. In 1958 US FOR sent **Bayard Rustin** to the first **Campaign for Nuclear Disarmament** Aldermaston march, helping European and American pacifists to learn from each other's tactics, and in the 1960s, as the cold war became entrenched, FORs in Europe and the USA started working toward East-West reconciliation. As the war in Vietnam escalated in the mid-1960s FOR established the International Committee of Conscience on Vietnam, bringing together ten thousand clergy from forty countries to work for peace and understanding: in 1967 executive secretary Alfred Hassler established contact with the peace movement in Vietnam and sponsored a world tour by Buddhist monk and peace leader **Thich Nhat Hanh**. In the Philippines in the 1970s and 80s, International FOR nonviolence trainings were a powerful contribution to the popular movement that overthrew the Marcos regime. International FOR, based in Alkmaar in The Netherlands, now has affiliates in more than thirty countries: some maintain a distinctly Christian orientation; some like US FOR are Jewish and Buddhist as well. Though they focus on education and training in noviolent direct action, national FORs have created a variety of structures and programmes: in Latin America FOR is a wide federation of peace and nonviolent liberation movements called Servicio Paz y Justicia.

Lilian Stevenson, *Towards a Christian International: The Story of the International Fellowship of Reconciliation*, Fellowship of Reconciliation, 1941

Caroline Moorehead, *Troublesome People: The Warriors of Pacifism*, Adler and Adler, 1987

Cyril Wright and Tony Augarde, *Peace Is the Way*, Lutterworth, 1990

David Walls, *The Activist's Almanac: The Concerned Citizen's Guide to the Leading Advocacy Organizations in America*, Simon and Schuster, 1993

Friends of the Earth [FoE]
1969–
environmental campaigning organisation

When the popular environmental movement erupted in the USA in the mid-1960s following the publication of books like **Rachel Carson's** *Silent Spring* (1962) and Paul Ehrlich's *The Population Bomb* (1967), traditional conservation groups such as the widely-respected but staid Sierra Club found it hard to adapt to changing concerns and tactics. While the Club's management wanted to maintain the preservationist principles of its founder, John Muir, its newly-appointed and charismatic executive director David Brower strove to place the Sierra Club at the forefront of environmental activism, vigorously opposing plans to build major dams and nuclear power stations. Although its membership grew tenfold during the 1960s, the Club's charitable status was removed and its traditionalist wing complained loudly: early in 1969 Brower was told to leave. He responded immediately by founding Friends of the Earth, an organisation which would campaign actively against environmental destruction and for the wise use of natural resources. In the USA it was to make a slow transition from San Francisco-based grassroots action group to Washington-based lobby group, but in Britain it quickly capitalised on the newsworthiness of direct action. In May 1971 members dumped empty Schweppes bottles outside the company's front door as a protest against the introduction of non-returnable bottles: they became media celebrities overnight. FoE's campaigning in the 1970s was built on two major issues: whaling and nuclear power. While **Greenpeace** confronted whalers on the high seas, FoE action in parliament and on the high street led to a plummeting market for whaling industry products and to demands for political bans. FoE's case at the public inquiry into plans for expansion of the Windscale (now Sellafield) nuclear reprocessing plant was important not just for what it said, but also for the way it brought together scientists and economists prepared to challenge government policy line by line. In the early 1980s FoE UK lost impetus and direction, with many potential members signing up to Greenpeace and the reborn **Campaign for Nuclear Disarmament**, but its new director **Jonathon Porritt** led a steady expansion from 1984 to the end of the decade. FoE in the USA also had financial and organisational problems, with David Brower leaving in 1986 after a threatened lawsuit: it thereafter became more an expert lobby group than a grassroots activist organisation. By 1988 FoE International had grown into a global organisation with more than thirty national groups and was able to coordinate effective environmental action around the world, being particularly vocal and successful in Malaysia, where Sahabat Alam Malaysia has led the fight to save forests and forest peoples. In 1989, when environmental concern rose rapidly, FoE became very popular, especially with its core audience of the well-educated who felt safe with its well-argued and well-researched campaigns. Action to ban CFCs in aerosols put FoE back on the front pages of the popular press; Prince Charles appeared at its fundraising events. FoE's strategy remains campaign-based, with a well-tested combination of global concerns and local group activities. Many of the world's sharpest environmental campaigners of the 1980s and 90s owe their apprenticeship to the organisation which insists that, with environmental threats mounting on every side, the earth needs all the friends it can get.

David Brower, *Friends of the Earth: The First Sixteen Years*, Earth Island Institute, 1986

Fred Pearce, *Green Warriors: The People and the Politics behind the Environmental Revolution*, Bodley Head, 1991

GABRIELA [General Assembly Binding Women for Integrity, Equality, Leadership and Action]
1984–c.1990
women's liberation organisation

The decade from 1975 to 1985 was designated the United Nations Decade for Women, and saw the establishment of women's rights organisations in a number of countries which until then had had only semi-official women's organisations or none at all. At the Nairobi conference which marked the end of the Decade, the Philippine women's organisation GABRIELA made a major impact. GABRIELA's history, and the issues it faced in its short life, at the same time illustrate the experience of women's organisations in developing countries, and reflect the uniqueness of the Filipino situation as the country emerged from the Marcos dictatorship into a democracy led by one of the world's few women national leaders. GABRIELA (the name being both an acronym and a memorial for the eighteenth-century anti-colonial campaigner Gabriela Silang) was established as a radical anti-Marcos alliance of grassroots women's organisations; its founders included community leaders and Catholic nuns. High on its agenda were the sexual exploitation of women detainees, availability of safe abortion, and reform of the laws which made divorce impossible. On **International Women's Day**, March 8th 1985, GABRIELA published a radical manifesto for women's rights, ending with the words 'Dismantle the US-Marcos dictatorship!' Throughout the following year, at the end of which the Marcos regime was finally deposed and the democratically elected president Cory Aquino took office, GABRIELA members organised marches, demonstrations and prayer rallies to express their opposition to torture and detention, sexual exploitation by both Filipino and foreign soldiers stationed on the islands, and the exploitation of Filipina women by multinational companies. As with all such alliances, there were differences of opinion within GABRIELA. In 1985 founder member Mita Pardo de Tavera resigned over the alliance's unwillingness to talk to the Philippine Communist Party for fear of upsetting the Aquino election campaign, while abortion reform caused further divisions. Ultimately, GABRIELA's breadth of support also led to lack of cohesion on key issues and, as its most active members became involved in other forms of lobbying and activism, the alliance faded away, but it had undoubtedly played a vital role in politicising Filipina women during an important period in Philippine liberation.

Marian Simms, 'Democracy, Freedom and the Women's Movement in the Philippines', *Politics of the Future: The Role of Social Movements* (ed. Christine Jennett and Randal Stewart), Macmillan Australia, 1989

Gay and Lesbian Liberation Movement
1969–
liberation movement

Many modern historians divide the history of gay and lesbian rights into three broad periods: a period of emergence from the 1890s to the second world war; the 'homophilic movement' of 1950 to 1969, characterised by organisations like the **Mattachine Society** and the **Daughters of Bilitis**; and the period of gay and lesbian liberation which started with the **Stonewall Riots** in New York. Organised shortly after Stonewall, the politically activist Gay Liberation Front (GLF) sought to link gay and lesbian rights with the other major social struggles of the day – antimilitarism, black rights, and the Cuban Revolution. The Gay Activist Alliance, founded in 1970, complemented the GLF by emphasising the particular demands of the gay and lesbian community, and worked hard to challenge discriminatory legislation and labour practices. In Britain, meanwhile, 1969 saw the establishment of the Campaign for Homosexual Equality (CHE), which changed its name to Campaign in 1971 and a year later boasted sixty local groups, and in October 1970 the first GLF meetings were held in London. Though the London GLF lasted only eighteen months, its inventive activism attracted much attention. The CHE on the other hand was decidedly apolitical, seeking integration rather than radical activism, and by the late 1970s was much criticised for its narrow bureaucratic and overly-male stance. In 1977 all of CHE's women members left to form the National Organisation of Lesbians, but this lasted less than a year. Crucial to the progress of the movement in the USA was the 1973 declaration by leading psychological and psychiatric bodies that homosexuality was not in itself an illness or an aberration; the landmark event in the fight to raise gay activists to public office was the 1977 election of **Harvey Milk** as San Francisco city supervisor. Milk's murder the following year, and the ridiculously light sentence given to his killer, did much to radicalise the US gay rights movement. In Britain the 1976 blasphemy case against *Gay News* by anti-gay agitator Mary Whitehouse had similar results. By the end of the 1970s many thousands of gay and lesbian groups were in existence across America, Europe and Australasia, affiliated to a wide range of organisations and networks. A major debate within the lesbian movement during the 1970s and 80s arose over the extent to which lesbian womens' concerns were congruent with those of the wider **women's liberation movement**, many radical lesbians seeing the whole straight world, including straight women, as 'the enemy'. A more intractable question was whether gay men and lesbian women could organise effectively together, or whether men would always see their own issues as paramount. By the mid-1980s the gay and lesbian liberation movement was having a tangible effect on public attitudes and official policies. 1985 saw the opening of Britain's first lesbian and gay centre in London, a gay pride march attracted 15,000 people, and the Labour Party conference passed a lesbian and gay rights resolution. Democrat presidential candidate Jesse Jackson addressed 600,000 demonstrators during the October 1987 National March on Washington for Lesbian and Gay Rights, and made such rights an important plank of his campaign. During the 1980s a major unifying force within the gay and lesbian liberation movement has been the spectre of AIDS and the need to fight for the rights of those with AIDS and HIV: the **AIDS Coalition to Unleash Power**, founded by gay rights campaigner **Larry Kramer** in 1987, represents one of the best examples of effective self-help and self-empowerment in modern US history. The 1980s also gave rise to a considerable anti-gay and lesbian backlash: in Britain 1988 saw the passing of the infamous Section 28 of the Local Government Act, forbidding local councils to 'promote homosexuality', though the campaign against Section 28 succeeded in mobilising the gay and lesbian movement into renewed activism. The lesbian and gay direct action group OutRage began to organise marches and 'zap actions', and the lobby group Stonewall to campaign strongly for gay rights. In the USA the election of Bill Clinton as president gave a new visibility to the American lesbian and gay lobby, though the administration was unable to deliver much of what it had promised. The gay and lesbian liberation movement continues to record successes, however: between 1990 and 1995 constitutional challenges supporting gay equality succeeded in Canada, Australia and New Zealand, and in South Africa in 1994 the **African National Congress** incorporated lesbian and gay rights into its charter.

Gerre Goodman *et al*, *No Turning Back: Lesbian and Gay Liberation of the '80s*, New Society, 1983

Barry Adam, *The Rise of a Gay and Lesbian Liberation Movement*, G.K. Hall, 1987

Bob Cant and Susan Hemmings (eds), *Radical Records: Thirty Years of Lesbian and Gay History, 1957–1987*, Routledge, 1988

Margaret Cruikshank, *The Gay and Lesbian Liberation Movement*, Routledge, 1992

Eric Marcus, *Making History: The Struggle for Gay and Lesbian Equal Rights, 1945–1990*, Harper Collins, 1992

Leigh Rutledge, *The Gay Decades: From Stonewall to the Present: The People and Events that Shaped Gay Lives*, Plume, 1992

Mark Thompson (ed.), *Long Road to Freedom: the Advocate History of the Gay and Lesbian Movement*, St. Martin's, 1994

Gensuikyō [Gensuibaku Kinshi Nihon Kyōgikai, Japan Council against Atomic and Hydrogen Bombs]
1955–
peace organisation

Ten years after the atomic bomb attacks on Hiroshima and Nagasaki which claimed 200,000 Japanese civilian lives, the USA decided to expand its nuclear testing to Bikini Atoll in the Marshall Islands, close to popular Japanese fishing grounds. Coupled with a growing understanding of the genetic deformities caused by the 1945 atomic bombs, the US decision sparked the birth and rapid growth of the Japanese peace movement. In 1955 the all-party antinuclear group Gensuikyō was formed, and in Hiroshima on August 6th, the anniversary of the bombing, it held the first World Conference against Atomic and Hydrogen Bombs. During the late 1950s and early 60s Gensuikyō became a powerful force, working with the labour movement to lobby for action to prevent the proliferation of nuclear weapons, and to organise events such as the annual peace march from Tokyo to Hiroshima. In 1965 the Socialist Party and the Sōhyō (Japanese Council of Trade Unions) felt that Gensuikyō had become 'soft', refusing for example to condemn all nuclear testing; they established their own organisation, Gensuikin (Gensuibaku Kinshi Nihon Kokumin Kaigi), though the two often worked together. By 1977 there was sufficient political support for a non-nuclear stance to persuade the government to issue a declaration against the manufacture and deployment of nuclear weapons on Japanese soil. Buoyed by their joint success and their ability to work together, Gensuikyō and Gensuikin decided to cooperate more closely, and have since jointly organised the annual peace conferences and marches. As with many Japanese organisations, the peace movement has always been characterised by splinter groups and religious sects. Thus Gensuikyō embraces Buddhist sects like the strictly pacifist Fujii Nittatsu (which since the 1970s has established an international network of 'peace pagodas'), groups like Rissho Kosei Kai (Society for the Establishment of Righteousness and Friendly Intercourse) whose temple in Tokyo attracts thousands to its daily morning service, and a variety of labour movement groups from the militant to the contemplative. In recent years Gensuikyō has waned in importance, to the extent that when in 1984 Prime Minister Nakasone Yasuhiro floated the idea (with American prompting) of rearming Japan, it was the parliamentary Conservative Women's Group that led the protest rather than the Japanese peace movement.

Caroline Moorehead, *Troublesome People: The Warriors of Pacifism*, Hamish Hamilton, 1986

Greenham Common Women's Peace Camp
1981–
peace action

In 1980, almost out of nothing it seemed, the British peace movement erupted into protest over the deployment of nuclear weapons on British soil. The two catalysts were E.P. Thompson and Dan Smith's 1980 exposé, *Protest and Survive*, of official nuclear defence policy, and the 1979 decision by the US military to base 140 cruise missiles in Britain. Early in 1981 peace campaigner Ann Pettit, living near Carmarthen in south-west Wales, read about a women's peace march from Copenhagen to Paris. Within a few months Ann and a group of likeminded women calling themselves Women for Life on Earth (WFLOE) had planned a similar march from Carmarthen to the largest of the missile sites, at Greenham Common US Air Base near Newbury in Berkshire. Greenham, built by the British army on Newbury's common land during the second world war, was believed by many civil rights groups to have been illegally handed over to the US military in 1951. With support from national organisations and local peace groups along the route, the women's peace march set out from Wales on August 27th and arrived at the gates of Greenham on September 5th. Ann Pettit repeatedly asked minister of defence John Nott for a public debate and, when it was clear that he planned to ignore the women, the few marchers who had remained camped outside the base decided to establish a permanent peace camp until the missiles were removed. To begin with the camp involved both women and men, but from February 1982, amidst considerable acrimony, it became women-only. The establishment of a new Women's Peace Alliance (involving WFLOE, **Women's International League for Peace and Freedom** and many other national and local groups) ensured that pacifist women all over the country knew about and were encouraged to support and visit the Greenham Common Women's Peace Camp. During 1982 similar peace camps were established outside other military bases throughout Britain and in other countries, many of them women-only or organised mainly by women. Greenham, however, remained the focus of greatest attention, and as the growing number of women developed a range of courageous and moving direct action tactics so their influence and inspiration widened. The women who lived in and visited the peace camp hung photographs and baby clothes on the high fences surrounding the base to symbolise the nuclear threat to their loved ones, and in November 1982, on the third anniversary of the decision to deploy cruise missiles at Greenham, 30,000 women held hands around the nine-mile perimeter fence in an impressive 'Embrace the Base' action. On New Year's Day 1983, with camps established ouside each of the base's eight gates, 44 women breached the fence and danced on top of one of the half-built missile silos. Between the first arrests in November 1982 and the end of 1984, more than a thousand Greenham women were arrested: many used their court appearances to stress the illegality of weapons of mass destruction. The first cruise missiles arrived at Greenham in November 1983, to be met by wailing women and more mass demonstrations. The local council served the peace camp with eviction orders and removed vehicles and caravans, but the women resorted to tents and 'benders' made of branches and polythene. A ten-day protest in September 1984 brought thousands of women to to the camp from all over the world: by now many tens of thousands of British women had played a part in supporting the Greenham protest. There were inevitably differences of opinion and tensions between the women involved in the Greenham actions, and these reached a head in 1988 with bitter disagreements between WFLOE, which wanted the camp to remain open to any woman working for peace, and more radical groups, but the camp survived intact. In 1989 the US government announced its intention to withdraw from Greenham, but a small group of peace campers vowed to stay until all the missiles were gone and the land returned to common ownership. The last missiles left in 1991, and in November 1994 the British ministry of defence offered to sell most of the now-disused base back to Newbury district council. A handful of protesters still live outside the base, determined to stay until Greenham Common returns to peaceful use once again.

Lynne Jones, *Keeping the Peace*, Womens Press, 1983
Barbara Harford and Sarah Hopkins, *Greenham Common: Women at the Wire*,
      Womens Press, 1984
Jill Liddington, *The Long Road to Greenham*, Virago, 1989

Greenpeace
1969–
environmental campaigning organisation

On October 2nd 1969 the US Atomic Energy Commission, despite massive protests under the banner Don't Make a Wave, detonated a large under-water nuclear bomb in the ocean near earthquake-prone Amchitka in Alaska. Among the organisers was veteran Canadian peace campaigner Jim Bohlen, who organised a group to find a suitable vessel to sail to Amchitka to protest against further testing: social worker Bill Darnell provided the group with the name Greenpeace, and in September 1971 the first Green-peace ship, the *Phyllis Cormack*, sailed to the Aleutian Islands. The planned tests were postponed, so the same tactics were applied to French tests on the Muroroa Atoll in 1972 and 1973. When the French detonated a bomb with the Greenpeace vessel *Vega*, captained by the indomitable David McTaggart, only fifteen miles away, considerable publicity was attracted for the antinuclear cause. In 1975 a revamped Greenpeace, now with an office in Vancouver, expanded its concerns beyond nuclear testing: its two ships set off to intercept the Japanese whaling fleet, initiating the anti-whaling campaign for which the organisation is probably best known. During the mid-1970s Greenpeace developed its strategy of audacious, well-documented, nonviolent actions against environmental destroyers and polluters, and in 1976 organised a successful and highly visible campaign against Arctic sealing. The following year Greenpeace estab-lished a solid European presence, and in July 1978 the *Rainbow Warrior*, Greenpeace's first custom-converted ship, was launched. By the end of the decade, despite widespread support, Greenpeace's organisation and fi-nances were in chaos; yet out of the ashes rose Netherlands-based Green-peace International, with McTaggart as its chief executive officer, together with a network of national groups. In 1985, during a voyage to the French Pacific territory of Rongelap to protest against nuclear testing, the *Rainbow Warrior* was blown up by French secret agents in Auckland harbour, New Zealand. The ensuing international incident deeply embarrassed the French government and gave Greenpeace enormous grassroots public support. Important subsequent Greenpeace campaigns have been aimed at pressing for the designation of Antarctica as a World Park, preventing the incineration of toxic chemicals at sea, and stopping harmful air pollution.

Robert Hunter, *Warriors of the Rainbow: A Chronicle of the Greenpeace Movement*, Holt, Rinehart and Winston, 1979
David McTaggart and Robert Hunter, *Greenpeace III: Journey into the Bomb*, Collins, 1978
Michael King, *Death of the Rainbow Warrior*, Penguin, 1986
Michael Brown and John May, *The Greenpeace Story*, Dorling Kindersley, 1989

Die Grünen [German Green Party]
1980–
political party

The 'environmental revolution' of the 1970s was nowhere as deeply felt as in West Germany. Decades of industrial pollution and an active antinuclear campaign combined with residual cultural guilt and youthful frustration to make Germans take the warnings of socialist politician Herbert Gruhl's bestselling *Ein Planet wird Geplundert* (*Plundered Planet*, 1975) very seriously. Small environment groups sprang up across the country, and many community councils stressed the urgency of environmental action. In 1977 a local green party, the Grüne Liste Umweltschutz (GLU, Green List for Environmental Protection), gained 3.9% of the votes in the 1978 election, and in July 1978 Gruhl established the Grüne Aktion Zukunft (GAZ, Green Action Future) with the memorable slogan 'Neither right nor left: we are in front'. In February 1979 GLU and GAZ joined with several other local green parties to contest the European Elections, and the following month the Sonstige Politische Vereinigung-Die Grünen (SPV-Die Grünen, Alternative Political Green Alliance) was formed at a meeting in Frankfurt: antinuclear campaigner **Petra Kelly** was a founder member and many prominent radical figures including **Heinrich Böll** and **Rudi Dutschke** became active supporters. In the European Election Die Grünen won an unexpected 3.2% of the vote: membership rose rapidly, offices were opened in many cities, and previously suspicious Marxist-communist groups joined forces with the growing green movement. The Offenbach Congress of October 1979 produced Die Grünen's policy programme, based on the 'four pillars' of ecology, social responsibility, grassroots democracy and nonviolence. The party first passed the qualifying 5% threshold for representation in government in the Bremen regional elections the same month, and by the end of 1982 there were nearly fifty green representatives sitting on regional legislatures. Although Swiss and French Greens made it to national legislatures before Die Grünen (in 1979 and 1981), the election of 28 Greens to the West German Bundestag in March 1983 with 5.6% of the national vote was seen by green parties the world over as a major breakthrough. When four years later Die Grünen won 8.3% of the vote and 42 Bundestag seats their success seemed assured. As with all political alliances, however, differences of opinion about policy, strategy and, above all, philosophical foundations, constantly threatened the fragile consensus. Early disagreements centred on the role of Marxist socialism within the green movement, but by the mid-1980s the main – and increasingly bitter – debate was between the 'realos' (realists) with their emphasis on parliamentary politics and achievable reform, and the 'fundis' (fundamentalists) who wanted the party to retain its radical character and grassroots focus. The issue came to a head with the dramatic resignation of green leader **Rudolf Bahro** at the party's annual congress in June 1985. In 1990 the issue of German unification transformed the country's politics, and in September Die Grünen finalised an electoral pact with their natural East German allies, Bündnis '90. In the first all-German national elections in December, however, Die Grünen won only 4.8% of the vote in former West Germany, thus losing all their Bundestag seats. Some consolation came from a 6.1% vote in fomer East Germany, winning the Bündnis '90/Die Grünen eight seats. The unexpected defeat shook Die Grünen and green parties throughout Europe. The realo/fundi argument resurfaced with a vengeance, with the issue of effective leadership high on the agenda. With the assured and pragmatic realo Joschka Fischer as party leader and the outspoken Petra Kelly eased out as party speaker, Die Grünen started to claw back previous gains in regional elections. The death of Petra Kelly in October 1992, though much mourned, was seen by many as marking a transition within Die Grünen from adolescence to maturity. Continuing electoral successes at regional level were consolidated in the October 1994 general election, where the Bündnis '90/Die Grünen coalition received 7.3% of the vote and 49 seats in the Bundestag, making it the country's third largest party.

> Die Grünen (trans. Hans Fernbach), *Programme of the German Green Party*, Heretic, 1983
> Sara Parkin, *Green Parties: An International Guide*, Heretic, 1989
> Gene Frankland, *Between Protest and Power: The Green Party in Germany*, Westview, 1992
> William Coleman, *A Rhetoric of the People: The German Greens and the New Politics*, Praeger, 1993
> Dick Richardson and Chris Rootes (ed.), *The Green Challenge: The Development of Green Parties in Europe*, Routledge, 1994

Heiminsha [Society of Commoners]
1903–1907
socialist organisation

Heiminsha, which takes its name from the class of *heimin* or commoners (as opposed to the nobles and the *samurai*), was the centre of Japanese socialist activities during the first decade of the twentieth century. It was founded by two antiwar journalists, Sakai Toshihiko and the veteran socialist campaigner **Kōtoko Shūsui**, who both resigned from the newspaper *Yorozu Chōzō* in protest against its belligerent stance on the eve of the Russo-Japanese War of 1904–05. Heiminsha grew quickly, attracting anarchist activists like **Ishikawa Sanshirō**, and published an influential newspaper, *Heimin Shimbun*, which served as a vehicle for socialist and pacifist news and opinion. As pro-war sentiment increased, however, its circulation began to fall; critical editorials by Kōtoko and Ishikawa early in 1904 resulted in their being arrested and indicted, and when *Heimin Shimbun* published the first Japanese translation of *The Communist Manifesto* in November 1904 the government suspended its publication. In January 1907 Heiminsha joined forces with the newly-established Japan Socialist Party and *Heimin Shimbun* was relaunched, but both organisation and newspaper lasted less than a year.

Haruhara Akihiko, 'Heiminsha', *Kodansha Encyclopedia of Japan*, 1983

Highlander Folk School [Highlander Research and Education Center]
1932–
resource centre

Highlander Folk School was founded in Monteagle, Tennessee, in 1932. One of 250 labour colleges in existence at the time, it was distinguished by its belief that people know for themselves what they need to learn. Myles Horton, the brilliant organiser and educator who was Highlander's director from 1932 to 1973, defined its purpose as not to solve problems, but to use problems and crises as the basis for educating people about a democratic society. Highlander focused initially on union organising, asserting that to be strong a union had to be democratic, which meant organising across barriers of race and sex. As a residential adult education centre for poor working and unemployed people, it provided its students with opportunities to socialise and work together that they could find nowhere else at the time. In the early 1950s Highlander decided to focus on public aspects of segregation. Committed to supporting black people's own agenda, the school brought black and white together to talk about racism and what could be done to counter it. One of Highlander's most successful efforts, resulting from the recognition that literacy requirements were denying black people access to the vote, was the fostering of citizenship schools. From this project, which developed into a wide-reaching grassroots adult education programme, came much of the leadership for the civil rights movement. Because Highlander transgressed the social norms – and laws – enforcing racial segregation, it was subjected to persistent and increasingly violent harassment by vigilantes and local authorities, who succeeded in shutting it down in 1959. Renamed the Highlander Research and Education Center, first in Knoxville and then in New Market, Tennessee, the school reopened and worked locally for some time with Appalachian people engaged in land rights and pollution struggles, but in the mid-1980s it again began extending its focus to encompass the rest of the south.

Frank Adams and Myles Horton, *Unearthing Seeds of Fire: The Idea of Highlander*, Highlander, 1975

John M. Glen, *Highlander: No Ordinary School, 1932–1962*, University of Kentucky, 1988

Indigenous Women's Network [IWN]
1984–
self-determination network

Established in 1984 by a group of North American and Pacific indigenous women, IWN has since become a worldwide network holding regular meetings and conferences where women can share their experiences and campaigning skills, and covers a wide range of issues including traditional family structures, domestic abuse, legal defence and natural resource management. The first of a series of International Indigenous Women's Conferences was held in July 1989 in Adelaide, Australia, where 1,500 women from fifteen countries agreed upon a 'Declaration of Unity', affirming solidarity with each other and with the land, 'our mother, who through generations has witnessed our struggles drenched with blood'. IWN is based in Austin, Texas, with affiliated groups around the world.

Industrial Workers of the World [IWW; Wobblies]
1905–
labour organisation

'The working class and the employing class have nothing in common. There can be no peace so long as hunger and want are found among millions of working people, and the few, who make up the employing class, have all the good things of life. Between these two classes a struggle must go on until the workers of the world organize as a class, take possession of the earth and the machinery of production, and abolish the wage system.' Thus began the preamble to the constitution of the IWW (as amended in 1908), the 'one big union' created in Chicago in 1905 to protect all workers from the arbitrary oppression of uncaring employers. The IWW, unlike the exclusive craft unions affiliated to the American Federation of Labor (AFL), sought to involve unskilled workers as well as the skilled, and stressed the importance of solidarity between poor immigrants, nonwhites, women and migrant workers. Among its founders were veteran trade unionist William ('Big Bill') Haywood from the Western Federation of Miners, **Eugene V. Debs** of the American Socialist Party, the legendary **Mother Jones**, and Haymarket martyr widow Lucy Parsons. The Wobblies (the nickname appears to have arisen from the initials I-Wobble-U-Wobble-U) soon made a name for themselves through their direct actions, dynamic leaders, and inspiring songs and posters. Fees and dues were kept low so as not to be a barrier to poorly-paid workers, and since labour-management contracts were viewed as an interference with the unconditional right to strike the IWW refused to sign such contracts, a controversial position it did not abandon until the 1930s. Strikes were the fuel for IWW militancy, for strikes built the experience and perspective needed for the general strike that Wobblies believed would overthrow the capitalist system. The IWW played a large part in breaking down barriers of sex and race within the working class: several of its branches were fully integrated, and women leaders like **Elizabeth Gurley Flynn** and Matilda Rabinowitz travelled the nation speaking on labour issues. As the first world war loomed the IWW maintained its pacifist stance in contrast with the pro-war-effort policy of the AFL. It continued to organise and support strikes where necessary, which gave employers and the government the opportunity to accuse the IWW of treason. In September 1917 justice department agents raided IWW offices throughout the country with warrants to arrest nearly two hundred officials as subversives: more than half were sentenced to long prison terms and hefty fines. Defence and amnesty campaigns sapped the organisation's strength, and controversy over Wobbly support for the Soviet Union divided its membership. Despite these setbacks IWW continued to fight for its members' rights: in 1928 it led an important strike in the Colorado minefields, and during the Depression the IWW helped to establish 'unemployed unions' to provide housing and food for the jobless. The IWW provided an important training ground for many of the direct action tactics which proved so effective in the civil rights movement of the 1950s and 60s, a period which also saw a revival of interest in the radical history of the USA. Today the IWW is still based in Chicago, but its membership can be counted in hundreds and its active branches in tens. In relation to its size however (even at its peak in 1914 it had only 100,000 paid-up members) the Wobblies did much to carry the empowering torch of workers' rights through the dark decades between the two world wars.

Philip S. Foner, *The Industrial Workers of the World, 1905–1917*, International
    Publishers, 1965
Melvyn Dubofsky, *We Shall Be All*, Quadrangle, 1969
Fred Thompson and Patrick Murfin, *The IWW: Its First Seventy Years, 1905–1975*,
    IWW, 1976
Joyce L. Kornbluh (ed.), *Rebel Voices: An IWW Anthology*, Charles H. Kerr, 1988

International Woman Suffrage Alliance [IWSA]
1904–1942
women's suffrage campaigning organisation

In 1888, on the fortieth anniversary of the Seneca Falls Convention (which marked the start of the organised women's suffrage movement in the USA), American feminists welcomed women from nine foreign countries and from more than fifty American women's organisations to an international suffrage conference in Washington. The initiative for this pioneering gathering came from **Elizabeth Cady Stanton** and **Susan B. Anthony** of the National Woman Suffrage Association: Stanton welcomed the delegates, explaining that 'we do not feel that you are strangers and foreigners, for the women of all nationalities, in the artificial distinctions of sex, have a universal sense of injustice that forms a common bond of union between them.' The conference agreed to establish the International Council of Women (ICW) to become the umbrella for women's organisations from all countries. As early as 1899, during the ICW's third congress in London, its fragile unity was shattered when ICW organisers decided that women who opposed suffrage were to be barred from attending. Two women from the German delegation, Anita Augspurg and Lida Gustava Heymann, convened an alternative meeting, which advocated the foundation of an international alliance specifically for women's groups campaigning for suffrage. The ICW went on to fulfil its important but mainstream role as a focus for women's voluntary organisations (today it is based in Brussels, and has affiliates in more than seventy countries), while the German proposal resulted in the foundation of the International Woman Suffrage Alliance. The American feminist Carrie Chapman Catt organised the first IWSA congress in Berlin in 1904, and remained president until 1923. Susan B. Anthony held the chair at the Berlin conference and the Australian **Vida Goldstein** was recording secretary. The eight countries with national suffrage associations (Australia, Denmark, Germany, Great Britain, The Netherlands, Norway, Sweden and the USA) sent delegations to Berlin, and four other countries – Austria, Hungary, New Zealand and Switzerland – were represented. The Dutch women presented a particularly impressive group, the delegation including the courageous doctor and birth control pioneer Aletta Jacobs and the efficient organiser Rosette Manus; the Hungarian feminist **Rosika Schwimmer** also cut her international teeth at IWSA meetings. During the first ten years of its existence the Alliance grew steadily: Carrie Chapman Catt and Aletta Jacobs made a world tour in 1911–12 to publicise the Alliance's goals, and the IWSA's seventh congress in Budapest in 1913 was attended by four hundred delegates from 24 countries. Gradually the suffrage movement started to achieve results: Norwegian women won the vote in 1913, Danish women in 1915, and in 1918 the IWSA changed its name to the International Alliance of Women for Suffrage and Equal Citizenship, in recognition that winning the vote was but a step on the road to equality. As more and more women won the vote (Austria, Germany and The Netherlands in 1919, the USA in 1920, Britain in 1928) the energy that had gone into the IWSA gradually moved into other campaigns, and the Alliance was wound up in 1942, but there was no doubt that the international sisterhood and solidarity experienced by its members had played a crucial part in winning increasing equality for women the world over.

International Council of Women, *Women in a Changing World: The Dynamic Story of the International Council of Women Since 1888*, Routledge and Kegan Paul, 1966

Mineke Bosch and Annemarie Kloosterman (eds), *Politics and Friendship: Letters from the International Woman Suffrage Alliance, 1902–1942*, Ohio State University Press, 1990

International Women's Day
1908–
women's solidarity event

Although Women's Day was first publicly celebrated in the USA in 1908, the 1908 march marked the anniversary of a nationwide women's demonstration held on March 8th 1857 to protest against low wages and poor working conditions. Following the 1908 march, the last Sunday in February was declared National Women's Day, and in 1910, at the Second Conference of Socialist Women in Copenhagen, **Clara Zetkin** proposed the establishment of an International Women's Day on March 8th. European women celebrated the day for the first time in 1911, when rallies and demonstrations were held in Germany, Denmark, Switzerland and Austria. In 1914 French women held antiwar demonstrations on Women's Day, and in Russia, where Women's Day had been celebrated since 1913, the 1917 women's march sparked the 'February Revolution' (at that time Russia was still using the Julian calendar, so March 8th in Western Europe and the USA was February 23rd in Russia). International Women's Day was widely celebrated through the 1920s, (the first British Women's Day was held on March 8th 1926 and Australia's on March 25th 1928), but by the end of the 1930s the celebrations had petered out. The birth of the modern **women's liberation movement** in the late 1960s revived interest in International Women's Day; by the late 1970s it was being celebrated all over the world, and was officially recognised by the United Nations in 1977. An official holiday in Russia and China, March 8th is for many women an opportunity to celebrate women's achievements and press for women's rights.

Internationals
1864–*c*.1970
international communist workers' organisations

The 'Internationals' in socialist circles refer to the four major incarnations of the international labour organisation first established in London and Paris in 1864 as the International Working Men's Association (IWMA). **Karl Marx** and **Friedrich Engels** quickly became leaders of the First International (as the IMWA came to be known), and the Paris Commune of 1871, during which the International's French supporters played an important part, provided the impetus for the transformation of the IMWA into a working class political party. The Hague Congress of 1872 brought together 65 delegates from thirteen European countries, Australia and the USA, but by 1881 a split between the Marxists and **Mikhail Bakunin**'s anarchist faction had divided the International beyond redemption. Its successor, the Second International, was established at the Marxist-organised International Workers' Congress in Paris in July 1889, and by 1904 its affiliated parties were operating in 21 countries, winning nearly seven million votes and 261 parliamentary seats. The Second International was a loose federation of Marxist-oriented parties and trade unions with a bureau in Brussels. It hosted congresses every two to four years, much of the business hinging on semantic and tactical differences, but the 1907 Stuttgart Congress, meeting as warclouds threatened to engulf the continent, debated and passed an amendment (submitted by **Lenin**, Lenin's colleague Yuriy Martov, and **Rosa Luxemburg**) urging 'every effort in order to prevent the outbreak of war,' and if war should be waged, 'to intervene in its speedy termination, and to utilise the economic and political crisis created by the war to rouse the masses and thereby to hasten the downfall of capitalist class rule.' When war came, however, most parties affiliated to the International gave their support to the war effort (those in Russia, Italy and the USA were notable exceptions), and by 1915 the Second International was all but moribund. The Third International, which was founded in Moscow in March 1919, became the ever more dogmatic and pro-Stalinist Communist International (shortened to 'Comintern'), which by 1930 had alienated all but the most hardline pro-Soviet parties outside the Soviet bloc. Though it enjoyed a brief reawakening in response to the German fascist threat in the early 1930s, its 1935 Congress, attended by delegates from 65 affiliated parties, was to be its last. In 1938 **Leon Trotsky**, a harsh critic of the 'counter-revolutionary' Third International, established the Fourth International with its founding document 'The Death Agony of Capitalism and the Tasks of the Fourth International' (more usually known as 'The Transitional Programme'). Trotsky's assassination in 1940, the second world war and constant factional infighting ensured that the Fourth International never had very much influence. Although a number of small socialist groups, most notably the Socialist Workers Party, were nominally affiliated with the Fourth International during the 1960s, by 1970 a century of socialist Internationals was little more than a memory.

Julius Braunthal (trans. Henry Collins and Kenneth Mitchell), *History of the International*, Praeger, 1967–1980
A.I. Sobolev *et al* (trans. Bernard Isaacs), *Outline History of the Communist International*, Progress Publishers, 1971
Tom Bottomore (ed), *A Dictionary of Marxist Thought*, Blackwell, 1983

Las Madres de Plaza de Mayo
1977–
civil liberties organisation

In March 1976 a military coup in Argentina suspended all civil liberties and set in motion a cycle of kidnapping, torture and murder which, within six years, had created a network of 340 concentration camps and 'disappeared' an estimated 30,000 people, including a large number of children. While its primary function was to eliminate opposition, this policy of terror also succeeded in silencing media and legal concern – at least 109 lawyers and 100 journalists were among the *decaparecidos*. Where mainstream tactics failed, however, women's subversion thrived. Starting early in 1977, mothers and grandmothers of the disappeared gathered silently each Thursday afternoon in one of the main squares of Buenos Aires, the Plaza

Mayo, opposite the presidential palace. Under the eyes of security police, they identified each other by carrying a leaf or a flower, and passed messages about the *decaparecidos* from hand to hand. In October 1977 Las Madres (The Mothers) made their campaign public; they started to wear white headscarves embroidered with the words *aparicíon con vida* (return our children alive), and published a large advertisement demanding information about the *decaparecidos*. Two months later the military retaliated, kidnapping thirteen demonstrators including Azucena de Villaflor, Las Madres' main organiser – none of them were seen again. Although little support was forthcoming from the church or the legal profession, Las Madres continued to organise, using the 1978 World Cup (held in Argentina) to make contact with foreign journalists. In 1979 Las Madres de Plaza de Mayo was registered as a legal organisation, and in 1981, when yet another military coup installed Leopoldo Galtieri, it organised its first 24-hour March of Resistance. Military rule finally ended with the election of Raúl Alfonsín in 1984, who pledged to search for the *decaparecidos*; it soon became clear, however, that most had been killed. Las Madres now concentrated on demanding the prosecution of those responsible for the disappearances, and the return of children who had been kidnapped in order to be illegally fostered. The Alfonsín government, wanting to put the military junta's excesses behind it, found Las Madres' continued demands an embarrassment, and set a time limit of April 1987 for new prosecutions; meanwhile Las Madres themselves had divided over methods of making their continued demands effective. Despite many setbacks, Las Madres have continued to campaign for information and justice: successes include the setting up of a national genetic data bank to establish links between kidnapped children and their families, and (despite a series of facesaving amnesties) a number of successful prosecutions. The Thursday afternoon demonstrations in Buenos Aires' Plaza de Mayo, although much smaller today than in the early 1980s, continue.

Jo Fisher, *Mothers of the Disappeared*, Zed, 1989
Marysa Navarro, 'The Personal is Political: Las Madres de Plaza de Mayo', in *Power and Popular Protest*, University of California Press, 1989

Liberty [National Council for Civil Liberties; NCCL]
1934–
civil rights organisation

The British civil rights organisation the National Council for Civil Liberties (renamed Liberty in 1989), was founded in February 1934 at a meeting called by London solicitor Ronald Kidd. Like many other people in central London in November 1932, Kidd had watched with great concern as police harassed crowds of hunger marchers, and had taken up the matter with the Metropolitan Police Commissioner. Though he extracted an assurance that severe action would follow any similar occurrence, Kidd and a group of like-minded people felt that an independent monitoring group was needed, not only to monitor police harassment but also to ensure that the whole range of civil liberties from freedom of assembly to freedom of speech was being respected. Other founder members of NCCL included **Vera Brittain**, writers H.G. Wells and A.P. Herbert, and Labour politician Clement Attlee. NCCL members monitored subsequent hunger marches, and by 1936 the organisation was also fighting police bans on antifascist rallies, challenging cinema censorship, and protesting against new public order legislation. During the second world war NCCL consistently upheld the right to free speech, condemning unnecessary emergency powers and the arbitrary blacklisting of those who held antigovernment views. After the war NCCL campaigned vigorously on behalf of the thousands of people being held in mental health institutions with no rights over their own lives: the 1959 Mental Health Act incorporated many of its suggestions. In the 1960s the Council placed an emphasis on travellers' rights and working against racial discrimination and, with the introduction of politically-motivated internment in Northern Ireland in 1971, the rights of protesters in this British province became a major NCCL concern. In 1974 the Council established a Gay Rights Committee, and six years later appointed its first gay rights officer. Following the change of name to Liberty, the organisation published its version of a Bill of Rights for Britain (a supposedly free country yet with no universal civil rights legislation) entitled *A People's Charter*. Like its US counterpart, the **American Civil Liberties Union**, London-based Liberty continues to fight for the rights of citizens across a broad range of issues, working particularly hard for those whose voices are heard the least.

> Sylvia Scaffardi, *Fire Under the Carpet: Working for Civil Liberties in the 1930s*, Lawrence and Wishart, 1986
> Carol Harlow and Richard Rawlings, *Pressure Through Law*, Routledge, 1992
> Liberty, *Liberty 1934–94: Sixty Years of Action*, Liberty, 1994

Livermore Action Group [LAG]
1981–1984
antinuclear protest

The Livermore Action Group was organised in 1981 with the idea of closing the Lawrence Livermore National Laboratory, a producer of nuclear weapons affiliated with the University of California. Modelled on the **Clamshell** and **Abalone Alliances** (nonviolent direct action based on affinity groups, each sending a member to a central council, with all levels of decision-making being by consensus) LAG created working groups to carry out organisational functions. It also fostered the clustering of like-minded affinity groups, encouraging a variety of autonomous and imaginative actions expressing the diversity of people in the coalition. The first mass action, in June 1982, had more than 1,300 blockaders, all trained in nonviolence, on the four roads into the laboratory, along with a support demonstration of over 5,000 people. Over the next year, LAG clusters carried out three actions which succeeded in delaying MX missile launches. LAG's second mass blockade of the laboratory in June 1983 was successful as an action – including the experience of community that arrested blockaders shared in detention – but the number of participants was clearly smaller, and no direction for re-energising LAG emerged from subsequent debates. In the course of the next year, with many of its activists moving to anti-intervention work in response to US policy toward Central America, LAG ceased to function.

> Barbara Epstein, *Political Protest and Cultural Revolution: Nonviolent Direct Action in the 1970s and 1980s*, University of California, 1991

Mattachine Society
homosexual rights group
1950–c.1970

In February 1950 reactionary US senator Joseph McCarthy openly accused the Truman administration of harbouring 'loyalty and security risks' in government service, these being 'in no small part sex perverts'. The veteran Los Angeles gay rights activist Harry Hay responded by establishing, with a few colleagues, the Mattachine Society, named after the French medieval masque group La Société Mattachine to reflect the fact that 'gays were a masked people, unknown and anonymous'. Mattachine organisation was strictly hierarchical, based on masonic and communist models, with local groups relating upwards through a structure of 'orders' but having little or no contact with other such groups. The Mattachines believed that the injustice and oppression which they suffered stemmed from relationships deeply embedded in the structure of American society; homosexuals constituted a social minority unaware of its own status, a minority that needed to develop a group consciousness that would give it pride in its own identity. By promoting such a positive self-image the founders hoped to forge a unified national movement of homosexuals able to fight against oppression. The movement grew rapidly along the California coast, and in mid-1952 (in its public guise as the Citizens Committee to Outlaw Entrapment) won a historic court case when one of the original Mattachines, Dale Jennings, was entrapped by a Los Angeles plainclothes policeman. While he was happy to admit his homosexuality, Jennings denied all the charges brought against him, and following a deadlocked jury the charges were dropped. Emboldened by the positive response to the Citizens Committee, Hay decided to incorporate the Mattachine Foundation as a not-for-profit educational organisation, which would attract more members and provide an acceptable front for the gay community to relate to the wider society. In March 1953 a Los Angeles newspaper ran an article equating 'sexual deviates' with 'security risks' who were banding together to wield 'tremendous political power': in response the Mattachines called a series of meetings at which the organisation moved decidedly rightwards towards political safety. A despondent Harry Hay moved out of the leadership and never again played a central role. The restructured Mattachine Society now sought assimilation and collaboration, which led to a bitter struggle with the organisation's more radical members and a rapid decline in membership and influence. Though its California base continued to decline, the Mattachine journals *One Magazine* and *Mattachine Review* reached many previously isolated individuals in the late 1950s. Chapters functioned through the 1960s in several American cities, where they operated as gay support and information centres. They failed to adapt to the militant radicalism of the post-**Stonewall** years after 1969, however, and by the early 1970s the Mattachine Society had ceased to function.

Stuart Timmons, *The Trouble with Harry Hay: Founder of the Modern Gay Movement*, Alyson, 1990

John D'Emilio, *Sexual Politics, Sexual Communities: The Making of a Homosexual Minority in the United States, 1940–1970*, University of Chicago Press, 1983

Warren Johansson, 'Mattachine Society', *Encyclopedia of Homosexuality* (ed. Wayne Dynes), Garland, 1990

May 1968
1968
youth protest movement

To conventional cultural historians the month of May 1968 warrants little mention beyond that of a student revolt at the Sorbonne in Paris which resulted in an overhaul of the French higher educational system. Yet the turbulence which peaked in Paris was only a small part of a youth revolt which rocked cities from San Francisco to Berlin, Chicago to Rome, London to Tokyo, and which challenged the international political order to an extent rarely equalled in this or any century. The two linked and unifying factors in the insurrections of 1968 were the escalating war in Vietnam, increasingly judged a criminal exercise in neocolonial domination, and the growing unwillingness of young people to trust those in power, be they politicians, teachers or police. By the end of 1967 antiwar sentiment amongst young Americans had reached a new peak with the massive Pentagon Action of October 21st, when the **Yippies** and **Students for a Democratic Society**, the **Congress of Racial Equality** and the **American Friends Service Committee**, **Martin Luther King**'s Southern Christian Leadership Conference and **David Dellinger**'s Mobilization Committee all joined forces in a massive peaceful demonstration against US military imperialism. The Pentagon Action struck a chord with students the world over, and during the early months of 1968 large anti-authority demonstrations erupted in Poland, Spain, England, Italy, Germany and France, all of them met with more or less violent police intervention. The linked events which set the immediate scene for the May riots were the March occupation of the French University of Nanterre following the arrest of student leaders including **Daniel Cohn-Bendit**, the April 4th assassination of Martin Luther King, the April 11th attempt on the life of the German student leader **Rudi Dutschke**, and the April 23rd occupation of New York's prestigious Columbia University in protest against the draft, all seen as part of the same oppressive militaristic world order which in April sent a record number of bombing raids against North Vietnam. This highly volatile mixture boiled over in the second week of May, when the streets of Paris witnessed clashes not experienced since the Commune of 1871. Meanwhile the people of Prague were enjoying **Alexander Dubček**'s 'Prague Spring', 'free universities' were flourishing in New York, Berlin and London, radical theatre was thriving and student publications multiplying. The promise of love and peace was, in most quarters, to be short-lived. Russian tanks rolled into Prague in August to stifle Czechoslovakia's fledgling democracy, the London School of Economics (the centre of youth protest in Britain) was temporarily closed down in January 1969, student leaders and radical activists in the USA, Japan, Germany, France and Italy were given harsh prison sentences. It was perhaps inevitable that some of the idealism and anger which had fuelled the 1968 rebellion, now harshly repressed and punished by reactionary governments who seemed to care little for true democracy, should reemerge as the gun-and-dynamite tactics of the Weathermen, the Red Army Faction and similar underground movements.

David Caute, *Sixty-Eight: The Year of the Barricades*, Hamish Hamilton, 1988

May 4th Movement
1919
civil rights protest

In early May 1989, as thousands of democracy movement students demanded freedom in Beijing's Tiananmen Square, an older generation remembered a similar protest in this same square exactly seventy years earlier. The May 4th Movement took its name from a demonstration in Beijing on May 4th 1919 when more than three thousand students marched to protest against the decision of Great Britain, France and Italy to assign defeated Germany's rights in the province of Shandong (the birthplace of Confucius) to imperialist Japan instead of returning it to China. Outraged by what they saw as a betrayal by the 'civilised' West, representatives of a number of student groups based at Beijing's Beida University had planned an orderly demonstration, but it ended in violence when a small group stormed the home of a pro-Japanese official, beat alleged traitors, ransacked the house and set it on fire. News of May 4th rapidly spread through the country, and newly-radicalised students demonstrated in Tianjin, Shanghai, Nanjing, Wuhan and other cities. Workers staged sympathy strikes and merchants organised an anti-Japanese boycott. Local student groups proliferated, and on June 16th 1919 the National Student Association was formed in Shanghai, consolidating the new-found power of young Chinese intellectuals. Interest in anarchism and socialism revived, and revolutionary Russia became very popular. The May 4th Movement inspired a new generation of leaders, who played a large part in the revival of support for **Sun Yat-Sen** and the Kuomintang and in the founding of the Chinese Communist Party.

Jeffrey N. Wasserstrom and Elizabeth J. Perry (eds), *Popular Protest and Political Culture in Modern China: Learning from 1989*, Westview, 1992

May Day
1886–
celebration of labour rights

An ancient holiday in celebration of spring and fertility, it was almost inevitable that May Day should become the revolutionary holiday of the nineteenth-century workers' movement. On May 1st 1886, as the Knights of Labor developed into the first national trade union in the USA, nearly half a million American workers left work to demonstrate for an eight-hour working day. At a machine works near Chicago police violently broke up a clash between strikers and blackleg workers, leaving several demonstrators dead. At the end of a protest demonstration in Chicago's Haymarket Square three days later a bomb was thrown into the excessively large contingent of police. Eight labour organisers were prosecuted for conspiracy to murder and four were hanged, though there was no evidence linking them with the bomb. The first May Day labour holiday and the 'Haymarket Martyrs' quickly become a vital part of labour history. In 1889 the International Socialist Congress in Paris designated May 1st as an eight-hour holiday for workers the world over, and elaborate ceremonies evolved with brass bands, songs, banners and uniforms: the banners often made reference to the Haymarket Martyrs. The first world war and the growing split between socialism and communism dampened May Day celebrations in the USA, and among mainstream labour unions its observation became muted or was dropped altogether. In the Soviet Union and its allies, meanwhile, May Day became a time for military parades, though many Western European countries continued to mark May Day with a holiday celebrated by trade unions and other labour organisations.

David Henry, *The History of the Haymarket Affair*, Russell and Russell, 1958
Eric Hobsbawm and Terence Ranger (eds), *The Invention of Tradition*, Cambridge University Press, 1984
David Roediger and Franklin Rosemont (eds), *Haymarket Scrapbook*, Charles H. Kerr, 1986

Men's Liberation Movement
1969–
liberation movement

Given that many women in the late 1960s started looking with newly-opened political eyes at women's role in society, it was unsurprising that many of the men with whom they related and discussed feminist issues also wanted to liberate themselves from oppressive stereotypes. The first male consciousness-raising groups were established in New York, attracting mostly young middle class white men with leftist sympathies who wanted to share the insights of feminism, and the antisexist men's movement quickly established groups across the country. Of the many groups and organisations within the movement, one of the most important is the National Organization for Changing Men (NOCM), founded in 1975; a number of men's resource and meeting centres were also established, including the Berkeley Men's Center, Boston-based Men Sharing, and the Knoxville Men's Resource Center. Wherever profeminist men met in groups the newsletters and journals quickly proliferated: in the USA the NOCM journal *Changing Men* was one of the first, but there are or have been more than two hundred other American men's liberation publications, including the *Journal of Men's Studies*, *M.: Gentle Men for Gender Justice*, *Wingspan*, *Man!*, *Man Alive*, *Journeyman*, *Thunder Stick* and *MENtor*. In Britain the first Men Against Sexism (MAS) group was established in Brighton in 1971, and during the next decade MAS groups were established in many cities: the leading British publications are *Achilles Heel*, first published in 1976, and the *Men's Antisexist Newsletter*. There are also active antisexist men's movements in other countries, most notably Germany and Australia. Of the many voices of the men's liberation movement, probably the most influential is John Stoltenberg, a New York-based editor and journalist who has written many articles about sexual politics, and books including the thought-provoking collection of essays *Refusing to be a Man* (1989).

Jon Snodgrass (ed.), *For Men Against Sexism: A Book of Readings*, Times Change Press, 1977
John Stoltenberg, *Refusing to be a Man*, Breitenbush Books, 1989

Movimiento Campesino Paraguayo [MCP]
1980–
self-help movement

For thirty-five years from 1954 until 1989 General Alfredo Stroessner ruled Paraguay, becoming Latin America's longest-surviving dictator, and for most of that period Paraguay was the only South American country without an independent peasants' movement. A Christian cooperative movement called the Peasant League was crushed in 1976 and many of its leaders murdered, yet despite the dangers peasant leaders continued to organise and in 1980 established the independent Movimiento Campesino Paraguayo (Paraguayan Peasants' Movement). During the early 1980s Paraguay's economic crisis deepened, leaving more than 350,000 rural poor landless by 1985. Meanwhile Paraguayan women, who are still subject to repressive and archaic discriminatory legislation, began to organise, and in November 1985 more than a thousand peasant women from 48 communities met in Caaguazú to establish the Coordinación de Mujeres Campesinas (Peasant Women's Commission), initially to work within and alongside the MCP for land rights, but later to campaign specifically for women's rights. In 1986 the first 120 landless families were given provisional title to land which had belonged to Brazilian entrepreneurs. The MCP also helped to organise the Asunción street protests of 1986, which marked a turning point in Paraguayan civil resistance to the Stroessner autocracy, and three years later the hated regime fell. Since then the organisation has continued to grow, establishing seven new rural resettlement schemes and attracting more than 100,000 members. For a country steeped in machismo and repression of women's rights, it was encouraging that by 1993 eight members of the fifteen-strong MCP national executive were women.

Jo Fisher, Women, *Resistance and Politics in South America*, Latin America Bureau, 1993
Petrona Coronel, 'Women Leading the Paraguay Peasants' Movement', in *Compañeras* (ed. Gaby Küppers), Latin America Bureau, 1994

Movimiento de Mujeres Pobladoras [MOMUPO]
1982–
self-help movement

The military government of Augusto Pinochet which ruled Chile from 1974 to 1988 brought both fear and extreme poverty to millions. As the economic crisis deepened in the early 80s, family life began to break down, especially in the densely-populated suburbs (*poblaciones*) of cities like Valparaiso and Santiago. Recognising that community organising was the only way to guarantee basic needs like education, health and food, more than five hundred community-based organisations were established in Santiago alone between 1980 and 1982; in the majority of them women were the main instigators and organisers. By 1982, however, the military government had established a network of 'mothers' centres' to counter such initiatives, and male-dominated church and trade union organisations threatened to undermine the practical and consciousness-raising work being done by Chilean women, so a network of women within the community movement established MOMUPO – the Movement of Women *Pobladoras* – in order to maintain an independent organisation which would recognise the contribution and particular needs of ordinary women in the *poblaciones*. Among its early initiatives were communal kitchens and independent craft cooperatives. As the economic crisis deepened, MOMUPO started to organise nationwide campaigns: in 1984 it coordinated a Hunger Campaign, when dozens of women wearing black and carrying empty saucepans marched in silent protest to local government offices. In 1985 it organised a health and reproductive rights campaign, and ran its first summer school on women and politics. By 1987 a potential split in the organisation was emerging: those who wanted it to remain a grassroots social movement were concerned that middle class issues were taking the organisation away from its primary purpose of empowering disadvantaged women. One of the founders, Luz María, left to establish a women's centre in one of Santiago's poorest *poblaciones*, and MOMUPO distanced itself from middle class Chilean feminism, which often alienated poorer women by concentrating on issues like lesbianism and equal rights within privileged professions. Following Chile's free election in 1989 women's groups continued to proliferate within the *poblaciones*, and MOMUPO has to a large extent succeeded in maintaining its networking status, forging new alliances between a wide variety of women's organisations.

Jo Fisher, *Out of the Shadows: Women, Resistance and Politics in South America*, Latin America Bureau, 1993

National American Woman Suffrage Association [NAWSA]
1890–1920
women's suffrage campaigning organisation

When NAWSA was formed through the merger of the two main wings of the US suffrage movement, the campaign for women's voting rights was already nearly half a century old. Organised campaigning had started with the Seneca Falls Convention of 1848, which resulted in the establishment of the National Woman Suffrage Association (NWSA) by the veteran women's rights campaigners **Elizabeth Cady Stanton** and **Susan B. Anthony**. In 1869, concerned that NWSA was alienating middle class Americans with its militancy and 'advanced' views about issues such as free love and divorce, Lucy Stone and Henry Blackwell founded the relatively conservative American Woman Suffrage Association (AWSA), open to both women and men. By the mid-1880s Stanton and Anthony had moved apart, the former holding to the NWSA's radical origins while the latter sought strategic alliances with less explicitly feminist organisations, thus edging closer to the AWSA position. The 'National's movement away from radicalism enabled the merger with the 'American' in 1890 to form the 'National American': Elizabeth Cady Stanton was its first president, and by 1896 Susan B. Anthony had been completely edged out. Although the merger healed old rifts and presented a united front for suffrage, many older feminists like **Matilda Joslyn Gage** withdrew, and it was soon clear that the movement had entered a stagnant period. Arriving home in 1910 from England, where she had learned much from the militant suffragettes of the **Women's Social and Political Union**, young feminist Alice Paul promised to revive the NAWSA fight for a federal woman suffrage amendment. Paul's militancy occasioned yet another split, this time between NAWSA's more conservative members and its radical wing, which under Alice Paul called itself the Congressional Union. The turning point came at the end of 1915, when the diplomatic and efficient organiser Carrie Chapman Catt again agreed to become the NAWSA president (she had held the presidency from 1900 to 1903, but had resigned when her husband became ill). She quickly turned NAWSA into a genuine political force and used a mixture of charm and threat to persuade President Woodrow Wilson to take women's suffrage seriously. Success finally came in 1920 with the passing of the Nineteenth Amendment to the US constitution, and American women first voted in a presidential election in 1921. After the vote had been won the NAWSA became the much more conventional and ineffectual League of Women Voters: Carrie Catt turned her attention towards pacifism and Alice Paul to the National Women's Party and the **Equal Rights Amendment**.

Jacqueline Van Voris, *Carrie Chapman Catt: A Public Life*, Feminist Press, 1987

Christine Bolt, *The Women's Movements in the United States and Britain from the 1790s to the 1920s*, Harvester-Wheatsheaf, 1993

National Organisation for Women [NOW]
1966–
women's rights advocacy and campaigning organisation

As the civil rights movement began to secure tangible victories in the early 60s, a growing number of feminist women felt that it was time for parallel changes in the laws sanctioning sexual discrimination. In 1961 Esther Paterson succeeded in persuading President Kennedy to establish a President's Committee on the Status of Women, in 1963 the US Congress passed an Equal Pay Act, and the historic Civil Rights Act of 1964 theoretically illegalised sex discrimination in employment, though the new Equal Employment Opportunities Commission did little to enforce it. In July 1966 a group of 28 women including **Betty Friedan**, Aileen Hernandez and Pauli Murray, annoyed with the government's unwillingness to enforce its own laws, founded the National Organization for Women. Its goal was 'to take action to bring women into full participation in the mainstream of American society now, exercising all the privileges and responsibilities thereof in truly equal partnership with men.' NOW soon became the largest feminist civil rights organisation in the USA, but divisions quickly rose to the surface between its more respectable and traditionally liberal members and a growing number of young activists. Typical of the debates which threatened to divide NOW was the attempt by its conservative wing, under Betty Friedan, to exclude lesbians from standing as NOW officers: the proposal was defeated by a large margin, but left many in the nascent **women's liberation movement** unhappy with NOW's stance. In 1977 NOW made ratification of the **Equal Rights Amendment** its top priority, and until the Amendment's defeat in 1982 it was effectively a single-issue organisation. In the 1980s NOW entered mainstream politics, endorsing national candidates and working with state and national legislatures to secure equal rights for women. Its increasing emphasis on electoral politics has led to a loss of its more radical members, but there is no doubt that NOW has led to a widespread public recognition of women's issues, and to official acceptance of the need to involve women at all levels of decision-making. In the 1990s there are signs that NOW is again becoming more radical: it has been particularly active in campaigning for reproductive rights, and in 1991 NOW president Patricia Ireland made it clear that its members would fight for women's right to safe, legal abortions. Membership of NOW, which is open to both women and men who believe in equal rights for women, is in excess of a quarter of a million, organised in 750 chapters across the USA.

David Walls, *The Activist's Almanac: The Concerned Citizen's Guide to the Leading Advocacy Organizations in America*, Simon and Schuster, 1993

New Left
*c.*1958–1971
radical political movement

During the 1950s many radicals came to realise that the socialist arguments, tactics and policies which had sustained the left up to mid-century
– mainstream Marxist analysis, Soviet-style communism and a trade union
movement based largely on primary industries – were rapidly losing touch
with the realities of changing circumstances. On both sides of the Atlantic
small groups of young intellectuals started referring to themselves as the
'new left', to distinguish and release themselves from what was perceived
as the political and cultural straitjacket of the 'old left'. In Britain the new
left dated from the establishment in the late 1950s of a network of
university-based New Left Clubs, whose founders included **Stuart Hall** and
Raymond Williams. Many members were disaffected Marxist intellectuals
critical of Soviet policy, though many of the wider issues of human rights,
environmental concern and social equality were aired in the pages of the
New Left Review, which started publication in 1959 following a merger
between **E.P. Thompson**'s *The New Reasoner* and Hall's *Universities and Left
Review*. In the USA the parallel movement grew from activists who had
broken with the Socialist Workers Party. Common concerns such as civil
rights, antimilitarism, the Chinese stand against the Soviet Union, the
Cuban Revolution and banning the bomb ensured that the grouping of
those with forward-looking socialist sympathies grew rapidly. By the time
the Catholic activist Tom Hayden drafted the radical Port Huron Statement
in 1962, adopted as the manifesto of **Students for a Democratic Society**
(SDS), large numbers of alienated young Americans were ready to rally
behind the new left banner. The heroic struggles of the **Student Nonviolent
Coordinating Committee** (SNCC) and **Martin Luther King**'s rallies and
marches against racism in the early 1960s empowered young people
throughout the country, and in 1964 students demanding freedom of
speech at the University of California at Berkeley succeeded for the first
time in paralysing a prestigious educational establishment. The escalating
US invasion of Vietnam after 1965 politicised many more young people,
and antiwar protests, marches and teach-ins brought the ideas of the new
left to campuses across the country. While US radicals protested, the
European new left seemed at first to prefer writing and lecturing, but by
the end of 1967 the scene was set for the French university protests which,
in May 1968, suddenly spread across the continent, being mirrored as far
afield as Japan and Australia. Though police and politicians were quick to
suppress rebellious young leaders including **Daniel Cohn-Bendit** and **Rudi
Dutschke**, it was clear by the end of the decade that many who had cut
their teeth on the new left of the 1960s recognised that their demands and
peaceful protests were regularly being met with official lies and violence,
and had themselves chosen a more violent route towards social and
political change. The German Red Army Faction was founded in 1968; in

1969 the SDS split, spawning the militant Weathermen; and in 1970 the
SNCC merged with the **Black Panther Party**. The new left of the 1960s
which had sought change through peaceful means was left largely defeated
and disillusioned, though many of its adherents kept faith with the radical
socialist vision and linked their ideas and activism with the growing
women's and **gay liberation movements**, and with the nascent green
movement. In Europe, and particularly in Britain, many of the ideas
developed by the new left have been incorporated into contemporary
socialist thinking: the London-based *New Left Review* continues to publish
groundbreaking work in socialist history, ideas and contemporary practice.

Carl Oglesby (ed.), *The New Left Reader*, Grove Press, 1969
Todd Gitlin, *The Sixties: Years of Hope, Days of Rage*, Bantam, 1987
Ronald Fraser *et al* (eds), *1968: A Student Generation in Revolt*, Pantheon, 1988
Irwin Unger, *The Movement: A History of the American New Left, 1959–72*,
     University Press of America, 1988
Lin Chun, *The British New Left*, Edinburgh University Press, 1993

Nuclear-Free and Independent Pacific
1975–
peace and self-determination movement

The Nuclear-Free and Independent Pacific movement is an indigenous
peoples' organisation working toward building a nuclear-free, superpower-
free and unpolluted Pacific. It was established in Fiji in 1975 in response
to growing US and French military presence in the area, following a long
history of cultural and environmental abuse – as a result of US nuclear
testing in the 1950s and 60s, for example, six of the Marshall Islands were
completely destroyed and a further fourteen left uninhabitable. The movement adopted a People's Charter for a Nuclear-Free Pacific, which has since
been adopted by many church groups, trade unions, and (in large part) by
the South Pacific Forum, a regional grouping of thirteen Pacific states. In
1980, against strong opposition from the USA, a group of women from
Belau Island insisted on the world's first antinuclear constitution, and in
1982 the Kwajalein Islanders were forced to move to Ebeye Island, a ghetto
colony, because of the damage done by the US long-range missile tests
fired into the atoll. They protested with a series of 'sail-ins' called 'Operation Homecoming' to reoccupy their land. Recognising that freedom from
nuclear weapons requires independence from outside powers, in 1983 the
People's Charter incorporated into its aims the withdrawal of all colonial
powers from the area. The nuclear-free movement has united nearly all the
Pacific islands with considerable success: the Treaty of Rarotonga (1985),
negotiated by the South Pacific Forum, prohibits the ownership, use,
stationing and testing of nuclear weapons and the dumping at sea of
nuclear waste. By 1990 eight Pacific states had signed the treaty, and so
had China. The USSR has signed two of the protocols, but the main regional
colonial powers, the UK, the USA and France, have yet to sign.

Julian Burger, *The Gaia Atlas of First Peoples*, Robertson McCarta, 1990

Nuclear Freeze [National Nuclear Weapons Freeze Campaign]
1979–1983
disarmament campaign

The US counterpart to the **Campaign for Nuclear Disarmament** (CND) is SANE, the National Committee for a Sane Nuclear Policy, which was established in mid-1957. Its founding group of 27 included journalist Norman Cousins and Clarence Pickett of the **American Friends Service Committee**, and the acronym was suggested by radical psychologist **Erich Fromm**. SANE's early successes included major rallies, including one in New York's Madison Square Gardens in May 1960 which drew a record twenty thousand people. In the early 1960s SANE was one of the major lobby groups behind the creation in 1961 of the Arms Control and Disarmament Agency and the success of the Limited Test Ban Treaty of 1963. Controversy resulted from the appointment of paediatrician and political activist Benjamin Spock to the SANE executive: Spock was also cochair, with **Martin Luther King**, of the April 1967 Spring Mobilization to End the War in Vietnam, an event which the SANE board declined to endorse: Cousins and executive director Donald Keyes resigned believing that SANE was becoming too radical and Spock because he believed it was becoming too conservative. Although SANE, like CND, declined in membership during the 1970s, the nuclear race continued apace. By the late 1970s the USA and the Soviet Union were deploying 4,500 nuclear delivery systems containing 17,000 warheads, together having the firepower of more than half a million times the atomic bomb dropped over Hiroshima in August 1945. Such nuclear madness – and the means to counteract it – were beyond the comprehension of many people, but in 1979 Randall Forsberg, director of the Institute for Defense and Disarmament Studies at Brookline, Massachusetts drafted *The Call to Halt the Nuclear Arms Race*, outlining a bilateral nuclear weapons freeze between the USA and the Soviet Union. In March 1981 US peace groups and arms control experts held a national conference to approve the strategy, now known as the National Nuclear Weapons Freeze Campaign (or simply 'Nuclear Freeze'). Major national religious, civic, and political organisations endorsed the freeze proposal, and a national office opened in St Louis in December 1981, with veteran peace activist Randy Kehler as its first national coordinator. A Disarmament Week was held in October 1981, culminating in a national 'call-in', encouraging Americans to call the White House and urge Ronald Reagan to propose a mutual freeze. On June 12th 1982 the Freeze Campaign organised the largest peace demonstration in US history, bringing nearly a million people to New York to support the proposal, and during the autumn of 1982, in the closest equivalent to a national referendum in the history of American democracy, 30% of the American electorate voted for a bilateral freeze. In the November 1982 elections voters in eight states and a number of major cities approved freeze referendums, which also won support from leading Democratic politicians. In March 1983, however, Reagan called for the development of a space-based defence system that would render nuclear missiles 'impotent and obsolete': the ludicrous $30 million 'Strategic Defense Initiative', which was eventually called off by president Bill Clinton in 1994. In May 1983 Roman Catholic bishops issued a pastoral letter condemning nuclear war, and the House of Representatives approved a resolution calling for a 'mutual and verifiable freeze' on nuclear weapons, but in October 1983 a similar resolution was rejected by the Senate. During the period when the Freeze campaign was most active SANE membership grew rapidly, from 17,000 in 1982 to 130,000 by 1986, and in December 1986, following lengthy negotiations, a formal merger was announced between SANE and the Freeze campaign. In the event it was Gorbachev's rise to power and the collapse of the Soviet bloc that led to the first major reductions in the world's nuclear arsenals, based on two major Strategic Arms Reduction Treaties (START I and II): from the American viewpoint, however, the groundswell of public antinuclear sentiment generated by SANE and the Freeze campaign undoubtedly paved the way for US involvement in active nuclear arms control.

Daniel Ford, Henry Kendall and Steven Nadis, *Beyond the Freeze: The Road to Nuclear Sanity*, Beacon Press, 1982
Robert Seeley, *The Handbook of Nonviolence*, Lawrence Hill, 1986

Peace Pledge Union [PPU]
1934–
peace organisation

The Peace Pledge Union in Britain developed from a letter that Dick Sheppard, a charismatic Anglican clergyman who had served as a chaplain in World War I and whose broadcast sermons had made him well known, wrote to the press in 1934. In his letter he wrote 'I renounce war and never again, directly or indirectly, will I support or sanction another,' and asked men who supported this statement to send him a postcard. Within two days he had received 2,500 cards. The PPU was formally named and established in 1936, and opened to women, who became active campaigners on its behalf. By October 1937, when Dick Sheppard suddenly died, pledges totalled 120,000; the number peaked in April 1940 at 136,000. During the war, the PPU housed the Central Board for Conscientious Objectors in its London headquarters, and set up the Pacifist Service Bureau. Postwar studies of Gandhian nonviolent resistance led in 1952 to the first actions protesting against the atomic bomb. Affiliated with **War Resisters International** and other organisations including the Campaign Against Arms Trade, which it helped to establish in 1974, the PPU's present work includes peace education and the support of conscientious objectors. Based in London, its publications include *The Pacifist* and *Studies in Non-Violence*.

Sybil Morrison, *I Renounce War: The Story of the Peace Pledge Union*, Sheppard, 1962

Caroline Moorehead, *Troublesome People: The Warriors of Pacifism*, Adler and
    Adler, 1987

Plowshares
1980–
peace action

The first of many Plowshares actions was carried out on September 9, 1980,
when eight people entered the General Electric Plant in King of Prussia,
Pennsylvania, struck two MX missile nosecones with hammers and poured
their own blood over documents. Physical damage to weapons systems and
the pouring of blood to symbolise the deadly nature of those weapons
characterize 'plowshares actions', named after the Biblical exhortation to
'hammer swords into plowshares'. Most participants, though not all, have
been committed Christians. Most courts have not allowed Plowshares
activists to present their defence for the destruction of property – that the
action is justified in calling attention to the devastating effects of nuclear
war and the costs of the arms race. When a full defence and expert
witnesses have been allowed, the trials have been powerful testimonials.
Plowshares activists are prepared to spend time in prison, and almost all
do. In the USA they have been given sentences ranging from one to
eighteen years, although sometimes public support has resulted in charges
being dropped. By the mid-1990s, more than fifty Plowshares actions had
taken place in the United States, Germany, Britain and Australia.

Arthur J. Laffin and Anne Montgomery, eds, *Swords into Plowshares: Nonviolent
    Direct Action for Disarmament*, Harper & Row, 1987
Michael True, *To Construct Peace*, Twenty-Third Publications, 1992

Rosenberg Case
1950–1953
prisoners' defence campaign

By the middle of 1950, when Julius and Ethel Rosenberg and Morton Sobell
were arrested and charged with espionage, the US government was at fever
pitch with anticommunist hysteria, and thousands of 'red subversives' had
fallen victim to Senator Joseph McCarthy's wave of political repression. To
add to American fears, the Soviet Union had recently tested its first atomic
bomb, and widespread civil defence preparations were under way in case
the Korean War 'turned atomic'. On February 2nd 1950 British physicist
Klaus Fuchs, who had worked in America on the A-bomb project, was
arrested in England as a Soviet spy: he confessed and received a fourteen-
year sentence. On May 23rd the FBI announced that Harry Gold, a Philadelphia chemist, was Fuchs's American accomplice, and on June 16th David
Greenglass, a New York machinist, was arrested for passing information to
Gold while stationed at Los Alamos. Julius Rosenberg, Greenglass's brother-
in-law, an engineer who had lost a government post two years earlier for
being an alleged communist, was arrested on July 17th. He insisted on his
innocence, but on August 11th his wife Ethel was also arrested. Finally, on

August 18th, Morton Sobell, a college classmate of Julius's, was arrested in Texas after supposedly having been kidnapped in Mexico City by FBI agents. The trial of the three for conspiracy to commit espionage opened in March 1951, and though it lasted only fourteen days it was to become the most famous political trial in American history. Despite the lack of any conclusive evidence and the defendents' strenuous denial of any involvement in espionage, all three were convicted. The Rosenbergs were sentenced to death and Sobell to thirty years in prison, the judge opining that 'their conduct in putting into the hands of the Russians the A-bomb' had already caused 'the Communist aggression in Korea, with the resultant casualties exceeding 50,000 and who knows but that millions more of innocent people may pay the price of your treason.' Within months a massive defence campaign was under way, led by the National Committee to Secure Justice in the Rosenberg Case. Albert Einstein made his concern public and 2,300 clergy endorsed an appeal. In Europe **Jean-Paul Sartre** and Pablo Picasso sent petitions of clemency to the Pope and the French president. The Supreme Court refused to review the case unless the Rosenbergs confessed and named other spies, and in June 1953 President Eisenhower denied a final clemency plea, declaring that 'by immeasurably increasing the chances of atomic war, the Rosenbergs may have condemned to death tens of millions of innocent people all over the world.' In New York, Paris, London and other major cities hundreds of demonstrators protested against the sentence, but on June 19th the Rosenbergs were executed. Meanwhile Morton Sobell had been sent to the notorious Alcatraz Penitentiary and, with his wife Helen as its leader, a Committee to Secure Justice for Morton Sobell initiated a defence campaign which won widespread support. The Rosenberg 'Spy Trial' continued – and continues – to polarise American opinion over the issue of patriotism and espionage. The case inspired a number of books, most notably that written by the Rosenbergs' sons Robert and Michael (Meeropol is their adoptive surname): *We Are Your Sons* used newly-available government files to prove the innocence of the Rosenbergs, even though many of the crucial documents remain censored or withheld.

Walter Schneir and Miriam Schneir, *Invitation to an Inquest*, Pantheon, 1983
Robert Meeropol and Michael Meeropol, *We Are Your Sons* (second ed.),
    University of Illinois Press, 1986

Sacco-Vanzetti Case
1920–1927
prisoners' defence campaign

During the postwar 'red scare' of 1919–20 the US government clamped down on anarchist activists and sympathisers, often arresting them on minor charges and delivering harsh sentences. The incident which encapsulates the atmosphere of those years was that of two working class Italians, Nicola Sacco and Bartolomeo Vanzetti. Both were committed activists in the Boston anarchist movement, and Sacco had been a conscientious objector during the first world war. On May 9th 1920 they were arrested for distributing circulars announcing a protest meeting for one of their anarchist friends, Andrea Salsedo, who had died in suspicious circumstances while being held by justice department officials. The day after their arrest Sacco and Vanzetti were charged with murdering a paymaster and guard three weeks earlier, during a payroll robbery at South Braintree, Massachusetts, a crime with which they almost certainly had no connection. The ensuing trial became more a test of freedom of political expression than one of criminal guilt, and rapidly developed into an international cause célèbre. On July 14th 1921 Sacco and Vanzetti were found guilty of robbery and murder, a verdict which marked the beginning of a lengthy legal struggle to clear the two men. The long process of petitions and appeals required immense sums of money, and the defence lawyers organised large-scale appeal funds to which many thousands of working people contributed regularly. Many well-known voices added their outrage and concern, led by Harvard law professor Felix Frankfurter, and the Sacco-Vanzetti case polarised US opinion between freedom and patriotism, the rule of law and 'American honour'. On April 9th 1927, after all recourse in the Massachusetts courts had failed, Sacco and Vanzetti were sentenced to death, and they were electrocuted on August 23rd. Their final statement is still often quoted by radical activists: 'Only two of us will die, but you, our comrades, will live by millions. We have won. We are not vanquished. Treasure our sufferings, our sorrows, our mistakes, our defeat, our passion, for future battles for the great emancipation. We embrace you all and bid you our extreme goodbye. Now and ever, long life to you all. Long live liberty.'

Herbert B. Ehrmann, *The Case That Will Not Die*, Beacon Press, 1969

Robert D'Attilio and Jane Manthorn (eds), *Sacco-Vanzetti: Developments and Reconsiderations*, Boston Public Library, 1979

Sanctuary Movement
1980–*c*.1987
human rights action

The sanctuary movement in the United States became publicly known on March 24th 1982, the anniversary of the assassination of **Oscar Romero**, when five churches announced that they were offering sanctuary to Central American refugees. The movement originated in Arizona during the spring and summer of 1980 when Jim Corbett, a retired rancher and Quaker, and John Fife, pastor of the Southside Presbyterian Church in Tucson, became aware of the situation of Salvadoran refugees who were fleeing death squads at home only to be arrested in the USA and returned to even greater danger. They and their communities responded by fundraising to post bond for some of the many refugees in detention, organising legal assistance with applications for political asylum, and developing an 'underground railroad' to assist and shelter refugees. It soon became clear that the legal process was futile, because 97% of Salvadorans were denied asylum. Deciding to break the law and offer sanctuary to Central American refugees, the Southside congregation invited other churches to join it. Once public, the movement grew quickly: by the mid-1980s an estimated three hundred churches and synagogues, nineteen cities, twenty universities and one state (New Mexico) had declared themselves sanctuaries, and some 70,000 US citizens were active in transporting, housing, and feeding refugees. The movement's purpose, besides protecting the refugees, was to challenge the US policy that supplied the military training and weapons the people were fleeing. North American sanctuary workers and churches testified repeatedly to a vital deepening of their own political awareness, inspired by the courage and hope of the refugees and their struggle for social justice. The sanctuary movement was subjected to harassment and intimidation, including the arrest and imprisonment of activists in Texas and Arizona.

Jim Wallis and Joyce Hollyday (eds), *Cloud of Witnesses*, Orbis and *Sojourners*, 1991

Arthur J. Laffin and Anne Montgomery (eds), *Swords into Plowshares*, Harper and Row, 1987

Sarvodaya Shramadana Movement [SSM]
1958–
self-help movement

An independent 1984 report called Sri Lanka's community-based self-help movement SSM 'a remarkable organisation, probably unique in the field of international development'. Founded in 1958 by the 26-year-old Ahangamage Tudor ('A.T.') Ariyaratne, who later became one of Sri Lanka's leading social activists, SSM's aim is to work with village communities to establish a balanced programme of development appropriate to each community – the name means 'sharing people's resources to achieve mutual awakening'. By 1985 SSM was active in more than a third of Sri Lanka's 23,000 villages, with more than 30,000 trained workers. When a village community decides to think creatively about its future, experienced SSM staff members visit the village and work with its inhabitants, first to establish what the community feels are its main needs, and then to organise the labour and resources to achieve those needs – this usually takes the form of a voluntary work camp or 'shramadana'. Once a village has developed sufficient experience in self-reliance, it forms itself into an independent SSM Society, and thereafter an elected committee of 25 runs the affairs of the society; of the 25 at least three must be children between seven and fourteen years old, three must be between fifteen and twenty-eight, and three must be women. SSM is today a large organisation, running savings schemes, training courses, welfare networks, legal aid services and small-scale economic enterprises. Sarvodaya and its founder are well aware of the dangers of creeping capitalism and political intrigue, and A.T. Ariyaratne has written and spoken at length about the importance of retaining SSM's Buddhist principles and political independence, even if that means losing financial and government support. SSM calls itself 'a non-political organisation', a line which has prompted criticism from both mainstream and opposition politicians in a country riven with violent inter-racial tensions, yet its commitment to working nonviolently with all religious and cultural minorities has won it much admiration. SSM regularly organises peace marches and actions, and even when faced with terrorist threats and racially-inspired violence, joint Tamil and Sinhalese SSM teams work together for reconciliation and mutual self-help. As in so many poor southern countries, SSM has found it hard to counter the dual threats of Western-style capitalism and internal ethnic unrest. Despite achieving so much and affecting the lives of so many Sri Lankans, SSM has not succeeded in stemming the growing tide of bloodshed that has engulfed the country in the last decade, but without its inspiration and commitment to non-violence the situation today could be much worse.

Scottsboro Case
1931–1937
prisoners' defence campaign

On March 25th 1931 nine young black men (Olen Montgomery, Clarence Norris, Haywood Patterson, Ozie Powell, Willie Roberson, Charlie Weems, Eugene Williams, and Andy and Roy Wright) were arrested and accused of raping two white women on a train near Paint Rock, Alabama. They were tried without proper counsel, hastily convicted, and all but Roy Wright were sentenced to death. Already involved in a large-scale antilynching campaign begun a year earlier, the Communist Party-dominated International Labor Defense (ILD) gained the confidence of the defendants and their parents, initiated a campaign for their freedom, and in the process waged a fierce battle for control over the case with the National Association for the Advancement of Colored People (NAACP), who accused the communists of using the case as propaganda. The ILD argued that the Scottsboro case was not simply an isolated instance of injustice, but represented widespread oppression and white rule throughout the South. Protests erupted throughout the country, and the governor of Alabama was bombarded with telegrams, postcards and letters demanding the immediate release of the 'Scottsboro Boys'. Although the Scottsboro defendants never publicly identified with the ILD, they became cultural symbols of the radical left, and the subject of many poems, songs and plays. In March 1933 the ILD secured a new trial, yet, despite a brilliant defence by renowned lawyer Samuel Leibowitz and the repudiation of the rape charge by one of the women, the all-white jury found the Scottsboro defendants guilty. Several months later, however, in an unprecedented decision, Alabama circuit judge James E. Horton overturned the March 1933 verdict and ordered a new trial. By this time the ILD's influence was on the wane, and in 1934 Leibowitz founded the American Scottsboro Committee (ASC). The ILD and NAACP joined forces and, together with the ASC and the **American Civil Liberties Union**, formed the Scottsboro

Defense Committee (SDC), which opted for a more reformist campaign. After failing to win the defendants' release in a 1936 trial, in 1937 the SDC agreed to a plea bargain whereby four were released and the remaining five endured lengthy prison sentences – the last was not freed until 1950. The campaign to free the Scottsboro defendants had tremendous legal and political implications, and showed many civil rights campaigners that successful interracial action was possible.

Dan Carter, *Scottsboro: A Tragedy of the American South* (second ed.), Louisiana State University Press, 1984

Hugh Murray, 'The NAACP versus the Communist Party: The Scottsboro Rape Case, 1931–1932', *Phylon*, 28 (1967)

Charles Martin, 'The International Labor Defense and Black America', *Labor History*, 26 (Spring 1985)

Seikatsusha [Security Society]
1965–
economic self-help organisation

Japan is often thought of as the world's ultimate market economy, but the trend towards blind materialism has not gone unchallenged and Japan is also the home of one of the world's most successful grassroots challenges to the consumer society – the Seikatsusha or Seikatsu Club. Seikatsusha started as a small milk-buying cooperative in Tokyo; gradually the initiative extended to other products such as *shoyu* (soya sauce), soap, orange juice and dried fish, all carefully sourced to ensure their quality and that the growers and producers receive a fair price. Where the club could not easily find products it resolved to start its own enterprises; in the late 1970s it established two organic dairies and a factory manufacturing soap from recycled cooking oil. In 1989 the organisation had a membership of 170,000 households in eleven Japanese prefectures, and by 1992 this had grown to nearly 400,000 households; the number of different products being traded is around four hundred. The Club employs several thousand people and has an annual turnover in excess of 100 billion yen (£500 million). Seikatsusha is overtly political, with the aim of empowering its members to have more control over their daily lives. Its organisational structure (based on small local groups or *han* of six to ten members, grouped in branches of fifty to one hundred *han*) is designed to make decision-making as accessible as possible to its grassroots membership; the majority of the active members are women, and this is reflected in Seikatsusha's board of directors, of whom eighty per cent are women. Linked with the Seikatsusha is a network of community-based political groups whose platform is based on local democracy, conservation, peace and the advancement of women. In the 1987 Japanese local elections 33 Seikatsusha candidates, all of them women, were elected to municipal councils; in the 1991 elections the number more than doubled to seventy.

Paul Ekins, *A New World Order: Grassroots Movements for Global Change*, Routledge, 1992

Seitōsha [Bluestockings Society]
1911–1916
feminist organisation

The most prominent early feminist group in Japan was named after an influential eighteenth-century salon of British intellectual women, since its initial goal was to provide a literary outlet for talented women writers through its journal *Seitō*. The group's founder, **Hiratsuka Raichō**, became one of Japan's foremost suffragists and, until the 1940s at least, the country's best-known feminist leader. *Seitō* soon became a vehicle for feminist criticism, covering issues as wide-ranging as the role of motherhood and the campaign for women's suffrage, and attracted many talented writers including **Yosano Akiko**. From 1914 onwards the influence of *Seitō* began to wane, partly because of public criticism and partly because many of Seitōsha's members, including Hiratsuka Raichō, were occupied with family concerns. In 1915 the anarchist feminist **Itō Noe** took over the editorship of *Seitō*, which continued to publish articles on issues such as prostitution, abortion and chastity, but financial and organisational problems forced its closure in February 1916.

> Nancy Andrew, 'The Seitōsha: An Early Japanese Women's Organisation', *Papers on Japan*, East Asian Research Centre, Harvard University, Vol. 6 (1972)

September 19th National Union of Garment Workers
1985–
trade union

When a massive earthquake struck Mexico City early in the morning of September 19th 1985, the damage it wreaked included the deaths of more than a thousand garment workers in the ruins of eight hundred small garment factories in the neighbourhood of San Antonio Abad, and the loss of 40,000 jobs. Seamstresses arriving for work climbed on to the rubble of one building to rescue women already in the factory, but were pushed back by soldiers, who cordoned off the site. When the owners and the army arrived with a crane, the women soon realised that it was sewing machines, not women, that were being rescued. In their horror and anger some blockaded the equipment while others confronted the owners, demanding pay and compensation. The seamstresses held to their demands, maintaining vigils and blockades until the government, embarrassed by media attention, pressured the factory owners to offer compensation. Within weeks the September 19th Garment Workers Union was founded, so structured that seamstresses themselves would run it, formulating policies which would fulfil the workers' real needs. Having initially accredited the union, the Mexican government rescinded certification once international attention had waned, and the ruling party hired thugs to threaten activists at work. In response the union worked with local feminists to make links with US feminists and union activists, and garment workers met with their Latina and Chinese-American counterparts in US cities. As an organisation of and for women, the union has become a forum which honours the need to debate and integrate its members' needs as wives, mothers, workers and union activists.

Cynthia Enloe, *Bananas, Beaches and Bases: Making Feminist Sense of International Politics*, Pandora, 1989

Silvia Tirado, 'Weaving Dreams, Constructing Realities: The Nineteenth of September National Union of Garment Workers in Mexico', *Dignity and Daily Bread: New Forms of Economic Organising among Poor Women in the Third World and the First* (ed. Sheila Rowbotham and Swasti Mitter), Routledge, 1994

Solidarność [Solidarity]
1980–
trade union, political party

In 1970 Edward Gierek became First Secretary of the Central Committee of the Polish Communist Party, and over the next decade did much to modernise the Polish economy. His regime was marked, however, by widespread corruption, waste and inefficiency, and in 1980 a series of strikes protesting about poor working conditions and low wages spread through the country. One such strike was that at the Lenin Shipyard in Gdańsk, where **Lech Wałęsa** was head of the interfactory committee which at the end of August signed the Gdańsk Accords with Gierek, for the first time allowing free trade unions in Poland and the right to strike. The trade union Solidarność (Solidarity) was established a month later with Wałęsa as its leader, and the farmers' union Rural Solidarity was founded in April 1981. By the time of Solidarność's first conference in September 1981 there was much tension both within Solidarność and between the union and the government, and when in December a referendum on ending communist rule was proposed the authorities declared martial law: Wałęsa was detained for eleven months. Solidarność functioned as an underground movement for several years, but in October 1984 the murder of the popular pro-Solidarność priest Jerzy Popiełuszko by the Polish secret police brought the organisation back into the public eye. In 1986 the government declared an amnesty for more than twenty thousand detainees including many Solidarność activists, in November 1988 Wałęsa appeared in a television debate to set out the case for social and economic change in Poland, and in the parliamentary elections of June 1989 Solidarność candidates and their allies won a resounding majority: during this period the union had more than ten million members. Tadeusz Mazowiecki, a veteran politician from the Catholic opposition party, was appointed prime minister, and Lech Wałęsa became the president of Solidarność. During 1990, however, Mazowiecki and Wałęsa were seriously at odds over government powers and economic policy, and as new elections approached in November of that year many Solidarność leaders accused Wałęsa of behaving like a dictator in order to convince the Polish people of his presidential qualities. Wałęsa nevertheless won the presidency by a large margin, and resigned from the leadership of Solidarność. The next three years saw the fall of successive coalition governments led by Soli-darność candidates, and by the end of the fourth Solidarność government led by lawyer Hanna Suchocka in March 1993 the former freedom party had lost much of its support and was being openly criticised by its erstwhile leader. In the Polish elections of September 1993 former communists gained a surprising majority, and formed a coalition under Waldemar Pawlak. Solidarność, however, with Wałęsa's renewed support, made a marked comeback during 1994, organising pro-democracy marches and demonstrations in several Polish cities: 1994 membership was estimated at 1.6 million.

Michael Dobbs, *Poland, Solidarity, Walesa*, McGraw-Hill, 1981
Jarosław Kurski, *Lech Walesa: Democrat or Dictator?*, Westview, 1993
Roger Boyes, *The Naked President: A Political Life of Lech Walesa*, Secker and
    Warburg, 1994

Spanish Civil War
1936–1939
democracy struggle

Following the fall of the royally-appointed dictator Primo de Rivera and the abdication of King Alfonso XIII in 1931, Spain was critically divided. On one side were the landowners, the church, the military and the increasingly reactionary El Falange Española; on the other were Catalan and Basque separatists, socialists, communists and anarchists. The elections of Febru-ary 1936 established a leftwing Popular Front Republican government under Manuel Azaña y Diaz, but in July 1936 generals José Sanjurjo and Francisco Franco led a military uprising against the Republic, and civil war ensued. Most of Castilia declared for the rebel Nationalists, while Valencia, Andalusia, Barcelona and Catalonia, together with Basque Bilbao, remained loyal to the Republic. As the war intensified the fascist regimes of Germany and Italy sent massive forces to fight alongside Franco's army; although the Soviet Union sent advisers and supplies to the Republicans, other European governments did little to support the elected regime and avert the growing crisis in which tens of thousands of civilians were being tortured and killed. Socialist and libertarian sympathisers from many countries were quick to offer whatever help they could: the English poet W.H. Auden spoke for many when, in his poem 'Spain 1937', he declared 'Yes, I am Spain', and the list of radicals who spent time in Spain supporting the Nationalist cause included **Emma Goldman**, Ernest Hemingway, **Pablo Neruda**, **George Orwell**, **Paul Robeson** and Stephen Spender. The Republican government moved from Madrid, a city of split loyalties, to Valencia, and in 1937 to Barcelona: Madrid now became the main target of Nationalist attack, being besieged for more than two years. In 1937 Franco's Nationalist troops divided the Republican forces by controlling the territory between Valencia and Barcelona. The Republicans, weakened by internal disagreement and by the 1938 withdrawal of Soviet support, attempted a desperate counter-attack in the Battle of the Ebro, spurred on by **Dolores Ibárruri**'s passionate 'no pasaran'. The stand failed, and Barcelona fell on January 26th 1939, quickly followed by Madrid on March 28th. The war was over, but it had cost three quarters of a million lives, and plunged Spain back into a dictatorship which was to last until Franco's death in 1975.

> Hugh Thomas, *The Spanish Civil War*, Eyre and Spottiswoode, 1961 (new ed. St Martin's Press, 1994)
>
> Michael Alpert, *A New International History of the Spanish Civil War*, St. Martin's Press, 1994

Stonewall Riots
1969
gay rights action

In the early morning of June 28th 1969 New York police raided the Stonewall Inn, a well-known gay bar in Greenwich Village. Although such raids on gay bars were common, the spontaneous rebellion that followed this particular raid represented a new response to oppressive police tactics. Ejected patrons congregated on the street outside the bar and, as police arrested them and led them to the police vans, a growing group of protestors – eventually numbering some two thousand – threw stones, bottles and garbage containers, lit small fires, and taunted the police with chanting. Several nights of rioting followed. In the days immediately following the raid, as moderate homophile groups and **new left** activists tried to harness this new gay militancy, the Gay Liberation Front (GLF) was born. Here for the first time was an organisation representing a politically radical and specifically gay point of view, and for the next five years the GLF stayed in the forefront of the movement for gay rights, spawning many other groups and networks that were to became important in gay politics. Several gay organisations have since used the name Stonewall to symbolise their solidarity with the 1969 protestors, most notably the London-based lobby group Stonewall. Established in 1989, Stonewall works with national governments and international agencies to build a coherent civil rights strategy based on tolerance of and responsibility for individual sexual choices.

> Margaret Cruikshank, *The Gay and Lesbian Liberation Movement*, Routledge, 1992
>
> Martin Duberman, *Stonewall*, Dutton, 1993
>
> Emma Healey and Angela Mason (eds), *Stonewall 25: The Making of the Lesbian and Gay Community in Britain*, Virago, 1994

Student Nonviolent Coordinating Committee [SNCC]
1960–1969
civil rights organisation

SNCC (pronounced 'snick') was formed at a conference in Raleigh, North Carolina, in April 1960, where civil rights veteran **Ella Baker** met with a group of (mostly black) students to coordinate the growing number of anti-segregation sit-ins in public places throughout the southern states. Advocating nonviolent direct action, it rapidly became the main activist thrust of the American civil rights movement. In many places SNCC 'field secretaries' moved into black communities, gained the confidence of local blacks, and encouraged nonviolent opposition to segregation and discrimination. Following bus-burnings in early 1961, SNCC helped to organise 'freedom rides', and during 1962–63 worked with other civil rights organisations to encourage voter registration. In 1964 SNCC invited more than a thousand northern students to help with voter registration in Mississippi and to teach in 'freedom schools'. SNCC members were fully aware of the power and hatred behind racism. Speaking during the massive 'March on Washington' in summer 1963, SNCC leader John Lewis, despite the disapproval of other black leaders, criticised the Kennedy administration for failing to defend black rights. In summer 1964 three SNCC activists were murdered in Mississippi, and in August the SNCC-inspired black Mississippi Freedom Democratic Party was rebuffed by the Democratic Party, which agreed to recognise only the white Mississippi delegation (though this did lead to reforms in the Democratic Party four years later). For five or six years SNCC was highly successful, its courageous stance winning a great deal of public sympathy. In 1966, however, a new leadership (including Stokely Carmichael as chairman) abandoned SNCC's commitment to non-violence, changed its name to the Student National Coordinating Committee, and in 1969 formed a shortlived alliance with the **Black Panther Party**. Many leading activists left the organisation, and SNCC started to disintegrate. During its brief life SNCC affected the thinking of many concerned Americans, both black and white. In its hostility to government policies (SNCC members were among the first draft resisters during the **Vietnam War**), its early raising of the issue of sexual equality (by young SNCC women in the Atlanta office), and its closeness to local communities, SNCC played a pioneering role in creating the radicalism of the 60s.

Clayborne Carson, *In Struggle: SNCC and the Black Awakening of the 1960s*, Harvard, 1981
Howard Zinn, *SNCC: The New Abolitionists*, Beacon, 1964

Students for a Democratic Society [SDS]
1960–1970
social change organisation

Students for a Democratic Society started in 1960 as an offshoot of a longstanding socialist group, the League for Industrial Democracy, but it was not until its 1962 convention, when it adopted the inspirational Port Huron Statement, that it fully articulated its philosophy and plan of campaign. Drafted by the young peace activist Tom Hayden, the Statement stressed the need for social action, participatory democracy, personal responsibility and integrity, thus providing the emerging American **new left** with a sound intellectual and moral underpinning. By its height in 1968 SDS had become, under Hayden's leadership, an influential national organisation with 350 official chapters and 100,000 members. SDS provided training and support for many white participants in the early civil rights

protests, numerous leaders of the Vietnam antiwar and antidraft movements, the bulk of those involved in demonstrations and strikes against
autocractic university administrations, the activists (formed as SDS's Economic Research and Action Project) who made poverty a national issue,
and many of the women involved in the ideas and early actions of the
women's liberation movement. SDS members developed a range of tactics
which were to become commonplace in the 1970s: teach-ins, direct
actions, consensus decision-making and small group organisation. The end
of SDS was heralded in mid-1969 by growing splits between increasingly
extremist elements including the Revolutionary Youth Movement, the
neo-Maoist Progressive Labor Party, the relatively mild Worker-Student
Alliance and a centralist tendency calling itself the Weathermen. When in
October 1969 selfstyled Weathermen commandos initiated a bombing
campaign the SDS went into terminal decline. Hayden, standing trial with
Yippies Abbie Hoffman and Jerry Rubin, denounced the Weathermen as a
'primitive neophyte army'. Despite its ultimate demise, the impact of SDS
throughout the 1960s was considerable, its legacy a radicalised generation
experienced in the ways and the successes of mass protest; many SDS
graduates are still active in American radical circles.

> Kirkpatrick Sale, *SDS*, Random House, 1973
> David Caute, *Sixty-Eight: The Year of the Barricades*, Hamish Hamilton, 1988
> Todd Gitlin, *The Sixties: Years of Hope, Days of Rage*, Bantam, 1987

Survival International
1969–
human rights organisation

There are estimated to be more than three hundred million people in the
world whose way of life is still tribal – they live in communal villages and
make a livelihood from traditional crops, but almost everywhere their land
and livelihood is at risk. Since the second world war the rate of 'civilised'
expansion into the world's wilder places has accelerated, putting more and
more tribal people at risk from logging, dams, mineral extraction, wildlife
depletion and disease. In March 1969 a journalist who had seen the plight
of the Amazonian Indians at first hand, Norman Lewis, wrote an article in
the British *Sunday Times Magazine*, and in reponse a group of people wrote
to the paper suggesting that an organisation be formed to protect tribal
people's rights. The group included naturalist Nicholas Guppy and anthropologist Francis Huxley, and among those who responded positively
were Conrad Gorinsky, a part-Amerindian doctor, and the explorer Robin
Hanbury-Tenison. Within months Survival International had been established, one of its first tasks being to investigate the situation of the
Yanomami in Brazil and Venezuela: the Yanomami support campaign was
to last for more than twenty years, but intensive lobbying by Survival and
Yanomami leaders eventually led in 1992 to the allocation by the Brazilian
and Venezuelan governments of large protected reserves. In its early years
Survival initiated support campaigns wherever it felt the need, but by 1974

tribal peoples themselves started approaching Survival for help. One of the first such campaigns enabled the Andoke Indians of Colombia to free themselves from seventy years of debt-slavery to rubber plantation owners. In 1975 Survival helped to organise the establishment of the World Council of Indigenous Peoples, which held its first meeting at Port Alberni in Canada. Survival International has been at the forefront of criticism of destructive dam schemes, and its successes include the stopping of the Upper Mazaruni Dam in Guyana in 1979 and a share in the halting of work on the Bodhgat Dam in the Indian state of Madhya Pradesh in 1988. In 1989 Survival International was awarded a Right Livelihood Award for its campaigning work with tribal peoples. With main offices in London, Washington, Paris, Milan and Madrid, Survival currently has a membership of 15,000 in 67 countries.

> Survival International, 'Survival: 25 Years of Standing By Tribal Peoples', *Survival Newsletter 33*, 1994

Vietnam Antiwar Protest Movement
1964–1975
peace and antimilitarism campaign

In the early 1960s the American military establishment was obsessed with the 'domino theory' of creeping world communism, and in August 1964 the US Congress passed the Tonkin Gulf Resolution allowing President Lyndon Johnson to send a massive contingent of marines to South Vietnam. It was to become a military and civilian nightmare, with more than half a million US soldiers fighting a protracted, dirty, unwinnable war against a largely imagined enemy. Opposition to US intervention was intense both in Vietnam and at home: in January 1968 the largely successful Vietcong 'Tet Offensive' proved that US forces were far from invincible, and it was also in 1968 that the antiwar protest movement began to have a marked effect on US policy. As early as April 1965, a month after the first US troops landed at Da Nang, a **Students for a Democratic Society** march in Washington DC mustered twenty thousand protestors, the largest peace demonstration to that date. The swelling of the peace movement, especially among students, quickly created the largest American radical surge since the labour movement of the 1930s. Throughout the Vietnam decade, despite the proliferation of peace organisations and coalitions and the many internal differences of opinion about tactics and political orientation, the peace demonstration remained the dominant manifestation of radical sentiment, and antiwar discourse the main channel for radical education. By early 1967 the protest movement had reached almost unimaginable proportions: the Spring Mobilization Committee's nationwide demonstrations in mid-April brought nearly half a million Americans onto the streets. Although peace organisations like the **Fellowship of Reconciliation** and SANE chose not to be official sponsors of the event, many thousands of their members were among the marchers. As the demonstrations continued a growing number of angry and traumatised Vietnam veterans joined the antiwar movement, as did progressive trade unionists and feminist women's groups such as Women Strike for Peace. By late 1967 the war in Vietnam had all but drained an anguished President Johnson, and the American peace movement was going from strength to strength, with more than a hundred peace vigils taking place between September and December and draft-counselling centres opening across the country to advise the growing number of men who refused to participate in such military madness. Opposition abroad was growing too, with large 'Stop the Vietnam War' demonstrations being held in Britain, France, Australia, New Zealand and many other countries. **Martin Luther King**'s assassination in April 1968 provided added impetus to the **new left**'s criticism of government tactics and deprived the peace movement of an important unifying force. The increasingly desperate FBI and CIA campaigns against 'left wing dissidents' reached a peak in the May 1970 killing of four peace demonstrators at Kent University in Ohio, which resulted in a wave of public sympathy and antiwar feeling across the country. By now the new president, Richard Nixon, had begun to withdraw US troops from Vietnam, urged on by an increasingly well-orchestrated protest campaign. The later antiwar movement was marked by several high-profile public-figure initiatives like Jane Fonda and Tom Hayden's Indochina Peace Campaign, whose roadshow attracted widespread mainstream support. By the time Nixon was forced to resign over the Watergate scandal in August 1974 the last US combat troops had returned home and the peace movement had come of age. There were now new struggles in which to engage, notably covert US military involvement in Latin America. The Vietnam protest movement had convinced many thousands of concerned Americans that the US government could not be relied upon to guarantee international peace and equity, and the lessons learned during Vietnam were put to good use in such activities as the **Sanctuary Movement** and the **Nuclear Freeze** campaign.

Fred Halstead, *Out Now! A Participant's Account of the American Movement Against the Vietnam War*, Monad Press, 1978

Lawrence Wittner, *Rebels Against War: The American Peace Movement, 1933–1983*, Temple University Press, 1984

Charles deBenedetti, *An American Ordeal: The Antiwar Movement of the Vietnam Era*, Syracuse University Press, 1990

Wages for Housework
1973–1979
economic rights campaign

The patriarchal (and Marxist) assumption that while men work for money, women work for love, and the economic oppression which arises from this convenient belief, were explored in some depth by early twentieth-century feminists including **Rosa Luxemburg** and **Mary Ritter Beard**. In 1973, however, the republication of a 1953 Selma James essay 'A Woman's Place' coupled with a new essay by Mariarosa dalla Costa entitled 'Women and the Subversion of the Community' under the title *The Power of Women and the Subversion of the Community*, brought together a group of women determined to press for housework to be considered just as real – and therefore just as deserving of financial reward – as paid employment. The campaign was strengthened by a 1970 Chase Manhattan Bank study, *What's a Wife Worth?*, which reckoned the average housewife's hundred hours of work a week as worth more than the average weekly wage of the time. Wages for Housework, which was by 1975 active in the USA, Britain, Italy, Germany and Canada, castigated mainstream Marxism for underrating women's labour and its value in underpinning capitalism, and in practical terms involved itself in welfare rights, reproductive rights, and working women's demands for higher wages and shorter working hours. Wages for Housework also championed the need of prostitutes to make a decent living. At several British Women's Liberation Conferences in the early 1970s the suggestion was made that wages for housework should be added to the movement's stated demands, but this was consistently rejected on the grounds that paying women for housecare reinforced the assumptions which keep women in the home. The Power of Women Collective, which for several years ran the British Wages for Housework Campaign, countered that if women refused to work in the home the collapse of the existing economic structure would quickly force a real shift in the balance of power towards women.

Mariarosa dalla Costa, *The Power of Women and the Subversion of the Community*, Falling Wall Press, 1973
Lise Vogel, *Marxism and the Oppression of Women*, Rutgers University Press, 1984

War Resisters International [WRI]
1921–
peace organisation

War Resisters International was founded in London in 1921 by radical pacifists who sought to support individual conscientious objection by organising collective public resistance to war. Among its founder members were the pacifist Labour politician Fenner Brockway and first world war conscientious objectors Herbert Runham Brown and Harold Bing. Bing, as WRI secretary, travelled throughout Europe in the postwar period, reporting to a growing membership the hitherto unpublished atrocities of the 'great' war. During the late 1920s WRI started to organise its international conferences, still held every three years, and as the threat of another world war loomed it became an important link between national and local peace organisations and campaigns. Today, as a London-based yet global anti-militarist network which links and coordinates more than sixty pacifist and nonviolent action organisations, WRI continues to provide solidarity and support for people who refuse to take part in war, and actively promotes the understanding and practice of nonviolent means of resolving the conflicts that can lead to war. In 1971 WRI initiated a series of women's gatherings on feminism, nonviolence and militarism, and the 1960s and

70s saw the establishment of a number of important regional peace campaigns, including Operation Omega in Bangladesh, a project challenging Pakistan's occupation of what was then East Pakistan, and an international march for demilitarisation across Europe's armed frontiers in order to spread the practice of nonviolence training and affinity groups. Each year on May 15th, International Conscientious Objection Day, WRI holds demonstrations of solidarity, and each December 1st it publishes an honour roll of imprisoned conscientious objectors and nonviolent antiwar activists.

Grace Beaton, *Twenty Years' Work in the War Resisters International*, War Resisters International, 1945

Caroline Moorehead, *Troublesome People: The Warriors of Pacifism*, Adler and Adler, 1987

Cyril Wright and Tony Augarde, *Peace Is the Way*, Lutterworth, 1990

Women's Freedom League [WFL]
1907–1961
women's suffrage organisation

The British suffrage organisation the WFL was formed in 1907, following a split between the loyal followers of **Emmeline Pankhurst's Women's Social and Political Union** (WSPU) and those with a greater commitment to democracy and the needs of working-class women. The WFL's founders, led by a group of women including **Charlotte Despard** and **Teresa Billington-Greig**, at first claimed to be the true WSPU, but soon let the original organisation go its own way. Charlotte Despard was elected president and, despite accusations that she wielded too much power, the WFL was run democratically. WFL tactics, though sometimes militant, were lower key that those of the WSPU, and included boycotting the 1911 census and organising the Women's Tax Resistance League. Its newspaper, *The Vote*, carried many important articles about women's rights. During the first world war, while Emmeline and **Christabel Pankhurst** campaigned for 'women's right to serve', the pacifist WFL argued that war showed 'the supreme necessity of women having a voice on the councils of the nation'. It established the Women's Suffrage National Aid Corps, campaigned against the reintroduction of the section of the Defence of the Realm Act under which women found to be suffering from venereal disease could be sentenced to six months hard labour, and, with **Sylvia Pankhurst**, established the League of Rights for Soldiers' and Sailors' Wives and Relations. WFL membership dropped rapidly after the vote was granted to women in 1928, but the League declared that its work was not yet finished and adopted a wider-ranging programme that included demands for equal pay, equal opportunities, better housing and childcare, and a national minimum wage. The WFL celebrated its golden jubilee in 1957 but, having attracted no new members since 1939, it disbanded when its last president, Marian Reeves, died in 1961.

Jill Liddington and Jill Norris, *One Hand Tied Behind Us: The Rise of the Women's Suffrage Movement*, Virago, 1978
Christine Bolt, *The Women's Movements in the United States and Britain from the 1790s to the 1920s*, Harvester-Wheatsheaf, 1993

Women's International League for Peace and Freedom [WILPF]
1915–
peace organisation

Soon after the start of the first world war, the European suffragists and pacifists Emmeline Pethick-Lawrence and **Rosika Schwimmer** travelled to the USA to enlist American women's support for the European peace movement. They met **Crystal Eastman**, who suggested a meeting with **Jane Addams** of the Hull-House project in Chicago. In January 1915 Addams called a national women's meeting in Washington DC, where the Women's Peace Party (WPP) was founded, and three months later a delegation from the WPP travelled to The Hague in the Netherlands, where Pethick-Lawrence, Schwimmer, and more than 1,400 other delegates from twelve countries met to share their ideas about how best to stop the war by mediation, international lobbying and other nonviolent means. This International Congress of Women decided to form a committee which would make approaches to European statesmen in the cause of peace and, although the war continued, Congress delegates were received by a number of senior politicians. When the second International Congress of Women met four years later in Zürich, delegates from the victorious nations were stunned to find their friends from defeated nations nearly unrecognisable, ravaged by exhaustion and malnutrition. Seeing in the proposed Versailles Treaty the seeds of a future war, the Congress criticised the harshness of terms against Germany and Austria and urged an end to the food blockade by means of which the Allies were forcing a settlement. Like its predecessor, this Congress sent delegates to talk with politicians, but only US president Woodrow Wilson acknowledged their concern. It was at the 1919 Congress that WILPF took its name, establishing its headquarters in Geneva and electing Jane Addams as its first president, a post which she held until 1929. By the 1930s WILPF membership had declined sharply, and there was considerable disagreement within its members between those who believed in peace at all costs and those convinced that the evil of fascism required active support for militant revolutionary movements. After the second world war Mildred Scott Olmsted, executive secretary of the US section from 1934 to 1966, rebuilt the various national groups into an international organisation, which gained nongovernmental organisation status with the United Nations in 1948. During the 1960s WILPF was much criticised by conservatives for initiating dialogue with women in the Soviet Union, and in 1970 held its first major meeting in a Third World country: its eighteenth international congress at New Delhi in India. This saw the beginning of a period of greater dialogue between women of the First and Third Worlds. WILPF played a major part in the UN Decade for Women (1975–85), and has continued to make economic and political justice for women a major part of its work. WILPF's primary objectives are total universal disarmament, the abolition of violence as a means of settling conflicts, and the creation of social, economic, political, and psychological conditions such that the causes of war are abolished. With a worldwide membership of 50,000 in thirty countries, WILPF convenes an international congress every three years and publishes a quarterly journal, *Pax et Libertas/Peace and Freedom*.

> Harriet Hyman Alonso, *Peace as a Women's Issue: A History of the US Movement for World Peace and Women's Rights*, Syracuse University Press, 1993
> Jill Liddington, *The Long Road to Greenham: Feminism and Anti-Militarism in Britain since 1820*, Virago, 1989

Women's Liberation Movement [WLM]
*c.*1968–
liberation movement

During the late 1960s many feminist women who were active in the civil rights and peace movements began to ask difficult questions about the predominance of men in leadership positions and men's unwillingness to address important issues of sexual equality, despite the supposed egalitarianism of organisations like the **Student Nonviolent Coordinating Committee** (SNCC), **Students for a Democratic Society** (SDS), and other **new left** groups. In 1964 Casey Hayden and Mary King raised the issue of the inferior status of women within SNCC, eliciting Stokely Carmichael's notorious reply that 'The only position for women in SNCC is prone'. Feminist women unsuccessfully raised the issue of women's rights at SDS conventions in 1965 and 1966, and at the National Conference for New Politics in Chicago in 1967. Here the predominantly male delegates insisted that the crucial issue was racism; when a group of women led by Jo Freeman and **Shulamith Firestone** attempted to present a resolution that, in order to reflect the proportion of women in the world, women must be allowed half the conference votes, they were refused access to the microphones. In response the women held a meeting in Chicago the following week, circulating a paper entitled 'To the Women of the Left' which called on women to organise an autonomous movement for their liberation. The new movement went under several names, including the 'radical women's movement' and simply the 'women's movement', but Jo Freeman, now editor of *Voice of the Women's Liberation Movement*, insisted with many others that the primary issue was women's liberation, and that calling it the 'women's liberation movement' gave immediacy to the movement's aims and intentions. The WLM made its tactics very public during the September 1968 Miss America pageant in Atlantic City, New Jersey, where demonstrations against sexism and the objectification of women received widespread media attention. In Britain, as in America, experience of being excluded from leftwing groups prompted many activist women to question the new left's attitude towards feminism. **Juliet Mitchell**'s 1966 essay, 'Women: The

Longest Revolution', provided an important position paper, and by 1969 a number of pioneering consciousness-raising groups had come together as a loose collective called the London Women's Liberation Workshop and were publishing the magazine *Shrew*. The first of several British National Women's Liberation Conferences was held in 1970 at Ruskin College, Oxford. The first Canadian women's liberation collective was formed in September 1967, and in Australia the first women's liberation (there often called 'wl') conference was held in May 1970. The idea of women's liberation spread quickly, and many thousands of women began to meet in groups for consciousness-raising sessions and to plan campaigns and actions. Many who had experienced the more mainstream women's rights organisations, like the **National Organization for Women** in the USA and the Women's Electoral League in Australia, as overly hierarchical and restrictive, now questioned the need for any sort of leadership within the WLM, hence much of the movement was loosely organised. From this unrestrained and ever-shifting composition came much of its strength. While many groups experimented with a wide range of participatory structures, some found the 'tyranny of structurelessness' frustrating and ineffectual. One of the most visible aspects of the WLM was the growing number of women's centres, offering a meeting place and information resource for women in a town or city: many also offered workshop space and counselling, and some of the larger centres housed bookshops and cafés. By 1990 the number of women's centres had peaked, but there are still some three hundred in the USA and more than thirty in Britain. Another result of the movement was the burgeoning of women's studies, with more than 350 programmes being offered by US universities and colleges in the early 1980s. Women's publishing also blossomed, with hundreds of women's presses producing thousands of titles, and women's music, women's art and women's theatre all reflected the new possibilities offered by liberation from patriarchal standards. Many women who considered themselves part of the WLM were involved in other campaigning work: for peace, health and reproductive rights, the environment, economic justice and human rights. During the 1980s and 90s the boundaries between the movement and linked campaigns became ever more blurred, so that by the mid-90s it was hard to define the contemporary women's movement, and even harder to distinguish its constituent parts. There is no question, however, that for the hundreds of thousands of women touched by what is sometimes called 'second wave feminism' the world has changed as a result of the women's liberation movement, and though the struggle has been (and still is) sometimes hard, the rewards more than justify the effort.

Sara Evans, *Personal Politics: The Roots of Women's Liberation in the Civil Rights Movement and the New Left*, Vintage, 1980

Marian Sawer and Marian Simms, *A Woman's Place: Women and Politics in Australia*, Allen and Unwin, 1984

Sheila Rowbotham, *The Past is Before Us: Feminism in Action since the 1960s*, Pandora, 1989

Michelene Wandor (ed.), *Once a Feminist: Stories of a Generation*, Virago, 1990
Sheila Rowbotham, *Women in Movement: Feminism and Social Action*, Routledge, 1992

Women's Social and Political Union [WSPU]
1903–1917
women's suffrage campaigning organisation

During the early 1900s **Emmeline Pankhurst**, the British women's suffrage pioneer, set as her goal the changing of Independent Labour Party (ILP) policy towards votes for women. Though other suffrage campaigners, including Emmeline's daughter **Christabel**, saw this as too narrow an objective, Emmeline believed that it was the quickest way to get women into politics, and typically went ahead singlemindedly with the formation of a pressure group for this purpose. She had originally planned to call it the Women's Labour Representation Committee but, when Christabel and Labour politician **Keir Hardie** pointed out that Representation Committees of militant suffragists were already active in Lancashire and elsewhere, Emmeline reluctantly changed the name to the WSPU, and it first met in the Pankhurst's Manchester home on October 10th 1903. During the early years none of the Pankhursts held formal office for fear of the organisation being seen as a family affair, but inevitably the WSPU was very much a Pankhurst initiative, and the Pankhurst connection quickly raised it to the role of national lobby group. In 1905, following arguments between the WSPU and the ILP, the WSPU loosened its support for Labour and turned its sights on the Liberal Party: unfurling their 'Votes for Women' banner at a Liberal meeting in Manchester's Free Trade Hall in October 1905, Christabel and her colleague Annie Kenney managed to get themselves arrested and imprisoned. The WSPU had become militant, newsworthy, and much admired in radical circles. In 1906 the WSPU moved its headquarters to London, and the suffrage campaigners' growing success and support encouraged the 'suffragettes' (as they were dubbed by the press) to take further audacious actions which would draw attention to their cause. It worked extremely well. As more and more suffragettes were arrested, refused to pay fines and were sent to jail, the newspaper coverage attracted public sympathy and outrage, the WSPU grew, and 'the woman question' was taken increasingly seriously by politicians. By August 1907 the WSPU had seventy branches throughout Britain, but many women in the suffrage movement were worried about the role of Emmeline Pankhurst, who still decided much of the the Union's policy. Disturbed by this degree of autocracy, a group of democratically-minded women including **Charlotte Despard** and **Teresa Billington-Greig** left the Union to form a new organisation called the **Women's Freedom League**. Despite the increasing visibility of the suffragettes, most politicians, including Prime Minister Herbert Asquith, continued to insist that the majority of women did not want the vote. Hoping to prove him wrong, the WSPU held a mass meeting in Hyde Park on June 21st 1908. Thirty thousand women marched, many wearing the suffrage colours of purple, green and white, and more than a quarter of a million people gathered to approve by acclaim a statement that called on the government to grant votes to women without delay. Asquith did nothing, and Christabel and other militants, through speeches and the Union's new journal *The Suffragette*, urged women to take the matter into their own hands, using violence (but only against property) if necessary. From the beginning of 1913 the WSPU initiated a campaign of window-breaking, stone-throwing, burning slogans onto public lawns, cutting telephone and telegraph lines, and burning pillarboxes and empty buildings 'to make the electors and the Government so uncomfortable that, in order to put an end to the nuisance, they will give women the vote.' The campaign of militancy came to an end with the first world war, when Christabel joined her mother to campaign for 'women's right to serve'. WSPU membership rapidly declined and, though there was an attempt to revive it in 1917 under the name The Women's Party, by 1919 it was defunct.

> Jill Liddington and Jill Norris, *One Hand Tied Behind Us: The Rise of the Women's Suffrage Movement*, Virago, 1978
> Christine Bolt, *The Women's Movements in the United States and Britain from the 1790s to the 1920s*, Harvester-Wheatsheaf, 1993

Working Women's Forum [WWF]
1978–
self-help movement

Disillusioned by the Indian Congress Party's inability to help the country's poorest people, Jaya Arunachalam resigned from the party in 1977 and in 1978 established the WWF with an initial membership of eight hundred poor working women. By the end of 1984 her initiative had spread throughout the country, and WWF had 36,000 members; six years later this number had quadrupled to over 150,000. Only poor working women, suffering under the multiple oppressions of marginal work status, gender, caste and poverty, can become members of WWF. Because WWF concentrates solely on the needs of the poor and promotes leadership from within its grassroots membership, it has been remarkably successful in building a high degree of trust and solidarity. Almost uniquely among development organisations, all WWF staff come from the same poor working class as its membership. When WWF started it was clear that a primary need was for small financial loans at manageable interest rates, and this remains one of the Forum's core services, but today is just one service among many. It is active in the areas of healthcare and education, child labour rehabilitation and family planning. It also remains a powerful activist force, where necessary organising marches (as in Madras in 1985, where thousands of poor women marched in pursuit of their rights), mass inter-caste weddings to break down discriminatory marriage practices, and meetings with senior politicians and officials – a measure of WWF's political clout is that in 1988 it twice requested, and received, a day-long audience with prime minister Rajiv Gandhi.

WWF, *A Decade of the Forum*, WWF, Madras, 1988

R. Chambers, *The Working Women's Forum: A Counter-Culture by Poor Women*, UNICEF, 1985

Paul Ekins, *A New World Order*, Routledge, 1992

Yippies
1967–1969
cultural protest movement

When Jerry Rubin and **Abbie Hoffman** launched the Youth International Party (almost invariably shortened to 'Yippies') in Washington DC in January 1968, their aim was to win the struggle for personal and political liberation by using humour and play to expose the stupidity of war and oppression. Other Yippies included Allen Ginsberg and singer Phil Ochs, who described the Yippie approach as 'merely an attack of mental disobedience on an obediently insane society'. Abbie Hoffman had already used theatrical tactics in organising a mass 'exorcism of demons' during the Pentagon Action in October 1967, and Yippie strategy was used to great effect during the Festival of Life held outside the 1968 Democratic National Convention in Chicago, when a pig called Pigasus was nominated as the Yippie presidential candidate. The Festival of Life was broken up by violent police action: The Chicago Eight (Yippies Abbie Hoffman and Jerry Rubin, Tom Hayden of **Students for a Democratic Society**, **David Dellinger** and Rennie Davis from National Mobilization to End the War in Vietnam, and three others including – incongruously given the mutual loathing between the Yippies and the **Black Panther Party** – BPP leader Bobby Seale) were charged with conspiracy to commit violence. The Yippies proceeded to turn the Chicago Conspiracy Trial into a showcase for hip culture and antiwar politics, mocking judicial decorum and refusing to follow court procedure. Rubin and Hoffman were both given prison terms, reduced on appeal, and became international heroes. The Yippies achieved massive press coverage, and Jerry Rubin's anarchist celebration *Do It!* and Abbie Hoffman's *Revolution for the Hell of It* became international bestsellers. The Yippie movement subsided shortly thereafter, but an organisation called the Yippies continued to publish protest material for almost twenty more years.

Jerry Rubin, *Do It!*, Simon and Schuster, 1968

The New Yippie Book Collective, *Blacklisted News, Secret History: From Chicago '68 to 1984*, Bleecker, 1983

David Caute, *Sixty-Eight: The Year of the Barricades*, Hamish Hamilton, 1988

Charles deBenedetti, *An American Ordeal: The Antiwar Movement of the Vietnam Era*, Syracuse University Press, 1990

Yūaikai [Friendship Association]
1912–1919
workers' organisation

Yūaikai was Japan's first workers' association, and played an important role in the Japanese labour movement. Established by the pioneering labour leader Suzuki Bunji and fourteen of his colleagues in August 1912, its guiding principles were mutual aid through friendship and cooperation, education and workers' rights. At first Yūaikai was opposed to socialism and emphasised joint efforts involving both employers and their employees, but by 1917 the organisation was becoming involved in a growing number of labour disputes and gradually took on the characteristics of a trade union. By 1918 Yūaikai had more than 30,000 members, and after the first world war became more politically active. In August 1919 it changed its name to Dai Nippon Rōdō Sōdōmei Yūaikai (Japan General Labour Federation), switched from an executive administration to a representative council, and included in its platform a call for free trade unions and an eight-hour working day. Suzuki Bunji, who was elected to the Diet (Japanese parliament) in 1928, was its leader until 1930.

Zengakuren [Zen Nihon Jichikai Sōrengō, All-Japan Federation of Student Self-Governing Associations]
1948–
student organisation

The basic unit of student organisation in Japanese universities and colleges is the Jichikai or Self-Governing Association, and each of these (of which there are some one thousand, with a total membership numbering hundreds of thousands) can choose to belong to one of several federations or Zengakuren. The original Zengakuren was founded in September 1948 by student members of the Japan Communist Party (JCP), and for its first decade of existence was an integral part of JCP politics. During the ten years from 1958 the Zengakuren was repeatedly subject to schism and factionalism over issues such as leadership, direction and alignment. By January 1968, when many Japanese students, like their European and American counterparts, were protesting against the **Vietnam War** and capitalist complacency, there were at least a dozen factions. The largest number of students belonged to the pro-Communist Minsei (Democratic Youth League), but the activist lead was provided by the Marxist groups Sampa Rengo (Three-Faction Alliance) and Kakumaru (Marxist Students League). Sampa Rengo again divided in July 1968, and since then there have been a number of rival Zengakuren groupings, with Minsei retaining its numerical dominance. Although membership of a Jichikai is automatic on becoming a student member of a faculty in a Japanese university, which provides the Zengakuren with a guaranteed income, only a small minority ever become actively involved in campaigns for student and other civil rights.

Stuart J. Dowsey, *Zengakuren: Japan's Revolutionary Students*, Ishi Press, 1970
David Caute, *Sixty-Eight: The Year of the Barricades*, Hamish Hamilton, 1988

APPENDIX A
RADICAL ACTIVISTS
BY COUNTRY

Following Thomas Paine's dictum that 'My country is the world' we have deliberately not included a reference to a country at the head of each person's entry, choosing instead to put such information an an appendix, showing both where each person was born and the countries in which they were most active. The asterisk symbol (*) indicates that the person was active in this country, though was not born there, while a dagger (†) indicates a person's country of birth though that person is better known for their activities elsewhere.

ARGENTINA
Augusto Boal*
Che Guevara†

AUSTRALIA
Bob Brown
Jim Cairns
Helen Caldicott
Vida Goldstein
Germaine Greer†
Bill Mollison
Bill Morrow
John Pilger†
Rose Scott
Dale Spender
Jessie Street
Peter Tatchell†

AUSTRIA
Martin Buber†
André Gorz†
Ivan Illich†
Leopold Kohr†
Freda Meissner-Blau
Adelheid Popp
Wilhelm Reich†
Bertha von Suttner

BANGLADESH
Taslima Nasrin

BOLIVIA
Régis Debray*

BRAZIL
Augusto Boal†
Helder Camara
Paulo Freire
Carolina Maria de Jesús
José Lutzenberger

Chico Mendes
Paulinho Paiakan

BURKINA FASO
Thomas Sankara

CANADA
Leopold Kohr*
Emily Murphy

CHILE
Salvador Allende
Vilma Espìn†
Victor Jara
Manfred Max-Neef
Pablo Neruda

CHINA
Chai Ling
Ding Ling
Fang Lizhi
Hu Feng
Jiu Jin
Kang Yuwei
Li Fei-Kan
Lu Xun
Mao Zedong
Agnes Smedley*
Sun Yat-Sen
Wei Jingsheng
Xiang Jingyu

COLOMBIA
Camilo Torres

CROATIA
Slavenka Drakulić

CUBA
Régis Debray*

Vilma Espìn*
Che Guevara*

CZECH REPUBLIC
Alexander Dubček*
Václav Havel

EAST TIMOR
Carlos Belo

EGYPT
Eric Hobsbawm†
Nabawiya Musa
Saiza Nabarawi
Nawal el Sa'dawi
Amina Said
Huda Shaarawi

EL SALVADOR
Oscar Romero
Marianella García-Villas

ENGLAND
Elizabeth Garrett Anderson
Eve Balfour*
Aphra Behn
Tony Benn
John Berger
Annie Besant
Teresa Billington-Greig
William Blake
Vera Brittain
Beatrix Campbell
Thomas Carlyle*
Edward Carpenter
G.D.H. Cole
Charlotte Despard
Crystal Eastman*
Paul Ekins*
George Eliot

Havelock Ellis
Ralph Waldo Emerson*
Friedrich Engels*
William Godwin
Germaine Greer*
Radclyffe Hall
Stuart Hall*
Keir Hardie*
Hazel Henderson
Eric Hobsbawm*
Ebenezer Howard
C.L.R. James*
Derek Jarman
Helen Joseph†
Petr Kropotkin*
R.D. Laing*
George Lansbury
Karl Marx*
H.J. Massingham
Juliet Mitchell*
William Morris
A.S. Neill*
Ann Oakley
George Orwell*
Tom Paine
Christabel Pankhurst
Emmeline Pankhurst
Sylvia Pankhurst
Sara Parkin*
John Pilger*
Jonathon Porritt
Sheila Rowbotham
Bertrand Russell
Dora Russell
Fritz Schumacher*
Percy Bysshe Shelley
Ethel Smyth
Dale Spender*
Elizabeth Cady Stanton*
Marie Stopes*
John Stuart Mill
Peter Tatchell*
Harriet Taylor
E.P. Thompson
Robert Tressell*
Beatrice Webb
Sidney Webb
Rebecca West
Oscar Wilde*
Raymond Williams*
Gerrard Winstanley
Mary Wollstonecraft
Virginia Woolf
Fanny Wright*

ETHIOPIA
Sylvia Pankhurst*

FRANCE
Hannah Arendt*
Raymond Aron

Mikhail Bakunin*
Henri Barbusse
Simone de Beauvoir
John Berger*
Augusto Boal*
Daniel Cohn-Bendit
Régis Debray
Isadora Duncan*
Frantz Fanon*
Michel Foucault
Charles Fourier
Natalya Gorbanevskaya*
André Gorz*
Petr Kropotkin*
Thomas Merton†
Tom Paine*
Sara Parkin*
Madeleine Pelletier
Pierre-Joseph Proudhon
Jean-Jacques Rousseau
Jean-Paul Sartre
Léopold Senghor*
Thich Nhat Hanh*
Louise Weiss

GEORGIA
Roy Medvedev†

GERMANY
Theodor Adorno
Hannah Arendt
Uri Avnery†
Rudolph Bahro
Mikhail Bakunin*
Ernst Bloch
Karola Bloch-Piotrkowski*
Heinrich Böll
Dietrich Bonhoeffer
Bertolt Brecht
Daniel Cohn-Bendit*
Rudi Dutschke
Friedrich Engels
Hans Magnus Enzenberger
Erich Fromm†
Jürgen Habermas
Magnus Hirschfeld
Max Horkheimer
Karen Horney†
Ivan Illich*
Petra Kelly
Rosa Luxemburg*
Herbert Marcuse†
Karl Marx
Ulrike Meinhof
Fritz Schumacher
Agnes Smedley*
Clara Zetkin

GHANA
W.E.B. Du Bois*
Kwame Nkrumah

Efua Sutherland

GUATEMALA
Che Guevara*
Rigoberta Menchú

GUINEA-BISSAU
Amilcar Cabral

GUYANA
Walter Rodney

HAITI
Jean-Bertrand Aristide

HUNGARY
Rosika Schwimmer
Thomas Szasz†
János Vargha

INDIA
Annie Besant*
Vinoba Bhave
Kamaladevi Chattopadhyay
Mahatma Gandhi
Aurobindo Ghose
Sarojini Naidu
J.P. Narayan
George Orwell†
Pandita Ramabai
Manabendra Nath Roy
Vandana Shiva
Tenzin Gyatso*

INDONESIA
Paul Ekins†
Raden Ajeng Kartini
Pramoedya Ananta Toer

IRAN
Homa Darabi
Kate Millett*
Ali Shari'ati

IRELAND
Mairead Corrigan McGuire
Charlotte Despard*
Mary Jones†
Jonathan Swift
Robert Tressell†
Oscar Wilde

ISRAEL
Shulamit Aloni
Uri Avnery*
Matti Peled*

ISRAELI OCCUPIED TERRITORIES
see Palestine

ITALY

Mikhail Bakunin*
Danilo Dolci
Antonio Gramsci
Errico Malatesta
Maria Montessori
Percy Bysshe Shelley*

JAMAICA

Marcus Garvey*
Stuart Hall†

JAPAN

Arahata Kanson
Hiratsuka Raichō
Ichikawa Fusae
Ishikawa Sanshirō
Itō Noe
Kagawa Toyohiko
Kiryū Yūyū
Kōtoku Shūsui
Kuroda Joichi
Matsumoto Jiichirō
Ōsugi Sakae
Ōyama Ikuo
Tanaka Shōzō
Tsuda Umeko
Yosano Akiko

KENYA

Jomo Kenyatta
Wangari Maathai
Ngugi wa Thiong'o

LITHUANIA

Emma Goldman†
Joe Slovo†

MALAYSIA

Harrison Ngau

MARTINIQUE

Frantz Fanon†

MEXICO

Erich Fromm*
Ivan Illich*
Vicente Lombardo Toledano
Ricardo Flóres Magón
John Reed*
Manabendra Nath Roy*
Leon Trotsky*
Emiliano Zapata

MOROCCO

Fatima Mernissi

MOZAMBIQUE

Samora Machel
Lina Magaia

MYANMAR (BURMA)

Aung San Suu Kyi
U Thant

NAMIBIA

Sam Nujoma

NETHERLANDS

Maria Montessori*
A.J. Muste†

NEW ZEALAND

Sylvia Ashton-Warner
Ormond Burton
Juliet Mitchell†
Kate Sheppard*
Marilyn Waring

NICARAGUA

Daniel Ortega

NIGERIA

Chinua Achebe
Nnamdi Azikiwe
Flora Nwapa
Molara Ogundipe-Leslie
Wole Soyinka

NORTHERN IRELAND

see Ireland

NORWAY

Gro Harlem Brundtland
Erik Dammann
Henrik Ibsen

PALESTINE

Hanan Ashrawi
Matti Peled
Edward W. Said†
Issam Sartawi

PERU

Hugo Blanco
Augusto Boal*
Gustavo Gutiérrez
José Carlos Mariátegui

POLAND

Karola Bloch-Piotrkowski†
Jerzy Grotowski
Rosa Luxemburg
Lech Wałęsa

PUERTO RICO

Leopold Kohr*

RUSSIA

Mikhail Bakunin
Alexander Berkman†
Yelena Bonner
Emma Goldman*
Natalya Gorbanevskaya
Dolores Ibárruri*
Vladimir Ilich Lenin
Aleksandra Kollontai
Petr Kropotkin
Roy Medvedev*
Irina Ratushinskaya
John Reed*
Manabendra Nath Roy*
Andrey Sakharov
Aleksandr Solzhenitsyn
Leo Tolstoy
Leon Trotsky*

SÃO TOMÉ E PRINCIPE

Alda do Espirito Santo

SCOTLAND

Eve Balfour†
Thomas Carlyle†
Keir Hardie
R.D. Laing†
John Maclean
A.S. Neill†
Robert Owen*
Sara Parkin†
Kate Sheppard†
Marie Stopes†
Fanny Wright†

SENEGAL

Mariama Bâ
Léopold Senghor

SIERRA LEONE

Adelaide Casely-Hayford

SLOVAKIA

Alexander Dubček†

SOUTH AFRICA

Steve Biko
Mahatma Gandhi*
Helen Joseph*
Ellen Kuzwayo
Albert Luthuli
Nelson Mandela
Winnie Mandela
Olive Schreiner
Walter Sisulu
Joe Slovo*
Helen Suzman
Oliver Tambo
Desmond Tutu

SPAIN

Emma Goldman*
Dolores Ibárruri
Pablo Neruda*

SURINAM

Aphra Behn*

SWEDEN

Selma Lagerlöf

SWITZERLAND

Mary Daly*

TANZANIA

Julius Nyerere

THAILAND

Seksan Prasotkun

TIBET

Tenzin Gyatso

TRINIDAD

C.L.R. James†

TUNISIA

Munsif Marzuqi

TURKEY

Ayse Bircan

UKRAINE

Leon Trotsky†

UNITED KINGDOM

see England, Northern
    Ireland, Scotland, Wales

USA

Chinua Achebe*
Jane Addams
Theodor Adorno*
Saul Alinsky
Jessie Daniel Ames
Susan B. Anthony
Hannah Arendt*
Sylvia Ashton-Warner*
Joan Baez
Ella Baker
Mary Ritter Beard
Edward Bellamy
Alexander Berkman*
Daniel Berrigan
Philip Berrigan
Wendell Berry
Murray Bookchin
Rita Mae Brown
Susan Brownmiller

Helen Caldicott*
Ernest Callenbach
Rachel Carson
Judy Chicago
Noam Chomsky
Kate Chopin
Herman Daly
Mary Daly
Angela Davis
Dorothy Day
Eugene V. Debs
David Dellinger
Barbara Deming
Frederick Douglass
W.E.B. Du Bois
Isadora Duncan
Andrea Dworkin
Crystal Eastman
Max Eastman
Ralph Waldo Emerson
Fang Lizhi*
Shulamith Firestone
Elizabeth Gurley Flynn
Matthew Fox
Betty Friedan
Erich Fromm*
Margaret Fuller
Matilda Joslyn Gage
Marcus Garvey
Charlotte Perkins Gilman
Emma Goldman*
Paul Goodman
Judy Grahn
Susan Griffin
Angelina Grimké
Sarah Grimké
Fannie Lou Hamer
Michael Harrington
Hazel Henderson*
Eric Hobsbawm*
Abbie Hoffman
bell hooks
Max Horkheimer*
Karen Horney*
Ivan Illich*
C.L.R. James*
Mary Jones*
Martin Luther King, Jr
Larry Kramer
Frances Moore Lappé
Christopher Lasch
Sidney Lens
Audre Lorde
Joanna Macy
Ricardo Flóres Magón*

Manning Marable
Herbert Marcuse*
Abraham Maslow
Thomas Merton*
C. Wright Mills
Harvey Milk
Kate Millett
Robin Morgan
Toni Morrison
Lewis Mumford
A.J. Muste*
Holly Near
Scott Nearing
Robert Owen*
Ōyama Ikuo*
Tom Paine*
Fran Peavey
Marge Piercy
Bernice Johnson Reagon
John Reed
Wilhelm Reich*
Adrienne Rich
Paul Robeson
Carl Rogers
Theodore Roszak
Bayard Rustin
Edward W. Said*
Kirkpatrick Sale
Margaret Sanger
Upton Sinclair
Agnes Smedley
Gary Snyder
Aleksandr Solzhenitsyn*
Elizabeth Cady Stanton
Starhawk
Gloria Steinem
Thomas Szasz*
Henry David Thoreau
Sojourner Truth
Harriet Ross Tubman
Alice Walker
Walt Whitman
Fanny Wright*
Malcolm X

VIETNAM

Thich Nhat Hanh

WALES

Leopold Kohr*
Robert Owen†
Raymond Williams†

ZIMBABWE

Robert Mugabe

APPENDIX B
RADICAL ACTIVISTS BY MAIN AREAS OF ACTIVITY

It is almost impossible to categorise the 'main areas of activity' of many activists whose stories appear in this book, partly because many have been active in a wide range of areas, and partly because those areas are almost impossible to categorise. Almost every person is a 'writer', a 'human rights campaigner', a 'political activist' and a 'social critic'. We have, however, attempted to make the categories in this appendix as useful as possible without being either too narrow or too vague. A couple of specific points: the 'Indigenous People's Rights Campaigners' category has been made wide enough to include all anticolonialism and self-determination campaigns, while the 'Democracy Campaigners' category deliberately covers those working for democracy only in countries whose politics are or were characterised by state socialism.

ABOLITIONISTS (ANTI-SLAVERY CAMPAIGNERS)

Jessie Daniel Ames
Frederick Douglass
Ralph Waldo Emerson
Angelina Grimké
Sarah Grimké
Harriet Ross Tubman
Sojourner Truth

ACADEMICS

Chinua Achebe
Theodor Adorno
Hannah Arendt
Raymond Aron
Hanan Ashrawi
Wendell Berry
Ernst Bloch
Noam Chomsky
G.D.H. Cole
Herman Daly
Mary Daly
Homa Darabi
Angela Davis
W.E.B. Du Bois
Fang Lizhi
Michel Foucault
Erich Fromm
Jürgen Habermas
Stuart Hall
Eric Hobsbawm
Joanna Macy
Abraham Maslow

Fatima Mernissi
Toni Morrison
Ann Oakley
Molara Ogundipe-Leslie
Ōyama Ikuo
Matti Peled
Ali Shari'ati
Wole Soyinka
Thomas Szasz
Raymond Williams

ANARCHISTS

Mikhail Bakunin
Alexander Berkman
Murray Bookchin
Edward Carpenter
Ralph Waldo Emerson
Charles Fourier
William Godwin
Paul Goodman
Petr Kropotkin
Errico Malatesta
Thomas Paine
Pierre-Joseph Proudhon
Henry David Thoreau
Leo Tolstoy

ANTI-APARTHEID CAMPAIGNERS

Steve Biko
Helen Joseph
Ellen Kuzwayo
Albert Luthuli
Nelson Mandela
Winnie Mandela

Walter Sisulu
Joe Slovo
Helen Suzman
Oliver Tambo
Desmond Tutu

ARTISTS

John Berger
William Blake
Judy Chicago
William Morris

CIVIL RIGHTS CAMPAIGNERS

Joan Baez
Ella Baker
Angela Davis
David Dellinger
W.E.B. Du Bois
Marcus Garvey
Fannie Lou Hamer
Martin Luther King, Jr
Paul Robeson
Bayard Rustin
Pete Seeger

DEMOCRACY CAMPAIGNERS

Yelena Bonner
Chai Ling
Ding Ling
Fang Lizhi
Natalya Gorbanevskaya
Václav Havel

Hu Feng
Kang Yuwei
Roy Medvedev
Irina Ratushinskaya
Andrey Sakharov
Agnes Smedley
Aleksandr Solzhenitsyn
Lech Wałęsa
Wei Jingsheng
Xiang Jingyu

ECONOMISTS

Herman Daly
Paul Ekins
André Gorz
Hazel Henderson
Leopold Kohr
Manfred Max-Neef
Fritz Schumacher
Marilyn Waring

EDUCATIONAL REFORMERS

Sylvia Ashton-Warner
Mariama Bâ
Adelaide Casely-Hayford
Paulo Freire
Aurobindo Ghose
Ivan Illich
Raden Ajeng Kartini
Maria Montessori
Nabawiya Musa
A.S. Neill
Flora Nwapa
Tsuda Umeko

ENVIRONMENTAL CAMPAIGNERS

Rudolf Bahro
Eve Balfour
Wendell Berry
Murray Bookchin
Bob Brown
Helen Caldicott
Ernest Callenbach
Rachel Carson
Herman Daly
Erik Dammann
Paul Ekins
Hazel Henderson
Abbie Hoffman
Petra Kelly
Kuroda Joichi
José Lutzenberger
Wangari Maathai
Joanna Macy
H.J. Massingham
Freda Meissner-Blau
Chico Mendes
Bill Mollison
Scott Nearing

Harrison Ngau
Paulinho Paiakan
Sara Parkin
Jonathon Porritt
Theodore Roszak
Kirkpatrick Sale
Fritz Schumacher
Pete Seeger
Vandana Shiva
Gary Snyder
Starhawk
Tanaka Shōzō
János Vargha

ESSAYISTS

Wendell Berry
Heinrich Böll
Thomas Carlyle
Edward Carpenter
Slavenka Drakulić
George Eliot
Ralph Waldo Emerson
Hans Magnus Enzenberger
Charlotte Perkins Gilman
Germaine Greer
Carolina Maria de Jesús
Adrienne Rich
Theodore Roszak
Gary Snyder
Leo Tolstoy
Virginia Woolf

FEMINIST THEORISTS

Simone de Beauvoir
Susan Brownmiller
Mary Daly
Andrea Dworkin
Shulamith Firestone
Betty Friedan
Germaine Greer
bell hooks
Karen Horney
Fatima Mernissi
Kate Millett
Juliet Mitchell
Robin Morgan
Ann Oakley
Adrienne Rich
Sheila Rowbotham
Vandana Shiva
Dale Spender
Gloria Steinem

FILM DIRECTORS

John Berger
Derek Jarman
John Pilger

GAY AND LESBIAN LIBERATION

Rita Mae Brown

Edward Carpenter
Judy Grahn
Radclyffe Hall
Magnus Hirschfeld
Derek Jarman
Larry Kramer
Selma Lagerlöf
Audre Lorde
Harvey Milk
Kate Millett
Holly Near
Adrienne Rich
Ethel Smyth
Peter Tatchell
Walt Whitman
Oscar Wilde

HEALTH CAMPAIGNERS

Elizabeth Garrett Anderson
Havelock Ellis
Larry Kramer
R.D. Laing
Margaret Sanger
Marie Stopes
Thomas Szasz

HISTORIANS

Susan B. Anthony
Hannah Arendt
Mary Ritter Beard
Thomas Carlyle
G.D.H. Cole
W.E.B. Du Bois
Margaret Fuller
Matilda Joslyn Gage
Eric Hobsbawm
C.L.R. James
Christopher Lasch
Manning Marable
Karl Marx
Roy Medvedev
Lewis Mumford
Seksan Prasotkun
Walter Rodney
Sheila Rowbotham
Dale Spender
E.P. Thompson
Beatrice Webb
Sidney Webb
Raymond Williams

INDIGENOUS PEOPLE'S RIGHTS CAMPAIGNERS

Jean-Bertrand Aristide
Hanan Ashrawi
Aung San Su Kyi
Carlos Belo
Ayse Bircan
Amilcar Cabral
Alda do Espirito Santo
Frantz Fanon

Mahatma Gandhi
Marianella García-Villas
Tenzin Gyatso
Victor Jara
Jomo Kenyatta
Samora Machel
Munsif Marzuqi
Matsumoto Jiichirō
Rigoberta Menchú
Bill Mollison
Sarojini Naidu
Taslima Nasrin
Harrison Ngau
Sam Nujoma
Daniel Ortega
Paulinho Paiakan
Matti Peled
John Pilger
Oscar Romero
Issam Sartawi
Jessie Street
Emiliano Zapata

JOURNALISTS

Chinua Achebe
Arahata Kanson
Raymond Aron
Uri Avnery
Nnamdi Azikiwe
Henri Barbusse
John Berger
Alexander Berkman
Ayse Bircan
Vera Brittain
Susan Brownmiller
Beatrix Campbell
Ding Ling
Slavenka Drakulić
Hans Magnus Enzenberger
Margaret Fuller
Dolores Ibárruri
Kiryū Yūyū
Kōtoku Shūsui
José Carlos Mariátegui
Saiza Nabarawi
Ōsugi Sakae
Sylvia Pankhurst
John Pilger
John Reed
Amina Said
Gloria Steinem
Rebecca West
Walt Whitman

LABOUR ORGANISERS

Arahata Kanson
Alexander Berkman
Hugo Blanco
Eugene V. Debs
Elizabeth Gurley Flynn
Ishikawa Sanshirō

Mary Jones
Kagawa Toyohiko
Sidney Lens
Vicente Lombardo Toledano
Errico Malatesta
Chico Mendes
Bill Morrow
A.J. Muste
Adelheid Popp
John Reed
Lech Wałęsa

MUSICIANS

Joan Baez
Victor Jara
Holly Near
Bernice Johnson Reagon
Paul Robeson
Pete Seeger
Ethel Smyth

NOVELISTS

Chinua Achebe
Sylvia Ashton-Warner
Mariama Bâ
Henri Barbusse
Simone de Beauvoir
Aphra Behn
Edward Bellamy
Wendell Berry
Heinrich Böll
Vera Brittain
Rita Mae Brown
Ernest Callenbach
Kate Chopin
Régis Debray
Slavenka Drakulić
Andrea Dworkin
George Eliot
Charlotte Perkins Gilman
Radclyffe Hall
Larry Kramer
Selma Lagerlöf
Toni Morrison
Taslima Nasrin
Flora Nwapa
Ann Oakley
George Orwell
Marge Piercy
Theodore Roszak
Nawal el Sa'dawi
Jean-Paul Sartre
Olive Schreiner
Upton Sinclair
Agnes Smedley
Aleksandr Solzhenitsyn
Wole Soyinka
Efua Sutherland
Ngugi wa Thiong'o
Pramoedya Ananta Toer
Leo Tolstoy

Robert Tressell
Bertha von Suttner
Alice Walker
Rebecca West
Oscar Wilde
Virginia Woolf

PACIFISTS/
PEACE CAMPAIGNERS

Jane Addams
Shulamit Aloni
Hanan Ashrawi
Uri Avnery
Joan Baez
Ella Baker
Henri Barbusse
Daniel Berrigan
Philip Berrigan
Heinrich Böll
Vera Brittain
Ormond Burton
Jim Cairns
Helen Caldicott
Noam Chomsky
Mairead Corrigan McGuire
Dorothy Day
David Dellinger
Barbara Deming
Charlotte Despard
Danilo Dolci
Crystal Eastman
Mahatma Gandhi
Vida Goldstein
Paul Goodman
Tenzin Gyatso
Stuart Hall
Keir Hardie
Hiratsuka Raichō
Kagawa Toyohiko
Kiryū Yūyū
George Lansbury
Sidney Lens
Rosa Luxemburg
John Maclean
Joanna Macy
Thomas Merton
C. Wright Mills
Bill Morrow
A.J. Muste
Saiza Nabarawi
Holly Near
Scott Nearing
Ōyama Ikuo
Sylvia Pankhurst
Matti Peled
Madeleine Pelletier
Bertrand Russell
Dora Russell
Bayard Rustin
Issam Sartawi
Olive Schreiner

Rosika Schwimmer
Rose Scott
Jessie Street
Thich Nhat Hanh
E.P. Thompson
Bertha von Suttner
Louise Weiss
Virginia Woolf
Clara Zetkin

PHILOSOPHERS

Theodor Adorno
Hannah Arendt
Raymond Aron
Ernst Bloch
Martin Buber
Noam Chomsky
Ralph Waldo Emerson
Friedrich Engels
Michel Foucault
Aurobindo Ghose
Antonio Gramsci
Jürgen Habermas
Max Horkheimer
Ivan Illich
Herbert Marcuse
Karl Marx
John Stuart Mill
Pierre-Joseph Proudhon
Jean-Jacques Rousseau
Bertrand Russell
Harriet Taylor
Henry David Thoreau
Leo Tolstoy

PLAYWRIGHTS

Aphra Behn
Augusto Boal
Bertolt Brecht
Václav Havel
bell hooks
Henrik Ibsen
Larry Kramer
Wole Soyinka
Efua Sutherland
Ngugi wa Thiong'o
Oscar Wilde

POETS

Aphra Behn
William Blake
Augusto Boal
Bertolt Brecht
Edward Carpenter
Kate Chopin
George Eliot
Alda do Espirito Santo
Natalya Gorbanevskaya
Judy Grahn
Susan Griffin
Radclyffe Hall

bell hooks
Jiu Jin
Audre Lorde
Lu Xun
William Morris
Sarojini Naidu
Pablo Neruda
Marge Piercy
Irina Ratushinskaya
Adrienne Rich
Léopold Senghor
Percy Bysshe Shelley
Gary Snyder
Wole Soyinka
Efua Sutherland
Walt Whitman
Yosano Akiko

POLITICAL ACTIVISTS

Saul Alinsky
Arahata Kanson
Aung San Suu Kyi
Rudolf Bahro
Ella Baker
Mikhail Bakunin
Alexander Berkman
Vinoba Bhave
Steve Biko
Karola Bloch-Piotrkowski
Dietrich Bonhoeffer
Amilcar Cabral
Chai Ling
Noam Chomsky
Daniel Cohn-Bendit
Angela Davis
Charlotte Despard
Rudi Dutschke
Alda do Espirito Santo
Elizabeth Gurley Flynn
Mahatma Gandhi
Marcus Garvey
Aurobindo Ghose
Emma Goldman
Antonio Gramsci
Che Guevara
Stuart Hall
Fannie Lou Hamer
Michael Harrington
Abbie Hoffman
Itō Noe
C.L.R. James
Martin Luther King, Jr
Aleksandra Kollontai
Kōtoku Shūsui
Petr Kropotkin
Vladimir Ilich Lenin
Audre Lorde
Rosa Luxemburg
John Maclean
Ricardo Flóres Magón
Errico Malatesta

Nelson Mandela
Winnie Mandela
Mao Zedong
Herbert Marcuse
José Carlos Mariátegui
Karl Marx
Ulrike Meinhof
Freda Meissner-Blau
Kate Millett
William Morris
Bill Morrow
Robert Mugabe
Sarojini Naidu
J.P. Narayan
Scott Nearing
Kwame Nkrumah
Sam Nujoma
Julius Nyerere
Daniel Ortega
Ōsugi Sakae
Ōyama Ikuo
Tom Paine
Christabel Pankhurst
Emmeline Pankhurst
Sylvia Pankhurst
Sara Parkin
Fran Peavey
Marge Piercy
Seksan Prasotkun
Pierre-Joseph Proudhon
Irina Ratushinskaya
John Reed
Wilhelm Reich
Walter Rodney
Manabendra Nath Roy
Edward W. Said
Jean-Paul Sartre
Walter Sisulu
Joe Slovo
Agnes Smedley
Starhawk
Sun Yat-Sen
Helen Suzman
Oliver Tambo
Ngugi wa Thiong'o
Camilo Torres
Leon Trotsky
Desmond Tutu
János Vargha
Lech Wałęsa
Louise Weiss
Malcolm X
Xiang Jingyu
Clara Zetkin

POLITICIANS

Salvador Allende
Shulamit Aloni
Jean-Bertrand Aristide
Aung San Suu Kyi
Uri Avnery

Nnamdi Azikiwe
Tony Benn
Hugo Blanco
Augusto Boal
Bob Brown
Jim Cairns
Kamaladevi Chattopadhyay
Eugene V. Debs
Alexander Dubček
Keir Hardie
Václav Havel
Dolores Ibárruri
Ichikawa Fusae
Kagawa Toyohiko
Petra Kelly
Jomo Kenyatta
George Lansbury
Vladimir Ilich Lenin
Samora Machel
Nelson Mandela
Mao Zedong
Matsumoto Jiichirō
Roy Medvedev
Freda Meissner-Blau
Harvey Milk
Bill Morrow
Robert Mugabe
Sarojini Naidu
J.P. Narayan
Pablo Neruda
Kwame Nkrumah
Sam Nujoma
Julius Nyerere
Daniel Ortega
Ōyama Ikuo
Matti Peled
Pandita Ramabai
Thomas Sankara
Léopold Senghor
Walter Sisulu
Sun Yat-Sen
Helen Suzman
Tanaka Shōzō
Leon Trotsky
U Thant
Lech Wałęsa
Marilyn Waring
Sidney Webb
Louise Weiss
Clara Zetkin

PRIESTS/CLERGY

Jean-Bertrand Aristide
Carlos Belo
Daniel Berrigan
Philip Berrigan
Dietrich Bonhoeffer
Ormond Burton
Helder Camara
Matthew Fox
Gustavo Gutiérrez

Kagawa Toyohiko
Martin Luther King, Jr.
Thomas Merton
A.J. Muste
Oscar Romero
Jonathan Swift
Thich Nhat Hanh
Camilo Torres
Sojourner Truth
Desmond Tutu

PSYCHOLOGISTS

Frantz Fanon
Karen Horney
R.D. Laing
Abraham Maslow
Juliet Mitchell
Wilhelm Reich
Carl Rogers
Thomas Szasz

REPRODUCTIVE RIGHTS CAMPAIGNERS

Annie Besant
Shulamith Firestone
Madeleine Pelletier
Margaret Sanger
Marie Stopes

SOCIAL CRITICS

Theodor Adorno
Edward Bellamy
William Blake
Ernst Bloch
Augusto Boal
Heinrich Böll
Bertolt Brecht
Beatrix Campbell
Thomas Carlyle
Edward Carpenter
Chai Ling
Régis Debray
Max Eastman
Friedrich Engels
Hans Magnus Enzenberger
Frantz Fanon
Michel Foucault
Matthew Fox
Paulo Freire
William Godwin
Paul Goodman
André Gorz
Gustavo Gutiérrez
Jürgen Habermas
Michael Harrington
bell hooks
Max Horkheimer
Hu Feng
Ivan Illich
Kang Yuwei
Leopold Kohr

Petr Kropotkin
R.D. Laing
Frances Moore Lappé
Christopher Lasch
Lu Xun
Herbert Marcuse
Karl Marx
Roy Medvedev
John Stuart Mill
C. Wright Mills
Lewis Mumford
J.P. Narayan
George Orwell
Seksan Prasotkun
Pierre-Joseph Proudhon
Wilhelm Reich
Theodore Roszak
Jean-Jacques Rousseau
Bertrand Russell
Kirkpatrick Sale
Jean-Paul Sartre
Percy Bysshe Shelley
Upton Sinclair
Aleksandr Solzhenitsyn
Efua Sutherland
Jonathan Swift
E.P. Thompson
Henry David Thoreau
Pramoedya Ananta Toer
Leo Tolstoy
Walt Whitman
Oscar Wilde
Raymond Williams

SOCIAL REFORMERS

Jane Addams
Saul Alinsky
Salvador Allende
Vinoba Bhave
Hugo Blanco
Kamaladevi Chattopadhyay
Dorothy Day
Danilo Dolci
Alexander Dubček
Isadora Duncan
Havelock Ellis
Charles Fourier
Ebenezer Howard
Raden Ajeng Kartini
Mao Zedong
Manfred Max-Neef
Maria Montessori
Emily Murphy
A.S. Neill
Robert Owen
Fran Peavey
Manabendra Nath Roy
Thomas Sankara
Fritz Schumacher
Beatrice Webb
Sidney Webb

Fanny Wright
Emiliano Zapata

SOCIOLOGISTS

Theodor Adorno
Erich Fromm
Jürgen Habermas
Stuart Hall
Max Horkheimer
Ivan Illich
Herbert Marcuse
C. Wright Mills

SUFFRAGISTS

Jessie Daniel Ames
Susan B. Anthony
Mary Ritter Beard
Teresa Billington-Greig
Charlotte Despard
Crystal Eastman
Matilda Joslyn Gage
Charlotte Perkins Gilman
Vida Goldstein
Selma Lagerlöf
Emily Murphy
Christabel Pankhurst
Emmeline Pankhurst
Sylvia Pankhurst
Madeleine Pelletier
Kate Wilson Sheppard
Elizabeth Cady Stanton

THEATRE DIRECTORS

Augusto Boal
Jerzy Grotowski

UTOPIANISTS

Edward Bellamy
Ernst Bloch
Edward Carpenter
Charles Fourier
Robert Owen
Fanny Wright
Gerrard Winstanley

WOMEN'S RIGHTS CAMPAIGNERS

Shulamit Aloni
Elizabeth Garrett Anderson
Mariama Bâ
Ayse Bircan
Karola Bloch-Piotrkowski
Vera Brittain
Susan Brownmiller
Beatrix Campbell
Homa Darabi
Barbara Deming
Slavenka Drakulić
Andrea Dworkin
Vilma Espìn
Betty Friedan
Margaret Fuller
Hiratsuka Raichō
Ichikawa Fusae
Raden Ajeng Kartini
Aleksandra Kollontai
Ellen Kuzwayo
Lina Magaia
Winnie Mandela
Rigoberta Menchú
Fatima Mernissi
Kate Millett
Juliet Mitchell

Robin Morgan
Toni Morrison
Emily Murphy
Nabawiya Musa
Saiza Nabarawi
Taslima Nasrin
Holly Near
Ann Oakley
Molara Ogundipe-Leslie
Adelheid Popp
Pandita Ramabai
Adrienne Rich
Sheila Rowbotham
Dora Russell
Nawal el Sa'dawi
Amina Said
Olive Schreiner
Rosika Schwimmer
Rose Scott
Huda Shaarawi
Vandana Shiva
Agnes Smedley
Ethel Smyth
Dale Spender
Starhawk
Gloria Steinem
Jessie Street
Harriet Taylor
Sojourner Truth
Tsuda Umeko
Alice Walker
Marilyn Waring
Louise Weiss
Rebecca West
Mary Wollstonecraft
Xiang Jingyu
Yosano Akiko
Clara Zetkin

APPENDIX C
OTHER NOTABLE
AMERICAN RADICALS

This appendix provides details of more than eighty additional people active in the US radical movement: the rationale behind this listing is explained in the 'Criteria for Inclusion' section on pages xiv–xvi.

Louisa May Alcott
1832–1888
novelist,
women's rights advocate
Elaine Showalter, *Sister's Choice: Tradition and Change in American Women's Writing*, Oxford University Press, 1991
Elizabeth Lennox Keyser, *Whispers in the Dark: The Fiction of Louisa May Alcott*, University of Tennessee Press, 1993

Nelson Algren
1909–1981
socialist novelist and essayist
H.E. Donohue, *Conversations with Nelson Algren*, Hill and Wang, 1964

Oscar Ameringer
1870–1943
journalist, labour organiser
Oscar Ameringer, *If You Don't Weaken*, University of Oklahoma Press, 1983 (orig. pub. 1940)

Maya Angelou [Margeurite Johnson]
1928–
civil rights campaigner, writer, actor, singer
Maya Angelou, *I Know Why the Caged Bird Sings*, Random House, 1970
Sarah King, *Maya Angelou: Greeting the Morning*, Millbrook Press, 1994.

Virginia Apuzzo
1941–
feminist, gay and lesbian rights and health campaigner
Ginny Vida (ed.) *Our Right to Love: A Lesbian Resource Book*, Prentice-Hall, 1978

Herbert Aptheker
1915–
historian
Herbert Aptheker, *American Negro Slave Revolts*, International Publishers, 1963 (first pub. 1939)
Herbert Aptheker, *A Documentary History of the Negro People in the United States*, Citadel, 1951–1993

Ti-Grace Atkinson
1939–
feminist writer and organiser
Ti-Grace Atkinson, *Amazon Odyssey*, Links, 1974

Emily Greene Balch
1867–1961
feminist, pacifist, economist
Mercedes Randall, *Improper Bostonian: Emily Greene Balch*, Twayne, 1964

James Baldwin
1924–1987
author, civil rights activist
James Baldwin, *The Fire Next Time*, Dial, 1963

Ruth Benedict
1887–1948
anthropologist
Margaret Mead, *An Anthropologist at Work: Writings of Ruth Benedict*, Houghton Mifflin, 1959

Elizabeth Blackwell
1821–1910
abolitionist, doctor, women's health campaigner
Dorothy Clarke Wilson, *Lone Woman: The Story of Elizabeth Blackwell, The First Woman Doctor*, Little, Brown, 1970

Harriot Stanton Blatch
1856–1939
feminist, suffragist
Harriot Stanton Blatch and Alma Lutz, *Challenging Years: The Memoirs of Harriot Stanton Blatch*, Putnam, 1940

Kenneth and Elise Boulding
1910–1994 and 1920–
peace activists, social critics, writers
Kenneth Boulding, *Stable Peace*, University of Texas Press, 1976
Elise Boulding, *Building a Global Civil Culture: Education for an Interdependent World*, Syracuse University Press, 1990
Cynthia Kerman, *Creative Tension: The Life and Thought of Kenneth Boulding*, University of Michigan Press, 1974

Randolph Bourne
1886–1918
social critic, pacifist
Randolph Bourne (ed. Van Wyck Brooks), *The History of a Literary Radical, and Other Papers*, Russell, 1956

Anne and Carl Braden
1924– and 1914–1975
journalists, civil rights activists
Anne Braden, *The Wall Between*, Monthly Review Press, 1958

David Brower
1912–
environmental campaigner
David Brower, *David Brower: Environmental Activist, Publicist, and Prophet*, Regional Oral History Office, Bancroft Library, University of California, 1980

Lester Brown
1934–
environmental campaigner
Lester Brown, *Building a
Sustainable Society*, Norton,
1981

Carlos Bulosan
1911–1956
labour organiser
Carlos Bulosan, *The Power of the
People*, Tabloid Books, 1977

César Chávez
1927–
civil rights campaigner,
labour organiser
Mark Day, *Forty Acres: César
Chávez and the Farm Workers*,
Praeger, 1971
Jean Maddern Pitrone, *Chávez,
Man of the Migrants*, Alba
House, 1971

Voltairine de Cleyre
1866–1912
anarchist, pacifist
Paul Avrich, *An American
Anarchist: The Life of Voltairine
de Cleyre*, Princeton University
Press, 1978

Clarence Darrow
1857–1938
lawyer
Clarence Darrow, *The Story of
My Life*, Grosset and Dunlap,
1932
Kevin Tierney, *Darrow: A
Biography*, Crowell, 1979

John Dewey
1859–1952
philosopher, educator,
social reformer
Richard Bernstein, *John Dewey*,
Washington Square, 1966

John Dos Passos
1896–1970
novelist
Townsend Luddington, *John Dos
Passos: A Twentieth Century
Odyssey*, Dutton, 1980

**Bob Dylan [Robert Allen
Zimmerman]**
1941–
singer, songwriter
Robert Shelton, *No Direction
Home: The Life and Music of Bob
Dylan*, Beech Tree Books, 1986
Clinton Heylin, *Bob Dylan: Behind
the Shades: A Biography*,
Summit Books, 1991

Marian Wright Edelman
1941–
children's rights campaigner
Marian Wright Edelman, *The
Measure of Our Success: A Letter
to My Children and Yours*,
Beacon, 1992

**William Z. [Zebulon]
Foster**
1881–1961
labour organiser
William Z. Foster, *Pages from a
Worker's Life*, International
Publishers, 1939
Arthur Zipser, *Working-Class
Giant: The Life of William Z.
Foster*, International
Publishers, 1981

John Kenneth Galbraith
1908–
economist, social critic
John Kenneth Galbraith, *The
Affluent Society*, Houghton
Mifflin, 1958
John Kenneth Galbraith, *Annals
of an Abiding Liberal*, Houghton
Mifflin, 1979
Charles Henry Hession, *John
Kenneth Galbraith and His
Critics*, New American Library,
1982

William Lloyd Garrison
1805–1879
abolitionist
Walter McIntosh Merrill, *Against
Wind and Tide: A Biography of
William Lloyd Garrison*, Harvard
University Press, 1963
John Thomas, *The Liberator:
William Lloyd Garrison: A
Biography*, Little, Brown, 1963

Eugene Genovese
1930–
historian
Eugene Genovese, *The World the
Slaveholders Made*, Pantheon,
1969
Eugene Genovese, *From
Rebellion to Revolution:
Afro-American Slave Revolt in the
Making of the Modern World*,
Lousiana State University
Press, 1979

Carol Gilligan
1936–
feminist, writer
Carol Gilligan, *In a Different
Voice: Psychological Theory and
Women's Development*, Harvard
University Press, 1982

Woody Guthrie
1912–1967
singer, songwriter
Woody Guthrie, *Bound For Glory*,
New American Library, 1943
Joe Klein, *Woody Guthrie: A Life*,
Ballantine, 1980

**William ('Big Bill')
Haywood**
1869–1928
labour organiser
Joseph Conlin, *Big Bill Haywood
and the Radical Labor
Movement*, Syracuse University
Press, 1969
Peter Carlson, *Roughneck: The
Life and Times of Big Bill
Haywood*, Norton, 1983

Ammon Hennacy
1893–1970
anarchist, pacifist
Ammon Hennacy, *The Book of
Ammon*, Fortkamp, 1993 (orig.
pub. 1965)

Aileen Clarke Hernandez
1926–
feminist, women's rights
campaigner
Gayle Hardy, *American Women
Civil Rights Activists*,
McFarland, 1993

**Joe Hill
[Joseph Haegglund]**
1879–1915
artist, poet, labour activist
Philip Foner, *The Case of Joe Hill*,
International Publishers, 1965
Gibbs M. Smith, *Joe Hill*,
Peregrine Smith, 1984

Langston Hughes
1902–1967
novelist, poet, journalist
Faith Berry (ed.), *Good Morning
Revolution: Uncollected Social
Protest Writings by Langston
Hughes*, Greenwood, 1973
Arnold Rampersad, *The Life of
Langston Hughes*, Oxford
University Press, 1986 (Vol. I)
and 1988 (Vol. II)

Jesse Jackson
1941–
clergyman, politician
Jesse Jackson, *Straight from the
Heart*, Fortress Press, 1987
Barbara Reynolds, *Jesse Jackson:
The Man, The Movement, The
Myth*, Nelson-Hall, 1975

Jane Jacobs
1916–
sociologist, historian
Jane Jacobs, *Cities and the Wealth of Nations: Principles of Economic Life*, Random House, 1984

Helen Keller
1880–1967
socialist, pacifist, disability rights campaigner
Helen Keller, *Helen Keller: Her Socialist Years*, International Publishers, 1967

Abby [Abigail] Kelley [Foster]
1810–1887
abolitionist, women's suffrage campaigner
Dorothy Sterling, *Ahead of Her Time: Abby Kelley and the Politics of Anti-slavery*, Norton, 1991

Coretta Scott King
1927–
civil rights campaigner, singer
Coretta Scott King, *My Life with Martin Luther King, Jr*, Holt, Rinehart and Winston, 1969
Diane Patrick, *Coretta Scott King*, Franklin Watts, 1991

Robert M. [Marion] La Follette
1855–1925
politician, human rights advocate
Belle and Fola La Follette, *Robert M. La Follette*, Macmillan, 1953
David Thelen, *Robert M. La Follette and the Insurgent Spirit*, University of Wisconsin Press, 1985

Fiorello La Guardia
1882–1947
progressive politician
Thomas Kessner, *Fiorello H. La Guardia and the Making of Modern New York*, McGraw-Hill, 1989

Meridel Le Sueur
1900–
feminist, novelist, historian
Meridel Le Sueur, *Ripening: Selected Works 1927–1980*, Feminist Press, 1982

Denise Levertov
1923–
poet, pacifist
Denise Levertov, *The Poet in the World*, New Directions, 1973

Jack London
1876–1916
novelist, social activist
Andrew Sinclair, *Jack: A Biography of Jack London*, Harper and Row, 1977

Amory Lovins
1947–
environmental and energy issues campaigner
Amory Lovins, *Soft Energy Paths: Toward a Durable Peace*, Friends of the Earth, 1977

Staughton Lynd
1929–
civil rights and workers' rights campaigner, historian
Staughton Lynd, *Nonviolence in America: A Documentary History*, Bobbs-Merrill, 1966
Staughton Lynd, *Intellectual Origins of American Radicalism*, Pantheon, 1968

Vito Marcantonio
1902–1954
politician
Alan Schaffer, *Vito Marcantonio: Radical in Congress*, Syracuse University Press, 1966
Gerald Meyer, *Vito Marcantonio: Radical Politician*, State University of New York Press, 1989

José Martí
1853–1895
journalist, labour activist
Carlos Ripoll, *José Martí, The United States, and the Marxist Interpretation of Cuban History*, Rutgers University Press, 1984

Margaret Mead
1901–1978
anthropologist
Robert Cassidy, *Margaret Mead: A Voice for the Century*, Universe, 1982
Phyllis Grosskurth, *Margaret Mead*, Penguin, 1988

Bob [Robert Parris] Moses
1932–
civil rights campaigner
Eric Burner, *And Gently He Shall Lead Them: Robert Parris Moses and Civil Rights in Mississippi*, New York University Press, 1994

Lucretia Mott
1793–1880
abolitionist, women's rights campaigner
Otelia Cromwell, *Lucretia Mott*, Harvard University Press, 1958

John Muir
1838–1914
environmental campaigner
Michael Cohen, *The Pathless Way: John Muir and American Wilderness*, University of Wisconsin Press, 1984
Frederick Turner, *Rediscovering America: John Muir in His Time and Ours*, Viking, 1985

Ralph Nader
1934–
lawyer, consumers' rights campaigner
Robert Buckhorn, *Nader: The People's Lawyer*, Prentice-Hall, 1972
Charles McCarry, *Citizen Nader*, Saturday Review Press, 1972

Diane Nash
1938–
civil rights campaigner
Catherine Ingram, *In The Footsteps of Gandhi: Conversations with Spiritual Social Activists*, Parallax, 1990

Clifford Odets
1906–1963
playwright
Margaret Brenman-Gibson, *Clifford Odets: American Playwright*, Atheneum, 1981

Tillie Olsen
1913–
feminist, novelist
Tillie Olsen, *Silences*, Delta, 1978
Elaine Neil Orr, *Tillie Olsen and the Feminist Spiritual Vision*, University of Mississippi Press, 1987

Pat Parker
1944–
feminist, poet
Pat Parker, *Movement in Black: The Collected Poetry of Pat Parker*, Diana Press, 1978

Rosa Parks
1913–
civil rights campaigner
Rosa Parks, *Rosa Parks: Mother to a Movement*, Dial, 1992

Leonard Peltier
1944–
Indian rights campaigner
Peter Matthiessen, *In the Spirit of Crazy Horse*, Viking, 1983
Jim Messerschmidt, *The Trial of Leonard Peltier*, South End, 1983

A. Philip Randolph
1889–1979
civil rights campaigner
Jervis Anderson, *A. Philip Randolph: A Biographical Portrait*, Harcourt Brace Jovanovich, 1973

Walter Reuther
1907–1970
labour organiser
John Barnard, *Walter Reuther and the Rise of the Auto Workers*, Little, Brown, 1983

Elizabeth Robins
1862–1952
feminist, playwright, novelist
Elizabeth Robins, *Raymond and I*, Macmillan, 1956

Eleanor Roosevelt
1884–1962
human rights campaigner
Tamara Hareven, *Eleanor Roosevelt: An American Conscience*, Quadrangle, 1968

Muriel Rukeyser
1913–1980
poet, pacifist
Louise Kertesz, *The Poetic Vision of Muriel Rukeyser*, Louisiana State University Press, 1980

Kathie Sarachild [Kathie Amatniek]
1948–
feminist activist
Alice Echols, *Daring to be Bad: Radical Feminism in America, 1967–1975*, University of Minnesota Press, 1989

Sarah Schulman
1958–
lesbian journalist and activist
Sarah Schulman, *My American History: Lesbian and Gay Life during the Reagan and Bush Years*, Cassell, 1994

Barbara Smith
1946–
lesbian feminist poet and activist
Barbara Smith (ed), *Home Girls: A Black Feminist Anthology*, Kitchen Table, 1983

I. F. [Isidor Feinstein] Stone
1907–1989
journalist, pacifist
Robert Cottrell, *Izzy: A Biography of I.F. Stone*, Rutgers University Press, 1992

Lucy Stone
1818–1893
women's rights campaigner, abolitionist
Elinor Rice Hays, *Morning Star: A Biography of Lucy Stone*, Brace and World, 1961
Andrea Moore Kerr, *Lucy Stone: Speaking Out for Equality*, Rutgers University Press, 1992

Anna Louise Strong
1885–1970
journalist
Anna Louise Strong, *I Change Worlds: The Remaking of an American*, Seal Press, 1979 (first pub. 1935)

Norman Thomas
1884–1968
socialist, pacifist
W.A. Swanberg, *Norman Thomas: The Last Idealist*, Scribners, 1976

Carlo Tresca
1879–1943
labour activist, antifascist campaigner
Dorothy Gallagher, *All the Right Enemies*, Rutgers University Press, 1988

Mary Heaton Vorse
1874–1966
feminist, journalist, novelist
Mary Heaton Vorse (ed. Dee Garrison), *Rebel Pen: The Writings of Mary Heaton Vorse*, Monthly Review Press, 1985
Dee Garrison, *Mary Heaton Vorse: The Life of an American Insurgent*, Temple University Press, 1989

Ida B. [Bell] Wells[-Barnett]
1892–1931
civil rights leader
Ida Wells-Barnett (ed. Alfreda Duster), *Crusade for Justice: The Autobiography of Ida B. Wells*, University of Chicago Press, 1970
Mildred Thompson, *Ida B. Wells-Barnett: An Exploratory Study of an American Black Woman*, Carlson, 1990

Claude Williams
1893–1977
social activist, labour campaigner
Anthony Dunbar, *Against the Grain: Southern Radicals and Prophets, 1929–1959*, University of Virginia Press, 1981

William Appleman Williams
1921–1990
political writer and analyst
Henry Berger (ed.), *A William Appleman Williams Reader*, Ivan Dee, 1992

Richard Wright
1908–1960
novelist, historian
Constance Webb, *Richard Wright: A Biography*, Putnam, 1968
Michel Fabré, *The Unfinished Quest of Richard Wright*, Morrow, 1973

Howard Zinn
1922–
writer, historian, pacifist
Howard Zinn, *Disobedience and Democracy*, Random House, 1968
Howard Zinn, *A People's History of the United States*, Harper and Row, 1980

INDEX

An entry in **bold type** indicates the main entry for an individual or group.

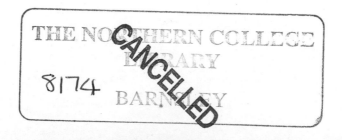
THE NORTHERN COLLEGE LIBRARY
CANCELLED
8174
BARNSLEY